The Oxford Centre for Staff and Learning Development

Proceedings of the 2001 9th International Symposium

Improving Student Learning

Improving Student Learning Using Learning Technology

Edited by Chris Rust

Published by
THE OXFORD CENTRE FOR STAFF & LEARNING DEVELOPMENT
Oxford Brookes University
Headington Hill Hall Campus
Headington
Oxford
OX3 OBP

Improving Student Learning
9 Improving Student Learning Using Learning Technology

ISBN 1 873576 68 4

British Library Cataloguing-in-Publication Data.
A catalogue record for this book is available from the British Library.

Printed 2002

Typeset in Palatino by Meg Richardson

Printed in Great Britain by
Oxonian Rewley Press Ltd
Oxford

Printed on paper produced from sustainable forests.

Contents

Part III
How can we successfully innovate/disseminate the use of learning technologies?

Part IV
How can we research student learning using learning technologies?

Part V
How can course design using learning technologies assist student learning?

Part VI
Symposia

Preface

For decades, technology in various guises – video, distance-learning packs, computers, the world-wide web – has been seen by some to either threaten or promise the demise of the teacher and the need for face-to-face instruction. And some have argued enthusiastically that it offers a new mode of learning. In recent years, many have argued for the potential of new information technologies to support student learning and improve teaching efficiency. Funding councils and educational institutions have invested heavily in this belief, illustrated, for example, by their support for the spread of web-based technologies.

It was in the light of these developments that the theme for the 9th annual International Improving Student Learning Symposium (ISL) was chosen as Improving Student Learning Using Learning Technologies. It was held at Heriot-Watt University, Edinburgh, Scotland, in September 2001 and the Symposium was the biggest yet, attracting 240 participants from 16 countries. The major aim of the Symposium is to provide a forum which brings together those who are primarily researchers into learning in higher education and those who are primarily practitioners concerned more pragmatically with improving their practice. From whichever starting point, papers are only accepted if they take a sufficiently scholarly research-based approach. The main intention in this Symposium was therefore to see what research evidence there was to indicate that the use of learning technologies was successful (or unsuccessful!) in improving student learning and/or teaching efficiency.

The Symposium was organised around four sub-themes:

- how do students learn using learning technologies?
- how can we successfully innovate/disseminate the use of learning technologies?
- how can we research student learning using learning technologies?
- how can course design using learning technologies assist student learning?

These sub-themes can be found as the various sections from Part 2 to Part 5 of these proceedings.

The symposium also included a series of 6 symposia where three related papers were presented together in an extended session. These can be found in Part 6.

The three keynote presentations at the symposium are also included in these proceedings, in Part 1. Steve Ehrmann from the USA opened the conference. The theme of his keynote was the pattern of initial enthusiasm and subsequent disappointment and waste associated with innovations in educational technologies, and more particularly, ways to break the cycle. He described a phenomenon he calls "rapture of the technology" whereby the technology itself is overemphasised, and the strategic ingredients needed for meeting the educational/institutional objectives neglected. "Rapture of the technology also is a kind of amnesia" and "self-defeating, like a tapeworm so greedy it kills its host" (Ehrmann 2001b).

In her keynote, Robin Mason from the UK addressed the question of learning technologies leading to new modes of learning. She said that she believed that online teaching and learning has been "over-emphasised as a new paradigm". Rather, "training is needed as much because of lack of emphasis on teaching in HE generally as because online teaching is different". For Mason, the technology is only a tool, a "delivery vehicle". It is human-dependent, and it can be used "badly or brilliantly" (Mason, 2001). Addressing the problem of researching the use of new learning technologies, Mason sparked lively discussion in the corridors, dinners and process groups about this. She questioned the seeming proliferation of very small-scale action research projects, stating that there has been a "lack of research in online learning" and a preponderance of the detailed "'this is how it was for me' approach" (Mason, 2001). She called instead for an effort to conduct large-scale longitudinal studies.

In the closing keynote, Ron Oliver from Australia noted the paucity of examples of good practice in the use of online learning environments. In particular he spoke with disdain about a "content-driven", approach which primarily involves reading; communication is largely restricted to individual reflection; and assessment is conventional and often lacks authenticity, much less validity. Instead, Oliver proposed a design framework for online learning that shifts the emphasis away from content delivery and onto student activity, or the "learning design". He offered the perspective of relatively "content-poor" online learning environments that can nevertheless offer the student high levels of engagement and richness of learning.

The symposium was designed to run in conjunction with the Association for Learning Technology conference which took place immediately after ISL, also in Edinburgh, and I acknowledge with gratitude their co-operation in the organisation of this. Finally, I would like to use this opportunity to also publicly acknowledge the invaluable work of the OCSLD/ISL team – Fiona Smith, Marje Bolton, and Nina Woods – in making the Symposium a success, and also to wish Nina every happiness in her new job.

Chris Rust

Oxford Centre for Staff and Learning Development, Oxford Brookes University, March 2002

1 Using technology to improve the outcomes of higher education: learning from past mistakes

Stephen C. Ehrmann
Teaching, Learning & Technology Group, USA

1.1 Overview

Over the last forty years, many technology investments have been justified partly by hopes that educational outcomes would be improved. By outcomes, I mean who graduates from a degree or certificate programme, what they know and can do by the time they graduate, and what it cost to educate them. Learning computer programming would teach them more sophisticated skills of logical thinking and design. Simulations would create a new world of skilled, insightful graduates. Email and computer conferencing would result in graduates with notably better skills in collaboration and insights into different cultures. The most consistent promise was that the computer-aided tutorials would enable students to learn faster, better and at less expense.

Although computers have often been of great educational value in other ways (e.g. new content, access for more learners, personal efficiency), many hopes for improved teaching-learning effectiveness have been frustrated since the 1960s. When it's been noticed, each failure was usually blamed on inadequate technology (the same technology that had been greeted with such hope when it first appeared only a few years earlier). Actually the problem lies more with the ways we acquire and use technology to improve outcomes.

- Enraptured by technology, we fail to budget enough attention and money for the other 'ingredients' needed to support large-scale improvements in teaching-learning practice and educational outcomes.

- Each new technology brings with it a different agenda for improvement. But it takes a long time to achieve improvements in outcomes, often longer than the life span of the technology that had triggered the initial hope. As technologies come and go, institutions and governments twitch from one educational vision to another, rarely sticking with any one goal long enough to achieve noticeable improvement in outcomes.

- Not all improvement agendas alter with every new technology. One such vision has been a constant for almost every new technology for the last 40 years: the development of large bodies of interactive, self-paced, cost-effective courseware. Yet after many fresh starts, we have not been able to achieve that vision either.

Using technology to make real progress in outcomes is difficult but it's probably not impossible:

- Select an educational outcome that is likely to be valued strongly enough and long enough to be accomplished (5–8 years in some cases), an outcome for which technology can be used to carry out key activities in new and better ways.

- Choose technologies likely to progress incrementally while helping to implement the evolving 'recipe'.

- Focus mostly on courseware formats that the average instructor can easily, inexpensively and quickly create, adapt, share and, when appropriate, abandon, while helping communities of instructors make progress.

- Use longitudinal study to help maintain focus and resources on the programme of improvement.

- Use diagnostic studies to help spot problems at the large and small scale that might otherwise slow or derail the desired improvements.

- Develop coalitions that can advance the programme. Teaching, Learning, and Technology Roundtables provide a setting for such coalition-building.

1.2 A story of failure and hope

Once upon a time, two hunters hired a pilot and light plane to fly them into the back country of Canada for some moose hunting. After an hour of flying, the little plane arrived over a small clearing high in the mountains. As he circled, the pilot announced his intention to land. The hunters were alarmed. The tiny meadow didn't look big enough for a successful takeoff, especially not with the added weight of a moose. 'Don't worry,' the pilot reassured them, 'I've landed in that very spot half a dozen times already!'

So they landed, hunted, bagged a moose, loaded it in the plane, and prepared for takeoff. With throttle at full power, the brakes were released and the tiny craft began bouncing over the rough ground. At the last minute, the pilot hauled back on the controls, the nose lifted, and the plane just barely cleared the nearest trees. Their problems were not over, however. The overloaded aircraft climbed with painful slowness, engine labouring in the thin air, and a series of ridges were coming up fast, each one higher than the last. Quickly a second stand of trees passed just beneath their straining wings and then a third. It didn't seem possible that they could climb fast enough to avoid the next ridge with its crown of trees. The pilot gave a final pull at the controls, the propeller snapped into the branches, and then there was a thunderous crash!

Silence returned to the forest and, after a moment, birds began to sing again. The battered plane balanced precariously in the branches of a tall tree. Finally, moans were heard as the three occupants of the plane recovered consciousness, tested their limbs, and called out to one another. The loudest voice was that of the pilot. 'This is great!' he shouted, peering from a shattered window. 'We got at least 30 yards further than the last time I tried to take off from that clearing!'

1.3 Generations of technology, achievement and waste

Trite statements often become trite because they are true. Take the statement 'Digital technology can revolutionise education.' Experiments and small-scale applications long ago provided convincing evidence of that promise. In fact, every few years, a major new computer chip, visual medium or telecommunications channel comes along. Often, new successes are quickly attained by early adaptors, and vendors help spread the word. The revolution really does seem about to happen. And in the next few years some larger, important improvements are usually made. But after a while, it becomes clear that many of those hopes were not realised. It has happened time after time, and there seems to be a pattern to the failures.

Table 1.1 is just a partial sketch of some of the educational hopes aroused by successive generations of new electronic technology since the 1960s.

A New Electronic Technology (period in which excitement about it was at its height)	A Few of the Educational Reasons for Investing in New Technology		
	Self-paced, interactive courseware that makes learning better, faster, and cheaper	Plus a distinctive educational agenda that is illuminated in powerful ways by this particular technology	Tools and resources developed for the wider world but also used for teaching and learning ("Worldware")
Mainframe Computing and time-sharing (1970-1980) [variety of operating systems changing over time, not usually compatible with one another]	Computer-assisted tutorials and assessment (interactive, self-paced, branching)	Simulation	Word processors; engineering and scientific programming and software packages for design, analysis, data retrieval, etc.
Computers with videodisc players (late 1970s – late 1980s)	(See above)	Visualization	Image archives in fields such as biology, art
Microcomputer (standalone) (early1980s – late 1980s)	(See above)	Learning Basic, Logo, etc. in order to learn computer skills, new skills of reasoning	Better word processors, spreadsheets, statistical software, paint program, widening range of tools from various disciplines
HyperCard (late 1980s – early 1990s)	(See above)	Students learn by creating hypertext resources	Students learn by creating hypertext resources
Computer conferencing systems (Late 1980s – early 1990s)	(See above)	1) Collaborative learning, 2) access for more kinds of learners	E-mail, asynchronous conferencing; chat
Web (late '90's to the present)	(See above)	1) Access for more kinds of learners; cut costs; 2) expanding the library	Global collection of information from business, entertainment, education, etc. Advances in some of the earlier forms of worldware

Table 1.1   Generations of technology, and educational reasons for buying it

People who focus on hardware, software and connectivity (the first column) have a right to be proud of the progress in the power and pervasiveness of our technological infrastructure in higher education over the last forty years.

However, observers who know the history of the second ('interactive courseware') column might wince because such software has never become the source of visible, international improvements in the outcomes of education at any level.

The distinctive educational goals described in the third column only rarely led to changes visible at the institutional and national levels. 'Access for more kinds of learners' (via distance learning) seems a rare and recent exception to that record of frustration.

The 'worldware' agenda (column 4) has shown more cumulative achievement in educational practice. Libraries of biology slides originally created for videodisc were often translated to CD-ROM and then sometimes to the Web. Educators using spreadsheets as mathematical construction kits were able to make steady progress in the 1980s, 1990 and early 2000s, even when spreadsheet software and vendors appeared and disappeared; they could always run last year's files with this year's machines. Educators and learners use worldware sometimes for reasons of efficiency (word processors instead of typewriters) and sometimes to tackle academic materials they couldn't or wouldn't deal with otherwise (e.g. molecular modelling in chemistry; computer graphics; analysis of large bodies of political science data). The outcome improvements easiest to document are all in this column: new competences and new degree programmes that are technology-dependent, starting with computer science and spreading across the curriculum (digital music, many of today's skills in political science etc.).

The good news is that there has (probably) been cumulative, national progress in educational outcomes in at least those three directions: new technology-relevant content; personal efficiency and (recently) access for large numbers of learners, including some types of learners (those with non-traditional schedules or locations) who were less well served before. (For a longer list of some of these dreams, many of which have succeeded at the level of individual courses and some of which have had success on a larger scale as well, see Steve Gilbert's recent paper, 'Why Bother?' http://www.tltgroup.org/gilbert/WhyBotherHOME.htm)

What about those other dreams, some in the table, some not: dreams of more active, collaborative learning, of improved learning outcomes, of better assessment of learning, of internationalising the curriculum, of improving quantitative literacy, communications skills, information literacy, and skills for doing creative work? They seemed realistic at the time - as a staff member in funding programmes I argued that many such proposals be supported over twenty years and exulted at early, promising evaluation results. In fact, I *still* believe many of those dreams were realistic in their descriptions of what the technology of the day could be used to achieve. So why didn't those dreams come true, too?

Each new technology rides in on claims about the inadequacy of earlier technologies. 'Buy the new technology to augment or replace the old technology and your dreams will come true.' But it now seems to me that the dreams have each been frustrated for reasons that have little to do with the strengths of the new 'new technology' or the weaknesses of the old 'new technology'.

There are at least three basic problems that have dogged most attempts to translate technological improvements into educational improvements:

- Confusing one ingredient (technology) with the whole recipe (educational improvement). As a result, when too much attention is invested in just one ingredient and, when initial improvement results are disappointing, the response has usually been to buy a newer, better version of the treasured ingredient while continuing to ignore the rest of the recipe.

- Forgetting that the lifespan of many new technologies is far shorter than the time it takes to implement that recipe for improving educational outcomes. Thus, long before outcomes improve, new technologies begin distracting attention from the 'old' improvement agenda. Worse, course materials and skills developed for (what is now) old technology may not fit the new technology.

- Ignoring the fact that one of those educational recipes – large-scale reliance on interactive, self-paced, cost-effective courseware – has been tried with almost every new technology of the last four decades.

- Let's look at these three problems separately (even though they overlap).

1.4   An ingredient, not a recipe – rapture of the technology

I sometimes imagine that yeast was first discovered as a foodstuff when someone accidentally found it could be used to make a primitive form of bread – a kind of puffy cracker, perhaps a little soggy in spots, but tasty and very promising.

The yeast-masters took over the baking of these new puffy crackers because they knew about yeast, without which puffy crackers couldn't be made. Also yeast was mysterious to most folks, so the yeast-masters became the 'Priests of the Puffy Crackers'. After a time, people became disappointed with this primitive bread; puffy crackers didn't taste as good nor were they as plentiful as the yeast-masters had predicted a few years earlier. Fortunately the yeast-masters had an answer: a new and more expensive form of yeast had just become available. And this new yeast really *was* better. But, when it was used, somehow the puffy crackers didn't get better. No one noticed that at first, because the new yeast was so exciting. By the time hungry people did notice that puffy crackers were still disappointing, the yeast-masters had fortunately discovered the answer. Better yeast!

Let's return to education. Imagine, for example, that a department wants to internationalise its curriculum. Obviously, the World Wide Web can play a crucial role if enough money is spent on computers and connectivity for faculty members, the library, students and other key staff. But it should be obvious that spending money on hardware and connectivity is not sufficient to internationalise the curriculum. Nor is it sufficient to add a small budget to make sure that everyone knows how to turn on the hardware and use the basic commands of the software. Obviously, it's equally crucial to fund appropriate faculty development regarding those other cultures and about ways to teach about unfamiliar cultures. The programme will need to buy and produce new curricular materials, not all of them technological. Many books will be needed for the library: paper is a good reading surface and, more important, many crucial materials are not available electronically. These days, to take advantage of the potential of the technology for internationalising the curriculum, the institution will also need to create or join a network of people and organisations in the countries under study.

That set of diverse ingredients is what I mean by the metaphor of a 'recipe'. In order to have a hope of using technology to improve educational activities and their outcomes, institutions need more than just that technology.

Unfortunately, rapture of the technology often siphons money and attention away from those other ingredients as the institution strives to buy the best computers and the fastest connectivity. Later, we find it easy to believe that dreams aren't coming true because the technology (that looked so good only a few years earlier) isn't good enough.

Even worse, rapture of the technology leads people to believe that, each time technology changes, the experiences of the past become irrelevant. Who needs to learn about 35 years of past experience with educational uses of technology now that we have the World Wide Web? Isn't that history of success and failure now irrelevant? For this reason, and because so many new people are drawn in by each new technology, rapture of technology creates a kind of amnesia.

For all these reasons, rapture of the technology is self-defeating: a tapeworm so greedy that it kills its host. When it comes to using technology to improve outcomes, computers may or may not be their own worst enemy but computer zealots often are.

1.5 A brief window of opportunity: Moore's Law

Whether you are in 1968, 1988 or 2008, only 12–18 months 'ago' computer chips were only half as powerful; 12–18 months from 'now' they will be twice as powerful. That's Moore's Law.

Each predictable doubling of chip power enables the development of surprising new tools for thinking, analysing, studying, creating, and communicating in the world. Products and professions erupt, altering the content of some disciplines, creating new fields, and compelling new forms of interdisciplinary collaboration in the wider world. The level of education required for many jobs is increasing as well. So technological change in the wider world both increases the number of people who need an education and changes what they need to learn.

Moore's Law has also created waves of improvement in the processes on which education most relies: how people can get and use information and how they can communicate with one another. That's one reason why each new generation of technology seems capable of producing unprecedented changes in how students learn and what they learn.

Moore's Law, unfortunately, is a double-edged sword. With advances in chips and other computer equipment (memory, disk drives, connectivity, displays) come changes in operating systems. When hardware and operating systems change, older software may no longer work unless it's upgraded, and the costs to upgrade it are often enormous. Even if the course material does still work with the new operating systems, it may look so old-fashioned that institutions and students are reluctant to use it.

New technology often doesn't stick around for long: sometimes only a year or two, sometimes five years, occasionally seven years or more. Let's be charitable and say 'seven years'. Even seven years is often just barely enough to implement that complex recipe (e.g. faculty development, course development, faculty skills, library resources, organisational partnerships, the programme's image and recruiting processes, and so on). It can easily take five or six years before we can glimpse the first valuable improvements in what students are doing after graduation. If the technology is going to become obsolete in seven years, that doesn't give us much time to accomplish the improvement before the technology is ripped away and we have to start over. Does that sound bad? The reality is even worse – we usually don't have seven years because other factors prevent us from using the full life cycle of the technology to make progress.

1.5.1 Temporary pedagogical regression

A curious kind of dance step characterises the educational capabilities of each new generation of technology in its early years of use: a small pedagogical step backward precedes the larger step forward. Each of these temporary regressions has several typical causes.

(a) *At first, fewer people have the new technology than the old one, even though the new technology will eventually become more widely used than its predecessor.* During this period when few people have the new technology, it's hard to spread new ideas about changing education with it. People often can't visualise the improvement until they have the equipment and have become comfortable using it for more traditional purposes.

(b) *Initially, the new technology is not as good or flexible for instruction as the old technology*

- The old technology had been around long enough to develop the capability to handle, for example, non-Western alphabets, mathematical expressions and writing from right to left or from top to bottom. Probes were probably developed that could enable the computers of the day to collect data from science experiments. Bar-code readers were developed that could link teachers to get random access to images. Screen readers help blind students and faculty to use the hardware. But those handy devices don't work with the new computers. After a period of time, the new technology will develop these capabilities and more. For a few years, however, its basic capabilities may be quite uneven.

- The old technology also had time to breed sophisticated authoring aids for courseware development. A generation of authors then became skilled in the use of those tools. At first, however, the new hardware has no such authoring tools and no group of experienced authors. In time they too will appear.

As a result of these backward steps, each new generation of technology begins its teaching–learning life in a promising but relatively primitive state. In two to four years all that will have changed. But, you can hear the ticking of Moore's clock as we wait for the zag to reverse the initial zig. By the time the non-Roman alphabets, screen readers, and authoring tools arrive, the 'new' generation of technology often doesn't have many more years to live and when it goes, the courseware developed to run on it often disappears, too.

1.5.2   Moore's Babel

Moore's Law also makes it harder for technology support staff and technology users to speak the same language. If technology remained the same for decades, many faculty members would learn to help themselves (as they have with VCRs), and at least some technology support staff would develop a more sophisticated understanding of education. But thanks to Moore's Law, users periodically find themselves beginners all over again. Just as bad, that constant technological change helps to ensure that many technology support staff are new, in that people are hired because they are among the few who understand the new systems. These new staff members haven't had much time to learn to look at the world through the eyes of an instructor.

1.6   The interactive courseware mirage

Since the days of the mainframe computer, many hopes for technology have been based on the promise of interactive, branching curricular courseware for making learning faster and less expensive. Based on principles of self-paced instruction, this interactive software features frequent assessment of student responses that guide the next instruction that the student sees.

If the assessment shows low performance, the next step might be remedial. If the assessment is unexpectedly strong, the student may be leapfrogged to more ambitious material.

Research showed decades ago that self-paced instruction has the power to improve and accelerate learning by about one-third, compared with lectures and conventional assignments on the same topic. (For references on this research, see section 1.9, Resources and further reading, at the end of this chapter.) Further, because interactive courseware can substitute for at least some teacher time and is inexpensive to copy, the more students who use a particular courseware package, the lower the cost per student.

Interactive self-paced courseware is no panacea, of course. Such courseware only works well in areas where learning can be organised into chunks, and sequences of chunks, and where answers can be predicted and marked right/wrong. Even so there are many areas where interactive courseware is appropriate. That's why self-paced instruction's lure of improved results and decreased unit costs has been powerful for so long. But so far, as a means of improving the outcomes of a higher education on a national scale, interactive courseware has proved to be a mirage, always imminent, never quite here.

The problems begin Moore's Law – such courseware becomes obsolete when the underlying hardware, operating systems, languages and authoring systems change. When computers shift from MS-DOS to Macintosh, or when authors shift from PLATO to Basic to Java applets, they need to start over, developing courseware from scratch. If version 1.0 of a teaching concept was expensive to develop on last year's technology, version 2.0 may cost as much or more to 'upgrade' so that it works on this year's system.

There are other barriers, too.

For example, interactive courseware remains expensive to develop and update. With each new generation of technology and authoring aids, we hear promises that, at last, interactive courseware will become far cheaper to create. But that hope is based on the false premise that slow computers were to blame for higher development costs of the last generation of courseware. The real costs, however, come from the time it takes humans to conceive, design and debug all those branching educational pathways: the more branches, the greater the pedagogical complexity of the task.

Secondly, each new generation of technology brings a more sophisticated 'look and feel' than its precursor. So there are new development expenses (including new design skills and tools) to buy each time the underlying technology advances. For these and other reasons, it still usually takes hundreds or thousands of hours of producer time, and a lot of money, to create reliable, distributable courseware that students go through in just an hour or two.

Meanwhile time is passing and with each passing month the window of opportunity for this generation of technology closes a little farther. It takes time:

- to raise the money needed to create the courseware;

- to create pilot versions and sometimes to evaluate them;

- for potential users to 'skim' unfamiliar interactive courseware, far longer than the time needed to size up a textbook.

Once users grasp what the new technology offers, they may not instantly leap to obtain it. In fact, the more revolutionary the courseware's implications for transforming the instructional programme, the more cautious potential users become: making a change in their teaching this big could lead to unforeseen problems so why not wait until someone else has done it first?

To sum up, it can easily take several years to develop courseware with the potential to transform the way a difficult topic is taught, and still more years for that courseware to find national acceptance. In fact, it takes so many years that version 1.0 has begun to look rather old-fashioned before it ever does find wide use.

That *might* be fixed by creating version 2.0 of the courseware. But version 2.0 appears much later, if at all. No one has the motivation. Developers on a tenure track are rarely promoted for doing a second edition – it isn't enough of an advance in the state of the art – and foundation programme officers don't get much credit for funding second editions either. Another motivation is money, but publishers are unlikely to put up the money because they almost never realise sufficient return on their investment in version 1.0, so they're feeling burned. It takes a lot of money, too, to create version 2.0. Good second editions of courseware often cost as much as the first edition, in part because computers themselves have changed so much in the intervening years (Moore's Law again).

So instead of triggering an educational revolution in its discipline, the award-winning version 1.0 of the courseware fades away. Of course new interactive courseware will spring up, designed from the start for the new generation of technology. But it's often so different from the old courseware that everyone must start over or stop using interactive courseware. Many choose this second option.

Perhaps this explains why this exciting effective type of software has thus far produced so little improvement in the outcomes of higher education after so many decades of predictions that courseware-enabled improvements were just about to change everything.

1.7 Six strategies for using technology to improve outcomes on a large scale

Progress, far from consisting of change, depends on retentiveness. Those who do not learn from the past are condemned to repeat it. (George Santayana)

Moore's Law is real, and there is no way completely to escape the battering. The world's use of technology will continue to change, and if we tried to ignore that fact, we'd be making the biggest mistake of all: allowing education to fall behind the world in which its students must live.

The key is for education itself to learn to live with the rapid pace of change and make choices that enable us to improve effectiveness and outcomes. Here are six interrelated considerations for selecting and implementing a long-term programme of improvement.

1. long-term focus on a direction for *educational* improvement that several generations of technology can help to advance;
2. technology platforms for the long term;
3. courseware formats for the long term;
4. longitudinal study to focus attention and guide strategy;
5. diagnostic studies to guide tactics and reduce costs, stress; and
6. coalitions that span traditional barriers in order to support the programme.

1.7.1 Long-term focus on selected outcomes and the activities needed to improve them

The single most important message of this chapter is that educational outcomes take far longer to improve than the likely lifespan of a single generation of technology. Therefore, if an institution or a nation is to make educational and technological progress, its technological choices must to some degree be subordinated to some long-term educational priorities.

That's easy to say and almost impossible to accomplish in an environment shaken by the winds of Moore's Law as well as political change in institutions and governments. However, looking at 40 years of waste and frustration may stiffen our resolve. Other strategies outlined here are designed to help make such long-term focus more feasible.

What types of outcomes can technology help your department, institution, system or nation improve? Here are some examples where technology has already shown promise; some of these overlap and they are not in any particular order:

- collaborative skills and linkages to wider communities of practice; graduates who excel in collaborative and community building skills useful in the face to face and online worlds;

- international and intercultural understanding;

- learning practices and outcomes that are advanced by greater numbers of students, and a greater diversity of students (just as today's libraries are better when they have more books);

- graduates who excel in designing and composing in one or more fields; graduates who have learned to basic skills of designing and composing as skills as part of their general education (e.g. creating newsletter, designing a living room, composing music for pleasure);

- graduates who excel in quantitative analytic approaches and model-making strategies;

- institutions that excel in assessment of learning, and thereby advance their educational agendas;

- systems and governments that offer unprecedented arrays of specialised study options and staff to all students;

- access to education for specific types of students;

- shift towards active, constructivist learning strategies (e.g. projects that are sometimes developed by teams) and away from over-reliance on lectures, page-turning and other relatively passive teaching strategies. Outcomes should include more lasting understanding and ability to apply learning after graduation.

Obviously institutions and nations made progress in each of these directions long before computers became available. But today there are decades of experience suggesting that technology has already helped improve outcomes, at least on a small scale, in each of these areas. For example, the educational use of technology for collaboration and community building dates back at least to the PLATO mainframe instructional system of the 1970s, the EIES computer conferencing system of the early 1980s, and early uses of Internet and Web mail in the 1990s.

1.7.2 Choose technology that can contribute to long-term, cumulative improvement in the chosen activities

At the same time that goals are being chosen, the institution needs to be thinking about technology. And the question of technology needs to be readdressed each time the buzz rises about the newest new thing.

At least four questions ought to be asked about any major purchase of technology after the institution has begun to get a sense of educational direction:

1. *Value-added?* Does this new technology promise to help make major progress towards improving learning outcomes in the chosen area, compared with other ways of spending money for that purpose (including but not limited to other old and new technologies)?
2. *Reasonable operating costs?* It is difficult to build cutting-edge education on cutting-edge technology: truly new technology is usually brittle, expensive, and hard to support. That's fine for experiments but not fine for advancing mainstream educational practices and materials. And there's the pedagogical regression we talked about earlier. Has enough time elapsed so that this new technology is 'ready for prime time'? Are other institutions beginning to use the same new technology for the same purposes as your institution so that your faculty members won't have develop all the new materials and practices by themselves?
3. *Transition costs this time?* If so, what are the chances that the change in underlying technology will disrupt the strategy that has been taking shape? Will curricular materials need to be discarded or are they likely to be translated easily? Will faculty need to learn a whole new set of skills? Will institutional spaces need to be substantially rebuilt?
4. *Transition costs next time?* Finally, in a few years, as this technology ages and becomes obsolete, will there likely be another family of technologies that will also have manageable costs of transition? If this technology has low initial transition costs 'in', it may well also have low transition costs 'out'.

Where should we look for such technology for the long term? One direction is 'worldware'. Let's define worldware to be hardware or software that is used for education but that was not developed or marketed primarily for education. Examples include computers, the Web, productivity tools such as word processors and spreadsheets, and research tools such as computer-aided design software and online census data.

Worldware usually has several features that help it support incremental, long-term educational improvement. Because of worldware often has a larger market than software designed only for instruction, it often advances incrementally and faces competition. An important side-benefit – a new vendor's software can often read files created by its larger and older competitors. That's why any faculty member who began using spreadsheets as a mathematics construction kit in physics courses in 1979 could improve her teaching for the next twenty years, taking advantage of new spreadsheet features and new ideas in physics. She would never have been forced to abandon assignments or handouts simply because a spreadsheet vendor had gone out of business. Without missing a beat, such instructors could move their spreadsheets from MS-DOS to Macintosh, from Windows 3.1 to Windows98. In contrast, colleagues who reformed their courses by relying new interactive courseware in

1979 (or 1989 or 1994) might well have been marooned when computer operating systems changed, rendering their packages obsolete.

Worldware has other educational advantages, also, such its familiarity to faculty (they use it in their research), motivation for students to master its use (they know they'll need to learn to use it for future jobs), and a market base that is large enough to help provide good support materials and outside training. In these ways, worldware can reduce stress on the exhausted, understaffed technology support units at your institution.

Worldware may lack of some of the short-term value of interactive courseware but it more than makes up for it in long-term viability and ease of support.

1.7.3 Emphasise forms of instructional material that most faculty members find it quick and easy to create, adapt and share

Interactive courseware can be extraordinarily powerful but, as pointed out above, such courseware rarely has enough users to keep it alive for long. Highly interactive courseware has another problem, too. The bigger and more complex the courseware, the more rigid it usually is: a challenge for instructors who want to adapt it to a particular set of students, a particular day's events, or their own slant on how a skill or topic might best be learned. Such courseware formats work best for widely taught, large enrolment courses where there is a widely held, lasting agreement about how to teach the course. For such courses, costs per student can be kept down, too, especially if the courseware lasts long enough to make enough a success for its investors to justify upgrading it as operating environments advance.

Obviously that course format doesn't work for most faculty and most courses. For them, a 'small is beautiful' strategy may be more to the point.

These instructors (whether working alone or in relatively small communities that may span institution boundaries) need course materials that they can easily, quickly, and inexpensively modify. For example, a word-processed syllabus is easier, quicker and cheaper to modify than a typed one; a Web syllabus can be even better for those purposes because all students can see the changes at once. The challenge is to come up with materials and assignments that are educationally powerful, but still inexpensive for the typical academic staff to develop, modify and share.

A second requirement is resources be invested in a continuing way to help faculty organise, edit and share their incremental improvements. Progress can be made without such processes, but it will almost certainly be slower.

1.7.4 Track the progress of the strategy to get the data (and money) needed to stay on course

If we want to describe how technology can improve the outcomes of a higher education programme, we need at least three elements:

1   a set or sequence of technologies that are used over the years, plus other ingredients for the 'recipe';
2.   the educational activities for which people use those technologies and other ingredients; and
3.   The outcomes that those activities are intended to improve, as well as other results of the effort.

Let's call this three-part vision a 'triad'.

The challenge facing the instructional programme (or institution, or nation) is to maintain focus on the triad for enough years to achieve meaningful improvements in the outcomes. Longitudinal (periodic) studies of the triad-in-use can help maintain focus and advance the 'recipe' in at least three different ways.

First, in the early phases of an improvement programme, evaluation can help maintain focus by reporting on whether the ingredients of the strategy are coming into place and working well, and whether the activities have begun to change. It's too early to expect changes in outcomes – students have not taken enough of the altered courses and few, if any, have graduated. Providing feedback indicating that the early steps are going well can help maintain energy.

Of course, the early steps may not be going as planned, which leads us to the second use of longitudinal studies. Such studies can provide data useful for guiding and fine-tuning the strategy. For example, the initial strategy might have neglected the importance of enlarging the library's collection or the need to form new external partnerships. Early evaluative study may show that teaching activities are not changing as expected and that these gaps are one of the reasons. By drawing attention to a problem, the study can help solve it.

Thirdly, documented achievements can be used to solicit support and raise money for institutions. That may be crucial. Institutions are rarely rewarded for improving teaching effectiveness. In fact, if one or more institutions in your state or nation became 10 per cent more effective, or less effective, it's quite possible no one would notice. That's one reason why institutions so rarely provide adequate rewards for faculty who take risks to improve their own courses – where are those rewards to come from? If the institution is no better off as a result of the collective efforts of such risk-taking faculty, then rewards must be cannibalised from other budgets. That's pretty risky, politically. So this third reason to evaluate progress is so that evaluation data can be used to help make the invisible progress more visible to the outside world. If data can help draw new resources to the institution, then risk-takers can be rewarded without penalising others.

1.7.5 Diagnose problems 'on the ground' as they occur in order to increase your chances of success while reducing stress and other costs

Continued turbulent change almost guarantees that individuals and units will miss important opportunities and, worse, will be ambushed by problems they failed to see in time.

Imagine, for example, that your programme has selected 'collaborative skill and academic community' as a guiding theme for a decade of progress. You've redesigned the course in ways that depend upon students using the Web to collaborate on homework projects. You've never asked students to do much work together on homework before. It's now week two of the term. It's hard to know for sure but you fear that students are not collaborating on line as much or as well as you'd hoped. The course's schedule and success might be in jeopardy. Or maybe everything is OK. Is there really a problem? If so, why?

- Perhaps some students lack adequate hardware and software?
- Do some students believe that collaborative learning is a waste of time?
- Do some students fear that if they work together they will be labelled as cheats?
- Are your assignments so easy for a student to do alone that it's not worth his or her effort to collaborate?

- Did some students not take the training in how to use email and computer conferencing?

These and literally dozens of barriers *could* hinder collaboration online. But which of these barriers are actually hindering your students? Unless you can find out quickly, you may soon be in real trouble.

Our intuition often doesn't do us much good in such situations because our insights were shaped by stable times. 'Muddling through' isn't good enough anymore. The clock is likely to strike midnight before we have time to learn what is hitting us, within a course or as an institution.

The answer seems to lie with increased use of diagnostic tools. Some of these strategies are quite simple and generic, such as 'minute papers'. Other tools could be developed for specific purposes, e.g. a set of diagnostic procedures designed to help educators and their institutions improve online collaboration among students.

One area most in need of diagnostic help involves the costs and other stresses created by our emerging uses of technology. I once sat briefly with a group of faculty and staff who were analysing the total costs involved when support staff helped faculty use technology in their courses. It's fair to say that everyone in this little group was appalled, despite the fact that all of them had been intimately involved in the process for years. They were so surprised even though each had known that his or her piece of the work was stressful, expensive and/or time-consuming. However, each had also assumed that everyone else was doing work that was simpler, easier, and cheaper. Diagnosing the stresses created by the current activities is the first step toward redesigning them in time – before large-scale burnout and busted budgets derail the improvement programme.

1.7.6   Create coalitions to make sure that your programme has all the ingredients needed in your recipe for improving outcomes

One of the most unnatural acts in making a technology-enabled improvement of outcomes is for the technology lovers to make common cause with others who also care about the goal and activity but who are neutral or 'anti' when it comes to hardware. If these groups succeed in creating a coalition, however, they can campaign to build support for the whole recipe together.

Think of the math this way. Imagine an institution with 100 staff members. Imagine that five of them care passionately about computing, five care equally about collaboration, about internationalisation, and or about academic community. At budget time, or policy-making time, five of them would normally battle for what they want against the opposition or apathy of 95 others. Predict the outcome. Now assume that these 20 people make common cause in order to use technology and other ingredients to create an international community of learners, and learning. For each budget issue and policy choice (whether about a hardware buy or a change in course requirements) 20 of them make themselves heard. That's a different situation entirely.

The greater the value of the improved outcomes, by the way, the easier it may be to assemble a coalition of groups who wouldn't collaborate if the stakes were lower. Most improvement efforts don't attract big coalitions because there is little at stake.

Such collaboration was once rather rare in educational institutions. People didn't have to collaborate in order to function. For that and other reasons, higher education attracted people who valued their autonomy and who 'did not work and play well with others'. That's one reason why traditional universities are relatively poor at information sharing, especially 'diagonally' across administrative units and vertically across levels of authority.

With technology and the world changing as fast as they do today, failure to share information, cooperate, and collaborate can have unhappy consequences for an institution. 'We must indeed all hang together or, most assuredly, we shall all hang separately,' said Benjamin Franklin on 4 July 1776. His remark applies to institutions of higher education today. Collaboration, within and among institutions, is becoming a survival skill. This is not without precedent. Only a few hundred years ago, most scholars did their work alone. Then the emerging universities enabled scholars to enter a new world, if they were willing (or eager) to specialise and surrender some of their autonomy. Meanwhile, the scholars who remained completely independent faced increasingly limited options for research and teaching.

Today, collaboration is slowly and sometimes painfully increasing among institutions who realise that working closely together on creating virtual learning environments, managing online information, marketing their services to students and other tasks, give them advantages over institutions that continue to go it alone.

The survival value of collaboration within institutions is also one reason why the notion of 'Teaching, Learning, and Technology Roundtables' has spread so rapidly since Steven W. Gilbert introduced it in the mid-1990s. Over 400 institutions have created TLT Roundtables that meet regularly to share information, to coordinate activities and, often, to create small action teams to work on problems that are not within the province of any single unit or individual in the institution. Most successful TLT Roundtables are actively supported by the chief academic officer and other leaders, to whom the TLTR makes recommendations on key budget and policy decisions.

It's no coincidence that TLT Roundtables began to appear the same year that studies by Kenneth Green revealed the beginning of the current mainstreaming of computers for teaching. And recently a dissertation by Daryl Nardick revealed that one gain associated with successful TLT Roundtables is an increased ability to move information quickly from outside the institution to all those inside who most need it.

My main point here is that Roundtables and some of these consortial structures provide suitable settings for discussing long-term programmes of educational improvement and the strategies needed to accomplish them over five or ten years.

1.8   Closing thought

Today's world relies upon rapidly changing computer technology in almost every phase of life. That creates a breakneck pace of change for the academy. In this new world, the old 'muddling through' approach to educational improvement doesn't work well any more. The window of opportunity associated with each new generation of educational technology closes too quickly.

Ironically the solution is not move faster. Nor does it work to follow our instincts about what will work and what will fail. Instead, this time, we need to study 40 years of past failures and successes. This time, we need to get it right.

1.9 Resources and additional reading

For more background on 'worldware' and the courseware mirage, see P.M. Morris, S.C. Ehrmann, R.B. Goldsmith, K.J. Howat and M.S. Vijay Kumar (eds) (1994) *Valuable, Viable Software in Education: Case Studies and Analysis*. New York: McGraw-Hill.

One example of a meta-analysis of the research on interactive, self-paced courseware is R.E. Clark (1983) Reconsidering research on learning from media, *Educational Research* **53** (Winter): 445–59. Clark pointed out that self-paced instruction, whether computer-based or not, tends to enable learners to learn much faster and better (in those content areas where assessment can be automated and where content can be organised into sequence of bits that can be organised into sequences and branches). For a paper focused more directly on courseware, see C-L.C. Kulik and J.A. Kulik (1991) Effectiveness of computer-based instruction: an updated analysis, *Computers in Human Behavior* **7**(1–2): 75–94. The Kuliks have done such analyses for some time, and earlier papers are referenced in this 1991 summary.

The *Flashlight Program*, directed by Dr Ehrmann, provides tools, resources, coaching and consulting for doing the longitudinal and diagnostic studies outlined in this chapter. For more information on The Flashlight program see
http://www.tltgroup.org/programs/flashlight.html.

For an earlier, more detailed version of the evaluation suggestions in this essay, see S.C. Ehrmann (2000) Computer-intensive academic programs: how to evaluate, plan, support and implement (in that order) your campus technology investments, *AAHE Bulletin* **53**(3) (Nov.): 7–11. Draft at http://www.tltgroup.org/resources/F_Eval_Computer-Intensive.htm.

For more on TLT Roundtables, see http://www.tltgroup.org/programs/round.html.

About the author: While doing his doctoral dissertation research in the early 1970s, Stephen C. Ehrmann began his study of educational uses of computing with an analysis of 1960s applications in the MIT Department of Civil Engineering. In 1978 he became Program Officer with the Fund for the Improvement of Postsecondary Education (FIPSE) of the US Government, where he spent much of his time reviewing technology-related proposals and monitoring funded projects. In 1985, he left FIPSE to become Program Officer for Interactive Technologies with the Annenberg/CPB Project, where he helped fund and monitor projects involving innovation and research on educational uses of technology. In 1992, while with Annenberg/CPB he began a process leading to the creation of the Flashlight Program for the Study and Improvement of Educational Uses of Technology, a programme he still directs in his role as Vice President of the non-profit Teaching, Learning, and Technology Group in Washington DC. For more information on the TLT Group, Teaching Learning and Technology Roundtables and the Flashlight Program, see http://www.tltgroup.org

2 E-learning: what have we learnt?

Robin Mason

The Open University, UK

2.1 Introduction

Despite a deluge of conferences, case studies and journal articles about computer conferencing and online courses over the last ten years, remarkably little evidence has emerged about best practice, how to design successful online environments, and what works well and what does not. One problem has been that practitioners and researchers have been experimenting on a moving target, as online technologies have developed from command line software to the wonders of multimedia on the Web! As the scope of online learning has broadened with the technology, confusion has arisen about what is meant by the term e-learning, and other terms, such as online learning, web-based training, virtual environments and telelearning, are often used interchangeably which complicates the field still further. Another factor is endemic to all educational research: learners can not be manipulated like substances in a scientific laboratory. Ethical considerations, data protection regulations and online etiquette all add to the difficulties of researching electronic communication. Nevertheless, this chapter attempts to address the (apparently simple) question, 'What have we learnt about online learning?' My aim is not to review the research literature, but to try to identify what we, as a community of practitioners, researchers and learners, have come to be reasonably sure is applicable to teaching and learning in the electronic environment. From the extensive collection of books, papers and websites that exist in this field, I have chosen to draw primarily on four sources which I consider relatively representative of writings about e-learning:

- an authored book: Collis and Moonen (2001);

- an edited book: Stephenson (2001);

- a research study: Networked Learning, funded by JISC and available at: http://domino.lancs.ac.uk/edres/csaltdocs.nsf

- an online book by practitioners, available at: http://otis.scotcit.ac.uk/onlinebook

2.2 What is meant by e-learning?

A review of the e-learning literature reveals considerable ambiguity and often contradictory conceptions about what e-learning actually is. This is particularly true in the training and workplace use of the term. Some definitions of e-learning carry strong overtones of computer-based training transferred to the Internet. The emphasis is on the electronic nature of the content, not the communicative potential of the Web. The UK's Chartered Institute of Personnel and Development takes a different view, however, emphasising the importance of connectivity over stand-alone approaches such as CD-ROMs, satellite broadcasts, video and audio cassettes:

> Learning that is delivered, enabled or mediated by electronic technology, for the explicit purpose of training in organisations. It does not include stand-alone technology-based training such as the use of CD-ROMs in isolation. (CIPD 1999).

In the higher education literature, there is greater consensus that online learning or e-learning means electronic access and interaction with learning materials, fellow learners and tutors. The focus here is on the communicative potential of e-learning, rather than content delivery.

Practitioners of e-learning who emphasise the communicative nature of e-learning draw on constructivist and social practice theories of learning, often very overtly aiming to transform the role of the instructor to that of a facilitator of knowledge construction, and to create a social environment in which learners learn from each other online. Practitioners who emphasise the content delivery side of e-learning very often have a behaviourist or cognitive conception of learning, whether consciously or not. They focus on the development of clearly presented content, facilities for testing the learner and multimedia materials for increasing learner motivation. Access to training, reduced costs, and speed and retention of learning are the attractions of e-learning for them.

In higher education, the majority of the content of an e-learning course may be delivered through lectures or through distance-education textual material, but the course is categorised as e-learning because interaction with the tutor, dialogue with other students, the searching for resource materials, conduct of collaborative activities, access to course outlines and supporting material are conducted online.

2.3   Contradictory findings

In reading through a vast amount of e-learning and e-training literature recently, I was struck by how much apparently contradictory evidence was available, both in subjective matters which is understandable, but also in objective measures. For example:

- whether online courses were or were not engaging to learners;

- what are the key success indicators which reduce drop-out and lead to positive learning outcomes;

- evidence – or not – of cost savings;

- whether or not learners are choosing to sign up for e-learning courses.

It seems to me that there are a number of explanations for the contradictory findings. In some cases the findings are based on the web-based training model, where tutorial support is minimal or non-existent, and in others the findings come from courses using supported online learning. Much of the visionary literature draws on the e-community concept, while much of the negative doomsday writing has the CBT-on-the-Web concept of e-learning in mind. All are commonly referred to as e-learning, yet they are very different kinds of learning experiences and serve different markets and purposes. Even within higher education, there are different markets and purposes: for example, 18–22 year olds versus mature, working adults; campus learners versus remote learners and technical, mathematical and scientific areas of the curriculum versus arts, social science and education subjects. The confusion over what is meant by an e-learning course underlies other apparent contradictions: some findings refer to the online content of the course; others refer to the online communication. Lists of best practice may be based on a model of totally online courses where the learners never meet, or they are based on a course model which is only partially online. Finally, there is a plethora of literature based on conclusions from very small, contextualised case studies. There is a real dearth of large-scale research based either on large numbers of students or large numbers of courses. In my opinion, far too few studies recognised these differences in drawing conclusions and making generalisations about what works and what does not work online.

2.4   Designing online courses

Despite these critical remarks about the substance of the field, I do consider that we have advanced both in our understanding and in our practice. My first area for analysis is broadly centred on the design of online courses. It is clear to me from my four primary sources that we are agreed on the following:

- the need for clear, unequivocal instructions for online learners – free-for-all discussion conferences and vague suggestions from the tutor rarely produce high quality learning outcomes;

- e-learning content – whether originally a lecture or printed course material – needs to be re-thought as activities with active and interactive components;

- e-learning course design is best conceived as a team approach, as it is rare for one person to have comprehensive content expertise, graphic and web production skills as well as the impartiality to edit their own work.

There is widespread condemnation of the practice of putting overheads or lecture notes on the Web and calling the course e-learning. Online course content should capitalise on the unique features of the Web:

- a balancing of hyperlinked and linear conceptions of the course content;

- links to additional external web resources to enrich the student experience;

- up-to-date material and links which are modified as required even during the course;

- multimedia features such as webcasting, simulations, video/audio clips as appropriate to the access context of the learners.

2.5 Online assessment

One of the areas of real opportunity opened up by e-learning technology is online assessment, and this is reflected in the growth of papers and research studies about applications and findings of practitioners.

As with the term e-learning, there is a parallel confusion over the term online assessment. At one end of the spectrum, there is web-based assessment, which usually describes various types of multiple choice questions delivered on the Web and marked electronically. The types of questions have become very sophisticated and the presentation can draw on the full graphical and multimedia potential of the Web (e.g. matching concepts or images, assertion/reason formats, ranking and sequencing of concepts, and of course multiple right answers). While these innovative approaches can be very challenging for learners, the immediate marking especially when feedback is provided make them very popular with students. They also tend to be fairly demanding to design. At the other end of the spectrum are individual learning contracts, negotiated online with the tutor. These are generally regarded as hard work by students, but immensely rewarding. They are also very time-consuming for tutors to manage and to mark. In the middle are various forms of collaborative assignments which build on both the communicative and the resource-based potential of the Web. Students can be asked to construct a joint website, or write a collaborative project. Collaborative assignments are not popular with all students, but are not overly demanding to design or to mark.

Three conclusions seem clear to me from the literature:

- Designing an assessment strategy for e-learning is an art involving a triple challenge: feasibility (both for the student and the institution), reasonable approaches to marking reliability (especially if more than one marker is involved) and the desire to set challenging assignments which have real learning (rather than just testing) outcomes for the learners.

- While many practitioners want to use a student-centred approach to assessment in keeping with their overall approach to the design of the course, this needs to be tempered with the institution's responsibility for certifying achievement.

- The more innovative assignments tend to be more open to cheating and to plagiarism.

Best practice approaches indicate the following:

- use a variety of assessment methods over the course as a whole, because any particular method advantages particular types of learners;

- the approach to assessment must be related to the pedagogical approach of the course as a whole;

- make the aims, criteria and standards explicit to the learners;

- use authentic and holistic tasks wherever possible;

- provide opportunities for feedback and even opportunities for students to redo assignments taking the feedback into account.

2.6   Models of course design

It is increasingly evident that standard practice in higher education will always involve some combination of face-to-face meetings and online delivery. It seems safe to predict that purely face-to-face and purely online courses will increasingly be reserved for specialist uses. In fact, the term e-learning is beginning to evolve in harmony with this observation and is often referred to as meaning 'enhanced learning' (that is, learning enhanced by electronic technologies, rather than the original 'electronic learning'). Those of us who were early pioneers in online teaching as well as those who are recent practitioners are coming to see that online learning has been over-sold as a new paradigm in education. The demands for academic staff training in e-learning techniques is, in my opinion, as much a reflection of the lack of emphasis on teaching in higher education generally as it is of online teaching as a new paradigm. Online education is much more revolutionary for campus education than for distance education where course teams, separation of content and support and a different conception of the role of the academic have been standard practice before the advent of e-learning. Nevertheless, it is evident that online teaching has upset the apple-cart and increasingly demands a rethink of what is taught, by whom and with what aims.

Before leaving the issue of course design, there is one factor about which there is almost no conflicting evidence in the literature: the time-consuming nature of online teaching both in course preparation and in online tutoring. This relates to the higher regard given to research and the relatively lower status accorded to teaching by most higher education institutions, along with the consequent lack of time to design online materials and the lack of reward for devoting time to it. These arguments are all well rehearsed in the literature. A more interesting question is – given adequate time, reward, training and status, and given practice and a body of expert analysis and good practice on which to build, will online learning always be 'overly' time-consuming relative to the learning outcomes? In short, is the present preoccupation with 'the time factor' a current phenomenon that will pass or at least ease in another generation? Perhaps this is not susceptible to answering, as it is an evolutionary process with new factors intervening along the way.

In any case, it is surely safe to conclude with the observation that good teaching, whatever the medium, never happens 'on the cheap'.

2.7   Learning online

Course design is one half of the process; the other half involves the interaction and support of the learners. Here I would say that the evidence has not changed over nearly 15 years: the more 'adult', the more 'learning mature', the more motivated, the more self-confident the learner, the better they enjoy and benefit from online learning.

My four primary sources provide many studies of campus-based uses of online learning. One strong impression from this data is that campus students often feel they are being 'fobbed off' with online education. Contrary to this, are studies which cite learners' contentions that they experience much more interaction, more real contact with their peers and their teachers in online courses than they ever did in lecture courses. On the whole, it seems somewhat more difficult to generate online discussion where students are co-located on a campus than where students are geographically distributed, though this may be another short-term phenomenon related to campus-based course designers having less experience and fewer models of how to make online courses work in campus settings. Studies based on distance students usually show very positive results with more interaction online and a greater feeling of community. Nevertheless, there remains a hard core of distance students who resist online interaction or who want to retain face-to-face tutorials.

2.8   Collaborative learning

Studies of collaborative learning in the online environment are extensive, and perhaps because of this, I found reasonable agreement about 'what we know'. Three conclusions stand out:

- E-learning collaborative activities require good organisation, good design and strong leadership by the online tutor especially at the beginning.

- Students generally need help and scaffolding support from tutors in accepting collaborative approaches.

- Collaborative learning can work extraordinarily well but not for everyone – there is evidence of significant learning gains for some students.

2.9   Resource-based learning

As with collaborative learning, students need considerable support in coming to see the benefits of being more self-directed in their learning. The primary sources indicate that when asked, students claim they don't like resource-based learning because:

- it is more work;

- it is more difficult to study for exams;

- it is often poorly supported;

- it can appear that the teacher has abrogated the instructor role.

It is an obvious conclusion from many studies that motivation and openness to learning matter more than any experience or prior learning. However, many practitioners predict that the effect of prior experience with the Internet and mobile phones will lead to greater demand for online courses and more student-centred forms of learning.

2.10   What works for learners

It is a truism that good course design engages the whole learner, not just their cognitive centre. The question is, 'how to engage the whole learner?' It is still very difficult to 'get it right' the first time. There are so many variables: the nature of the learners' access (home, campus, workplace), their learning maturity, the right size for group discussions. The particular context within which an e-learning course takes place is critical to identifying the appropriate elements of the design and support for students. The best advice, therefore, seems to involve trials or pilots which offer the opportunity to put a 'toe in the water', to experiment with various kinds of online activities, to try different group sizes and to introduce some elements of collaborative or resource-based learning.

2.11   The technology

I put the discussion of the appropriate technology last because it is so evident from the research that the technology is the least important part of the learning experience for students. It is true that serious technical problems will certainly lead to failure, but 'good technology' contributes very little to the success of a course. Without a doubt, this confirms the warning against being technology-led!

2.12   Best practice

One of the chapters in the edited book from my four sources reviews a hundred research papers about e-learning in higher education. Four major features of good practice are identified:

> Dialogue: using e-mail, bulletin boards, 'real-time' chat, asynchronous chat, group discussions and debate, the tutor or moderator structures interactive opportunities into the content of the course.
>
> Involvement: includes responses in structured tasks, active engagement with material, collaboration and small group activities.
>
> Support: includes periodic face-to-face contact, online tutorial supervision, peer support, advice from experts, feedback on performance, support services and software tools. This is the most important feature of successful online courses, as reported in nearly all of the 100 papers surveyed.
>
> Control: refers to the extent to which learners have control of key learning activities and are encouraged to exercise that control. Responses to exercises, pace and timing, choice of content, management of learning activities, navigation through course content, overall direction and assessment of performance. (Coomey and Stephenson, 2001)

This list provides a useful framework for considering the design and support of online courses.

2.13   Conclusions

The following are my conclusions from the literature about what we know. I consider that there is considerable consensus:

- around the desirability of student-centred learning (although this is markedly less so in the sciences);

- around the need for structuring the online environment;

- around the value of interactivity;

- around the need for support and scaffolding to help students adjust to the online environment.

I think we are sadly lacking in understanding and practice in:

- how to engage students affectively;

- how to design relevant, appropriate assessment;

- how to create exciting, relevant online activities in many curriculum areas;
- how to conduct longitudinal research into the effects of e-learning;
- how to teach more students in less resource with higher quality!

I doubt we will find solutions to this last omission ...

2.14   References

CIPD (1999) *Workplace Learning, Culture and Performance.* London: Chartered Institute of Personnel and Development.

Collis, B. and Moonen, J. (2001) *Flexible Learning in a Digital World.* London: Kogan Page.

Coomey, M. and Stephenson, J. (2001) Online learning: it is all about dialogue, involvement, support and control – according to research. In J. Stephenson (ed.) *Teaching and Learning Online.* London: Kogan Page.

Stephenson, J. (ed) (2001) *Teaching and Learning Online.* London: Kogan Page.

3 Winning the toss and electing to bat: maximising the opportunities of online learning

Ron Oliver

Director of CRITC, Centre for Research in Information Technology and Communications, Edith Cowan University

Keywords:
online learning; open-ended learning designs; instructional design; knowledge construction; constructivism

3.1 Overview

There are now many educational organisations and institutions that are strategically moving to adopt flexible delivery and online learning. The factors that have influenced these moves are typically based on such imperatives as the need to deliver programmes more efficiently, the desire to provide more flexible programmes for existing students and the opportunities online settings provide for creating new markets. But the online delivery of programmes offers potentially far more than these outcomes alone. Online delivery supports and encourages very powerful learning environments and has the prospect to transform education if approached in the correct fashion.

It would not be unfair to say that most forms of online delivery, across all sectors of education throughout the world, tend not to be that impressive when viewed from a learning perspective. The bulk of online units tend to be based around very narrow instructional design models and tend to be testament to the economic, efficiency and marketing imperatives on which they are based. But with online delivery it is possible to pursue these imperatives and at the same time to pursue other goals such as the improvement of teaching and learning. Strategies supporting the pursuit of these other goals is the focus of this chapter.

3.2 Introduction

There are now many educational organisations and institutions that are strategically moving to adopt flexible delivery and online learning. The factors that have influenced these moves are typically based on such imperatives as the need to deliver programmes more efficiently, the desire to provide more flexible programmes for existing students and the opportunities online settings provide for creating new markets (e.g. Fraser and Deane, 1997; Holt and Thompson, 1998; Nunan, 1996). But the online delivery of programmes offers potentially far more than these outcomes alone. Online delivery supports and encourages very powerful learning environments and has the prospect to transform education if approached in the correct fashion (Biggs, 2001).

It would not be unfair to say that most forms of online delivery, across all sectors of education throughout the world, tend not to be that impressive when viewed from a learning perspective. The bulk of online units tend to be based around very narrow instructional design models and tend to be testament to the economic, efficiency and marketing imperatives on which they are based (e.g. Burbules and Callister, 2000; Dehoney and Reeves, 1999; Mioduser, Nachmias, Oren and Lahav, 1999). But with online delivery it is possible to pursue these imperatives and at the same time to pursue other goals such as the improvement of teaching and learning. Strategies supporting the pursuit of these other goals is the focus of this chapter.

3.3   How students learn

The growth of the popularity of new learning technologies appears to have coincided with a growing awareness and recognition of alternative theories for learning, theories that suggest many problems and inefficiencies with conventional forms of teaching. The theories of learning that hold the greatest sway today are those based on constructivist principles (e.g. Duffy and Cunningham, 1996). These principles posit that learning is achieved by the active construction of knowledge supported by various perspectives within meaningful contexts. In constructivist theories, social interactions are seen to play a critical role in the processes of learning and cognition (e.g. Vygotsky, 1978).

The strengths of constructivism lie in its emphasis on learning as a process of personal understanding and meaning-making which is active and interpretative. In this domain learning is viewed as the construction of meaning rather than as the memorisation of facts (e.g. Jonassen and Reeves, 1996; Lebow, 1993). Technology-based approaches to learning provide many opportunities for constructivist learning through their provision and support for resource-based, student-centred settings and by enabling learning to be related to context and to practice (e.g. Barron, 1998; Berge, 1998).

Many writers have in the past provided guidance for the design of constructivist learning settings by articulating the underpinning characteristics. For example, Cunningham, Duffy and Knuth (1993) argue that constructivist learning environments are characterised by seven pedagogical goals. They suggest that constructivist learning settings are those which concurrently:

- provide experience in the knowledge construction process;
- provide experience in and appreciation for, multiple perspectives;
- embed learning in realistic and relevant contexts;
- encourage ownership and voice in the learning process;
- embed learning in social experience;
- encourage the use of multiple modes of representation;
- encourage self-awareness in the knowledge construction process.

In a similar vein, Savery and Duffy (1995) argue that the following four principles necessarily underpin learning in constructivist settings:

- learning is an active and engaged process;

- learning is a process of constructing knowledge;
- learners function at a metacognitive level;
- learning involves social negotiation.

In an attempt to ground these principles in ways that can support instructional design, Grabinger (1996) discusses these forms of learning design from the perspective of learners. He provides a list of the assumptions of learning that are aligned with contemporary constructivist views and discusses how these assumptions can impact on the role of learners. He argues what:

- people transfer learning with difficulty and need both content and contexts for learning;
- learners are active constructors of knowledge;
- learning is cognitive and in a constant state of growth and evolution;
- learners bring their own needs and experiences to learning situations;
- skills and knowledge are best acquired within realistic contexts; and
- assessment must take more realistic and holistic forms.

The descriptions which authors provide of the elements required for constructivist learning settings can help designers to understand the forms of learning activity which are required but often fail to provide adequate guidance for the actual learning designs that can encapsulate such principles in cohesive and supportive ways. Hannafin, Hall, Land and Hill (1994) suggest that appropriate forms of learning settings are that they call *open-ended* learning environments. These are characterised by learner engagement in cognitively complex tasks involving such activities as problem-solving, critical thinking, collaboration and self-regulation.

There are a number of discrete learning designs that support constructivist learning and whose forms can provide designers with guidance and structure in the design of actual learning settings as suggested by Hannafin, Hall, Land and Hill (1994). In the literature many of these designs remain ill-structured in their definitions and descriptions which can limit teachers in their choice and use of them.

3.4   Designing effective learning settings

The forms of learning setting that stem from the application of constructivist learning principles are similar in many respects to, and also quite different from, conventional settings. The designs tend to be based on forms of learning that are based on learners undertaking various forms of activity that are open-ended and student-centred. The forms of environment tend to be those that require learners to work with others and to share the results of their work and to reflect on the outcomes. They tend to be settings where there are no fixed resources or content to be learned and where the emphasis is on learning *how* rather than learning *about*. There are a number of discrete learning designs that accommodate these needs. Some of the more common forms of design include problem-based, case-based, project-based and inquiry-based learning.

3.4.1   Problem-based learning

Problem-based learning (PBL) is a learning design that found popularity in the mid 1980s in medical schools as an alternative to traditional forms of learning in this domain. A problem-based setting is one where students work in small groups under the guidance of a facilitator. For example, in a problem-based setting students may be required to diagnose a patient's medical condition and to provide a rationale for their diagnosis and treatment. PBL involves presenting students with a real-life problem immersed in a context which is relevant to professional practice. Problem-based learning designs involve complex problems which provide a stimulus for learning. They provide students with the opportunity to immerse themselves into a context which requires more than memorisation and understanding of concepts and challenge them to apply their knowledge to determine the best outcome (e.g. Bligh, 1995).

In PBL settings students apply their conceptual knowledge as well as processes and effective action learnt in solving the problem. Problem-based learning usually incorporates cooperative learning groups. Students work cooperatively in small groups identifying their prior knowledge and what they need to know to effectively solve the problem. Problems did not encourage simple, lower level solutions but demand that students pursue new knowledge through the process of solving the problem. The application of knowledge and skills is essential during the process of problem solving. The teacher's role is to facilitate a positive, encouraging cooperative learning environment and provide scaffolding at crucial times, as determined by the dynamic process of solving the problem (Boud and Feletti, 1995).

3.4.2   Case-based learning

Case-based learning is a form of problem-based learning but with a different and characteristic form. In case-based learning, students typically work through a problem setting which is usually a realistic case relevant to their course, for example, medicine or business. Students work through the case, either collaboratively or individually, and make decisions as to what would be the best course of action. A case is an abstract of an event and interpretations of experiences. It can either be a previously encountered and solved problem, or a typical way of solving a problem.

The characteristic feature of this type of learning activity is case-based reasoning. Case-based reasoning is a problem-solving paradigm which utilises the specific knowledge of previous experiences within concrete problem situations such as cases. A new problem is solved by finding a similar past case, and applying its solution to the new problem situation. Cases can have several components. If each component of the case is interpreted correctly the more useful it will be when it is necessary for the student to recall and apply similar knowledge and processes to another case (Kolodner and Guzdial, 2000).

3.4.3   Project-based learning

Project-based learning engages students in the process of designing and creating products that meet authentic needs. It can focus on the central concepts and principles of a discipline through involving students in problem-solving investigations. Project-based learning lends itself to cooperative learning environments which enable students to discuss, explore, test ideas and concepts supported by a team environment. Projects can may even be completed individually. Project-based learning environments are typically authentic in nature and provide a learning environment which stimulates and encourages students to construct their own knowledge and pursue their own interests resulting in the creation of realistic products (Guzdial, 1997).

Project-based learning tends to be used in instances where the course supports the construction of some product or artefact. For example, the development of a design or a model; or the development of a script or a description. The development of the product forms the basis of the learning experience and students are supported in their learning by the guidance and feedback they gain from the project experience.

3.4.3   Inquiry-based learning

Inquiry-based learning describes a learning design where students are faced with an open-ended task for which they must formulate investigative questions, obtain factual information, and then build the knowledge that enables them to answer the original question. The form of learning is a hybrid of problem-based learning with its own idiosyncratic features. Students are often required to observe and question, present explanations, devise and conduct tests to test their theories; analyse data; draw conclusions, or design and build models. Inquiry-based learning emphasises research, critical thinking and multi-disciplined study to achieve course outcomes. Inquiry-based learning is sometimes discussed in conjunction with problem-based learning. Jakes, Pennington and Knodle (2001) describe inquiry-based learning as a process where students formulate questions or the teacher provides questions to stimulate investigative processes to obtain information to help build knowledge to effectively determine a solution. Typically students are aided with questions or scaffolds provided by the teacher or other students.

Inquiry-based learning differs from problem-based learning by virtue of its use of a greater range of learning methods, high levels of teacher support and scaffolding, and an emphasis on an interdisciplinary approach to learning, critical thinking as well as students assuming responsibility for their own learning (Magnussen, Ishida and Itano, 2000). Inquiry-based learning can involve other forms of learning design including discussions, group exercises and role plays. The strategy makes strong use of student interactions, their previous knowledge and life experiences (Cerny, Amundson, Mueller and Waldron, 1996).

3.5   Implications for teaching

The learning designs described above are discrete and recognisable entities. They represent forms for the design of any type of learning environment but are also very well suited to online settings. There are many academics and teachers who are finding very effective ways to apply these design strategies in their classes in higher education, but for many the learning design is unknown and its potential for application in their classroom teaching is quite distant.

Designing online learning settings based on open-ended tasks and activities is often a difficult process for teachers accustomed to more content-centred approaches to instructional design. In our activities we have explored strategies to guide the development of learning environments based on the forms of open-ended learning settings described above. A framework which we have found to be very useful and supportive for the instructional design is one which isolates the discrete elements for which design and development is required. The three discrete elements, which form the framework, are the learning activities, the learning supports and the learning resources (Oliver, 1999). These

Learning design elements	Description	Examples
Learning activities	The tasks, problems, interactions used to engage the learners and upon which learning is based	Reading activities, computer-based interactions, simulations, inquiry tasks, projects, open-ended problems, inquiry tasks, collaborative tasks
Learning resources	The content, information and resources with which the learners interact in completing the tasks	Web pages, readers, textbooks, computer-based tools, web links, notes, documents, workplace manuals, case studies, databases
Learning supports	The scaffolds, structures, motivations, assistances and connections used to support learning	Learning guides, discussions, chats, suggested learning pathways, mentors, buddies, workplace trainers

Table 3.1   Framework describing critical elements of online learning settings

elements provide a strong framework for instructional design and highlight the importance of planning specific roles for learners, the teacher and the technology in the learning environment (see Table 3.1).

The framework provides a means to isolate and study the various elements within learning settings and suggests emphases which can be made in the instructional design process. Contemporary learning theories posit that the forms of learning design most appropriate to higher education are those based on constructivist learning principles. The above framework takes on particular and discrete forms when applied this way.

3.6   Exemplars of quality online learning design

The National Flexible Toolbox Project being conducted in the vocational education and training sector in Australia has provided a sound basis to explore some of the design principles that have been described in this chapter. Within this project online learning materials are being developed for National Training Packages. These packages are nationally endorsed training materials which describe an integrated set of nationally endorsed competency standards and assessment guidelines. By their very nature Training Packages seek to develop learners' competencies and it is this feature that makes the selection and design of learning activities an important and critical component of the online learning settings. In more general terms, Training Packages are very much about *learning how* as distinct from *learning about*.

3.6.1   Learning activities

In the design of learning activities for Toolboxes, developers are encouraged to consider the competencies being developed and the forms of learner activity that will support this development. This approach to instructional design takes the emphasis away from content as the organising framework for learning and places it squarely with learner activity. The design of activities that can develop competency requires a high degree of knowledge and understanding on the part of the designer. The activities need to engage the learners, to encourage reflection and articulation and to promote higher order thinking. Activities which lack these elements rarely help students to learn in any meaningful way. Typical learning designs that have informed the development of Toolbox learning activities are problem-based learning, case-based learning and inquiry-based learning.

Figure 3.1   A learning activity exemplar: project based learning in the Tourism Flexible Learning Toolbox

3.6.2   Learning supports

Many of the early online learning developments attempted to create reduced roles for teachers and tutors as a means to create economies of scale and delivery. More recently online learning settings have been characterised by high levels of teacher support through the use of discussion boards and other forms of online communication. Most designers recognise the need to provide supports and guidance for learners in online settings and include an array of tasks for this purpose. In the Flexible Learning Toolboxes, designers have been encouraged to explore ways to provide feedback and support for learners through processes that promote students' self-directed learning. The intention is to provide strategies for support that reduce the need for direct teacher intervention and activity while still ensuring learners have access to the forms of help needed to progress.

Figure 3.2   The use of peers and mentors as learning supports in the Multimedia Design Flexible Learning Toolbox

The forms of learning support that have been included in many of the Flexible Learning Toolboxes are those which provide scaffolds for the students and which can be faded as the learning occurs. The strategies that have been used include the use of buddies and mentors as human supports, innovative bulletin borads and postings as electronic supports and adaptive guides and online supports that students can use at their will when required (see Figure 3.2). In most instances, the Toolboxes enable teachers a number of choices and options in the forms of support they will use with their students, a factor which recognises the importance of the teacher in the online setting while accommodating the needs of the individual and self-directed learners.

3.6.3 Online learning resources

A common approach in the development of online settings is through content-centred approaches where course content and its delivery is used as the basis of the learning materials. This approach is limited in the learning it can support by virtue of the fact that learners often have no explicit purpose or reason to interact. Such settings tend often to be lacking in context and relevance. In the Flexible Learning Toolboxes, designers are encouraged to select and design learning resources in response to learners' needs. These needs arise from the learning activities they are given and the resources matched to the forms of learning outcomes being sought. The consequence of choosing resources based on

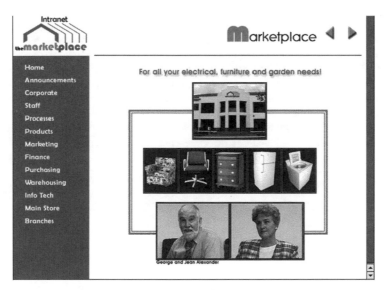

Figure 3.3   Learning resources examples from the Systems Analysis flexible Learning
     Toolbox

the needs of learning activities creates a number of advantages for the learning environment. These advantages stem from the fact that the resources can be organised in meaningful ways for access and retrieval and that developers can use existing resources without specifically having to tailor them for their needs. The resources can be taken from actual settings and can be documents and manuals from workplace settings.

The separation of resources from learning activities that is encouraged in the Toolbox development, supports their customisation and reuse. The use of consistent metatags and organisational strategies that support disaggregation also provides advantages for storage in repositories and the concept of reusable learning objects. Figure 3.3 demonstrates the use of an Intranet within an online learning setting as an organising strategy for a variety of relevant and authentic learning resources. There are many strategies that can be used to present learning resources in online settings and a variety of options exist for resource organisation to support student learning and the transfer of this learning to the workplace.

3.7 Summary and conclusions

This chapter has discussed the form of conventional online learning settings and has suggested design strategies that can be used to develop learning settings able to support knowledge construction. In particular the chapter has described strategies by which open-ended learning designs can be developed to support learning in online settings. Conventional approaches to online learning are often impeded by a tendency for designers to use a content-oriented approach to design. In this chapter strategies have been proposed that focus the design process on the choice of learning activities as the basis for the learning process.

There is now a growing awareness of the need for online design to support more student-centred learning approaches. The use of a design process that focuses on learning activities provides strong support for this. Such approaches have the capacity to provide more flexibility in terms of learner pathways and learner voice in the learning process. In the future we can expect to see many more examples of online learning organised around authentic activities and tasks. Teachers and learners are coming to recognise the value in more open-ended settings and there is an increasing level of this form of design and development leading these activities across all sectors of education.

3.8 References

Barron, A. (1998) Designing Web-based training, *British Journal of Educational Technology* **29**(4): 355–71.

Berge, Z. (1998) Guiding principles in web-based instructional design, *Education Media International* **35**(2): 72–6.

Biggs, J. (2001) The reflective institution: assuring and enhancing the quality of teaching and learning, *Higher Education* **41**(3): 221–38.

Bligh, J. (1995) Problem-based learning in medicine: an introduction, *Post-Graduate Medical Journal* **71**(8): 323–6.

Burbules, N. and Callister, T. (2000) Universities in transition: the promise and challenge of new technologies, *Teachers College Record* **102**(2): 271–93.

Boud, D. and Feletti, G. (1997) Changing problem-based learning. Introduction to the Second Edition. In D. Boud and G. Feletti (eds), *The Challenge of Problem-based Learning* (2nd edn, pp. 2–16). London: Kogan Page.

Cerny, J., Amundson, M., Mueller, C. and Waldron, J. (1996) Inquiry-based learning, nursing, student attitudes and the HIV patient, *Journal of Nursing Education* **35**: 219–22.

Cunningham, D., Duffy, T. and Knuth, R. (1996) Textbook of the future. In C. McKnight (ed.), *Hypertext: A Psychological Perspective*. London: Ellis Horwood.

Dehoney, J. and Reeves, T. (1999) Instructional and social dimensions of class web pages, *Journal of Computing in Higher Education* **10**(2): 19–41.

Duffy, T. and Cunningham, D. (1996) Constructivism: implications for the design and delivery of instruction, *Handbook of Research for Educational Telecommunications and Technology* (pp. 170–98). New York: Macmillan.

Fraser, J. and Deane, E. (1997) Why open learning?, *Australian Universities Review* **40**(1): 25–31.

Grabinger, S. (1996) Rich environments for active learning. In D. Jonassen (ed.), *Handbook of Research for Educational Telecommunications and Technology* (pp. 665–92). New York: Macmillan.

Guzdial, M. (1997) Creating a Project-Based Learning Focus in *Undergraduate Engineering Education: Why Project-Based Learning in Undergraduate Engineering Education.* http://guzdial.cc.gatech.edu/repp/draft.html (accessed Oct. 2001).

Jakes, D., Pennington, M. and Knodle, H. (2001) *Using the Internet to Promote Inquiry-based Learning: An Epaper about a Structured Approach for Effective Student Web Research.* http://www.biopoint.com/inquiry/ibr.html (accessed Oct. 2001).

Holt, D. and Thompson, D. (1998) Managing information technology in open and distance higher education, *Distance Education* **19**(2): 197–227.

Jonassen, D. and Land, S. (eds) (2000) *Theoretical Foundations of Learning Environments.* Mahwah, NJ: Lawrence Erlbaum Associates.

Jonassen, D. and Reeves, T. (1996) Learning with computers: computers as cognitive tools. In D. Jonassen (ed.), *Handbook of Research for Educational Communications and Technology* (pp. 693–719). New York: Macmillan Library Reference.

Kolodner, J. and Guzdial, M. (2000) Theory and practice of case-based learning aids. In D. Jonassen and S. Land (eds), *Theoretical Foundations of Learning Environment.* Mahwah, NJ: Lawrence Erlbaum Associates.

Lebow, D. (1993) Constructivist values for instructional systems design: five principles toward a new mindset, *Educational Technology, Research and Development* **41**(3): 4–16.

Magnusson, L., Ishida, D. and Itano, J. (2000) The impact of the use of inquiry-based learning as a teaching methodology on the development of critical thinking, *Journal of Nursing Education* **39**(8): 360–4.

Mioduser, D., Nachmias, R., Oren, A. and Lahav, O. (1999) *Web-based learning environments: current states and emerging trends.* Paper presented at the Ed-Media 1999. World Conference on Educational Multimedia, Hypermedia and Telecommunications, Seattle, USA.

Nunan, T. (1996) Flexible delivery – what it is and why is it a part of current educational debate? In *Higher Education Research and Development Society of Australasia.* Perth: HERDSA.

Oliver, R. (1999) Exploring strategies for on-line teaching and learning, *Distance Education* **20**(2): 240–54.

Savery, J. and Duffy, T. (1995) Problem-based learning: an instructional model and its constructivist framework, *Educational Technology* 35, **35**(5), pp. 31-38.

Vygotsky, L. (1978). *Mind in Society.* Cambridge MA, Harvard University Press.

4 The importance of lecturer conceptions of teaching and learning for facilitating student learning online: changes in conceptions following an online course about developing courses online

Barbara de la Harpe and Alex Radloff

RMIT University, Melbourne, Australia

Keywords

conceptions; online course; professional development; constructivism; student-centred learning

4.1 Overview

Universities all around the world are rapidly embracing new learning technologies. The development of teaching and learning using these technologies has required a rethinking of lecturer roles and has highlighted the need for staff development. An important challenge for staff development is to address the conceptions of teaching and learning that lecturers hold and to help them to change these in line with a student-centred constructivist approach to teaching and learning.

In this chapter, we outline the role of conceptions of teaching and learning for improving student learning and their importance for effective use of the new technologies; describe the development and implementation of an online course to help lecturers to develop courses online that had as one of its aims changing conceptions of teaching and learning; report outcomes in terms of shifts in conceptions of teaching and learning from data gathered as part of the course using both quantitative and qualitative methodologies; and discuss implications for supporting teaching and learning online.

4.2 Background

In order to improve student learning using new learning technologies, a focus is needed on the lecturers who are the developers, facilitators and assessors of courses that use these technologies, and on how they conceptualise their roles. The current institutional emphasis on 'getting courses online' and the design features of many proprietary software packages developed for this purpose often ignore the role that conceptions of teaching and learning play in how new technologies may be used to support student learning. Indeed, they may be reinforcing inappropriate conceptions such as a teacher-centred, content-oriented transmissive approach to the design of learning environments. Thus, the conceptions that lecturers hold need to be addressed, and if necessary, lecturers helped to change these so that they are more in line with a learner-centred, process-oriented constructivist approach to teaching and learning.

Conceptions of teaching and learning refer to the beliefs that teachers hold about what teaching and learning mean and their role as teachers in facilitating learning. Research on university teachers' conceptions of teaching has identified a number of different conceptions ranging from transmissive to constructivist (Gow and Kember, 1993; Prosser and Trigwell,

1999; Samuelowitz and Bain, 1992; Trigwell and Prosser, 1996). In a synthesis of the literature in this area, Kember (1998), suggests that teacher beliefs about teaching can be organised along a continuum from teacher-centred/content-oriented to student-centred/learning-oriented.

Conceptions about teaching are important since research suggests that lecturer conceptions influence the teaching approaches and strategies they adopt, and these, in turn, influence their students' learning approaches and the quality of their learning outcomes (de la Harpe, Radloff and Wyber, 2000; Gow and Kember, 1993; Trigwell and Prosser, 1996). Similarly, Kember (1998, p. 17) points out 'there is evidence of links between the teaching beliefs and teaching strategies and, more significantly, with the learning approaches of students'.

Thus, lecturers need to have or to develop approaches to their teaching which are learner-centred and learning-oriented, if they are to be able to promote quality learning. In fact, it has been shown that lecturers '...who adopt a teacher focused strategy are more likely to encourage students to adopt a surface approach to learning than those who adopt a student-focused strategy' (Trigwell and Prosser, 1996, p. 79).

Lecturer conceptions of teaching and their importance for student learning are equally important irrespective of the mode of instruction. However, in online teaching and learning, the emphasis on the mastery and use of the technology has been the primary focus of many staff development initiatives. The need for lecturers to examine their existing conceptions of teaching and to consider more appropriate ways of thinking about teaching and learning is often ignored in such staff development initiatives. To make full use of the promise of the new technologies, learner-centred conceptions of teaching that emphasise a social constructivist pedagogy are needed (McLoughlin, 2000). Thus, staff development for online teaching and learning needs to focus on conceptions of teaching that underpin the pedagogy as well as on the use of learning technologies (Wissink, 2001).

4.3   An online course for developing courses online

Developing an online course about teaching online, a project[1] funded by AusAid, provided an opportunity for staff development that included an explicit focus on supporting conceptual change. The course was developed by four staff (including the two authors) from an academic development unit in collaboration with key senior staff from the University of the Philippines Open University (UPOU). The aim was to develop an online course for university teachers in order to further the development and use of learning technologies for courses offered at a distance.

The project brief outlined a number of parameters that provided the basis for the development and implementation of the online course. These included meeting the expectations of UPOU, focusing the course on teaching and learning, and incorporating a one week face-to-face component in Australia at the end of the eight week online course. Although the course was not designed 'for credit', participants were required to show evidence of their learning through for example, a Learning Portfolio and the development of a component of a course online.

The participants in the course were 16 university teachers from UPOU engaged in distance teaching – 13 females and 3 males, ranging from 26 to 51 years in age. They came from a range of discipline backgrounds including Management, Education, Social Sciences and Humanities, Health Sciences and Technology, and had varying levels of teaching experience. None had developed a course online.

As outlined in Herrmann, de la Harpe, Fox and Radloff (2000), the course was designed around participants' developing and evaluating a component of a course of their choosing, for teaching and learning online. The course was divided into seven themes – Learners, Learning process, Learning outcomes, Breaking the mould: technology in teaching and learning, Thinking outside the square: selecting appropriate media, Good online teaching and learning, and Evaluating online courses.

Participants worked in groups of three to five. Contact between participants was facilitated through team discussion groups, general discussion groups and allocating a mentor for each group. Co-operation was encouraged by setting group tasks and reinforcing the value of collaborative learning. Challenging learning tasks were set and teams encouraged to strive to meet these. Participant feelings about their learning were monitored through prompting reflection at the end of each theme and requiring participants to complete an affect checklist indicating their positive and negative feelings to learning online.

In order to encourage a focus on student-centred learning-oriented conceptions of teaching and in line with the needs of adult learners, the guidelines underpinning the design, format and content of the course included:

- adopting a social constructivist approach to teaching and learning;

- addressing conceptions of teaching and learning;

- focusing on content and process outcomes;

- aligning course aims, activities and assessment; and

- creating a context that supported effective teaching and learning online.

The *social constructivist approach* was operationalised through an emphasis on the participants working in teams, constructing their own understanding of key educational principles through searching, reading, writing, discussion and reflection. Content in the form of extended course notes, lectures or set texts was de-emphasised in line with von Glasersfeld's (1987) view that '[k]nowledge is not a transferable commodity and communication not a conveyance'. In addition, facilitators conceptualised their role as guide rather than as instructor. Thus, the course emphasised the active role of learners in making sense of information and building their own understanding. Learning was seen as an active process of constructing personal meaning or restructuring prior knowledge rather than as the passive reception of teacher determined information (Derry, 1996; Doolittle, 1999; Murphy, 2000; Umass Physics Education Research Group, 1999).

The course addressed *conceptions of teaching and learning* in a number of ways. Participants were asked to identify and discuss the take home messages from key articles such as that of Barr and Tagg (1995), addressing the need for a shift from an instruction to a learning paradigm and Kember (1998), addressing the need to shift from a teacher focused, content-centred approach to a learner centred process-oriented one. Participants also developed their knowledge and understanding of conceptions of learning and their importance for how students approach their learning through activities and self-reflection. An example of an activity is illustrated in Figure 4.1.

In addition, participants were required to complete at the beginning and end of the course, the Approaches to Teaching Inventory, a 16-item questionnaire which measures teachers' approaches to teaching (Prosser and Trigwell, 1999; Trigwell and Prosser, 1996).

The course was designed to include an emphasis on both *content and process* – the 'what' as well as the 'how' of teaching and learning online. In particular, the course addressed

Categorising definitions of learning

At the start of this theme, you recorded your personal definition of learning and that of at least three other people. Now, post these definitions to your team discussion group (please limit each definition to 50 words).

Then, as a team, using the **'Conceptions of learning'** categories listed below, classify each definition on a level from 1 to 6. We suggest that you print out the list below so that you have it available when you classify the definitions in your team discussion group.

Figure 4.1   Learning activity

explicitly the process of learning, that is, how participants learned online. This was in line with Shuell's (1986) reminder that 'what the student does is actually more important in determining what is learned than what the teacher does'. Therefore, the course included carefully planned learning activities, provided tips and strategies for effective learning in teams and online, and required participants at the end of each theme to reflect on their learning, as shown in Figure 4.2.

L E A R N E R S | On-Line TEACHING & LEARNING

Reflect on this theme

Remember – you will need to include some of your reflections in your portfolio.

Think back on the theme – learners and the four questions you have worked through about learner characteristics, conceptions of learning and approaches to learning, and levels of cognitive and ethical development.

Now, respond to the following questions in your personal archive.

1. What have I learned in answering each theme question? (Write three to five points per theme question)
2. How can I use what I have learned when developing an online course?
3. What other issues do I need to think about?
4. What have I learned about learning and myself as a learner? (Include comments about approach to learning and feelings about learning online)

Back to theme, 'learners'

Figure 4.2   Reflection

Given the importance of *aligning* aims, teaching and learning activities and assessment tasks (Biggs, 1996; 1999), the course as a whole, and each theme, included aims expressed as student learning outcomes, theme outlines which detailed how these could be achieved and learning activities that supported their achievement.

The *learning context* was modelled on the Seven Principles for Good Practice (Chickering and Gamson, 1987), representing a synthesis of educational research that shows that good practice encourages contact between learners and teachers, develops reciprocity and cooperation among learners, uses active learning techniques, provides prompt feedback, emphasises time on task, communicates high expectations, and respects diverse talents and ways of learning. These principles formed a useful framework for matching teaching and learning activities with the appropriate technology (Chickering and Ehrmann, 1996).

4.4   Data gathering strategies

Data on lecturer conceptions of teaching were gathered using both quantitative and qualitative methods. The quantitative data was gathered using the Approaches to Teaching Inventory. The Inventory consists of two sub-scales – the conceptual change / student-focused approach (CCSF) sub-scale and the information transmission / teacher-focused approach (ITTF), each of which comprises 8 items. Four items refer to the motive of the approach and four to the strategy. Table 4.1 shows the scales and subscales with example items.

Scale	Subscale	Item
CCSF	Intention	I encourage students to restructure their existing knowledge in terms of the new way of thinking about the subject that they will develop.
	Strategy	Formal teaching time is made available in this subject for students to discuss their changing understanding of the subject.
ITTF	Intention	I feel that it is important to present a lot of facts in classes so that students know what they have to learn for this subject.
	Strategy	I structure this subject to help students to pass the formal assessment items.

Table 4.1   The scales, subscales and examples of items in the inventory

The Inventory items were developed from data derived from a phenomenographic study of 24 university science teachers teaching first-year physics and chemistry courses (Trigwell and Prosser, 1996). Participants completed the Inventory online at the beginning and end of the course, some nine weeks apart.

Qualitative data was gathered from Learning Portfolios. Participants were required to develop an electronic Learning Portfolio (Wiedmer, 1999) in which they documented their goals for learning, learning experiences, reflections, and action plans, and assessed progress and identified areas for personal development. Mandatory items for the Learning Portfolio included the following:

- participant's home page;
- reflections on achievement of course aims (aims listed on home page);
- reflections on conceptions of teaching and learning;
- reflections on technology skill development; and

- a summary of key learning based on responses to questions from the reflection section of each theme, namely *What have I learned in answering each theme question?; How can I use what I have learned when developing an online course?; What other issues do I need to think about?*; and *What have I learned about learning and myself as a learner?*

Learning Portfolio entries were examined and comments about conceptions or conceptual change were identified.

4.5   Changes in conceptions of teaching

Results from the quantitative and qualitative data analysis are presented below. In terms of the quantitative data, the responses of the 13 participants who completed the Inventory on both occasions were collated and pre-post scores compared using effect sizes (see Table 4.2). In line with Cohen (1969), an effect size of less than 0.2 was considered trivial; effect sizes between 0.2 and 0.5, small, effect sizes between 0.5 and 0.8, moderate and effects sizes in excess of 0.8, large.

For the CCSF scale, for both intention and strategy subscales, all changes, other than for item 15 which relates to students generating their own notes, were in a positive direction. There were educationally significant effect sizes for item 8, which relates to encouraging students to restructure existing knowledge and for item 6, which relates to giving students time in class to discuss difficulties.

For the ITTF scale, for both intention and strategy subscales, all changes, other than for items 11, 1 and 10, were in a negative direction, suggesting that participants were less teacher focused at the end of the online course than at the beginning. There were significant effect sizes for item 2 which relates to focusing only on objectives relating to formal assessment, item 4 which relates to presentation of facts, item 13 which relates to knowing the answers to all questions students might ask, item 7 which relates to concentrating on using a set text and item 12 which relates to providing only information that relates to formal assessments.

In general, mean pre scores for the CCSF approach for both intention and strategy subscales were higher than the ITTF approach mean scores. Further, for both approaches, the mean scores for the intention items were higher than the mean scores for the strategy items.

Overall, the quantitative data suggest that there were changes in some aspects of participants' conceptions of teaching and learning relating to what they wanted to do in their teaching and the way they went about teaching. These changes were generally towards more student-centred approaches. Specifically, in terms of intentions, participants showed most change in helping students to restructure their knowledge and developing a new way of thinking about the subject. In terms of strategy, participants showed most change in providing class time for student discussion. This finding may be associated with the fact that participants themselves found engaging in discussion as one of the novel aspects of their learning experience as indicated in their feedback at the end of the course. Participants also indicated that they were less likely at the end of the course to be textbook bound and to focus on information 'to pass the test'. These changes are in line with the aims of the online course and what was modelled by the facilitators.

On the other hand, participants expressed a stronger feeling at the end of the course that they give students notes rather than let them generate their own notes. This finding may reflect participants' own discomfort with the online course's deliberate exclusion of extended course notes, lectures or set texts.

Item	Description	Means		ES
		pre	post	g
	CCSF approach – Intention (items 5, 8, 15 and 16)			
5	I feel that the assessment in this subject should be an opportunity for students to reveal their changed conceptual understanding of the subject.	4.77	4.77	0.00
8	I encourage students to restructure their existing knowledge in terms of the new way of thinking about the subject that they will develop.	4.08	4.38	0.28 *
15	I feel it is better for students in this subject to generate their own notes rather than always copy mine	4.46	4.00	-0.42 *
16	I feel a lot of teaching in this subject should be used to question students' ideas.	3.46	3.50	0.03
	Total	**4.19**	**4.16**	**-0.03**
	CCSF approach – Strategy (items 3, 6, 9 and 14)			
3	In my class/tutorial for this subject, I try to develop a conversation with students about the topics we are studying.	4.46	4.54	0.10
6	We take time out in classes so that the students can discuss, among themselves, the difficulties that they encounter studying this subject.	3.77	4.23	0.42 *
9	In lectures for this subject, I use difficult or undefined examples to provoke debate.	2.69	2.92	0.19
14	Formal teaching time is made available in this subject for students to discuss their changing understanding of the subject.	3.31	3.31	0.00
	Total	**3.56**	**3.75**	**0.17**
	ITTF approach – Intention (items 2, 4, 11 and 13)			
2	I feel it is important that this subject should be completely described in terms of specific objectives relating to what students have to know for formal assessment items.	4.38	4.15	-0.18
4	I feel it is important to present a lot of facts in classes so that students know what they have to learn for this subject.	3.46	3.23	-0.20 *
11	I think an important reason for giving lectures for this subject is to give students a good set of notes.	2.00	2.15	0.13
13	I feel that I should know the answers to any questions that students may put to me during this subject.	3.62	3.31	-0.23 *
	Total	**3.37**	**3.21**	**-0.12**
	ITTF approach – Strategy (items 1, 7, 10 and 12)			
1	I design my teaching in this subject with the assumption that most of the students have very little useful knowledge of the topics to be covered.	2.69	3.00	0.18
7	In this subject I concentrate on covering the information that might be available from a good textbook. vassessment items.	2.54	2.31	-0.25 *
10	I structure this subject to help students to pass the formal assessment items.	3.08	3.38	0.21 *
12	When I give this subject, I only provide the students with the information they will need to pass the formal assessments.	2.08	1.69	-0.36 *
	Total	**2.60**	**2.60**	**0.00**

Note. Large effect size = *** Medium effect size = ** Small effect size =*

Table 4.2   Effect sizes for participants' (*n* = 13) pre-post scores on the inventory

In terms of the qualitative data, 25 comments relating to conceptions or conceptual change were identified from Learning Portfolio entries. These comments supported the quantitative data.

Comments focused on reflecting on learning experiences, on the self as learner, on teaching approaches, and on the role of technology in teaching and learning, as illustrated by the following quotes.

> The course is rather enlightening such that I am now more aware of other things that must be considered in offering an online course. [O]

> I learned that I have some good learning habits but can be better. I also learned that the tutor must teach not only content but how to learn content. [S]

> I've learned that the important thing is to remain grounded, that we are only using the technology for what it does best and that we must not let it dictate what we want to do with our courses...our learners and their needs and how the technology best be used to answer those needs is what we need to carefully look at. [C]

In addition, there were comments illustrating a student-centred, constructivist approach to teaching, as illustrated by the following quotes.

> I think that it is important to be learner-centred, to understand the experiences that our learners have already had, and then to assist them in acquiring skills to build on these experiences. [Le]

> I have learned ... that learning is not only acquisition but also reconstruction of knowledge, that qualitative conceptions of learning should be promoted through appropriate learning contexts. [Lo]

Also, there were comments on the importance of pedagogy in teaching, as illustrated by the following quotes.

> The principles of evaluation are important, whether online or not. [Y]

> [My long term goals are to] apply the principles of learning as I work, ...apply the learning and teaching principles as I develop an online component of Chem A. [C]

Finally, there were comments that focused on changes in beliefs and attitudes about teaching and learning, as illustrated by the following quotes.

> My goal then shifted to understanding these teaching and learning principles, to reflect about my own teaching and learning practices, and plan how to apply the new knowledge into my future courses. [F]

> I feel inspired to be more actively involved in doing 'things' online, to reach more students and to be more effective in delivering course content and providing student support. [O]

The comments from Learning Portfolios were in line with the aims of the online course in that they showed a high degree of reflection and a focus on students and on learning.

It should be noted that the participants were a highly motivated group of teachers who generally held student-centred views at the start of the online course. Moreover, the Approaches to Teaching Inventory was administered at the end of the online course before participants had had an opportunity to fully develop and teach a course in which they could apply the principles they had learned. Therefore, they would not have been able to answer the strategy items based on actual practice. On reflection, this may not have been the most appropriate instrument, given its focus on more traditional modes of teaching.

Finally, given the small number of matched cases, any generalisations must be made with caution.

4.6   Reflections on the online course

The changes in lecturer conceptions following the online course, while small, are, nevertheless, encouraging in that they suggest that it is possible to support staff to reflect on their conceptions and make changes. The online course provided a context in which participants were immersed in an intensive learning experience that modelled and reinforced a constructivist, student-centred learning-focused approach to teaching. They worked on an authentic task in groups over an extended period of time both online and face-to-face and showcased the course components they had developed. Opportunities for regular reflection were built into the course and participants shared their reflections in the face-to-face component.

Developing such an online course was a challenge. Factors that impacted on the design included a lack of similar courses to use as possible models, the lack of suitable online resources to use as links, the need to provide discipline-specific examples of teaching and learning activities for participants from a wide range of disciplines, finding a suitable programmer and graphic artist, and the time to develop the course in addition to a full time workload.

There were also obstacles in implementing the course. These included participants being unable to dedicate the time required to engage in the course activities online even though time release was promised, varying levels of motivation and ability among participants to work in groups, the design of the course which required individuals to work through the themes at a group pace rather than individually, the fact that the course was not credit-bearing and thus tasks were not assessable and there were no consequences for non-completion of set tasks, problems with the technology in terms of access to the online course especially from home and the associated costs, the lack of choice on the part of participants in doing the course, concerns about the status and future of distance education as an educational medium in the local context, and different expectations about the focus of the course with some participants wanting a greater focus on the technology skills. While attempts were made wherever possible, to overcome these obstacles, this was not always possible given the time and resource constraints. All of these factors may have reduced the impact of the course.

4.7   Implications for supporting teaching and learning online

The experience from designing an online course for teachers to help them teach online has a number of implications for supporting teaching and learning online.

The technology can be seen as both a friend and an enemy – a friend in that developing courses using the new technologies provides an opportunity for lecturers to address their teaching and learning conceptions and practices. This focus on technology in teaching can serve as the trigger for lecturers to identify conceptions and rethink their applicability and influence on student learning.

The focus on technology can be an enemy because it can dominate the educational agenda. Lecturers may be constrained by their lack of skill in using the technology and the time and effort needed to develop such skills. As a result, they may adopt strategies unquestioningly such as putting lecture slides online. Or they may uncritically accept proprietary software or advice from technical experts who have little or no background in educational theory or practice. There is also the danger that they may be seduced by the technology and lose sight of the educational implications of teaching and learning online. Moreover, this limited view of technology can be exacerbated by an emphasis at the institutional level on 'getting courses online' that may reinforce a transmissive view of teaching and a surface approach to the task.

Furthermore, while many of the proprietary learning management systems currently being promoted and adopted at least in Australian universities, have excellent course management features, they may unfortunately reinforce a traditional, linear, segmented and transmissive approach to teaching and learning. Such systems reinforce prevailing conceptions and make it very difficult to develop courses that are based on a constructivist student-centred learning-focused approach.

Attempts by universities to help staff achieve the goal of moving online often focus on poorly designed and low level 'technology training' programmes. While the development of appropriate skills in the technology is essential, such development must be done in the context of developing a course online and include a focus on the educational aspects of the technology. In order for student-centred approaches to teaching and learning to be implemented, teachers need support and encouragement to focus not only on using student-centred strategies but also on the underlying conceptions of teaching that they hold. As Trigwell and Prosser (1996, p. 85) point out, 'just helping academic staff become aware of, or even practicing [sic], particular strategies will not necessarily lead to substantial changes in teaching practice'.

The new technologies hold out the promise of expanding the focus on teaching and learning so that what is known about effective teaching and learning can be used to create exciting and engaging learning experiences online. The best way of achieving such a transformation is to combine the power of the new technologies with a constructivist student-centred conception of learning through well designed, well resourced and well supported staff development activities that focus on changing conceptions of teaching and learning. The type of course online described in this chapter, provides one tool to achieve this goal.

4.8   Conclusion

Learning technologies provides an opportunity for highlighting, discussing and reflecting on the role that conceptions of teaching and learning play in facilitating student learning online. This chapter has identified the importance of lecturer conceptions for facilitating teaching and learning online and described an online course underpinned by a constructivist learner-centred approach to teaching and learning aimed at helping staff to address their conceptions of teaching and learning. Findings show that it is possible to help lecturers change their conceptions albeit to a limited degree through participating in such a course. The major implication for teaching and learning effectively with technology highlighted in the chapter is the need to address staff conceptions of teaching and learning. Only then will lecturers be able to harness the power of technology to enhance student learning.

Note

1. This Philippines Australia Short Term Training (PASTT) project was a Curtin Consultancy Services project, funded by AusAID through SAGRIC International.

4.9   References

Barr, R.B. and Tagg, J. (1995) From teaching to learning: a new paradigm for undergraduate education, *Change* **27**(6): 12–25. Also available:
http://etip.unco.edu/etipweb/ETIPresources/LEARNING.htm.

Biggs, J.B. (1996) Enhancing teaching through constructive alignment, *Higher Education* **32**: 347–64.

Biggs, J.B. (1999) *Teaching for Quality Learning at University: What the Student Does.* Buckingham: SRHE and Open University Press.

de la Harpe, B., Radloff, A. and Wyber, J. (2000) What do professional skills mean for different disciplines in a business school? Lessons learned from integrating professional skills across the curriculum. In C. Rust (ed.), *Improving Student Learning: Improving Student Learning through the Disciplines (pp. 9–23). Oxford: The Oxford Centre for Staff Development, Oxford Brookes University.*

Chickering, A.W. and Ehrmann, S.C. (1996) Implementing the seven principles: technology as lever, AAHE Bulletin *(October) [online]. Available:*
http://www.aahe.org/Bulletin/Implementing%20the%20Seven%20Principles.htm

Chickering, A.W. and Gamson, Z.F. (1987) Seven principles for good practice in undergraduate education, AAHE Bulletin *(March).*

Cohen, J. (1969) Statistical Power Analysis for the Behavioral Sciences. *New York: Academic Press.*

Derry, S. (1996) Cognitive schema theory in the constructivist debate, Educational Psychologist **31**(3/4): 163–75.

Doolittle, P.E. (1999) Constructivism and online education. Paper presented at the 1999 Online Conference on Teaching Online in Higher Education. [online]. Available:
http://www.chre.vt.edu/f-s/doolittle/tohe/tohe2.html

Gow, L., and Kember, D. (1993) Conceptions of teaching and their relationship to student learning, British Journal of Educational Psychology **63**: 20–33.

Herrmann, A., de la Harpe B., Fox, R. and Radloff, A. (2000) Partnerships between pedagogy and technology: designing an online course about putting courses online. [CD-ROM] Proceedings of the 14th Annual Conference & Exhibition: Asian Association of Open Universities, Open learning & Distance Education Ideology, Pedagogy and Teaching, *Manila, Philippines, 25–27 October.*

Kember, D. (1998) Teaching beliefs and their impact on students' approach to learning. In B. Dart and G. Boulton-Lewis (eds), Teaching and Learning in Higher Education (pp. 1–25). Camberwell, Victoria: ACER.

Kember, D. and Gow, L. (1994) Orientations to teaching and their effect on the quality of student learning. *Journal of Higher Education* **65**(1).

McLoughlin, C. (2000) Beyond the halo effect: investigating the quality of student learning online. Paper presented at the Moving Online Conference, Grand Mercure Hotel, Gold Coast, Southern Cross University, , August. [online]. Available: http://www.scu.edu.au/schools/sawd/moconf/mocabstracts/moc16ab.html

Murphy, E. (2000) Constructivism: From philosophy to practice [online]. Available: http://www.stemnet.nf.ca/~elmurphy/emurphy/cle.html

Prosser, M. and Trigwell, K. (1999) *Understanding Learning and Teaching: The Experience in Higher Education*. Buckingham: SRHE and Open University Press.

Samuelowicz, K. and Bain, J.D. (1992) Conceptions of teaching held by teachers, *Higher Education* **24**: 93–112.

Shuell, T.J. (1986) Cognitive conceptions of learning, *Review of Educational Research* **56**: 411–36.

Trigwell, K. and Prosser, M. (1996) Congruence between intention and strategy in university science teachers' approaches to teaching, *Higher Education* **32**: 77–87.

UMass Physics Education Research Group (1999) A constructivist view of science education [on-line]. Available: http://www.perg.phast.umass.edu/perspective/Constructivism.html

von Glasersfeld, E. (1987) Learning as a constructive activity. In C. Janvier (ed.), *Problems of Representation in the Teaching and Learning of Mathematics (pp. 3–17). New Jersey: Lawrence Erlbaum Associates.*

Wiedmer, T.I. (1999) *Portfolios: a means for documenting professional development,* Journal of Staff, Program, & Organizational Development **16**(1): 21–37.

Wissink, H.F. (2001). *Education and training programmes in public administration: alternatives and guidelines for the implementation of online education delivery systems.* Paper prepared for Working Group 1 at the Annual International Conference of the International Association of Schools and Institutes of Administration, Athens, Greece, July.

5 Some implicit issues of educational philosophy involved in learning through web resources

Peter Ashworth

Learning and Teaching Research Institute, Sheffield Hallam University, UK

Keywords

authority; critical thinking; educational philosophy; Hannah Arendt; Internet

5.1   Overview

The use of the Internet within courses in the 'open resource' model allows the student absolute autonomy, but in what sense is it *educational*? Adopting the approach to educational philosophy of Hannah Arendt, who integrates 'radical' and 'conservative' concerns, we consider both the induction of the novice into the tradition (and the associated issues of authority) and the evocation of critical thinking (with the concomitant question of the openness of resources to critique).

5.2   Introduction

There are a number of major gaps in the literature of educational innovation. In particular, there has been little attention to the educational assumptions which underlie innovations. Admittedly, there have been some small attempts to engage in reflection on specific issues such as the question of transfer and the notion of competence, but very rarely do we have any analysis of the very nature of education implied by novel introductions (Gergen, 1995, is one exception). What I am doing in this chapter is related to this missing realm of literature, for I want to find a way of uncovering some unconsidered aspects of learning that lie hidden within certain educational innovations. These unconsidered issues seem to me to matter fundamentally because they have to do with the very nature of education - what we want to have our students become as a result of the learning experiences to which we guide them.

In this chapter, then, I focus on the use of Internet resources within courses. The kind of situation to be considered is where students are given free reign - analogous to being directed to the (once) conventional library – to seek information by browsing the Web in order to develop their awareness of a certain area of the curriculum. Like Hall and Dalgleish (1999), my focus is *not* on the use by students of 'information provided by academic staff nor on any form of computer-aided learning, but rather, on the information sought and used by students which [is] freely available on the Web ... the use of the Web to support their studies' (p. 334). So my concern is with what Hall and Dalgleish characterise as the 'open resource model'.

As Hall and Dalgleish make plain, the practice of encouraging students simply to browse the Internet for material relevant to their studies is widespread among teachers in HE.

> Many of the students had the experience of at least one lecturer mentioning the Web although the reference made to it was usually not a specific address: 'Lecturers mention you can look on the Internet but this is as far as it goes'. To quote another student: 'When she gives out the assignment she may say, there is quite a bit on the Internet about this.' (p. 342)

It is expected that such tasks will have the good effects of student centeredness – flexible delivery; a learning rather than a teaching emphasis, and autonomous learning (although Honey, 2000, is one critic of this assumption). But what does such a use of Internet resources imply concerning the meaning of education as such? The way I want to tackle this question is to draw on one aspect of the educational thought of Hannah Arendt (I have covered wider ground in Ashworth, 2001), and then interrogate the open resource model of Internet use in terms of her understanding of education. I believe that Arendt provides a very sophisticated, though not incontrovertible, commentary on the conservatism/radicalism dichotomy in educational thinking, and it is for this reason that I wanted to apply her thought to the issue of the chapter.

5.3   Conservative and radical educational thought

A basic dimension, which differentiates educational philosophies, can be given the shorthand designation *traditional, conservative* versus *liberal, progressive*. Hare (1994) states the conservative position as follows:

> The view in question is frankly sceptical about what many have claimed to be [education's] task of fostering critical thought, autonomy, open-mindedness and similar attributes, urging instead, the acquisition ... of a body of shared information.

There is variation over time regarding what exactly the focus of this debate is taken to be, but generally conservative thinking – at both the school level and in Higher Education – is supposed to emphasise the maintenance of standards of student performance, with a special concern that all students assimilate some key elements of knowledge – for example, there is a kind of panic in the UK whenever there is a suggestion that school pupils may not be made to read Shakespeare. Radical thinking is characterised as paying less attention to syllabus content than to the development of creative expression in students or more generally, their personal development. In Higher Education there are instances of this divide in (for example) the debates surrounding learning outcomes. The preservation of the knowledge content of the syllabus of a discipline on the one side, as against the specification of skill-based outcomes that can be met in terms of various syllabuses on the other, is one form of this divide. The essence of the conservative/radical dichotomy, then, is between concern with a disciplined induction into a particular scholarly culture on the one side and the encouragement of student development in personal and academic skills on the other.

Related to this is the question of pedagogy as enhancing freedom or as a regime of constraint. The radical interest in the personal expressive development of the student is supposed by conservatives to lead to lack of control and a threat to standards. In contrast, the conservative anxiety to inculcate the historical deposit of what is taken to be the best of the scholarly culture in the student is supposed by radicals to be tantamount to the suppression of the individual – a pedagogic authoritarianism.

I find myself unable to identify with either pole of these binary oppositions, and was overjoyed to see, in coming to read Hannah Arendt, that we have a conceptualisation of the educational scene which cuts through at least some of them.

5.4 Hannah Arendt, the political divide and its relation to the educational one

Arendt (1998) had a view of the realm of politics, motivated, it seems, by twin concerns.

- First, an understandably great *fear for the fragility of democratic civilisation* lends her thought an apparently *conservative* tinge in that she wanted to protect and maintain the institutions which support the activity of politics, and also to maintain the historically-sedimented bodies of knowledge and practice out of which, or against which, creative innovation has meaning.

- This conservatism crosses over, as it were, to a *radical concern for full openness in debate*. For her, politics was precisely centred on the function of providing a forum or field for discussion, for self-expression, action. The defining characteristic of politics was the process of full openness of debate – rather than, for instance, the provision of a mechanism for maximising either capitalist or socialist managerial competence in national economic affairs. And this should be understood very widely – not just within the arena of professional politics but in situations of everyday living. Closure of debate in totalitarianism of any sort is non-politics.

In fact Arendt's political position seems to me to balance rather nicely the claims of radicalism and conservatism in politics. For instance, she writes:

> In politics this conservative attitude – which accepts the world as it is, striving only to preserve the status quo – can only lead to destruction, because the world, in gross and in detail, is irrevocably delivered up to the ruin of time unless human beings are determined to intervene, to alter, to create what is new. ... Because the world is made by mortals it wears out; and because it continuously changes its inhabitants it runs the risk of becoming as mortal as they. To preserve the world against the mortality of its creators and inhabitants it must be constantly set right anew. (Arendt, 1968, p. 192)

Arendt's (1998) concern in political philosophy is partly to maintain the possibility of a stable communal political life within which innovation is possible, but also partly to urge for the constitution of the political arena as one in which freedom of debate and self-presentational personal social action is possible.

This thinking is paralleled precisely in her discussion of education. However, she enhances the analysis through the notion of *natality*. Natality refers to individuals coming to birth, and therefore constituting an upsurge of novices, a novitiate, a refreshing of the population. It also refers to the unclutteredness and freedom from ideas and ways of acting that are old and tired. Natality is about new beginnings. So, for Arendt, education – and I am sure this includes Higher Education as now constituted – is to be regarded as a cultural response to natality. Students constitute the birth into the culture of 'new people' who both threaten existing structures and are a power for innovation. The world is precious, and so are the 'new people'. The tradition is not to be spurned – the world as it is, is the only world there is, and it is within this world and against aspects of it that the next generation will find their very selves. On the other hand Arendt does not entirely dismiss the student centeredness of radical education, and says, approvingly:

> Modern education ... maintained that its exclusive aim was to serve the [student] and rebelled against the methods of the past because these had not sufficiently taken into account the [student]'s inner nature and ... needs. (Arendt, 1968, p. 187)

Education, then, must both *socialise* the 'new people' and maintain their freedom. Here we have the basis for a rejection and unfreezing of the dichotomy radical/conservative. This entails both what is usually regarded as conservative and radical. Gordon (1999), in a paper to which I am especially indebted, has pointed out tellingly the fact that there is a Janus-facedness to the role of education in Arendt's account:

> *The problem is simply to educate in such a way that a setting-right remains actually possible,* even though it can, of course, never be assured. Our hope always hangs on the new which every generation brings; but precisely because we can base our hope only on this, we destroy everything if we so try to control the new that we, the old, can dictate how it will look. Exactly for the sake of what is new and revolutionary in the [student] education must be conservative; it must preserve this newness and introduce it as a new thing into an old world ... (Arendt, 1968, pp. 192, 193, my italics)

5.5 Contemporary analyses which make the description of education in terms of the perspectives of conservatism and radicalism difficult

Let us assume Arendt's perspective then, and take the erstwhile dichotomy conservative/radical, not as opposed ideologies of education, but rather as complimentary perspectives on the field – one emphasising freedom through acquisition of the tradition, the other emphasising the freedom of personal innovatory power, natality. (Incidentally, a much later philosopher makes something of the same analysis of education. See Rorty, 1999.)

To apply this aspect of the thinking of Hannah Arendt to the question of the use of the Internet, one must take note *both* of the conservative concern for the tradition *and* the radical interest in the student as autonomous innovator. But before this is possible, we need to acknowledge three contemporary lines of social and educational analysis which hamper the easy application of concepts of tradition and the student. What is 'the tradition' which is so precious to conservative thought? Who is 'the student' which radicals wish to place at the centre of the educational process?

5.5.1 Constructivism

The contemporary understanding of learning is that learners have necessarily to *construct* their understanding of any item of knowledge (e.g. Gergen, 1995; von Glaserfeld, 1987; Jonassen, 1991, but in fact, St Augustine, in AD 389, knew that direct transmission of knowledge from teacher to student is a myth and that teaching is the activity of facilitating learning by the student). Constructivism is characterised by Tennenbaum, Naidu, Jegede and Austin (2001) as follows:

The continuing development of knowledge and learning is viewed as a cognitive activity involving the ongoing construction of mental representations of reality. This evidences a shift in dominant educational philosophy in which learning had been equated primarily with the attainment of behavioural outcomes. (p. 88)

The constructivist approach ...: views knowledge as an entity, which is mentally constructed via the actions and experiences that the learner undergoes with the immediate learning and broader social environments. Knowledge is actively constructed by the interaction between the learner and external objects through adaptation of and to the experiential world. (p. 89)

Tait (2000, pp. 61–2) has a 'set of principles that have been promoted by various authors', viz:

- learning involves the active construction of personal, conceptual knowledge by the learner relating new to existing knowledge;

- learning is reflective and builds on and also develops the learner's existing knowledge by identifying concepts. It benefits from multiple views of the subject area;

- learning is facilitated by authentic activity, relevant to the situation in which it will be applied;

- learning requires personal contact and social interaction between learning and tutor and between learners.

Tait's account is a little odd, in that it reads as if constructivism were a set of empirical generalisations leading to maxims of good practice in pedagogy rather than a theory of the learner (cf. Lunenberg, 1998). The point is, that this is a model of the learner as well as the learning process, and stresses the agency of the learner in constructing knowledge on the basis of an active interpretation – within his or her own life concerns and wider spheres of understanding – of the information to hand. The fundamental nature of this view is rarely, it seems, understood. Constructivism, in principle, allows the possibility that each learner will come to a quite distinct view of the material to be learned. In fact I believe there are constraints on this idiosyncrasy, but teachers need to understand that constructivism embeds the material within the understanding of the student – facing the teacher of the calculus (for example) with the task of facilitating an understanding of differentiation in 'Ben Jones' which is *his* understanding but yet means that Ben has, for practical purposes, that mind which Newton or Leibniz had in coming to that form of mathematical reasoning. This makes of teaching or learning facilitation an immensely noble and challenging activity.

In terms of our question of the adequacy of the conservatism/radicalism realm of discourse to cover the relevant area of educational debate, constructivism hampers easy application because it insists that no element of the tradition can be learned by someone and remain unchanged. Ben Jones's calculus is not Newton's – even if Ben calculates well. Learning is not a transmission of some aspect of the culture, but a *guided reinvention* of it.

5.5.2   Postmodernism

The contemporary scene, of course, is one in which 'the tradition' as such is problematical – not just that there is dispute over the content of the tradition in many areas, but that it is highly contentious whether there can now be a tradition, an agreed syllabus for novices (Lyotard, 1984; Rand, 1992).

In particular, postmodern thought (for a summary, see Ashworth, 2000, chapter 7) draws attention to the fundamental lack of unity within the culture in general and, in particular, within 'the disciplines' (whatever they remain as). Within the disciplines there is dispute as to criteria of relevance and adequacy. In the face of this situation, issues concerning the syllabus get decided, not in terms of rational criteria but in terms of the marketplace. What people (students, employers) will 'buy' determines the running of courses or the construction of the curriculum.

Again, postmodernism threatens the premises on which the dichotomy radical/conservative is based by challenging the idea of the 'tradition' – this time, not because of the transformation that it suffers in being learned by the new generation, but more fundamentally – its nature is not clear-cut in the way conservatives suggest.

5.5.3   Social construction of identity and of psychological processes

One strand of postmodernism is an extreme relativism which insists that the ways of thinking and the modes of being open to a person are given, and limited, by whatever is available within the culture (socially-available discourses). In the context of learning, this means that what learning is, and what the learner is, are not fixed but will vary with the history of the culture. To give a personal example, I believe it likely that my grandfather was dyslexic, though the absence of compulsory education meant that his consequent illiteracy did not matter, and he learned sufficient to develop a thriving building firm in which his wife kept the books and he did the quantity surveying by practiced mental maxims and rules. My son, in contrast, is dyslexic, a 'fact' which constitutes an element of his personal identity and his self-definition as a learner. In effect, dyslexia only exists in a culture in which learning is by reading and a student 'by definition' reads. Essentialists would say that these are the conditions for dyslexia to emerge and become important; social constructionists would say these are the conditions for there to be any such thing as dyslexia.

In any case, the social constructionist view of identity and of psychological processes is a third thing which hampers the easy application of the conservative/radical perspectives on education, for it undermines the assumption that the learner and learning have essential characteristics, true for all times and all cultures. In fact, we could say that, if e-learning is truly different and will in time present alternative ways of coming to grips with material to be learned, then this will mean that – subtly or maybe very obviously – the nature of the learner will change, the nature of the material to be learned will change, and what we regard as psychological characteristics and personal skills conducive to good learning will be different, and new problems of learning will emerge.

Three important limitations on the analysis of education in terms of the field of debate laid out by radical/conservative perspectives, then. However, always provided that we note that both emphases are to be respected and their intrinsic limitations are to be borne in mind, I am going to take the liberal and the conservative emphases as a framework.

5.6   Arendt's conservative concerns and the use of Internet resources

From the conservative direction, I want to consider issues of authority and legitimacy. Alexander (1995) is one of those who has seen Plato's concerns regarding 'writing' as relevant to all resource-based learning, not just the book.

In the *Phaedrus* (1961), Plato has Socrates in dialogue with Phaedrus, in which Socrates puts forward some very definite views about the value of the human teacher in contrast to resource-based learning.

SOCRATES: You know, Phaedrus, that's the strange thing about writing ... [written words] seem to talk to you as if they were intelligent, but if you ask them anything about what they say, from a desire to be instructed, they go on telling you just the same thing forever. And once a thing is put in writing, the composition, whatever it may be, drifts all over the place, getting into the hands not only of those who understand it, but equally of those who have no business with it; it doesn't know how to address the right people, and not address the wrong. And when it is ill-treated and unfairly abused it always needs its parent to come to its help, being unable to defend or help itself.
PHAEDRUS: Once again you are perfectly right.
SOCRATES: But now tell me, is there another sort of discourse, that is brother to the written speech, but of unquestioned legitimacy? Can we see how it originates, and how much better and more effective it is than the other?
PHAEDRUS: What sort of discourse have you now in mind, and what is its origin?
SOCRATES: The sort that goes together with knowledge, and is written in the soul of the learner, that can defend itself, and knows to whom it should speak and to whom it should say nothing.
PHAEDRUS: You mean no dead discourse, but the living speech, the original of which the written discourse may fairly be called a kind of image.

(Plato: Phaedrus, 275d–276)

Socrates then enunciates a set of communicative criteria which puts interactive (not ex-cathedra) speech clearly as preferable to writing. For Socrates, as portrayed by Plato, then, speaking-and-listening in full social interaction is different in kind to written material and other non-interactive forms of communication. Speech is paradigmatic in academic communication and writing is a defective form (ICT modes of writing fall into this category – though it may be argued that the more 'interactive' they are, the more they approximate human spoken communication). This has to do with the idea that *understanding* demands a multi-directional interrogation of the material, which is a matter of human interaction not 'reading' in the usual sense. Plato's concerns would plainly have particular importance for the 'open resource' model of Internet use, specifically, were the authority of the website to replace the authority of the teacher.

The teacher has, in the past, obtained their authority from membership of an educational institution. Arendt notes that this does not remain unchallenged. Postmodernism, together with the democratic spirit, is inimical to authority of this kind. Arendt, very interestingly, argues that educational authority should be privileged in order to serve the conservative educational function:

> We must decisively divorce the realm of education from the others, most of all from the realm of public, political life, in order to apply to it alone the concept of authority and an attitude toward the past which are appropriate to it but have no general validity and must not claim a general validity ... (Arendt, 1968, p. 195)

Leaving this very contentious opinion (Ashworth, 2001) to one side – and it is not certain that she would want to extend it to Higher Education in any case – in the current state of the art, the conventional account of the problem of authority of the website finds the difficulty to be rather different, in that (maybe modified by student credulity), the intellectual quality of web materials is rather strongly open to doubt (Grassian, 1998; Kirk, 1999; 2000; Lively, 1997; Tillman, 2000). In their interviews, Hall and Dalgleish (1999) found that

> nearly all the students commented on the accuracy and impartiality of the information available on the Web. As one student said, 'Anybody can set up a Web site.' The same student went on to say: 'If you've got some information about something you don't know if they've made it up or not.' (p. 341)

The very full guidance provided by Kirk (1999; 2000) for the evaluation of web resources discusses authorship, 'publishing' mechanism, how to test for unannounced point-of-view, the currency of information, and search engine characteristics.

Here we have a most interesting irony of the Web. Its virtue is its accessibility for the publication of information without censor and without needing authority. It is postmodern, especially in the sense of being free of universal criteria of publishability. It is anarchic. But Arendt's point about authority is very clearly made by the importance that is attached by many to the necessity of acquainting students with ways of judging the academic value or credibility of websites. This can be a major criticism of the open resource model of Internet use. If the conservative emphasis on the transmission of tradition is to be served, then staff must either control access to the Web by guiding students to authoritative sites, or students must be taught the rules by which they can themselves judge sites.

Finally – and this is linked strongly with the other issues of authority – we have the under-considered matter of the capacity of web resources to fulfil the socialising function of education. The student, in becoming the repository of the tradition, is not just a learner of it, but becomes a *member* of the culture, or of the disciplinary or professional group. This surely seems to require human interaction rather than any medium, be it ICT or the book.

5.7 Arendt's radical concerns and the use of Internet resources

We now turn to the radical side of Arendt's thought, for which education is preserving the innovatory spirit of natals – people who would be fresh blood, a source of rejuvenation, by whom the tradition would be preserved *by being transformed*. Arendt, and (to a diminishing extent the further he moved from Socratic thinking) Plato, too, regarded *democracy* and *critique* as imperative. Students must grasp the conventional material of their discipline (and understand it by interrogating the teacher's account) but also practice critique (an emphasis which we have seen to be stereotypically liberal/progressive).

From the liberal side, then, I wish in particular to consider the Web as supporting student liberty and autonomy, and the value of critique. The autonomy of the student in learning – learning by discovery; undertaking learning tasks under light guidance – is a 'value' which is said to justify the use of web resources in education. For liberals, the question is whether web information can be interrogated as to the discourse within which it is situated, and is sufficiently open to dispute. This latter consideration relates the concern for critique which I do not need to reiterate since we have already seen it in discussing the passage from the *Phaedrus*. Ideally – I recognise the assumption of good teaching here – human interaction may allow the student the insight that knowledge is always contestable, which even the most interactive of websites seems to preclude. In this context, it may be that the architecture of those web pages that are well designed for usability by students lead to *greater* vulnerability to Plato's concern (I draw on Forsyth, 1998, for design features of good sites).

However, in contrast to the idea that Internet use may lead to a stifling of natality because the material seems closed to critique, Hall and Dalgleish (1999) have some evidence that creativity, which is certainly one aspect of the complex of activities which can be called critique, may be enhanced by some features of even the 'open resource model' of web use. Hall and Dalgleish see the sheer quantity of information available on the Web as providing conditions for creativity. A student commented,

> It's just the amount of information that it there. ... It makes you aware of things that you may want to look into further – either through the Internet or through other means – that you might not have thought of before. ... It sparks off ideas that perhaps would not have emerged in your head otherwise. (p. 341)

Some students saw this feature of the Internet as tempting the user to inefficient side-tracking, but others saw it as serendipity, leading to otherwise unlikely discoveries and lines of productive thought.

5.8 Conclusion

In sum, the issues as explicated by Hannah Arendt demand that we interrogate Internet resources both for their capacity to induct the novice into the tradition and for their evocation of critical thinking. In saying this, however, we must remember the extent to which the valuable emphases of both radical and conservative thought in education are challenged by constructivism, postmodernism, and the social construction of the learner and the process of learning.

5.9 References

Alexander, S. (1995) Learning on the World Wide Web.
   http://www.scu.edu.au/sponsored/ausweb/ausweb95/papers/education2/alexander/
Arendt, H. (1968) The crisis in education. In *Between Past and future: Eight Exercises in Political Thought*. New York: Viking Press (pp 173–96).
Arendt, H. (1998) The Human Condition (2nd edn, orig. 1958). Chicago: University of Chicago Press.
Ashworth, P. (2000) *Psychology and 'Human Nature*. Hove: Routledge/Psychology Press.
Ashworth, P. (2001) 'Natality' in education: reflections based on work of Hannah Arendt. 20th International Human Science Research Conference, Taisho University, Tokyo.
Forsyth, I. (1998) *Teaching and Learning Materials and the Internet* (2nd edn). London: Kogan Page.
Gergen, K. (1995) Technology and the transformation of the pedagogical project
   http://www.swarthmore.edu/SocSci/kgergen1/text12.html
von Glaserfeld, E. (1987) Learning as constructive activity. In E. von Glaserfeld, *The Construction of Knowledge: Contributions to Conceptual Semantics*. California: Intersystems (pp. 212–14).
Gordon, M. (1999) Hannah Arendt on authority: conservatism in education reconsidered, *Educational Theory* **49**: 161–80.

Grassian, E. (1998) Thinking critically about World Wide Web resources.
  http://www.library.ucla.edu/libraries/college/help/critical/index.htm

Hall, R. and Dalgleish, A. (1999) Undergraduates' experiences of using the World Wide Web as an information resource, *Innovations in Education and Training International* **36**: 334–45.

Hare, W. (1994) Content and criticism.
  http://www.chss.montclair.edu/inquiry/spr95/hare.html

Honey, P. (2000) E-learning – could do better!
  http://www.peterhoney.com/articles/Article.63

Jonassen, D.H. (1991) Objectivism versus constructivism: do we need a new philosophical paradigm?, *Educational Technology Research and Development* **39**: 5–14.

Kirk, E.E. (2000) Evaluating information found on the Internet.
  http://milton.mse.jhu.edu:8001/research/education/net.html

Kirk E.E. (1999) Practical steps in evaluating Internet resources.
  http://milton.mse.jhu.edu:8001/research/education/practical.html

Lively, S. (1997) How to analyse web sources.
  http://www.stedwards.edu/hum/drummond/webanal.html

Lunenberg, F.C. (1998) Constructivism and technology: instructional designs for successful educational reform, *Journal of Instructional Psychology* **25**: 75–82.

Lyotard, J.-F. (1995) *The Postmodern Condition: A Report on Knowledge*. Minneapolis: University of Minnesota Press (especially pp 47–53).

Plato (1961) *The Collected Dialogues of Plato*. Bollingen Series LXXI. Princeton, New Jersey: Princeton University Press.

Rand, R. (1992) *Logomachia: The Conflict of the Faculties*. Lincoln: University of Nebraska Press

Rorty, R. (1999) *Philosophy and Social Hope*. London: Penguin.

Tait, B. (2000) Theory and practice in web based tuition, *Research and Innovation in Learning and Teaching* **1**: 61–71.

Tennenbaum, G., Naidu, S., Jegede, O. and Austin, J. (2001) Constructivist pedagogy in conventional on-campus and distance learning practice: an exploratory investigation, *Learning and Instruction* **11**: 87–111.

Tillman, H.N. (2000) Evaluating quality on the Net.
  http://www.hopetillman.com/findqual.html

6 Attitudes, confidence, strategies and knowledge: searching for answers on the Internet

Julia Gaimster
London College of Fashion, The London Institute, UK
Keywords
Internet; constructivist theory; instructional design; pedagogy; qualitative research; textiles; World Wide Web

6.1   Overview

This chapter will present the initial findings of a research study into the challenges faced by fashion students when they try to use the Internet and World Wide Web (WWW) as sourcing tools for textiles. Gagne's taxonomy was used as a framework for structuring the study. The advantages and disadvantages of instructional and constructivist approaches to learning are discussed. The research used a case-study approach and a combination of research tools. Themes and categories that arose in the data were identified and the relationships between them examined. This research shows that there are several related areas that underpin a successful Internet search. These categories are Attitudes, Confidence, Strategies and Knowledge. Each category is interrelated and contains sub-categories such as access, literacy, experience and support. The study reveals a complex set of factors that can lead to the success or failure of a search strategy. This interdependency of factors from the affective, cognitive and behavioural domains is discussed and used to provide a checklist of factors that tutors may wish to consider when integrating research on the Internet into a learning experience.

6.2   Background to the study and its objectives

In fashion education there has been a long-standing problem with providing students with up-to-date research materials. Because of the speed at which fashion evolves magazines can be three months out of date by the time they are published and books become fashion history as soon as they appear on the library shelves. The Internet and WWW seem to be the ideal research tools for fashion students the information is current, easily accessible and available almost in real time. This research study shows that access to all this information does not necessarily mean that students are using it effectively or indeed using it at all, so how can we effectively integrate this resource into the fashion curriculum?

A change in emphasis towards a student centred approach to learning has created the need for an examination of how best to support independent learning and debate continues about the effectiveness of new technologies in the facilitation of this process (Fischer and Scharff, 1998). This chapter will examine the role of the Internet and WWW in supporting one area of the fashion curriculum, fabric sourcing. Fabric trends are constantly changing and innovations in textiles are the key to some of the most important trends in fashion.

Employers in the fashion industry are looking for students with a sound knowledge of textiles and the ability to source fabrics from wholesale suppliers yet this is an area of the curriculum in which fashion departments are perceived to be failing (Denza, 1996). Students find it difficult to access information and to gain samples from wholesale suppliers many of whom do not respond positively to student enquiries and many students lack the confidence to approach them preferring to rely upon retail outlets. This study set out to examine whether the Internet and WWW can support students in the development of the research and communication skills they require for fabric sourcing.

The objectives of the study were:

- to examine the ways in which students[1] interact with the Internet/WWW;

- to determine their levels of confidence and ability in using the Internet/WWW;

- to analyse the students ability to apply appropriate strategies for independent learning;

- to identify areas in which students have difficulty in using or applying the technology and to propose strategies that may be useful in overcoming these problems;

- to propose strategies for the integration of the Internet/WWW with other traditional[2] teaching methods;

- to apply the knowledge gained to the development of other resources that can be utilised by fashion students undertaking independent research;

- to identify whether the Internet and WWW are useful resources for fabric sourcing.

6.3 Methodology

The research employed a case study approach and was conducted in three stages.

Stage 1   Research Activities Task
Stage 2   Observations
Stage 3   Interviews

This combination of methods enabled triangulation of the data thus strengthening the study design (Patton, 1990). In Stage 1 the Research Activities Task was used to identify the resources students were using for independent research. The respondents were asked to identify the research resources and activities that they would normally use and the order in which they would use them. The data from this part of the study was used to create a framework for the observations and interviews. The observations identified what was actually happening when students logged on to the Internet to perform a search and the interviews were designed to provide an insight into the students' attitudes and perceptions of the WWW as a research tool.

An assignment set for the second year HND Fashion Design and Technology students in July 1999 was used as the vehicle for conducting the research. One of the key aims of this assignment was to encourage the students to utilise wholesale sources for fabrics, thus increasing their knowledge of the range of fabrics available to them, developing confidence in professional communication, and utilising the knowledge gained in their textile technology classes. The students were supported during the assignment by a series of workshops, lectures and demonstrations including a series of three sessions on Internet skills and an introduction to course website created using software developed by Blackboard (2001).

Table 6.1 shows the stages of the study and the sample size at each stage.

Stage1 Research Activities Task Teaching Session 1	Stage 2 Observations Teaching Sessions 2&3	Stage 3 Interviews
19 Respondents	11 Respondents	6 Respondents

Table 6.1   Stages of the study and sample size

From 19 randomly selected students[3] who completed Research Activities Task (RAT) 11 students were observed. The students selected for observation had given a variety of responses to the questions relating to the use of IT in the first stage. These students were observed while using the Internet to try and find fabric suppliers for their project, during the sessions notes were taken and a tape recorder was used to record a series of questions, commentary and verbal feedback from the students. From the observations a chart was compiled to identify categories and themes within the observation data.

An interview schedule was constructed based upon the categories that arose from the RAT and the observations. The schedule was piloted using students who were not in the study and adjustments were made to focus some of the questions and take account of responses that had not been anticipated. A further sample of seven respondents was selected for interview. The selection was based on the respondents' performance in the observations and was designed to include respondents who demonstrated a range of confidence and experience with the technology. The interviews were taped and transcribed. The data from the interviews was then coded and categorised using a simultaneous process of data reduction and analysis (Miles and Huberman, 1994). One of the interview tapes was inaudible so this data was not included in the study.

It was recognised that a study of this type and scale would not permit statistical generalisations. The main focus of the study was to gain an insight into the experience of the individual student and recognised that 'individuals have different needs and will gain different outcomes even when engaged in the same activity' (Patton, 1990). Where quantitative methods were applied it was with the intention of identifying patterns or themes within the data rather than demonstrating any kind of statistical significance.

The hypothesis and theory were developed from the data as it was collected and analysed based upon the principles of grounded theory as described by Glaser and Strauss (1967). As the analysis proceeded adjustments were made to the study in order to accommodate issues and problems as they arose. The inductive approach enabled new patterns to be taken into account as they emerged and for multiple interrelationships to emerge from the data (Patton, 1990). It was not intended to make measurements but to draw together threads within the data that were interconnected and relevant to the individual. The inquiry was designed to be open-ended and to enable further research to be undertaken to gain a deeper understanding of the themes as they began to develop. A second sample of students at the same stage in their programme is to be observed and interviewed in Autumn 2001 this will:

- add depth and texture within the data;
- identify whether two years on the same issues are relevant;

- check the validity and reliability of the original analysis;
- enable the collection of further data relating to themes which arose as the study proceeded.

6.4   Gagné's taxonomy

In this study Gagné's taxonomy was identified as a means of classifying the different skills that the students required in order to be able to access the information on the Internet and process it in a meaningful way. The taxonomy uses five categories of learning outcomes to describe different types of performance these categories are verbal information, intellectual skills, cognitive strategies, attitudes and motor skills. In applying this hierarchy the instructional designer identifies the prerequisites required for each level of instruction by analysing the learning task thereby formulating a sequence or Instructional Curriculum Map for the task. Fundamental to the theory is the notion that each type of learning requires different conditions and a different type of instruction. The taxonomy also suggests a hierarchy of intellectual skills organised according to their complexity: discrimination, concrete concepts, rules and defined

Motor skills	Cognitive strategies	Intellectual skills	Verbal information	Attitudes
Control mouse	Use Boolean terms/advanced search techniques to refine or expand search	**Discrimination:** identify fibres/type of website	Textile terminology	Wanting to use computer
Use Keyboard	Utilise and transfer existing knowledge of fabrics/products	**Concrete concepts:** Identify properties characteristics of fabrics/Identify fabric types/structures	Name parts/ functions of computer	Confidence to experiment
	Experiment with alternative search engines/	**Rules and defined concepts:** How to: use basic keyboard commands, add bookmarks, read URLs, create files and folders, Save information, Print/Download files, Classify fabrics	Name market and consumer requirements	Inquisitiveness: What happens if?
	Evaluate search results, Scan reading/scroll through information	**High order rules:** Organise Bookmarks select appropriate search engines and gateways	Use appropriate garment/apparel terminology	
	Organise information	**Problem solving:** identify appropriate key words, relate existing knowledge to new situation, seek alternative solutions		
	Use synonyms, alternative keywords			

Table 6.2   Learning outcomes identified through the observations and organised into the five categories described in Gagné's taxonomy

concepts, high order rules and problem-solving. The five categories of learning outcomes were useful in helping to identify the range of skills that students using the Internet for research would require. The learning outcomes were identified from the observation data and proved to be a complex mix of skills as shown in Table 6.2.

Gagné points to the need for the conditions of learning to be met. The conditions may be internal, within the individual learner or external events and stimuli that are supportive of learning. These conditions need to take into account the previous knowledge of the learner and the instruction that is to be given. From the observations a list of external factors that might influence the outcome of a search were identified and categorised as shown in Table 6.3.

Hardware	Software	Content
Access to a computer with an Internet link on a regular basis	Stability of network connections	File not found messages
Specification of equipment (memory, modem speed)	Browsers require appropriate plug-ins	Sites that are more promotional than informative
Access to printers	Search engines that do not make it clear which Boolean term they accept	Contact details missing off sites
Access to zip or other storage facilities	Different advanced search facilities offered by different engines	Advertising banners that are misleading and confusing
Access to technical support		Search engines pages that are so cluttered it is difficult to find the results of your search
		Images of fabrics, price lists and product descriptions very difficult to find
		American dominance of web content
		Sites that are no more than lists of links

Table 6.3   External conditions that might influence the activity identified through the observations

In order to meet the Internal conditions the students would need to see the value of the activity. They would also need to have a positive motivation to use the computer because they would understand its value as a research tool. They would also need to have a certain level of confidence and experience in using the Internet and a basic understanding of how it works.

The taxonomy was useful as a means of structuring an activity and identifying the learning outcomes that needed to be met. It became apparent that it was extremely difficult to apply the taxonomy to a task that requires a holistic approach, is non-linear, concerned with open-ended enquiry and where the desired learning outcomes may not always be observable and measurable. These limitations have been commented upon by Crawford (1999); Keegan (1986); Laurrilard (1993). For the type of learning that the study was concerned with it seemed more appropriate to look at constructivist and cognitive theory.

6.5   Constructivist and cognitive theory

Constructivist theory takes the position that the learner is actively involved in the process of learning and uses their existing knowledge to develop or construct new ideas utilising a cognitive structure. The theory states that learning should be within a context, which enables the student to actively engage in the process. Experimentation and reflection are both critical factors in enabling students to further their understanding and construct new meanings (Strommen, 1992). Many commentators (Bransford, 1990; Brown, Collins *et al.*, 1989; CTGV, 1990; Lave and Wenger, 1990) have pointed to the importance of constructing learning activities that are authentic in order to assist the learning process. In applying the study to a real-world activity and context it was hoped that the students would be positively motivated to engage with the technology. It was also important for them to be able to build upon existing knowledge and to be presented with challenges that they were capable of achieving (Bruner, 1966). The work of Vygotsky (1962; 1978) on the zone of proximal development is also relevant. The zone is the area of skill or knowledge that can be developed with support from others as opposed to what the learner is able to achieve on their own. The Internet has been identified as a useful resource in the development of social skills (Benson Soong, Chuan Chan *et al.*, 2001; Crook, 1994; Seale and Cann, 2000; Windschitel, 1998) and may therefore have a role in enabling students to extend their skills and knowledge through collaboration.

In the fashion industry change is constant and the speed of change is being accelerated by the impact of technology. This means that the knowledge and skills required by students are not static. They need to develop the skills to access and build new knowledge on a continuing basis and to transfer these skills to complex domains and problems (Spiro, Feltovich *et al.*, 1992). Crawford (1999) believes that the teaching and learning of IT are 'inherently constructivist activities' and that a new pedagogy based upon constructivist methods will provide students with the opportunity to build the cognitive structures they will need in order to function in a society where 'knowledge is relative and understandings fluid and flexible'. It is hoped that this research study will make a contribution to the construction of this new pedagogy and to discover issues that are relevant to the design of learning activities that utilise the Internet and WWW.

6.6   Themes that arose from the data

The main categories that arose from the data in this study were Attitudes, Confidence, Strategies and Knowledge. These categories while separate were interrelated, as were the sub-categories. Table 6.4 shows the relationships between the categories and sub-categories.

6.6.1   Attitudes

Respondents displayed a mixture of positive and negative attitudes towards the medium. All could see the value of the Internet and its relevance to their future careers but most of them cited barriers that prevented them from using it effectively and confidently. Positive attitudes seem to be most prevalent among the respondents who have access to the Internet at home or other previous experience with the medium; they tend to use it socially and feel at ease using it for a variety of purposes.

> I love the Internet. I haven't come across any negative side. I visit a lot of sites. I'm very interested in music, so I look up a lot of bands, obviously fashion sites, cheap tickets for going home. (Respondent H)

	Attitudes	Confidence	Strategies	Knowledge
Time	Perceptions of wasting/saving time by using the technology		Lack of a strategic approach could lead to wasted time	Lack of knowledge of textile terms or computers could lead to wasted time.
Access	Negative attitudes reinforced by lack of access	Perception that if they had more access to computers they would find them easier to use		
Anxiety		Anxiety about using a computer lead to avoidance of IT		
Technical information		Knowing how to deal with technical issues like a crash can help the learner to be more confident		A basic knowledge of technical issues is needed for effective use of IT
Experience	Experience with the technology usually has a positive effect upon their attitude toward IT		Experience does not necessarily lead to the use of effective strategies	
Literacy		Literacy problems, dyslexia, EFL, poor spelling and lack of confidence in written communication were a key factor in confidence with the medium	Search strategies are text based and rely upon good literacy skills	
Social use of IT	Students had a positive attitude to the social use of IT			
Collaboration			One of the strategies for dealing with problems was to enlist the help of others	Others were used to fill in knowledge gaps
Content	Views about the content of sites were both positive and negative			Knowledge of how to identify & evaluate the source of information
Knowledge of advanced search techniques			Appropriate use of advanced techniques could lead to a more successful outcome	Knowledge of these techniques is required for effective searching

Table 6.4   Relationships between the categories and sub-categories

	Attitudes	Confidence	Strategies	Knowledge
Use of Related resources			Referring to course notes/library guides /trade associations etc to assist in the search	Lack of knowledge of useful resources
Subject knowledge		Knowledge of the subject helps build confidence in dealing with suppliers and engaging in the search	Subject knowledge enabled students 'to pass themselves off' as professionals	Knowledge of correct terminology characteristics and properties of fabrics is required for effective searching
Navigation & information seeking skills		The ability to navigate effectively and employ evaluation skills to information found	Knowledge of information evaluation techniques-reading URLs etc.	
Knowledge of Search engines, gateways etc			Ability to use appropriate search engines/gateways	Knowledge of how search engines function- knowledge of relevant gateways , portals and directories
Content	Accuracy/ usefulness of content		Volume of data can be over whelming- ability to evaluate quality	
Support		Students were more confident when they had access to support	Use of technical support, tutor, others for support	

Table 6.4 (continued)   Relationships between the categories and sub-categories

Respondents without access at home and with no or little previous experience displayed more negative attitudes toward the medium.

> Probably if I had more access to it earlier in my life, maybe I would be more used to using it. It's becoming more normal now, but it's a hassle sometimes to figure how it's working. (Respondent F)

6.6.2   Confidence

Levels of confidence in using the medium varied from feeling extremely at ease in the environment to acute anxiety. A lot of this anxiety was related to a lack of technical knowledge and problems with literacy. The Internet is a text-based medium and students' problems varied from feeling unconfident about spelling and selecting keywords to severe dyslexia which made the adoption of normal search strategies virtually impossible. Limited access and previous experience also had an impact upon their ability to practice and gain confidence.

the other problem I have, I know it sounds stupid, but it's the idea of coming into college and using the computers in college, I don't have access to e-mail at home, not down here anyway, we do at home. It puts me off the thought of it. I don't like coming into college, into the library to do it. (Respondent M)

I always try and stay away from computers or computer games, I've never really been into it. But now I try and get myself to be more familiar with the Internet and e-mails. I'm not confident enough about using them. I feel I need to go on it and use it. I don't think it is difficult, I just need to get used to using the system. (Respondent L)

Experience in using or contacting wholesale suppliers and knowledge of fabrics could also have an effect upon their confidence in undertaking the task, even when they found an appropriate supplier some respondents were hesitant about e-mailing them for information, either because of literacy issues or a feeling that they did not know how to ask for what they wanted. Respondents felt that they had a basic knowledge of fabrics but that was often insufficient for their needs.

6.6.3　Strategies

The strategies that students employ when using the Internet can also impact upon their confidence in using the medium and their attitude towards it. Only one of the students observed seemed to have developed a strategic approach to searching. Respondents stated that they used a variety of related resources including lecture notes and suppliers lists provided by tutors, however only one student was actually observed utilising these resources to inform his search strategy. Respondent H referred to a list of suppliers he wanted to find and was also aware of business directories on the WWW that made locating these suppliers easier. Most of the respondents went directly to either one of the search engines demonstrated in the sessions or one with which they were familiar and felt confident. Students did not seem to approach the search with any kind of plan as to how they were going to search or which keywords or portals might be of use. Some students had no idea how to evaluate the relevance of the sites that were listed or how to refine or expand a search, although book marking was one of the areas covered in the sessions many of the students did not use this facility. One respondent was able to use the relevance ratings to determine how useful the sites might be, another used scan reading but others read through everything or clicked on each link as it appeared. Two respondents said that they pretended to be working designers in order to overcome suppliers' negative attitude toward students.

Collaboration was one of the strategies students used when they became stuck or did not know how to do something, calling upon friends and family or members of their peer group to support them.

Experience in using the WWW did not necessarily translate into effective information seeking strategies respondent D although extremely confident and experienced in using the WWW did not display the use of any more effective strategies than some of the most inexperienced users.

6.6.4　Knowledge

In order to use the Internet effectively for the task students required an existing knowledge in several areas:

- textile terminology in order to make an effective search and to communicate with suppliers;

- a basic understanding of how computers and search engines work;
- knowledge of useful sources of information on the WWW;
- how to evaluate the information they found.

Time was one of the sub-categories that had a complex relationship with the main categories. The inexperienced user who does not know about or understand different search strategies is likely to spend more time searching for information or become frustrated and resort to more traditional sources. Time issues are related to other categories such as content, literacy and access, the student who has literacy problems or for who English is a second language takes longer to find the information that they are looking for. The student who has limited access is under more pressure to use time on the Internet effectively. The amount of content on the WWW can also lead to students feeling that they are wasting time trying to find what is relevant.

6.7 Discussion

In answer to the question is the WWW a useful resource to help students develop fabric-sourcing skills there are several factors to be considered. Some of the students managed to obtain samples using the WWW. Respondent H sourced all of his fabrics this way. Even if they were not so successful in sourcing fabrics the respondents still recognised the value of the exercise and the potential of the resource but there were many barriers for them to overcome in order to use it effectively. Experience in using the WWW did not necessarily translate into effective information seeking strategies this was also identified by Lazonder (2000) therefore it would seem appropriate to give students a basic grounding in how to apply these skills in a complex environment like the Internet.

The challenge of making the Internet more accessible for students with dyslexia and other learning difficulties requires further investigation and is beyond the remit of this study. It is generally accepted that there is a large population of dyslexic students in the field of art and design. These students will be disadvantaged if these problems are not addressed.

6.8 Limitations of the study

The scale of the study makes it difficult to identify any consistencies within the data that can be used for generalisation however it was possible to identify themes and issues that are relevant to more than one student within the sample and therefore may be relevant to others. Many of the themes identified are addressed by the literature so may be relevant and applicable in other subject areas. The follow-up study should enable further verification of the validity of the themes identified.

6.9 Implications for pedagogy

Further investigation into all of the issues identified is required. A larger scale study or further case studies may reveal sufficient data to make generalisations. There are connections with the data from the study and the literature in the field that indicate several areas for consideration when designing research activities using the Internet and WWW. The following guidelines will be useful to tutors when considering the use of the Internet as a research tool in a learning activity:

- ensure that external conditions support the learning environment, e.g. stability of the software and sufficient technical support;

- familiarise the students with the basic principles of search engine software before they begin, provide them with a list of starting points then allow them time to practise and build confidence;

- ensure there is sufficient access for those students who do not have their own computers;

- encourage them to draw up a search strategy, list of keywords, sites to visit etc. before they sit down at the computer and to consider the use of related resources;

- they should be made aware of the purpose of the task and its relevance to the real world;

- consider using collaborative strategies to help students build confidence;

- dyslexic students and those with literacy problems may require extra support;

- they may need guidance in how to interpret and evaluate their search results.

The issues identified in this study point to a need for tutors to understand the complexity of the factors that may impact upon a students ability to use the Internet successfully. They will need to devise strategies to ensure that students have the necessary skills and support in place to enable them to engage in independent research using the WWW. These strategies should be underpinned by an understanding of the various theories that can be used in the development of a pedagogy that supports the integration of information technology within the curriculum. There are elements of both instructional and constructivist theory that can usefully be applied to learning activities using information technology. Used in combination they can provide the tutor with a powerful set of theoretical tools that support independent learning.

Notes

1. .In this study students refers to HND Fashion Design and Technology students at the London College of Fashion.

2. Traditional techniques include lectures, workshops and tutorials.

3. The Lottery method was used; there were 55 students in the year group.

6.10   References

Benson Soong, M.H., Chuan Chan, H. *et al.* (2001) Critical success factors for on-line course resources, *Computers and Education* **36**: 101–20.

Blackboard (2001) Blackboard.com, http://www.blackboard.com. 2001.

Bransford, J.D. (1990) Anchored instruction: why we need it and how technology can help. In D. Nix and R.J. Spiro (eds), Cognition, Education and Multimedia.. Hillsdale, NJ: Erlbaum.

Brown, J.S., Collins, A. *et al.* (1989) Situated cognition and the culture of learning, *Educational Researcher* **18**(1): 32–42.

Crawford, R. (1999) Teaching and learning IT in English state secondary schools- towards a new pedagogy, *Journal of Education and Information Technologies* **4**: 49–63.

Crook, C. (1994) Computers and the Collaborative Experience of Learning. London: Routledge.

CTGV (1990) Anchored instruction and its relationship to situated cognition, *Educational Researcher* **19**(6): 2–10.

Denza, V. (1996) The impact of globalisation on design education. In *Image and Reality*: 2nd National Conference of the Association of Degree Courses in Fashion and Textiles Design, Brighton University, Fashion Textiles Dept, School of Design, University of Brighton.

Fischer, G. and Scharff, E. (1998) Learning technologies in support of self-directed learning, http://www-jime.open.ac.uk/98/4/fischer-98-4-01.html (accessed 2001).

Glaser, B.G. and Strauss, A.I. (1967) *The Discovery of Grounded Theory: Strategies for Qualitative Research* New York, Aldine.

Keegan, D. (1986) *Foundations of Distance Education*. London: Routledge.

Laurrilard, D. (1993) *Rethinking University Teaching: A Framework for the Effective Use of Educational Technology*. London: Routledge.

Lave, J. and Wenger, E. (1990) *Situated Learning: Legitimate Peripheral Participation*. Cambridge: Cambridge University Press.

Lazonder, A.W. (2000) Exploring novice users' training needs in searching information on the WWW', *Journal of Computer Assisted Learning* **16**: 326–35.

Miles, M.B. and Huberman, A.M. (1994) *Qualitative Data Analysis*. Thousand Oaks, California: Sage.

Patton, M.Q. (1990) *Qualitative Evaluation and Research Methods*. Newbury Park, Sage.

Seale, J.K. and Cann, A.J. (2000) Reflection on-line or off-line: the role of learning technologies in encouraging students to reflect, *Computers and Education* **34**: 309—20.

Spiro, R.J., Feltovich, P. J. *et al.* (1992) Cognitive flexibility, constructivism and hypertext: random access instruction for advanced knowledge acquisition in ill-structured domains. In T. Duffy and D. Jonassen (eds), *Constructivism and the Technology of Instruction*. Hillsdale, NJ: Erlbaum.

Strommen, E.F. (1992) *Constructivism, Technology, and the Future of Classroom Learning*. http://www.ilt.columbia.edu/k12/livetext-nf/docs/construct.html (accessed 2001).

Vygotsky, L.S. (1962) *Thought and Language*. Cambridge, MA: Harvard University Press.

Vygotsky, L.S. (1978) *Mind in Society*. Cambridge, MA: MIT Press.

Windschitel, M. (1998) The WWW and classroom research: what path should we take?, *Educational Researcher*: 28—33.

7   What do we mean by electronic literacy?

Colleen McKenna,
University College London, UK

Keywords
academic literacies; computer mediated communication; dialogic discourse; electronic literacy; hypertext; power

7.1   Overview

This chapter considers the concept of electronic literacy and attempts to define the range of activities within its scope and consider how and where they are located within the university curriculum. As this is a conceptual study, much emphasis is given to the themes emerging from the current literature of the field, in particular, the topics of power, reading and writing in digital environments, oral and visual literacies, and the relationship between C & IT and social change. Three theoretical frameworks for conceptualising electronic literacy are also explored.

7.2   Introduction

With the increased use in higher education of learning technologies, such as electronic communication, web-based resources and managed learning environments, students not only have to acquire a range of technical computing skills but they must also be able to use communication and information technologies (C & IT) to interpret, construct and express meaning. In other words, they must develop proficiency in 'electronic literacy', a rapidly changing area which involves practical, pedagogic and theoretical approaches to using digital media and networks for learning, teaching and research.

Practical activities within the field of electronic literacy include, but are not limited to, locating and evaluating electronic sources; interpreting multimedia; developing competence in computer-mediated communication (including electronic conferencing, and asynchronous and synchronous dialogues/discussions); reading and writing hypertext; electronic publishing; and devising strategies for addressing 'virtual' audiences across digital networks.

More theoretical areas of electronic literacy research include conceptualising the construction of new textual forms; investigating the ways in which C & IT (especially in the area of computer mediated communication) is transforming academic discourse; articulating changes in the concept of authorship and copyright; and exploring the impact of digital networks upon the development of scholarly communities.

This chapter aims to explore and define further the range of activities encompassed by electronic literacy, and to consider where the teaching of electronic literacy is best positioned within the academic (as opposed to the training) curriculum. The chapter will consider critical issues and theoretical models for electronic literacy proposed in the literature, and it will also ask whether electronic literacy represents a point of intersection within the curriculum between practice and theory in the use of learning technologies, particularly those which facilitate communication.

7.3   Background

My interest in this area began when I was asked to develop a credit-bearing course-unit which would give students opportunities to learn practical computer-based research and communication skills but would also enable them to reflect critically upon the use of computers to read, write and publish in an academic context. The ideas for this chapter came about as the course team struggled to understand who our audience might be, what a course syllabus would comprise, what readings would be used and how the practical activities (such as doing Internet-based searches, learning to participate in virtual learning environments, developing web projects, etc) would sit alongside more theoretical topics such as what is the relationship between reading and writing in such environments, with whom does power reside, and what does it mean to speak about gender and ethnicity in digital environments?

These questions led to an attempt to understand where such questions were currently being asked within the university curriculum and to locate theoretical frameworks in which to analyse such topics.

7.4   What is meant by electronic literacy?

As perhaps befits an evolving area of study, the naming of this 'field' is itself an unstable activity. Terms that cover some or all of the activities outlined above include 'IT/Information Skills', 'electronic communication', 'computer literacy', 'technology studies' and 'information literacy'. This chapter adopts the term 'electronic literacy', as defined by Shetzer and Warschauer (2000), who argue that the phrase combines aspects of information literacy (the ability to find, organise and make use of digital information) with issues of electronic communication, knowledge creation and research. Areas of study in electronic literacy would include:

- computer-mediated communication (including electronic conferencing and asynchronous and synchronous communication);
- interpreting multimedia;
- identifying and evaluating electronic sources;
- reading and writing hypertext;
- Internet publishing;
- developing strategies for addressing 'virtual' audiences, and understanding copyright.

However, such an account of electronic literacy perhaps implies that this is an unproblematic area. In fact, this is highly contested territory and recent work in the field has sought to challenge assumptions about power, democratisation and intellectual rigour. These will be considered in the following section.

7.5 Key themes from the literature on electronic literacy

There are several, broad discipline areas informing and influencing the development of electronic literacy. One of the most prominent set of voices in the literature belongs to researchers in the field of student writing and composition as the traditional notion of academic literacy segues into one of academic literacies (Lea and Street, 2000) or multiliteracies (New London Group, 1996), thereby encompassing student communication within digital environments. The second and quite distinct impulse is to be found within more traditional IT skills arenas. In the UK, the movement from IT skills to something more akin to information literacy is evident in government funding initiatives and sector-wide projects (JISC, 2000). The third is the influence of humanities computing, a field which has engaged with the technical and theoretical aspects of electronic literacy for some time with enquiries into issues of textuality, the future of the book, the construction of hypertext editions, the use of metalanguages etc. These three areas exert different forces upon the emerging area of electronic literacy and examples of the different ways in which these shape its development will be discussed in more detail below.

This section addresses four main topics from the literature in relation to the development and role of electronic literacy within the curriculum. These include issues of power (both in terms of teacher–student relationships and more broadly with respect to Internet usage outside higher education); reading and writing in digital environments; the rise or re-emphasis of new forms of literacy such as visual and oral literacies; and technology as socially applied knowledge (Kress, 1998) in the context of electronic literacy.

7.5.1 Issues of power

While at one time discourses about the use of email, the Web and virtual learning environments focused on the potential democratising properties of such media, now many of the more recent writings in the area challenge this assumption and consider more fully the advantages and disadvantages of the Internet from social, political and economic perspectives. Furthermore, a number of commentators would see this as an important area of inquiry within the teaching of electronic literacy itself. Extending standard arguments about power and conventional forms of literacy, Snyder (1998) argues that the very act of gaining proficiency in electronic literacy is riven with notions of power: 'power now is ... closely associated with access to and familiarity, affinity and dexterity with uses of new technologies for literacy purposes'. From a global perspective, access to new technologies is still limited to a relatively wealthy elite. Furthermore, the development of electronic literacy is complicated by the dominance of English on the Internet (Hawisher and Selfe, 2000; Warschauer, 1999).

In *Electronic Literacies: Language, Culture, and Power in Online Education*, Warschauer presents case studies which foreground the introduction of electronic literacy development to student groups whom he believes would otherwise be at risk of being 'marginalised' from the information society. He finds that not only does an understanding of the uses of new technologies support disciplinary study (in this case, undergraduate classes in writing, language and culture) but also that students from backgrounds with strong visual and oral histories (such as that of indigenous Hawaiians) can use new media to access and express pictorial, spoken and dance-based cultural communication. In the latter instance, proficiency in electronic literacy is empowering in both educational and personal contexts.

The discourse of electronic literacy must also take account of internal power relationships which inscribe learning and dialogue in digital environments. Lea (2000) asks whether computer mediated communication (CMC) exchanges enable different power relationships (particularly in terms of control and authority over course content) between students and lecturers. Analysing two different courses in which CMC was the primary method of interaction, she interrogates the assumption that the role of the academic moves from that of expert to facilitator who thereby cedes 'control' to students. She concludes that whether or not such a shift occurs depends more upon the model of teaching and learning within the course and less upon the introduction of technology. This finding supports Kress's position that electronic literacy and the dynamics of online learning situations are more a function of social application and context than of technology (Kress, 1998).

7.5.2   Reading and writing in digital environments

At the heart of research into electronic literacy is an enquiry into the impact (actual and theoretical) of C & IT upon reading and writing, particularly the production and analysis of hypertext. Much is made of teaching students how to present ideas-both textually and visually – in hypertext environments and, importantly, how to read and interpret such documents. But what often begins as discussions of coding and technique soon yields to the more theoretical problematising of reading and writing in hypertext environments, which sees students as potentially 'reader-authors' who construct their own pathways through material and potentially add text and links to a wider network of information (Pincas, 2000; Snyder, 1998). Both Pincas and Snyder argue that this blurring of boundaries between reading and writing potentially empowers the student and fosters a more interactive and explorative type of learning.

However, a number of critics (Snyder included) express concerns about the impact of hypertexts upon reading and interpretive practices. While not certain *how* reading practices will change, Burbules (1998) worries that current trends in electronic environments will encourage an insufficiently critical approach to reading hypertext, and he is especially exorcised by a lack of understanding of the rhetorical function of hypertext links. The link, rather than a neutral, functional device, in fact, potentially enacts a relationship (between objects, text, images) which reflect the ideological position of the site's author(s). Using poetic tropes as analogues, Burbules suggests that links construct associations and comparisons, the power of which is often underestimated by the cyber reader. The very act of associating information/pages/images to one another is laden with value-judgements which often go unrecognised and unacknowledged. A function of electronic literacy would therefore be to teach the reading or interpretation of hypertext in a manner similar perhaps to the reading of literature, history, visual art etc.

The rising prominence of new technologies and consequent literacies has prompted some scholars to revisit traditional forms of writing and ask critical questions about their use and position within the curriculum. Worried that the craft of sustained writing might be lost with shifts towards computer-mediated communication (CMC) and web-based writing, Doug Hesse argues powerfully for the preservation of 'essayistic literacy':

> There is an important value to reading and writing extended, connected texts whose author has managed the double pulls of complexity and order, producing works that convey their status as products of a certain experiential and intellectual nexus, not as objective truth. (Hesse, 1999)

Constructing what feels, at times, to be an artificial opposition between champions of 'network-based literacy' and those who support the essay, he does, none the less, offer persuasive arguments about the potential lack of criticality in web-based discourse, in which 'pointing' and linking is privileged over interpreting and analysing (Hesse, 1999). At the heart of this debate is role of the linear essay, in many ways the stalwart of academic communication, and a form which is seen to be threatened by the increased use of the Internet as a medium for constructing and publishing written texts. Yet, as Bolter (2001) observes, hypertext essays are able to accommodate multiple arguments and have the capacity to enable dialogue between writer and reader. Despite its use in teaching, however, the Internet has yet to yield a new form of scholarly essay adopted for professional publication (Bolter, 2001).

Moving from hypertext to more general CMC environments which enable synchronous and asynchronous interaction, it is clear that here, too, new technologies are fostering hybrid communication which resembles both written text and speech and also contains its own, unique features. Pincas (2000), who has termed such online discussion 'e-talk', observes that there are substantial differences in conversational behaviour (such as conventions involving turn-taking, sustaining themes, and listener feedback) between face-to-face and online discussion groups. Lea (2000), pursuing the question 'what kind of writing is this?', analyses CMC interactions linguistically, focusing upon issues of modality to investigate how students situate themselves, through their writing, in relation to the course content and how they are therefore able to 'negotiate their own personal construction of academic knowledge'. In contrast to much of the work in this area, Lea argues that computer mediated conferencing does not represent a homogeneous genre, but rather that the types of writing produced and the relationships that are engendered depend very much upon the overall academic context in which such writing occurs.

7.5.3 New literacies and social change

Perhaps the differentiation between essayistic literacy and network literacy discussed above is symptomatic of the range of different literacies which exist in relation to electronic literacy. Kress (1998) and Warschauer (1999) see digital environments as an opportunity to revive visual modes of communication, which, Kress believes, will 'rival' text-based communication. Warschauer, researching the impact of electronic literacy within a Hawaiian studies course, found that oral, visual and even dance and chant-based communications were key features of the Hawaiian language and education. He argues that the capacity to combine these multi-modal forms through computer-based media is both culturally and pedagogically appropriate:

> Many writers have claimed that network-based digital technologies are particularly congruent with many non-Western and oral cultures. They have pointed out that new technologies are restoring an attention to imagery and visual communication that pre-dates the print era (Bolter, 1996) and that is prominent in many non-western cultures (Lemke, in press). They have also stressed that the structure of computer -mediated texts harkens back to features of oral communication ... It was clear from my own study that many Hawaiian students and teachers feel that online communication is congruent with non-Western ways of learning and communicating. (Warschauer, 1999)

What is foregrounded here is the mode of learning and the content (art, sound recordings, dance) rather than the medium (computer network), and Kress (1998; 1999) and Warschauer (1999) argue that, in the context of considering changes associated with electronic literacy, less emphasis should be placed on the technologies themselves and more on the social contexts in which they are applied. Fundamentally, technology is not context-neutral (Burbules, 1998; Lea, 2000; Warschauer 1999) and shifts in communication and learning within electronic environments constitute social change not simply technological change:

When we look at the far-reaching and deep changes in forms of communication which characterise the present – e-mail and its changing forms of language, for instance – it is tempting to attribute these changes to some technological innovation but erroneous to do so ... Technology is socially applied knowledge, and it is social conditions which make the crucial difference in how it is applied. (Kress, 1998)

7.6 Theory and practice: three frameworks for electronic literacy

In her introduction to *Page to Screen: Taking Literacy into an Electronic Era*, Ilana Snyder argues for the development of theories of electronic literacies and suggests that they should accommodate the linguistic and socio-cultural impulses (among others) which are shaping the field. A number of commentators are beginning to theorise electronic literacy using existing linguistic and literary theories as well as devising, in the case of Shetzer and Warschauer (2000) and the New London Group (1996), critical frameworks that specifically address new technologies and pedagogy. The following section briefly considers three approaches to the conceptualisation of electronic literacy activities including a language-teaching approach, the application of Bakhtin's theory of dialogic discourse and the New London Group model of multiliteracies.

Shetzer and Warschauer's framework considers the movement from a conventional notion of literacy to electronic literacy, and using the categories communication, construction, reading and research, and learning paradigm, they map the changes between the two approaches and identify specific classroom activities. Of particular interest in their account of the shift towards electronic literacy is the increased emphasis on collaboration, the inclusion of new media (in terms of construction, interpretation and combination with text) and the movement from linear to non-linear (hyper)texts. In line with perspectives discussed above, Shetzer and Warschauer suggest that even seemingly transparent activities associated with electronic literacy should be viewed critically (see Table 7.1).

7.6.1 Bakhtin and dialogic discourse

Shetzer and Warschauer's framework marks out shifts effected through a consideration of electronic literacy from an activity-centred perspective. Dialogism offers a more linguistic approach to electronic literacy. Bakhtin's theory of dialogic discourse is premised on the notion that all meaning is constructed through dialogue – real or imagined. We write and speak with reference to a listener(s) (or addressee), and this listener's presence determines, at least in part, what we say. Thus, identity and discourse are shaped by engagement with others (Bakhtin, 1988). Furthermore, Bakhtinian theory is alert to voices, power relationships, difference and external utterances (for example, state, religious, slang, corporate discourses). Originally developed as a theory for explaining and analysing the dynamics of the novel, it is now being applied as a method to interpret and explain CMC transcripts and general network-based interaction.

Dialogic theory has been used as a framework in which to consider electronic literacy activities at three levels. At the finest level of granularity, it can be applied to the dialogue produced in electronic environments in much the same way it is used to analyse passages of fiction or poetry. In this instance, CMC transcripts are treated as texts. Batson (1998) applies this technique to exchanges between postgraduate students and identifies a range of utterances representing differences of tone, dialect, ideological positions etc. At a more general level, Bakhtinian theory helps to explain the dynamics of the 'networked classroom'

	Earlier approaches	**Electronic literacy approach**	**Electronic literacy activities**
Communication	Based on speaking and listening	Also includes computer-mediated communication	Communicating with individuals and groups; participating in collaborative projects; using asynchronous and synchronous technologies; understanding implications of CMC
Construction	Based on linear texts	Also includes hypertexts	create, store, maintain and manage web pages; publicise websites; be familiar with available web technologies; understand implications of web-based publications (copyright, intellectual property rights, censorship)
	Excludes non-print media	Combines texts and other media	
	Tends to focus on individual writing	Strong focus on collaboration	
Reading & research	Restricted to print sources	Includes online sources	Formulate questions; find online information; evaluate and analyse online materials and tools; determine authority and expertise; identify rhetorical techniques of persuasion; site online sources; select search technologies
	Focuses on linear texts	Also includes hypertexts	
	Excludes non-print media	Combines texts and other media	
	Tends to separate reading skills from critical evaluation skills	Views critical evaluation as central to reading	
	Focuses on library search skills	Includes searching and navigating online sources	
Learning paradigm	Often based on curricular learning paradigm	Based on interactive learning paradigm, with emphasis on autonomous learning	

Table 7.1   Electronic literacy Framework (from Shetzer and Warschauer, 2000)

and the pedagogy underpinning it. Galin and Latchaw's *The Dialogic Classroom* is wholly predicated on this premise:

> One way to understand the dynamics of the networked classroom is by seeing it in Bakhtinian terms ... This new rhetorical environment, in fact, could have arisen out of Bakhtin's imagination. His vision of the dialogic nature of language in novels – its simultaneously unifying and decentralising tendencies and its tendency towards stratification of discourse – has appeared much more clearly than ever in the networked classroom.

Such a reading is particularly relevant to the introduction of CMC in which students learn largely through discussion and debate with others. More broadly, the introduction of electronic literacy into a course is indicative of a larger paradigm shift in which the authoritative voice of the lecturer is replaced by dialogic interaction among participants who bring with them their own political, ideological and linguistic discourses which, in turn, shape the educational experience of others (Batson, 1998; Warschauer, 1999). The general movement in this model is from the dominance of a singular voice to the interaction of many voices.

7.6.2   New London Group – a pedagogy of multiliteracies

In some respects, what Bakhtin anticipates in his recognition and embrace of multiple discourses (including newspaper, song, dance, signs etc.) is the appeal of multiliteracies as defined by the New London Group (NLG) in 1996. The concept of multiliteracies was devised, in part, to describe the 'burgeoning variety of text forms associated with information and multimedia technologies' (NLG, 1996). It also is alert to the significance of visual literacy and, in particular, the relationship between text and image. In short, the NLG call for a re-conceptualisation of what it means to be literate in an era of cultural and linguistic diversity and one in which modes of communication are swiftly changing.

In order to enable the translation of their theories into classroom practice, the NLG devised a pedagogical model of multiliteracies, a version of which is advocated by Warschauer, 1999, as a framework in which to consider electronic literacy. The pedagogical model consists of four categories:

1. situated practice – the 'immersion in meaningful practices within community of learners'; the community includes experts and novices;
2. overt instruction – this involves 'active interventions' by teachers or other experts that 'scaffold learning activities'; one significant feature of this stage is the development of a metalanguage for reflection;
3. critical framing – this entails the repositioning of knowledge in broader contexts and enables learners to gain 'the necessary personal and theoretical distance from what they have learned'; in particular, this stage is alert to historical, social and political contexts;
4. transformed practice – this stage completes the loop. It puts the 'transformed meaning' back into a new context or cultural site. This represents the implementation of understanding acquired through phases two and three. The New London Group pays particular attention to doing this with discourses which may be at odds.

Although devised as a strategy for general literacy engagement, it is possible to see how such stages would enable students to become more proficient at communication within electronic environments as well as helping them to theorise the use of and interaction within such environments.

7.7   Discussion

The previous section considered how theoretical frameworks can usefully describe what happens when electronic literacy activities are introduced into the curriculum. A related question would be how would the teaching electronic literacy enable the intersection of theory and practice? A number of studies suggest that the actual teaching of electronic literacies occurs outside a critical framework. That is, while there exist texts which interrogate the social and political aspects of the widespread use of C & IT or which consider aspects of hypertextuality in theoretical terms, for example, these are frequently not incorporated into syllabi. I would argue that a course-unit on electronic literacy offers an ideal opportunity for marrying practice with theory and the types of topics one might consider include: contexts (historical, social, theoretical, political) for considering electronic communication; reading strategies within digital environments; interdisciplinarity – what constitutes electronic literacy in different subjects; issues of genre, voice and audience in CMC; comparison between traditional essayistic literacy and new forms; power and the Internet. Such topics could easily accompany more practical sessions on communicating and publishing online texts.

A further question might ask where in the curriculum should electronic literacy be taught? Activities associated with electronic literacy are positioned in a variety of departments and courses within institutions. In many of the examples discussed above, particularly those experiences from North American higher education, the context is often either language teaching (often in English as a second language courses) or writing/literacy teaching. In these instances, computers have generally been introduced to support the teaching of the traditional course and then, subsequently, the act of communicating and publishing in online environments has become a focus of teaching and analysis itself. Other sites of electronic literacy activity include English departments – which look at theoretical issues associated with textuality, hypertext fiction, and the use of hypertext environments to model associative characteristics of certain literary genres (Grigar 1998). Additionally, as suggested above, humanities computing has been considering both conceptual and technical aspects of electronic literacy (particularly in terms of textuality, the status of electronic editions, emerging literary genres, metalanguages etc.) for some time. Other areas offering aspects of electronic literacy provision are library and information science departments, central IT service groups (though these offerings tend to be skills-oriented) and some methods-based courses embedded in departments.

In the US, institution-wide writing programmes, which often have both centralised tuition (composition courses) as well as distributed components (writing across the curriculum, writing in the disciplines), perhaps provide a model for thinking about electronic literacy in the curriculum. In such programmes, there would appear to be scope for introducing electronic literacy quite widely and in discipline-specific contexts.

In the UK, where few such literacy programmes exist, the placement for electronic literacy teaching is likely to be located differently. While skills-based approaches to C & IT have existed, often in centralised units, there has been less emphasis on a more critical approach to electronic literacy. Yet recent government initiatives have actively promoted developments in this direction. A recent Joint Information Systems Committee (JISC) bid for funding differentiated between IT skills and 'information skills', calling the latter a 'broader' concept which is 'more directly related to the aims and processes of education as a 'knowledge creation' activity' (JISC, 2000). Both contributed to JISC's wider concept of 'information literacy' and the funding body has supported a study into how institutions (higher and further) would be providing the development of information literacy for students (and, to a lesser extent, staff).

To return to the original question posed at the start of this chapter, it would seem that on the one hand, issues of electronic literacy should be considered within subject-based contexts. (Such a philosophy underpins the writing in the disciplines movement in the US.) Nevertheless, the topic of electronic literacy is increasingly amassing a body of literature, so the development of academic modules which take electronic literacy as their topic, enable the subject to be interrogated and analysed to a high level. In particular, they allow the space and time for consideration of some of the more theoretical issues association with the field. Thus, while there is a desire for students to be conversant with electronic literacy activities in order to support their academic study, it is also the case that the field increasingly merits investigation and research in its own right.

This chapter has attempted to map the terrain of electronic literacy by considering the definition and naming of field, key topics in the literature (power, reading and writing in digital environments, the rise of new literacies enabled by C & IT, and technology as socially applied knowledge) and the development of relevant theoretical frameworks. It has also broached the issue of the positioning of electronic literacy within the university curriculum, and, hopefully, highlighted areas for further research into the impact and placement of electronic literacy within higher education.

7.8   References

Bakhtin, M.M. (1988) *Dialogic Imagination,* ed. M. Holquist, transl. C. Emerson and M. Holquist. Austin: University of Texas Press.

Batson, T. (1998) Rhetorical paths and cyber-fields: ENFI, hypertext, and Bakhtin. In J. Galin and J. Latchaw (eds), (1998) *The Dialogic Classroom.* Illinois: NCTE.

Bolter, J. D. (2001) *Writing Space: Computers, Hypertext, and the Remediation of Print.* New Jersey: Lawrence Erlbaum Associates

Burbules, N. (1998) Rhetorics of the Web: hyperreading and critical literacy. In I. Snyder, *Page to Screen: Taking Literacy into the Electronic Era.* London: Routledge, 102–22.

Galin, J. and Latchaw, J. (1998) *The Dialogic Classroom.* Illinois: NCTE.

Grigar, D. (1998) "What is seen depends on how everybody is doing everything: using hypertext to teach Gertrude Stein's *Tender Buttons.* In J. Galin and J. Latchaw (eds) *The Dialogic Classroom.* Illinois: NCTE, 27-42.

Hawisher, G. and Selfe, C. (2000) *Global Literacies and the World-Wide We*b. London: Routledge.

Hesse, D. (1999) Saving a place for essayistic literacy. In G. Hawisher and C. Selfe (eds), *Passions, Pedagogies and 21st Century Technologies.* Utah: Utah State University Press, 15–33.

JISC (2000) "C9/00 JCALT Programme 2000/01".

Kress, G. (1999) 'English' at the crossroads: rethinking curricula of communication in the context of the turn to the visual. In G. Hawisher and C. Selfe (eds), *Passions, Pedagogies and 21st Century Technologies.* Utah: Utah State University Press, 66–88.

Kress, G. (1998) Visual and verbal modes of representation in electronically mediated communication: the potentials of new forms of text, In I. Snyder, *Page to Screen: Taking Literacy into the Electronic Era.* London: Routledge, 53–79.

Lea, M. (2000) Computer conferencing: new possibilities for writing and learning in Higher Education. In M. Lea and B. Stierer (eds), *Student Writing in Higher Education.* Buckingham: SRHE and Open University Press, 69–85.

New London Group (1996) A pedagogy of multiliteracies: designing social futures, *Harvard Educational Review* **66**: 60–92.

Pincas, A. (2000) New literacies and future educational culture, *ALT-J* 8(2): 69–79.

Shetzer, H. and Warschauer, M. (2000) An electronic literacy approach to network-based language teaching. In M. Warschauer and R. Kern (eds), *Network-based Language Teaching: Concepts and Practice.* New York: Cambridge University Press.

Snyder, I. (1998) Beyond the hype: reassessing hypertext. In I. Snyder, *Page to Screen: Taking Literacy into the Electronic Era.* London: Routledge, 125–43.

Warschauer, M. (1999) *Electronic Literacies: Language, Culture, and Power in Online Education.* New Jersey: Lawrence Erlbaum Associates.

Enhancing the capacity of online discussions to support student learning

Jill Armstrong[1], Roger Clark[2] and Richard J. Varey[3]

1. LTSN Generic Centre; 2. Intellekt E-Learning Ltd; 3. University of Salford, UK

Keywords
computer based conferencing; conversation; critical discussion; Intellekt; online discussion

8.1   Overview

Online discussion systems have been adopted as elements of on-campus and off-campus learning delivery, but how far are we in creating effective learning environments through the use of such systems? This chapter argues that we need to start not with the technology, but with the use of discussion as a tool for learning, the need for taking a pedagogical point of view and for understanding discussion as a purposive conversation. We take the position that the teacher has a role as guide in supporting students' learning through discussions. Argument is made that current discussion forums, or the manner in which they are used, lead to certain problems for the learners. To help explore our thinking empirically, a research discussion system 'Intellekt' has been developed to include a number of features that support teacher activities in guiding online discussions. These features are explored and a trial of the use of the discussion platform described. We conclude, inevitably, that we have still much to understand about managing learning through on-line discussion.

8.2   Introduction

The use of discussion as a pedagogical tool in Higher Education in the UK is widespread, typically enacted as a 'seminar' or a 'tutorial'. It could be argued that this feature is almost definitional of 'Higher' as opposed to other educational settings, such as primary / secondary education or training. Few lecturers would design their courses without building in opportunities for discussion in one-to-one or tutor-to-group situations, and yet discussion as a pedagogical tool is rarely examined explicitly. Learning by discussing is a recognised educational strategy (see Bligh, 1985; Ments, 1990; and Rabow et al., 1994, for example). Brookfield and Preskill (1999) suggest that at the heart of discussion is the open and unpredictable creation of meanings through collaborative inquiry. But this may feel threatening to some tutors precisely because the course of a discussion then cannot be planned in detail (see, for example, Frederick, 1986, which bears the title 'The dreaded discussion: ten ways to start'). This characterisation exposes the dilemma that the tutor faces when using discussion as a teaching tool, which revolves around the role of the tutor and his/her 'superior' knowledge. Brookfield and Preskill (1999) comment 'For a discussion leader to have decided in advance what these meanings should be is intellectually dishonest

... we should never initiate [students] into predetermined conclusions or pre-selected meanings' (p. 19). But, we may feel, in some circumstances, that as teachers this is precisely what we should be doing.

The advent of web-based learning environments has added new dimensions of complexity to these issues by creating new forms of communication between tutor and students – mediated by a computer network. Just as the WWW 'revolution' has forced the business world to re-examine its assumptions about the way commerce operates, teachers are having to look at their own practices. Some of the opportunities afforded clearly have some relationship to what we are familiar with as 'discussion', facilitated by what are variously called 'message boards', 'conferences', or even online 'discussions'. In this chapter we begin to explore issues around the use and management of these technologies as an extension of the more familiar contexts in which academic discussion for pedagogical purposes takes place.

8.3   A pedagogical viewpoint

Not all disciplines value discussion as a pedagogical tool (Brookfield and Preskill, 1999), but many have used it centrally in their practices. As teachers, we sense the value in having discussion in seminars, tutorials, and one-to-one supervision, without necessarily explicitly understanding all that we are achieving or even trying to achieve. Brookfield and Preskill use the term 'discussion' to explore the theory and practice of group talk, blending previous descriptions of discussion, dialogue, and conversation. These previous attempts at definitions are not explored here, though they may be important to return to as we develop our understanding of what is happening and how to manage online discussion. Brookfield and Preskill have drawn ideas from the thinking about conversation, dialogue, and discussion, about reciprocity and movement, exchange and enquiry, co-operation and collaboration, formality and informality. While acknowledging some value in a simple exchange of views and some merit in entertainment, they define discussion as 'an alternately serious and playful effort by a group of two or more to share views and engage in mutual and reciprocal critique' (p. 5). They suggest a fourfold set of purposes for discussion (p. 5):

1.   to help participants reach a more critically informed understanding about the topic or topics under consideration;
2.   to enhance participants' self-awareness and their capacity for self-critique;
3.   to foster an appreciation among participants for the diversity of opinion that invariably emerges when viewpoints are exchanged openly and honestly;
4.   to act as a catalyst to helping people take informed action in the world.

Critical discussion is central to their model and arises from the tradition of critical social theory. Giroux (1987) argues for the need to make sites where students and teachers converge to make meaning by 'interrogating different languages or ideological discourses as they are developed in an assessment of texts' (p. 119). The power relationships and the voices rendered silent by particular linguistic, cultural, and philosophical traditions become of central concern within this view of critical discussion. Teachers and students probe their own taken-for-granted assumptions and connect their own experiences with those of wider social and political concern. Such discussion does not happen automatically, though. Brookfield and Preskill (1999) outline a set of dispositions (e.g. hospitality, humility, appreciation, mindfulness etc.) they see as creating appropriate conditions for effective engagement in discussion. We anticipate the need to develop an online culture for effective critical discussion, just as Brookfield and Preskill (1999) have sought to understand and implement conditions to engender appropriate classroom discussions.

When teachers and students are disposed to engage in critical discussion, certain benefits for learners arise (according to Brookfield and Preskill, 1999):

1. It helps students explore a diversity of perspectives.
2. It increases students' awareness of, and tolerance for, ambiguity or complexity.
3. It helps students recognise and investigate their assumptions.
4. It encourages attentive, respectful listening.
5. It develops new appreciation for continuing differences.
6. It increases intellectual agility.
7. It helps students become connected to a topic.
8. It shows respect for students' voices and experiences.
9. It helps students learn the process and habits of democratic discourse.
10. It affirms students as co-creators of knowledge.
11. It develops the capacity for the clear communication of ideas and meanings.
12. It develops habits of collaborative learning.
13. It increases breadth and makes students more empathetic.
14. It helps students develop skills of synthesis and integration.
15. It leads to transformation.

Brockbank and McGill (1998) develop a particular approach to discussion which they call 'reflective dialogue': 'For us, dialogue that is reflective, and enables critically reflective learning, engages the person at the edge of their knowledge, their sense of self and the world as experienced by them' (p. 57). They argue that although as teachers we may engage in dialogue all the time, this does not necessarily equate with critical reflective learning. Learning becomes reflectively critical they say, when the emergent ideas are related to existing senses of knowledge, self and the world, with new understandings emerging.

Discussion therefore, and in particular critical discussion, we conceive as a useful tool to promote learning. In addition we are concerned to begin with the basic principles as they are currently understood in relation to the conditions necessary to promote learning (National Research Council, 1999).

- Students come to the classroom with preconceptions about how the world works. If their initial understanding is not engaged, they may fail to grasp the new concepts and information that are taught, or they may learn them for purposes of a test but revert to their preconceptions outside the classroom.

- To develop competence in an area of inquiry, students must: (a) have a deep foundation of factual knowledge, (b) understand facts and ideas in the context of a conceptual framework, and (c) organise knowledge in ways that facilitate retrieval and application.

- A 'metacognitive' approach to teaching can help students learn to take control of their own learning by defining learning goals and monitoring their progress in achieving them.

In engaging learners in discussion online we need to focus centrally on what we are trying to achieve in this learning context, the broader stages through which online students tend to travel (Salmon, 2000) and the social act of discussion from a communication perspective.

8.4   A communication theory of discussion as purposive conversation

Part of the problem we face is in conceptualising discussion. Discussion is conversation for a purpose. For most of us, conversation is merely talk in which we use speech to interchange words and thoughts. Ramsey (1998) expands this to include spoken words, gestures, actions and documents that are meaningful for participants, and all are actions with which someone might co-ordinate (i.e. doing and making rather than naming or describing).

Heyman (1994) explains conversation as the use by people of ordinary language to make sense of each other. The meaning of language depends on the context (indexicality), while the context of language depends on the meaning (reflexivity). The meaning of words is narrowed down by the context in which they are used. Bass and Hosking (1998) stress that content ('text') cannot make sense outside a relation to context. The kind of talk we use makes a communicative event particular – the talk provides meaning for the context, and the context provides meaning for the talk.

What are the implications of the inherent indexicality and reflexivity of language? First, interactors (communicators) each have a responsibility for creating shared context for understanding. Secondly, we need to understand misunderstanding to create shared understanding founded on shared context through strategic talk. Thirdly, the teacher–learner encounter has to be a mutual context-creating interaction (we jointly create the world we experience).

8.4.1   Discussion as inter-action

Discussion as purposive conversation is a highly co-ordinated activity in which meaning is attained and affirmed using a number of mechanisms that have context-dependent functions. This conception is in contrast to the 'parcel-post' or 'transmission' model that has been rejected by Deetz (1992), Mantovani (1996) and others. Conversation is a complex, highly co-ordinated process in which conversants seek mutual understanding through the co-ordinated presentation and acceptance of a variety of lexical and non-lexical statements. Projections of the next conversational move and active listener response are crucial for this, as are the ability to make mid-course adjustments and abbreviated references.

The parcel-post model has items for communication ('messages') packaged and sent by the speaker and then unpackaged and decoded by the receiver. Mantovani (1996) heralds the obsolescence of this *old model of communication* as the transfer of information from one person to another. No longer should we be satisfied with an outmoded model which conceives of communication as 'the transportation of an inert material – the information that actors exchange with each other – from one point to another along a "pipeline"'. This posits the job of the originator of the 'message' to send via 'parcel-post' the facts, handling them as little as possible so as not to tarnish them. There is no account of the co-operation which stimulates reciprocal responsibility for interaction and the series of subtle adaptations which occur among 'interlocutors'. Nor does the 'old model' consider that communication is possible only to the extent that participants have some common ground for shared beliefs, that they recognise reciprocal expectations, and that they accept rules for interaction which anchor the developing conversation. The advocacy theory of communication treats knowledge as an object (i.e. as a body of information as independent facts to be processed) existing independently of the participants that can be carried through channels and possessed by a receiver when communication is successful. The *alternative conception of communication* is of a common construction of meanings through inquiry. Information is not moved from one place to another – it is always a means to an end, produced and used by social actors to attain their goals in daily life.

Thus we have seen that a discussion is a purposive conversation – a complex, highly co-ordinated process in which conversants seek mutual understanding through the co-ordinated presentation and acceptance of a variety of lexical (of the vocabulary of the language) and non-lexical statements (converse can mean opposite). Language use links our internal (thinking) with our external (doing). We argue that giving forth in enquiry through writing online has particular benefits in learning. In particular, a non-linear notion of learning must be adopted to avoid the belief that sending packages of information in messages will lead to any substantive learning.

However, online systems for communication are limited to what can be 'said' in written words – without audio and video facilities, the character of the communication is not the same as can be realised when people talk together with the spoken word in visual contact with each other. Can an online environment allow the kind of conversation in which information is given, exploration of ideas, beliefs, and so on is facilitated, support and challenge offered, risks taken, reassurance provided, and clarification sought?

8.5   Technologies to support discussion

An initial and simple distinction to make is between synchronous and asynchronous systems. The former is represented by the 'chat room' paradigm where participants have to participate simultaneously and their contributions are listed sequentially in a window that contains the discussion. This is rather like a text-only version of a telephone or video-conference, and software such as Microsoft's 'Net Meeting' conferencing software includes an optional chat facility. Chat rooms are very popular with young people and clearly do have some potential for teaching, but for serious, in-depth discussions the disadvantages outweigh any advantages.

The potential of asynchronous systems is clearly more flexible as it removes time constraints and allows a discussant to compose a contribution at their own pace. Asynchronous systems also free us from the constraints of normal conversation, which is a major strength as well as their most troublesome weakness. A normal conversation has a linear progression and a current focus, whereas some forms of asynchronous discussion are distributed over an ever-increasing 'surface' like an explosion. Navigating and digesting the discussion then becomes a difficult task. Nevertheless, asynchronous discussion systems clearly have great potential for pedagogical use.

There is no shortage of choice of asynchronous discussion software. David Wooley maintains a web resource which lists more than 150 commercial and freeware discussion systems, some of which are imbedded in the major Virtual Learning Environments in use in Higher Education.

The features of several systems as components computer supported cooperative learning (CSCL) are comprehensively described in McConnell (2000) . With such a large number of offerings it is difficult to make generalisations about the features that they offer, but they do divide into two basic types which Wooley (1998) calls 'threaded' vs 'linear', and McConnell

(2000) describes as 'branching' vs 'book' structures. The linear discussion resembles a chat room except that there is no constraint of synchrony. Contributions are added to the end of a list so there is a clear focus. All contributions are available on the one page, but discussions on other topics run in parallel. In the threaded model, also called tree or hierarchical, each contribution stands by itself and can be multiply responded to. Each response can then be the focus of a new set of responses. There are advantages and disadvantages of each type. In the hierarchical model, the issues in a contribution can be dissected and pursued down different threads, but navigation, reading connected contributions and understanding where the discussion currently stands get increasingly difficult as the discussion expands. The linear model has a more intimate feel, is easier to comprehend at a glance and tends to produce more activity. It is perhaps less suited to detailed analysis because the relationship of contributions to each other cannot be determined. More recent systems (e.g. WWW threads) have tended to confuse this distinction in being based around the threaded design but having the option of displaying contributions as a single book-like page.

It not clear that the systems made available to the academic community have been explicitly designed to support pedagogical purposes or whether they simply adopted the conventions of existing systems. It is clear that many of them have deficiencies from a teacher's point of view. Turoff (2000) offers a perspective both as a teacher delivering a course using a commercial conferencing system and as a software designer. He remarks that:

> To really be able to carry out the learning methodologies (sic) that one would like to apply depends on a great many functional features of the asynchronous CMC system being utilized. Often the instructor, as user, has to resort to clumsy substitutes in functionality and use them in ways the designers never conceived they would be used. Hopefully there will be a future generation of software that better understands the needs of instructors and the benefits of being able to handle large active collaborative classes.

and

> If users cannot comprehend a complex discussion because of the interface functionality, then it goes without saying that they will NEVER create or have one.

McConnell (2000) also acknowledges the constraints that design imposes on use, saying the 'logical structure of a CC [computer conferencing] system may largely determine the ways in which it is used'. Such systems, then, may have potential while currently being poorly designed to support pedagogical purposes. The question is then how do we go about the task of designing discussion systems better suited to our purposes as teachers in Higher Education?

8.6 A prototype web discussion system designed to support academic discourse

Discussion as a teaching medium can be used in a variety of ways even in traditional, face-to-face teaching. In one common usage the tutor leads a discussion around a topic which has, perhaps, been already introduced to the students through a lecture. The tutor may be aiming both to engage the students in the topic by expressing their own views, and to draw out what the tutor sees as the major issues. Various techniques are available to move the discussion along, including eliciting contributions, questioning, summarising and restarting. Even though a tutor may not be seeking to dominate the discussion they nevertheless have a capacity to 'shape' the discussion so as to maximise student learning from the session. By contrast, in many computer based conferencing systems a tutor has very limited means of influencing the direction of a discussion. They can, typically, set the discussion topic, delete or edit 'inappropriate' postings and contribute to the discussion in the same way as the other participants. The tutor may need to communicate outside of the discussion, by email, in order to manage it.

The first prototype 'Intellekt' discussion system was designed around the situation described above in order to support an academic style of sustained discussion, as well as giving a tutor some facilities to 'tend' or shape the discussion. Many of these features are available in existing systems, but not necessarily together. Other features seem to be unique to this prototype. The major features relevant here are summarised in Table 8.1. It should be noted that this is not a fixed and final product but a development platform for future, action-based research. The web-based discussion is linked to a method of email subscription, so that a link to the new contributions is sent at intervals. From the email link the item can be read and the discussion can be navigated in a limited way. To contribute in the discussion the discussant needs to login, which can be done from the email link.

Feature	Justification
Visual representation of the whole discussion, latest contributions highlighted, and current position marked	Can easily see relationships, lines of argument and currently active 'growing points'
'Highlighter pen' commenting in existing contributions	Comment and requests for clarification can be made about specific sections of text in a contribution without needing a separate contribution
Rich formatting of contributions	Arguments can be lengthy and be subdivided into points
Point & click to add live reference to other contribution	Supports the need to refer to several other contributions to make integrative arguments
Facilitator's/tutor's comments always available	The facilitator needs to comment about the discussion as well as contributing in the discussion. Also for summarising
Facilitator/tutor can reversibly hide/lock/freeze any part of discussion	To help focus efforts in productive directions. To summarise and re-launch the discussion into a new phase
Turn a contribution into the 'hotspot'	To direct attention and brainstorm potential avenues to explore

Table 8.1   Pedagogically relevant design features of the prototype

8.6.1   Rationale for features: viewing and contributing

The prototype envisages discussions being initiated by the tutor and continuing for a limited time, during which the tutor will devote time to 'tending' the discussion. The format is tree-structured but with a variety of mechanisms to make the tree easy to navigate and to be aware of the position of a contribution in the discussion, for example the newer contributions are marked in shades of green (the discussion growing points) and the tree is unfurled to reveal them. Clicking on an item on the tree will show that contribution in a separate viewing pane, but the whole tree is still visible and the currently viewed contribution is marked on the tree diagram (discussion map) with a flashing icon. On joining the discussion, the viewing pane contains the 'facilitator's comments' ensuring that contributors are aware of the tutor's latest suggestions. Contributors, it is argued, need to be able to compose relatively complex contributions, referring to existing contributions and other documents as well as commenting on existing items. The compose window, for composing and formatting a contribution is revealed or hidden by a click, and is independent of any existing contribution. The whole discussion can be navigated and viewed without changing the content of the compose window, and so quotations from existing contributions (or from Word/Excel/Web documents) can be pasted into the new contribution while preserving their formatting. A clickable link (reference) to another contribution can be inserted with a single click and will subsequently display the referred-to item in a separate window when clicked. An existing contribution can be annotated by selecting a passage and writing a comment. This inserts a comment marker which, when clicked, displays the comment and highlights the passage to which it refers.

8.6.2   Rationale for features: facilitating

In most existing systems the facilitator (or moderator as they are usually referred to) has little control over the shape of the discussion but in this prototype system the tutor can completely change the view that participants get of the discussion. The tutor's view as administrator is the same as the contributors' view but with some added tools.

- First, the tutor can add and delete items in their facilitator's comments, which will then be available to all contributors when they open the discussion. They might use this as a meta-discussion, that is to comment on the way the discussion is going, to suggest fruitful lines, to show appreciation and to give information.

Clicking the icon of a contribution opens a panel where the status of that contribution and any discussion line emanating from it can be changed.

- Locked/Frozen/Hidden status

    - Locked means that the item can no longer be replied to, though existing replies can continue to be developed. This can be used to focus the discussion on a few major lines of enquiry.

    - Frozen means the line is visible (shown in blue on the discussion map) and can be viewed, but no further development is possible. Again this can be used for focus, to divert effort to other lines of discussion or to restart the discussion at a higher level.

    - Hidden means the line is no longer visible at all. This can be used to simplify where the sophistication of a discussion has moved on and the hidden lines would be confusing.

- Hotspot status. This is a way of using the linear or page-based discussion within a threaded structure. Only one item can be the hotspot at any particular time, and it is then displayed automatically on entering the discussion. Replies to the hotspot are not threaded but added below the previous contribution in the same window. This is conducive to 'brainstorming' and getting quick responses on a topic so that productive lines for further discussion can be identified. This is further enhanced by allowing contributions to be anonymous (but traceable).

8.7 The prototype in use: trial run

Even at this early stage of development it is important to road-test a system to establish any unforeseen problems, and whether the design needs to be rethought in the light of experience. This can only be done in a real situation so the opportunity was taken when there was a need to establish a discussion between academics involved in Problem Based Learning prior to a working non-virtual conference. The PBL web conference was set up and facilitated by the conference convenor, one of the authors. From a design point of view, the main advantage of this first outing was identifying and solving problems but two features were specifically explored: the use of the facilitator's comments function, and the 'hotspot' feature. Email support was offered to participants and the support requests, the facilitator's experience and the conference contributions themselves inform this descriptive and impressionistic account.

Over 80 contributors registered on the discussion, from several countries. There were some requests for technical help in getting access to the system, but only one request for help with using the system, so it seemed to be reasonably user-friendly. Many registered contributors did not actively take part, but this is a common experience of computer-based discussions (McConnell, 2000), as well as some face-to-face discussions. The hotspot feature was activated twice, and while a hotspot was active all contribution to the discussion happened in the hotspot, accounting for nearly half of all the contributions. Since it is possible to contribute in the usual way while a hotspot is active, it is clear that designating a hotspot did in fact focus the participants' attention in this particular discussion. The facilitator's comments were used regularly for reviewing progress. When new comments are made, the email subscription system relays them to contributors so the facilitator felt her pleas for a higher level of contribution were at least being heard, if not achieving the desired effect.

Obviously it is not possible to draw wider conclusions from this limited experience, but it did feel that the discussion was being actively managed and that the tools provided were straightforward in use.

8.8 Conclusions and future directions

It is possible, then, to design and implement web-based discussion systems that support a high-involvement academic style of discourse more effectively, and which allow a tutor to manage a web discussion as they might manage a face-to-face discussion. The issue arises, however, whether it is a good thing to enable a tutor to intervene in the course of a discussion in this way. What we have presented as the shortcoming of existing systems could also be represented as a positive step to democratising education. What is required for this is a non-linear notion of learning and the commensurate conception of communicating as participation in inquiry, rather than as only advocacy of a fixed way of thinking. When there is limited tutor control, students can discuss in their own way, relating issues to their own experience and, importantly, drawing upon each other's experience and knowledge to learn cooperatively. This dimension relates to the important issue of the authority of the teacher, which is thrown into striking relief here because the presence of the teacher in web-based teaching is not as dominating as in face-to-face situations. On the other hand it can equally well be argued that it is a teacher's duty to guide the intellectual development of their students, to lead them gently towards new understandings that they would find difficult, if not impossible, to recreate for themselves. These alternative views of what it is to be a teacher – the authority on, and communicator of, knowledge, the intellectual guide, the support vehicle for someone else's intellectual journey – define our individual approaches to teaching. These approaches may have been largely unconscious and unexamined in the past, but this 'technology-opportunity' led 'revolution' in teaching is exposing them and forcing us to revisit our pedagogical assumptions. Even if the claims for technology turn out to be ill founded, this process will have been valuable and teaching in higher education may never be the same again. Understanding the role and potential in on-line discussion for learning is in its infancy.

8.9   References

Bass, A. and Hosking, D-M. (1998) Mistaken identity: never mind, *Career Development International* **3**(7): 277–82.

Bligh, D.S. (ed.) (1986) *Teach Thinking by Discussion*, Guildford: Society for Research into Higher Education/NFER-Nelson.

Brockbank, A. and McGill, I. (1998) *Facilitating Reflective Learning in Higher Education*. The Society for Research into Higher Education and Open University Press.

Brookfield, S D. and Preskill, S. (1999) *Discussion as a Way of Teaching: Tools and Techniques for University Teachers*. London: Open University Press/Society for Research into Higher Education.

Deetz, S.A. (1992) *Democracy in an Age of Corporate Colonization: Developments in Communication and the Politics of Everyday Life*. Albany, NY: State University of New York Press.

Deetz, S.A. (1995) *Transforming Communication, Transforming Business: Building Responsive and Responsible Workplaces*. Creskill, NJ: Hampton Press Inc.

Frederick, P. (1986) The dreaded discussion: ten ways to start. In D.S. Bligh (ed.), *Teach Thinking by Discussion*. Guildford: Society for Research into Higher Education/NFER-Nelson.

Giroux, A.H. (1987) Citizenship, public philosophy, and the struggle for democracy, *Educational Theory* **37**: 103–20.

Harvey, L. and Knight, P. (1996) *Transforming Higher Education*. Buckingham: SHRE and Open University Press.

Heyman, R. (1994) *Why Didn't You Say That In the First Place: How to Be Understood at Work*, .an Francisco: Jossey-Bass.

Mantovani, G. (1996) *New Communication Environments: From Everyday to Virtual*. London: Taylor & Francis.

McConnell, D. (2000) *Implementing Computer Supported Co-operative Learning*. London: Kogan Page.

Ments, M. van (1990) *Active Talk: The Effective Use of Discussion in Learning*. London: Kogan Page.

National Research Council (1999) *How People Learn: Bridging Research and Practice*. Washington DC, National Academy Press.

Rabow, J., Charness, M.A., Kipperman, J. and Radcliffe-Vasile, S. (1994) *Learning Through Discussion*, 3rd edn. London: Sage Publications.

Ramsey, C. (1998) Managing within conversation: influencing for change, *Career Development International* **3**(7): 293–9.

Salmon, G. (2000) *E-moderating: the Key to Teaching On-line*. London: Kogan Page.

Turoff, M. and Hiltz, S.R. (2000) *Effectively Managing Large Enrollment Courses: A Case Study*. CIS Dept., New Jersey Institute of Technology, Sloan ALN Workshop, September, Lake George, NY.

Wooley, D. (1998) *The Future of Web Conferencing*. Available at www.thinkofit.com

9 Enhancing learning with computer mediated communication: teacher intentions and student conceptions of online learning

Maggie Hutchings
Bournemouth University, UK

9.1 Introduction

Educational institutions, challenged with managing increasing student numbers within a shrinking resource base, are utilising information and communication technologies to support learning and teaching. Computer mediated communication (CMC) is one of the technologies being used to increase accessibility, offer more flexible modes of delivery, and to enhance learning. CMC offers teachers the opportunity to enhance student learning by encouraging debate and discussion, reflection, and the development of writing skills outside of the conventional classroom. The potential of CMC as a vehicle for the promotion of higher order cognitive skills like critical thinking and problem-solving is however influenced by the students' conceptions and approaches to learning and by the teacher's intentions in implementing CMC learning environments. This chapter will examine the factors contributing to online learning experiences of students and staff with the intention of identifying key learning and teaching strategies for subsequent development of effective online learning environments.

The chapter will investigate how CMC can be used to enhance learning. Concepts, theories and models associated with conceptions and approaches to student learning and teaching will be used to explore the complex relationship between the teacher's intentions and the students' conceptions and approaches to online learning. This analysis will be situated within the context of conventional undergraduate and postgraduate courses where students and staff are experiencing CMC environments. Possible influences in engagement with and interpretation of CMC will be examined in order to draw out some key principles for the management and implementation of CMC environments.

9.2 Establishing the territory: definitions and models

Technology for learning is not a neutral mechanism. Educational policies can be dominated by the rhetoric of 'naïve technological determinism' (Ramsden, 1992, p. 159). This can skew interpretations of what stakeholders – students, teachers, administrators and managers – do with these learning technologies and how their conceptions of learning may influence their perceptions and approaches to learning technologies. Ramsden suggests:

> It may be the potential for interaction and for encouraging deep approaches, or less charitably it may be the vision of an easier and cheaper form of information-transmission that looks up to date, that has led some authors to predict the imminent arrival of the 'completely electronic classroom'. (1992, p. 159)

The use of learning technologies is context-dependent, a human activity open to research which aims to draw qualitative insights into what people do with learning technologies based on their perceptions, values and experiences and the resources available to them in situated contexts. This study adopts a research methodology based on an inductive approach in order for student and teacher perspectives on how learning technologies are used to emerge from a variety of mainly qualitative approaches to data collection. By adopting this approach it is hoped to avoid the 'hype' associated with learning technologies by expressing them through the voices of the learners and their teachers.

Students experiencing the technology define CMC for us:

> I think it just gives people the opportunity *to discuss things in another way* as opposed to face to face. You use the computer and you're able to *put your views in words* and it's *all written down* so you can *store* it and *look back* at it.

> It's a way of *putting forward ideas to a group* without them *being present* and then you have to pick up their replies *at a time convenient to yourself.*

Distinctive features of CMC	Learning opportunities in CMC
Many-to-many communication	Group work, peer support collaborative learning, communication skills
Shared spaces	Knowledge representation
Message threading	Knowledge construction
Message organisation	Critical thinking
Public archive	Reflection
Message history	Feedback identification, tracking
Text-based	E-writing, written communication skills, academic writing development
Asynchronous	Access, flexibility, IT skills

Table 9.1   Key features of CMC and related learning opportunities

Table 9.1 identifies features of text-based conferencing together with the learning opportunities they support. Group spaces are created for interaction by means of written communication. Ideas can be shared through text messages as products or knowledge representations. These knowledge representations are available for review and reflection by students and teachers and can assist them in subsequent knowledge construction. CMC offers the potential of a learning medium for the process of knowledge construction and reflection, provided students are actively engaged in the process (Klemm and Snell 1996).

9.3   Online learning models

How does this relate to practice in the design of CMC environments? Paulsen (1995) provides a comprehensive framework for analysing a range of pedagogical techniques, which can be used in online learning environments. Table 9.2 identifies four paradigms and their associated interactions and learning resources. Different approaches to using online learning environments can encourage different kinds of learning. The *online resource paradigm* sees the student working alone with a variety of learning resources in an *independent learning* mode. The *e-mail paradigm* sees the student interacting with the lecturer, perhaps to ask questions or receive feedback, or interacting with individual students. Here the student is operating in a *personalised learning* mode. The *bulletin board paradigm* sees the lecturer presenting information to students in a *transmissive learning* mode. The *conferencing paradigm* sees small groups of students working together on specified tasks in a *collaborative learning* mode.

Paradigm	Online resource	E-mail	Bulletin board	Conferencing
Interaction	One alone Student > resource	One-to-one Teacher > student Student > teacher Student > student	One-to-many Teacher > students Student > students	Many-to-many Student > students
Communication sphere	With material	With individual	With many	Within groups
Learning resource	Online journals, Computer assisted learning packages	Learning contracts, Apprenticeships	E-lectures, Assignment guidelines	Peer group
Learning method	Self study	Supported study	Knowledge presentation	Teamwork
Learning mode	Independent learning	Personalised learning	Transmissive learning	Collaborative learning

Developed from Paulsen (1995)

Table 9.2   CMC paradigms and learning experiences

Paulsen's framework can be used to analyse different teaching strategies and learning modes operating in online learning environments. Although each may have a valid part to play within the student's learning experience, different strategies are likely to have differential impacts on learning. When linked to the tension between the value of learning technologies as a cheaper form of information-transmission and their potential to provide interaction and encourage deep approaches (Ramsden, 1992, p. 159), two key questions are raised: What is quality e-learning? What teaching strategies are best for supporting a deep approach in using CMC?

9.4   Student learning: concepts, theories and models

Key concepts, theories and models from the extensive literature on student learning and the role of teaching have particular relevance to the analysis of CMC's learning potential in higher education learning environments. Early work by Perry (1970) indicated a developmental trend in student thinking from a belief in *dualism*, where right answers exist, provided by teachers, for producing in assessments, to an awareness of *relativism*, where conclusions are based on evidence to be cautiously interpreted by learners.

Research by Säljö and Marton and subsequent work by Beaty led to the identification of six categories of learning (Säljö 1979, Marton *et al.*, 1993; Beaty *et al.*, 1997a). The categories represent qualitatively different conceptions of learning and form a hierarchy with higher conceptions based on the foundations of lower conceptions. In the three lower conceptions, learning can be viewed as something external to the learner, a product, which can be taken and absorbed by the learner. Learning outcomes are demonstrated by the learner being able to *reproduce* the information. In contrast, the three higher conceptions identify the role of the learner in making sense of the meaning, in internalising the learning and understanding it in the context of the real world. Learning outcomes are demonstrated by the learner being able to *transform* the information. People's conceptions of learning affect their approaches to learning. Marton and Säljö's work (1976; 1997) generated two key definitions based on students' descriptions of their approaches to learning, a *surface* approach and a *deep* approach (Gibbs, 1994, p. 2). These models of learning are appealing because they support Perry's idea of a process of learner advancement along a developmental continuum.

Approaches to learning are affected by approaches to studying. They are not characteristics of an individual person but represent how they will approach a particular task or set of tasks (Ramsden, 1992, p. 44). Students learn differently in different situations. The same student can adopt a *surface* approach for one task or subject area and adopt a *deep* approach to deal with another task or subject area (Gibbs, 1994). Entwistle and Ramsden (1983) identify the influence of assessment demands, producing a distinction between a *strategic* approach to studying and a non-academic or *apathetic* approach. This is related to student motivations in studying. Beaty *et al.* (1997b) distinguish between *intrinsic interest* in the context of the course and an *extrinsic concern* with the qualification to be obtained. The research demonstrates qualitative differences in learning outcomes are closely associated with different approaches to learning (Gibbs, 1994; Marton and Säljö, 1997; Prosser and Trigwell, 1999).

9.5   Conceptions and approaches to teaching

So what does this mean for the teacher and the teaching strategies they adopt? Prosser and Trigwell (1999) have found teachers' conceptions of teaching to be very similar to those describing conceptions of learning. These conceptions and approaches to teaching are represented in Figure 9.1 (Entwistle, 1998; Prosser and Trigwell, 1999; pp. 153–4). Some teachers hold a teacher-centred view, focusing on the content, syllabus and textbooks, and see their role as transmitting information based on their knowledge. Other teachers focus on their students in planning their activities and see their role as helping their students develop and change their conceptions. These teachers are likely to adopt different approaches to teaching with consequent effects on the quality of the student learning experience. The teacher's conceptions have a powerful influence on what and how students learn, with students adopting deep or surface approaches according to the demands of the task.

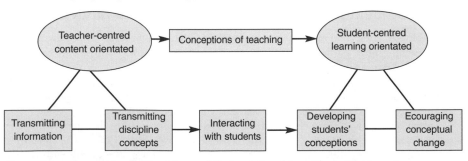

Figure 9.1   Conceptions of teaching and their relationship with student learning

How does this affect learning and teaching in a CMC environment? Writers on learning technologies confirm that learning outcomes are related more to how a particular medium is used than to the intrinsic characteristics of the medium (Ehrmann, 1995; Hiltz 1994; Laurillard, 1993). The context in which learning takes place will play a significant part in identifying pedagogical, social, and environmental factors, which can assist or impede the contribution of CMC to quality learning. Given the significance placed on how the medium is used, over and above its distinct features, in influencing learning, findings from two case studies will be used to situate CMC within a specific educational context and to develop and expand on the key themes identified above.

9.6 Research findings from case studies

The two case studies are based on student experiences of using CMC within all years of an undergraduate campus-based course in Leisure Marketing (BALM) and a final year option and postgraduate unit in Interactive Media Strategies (IMS). Focus groups were used initially as a means of exploring student perceptions and experiences of using CMC. Interviews and subsequent focus groups have been used to capture students' descriptions of learning, teaching, and learning technologies, to elaborate on and verify findings from the earlier focus groups and to compare the experience of undergraduates with postgraduates. Students' learning and study orientations were analysed by means of the Approaches to Studying Inventory (ASI) (Entwistle, 1981; Entwistle and Ramsden, 1983). The two teachers who implemented CMC in their courses were interviewed and completed the Approaches to Teaching Inventory (ATI) (Prosser and Trigwell, 1999).

9.7 Teacher's intentions and approaches to teaching

CMC was introduced to add value to the curriculum. It was intended to contribute to the development of student learning by providing active and collaborative learning opportunities outside the classroom. Additional reasons given for using CMC included novelty value, experimentation and it's potential in widening access. CMC's relevance to the discipline was viewed as an added bonus for IMS.

Both teachers engage their students in group work, face-to-face and online. They employ questioning to encourage students to think critically. They try to give students choice in topics they study and use learning agreements for individual assignments, though they recognise students express difficulties in making choices and developing learning agreements.

The ATI reflected the teaching approaches of the two teachers with high scores on their intentions and strategies to encourage conceptual change through a student-focused strategy, and much lower scores on the teacher-focused strategy with the intention to transmit information. It will be important to see how the teacher's intentions match the learning opportunities in CMC and the students' experiences and perceptions of CMC.

9.8 Mapping teacher's intentions against students' experiences

9.8.1 Collaborating rather than constructing

Students appreciated the value of collaborating face-to-face with other students. When asked to identify teaching approaches, which helped their learning, third-year undergraduate students mentioned the importance of discussing things in depth and questioning. But this valuing of face-to-face discussions does not necessarily transfer into online learning environments. Students saw benefits in using other people's ideas for reflection and helping them to change their conceptions online. There was some evidence that critical thinking, reflection and the development of e-writing skills were encouraged by the medium. But the sharing of ideas was not necessarily reciprocated with students preferring to read rather than post messages.

Collaborative learning was taking place but perhaps not in the way the teachers had intended. Contributions online were limited. Both undergraduate and postgraduate students seemed reluctant to actively engage in conferences. The experience of both teachers in BALM and IMS was that students collaborated on shared tasks outside the CMC medium and then posted a product, the results of their deliberations, in the appropriate conference.

9.8.2   Authenticated product rather than process orientation

One of the most useful features of CMC identified by students was its value as an information resource. This is summed up by a comment from one of the postgraduate IMS students:

> For me it wasn't the conferencing per se but the fact that we could get the lecture notes for the whole term, that it was stored in there, in FirstClass, and that was great for easy referencing. And just looking at that, it gave us a better idea of what we were going to learn for the whole term.

Students appear to be information hungry and value CMC as a tutor-constructed resource. But they are also very selective about what is valid information. Knowledge representations from peers do not seem to be valued in the same way as those of the tutor in CMC.

> You don't have that much trust in students because you can't guarantee what they're saying is right or wrong. You do put a level of faith in the lecturers, that what they're saying is right.

This comment is also reflected by the teachers' experiences online:

> They saw feedback from peers as being less valid than feedback from the teacher. They wanted me to respond to everything they posted.

This phenomenon is not confined to online experiences. Views on face-to-face seminars where students were presenting their ideas on particular questions, were similar with comments like:

> I don't mind listening to other students but I'd rather hear it from someone that I know and trust and know who's going to write the exam paper.

This valuing of CMC as a tutor-constructed resource follows Paulsen's online resource paradigm. Students appear less trusting of their peers' ideas and comments and need authentication from the teacher. Given these findings, we need to ask what are the possible influences on student approaches to and engagement with CMC?

9.9   Influences in engaging with and interpreting CMC

Although technical factors can influence engagement in CMC and participation rates were positively correlated with Internet access, social factors seemed more prominent in students' comments. Students appreciated the flexibility of the medium but this feature can be interpreted as both a strength and a weakness. The 'flexibility to neglect' the CMC environment when 'there are always other imperatives, other things to do' was identified by one of the teachers.

Written communication skills and academic writing development is recognised by the teachers as one of the most important learning opportunities in CMC:

> I think that's one of the main advantages of using it because everything we're doing is developing verbal skills and we're not really developing writing skills and that's what we're summatively assessing, they're getting no formative assessment on their writing skills.

This key rationale is supported by the literature (Kaye, 1989), but students identified difficulties in communicating and writing within an unfamiliar environment. This is summed up graphically in one student's description of trying to compose appropriate messages:

> I started writing them and then I thought 'oh no' and I kept writing them. When you write assignments you almost, you try and write it so it's perfect and you always go back and change bits because it makes more sense. I just kept doing that and in the end it was taking me so long I just didn't put very much on and I'd just leave it and not send anything.

Knowing and interpreting what they were supposed to do in the conferences seemed problematic for the students. They had differences of opinion as to the terms of engagement in the spaces with comments like:

> The discussions were not discussions. They were mini-essays.

The affective aspects of engagement in CMC seemed particularly significant and linked to the perception of the visibility of contributions in CMC. Comments included:

> I feel exposed in that environment because it has your name tagged to everything.

The archiving features of CMC enable a valuable store of information to be built up for subsequent review and reflection by students. Though valued by the students it has a significant downside as a public record leading to student feelings of vulnerability where they think their ideas are being judged by all their peers:

> It's quite nerve racking putting your work on it when you can have 40–50 people judging how you react.

There are also signs of peer sub-cultures operating within the CMC environment:

> In the first and second year … it had that sort of negative view that you're a bit sad if you wanted to put your opinion on a subject.

9.10 Can the educational models help us understand student behaviour in CMC?

Perry's intellectual development argument might suggest students, in the early stages of their course, are not intellectually mature enough to appreciate the collaborative/constructivist purposes of the conferencing environment. Comments from final year undergraduates suggest their conceptions of learning can change from dualism to relativism over the life-cycle of the course:

> Up until this year, I'd have said the learning was the way someone, a teacher, imparts some sort of knowledge to you [but now] there's various ways of interpreting things.

Valuing of CMC as resource rather than a space for active engagement in learning through discussion might suggest students would demonstrate high scores on the ASI reproducing orientation. However analysis of the ASI does not reveal any statistically significant relationships between numbers of postings and approaches to learning for three cohorts of BALM level 1 and 2 students. Though IMS postgraduates demonstrated higher meaning/transforming orientations and much lower ratings on reproducing orientations than national norms (Gibbs, 1992), they also commented on the value of CMC as a reference tool.

For many students approaches to studying appear to be motivated more by strategic considerations than by a deep or surface approach to their learning. Students make choices about use of time when marked assignments take priority over interaction in CMC. Students tend to be assessment driven, acknowledging the role it can play in encouraging participation in CMC:

> If there is encouragement to use it, maybe if things that we were set to do on there were part of an assignment and we were actually marked then it would encourage people to use it. Because it wasn't marked and people had other marked assignments to do at the time then those took priority.

These findings are supported by the results of the ASI on achieving orientations for BALM and IMS students which were found to be much higher than the national norms (Gibbs, 1992). However, perhaps the most significant finding was that of a positive correlation between number of postings and end of year average grades for BALM students. The better performing students will try to get involved, figuring there might be something in CMC if their teacher is encouraging them to use it. But they may not persevere with CMC, if they do not see continuing benefits, perhaps through the reward of grades or continuing interaction and feedback from peers and teachers.

9.11 Role of the teacher in student engagement and interpretation of CMC

Both teachers demonstrate a student-focused approach to their teaching with activities geared to helping students to develop and change their conceptions. They see their responsibility in setting up a framework in which students can work:

I act as a gateway or a signpost. There is a framework, a structure that sets the parameters for those 200 hours of learning rather than just the lecture/seminar programme, which is two hours a week.

They provide information in the form of lecture notes and references but see dangers in this approach of moving towards an information transmission model of teaching with CMC operating as Paulsen's bulletin board and online resource models:

I've fallen into the trap of ending up using it for online content because the students all identify that as an advantage of CMC. It's not communication. They're only retrieving. Occasionally the students will offer content, but very rarely do they do that.

Neither of the teachers assessed student participation or products in the CMC environment. This may seem surprising given the potential of assessment acting as a key motivational force to more active participation in CMC by students, who are largely strategically orientated in their approach to studying (Harasim, 1995). But the teachers may not be prepared to risk increasing the value of working in CMC from the student's perspective for sound reasons related to technology access and reliability issues, the wish to experiment, and their own confidence in the approach.

The authority of the teacher is paramount in CMC. Although students identify their individual responsibility for learning based on guidance, direction and a framework from the teacher, they are strongly influenced by teacher's opinions:

Teaching does influence your learning quite a lot and the way you interpret things.

Students value and need feedback when they are prepared to contribute online:

I felt I should contribute something and it was nice getting feedback from the teacher. She put feedback on and that was encouraging.

This reliance on the authority of the teacher does not bode well for encouraging a shift of focus from the teacher to the students sharing and collaborating online.

9.12 Conclusions

The conceptions and experiences of BALM and IMS students were very similar. CMC has the potential to develop academic writing and argumentation skills outside the classroom but only if individuals are prepared to engage collaboratively with the process of knowledge construction. On balance CMC may present more negative than positive aspects. Experiences of using CMC in distance courses seem positive (Salmon, 2000) but it does not appear to work as effectively in conventional courses where the dominant culture is an interactive teaching mode using face-to-face lectures and seminars.

The environment can feel alien when students and teachers are used to communicating face-to-face. One of the most significant findings from the focus groups was the degree of discomfort felt by students engaging with CMC. The students made comparisons between the comfort and familiarity of e-mailing friends and the discomfort and unfamiliarity of communicating within the conferencing environment. Figure 9.2 presents a model for understanding student engagement with and interpretations of online environments,

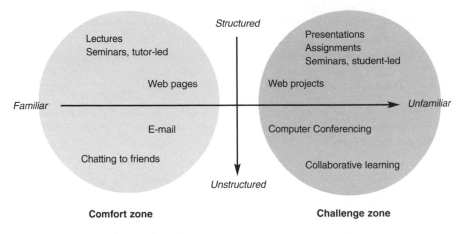

Figure 9.2   Comfort and challenge zones in conventional and online learning

applicable to CMC and VLE (virtual learning environment) interfaces. The model plots student experiences of the learning environment, both conventional and online, along two axes, one specifying degrees of *familiarity* and the other degrees of *structure*. The model suggests students are comfortable in lectures and seminars where these are structured by the teacher. Where these learning environments follow a particular structure and pattern, they can become very familiar to students along the same familiarity axis as chatting to friends, though chatting to friends will be unstructured. These experiences are positioned in what is termed the *comfort learning zone*. Learning environments can become more uncomfortable and less familiar as students have to engage more actively, as in presentations, student-led seminars, assignments and collaborative projects. This part of the model is termed the *challenge learning zone*, where students learn by doing, experimenting, taking risks and making mistakes.

When the associated learning technologies are added, it is possible to see the impact of CMC on student conceptions of online learning. These learning technologies have been placed in the four quadrants of the model. Web pages providing lecture and seminar material are structured though less familiar than face-to-face environments for both students and staff. E-mail may also be less familiar than face-to-face encounters and is unstructured. Students may be asked to design a web site for a presentation or assignment. This is likely to prove less familiar and perhaps less structured, in terms of accepted guidelines, than conventional assignments. However, it is the *conferencing* paradigm, which is potentially the most unfamiliar and unstructured learning environment for students and teachers. It can be used for e-lectures, online resources, seminars, assignments, student-led debates, discussions and group work tasks (Paulsen, 1995).

Deep learning is hard. Good conferencing is even harder, especially when it is intended to develop deep learning. The process is time-consuming. Everything takes longer than in a face-to-face discussion. When collaborating in CMC is set against student workloads it can be neglected, especially where it is not assessed. The authority of the teacher to influence student conceptions and approaches to learning is powerful but also fraught with risks. Students have strategic approaches to their learning. They appreciate CMC as a tutor-constructed resource in which the tutor provides knowledge, information resources, signposts, guidance, and feedback to help them manage their learning. What they may not appreciate is the challenge of working in an unfamiliar environment, where they are asked to construct knowledge among themselves, to accept ideas and give feedback to their peers, and to value peer-constructed products which are not always authenticated by the teacher. This would suggest difficulties in promoting CMC as a student-centred approach with the locus of control moving from the tutor to the students.

This has important implications for the design and development of online learning spaces. Does the teacher give the students what they think they want or what s/he knows they need in order to encourage deep approaches to their learning? Acknowledging different conceptions and approaches to learning and teaching provides a way of understanding and choosing appropriate learning and teaching strategies to meet the intended learning outcomes of the course. It is possible to adopt a support or wrap around model for CMC, which provides a framework, resources, and communication facilities in a VLE-type environment, while letting the classroom remain the main focus for debate and discussion (Mason, 1998). This would promote Paulsen's online resource, e-mail and bulletin board paradigms but not the conferencing paradigm. Alternatively it is possible to persevere with the potential of CMC to enhance deeper learning by building an integrated model, with the assistance of a VLE, into which CMC as conferencing and not just communication can be situated.

Innovations can be risky even in conventional settings of face-to-face lectures and seminars (Gibbs, 1992). Students' reactions to unfamiliar approaches can be negative. Staff prepared to experiment with innovations, hoping to improve the quality of student learning, are faced with many challenges, including the risk of failure. For CMC to have an impact on the quality of student learning, it needs to be:

- Contextualised

The tutor needs to:

- work with students' *comfort zones*, carefully considering *group sizes* and providing opportunities for *small group work* especially in the initial stages of working in the conferencing environment;

- provide *social as well as work spaces*, e.g. student cafés;

- include *essential information resources as incentives* to engage in the conferencing environment;

- be prepared to develop *communities of learners over a considerable period of time.*

- Structured

- *Learning activities* need to be carefully planned and linked to *learning outcomes, assessment strategies* and *student and staff workloads (course design issues).*

- Confidence building activities in small groups in the early stages of conferencing are important for developing *IT, social and e-writing skills* and should be *fun*. Knowledge construction will take longer (Salmon, 2000).

- *Models of good practice* in collaborative and constructivist interaction can assist students in understanding the intentions of the process and many of the sound pedagogic techniques we use in conventional settings can be applied in the CMC environment.

- If *e-learning outcomes*, including *critical questioning* and the development of *argumentation skills* are required, these need to be clearly specified.

- Integrated

    - CMC needs to be strategically integrated over the course of a programme, providing *opportunities to engage in different ways at different stages* of the course.

    - Efforts need to be made to ensure the innovation is *shared by the course team* and not just seen as the work of a lone champion.

    - Consideration needs to be given to the creation of an *integrated virtual learning environment (VLE)*, which contains information resources (lecture notes, web resources, notices) as well as a focus for communication and group interaction.

    - Students need to be *introduced to the VLE early* in their courses so that it is perceived as an integral part of their studies.

- Valued

    - By students, through linking it more closely to *assessment*, and giving primacy to the role of *feedback* in the early stages of discussions.

    - By staff, through ensuring it is *owned* by all the course team.

- Acknowledged

    - To achieve the *conferencing paradigm is difficult and challenging* for students and for staff.

    - Students tend to adopt *strategic approaches to studying*. This needs to be accounted for in positioning CMC in students' conceptions as a *peripheral or central activity*.

    - Students value *authentication of knowledge by teachers* over knowledge and feedback from their peers. Opportunities for developing *self and peer assessment* online need to be considered.

    - We are in a *transitional and developmental phase*, possibly unsure whether CMC should *supplement* or *replace* aspects of conventional teaching and constrained by *resourcing issues* (numbers of networked computers and proportions of students with Internet access from home) which act as powerful levers.

    - We will need to continue to address the issue of whether *the student goes to the learning* or *the learning goes to the student*, through opportunities to learn online.

Quality learning is about enabling students to apply and modify their own ideas; it is something the student does, rather than something that is done to the student. Bruner sums it up by saying: 'Knowing is a process, not a product' (1966, p. 72). Conferencing can help to deliver quality learning but it is not an easy option. Though it offers great potential as a learning medium, its implementation needs to be creatively managed within the context and structure of the course curriculum.

9.13   References and bibliography

Beaty, E., Dall'Alba, G. and Marton, F. (1997a) The personal experience of learning in higher education. In P. Sutherland (ed.), *Adult Learning*. London: Kogan Page, pp. 150–2.

Beaty, E., Gibbs, G. and Morgan, A. (1997b) Learning orientations and study contracts. In F. Marton, D.J. Hounsell and N. Entwistle (eds), *The Experience of Learning*. Edinburgh: Scottish Academic Press.

Bruner, J.S. (1966) *Toward a Theory of Instruction*. Cambridge, Mass.: Harvard University Press.

Ehrmann, S. (1995) Asking the right question: what does research tell us about technology and higher learning?, *Change: The Magazine of Higher Learning* **27**, Mar/Apr. http://www.learner.org/edtech/rscheval/rightquestion.html

Entwistle, N. (1981) *Styles of Learning and Teaching*. Chichester: Wiley.

Entwistle, N. (1998) *Conceptions of Learning, Understanding and Teaching in Higher Education*. SCRE Fellowship lecture, 5 November. http://www.scre.ac.uk/fellow/fellow98/entwistle.html

Entwistle, N. and Ramsden, P. (1983) *Understanding Student Learning*. London: Croom Helm.

Gibbs, G. (1992) *Improving the Quality of Student Learning*. Bristol: Technical and Education Services.

Harasim, L. *et al.* (1995) *Learning Networks: A Field Guide to Teaching and Learning Online*. Cambridge, Mass.: MIT Press.

Hiltz, S.R. (1994) *The Virtual Classroom: Learning without Limits via Computer Networks*. Norwood, New Jersey: Ablex.

Klemm, W.R. and Snell, J.R. (1996) Enriching computer-mediated group learning by coupling constructivism with collaborative learning, *Journal of Instructional Science and Technology* **1**(2), March. http://www.usq.edu.au/electpub/e-jist/vol1no2/article1.htm

Laurillard, D. (1993) *Rethinking University Teaching: A Framework for the Effective Use of Educational Technologies*. London: Routledge.

Marton, F. *et al.* (1993) Conceptions of learning, *International Journal of Educational Research* **19**: 277–300.

Marton, F. and Säljö, R. (1976) On qualitative differences in learning – I: outcome and process, *British Journal of Educational Psychology* **46**: 4–11.

Marton, F. and Säljö, R. (1997) Approaches to learning. In F. Marton, D.J. Hounsell and N. Entwistle (eds), *The Experience of Learning*. Edinburgh: Scottish Academic Press.

Mason, R. (1998) Models of online courses, *ALN Magazine* **2**(2).

Paulsen, M.F. (1995) *The Online Report on Pedagogical Techniques for Computer-Mediated Communication*. Norway, Oslo. http://www.nettskolen.com/alle/forskning/19/cmcped.html

Perry, W.G. (1970) *Forms of Intellectual and Ethical Development in the College Years: A Scheme*. New York: Holt, Rinehart & Winston.

Prosser, M. and Trigwell, K. (1999) *Understanding Learning and Teaching: The Experience in Higher Education*. Buckingham: Society for Research into Higher Education and Open University Press.

Ramsden, P. (1992) *Learning to Teach in Higher Education*. London: Routledge.

Säljö, R. (1979) Learning in the learner's perspective. I. Some common sense conceptions, *Reports from the Institute of Education* **76**. Gothenburg: University of Gothenburg.

Salmon, G. (2000) *E-moderating: The Key to Teaching and Learning Online*. London: Kogan Page.

10   A grounded theory investigation of students' perceptions of learning management systems

Graham Alsop and Chris Tompsett

Learning Technology Research Group, Kingston University, UK

10.1   Overview

This case study relates to the introduction of a learning management system (LMS) into a large modern UK university. Initial evaluation of one such system, Web-CT(tm), in the preceding year (1999–2000) led to the establishment of a longer three-year programme to establish another system, Blackboard(tm), across the university, starting in 2000–01. This represents a major change in the way in which the university manages and delivers its courses, with the potential for far-reaching consequences both in technological dependence, geographical availability and approaches to teaching and learning. The programme of deployment and technology transfer requires as much feedback as possible as the system is rolled out across subjects with a lower baseline of technical skills, or subjects that do not convert easily to a model of education based on static resources as opposed to interactive discourse. Even if the programme appears to be progressing satisfactorily in the initial stages it is critical to understand whether this is unduly successful because of the technical competence of the users, their staff, or the educational model, rather than the inherent flexibility and 'good' design of the LMS used. The Blackboard(tm) system was adopted as having a 'better' user interface and this provided the motivation for the research.

Most course development takes place without having first in place a research model to evaluate or interpret the changes in students' learning. Where the developments are technologically based there is an added danger that those responsible for the technology have little contact with students or the process of learning. In this study two cohorts of students that had experienced at least two different learning management systems afforded an unusual opportunity to research the design of these systems on a comparative basis. The intention was to provide understanding of the students' experience and provide direction to the evolution of the Learning Management System within the university.

Early evidence suggests that there is much to be learnt and to feed back both into extending the usage across the university and to any incremental development options that are planned.

10.2   Background

Students in this study initially used a faculty-based intranet (Sci-Net) during 1998–99, and two learning managements systems, WebCT(tm) from 1999–2000 and Blackboard(tm) from 2000–01. They were based in the Geographical Information Systems field and covered a limited range of courses and degree levels. Students were either in their second or final years of study and had all experienced both LMSs. In some cases students had experience of all three systems.

10.2.1   Defining a Learning Management System (LMS)

All three systems share the common facility to deliver information in the form of files (e.g. lecture notes and instructions for practical work) from a server to the user. The experience with WebCT(tm) supported the integration of course management and communication facilities but this was rejected in favour of Blackboard(tm), which was considered to provide a simpler interface. This presumption was a key motivation for the research reported here.

All systems were implemented to support rather than replace 'traditional teaching'. Students still experienced a full range of lectures, workshops and practicals. The scale of implementation and quantity of modules being put online increased over the three-year period and access was extended from an intranet model 'Sci-Net', to intranet and password protection in WebCT(tm), and then to Blackboard(tm) which was set up to allow password protected remote access.

10.3   Selecting a research model

A significant step in all research, though one too frequently taken by default or without full awareness that a model implicitly lies behind any research, is the adoption of a research model. In this case the decision to use a Grounded Theory approach was reached in two stages: the rejection of the 'scientific' framework, and then a refinement of our choice within the requirements of the cases available and the overall intention in the study (see Miles and Huberman, 1994; Silverman, 1997).

10.3.1   Science or social science?

The methodologies used to design and build LMSs are essentially scientific. A wide range of methods can be used from 'hard' methodologies such as Structured Systems Analysis and Design Method (SSADM) (e.g. Goodland and Ashmworth, 1995) through to soft methods including Soft Systems Methodology (e.g. Checkland, 1999) and other participative approaches. It is considered in this research that the basis for understanding the problems faced in implementation cannot be based on the traditional objective/scientific approach. If the use of the system is not as expected then the designers' views are already known to be at least partially incorrect.

These approaches share the realist view that knowledge of a system can be gathered by an 'outside' observer who can interact with the users and execute a design process. The knowledge/design that is derived from these observations is therefore the same as would be derived by any other trained 'observer/designer'.[1] This is not a generic critique of the design process but rather the continued use of the same principles to understand why the principles and or processes are inadequate.

Technically an LMS provides little more than a controlled membership, online community support system. This apparent limitation in an LMS nevertheless offers the potential to effect significant changes in the way in which students use it. If the core protocols are common to community systems designed for a variety of approaches then any educational redesign will lie within the interface between the protocols and the students.

The use of the system for educational purposes will be mediated through the conceptual model that is developed by the students. This model may be based on 'cosmetic' issues (the look and feel, the icons and vocabulary), or they could be institutional, affected by the approach taken to 'present' the system to the users (see, for example, Orlikowski (1992) for illustration of why this is important). It should be simpler to make changes in either of these aspects than to the underlying technology or Internet protocols!

This approach requires an understanding of the behaviour of the students from their own viewpoint. This is an exercise in social science research. It requires the selection of a particular methodology/philosophy (see the overview in Miles and Huberman (1994, pp. 5–11) or Silverman (1997) for more extended descriptions). The methodology used should establish, at the very least, why users see their behaviour as 'right'.[2]

The key change in moving from a scientific to a social science approach is that the observer has to be accounted for explicitly within the research process, i.e. the researcher is as much a part of the problem as the subjects who are being studied.

10.4   Selecting a social science methodology

An external observer describing a social phenomenon will be framing observations within a conceptual framework that the observer owns and believes is correct and independent of the process being researched. Yet the observer, in producing a description is also creating a new social phenomenon (part of which is this chapter by us, read by you today).

The researcher cannot be external to the problem that is being studied; they are an inextricable part of the problem itself – even the use of a term such as 'e-learning' presupposes that learning is the purpose of an event. Large-scale social science seeks to reduce these effects by statistical means but looses other detail in the same process. This is not an option at this point, so any approach must track the points at which the observer's influence could determine the conclusions reached.

10.4.1   Principles for selecting a methodology

While the natural sciences appear to be consistent about the nature of research, the domain of social science research seems fragmented. This dichotomy is more apparent than it really is (see, for example, Knorr Cetina, 1995; Potter, 1996).

If it is accepted that the researcher cannot be independent of the research process, then how can the work that is done be any more than a subjective impression that has no more predictive value than that of any other subjective observer? How can a description of one system have predictive power regarding a different system? At this point it is not possible to progress without examining some critical issues regarding the nature of social science research and use these to identify an approach based on methodologies that are, at the very least, consistent with what the research expects to achieve.

10.4.2   Selecting an appropriate methodology

These methodologies cover a multi-dimensional spectrum, ranging from large-scale statistical analysis of populations to ethnomethodological studies of microcosmic social activity (see e.g. Turner, 1974). Selection of a relevant methodology depends on understanding both what these critical dimensions are and, for any single methodology, either the particular philosophy of social science on which it is based, or the point at which it stands on each of the relevant dimensions.

The dimensions that are described below do not represent an open choice since many choices are interlinked. Unlike research in social science where adherence to a particular philosophy would frame the research question as part of the design, the structure and conditions of the research problem are used here to select an appropriate methodology. Once a methodology and philosophy has been chosen, the principles are then applied consistently throughout the research, including its design, development and the interpretation of the results. The key issues considered here are:

- the nature of the theory – from descriptive to predictive and from situated to generalised;[3]
- the scale at which the approach acts: populations, communities, groups, individuals;
- for those approaches that are reductionist, whether the theory accounts for the larger groups in terms of smaller groups, or vice-versa;
- the ontology or world in which these approaches act – events, beliefs, emotions, behaviour and discourse;
- from theory forming to theory testing.

In our context the methodology must be predictive in order to extrapolate from understanding the actions of the current students to future behaviour of other 'similar' students with related but redesigned systems. (The concept of 'similar' must be clearly elucidated in the research.)

Next, the research is concerned primarily with individuals, with their personal impressions and understandings, and how these determine how a system is used. This reflects the approach to education that is central to the university system, that it is the 'individual' who is educated. Even on degrees that aim to develop a collective understanding of a subject, students are awarded individual degrees. Though behaviour will be considered as based on individual decision-taking, this does not mean that it will be assumed, a priori, that there cannot be some aspects of behaviour that reflect group-like behaviour. Certain students may have a strong influence on most of the others (e.g. be seen as leaders) and there may also be more generalised social influences such as 'peer pressure' to conform to a common pattern of behaviour.

There is no sense though in which the research is attempting to explain the behaviour of students as a coherent social group that, a priori, must exhibit certain patterns of group behaviour. In particular it is not expected that the behaviour of individuals will be explained explicitly in terms of the groups to which they belong so the approach will not be reductionist moving from large to small scale.

The scale on which the research will operate must allow for more than a single individual's behaviour. If we were to work only at the scale of an individual, assuming that each individual requires a different explanation, it would not be possible to extend the theory to the behaviour of others in the future and the choice would be limited to purely descriptive approaches. The concern is to seek an understanding of how a student provides an explanation of their individual use of the LMS, in terms that can generally be related to other students, but which could include differences that are specific to individuals and groups within a subject and level of attainment. This would then allow for decisions regarding future use of the LMS to be targeted towards the groups that emerge.

As noted above, the scale of the research is limited by the number of students available and by the time-scale over which the research can take place, but there are stronger reasons for adopting an approach that must work on the small scale. While approaches that would attempt to generalise across a large number of students might be useful in certain settings it is unlikely that such results would be useful here. The choice of pilot groups is neither typical of the student body, nor the staff as a whole. So extrapolating from this research would be unwise. There would also be a danger in accepting that a 'percentage' analysis should be used to extend the LMS across the university on the current programme. This would accept that a percentage would be disenfranchised as not fitting the normal mode. However, such approaches may be important at a later stage.

The ontology of our research should allow for any aspect that is seen to be of importance to the students in their description. The literature on technology transfer and educational experience (in particular the research described in Bliss and Ogborn, 1977) includes many case studies in which emotions (e.g. fear), beliefs (e.g. 'it will never work'), have provided evidence that such aspects are used to account for the behaviour of users. There is no implication that these must feature in explanations but there is no suggestion that such aspects must be ignored or reduced to other non-emotional aspects.

The distinction between the behaviour of students and discourse is harder to assess. This distinction arises from acknowledgement that any explanation that is provided to account for a past action is not equivalent to the original motivation, reason or explanation for the past action, since it now constitutes a new social event with its own motivation, reason and/or explanation. This effect (more generally included within reflexivity, e.g. Ashmore, 1989) requires that any principles that are considered to apply to the subjects being studied should also apply to the research process and the researchers themselves. The way in which this potential recursion is broken will depend on the theoretical approach chosen. Some strong (extreme) approaches argue that the only aspect open to social investigation is the production of the current explanation (see Potter (1996) again on Discourse Analysis).[4]

Since the research will start from individualised accounts there are further restrictions in how the work can proceed. A direct observation account would not be feasible with previous systems and clearly intrusive if carried out in students' homes. This also removes the possibility of augmenting observation with direct reporting of students while using the LMS (protocol analysis). Protocol analysis is also vulnerable to the intrusion created by the parallel tasks of using an LMS (or not) and providing a commentary at the same time (see for example the discussion in Welbank, 1983). The method selected is therefore based on post-hoc explanations produced by the students for other students, but within an explicit research context. One positive reason for doing so is that such explanations should occur frequently with students in describing their own experiences to each other.

In summary, the research approach must be concerned with the explanations that students, as individuals, provide to account for their decisions in using/not using what is provided by any particular LMS. These explanations should be expressed within their own perceived notions of what the system offers and what it does not offer. This does not imply that the research should account for the subtleties of behaviour of individual students. The LMS should provide a system within which most of the students will experience similar opportunities. Rather the focus is on understanding the commonality between the individual accounts that are produced by students.

It is clear that the approach must be able to build a theory, but it cannot afford to begin with any theory. This dilemma proved a guide in selecting a process that was able, at the same time, to support the restrictions that were placed on the research.

The approach that has been adopted is that of Grounded Theory, which was originally described by Glaser and Strauss (1967) and more recently expanded, with illustrative examples, in Strauss and Corbin (1990). This meets the requirements described above. It should provide an understanding of the significant deficiencies in the current system and a model that can be used to understand how students might respond to future developments.

10.5   Grounded Theory – the process[5]

To achieve both theory forming and theory testing the data collection process is essentially integrated with the development of an ontology and a theory, and the theory is assessed for completeness. As the ontology is developed from the data collection process it is accepted that the process must be recursive in nature. Initial understanding guides continuing data collection until the process is considered 'saturated' (see Glaser, 1978, pp. 124–6) when further attempts to perturb the theory by using new cases fails to do so.

The process is explicitly dependent on the researcher and all aspects of the analysis are recorded and treated as part of the data. This implies that the results are accepted as viewed through the eyes of the researcher (and philosophically could not fail to be so) but that the process of the analysis could be rerun by another reviewer.

The intention is to build a general model that can account for all the cases that are taken (a case here being an individual account and not an individual student). The rigour is reached by establishing theoretical saturation resulting in a theory that could be agreed by other experts as a valid systematic account. This requires evidence of actively searching for new cases, as well as conflicts and contradictions, which could exist within the current model (cf. Popper's concept of falsifiability (1959)). Existing social models are not ignored within the data, nor are they used to guide collection of the data. Instead they are treated as an influence on the researcher and acknowledged when they intrude or become relevant from within the data (termed 'theoretical sensitivity').

In practice the methodology starts with a number of cases that are collected around the issue that is to be researched. These accounts are reviewed in a process termed 'open coding' (Glaser, 1978, p. 61). Searching for common language or common meaning between the different cases explains the meaning of 'grounded' in Grounded Theory.

These accounts (recursively new case studies) are collated to produce a common framework, based on the language used and terms that represent a higher level categorisation of these ideas. This level starts as descriptive but seeks to gain explanatory power by understanding, not just the context in which decisions are made, but also the potential for those decisions to have been different had the situation been different. Thus negative cases (why systems are not used) are as essential as positive accounts.

The second phase, 'axial coding' (ibid., pp. 96–7), provides a standardised framework for allocating the categories and relationships to a story-telling paradigm. A core category or phenomenon provides an overall focus for all the cases and is a generalisation to which all the cases relate. Within this core phenomenon the stories are codified to understand the 'causal conditions' (the situations that lead to the event occurring), the context (the significant variables within a story that are relatively fixed but affect the outcomes) and the consequences (the outcomes either positive or negative). One further element is critical which is the consideration of intervening conditions and action/interaction events. These are the choice points in the story where decisions are made, and these represent the focal points at which changes could be made in the future.

Further sampling is used to test the validity of the axial coding and the robustness of the action/interaction events. Generalisation is explicitly used to test alternative approaches to establish similarities across a wider field of relevant cases and some cases are developed in interviews to hypothetical situations (flip-flop and red-flag – ibid., pp. 84–95).

For completeness of testing the conditional matrix approach is used (Miles and Huberman, 1994; Strauss and Corbin, 1990). The overall outcome is to establish the ability to trace the conventional patterns of decisions and behaviour pertaining to a phenomenon.

This is not to suggest that the theory is attempting to produce a simple network of condition-action pairs, leading to new conditions and actions. The theory must work at a more detailed level. This should reveal the critical and or marginal changes in conditions that would lead to different actions being pursued.

10.5.1   The method

The initial stages of data collection and ontology building are complete. Surprisingly rapid convergence has taken place on the development of an axial model including a core phenomenon that could be established to cover most of the cases. Confidence in this convergence was reinforced through a variation of the standard method of case studies/interviews which is currently believed to be novel. In this approach the students act both as providers of the case study and also as researchers interpreting each other's cases.

In our study 49 cases were collected from the students. These initially focused on specific personal events presented in the form of written accounts. These were generated from two seed statements that requested: the 'most rewarding' and the 'worst educational' experience of using an LMS. These formed the major source of the cases with further accounts and comments collected subsequently. As students completed their individual accounts they were asked to write a summary statement which was kept separate from the story itself. They were then grouped into small sub-groups (4 or 5 if possible) and, without discussion (they were explicitly told that this was to avoid influencing each other's interpretation), they read and summarised each other's accounts with a similar term or brief statement. Finally each group was asked to reach an agreement on a single concept to encompass the complete set. This process of summarisation was intended to achieve a number of effects. The first was to focus the students on providing an account that another student would read (anonymity was built into the process as far as academic staff were concerned). Secondly, it was expected to demonstrate the degree to which a student's account would be interpreted consistently by the other students, and, finally, it was intended to provide an indication of the students' confidence in generalising the cases. This also offered the potential to identify whether any particular student had dominated a group during the process.

After these two case studies were collected, students were invited to describe the differences between the implementations they had used and asked to provide any matter that should be explicitly visited if it was not raised in any other case. There are further accounts that will be included in this study but, since they were not directly collected from students for the purpose of the study, permission remains outstanding from students to include these cases.

These cases (which were handwritten) were typed up and entered into NUD*IST[(tm)] (from Qualitative Solutions and Research Pty Ltd.). This followed, wherever possible, what was originally written. The only significant changes were inclusions of alternate correct spellings to ensure that keywords could be picked out from text searches. This change implies the existence of a prior external framework for the research, however, all original spellings were retained as well and the list of words that were changed can be audited. Any comments or observations by the researchers at this stage were also included within the case studies. The two researchers worked to an agreed coding structure as required by the software with each group represented as a document and the cases studies combined into a single NUD*IST[(tm)] project.[6] Both researchers then developed coding systems for the cases. This discussion covers the results of the coding process that are common between the two researchers.

10.5.2 Open coding

This stage is only reported in outline as a more detailed analysis is reported elsewhere (see Alsop and Tompsett, 2001 and 2002). This discussion covers the process of identifying a core phenomenon highlighting key issues that are central to the research process.

The key findings from the first reading of the accounts were that students interpreted each other's accounts consistently using a common vocabulary, providing a remarkable consistency in the responses (and summaries) to the seed questions. Positive descriptions were dominated by considerations of remote access rather than any one interface design. Negative descriptions focused on instances of failure to successfully download and make use of online materials.

The students did not perceive the system in terms of the underlying technology other than the evident use of the Internet and remote access. This reinforces the original thesis that the labelling and organisation of the interface can be used to control the students' perceptions. However, the interface appears to have a greater effect than this. The technology is used by the students 'as is described' by these labels but, despite the evident facility that the students have with computers, there is no evidence that students think and reason in terms of the underlying protocols or technology. In fact there is just as much indication that they fail to do so.

The researchers' anticipation that interesting comments would be made regarding education is rewarded with a virtual silence in the case studies. Few examples can be found that refer to processes that impact on learning and only three are mentioned more than once: printed notes being available to avoid note taking in lectures, catching up after illness and the need to fit study around paid employment. Other individual aspects are mentioned in only single cases: the use of the talk 'applet' in Blackboard, and the 'pinching' of ideas from spying on the discussion of other groups (where other groups failed to close their discussion to observers). The first appears to be a positive educational use but it is exploited by the student to save time over repeated telephone calls. Even the second is introduced as a quick way to find new solutions.

A negative view of these results could be that the students have little concern for the educational benefit that such systems do or could provide. Alternatively it could be seen that students are more concerned that their time studying is used effectively and that this must be balanced with all the other activities that are critical.

The consistency of language and outcomes, even though not as intended, provides validation for the research method that was adopted. However, this is only the first stage in the development of a 'theory' and the lack of direct discussion of an issue requires further aspects to be considered.

10.5.3 Axial coding

The move from open coding to axial coding requires identification of the core phenomenon. The central issue of remote access (both successes and failures) would suggest that this should be considered as the starting point. However, on review of accounts and other examples from the literature, it became clear that remote access was an aspect of the LMS that the students were able to exploit, rather than the focus of their activities (i.e. context not core phenomenon). The researchers' interest in the educational design of the interface (see comments above) was noted as a memo on the process but is still currently unmatched in the rest of the data.

Remote access has provided a significant opportunity for time to be used more effectively – to avoid unnecessary travel as long as the systems are dependable. For many, travelling is a significant element of unproductive time. Merely releasing time allows for more time to be used for whatever purpose, including study. That at least offers the potential for improving student learning. It is clear that remote access is seen as a fundamental transformation of the student experience. This occurs in a wide range of educational contexts and is also reinforced by negative comments about the 'intranet' implementation of WebCT[(tm)].

10.5.4   Identifying the core phenomenon

This review led to initial suggestions for the core phenomenon based around management of time as a resource with many references to saving/wasting time, having things available when needed and poor time management (examples of compensating for missing materials). These fit sensibly into a hierarchy:

poor time management → time management → resource management

providing three possible categories as the 'core phenomenon'. Review of the accounts (ibid.) using this as a first analysis indicated that a more complex network of categories (Figure 10.1) should be considered.

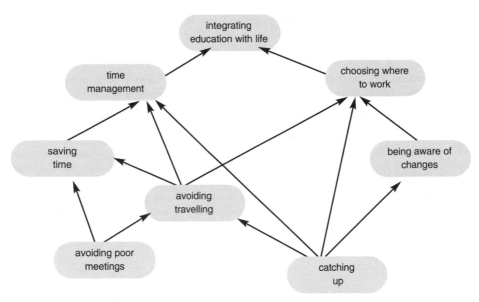

Figure 10.1   Network of benefits

The development of a full theory is cyclical in nature and involves the interleaving phases of data collection and theory building. The move from 'accessibility' to the 'network of benefits' represents two steps in this process.

However, there are two complications to consider. First, students complete their degrees and move on, and, secondly, the initial findings have led to changes in the way the system is supported by the University, so context, in terms of the use of the LMS, changes. Although this would seem problematic with some methodologies this is not considered so within

Grounded Theory. As each event is considered as a case in its own right, rather than a case being an individual student, the building of a valid theory should be capable of accounting for the variation that will be included through this process. The 'network theory' would remain valid, but new related, subtler iterations would become apparent.

Indeed it would be argued that the notion of completeness requires that the range of cases that should be included becomes increasingly well defined but that new cases remain within the scope of the current theory. The ability to build a viable theory may be harder, but it will be the only one that is worthwhile. As with action research, the value of this research is to guide development of the system.

The current network of benefits provides a set of potential issues for consideration as the core phenomenon. The hierarchical[7] structure that has been created provides a simple mechanism for ensuring that all the cases are eventually included within more general levels with the result that the topmost benefit provides an evident primary candidate.

However, there are two aspects of this that need more careful consideration. First, the concept, though labelled, has been created artificially to include the lower (more specific) levels. The relevance of this grouping will need to be elucidated through the exploration of the potential cases that would support this view. Since the process of creating this structure is mechanical, it is also critical to demonstrate that there are some cases that would need to be included at this level and could not be included at the lower level.

This raises the possibility that there is no single core phenomenon that naturally includes all cases in a straightforward process. In such cases the preferred approach is to develop alternate theories, both of which include all the cases, but in which each of the competing core categories is considered to take precedence with the other phenomenon included as a subsidiary aspect. This retains the principle that all cases are included within a theory but potentially revealing complementary views of which is the controlling factor. There is no indication that this will be the case in the current theory being constructed.

Extending to a wider set of cases will broaden the scope of the theory and provide an alternative approach of hypothetical variations on the existing cases. This will not eliminate the use of more detailed interview techniques to explore the critical factors that control action/interaction events. Although these techniques, e.g. flip-flop and red-flag waving, are not exclusive to Grounded Theory, the processes by which the techniques are controlled is significantly different.

The flip-flop technique is designed to generate cases or contexts in which one of the key features that is otherwise dominating the analysis is either inverted or removed. This can be used both in discussion of a single case (with the intention of identifying the subsidiary aspects which might otherwise be subsumed within the dominating factor) and also in the process of generalisation that is followed by the researcher. In this mode the researcher needs to be sensitive to a range of potential features that have not yet become significant. This is not so much to generate new cases, but more to exclude lines of enquiry. The normal model is to search for analogous activities to the current contexts in which the dominant feature is excluded and identify the range of issues that then become important.

For example, when the students mentioned 'access' it was both in a positive and negative light. Some saw the remote access as the key that allowed them to improve time management, whereas others described it as wanting to access a resource but failing to do so.

The second technique, red-flag waving, is more generic. This is intended to probe scenarios where a description is produced that includes extreme expressions, either terms such as 'never', 'always', 'essential', or, as in one of our cases, a scenario that is clearly written as 'tongue in cheek'. These cases are problematic to analyse, since they lack complexity and contribute little to the development of a detailed theory. Yet these cases are clearly of interest as some factor has become so dominant that the case precludes a balanced discussion of options. The intervention technique used is to challenge the scenario and seeks to identify just how far other factors can change before the single-minded approach would break down.

In Grounded Theory the influence that the researcher has must be both circumscribed and tracked. In moving away from scenarios that are presented into a hypothetical world it is too easy to generate virtual cases in which the researcher creates scenarios and decisions to meet their personal expectations. This issue requires that flexibility is both capably and clearly related to the existing view, yet not necessarily viewed as exclusively produced from a real view.

The most obvious control is to remain within the ontology that has been used within the complete set of cases. This is more generic than asking for simple comparisons between systems since the interest is in following the change through a series of action/interaction steps.

Although this approach provides a tight control mechanism, it can fail to explore some areas that are common to the majority of cases. The lack of reference to direct educational benefits, for example, although of significance in providing outcome in the first phase, must also be challenged. It is plausible that, far from suggesting a lack of relevance, it merely reflects a consistent view by all students which then does not require specific reference.

The theory will also need to be challenged in terms of the extent to which aspects that are specific to the group of students may be critical. Although these may be omitted from the ontology at present, this may be precisely because they do not have to be related to each other, each time, within the current group of students. In order to extend the range of issues that are currently reviewed requires a method for generating questions that is generic within the context of the class of discourse being reviewed.

Avoiding travel will usually save costs and save time; being aware of changes could save travel. Even if an LMS is less likely to produce an answer to a problem than going into university, and if both methods have a risk of failure, a solution with a higher risk of failure may still appear to be a preferable option if the 'cost' is lower.

The current axial model reflects an active management of resources, even if the nature of the resources is unclear. It is thus relevant (in terms of theoretical sensitivity), to assess the potential of a planning model in providing a semi-structured interview structure in order to explore some cases in detail (in particular see the analysis of explanations by Hughes (1986)). This approach, related more generally to the work of Shank at Yale (e.g. Shank 1986) provides a hierarchical structure to interpret explanations for behaviour, identifying classes of explanations and connections between these classes. This model, without imposing a new ontology to the students' scenarios, will provide a mechanism for encouraging students to provide more complex issues.

This will allow us to use the issues raised in one scenario to question the accounts raised in the other accounts, thus identifying a range of concomitant benefits that are not explicitly identified by the account writer. Rather we are presented with a range of questions that allow us to look for secondary issues that might be relevant in the accounts that do not fit in within the main story-line of that case.

10.6   Review of the research methodology

The five dimensions used in choosing a theory will now be returned to as a means of closure. Was Grounded Theory the appropriate methodology? Did it achieve worthwhile outcomes given the context?

- The use of Grounded Theory successfully allowed the move from descriptive to predictive and situated to generalised. Students' accounts already extend beyond the particular learning experience and include controls and influences that are derived from levels of authority that act on a much wider scale than a particular course.

- The current theory still allows consideration of both individual and group aspects. The elements of group behaviour and individual behaviour are distinct. A theory based on either individuals or groups alone would have been ineffective.

- The theory that is being developed neither supports a reductionist approach nor rejects one. This allowed sufficient flexibility for the application in this context.

- The methodology has allowed an ontology of high consistency to be developed that is significantly different from that anticipated by the researchers. This has allowed for the development of a theory that is clearly based on the views of the students. As noted above, improving the process of learning through technology does not appear to be the emergent theme. The students' framework is the focus of this work and the researchers' views have remained subservient.

- Although theory testing is not completed ('saturated'), the results are sufficiently detailed to have instigated changes in the implementation of Blackboard™. These are key to the students, but might seem otherwise trivial to the designers and implementers. This should provide the opportunity to test the theory that has been developed so far and provide more interesting aspects to be researched over the coming year in six different Faculties. This will allow a further iteration of the research cycle.

This review provides a clear indication that the principles on which the methodology was chosen have led to the use of a research model that is both robust and informative.

An after note

It might be argued that the research has missed the 'real' student model of how Blackboard^(tm) is used and how it could be improved. The reply to this (from this research perspective) is to point out politely that that implies a value judgement based on what the critic wanted to hear. To the seasoned educator and technological sceptic the conclusions above are not new. The rewarding result is that it was reached through careful examination of the research process from within the information systems domain.

Notes

1. The notion of realism suggesting that objects exist independently of existence – for a discussion of this see Moore (1903).

2. In contrast, most designers view the same behaviour as failure to use a system correctly!

3. Also paralleling problems faced by the philosophy of history, see Dray (1966; 1980) and Walsh (1967).

4. Thus bringing the researcher into equal status with the subject.

5. The outline principles of Grounded Theory are summarised from Strauss and Corbin (1990).

6. It became evident that the structure imposed by NUD*IST™ is limited and that an XML based editor would allow both more flexible coding and search techniques supported by XSLT, if the tracking facilities provided by NUD*IST(tm) could be reproduced.

7. The term is used loosely here; mathematicians would prefer the term lattice.

10.7   Bibliography

Alsop, G. and Tompsett, C.P. (2001) Interface Design in Learning Management Systems. Presented at ALT-C 2001 Edinburgh. Contact g.alsop@kingston.ac.uk for a username and password access to http://infosys.king.ac.uk/LTRG/.

Alsop, G. and Tompsett, C.P. (2002) Grounded Theory as an Approach to Studying Students' Uses of Learning Management Systems, *In Print ALT-J 2002*

Ashmore, M. (1989) *The Reflective Thesis*. Chicago: University of Chicago.

Bliss, J. and J. Ogborn (1977) *Students' Reactions to Undergraduate Science*. London: Heinemann.

Checkland, P. (1999) *Soft Systems Methodology: A 30-Year Retrospective*. Chichester: Wiley.

Dray, W. (ed.) (1966) *Philosophical Analysis and History*. London: Harper & Row.

Dray, W. (ed.) (1980) *Perspectives on History*. London: Routledge & Kegan Paul.

Glaser, B.G. (1978) *Theoretical Sensitivity*. Mill Valley, Ca.: Sociology Press.

Glaser, B.G. and Strauss, A.L. (1967) *The Discovery of Grounded Theory: Strategies for Qualitative Research*. London: Weidenfeld & Nicolson.

Goodland, M.S. and Ashworth, C. (1995) *SSADM Version 4: A Practical Approach*. Maidenhead: McGraw-Hill.

Hughes, S. (1986) Question classification. In M. Bramer, *Research and Development in Expert Systems III*. Cambridge: Cambridge University Press: 123–31.

Knorr Cetina, K.D. (1995) Laboratory studies: the cultural approach to the study of science. In S. Jasanoff *et al.*, *Handboook of Science, Technology and Society*. London: Sage.

Miles, M.B. and Huberman, A.M. (1994) *Qualitative Data Analysis: An Expanded Source Book*. London: Sage.

Moore, G.E. (1903) The refutation of idealism, *Mind* **12**.

Orlikowski, W. (1992) Learning from notes, *CSCW* **92**.

Popper, K.R. (1959) *The Logic of Scientific Discovery*. London: Hutchinson.

Potter, J. (1996) *Representing Reality: Discourse, Rhetoric and Social Construction*. London: Sage.

Schank, R. (1986) *Explanation Patterns*. London: Lawrence Erlbaum Associates.

Silverman, D. (ed.) (1997) *Qualitative Research – Theory, Method and Practice*. London: Sage.

Smith, H.W. (1975) *Strategies for Social Science – The Methodological Investigation*. London: Prentice/Hall International.

Strauss, A.L. and Corbin, J. (1990) *Basics of Qualitative Research: Grounded Theory Procedures and Techniques*. London: Sage.

Turner, R. (1974) *Ethnomethodology*. Harmondsworth: Penguin.

Walsh, W.H. (1967) *An Introduction to the Philosophy of History*. London: Hutchinson University Library

Welbank, M. (1983) *A Survey of Knowledge Elicitation Techniques*. Martlesham: British Telecom Research Laboratories.

11 Screen or monitor? surveillance and disciplinary power in online learning environments

Ray Land[a] and Siân Bayne[b]

a. University of Edinburgh; b. Queen Margaret University College, Edinburgh, UK

11.1   Overview

This chapter considers a little-discussed aspect of online learning - the surveillance or 'student tracking' capabilities of virtual learning environments (VLEs). In, at least, the two main commercially available VLEs – Blackboard and WebCT – sophisticated, powerful, easy-to-use means of collecting data on students' activities within the learning space are built in as part of its pedagogical functioning. Where such surveillance tools are often promoted, and accepted, as useful ways of evaluating course effectiveness through helping us to understand student usage of the online facility, we wish to probe a little deeper and think about some of the broader cultural and pedagogical implications of using these tracking devices.

The chapter uses a theoretical framework drawn from the work of Foucault and from more recent theoretical approaches to privacy within cyberspace. It begins by giving a brief overview of the kinds of surveillance tools which we have access to in WebCT and Blackboard, moving on to the application of Foucault's panopticon metaphor to such facilities, and finally examining the implications of their use for educational practice.

The unifying theme of our discussion relates to the way in which the individuality of our learners is affected by the use of cyberspace as a learning environment. We believe that the learning environments we use work to develop certain kinds of learners, thus the subjectivity of the online learner is our central concern.

11.2   Introduction: tracking students in virtual learning environments

Murray Goldberg, WebCT developer, asks in his online newsletter, 'It's 10pm, do you know where your students are?' (Goldberg, 2000). He goes on to describe how the rationale for the development of the student tracking tools in WebCT grew out of his own experience of teaching online. The tools are, indeed, extensive. WebCT allows tutors to track the date and time of students' first and last logins, which pages each individual student has accessed and when, the total number of times the student has accessed the system, and for every section of the course to track the number of discussion board articles each student has opened and the number and date of each student's own discussion board contributions (see Figures 11.1 and 11.2).

Show Distributions
Return to Track Students

Full Name: Student 1   User ID: studeone
First login: Feb 02, 2001 16:03   Last login: Jun 22, 2001 16:31
Total number of accesses: 968   Last page visited: Homepage

Show history of content pages visited

Distribution of Visits for Student 1

Page	Count	
Homepage	195	
Tool Pages	187	
Glossary	1	
Discussions	**Count**	
Articles Read	482	
Original Posts	31	
Follow-up Posts	72	

Figure 11.1   WebCT – date and time of one student's first and last login, total number of accesses and hits to each content page

History of Content Pages Visited by Student 1

[Prev 10 Visits] [Next 10 Visits]

	Page Name	Time of Access
4	Page Editor: Designer Buttons	Tue, 27 Jul 15:41:43 1999
3	Page Editor: Button Bar	Tue, 27 Jul 15:41:29 1999
2	Page Editor: Delete Path Pages	Tue, 27 Jul 15:41:26 1999
1	Page Editor: Designer Buttons	Tue, 27 Jul 15:40:04 1999

Figure 11.2   WebCT – history of pages visited by student, with dates and times

Class records can be generated allowing tutors to organise their students according to frequency of accesses to the course, by date of first or last access, or by the number of discussion board items opened or posted (see Figure 11.3).

WebCT's main out-of-the box virtual learning environment rival, Blackboard, has a similar suite of surveillance tools, enabling records to be generated showing for each individual user the total number of accesses to the course as a whole, the total number of accesses to each individual area and page of content, number of accesses over time, accesses per day of the week and by hour of the day. With both VLEs the tutor can also, of course, keep permanent records of the more obviously 'visible' activities undertaken by the student – the number, time and quality of contributions to discussion boards, emails exchanged between tutor and student, results from online quizzes (those intended for self- or formative assessment as well as those which are summative)

These tools are far more than the electronic equivalent of the attendance sheet. As in so many arenas, computers have enabled us to do things that were previously impossible or very difficult. VLE surveillance tools record every move a student makes within the learning

Student Records

To sort by a category, click the category heading
For more statistics on an individual student, click the student's name

Page: [All ▼] Previous Page Next Page

Personal Information		Access Information			Articles	
Full Name	User ID	First Access	Last Access	Hits	Items Read	Posted
Kirk, David	dkirk	Mar 23, 2001 17:11	Apr 24, 2001 14:07	33	17	0
Ross, Daniel	dross	Feb 09, 2001 14:24	Jul 13, 2001 14:37	127	52	3
Peacock, Dan	speacock	Feb 05, 2001 22:16	May 10, 2001 15:10	139	48	0
Laffan, Henry	hlaffan	Feb 10, 2001 06:18	Jul 03, 2001 12:20	146	114	21
Singh, Michel	msingh	Feb 05, 2001 13:52	Jun 04, 2001 13:31	153	112	19
Shirazadeh, Tony	tshirazadeh	Feb 07, 2001 11:05	Jun 15, 2001 16:35	219	115	9
Foongyap, Landy	lfoongyap	Feb 05, 2001 11:34	May 28, 2001 09:06	249	157	26
Madraj, Sham	smadraj	Feb 02, 2001 10:37	Apr 10, 2001 12:43	264	88	10
Diak, Abdi	adiak	Feb 06, 2001 19:43	May 18, 2001 15:01	316	179	17
Keenan, Kimberley	mdkeenan	Feb 05, 2001 12:43	Jun 15, 2001 13:25	332	181	15
McClugan, David	mcclugan	Feb 02, 2001 16:03	Jun 22, 2001 16:31	968	482	103

Figure 11.3 WebCT – list of students organised by number of times they have accessed course

By Date	Hits	%
Tue Jun 26, 2001	86	86.8
Fri Jul 13, 2001	13	13.1

By User	Hits	%
Lund, Ray	99	100

By Day of Week		Hits	%
Sunday		0	0
Monday		0	0
Tuesday	████████████████	86	86.8
Wednesday		0	0
Thursday		0	0
Friday	███	13	13.1
Saturday		0	0

Figure 11.4 Blackboard – number and date of hits to a particular section of course by one user

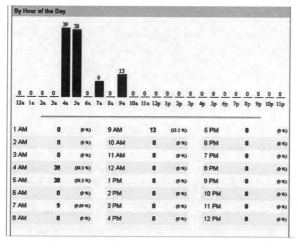

1 AM	0	(0%)	9 AM	13	(13.1%)	5 PM	0	(0%)
2 AM	0	(0%)	10 AM	0	(0%)	6 PM	0	(0%)
3 AM	0	(0%)	11 AM	0	(0%)	7 PM	0	(0%)
4 AM	39	(39.3%)	12 AM	0	(0%)	8 PM	0	(0%)
5 AM	38	(38.3%)	1 PM	0	(0%)	9 PM	0	(0%)
6 AM	0	(0%)	2 PM	0	(0%)	10 PM	0	(0%)
7 AM	9	(9.09%)	3 PM	0	(0%)	11 PM	0	(0%)
8 AM	0	(0%)	4 PM	0	(0%)	12 PM	0	(0%)

Figure 11.5 Blackboard – number of the user's hits to a particular section by hour of the day

space, and provide intimate details of every student's working hours and patterns of study. Where such a virtual learning environment (VLE) is integrated with wider institutional information systems to form what is currently generally called a managed learning environment (MLE), anyone wishing to generate a student record walks through an even richer information landscape. Similarly, system administrators may extract information at a similar level of detail from almost any networked activity, whether undertaken by students or staff. However, where previously to track activity within a web-based learning environment would have involved the deliberate, rather complex analysis of log files and server statistics (something for which the majority of us would have neither the time nor the inclination), within VLEs surveillance is a casual act – sophisticated and detailed reports on individual students can be obtained with a couple of mouse clicks. Further, such tracking tools are included in learning environments as an integral element of their *pedagogical* functioning. Goldberg, for example, describes how by enabling continual evaluation, such tools simply help him to be a better online educator, providing higher quality web-based courses:

> [the] benefit is all in the name of continually trying to improve my course offering, not only in response to direct student comments, but also in response to the way students are interacting with the course. Without this activity tracking I would be in the dark...
> (Goldberg, 2000)

The aim of this chapter is not to deny the usefulness to tutors of such facilities, and we wish to avoid succumbing to the techno-paranoia which sometimes accompanies explorations of the impact of 'dataveillance' (Clarke, 1991). Rather we wish to render strange an element of online learning which risks becoming banal, a matter of 'common sense', and to explore what we see as some important cultural and pedagogical implications of using such tools, from which we might hazard some tentative recommendations for practice. As McLuhan argues, technology is not neutral: 'technological environments are not merely passive containers of people but are active processes that reshape people and other technologies alike' (McLuhan, 1962, p. iv). The wish to avoid accusations of technological determinism should not prevent us from looking closely at how our technologies change the way we work and the way we experience ourselves and others.

The framework for our discussion is provided largely by Foucault, and it is his perspective which perhaps most usefully indicates our approach:

> My point is not that everything is bad, but that everything is dangerous, which is not exactly the same as bad. If everything is dangerous, then we always have something to do. So my position leads not to apathy but to a hyper- and pessimistic activism.
> (Foucault, 1983, pp. 231–2)

11.3   The panopticon as metaphor

The imagery of the panopticon is regularly drawn on in discussions of cyber-surveillance (for example see Bowers, 1988; Gandy, 1996; Lyon, 1993; Poster, 1996; Provenzo 1992; Spears and Lea, 1994; Zuboff, 1988)[1] and does indeed provide a powerful metaphor for thinking about the way in which power relations are constructed in online environments.

In 1791, the English utilitarian philosopher Jeremy Bentham conceived of the architectural innovation of the panopticon as a way of achieving conformity and order within a 'humane' prison system (see Bentham, 1962). The panopticon is a circular building, in which the cells of the prisoners occupy the circumference. The cells are divided from each other in such a way as to prevent any communication between prisoners. At the centre is the 'inspector's lodge' or observation tower from within which prison guards can see into every cell,

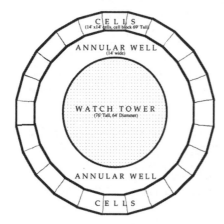

Figure 11.6   Plan view of the panopticon

without themselves being visible. The goal is the achievement of control through both isolation and the possibility of constant (invisible) surveillance (see Figure 11.6).

For Foucault (Foucault, 1979a) the panopticon encapsulates in its form the shift in the nature of power relations which took place during the seventeenth and eighteenth centuries. Where previously what Foucault refers to as sovereign power had exercised dominion through punishment of the physical body (physical torture, public execution), during this time a different, less visible, power mechanism emerged which Foucault calls disciplinary power. Disciplinary power is exercised over individual and collective bodies 'through surveillance and via a grid or network of material coercions which effected an efficient and controlled increase (minimum expenditure, maximum return) in the utility of the subjected body' (Smart, 1985, p. 80).

The panopticon, as one of the 'technologies of power' of this regime, functions less through the imposition of physical force than through its ability to bring about conformity through self-regulation. As subordinates are never sure when they are being observed, they have no alternative than to assume an unwavering surveillance and hence internalise the 'normalising regime'.

> He who is subjected to a field of visibility, and who knows it, assumes responsibility for the constraints of power; he makes them play spontaneously upon himself; he inscribes in himself the power relation in which he simultaneously plays both roles; he becomes the principle of his own subjection. (Foucault, 1979a, p. 203)

Disciplinary power is not only manifested in the workings of penal institutions. For Foucault it is identified with the power-knowledge nexus which is inherent in the workings of institutions throughout the social sphere, including educational institutions. It is important to note, however, that power is not, for Foucault, simply a matter of repression or domination, the property of a particular individual, or group, or class. Rather it is a constituent element of contemporary society – it circulates throughout social relations like an energy. Hence Foucault's famous claim that 'where there is power, there is resistance' (Foucault, 1979b) – an issue we would like to return to later. Power, like surveillance, is not necessarily 'bad', but it is dangerous, with effects which are both positive and negative. As Ball points out, for example, 'Education works not only to render its students as subjects of power, it also constitutes them, or some of them, as powerful subjects' (Ball, 1990, p. 5).

It is not surprising that those theorising the place of privacy in the information society have seized on Foucault's analysis and the panopticon metaphor, seeing in computerised and video surveillance a full realisation of the principles of the panopticon. Computerised student tracking systems like the ones described above do appear to represent the perfect disciplinary apparatus, the single gaze that constantly observes everything.

Surveillance for Foucault is an element of the hierarchical observation which is a key instrument of disciplinary power. Hierarchical observation binds the concepts of visibility and power. There is an unequal power relationship between the seer and the seen – the visibility of the seen enables the seer to 'know' them, to alter them. Access to this knowledge, to this power, is of course unevenly distributed.

We have to bear in mind that in the everyday functioning of the virtual learning environment, the tutor, or 'course designer', has access to extensive surveillance tools, and the student does not.[2] Whatever truth there may be in the much-vaunted claims that computer mediated communication has the potential to do away with many of the cues through which hierarchical relationships and status differentials are inscribed (Dubrovsky, Kiesler and Sethna, 1991; Kiesler and Sproull, 1992; Sproull and Kiesler, 1991; Wiesband, 1992), the relation between teacher and learner is still (and perhaps necessarily) a hierarchical one, not least where the teacher is also the assessor. How comfortable should we be, however, with such ready, casual access to tools which so starkly represent the 'power of mind over mind' (Foucault 1979a)?

11.4   The subject

Hierarchical observation is only one of the instruments through which disciplinary power exercises itself. The two main others – normalising judgement and examination – are also well known to educators. Their collective effect is one of classification and division, rendering the subject 'knowable' through the collection of data relating to them. For Foucault, the file, the document and the record are powerful tools representative of the exercise of disciplinary power. It is partly through these that the individual is constituted, the subject objectified. The power to classify, to collect data relating to students, is hardly new in education, yet in the use of online surveillance tools we see it reaching a new level of depth and detail, representing a further extension of what Foucault calls the 'progressive objectification and the ever more subtle partitioning of individual behaviour' (Foucault, 1979a, p. 178). As Provenzo points out, 'this desire to partition individual student behaviour into ever more subtle units – to systematically collect data – is built into the structure of many computer education programs' (Provenzo, 1992, p. 185).

Foucault writes against the idea of the sovereign subject, the world view which sees the individual – the subject – as the foundation of knowledge and meaning. For Foucault, the subject does not exist prior to the exercise of power, the process of subjectification. Hence, within the panopticon, individuals are made to internalise the gaze of power, to adopt its values as their own, to conform. They are thus formed by power – rather than seeing it as an external force being applied to a pre-existing, stable subject, it is power which makes us who we are. Disciplinary power is an element of what Foucault calls discourse, in which individual subjectivity is seen not as the possession of the conscious self, but as something which is dispersed throughout a network of external structures and practices:

> discourse is not the majestically unfolding manifestation of a thinking, knowing, speaking subject, but, on the contrary, a totality, in which the dispersion of the subject and his discontinuity with himself may be determined. It is a space of exteriority in which a network of distinct sites is deployed. (Foucault, 1966, p. 55)

It follows that discourse and practice are inseparable. Discourses are 'practices that systematically form the objects of which they speak' (Foucault 1974, p.49) – in other words, the discourses of pedagogy create both the teacher and the taught; the discourse/practice of technology-assisted learning creates both the online learner and the teacher or facilitator of online learning.

In this scheme we can see disciplinary apparatuses or 'technologies of power' (of which the virtual learning environment is an example) as being about creating a *certain type of subject*; in using these technologies we are therefore also involved in creating a certain type of subject, a certain type of learner. For Lyotard, predicting back in 1979 the impact of technology on education, the kind of learner being produced would be one who, in the name of enhanced performativity, would be an efficient, skilled user of information (Lyotard, 1979, p. 51). In the current discourse of learning technology we would be more likely to describe the kind of learner we are trying to produce as one who is 'active', 'independent', 'lifelong', 'flexible'. Applying the Foucauldian approach in any case problematises the notion that it is possible to place 'the learner' at the centre of the learning process. Instead, it would see the subjectivity of the learner as constituted through and by the learning environment and the discourses/practices within it. The practices of 'student centred learning', particularly perhaps in their online manifestations, normalise students through surveillance, observation and classification but rarely explicitly acknowledge that the developing individual is an 'object' produced by those same practices, rather than a secure, pre-existing subject.

11.5 The 'superpanopticon'

Cyberspace theory building on the work of Foucault highlights the way in which the virtual environment works to constitute the subjectivity of its users, restructuring the nature of individuality in the process. Poster (1996) analyses the particular impact on subjectivity of electronic databases, characterising the surveillance function of such technologies as a 'superpanopticon' (Poster, 1996). The superpanopticon constitutes individual 'subjectivities' according to its own rules. For example, within interlinked electronic databases, the fields and records containing an individual's details (name, age, sex etc.), highly limited by the determinations of the technology, actually become the 'retrievable identity' of that individual. In other words, the data held on an individual become, to borrow a term from Baudrillard, a 'simulacrum' of that individual – a copy which, as far as the imperative of the technology is concerned, has no original. For Poster therefore, computerised databases are 'nothing but performative machines, engines for producing retrievable identities' (p. 186). What is more, the individual has no control over, or even awareness of this 'other identity' which is circulating throughout the electronic network:

> Now, through the database alone, the subject has been multiplied and decentered, capable of being acted upon by computers at many social locations without the least awareness by the individual concerned yet just as surely as if the individual were present somehow inside the computer. (Poster, 1996, p. 184)

The data represented in the discourse of the database comes to stand for the subject in 'a highly caricatured yet immediately available form.'

> To the database, Jim Jones is the sum of the information in the fields of the record that applies to that name. So the person Jim Jones now has a new form of presence, a new subject position that defines him for all those agencies and individuals who have access to the database. (ibid., p.188)

Lyon (1994) characterises these representations as 'complementary selves' who are 'the sum, as it were, of their transactions'.

> New individuals are created who bear the same names but who are digitally shorn of their human ambiguities and whose personalities are built artificially from matched data. Artificial they may be, but these computer 'selves' have a part to play in determining the life-chances of their human namesakes. Thus are subjects constituted and deviants defined within the Superpanopticon. (p. 71)

We should not underestimate the extent to which this power to constitute and disperse the subject can be applied in virtual learning environments. While humanist ways of knowing might resist the idea that identity formation can take place outside the skin of the individual, we need to consider the possibility that the online student may be starkly objectified in her virtual construction, that 'the learner' may be, as far as our systems are concerned, to some extent constituted by records of their first login, last login, frequency of login, number of discussion board submissions, pattern of page visitation across the site, and so on. Such an identity might exist not only beyond the control of the individual learner, but its very existence – and the possibility of 'judgement' being applied to it either wittingly or not – might remain unknown to them. The literature is full of claims to the emancipatory potential of online communication in educational and other contexts, particularly in the way it enables us to reformulate ourselves and experiment with new identities. In our focus on the way in which we are able to 'make ourselves' in cyberspace however, we should not neglect the ways in which cyberspace technologies may also *make us*.

11.6 Implications for educational practice

11.6.1 Paradigmatic contradiction

The ethos of the MLE can be viewed in many ways as essentially managerialist. It is about order, efficiency, identified outcomes and control. The attraction of databases to the organiser of the MLE is not just their retrieval speed but their relational abilities and totalising nature. In its concern for control and managerial efficiency the MLE reveals its essentially modernist nature and its notion of an individualised rational and stable learner.

The cultural technologies on which it is predicated however (web-based learning environments, relational databases) give rise to discourses/practices which constitute the subject in a decidedly different fashion, as multi-faceted, heterogeneous and dispersed.

Despite such heterogeneity and multiplicity however, the archival permanence promised by MLE databases militates in the opposite direction. Within such archival fixity and retrievability students will never be able to escape their past. There is a loss of redemptive possibility from the digital database which, according to Poster (1996, p. 182) is 'perfectly transferable in space, indefinitely preservable in time' and 'may last forever everywhere'. There is here no Whitmanesque notion of the subject as a perpetually reinventing 'self', self-redeeming. 'Do I contradict myself? Very well then I contradict myself, (I am large, I contain multitudes)' (Whitman, 1975, p. 123).

Within a managerialist paradigm the learner may be individualised, a unified subject, but is not the Romantic self. What is offered, rather, is a disempowering and constraining constitution of the subject. And yet the poststructuralist interpretation of these technologies, as interpellating the subject within a primarily linguistic environment (in which even the databases themselves are a form of writing, of language) offers a multiplicity, fragmentation and re-signification of the subject which, in its uncertainty and instability is the antithesis of the certainty and permanence that managerialism endeavours to achieve.

11.6.2   Insouciance

Perhaps because our current theories of learning are inadequate to explain and analyse the discursive practices that are now emerging within new technologies there appears to be a lack of critique or even a certain insouciance in regard to the (often occluded) effects of these rapidly developing new practices. We are reminded of President Richard Nixon's confident assertion at the onset of Watergate that 'The country doesn't give much of a shit about bugging ... most people around the country think it's probably routine, everybody's trying to bug everybody else, it's politics' (cited in Marx, 1996, p. 193). Though the American public were later to demonstrate their concern about his political mendacity his observation about the public perception of surveillance may not have been inaccurate. Provenzo (1992), for example, suggests that:

> students learn that surveillance is part of their education. Mastering the new computer literacy implies the acceptance that information will be automatically collected and that in turn control will be exercised. (p.186)

He cites Bowers, who argues that this kind of student experience might be deemed 'essential to the development of the socially responsible citizen, and thus it could be expected to view it as a normal, even necessary, aspect of adult life'. (Bowers, 1988, p. 19). Our own interviews with practitioners in UK higher education reveal a similar outlook:

> Now students don't mind. We speak to students. They don't care. They expect ... they know they're being logged. They're quite astonished to find they're being logged as little as they are. There seems to be, at least with them, an idea that it's acceptable to be logged through their educational activities. There are other activities where they wouldn't, which are more social or more exploratory. But they expect, for every crossed knees and twitch they make, that we try and log that. (Interview Respondent, 2001)

We are reminded too of Poster's characterisation of such responses as 'a complicated configuration of unconsciousness, indirection, automation, and absentmindedness both on the part of the producer of the database and on the part of the individual subject being constituted by it' (Poster, 1996, p. 187 [SEB3]).

Insouciance notwithstanding, it is important to bear in mind that UK Universities have a responsibility to comply with the Data Protection Act of 1998, which raises the interesting issue of whether certain tracking activities within V/MLEs are actually legal under current European legislation. Discussions with University Data Protection Officers lead one to conclude that the, as yet, mainly untested application of the law to University practice remains something of a 'grey area'.

> The whole environment in which we're working is dynamically locking down on our responsibilities, on what we can and cannot do ... I have my doubts at three o'clock in the morning that we potentially could have a problem under the Data Protection Act because we don't have a full disclosure. We are very concerned about it. We keep ourselves as informed about it as possible. (Interview respondent, 2001)

11.6.3   Policies of acceptable use

The requirements of the Act, not to mention professional and ethical obligations, give rise to questions of what constitutes acceptable use of such technologies. Any code of practice, we suggest, would need to address a range of issues, principally to:

- adhere to the principle of informed consent;

- specify which activities are tracked and for what purpose;

- grant students (and staff) the right to see (their own) database;

- grant third party (External examiners?) the right to check usage of data (more inspection!);

- issue a clear statement/policy of how long databases would be kept (e.g. for appeal purposes only? for three months after resits?);

- reach agreement on who 'owns' the database and to which other parties it might be made available (e.g. would QAA inspectors/externals have right to view it? – and which parts?) and with which other databases it might be made 'relational';

- * address the legal implications of operating franchises and other web-based activities outside European boundaries

However these measures, if implemented, probably have limited value. Such ethical responses tend to be those of Marxist analysts or Liberal commentators such as Lyotard (1979) who, in their wish to democratise information, assume a relatively unblurred demarcation of private from public spheres, and a separation of knowledge from power. They posit the existence within these environments of learners who are centred, autonomous subjects, rational actors for whom rationality is equated with freedom or political emancipation. However, from a poststructuralist perspective, databases preclude such agency. There is no direct equation of increased access to data = increased knowledge = increased power.

Postmodern culture configures multiple, dispersed subject positions whose domination no longer is effected by alienated power but by entirely new articulations of technologies of power. The cultural function of databases is not so much the institution of dominant power structures against the individual as it is the restructuring of the nature of the individual. ..the viewpoint that I am proposing posits a different relation of knowledge and power, one in which knowledge itself is a form of linguistic power, the culturally formative power of subject constitution (Poster, 1996, p. 190[SEB4]).

11.6.4   Interpretation of tracking data

Interviews with practitioners provide salutary reminders that the interpretation of V/MLE surveillance data can often be misleading. What does the pattern of logging activity actually mean? What does the data really signify? Using the classifications and divisions provided by V/MLE tracking activity to make judgements of student performance or intention appears fraught with dangers of misreading, misinterpretation and assumption.

> The reporting is more important than the actual raw data ... It's not terribly useful for us and I really question whether it's particularly useful for Blackboard or WebCT because what you're actually capturing is not what's actually going on. You're capturing what you think's going on. The student may actually just look at a page, print it off, take it away or they can print off three copies for their friends or their friend is sitting next to them or they accidentally go to some pages or they do a quick flick through the pages to make sure they've covered all the things, the questions that they know there might be teaching about. You're not actually capturing what you think you're capturing. What you're capturing is only that that page has at any time been looked at by that student. That can be exceptionally misleading. (Interview respondent, 2001)

The need to minimise the degree of interpretability of data assumes particular importance when it is used as the basis of assessment or other formative judgements. Caution and active inhibition would appear to be the operative watchwords:

> Anybody you interview who's using WebCT or Blackboard, slap them round the face and say 'Do you know what you're doing?' – because I bet they don't! (*laughs*). (Interview respondent, 2001)

11.6.5   The role of the tutor

A final consideration is the way in which the subjectivity of the tutor becomes constituted through the discourses and practices of computer mediated learning environments. Though the discourse of flexible or student-centred learning might position or interpolate the tutor as 'moderator' or 'facilitator', the forms of agency inherent in practice within a surveillant online environment might include more problematic roles of monitoring, recording, interpreting and forwarding online data. Tutors, of course, are 'seers' of their students but 'seen' by managers.

> By means of surveillance, disciplinary power became an integrated system ... it also organized as a multiple, automatic and anonymous power; for although surveillance rests on the individual, its functioning is that of a network of relations from top to bottom ... and laterally this network holds the whole together and traverses it in its entirety with effects of power that derive from one another: supervisor perpetually supervised. (Foucault, 1979a, p. 177).

Another interview respondent described a situation in which study advisors' use of MIS systems revealed which tutors were registered to make use of new university databases to advise their students. One tutor was identified as having never registered or accessed the database and was deemed by managers to be potentially unsuitable to remain within the role, though such deliberations went on unknown to the tutor concerned. This reconstitution of the subject, through the *absence* of a data record, has a peculiarly postmodern complexion.

Academic staff also need to be aware of both the changes in authority and the more diverse forms of agency that can arise in online learning environments.

> There's a major underlying factor which I don't think they'd even admit to but they're afraid of losing their power. By introducing the [*name of VLE*] system we have introduced into the power equation issues of who controls, who monitors, who watches the [*name of degree*] progress. We've suddenly got developers in there, we've suddenly got the learning technology section in there who by holding on to, creating and capturing this information are suddenly incredibly powerful because that's the node to where everything goes. So in that respect there are major concerns about whether we should be there at all, about whether the power should be devolved. From personal positions of being threatened, of losing power, of losing influence and control of what's going on, both from their own personal point of view about advancement, responsibility and respect as well as professionally about 'Should we lose this power?'. So there's a fundamental point about when you introduce a V or MLE you are going to change power balances – you can't help doing that in quite a fundamental and significant way, that the power structures will change. (Interview respondent, 2001)

11.7   Conclusion

The preceding discussion gives rise to a more fundamental concern in relation to learning within virtual and managed learning environments. This concern relates to humanist tendencies within currently predominant theories of learning in higher education to posit learners primarily as unified and stable subjects. Such analyses tend to emphasise and privilege notions of interior processing (the 'deeper' the learning the better) and cognitive restructuring. Transformation is sought to a more *reflective*, i.e. more fully interiorised, individualised and unified subject. Currently available learning theory appears increasingly inadequate to deal with the complexities of agency, discursive practice, identity and subjectivity within virtual learning environments. We suggest, therefore, that we need to identify and understand forms of agency and learning appropriate to the dispersed, multiple subject characteristic of V/MLEs.

Interesting incursions have been made into such a project, for different purposes, by feminist theorists of technology. Haraway's concept of the cyborg self, for example, examines redefinitions of the power-knowledge-body equation through the possibility of the merging of self and machine. If, for Foucault, the body held a primary position within the regime of sovereign power (which exercised control through bodily punishment), which was then displaced to a secondary position by the emergence of disciplinary power, we see it relegated now to a tertiary position by the power of new technology to blur the boundaries between self and network, to disperse the subject in cyberspace, to remove 'subjectivity' from the body. For Haraway, it is this very blurring of boundaries which constitutes such technologies as sites for resistance. As she puts it:

[there are great] possibilities inherent in the breakdown of clean distinctions between organism and machine and similar distinctions structuring the Western self. It is the simultaneity of breakdowns that cracks the matrices of domination and opens geometric possibilities. (Haraway, 1989, p. 174)

We may, like Haraway, take comfort from the subversive possibilities of the cyborg self, or we may view with disquietude the way in which new technologies appear to represent an extreme manifestation of how a technology of power can achieve control by the total and thoroughly disempowering constitution of the subject. In either case, our chances of developing effective pedagogies for online learning will be greatly enhanced if we are prepared to recognise and work with the new modes of identity formation and new articulations of power/knowledge which cyberspace technologies represent.

Notes

1. The majority of these discussions focus on surveillance and privacy in the workplace, the marketplace and in the functioning of the State, rather than on education *per se*.

2. An interesting exception is the conferencing software FirstClass, in which the hardly extensive, but functional, 'message history' tool is equally available to both. 'Message history' allows users to track who has read any given message, and when.

11.8   References

Ball, S.J. (1990) Introducing Monsieur Foucault. In *Foucault and Education: Disciplines and Knowledge*. S.J. Ball. London: Routledge: 1–7.

Bentham, J. (1962). 'Panopticon; or the Inspection-House'. *The Works of Jeremy Bentham*. J. Bowring. New York, Russell and Russell.

Bowers, C. A. (1988). *The Cultural Dimensions of Educational Computing: Understanding the Non-Neutrality of Technology*. New York, Teachers College Press.

Clarke, R. (1991) 'Information Technology and Dataveillance'. *Controversies in Computing*, C. Dunlop and R. Kling (Eds.), New York, Academic Press.

Dubrovsky, V., Kiesler , S. & Sethna, B.(1991) 'The equalization phenomenon: Status effects in computer-mediated and face-to-face decision making groups.' *Human Computer Interaction*, **6**, 119-146.

Foucault, M. (1966). *The Order of Things: an archaeology of the human sciences*. New York, Pantheon.

Foucault, M. (1974). *The Archaeology of Knowledge*. London, Tavistock.

Foucault, M. (1979a). *Discipline and Punish: the birth of the prison*. Harmondsworth, Penguin.

Foucault, M. (1979b). *The History of Sexuality, vol. 1: an introduction*. London, Penguin.

Foucault, M. (1983). 'On the Genealogy of Ethics'. *Michel Foucault: Beyond Structuralism and Hermeneutics*. H. L. Dreyfus and P. Rabinow. Chicago, University of Chicago Press.

Gandy, O. H. (1996). 'Coming to Terms with the Panoptic Sort'. *Computers, Surveillance, and Privacy*. D. Lyon and E. Zureik. Minneapolis, University of Minnesota Press: 132-155.

Goldberg, M. (2000). 'Message from Murray: Student Activity Tracking'. OTL Newsletter. web page.

http://webct.com/service/viewcontentframe?contentID=2339320

Haraway, D. (1991) 'A Cyborg Manifesto: science, technology and socialist-feminism in the late twentieth century.' *Simians, Cyborgs, and Women: the reinvention of nature*. London, Free Association Books.

Kiesler, S., & Sproull, L. (1992) 'Group decision making and communication technology.' *Organizational Behavior and Human Decision Processes*, **52**, 96-123.

Lyon, D. (1993). 'An Electronic Panopticon? A sociological critique of surveillance theory.' *Sociological Review* **41**: 653-78.

Lyon, D. (1994) 'From Big Brother to Electronic Panopticon', Chapter 4, The Electronic Eye: The Rise of Surveillance Society Lyon.D. Minneapolis: University of Minnesota Press, 1994: 57-80.

Lyotard, J.-F. (1979). *The Postmodern Condition: A Report on Knowledge*. Manchester, Manchester University Press.

Marx, G. (1996) 'Electric Eye in the Sky: Some Reflections on the New Surveillance and Popular Culture' *Computers, Surveillance, and Privacy*. D. Lyon and E. Zureik. Minneapolis, University of Minnesota Press:193-208.

McLuhan, M. (1962). *The Gutenberg Galaxy*. Toronto, The University of Toronto Press.

Marshall, J. D. (1990). 'Foucault and Educational Research'. *Foucault and Education: disciplines and knowledge*. S. J. Ball. London, Routledge: 11-28.

Poster, M. (1996). 'Databases as Discourse; or, Electronic Interpellations'. *Computers, Surveillance, and Privacy*. D. Lyon and E. Zureik. Minneapolis, University of Minnesota Press: 175-192.

Provenzo, E. F. J. (1992). 'The Electronic Panopticon: Censorship, Control, and Indoctrination in Post-Typographic Culture'. *Literacy Online: The Promise (and Peril) of Reading and Writing with Computers*. M. C. Tuman. Pitsburgh, University of Pittsburgh Press: 167-188.

Smart, B. (1985). *Michel Foucault*. London, Tavistock.

Spears, R. and Lea, M (1994). 'Panacea or Panopticon? The hidden power in computer-mediated communication.' *Communication Research* **21**(4): 427-459.

Sproull, L. & Kiesler, S. (1991) *Connections: New ways of working in the networked organization*. Cambridge, MIT Press.

Whitman, W. (1975) 'Song of Myself' from 'Leaves of Grass' in *The Complete Poems of Walt Whitman*, (ed F. Murphy) Harmondsworth, Penguin.

Wiesband, S. P. (1992) Group discussion and first advocacy effects in computer-mediated and face-to-face decision-making groups. *Organizational Behavior and Human Decision Processes*, **53**, 352-380.

Zuboff, S. (1988). *In the Age of the Smart Machine: the future of work and power*. New York, Basic Books.

12 Variation in the experience of learning technologies in teaching in art, design and communication: implications for network dissemination strategies

Linda Drew and Christina Williams
University of Brighton, UK

This study explores the qualitatively different ways that teachers of art, design and communication experience learning technologies.

There has been empirical identification of qualitatively different ways of conceiving of, and approaching teaching in higher education. Relations have been discovered between teachers' approaches to teaching and their perceptions of the teaching context (Martin and Balla, 1991; Prosser and Trigwell, 1997, 1999; Trigwell, Prosser and Taylor, 1994). More importantly, relations have also been found between teachers' approaches to teaching and students' approaches to learning (Trigwell, Prosser and Waterhouse, 1999), linking the two previously separate research areas.

One element of the context of teaching is teachers' experience of learning technologies.

This study of teachers' perceptions forms the point of departure for this chapter. The data is from an interview study of 24 teachers and is explored with a phenomenographic approach. The chapter adopts a second-order perspective on perceptions of the use of learning technologies in the context of teaching in art, design and communication departments. Teachers were asked to describe their experience of using learning technologies; this chapter focuses mainly on describing key aspects of the variation in that experience.

The chapter commences with an exploration of research into learning and teaching which supports the student-focused approach. The principle of teachers' awareness of their learning and teaching situations to improve learning and teaching is examined in relation to this. The importance of teachers' becoming aware of their conceptions and context are key principles underpinning academic development (Prosser and Trigwell, 1999). The results reported in this chapter provide a mechanism for this action.

Implications for network dissemination strategies are discussed in the context of increasing awareness among teachers of art, design and communication where there has been less adoption of the uses of learning technologies.

The findings central to this paper are the categories of description of variation in the experience of learning technologies, these categories are described and further discussed with extracts from the interview data.

This chapter goes on to highlight strategies which explore approaches to teaching, or of becoming a facilitator of learning (Forsyth, 1996). The key conclusion is that academic development should include all members of a work group in order to generate a commitment to change and agree on ways to achieve this (Inglis *et al.*, 1999; Knight and Trowler, 2000).

12.1   Background

Many studies show that it is the way teachers conceive of and approach teaching (Gow and Kember, 1993; Kember, 1997; Prosser and Trigwell, 1999; Prosser, Trigwell and Taylor, 1994; Samuelowicz and Bain, 1992; Trigwell and Prosser, 1996; Trigwell, Prosser and Taylor, 1994; Trigwell, Prosser and Waterhouse, 1999; Walker and Entwistle, 1999) and the way they design courses (Ramsden, 1994), which encourages deep learning more significantly than the characteristics of individual learners. As a teacher develops they can become more aware of their conceptions of teaching, in fact it is an essential part of changing approaches to teaching to increase this awareness. Teachers' conceptions and experiences are stressed by Prosser and Trigwell (1999, p. 160) in their principles underpinning academic development, they argue that one of the primary roles of academic development is to expand teachers awareness of their learning and teaching situations. Those principles are:

- Teachers need to become aware of the way they conceive of learning and teaching within the subjects they are teaching.

- Teachers need to examine carefully the context in which they are teaching and to become aware of how that context relates to or affects the way they teach.

- Teachers need to be aware of and seek to understand the way their students perceive the learning and teaching situation.

- Teachers need to be continually revising, adjusting and developing their teaching in the light of this developing awareness.

In this analysis of teachers' experiences of learning technologies there is evidence to suggest that teachers could enhance their students learning experience and the quality of the learning outcomes if all of these principles were addressed in their development. It is to be regretted that so much emphasis is placed in institutional and departmental learning and teaching strategies on the development of staff to adopt learning technologies without fully considering the appropriateness to the learning situation.

12.2   Method

Phenomenographic interviews were conducted with 24 practice-based teachers of art, design or communication in four higher education institutions. Opportunity sampling was used to identify the four university departments of art, design and communication. The researchers were able to identify those departments as part of their remit in working for the Learning and Teaching Support Network for Art, Design and Communication. Within each of these departments the participants were selected in such a way as to ensure a spread across subjects and to maximise the variation in possible conceptions of learning technologies.

The interviews were semi-structured and consisted of questions designed to encourage the respondent to talk about their work strategies and the intentions behind them. Each respondent was interviewed for approximately 45 minutes. Teachers were asked about their experiences of learning technologies and their intention in using, or not using, them in their teaching. Their responses were continually followed up with prompts to probe for a better understanding of the meanings behind their statements. Prompts used included:

- Could you explain what you mean by that word?

- What is your role in this teaching situation?

- What do you hope your students will achieve by that?

- What is your intention when you do that?

The interviews were taped and transcribed verbatim, and both researchers read these transcriptions thoroughly, and repeatedly. The aim of phenomenographic analysis is to develop categories of description which illustrate the limited number of qualitatively different ways of experiencing a phenomenon, in this case the experience of learning technologies in teaching art, design and communication. The categories were devised by looking for the variation between responses, and the similarities between statements within categories. Then final descriptions were produced to reflect these similarities and differences. The descriptions of the categories were developed using two components - how the explanation is given and what is focused on (Trigwell, 2000, p. 74). In this research teachers' statements about learning technologies focused on either the technology itself, or on learning.

The categories of description, described in the next section, are internally related to each other. Categories were sorted into a meaningful order, with the 'lower', less complete conceptions first, moving into 'higher', more complete conceptions. The higher conceptions encompass the lower conceptions and are therefore more complete. This is known as a hierarchy of categories of description, the logical relations between these categories are shown in the outcome space. (Table 12.1)

12.3 Findings

At this stage we have identified six categories which describe the essential features of the variation in experience of learning technologies. The focus of the analysis was on how learning technologies were experienced by teachers in practice based subjects of art, design and communication. The categories are briefly described below.

12.3.1 Conception A: Learning technology is a method for information transmission

The teacher uses a range of learning technologies to either demonstrate skills (e.g. how to make an artefact) or transmit information to students. Learning technologies are regarded as an additional method to disseminate the teacher's course notes and subject knowledge. In this conception, teachers focus on their use of the technology and developing a competence with it.

> A lot of the lectures I try and do on Powerpoint demonstrations, to practise their lines, distil the key points and help them remember that. And I find it engages them more, although they understand on a whiteboard, although I do that too, it gives them something to latch on to, and with something like [media] law they have to remember things ... Unfortunately it comes down to you just have to know. So as well as introducing them to ethical questions there's some quite specific points that need committing to memory. So I try and use Powerpoint where I can to help them address those particular things. (Journalism)

Essentially, what you find is after a while you are telling the same thing to a whole group of students and you recognise that it is the time to get them all together with a slide projector in the studio and you say 'Well, let's have a look at this problem as a group' and what we need to explain is the difference between primary geometry and secondary geometry. We say 'Look at these examples', so we do a mini slide-show if you like, which can last for ten minutes if it is a simple point, but occasionally when I am introducing a project, because we give them projects to do also, it may last anything up to an hour which is a third of the studio time. (Design)

12.3.2   Conception B: Learning technology is a source of information

The teacher uses a learning technology (e.g. the Internet) as an additional teaching resource. The use of this technology is encouraged by the teacher as part of the information gathering process for their students. The teacher focuses on their own and their students use of the technology and may direct their students to particular approaches in respect of this.

My students use computers to get information, do research, Internet stuff, and they write emails to friends and stuff, but they use it for PhotoShop Illustrator.
But that is not part of your usual course?
No, it's media and not the learning tool. So students use everything. (Design)

The library, for resources, and they get to do research, they have to, they have to go research – they all, a lot of them use the Internet as well, different sources for different things. (Design)

12.3.3   Conception C: Learning technology is a method of communication

In this conception, the teacher uses a range of learning technologies to facilitate remote communication with students where it is considered to be more convenient than face to face communication. This can be teacher to student, e.g. project briefing, course administration; it can also be student to teacher, e.g. submission of project work, students on placement. Again, the teacher focuses on their own and their students use of the technology.

When I do their computer induction they all send me email and I set up a little user book. They all have my mobile phone number ... I have their mobile numbers, And I said to them that I would answer their emails within three working days, whatever, whatever happens you know, and not to use the mobile number unless they're really desperate, but I didn't mind text messages as long as they were short. So we do have a sort of subversive undercurrent of knowing each other really.
Right, so do you use the emails and the text messaging just for communicating or do you use it for teaching?
I don't use it for teaching ... no I think it's just about communication. (Fine Art)

One of the major changes that's happened in recent years is that every student now has an email address which doesn't change with their physical address. In other words they leave Carlisle, they go back home or take up jobs in Leeds or Manchester and you lose touch ... Now I have a mobile phone and I have email and I can stay in touch, and we're setting up a web page as part of the Media Production course which will enable students who've recently left to communicate with students who are still here. (Media)

12.3.4 Conception D: Learning technology is a medium for communicating concepts of the practice

The teacher encourages the use of learning technology (e.g. video, web pages) for students to produce their work and develop their practice. The work is in a medium which is accessible to tutors and peers, so it is not just a tool for making an artefact or developing a skill. In this conception, the teacher's focus is on the student's learning through the application of the technology. The teacher is more concerned about what and how the student learns, not on their skills in the use of the technology.

> We use the Internet a lot and that is probably it really ... We have found that more and more now we are using the Internet for dissertation work and for portfolio referencing as well. We have already found that a lot of students have website references. They are producing more of their own work on computers too. I mean, I have three who have done their own websites this year. So they are actually putting out a lot of their own work as individuals on to websites ... The way that they actually come up with the portfolio can be up to them, there is no set way... They can use [the Internet] for references, some students do the whole thing totally on the Internet. (Design)

> we encourage them to look differently on different kinds of modules, but to use the Internet as a kind of resource for information and also very much actually as a site for work and as a way of making work. (Design)

12.3.5 Conception E: Learning technology facilitates interaction with students

The teacher uses learning technology as a time flexible approach to engaging with and interacting with students. In this conception, the teachers' focus is on student learning and a concern for their development. The interaction with the students provides an opportunity for an exchange of ideas, often through formative feedback. In Conception C the emphasis is more on simply making the student work available in the medium; whereas in this conception the work can be referred to, engaged with and contested.

> one of the things that was a common aspect from the students that have gone away on exchange before was that they have had an absolutely fantastic experience with the modules but feel quite alienated from us when they come back. So the idea of this is to give them access to all of the things they would have access to here; tutors, student support, things like that, registration details, pass marks and things like that. So it is going to keep them interactive with each other, because you might have one going to Vienna, one going to Prague, wherever, so it is more of an idea of making a community ... over the last few years we have had web access for everybody who has been going on overseas exchange and then gradually they have been downloading work and sharing it. There is also a web board facility on there where they can communicate and swap information ... (Photography)

12.3.6 Conception F: Learning technology enhances students critical and conceptual abilities

In this conception the teacher also uses learning technology to engage and interact with students. The teachers' focus is on student learning, a concern for their development and enhancing the learning experience. The interaction with students by discussion and extended critique encourages the development of critical thinking and conceptual change.

> I have used a public folder system for my seminars ...
> *What is your intention of using technology rather than face-to-face?*
> A number of things I think. One is to familiarise students with that type of technology and make them realise that it can be used in a number of different ways. I think the second thing is probably to show them that kind of situation produces a whole set of dynamics and interestingly sometimes you have people who are really quiet in the seminar room and just sit there and you put them all in the same room at the same time, suddenly people speak differently and I think that is a very good experience for somebody who doesn't necessarily say very much in situations to suddenly think that they can. It is also good for other students to notice that. It is also really interesting in terms of authority, when I'm sitting in a room with everybody sitting there and it is very straightforward in terms of conventions, whereas if you go into an online seminar situation it is very, very different and I think that is a very valuable learning experience in terms of who has responsibility ... It serves a number of different functions. It explores space in a different way, it explores technology in a different way and it increases the facility of using certain kinds of technology and it opens up the whole kind of conceptual mind ... it gives them very immediate experiences, concepts and ideas and that is something that we want them to be aware of, setting them up for all kinds of engagements and discussions and interesting ideas. (Design)

> You have back-up examples to illustrate. Like they will, in the essay, if you use the visual, like they often make videos now as their essay, they have clips of examples of their points and it's very much getting them to be critical, I use video a lot for that. Also giving them some background history to something that is going to be developed later. On the whole it's training them to critique their way of looking. (Fine Art)

> Students can work and think visually, and the MLE/web site facilitates this as it is spatial rather than textual, and is navigated in a non-linear way. I see the use of this technology as additional rather than instead of face-to-face delivery of the course. I'm keen to ensure that technology is used because it improves on current ways of doing things. (Design)

12.3.7 Outcome space of categories of conceptions of learning technologies

	Referential (teachers' intentions)				
Structural (teachers' focus)	Demonstrate skills/ transmit information	Provide information resource	Communicate	Interact/ engage with concepts	Develop critical/ conceptual abilities
Technology	A	B	C		
Learning			D	E	F

Table 12.1   illustrates the structural relationships between the categories of description of conceptions of learning technologies.

12.4   Discussion

These qualitatively different conceptions of learning technologies can inform an institution's implementation strategy. In understanding teachers' experiences of technology we can attempt to ensure that it is introduced and used in order to improve student learning rather than for its own sake. What these conceptions tell us is that it is the *focus* of understanding that is important, rather than the type of technology.

In conception F, the highest level conception, teachers experience technology as a method of improving and enhancing their students' critical abilities and as a way to encourage conceptual development. The statements that illustrate this conception show that teachers with this conception are using not only new Internet technologies in this way, but also more traditional ones such as slides and videos. It is their focus on learning that makes this conception more complete and more supportive of quality student learning experiences.

In conception A, the lowest conception, the teacher's focus is on the technology rather than on learning. Here, a range of technologies is seen as a method for transmitting information or the teacher's knowledge to the student. Internet technology does not automatically in itself improve the quality of the learning experience, and in this conception the Internet might be used to display lecture notes – a form of transmission.

Forsyth (1996) suggests that the adoption of learning technologies in higher education has led to a paradigm shift in ways of thinking about learning and teaching. He proposes that a commitment to online education requires both teachers and students to make a leap in their understanding of their roles. Students must become responsible for their own learning while teachers must take on the role of facilitator of learning rather than the disseminator of information implied in the traditional lecture.

Our research reveals that some conceptions of learning technologies are not student-centred, and that the notion of the teacher transmitting knowledge to passive students is still embedded within them. It would seem that Forsyth's paradigm shift is as yet incomplete.

It is important that these different conceptions are recognised and addressed when learning technologies are introduced into learning and teaching in higher education. This adoption of technology can be used as an opportunity for conceptions of teaching and learning to be discussed and reviewed. In their research with teachers Littlejohn and Stefani (1999) found that the emphasis on new technologies in teaching 'was in essence providing an opportunity for academic staff to rediscover pedagogy' (p. 70).

It has also been specifically argued that teacher development will not be effective in the context of design courses if it does not take account of the ways that teachers perceive the use of computers (Martin and Balla, 1991).

This argument is further supported by Martin and Milton (1992), who explored teachers' conceptions of the role of computers in design education. The categories of conceptions they noted also demonstrate a focus on technique and technology, with higher level conceptions which relate to conceptual or problem solving skills. The strategy in most design departments is considered by them to be instrumentally focused on the technology and interaction with the students in its use rather than exploring conceptions with other academics or other scholarly approaches.

An awareness of teachers' conceptions of teaching, learning, and technologies, can encourage a positive change in those conceptions and a re-evaluation of teaching strategies and approaches.

Staff development programmes for teachers who wish to use new technologies can be a useful arena for stimulating this awareness of conceptions and re-evaluation of teaching.

Inglis *et al.* (1999) suggest that such staff development should take place in work groups, or teams, in order to generate a commitment to change and a common understanding of the direction of that change. Knight and Trowler (2000) further develop this theme when they argue that there are culturally prevalent views of learning, dominated by the main activity system in a teacher's experience, the department, or the sub-unit of it, the course. To focus on the main activity system, rather than on the individual, can be said to be a more effective way of influencing cultural changes leading to the improvement of learning and teaching. They emphasise that course and departmental focus is crucial to maintaining the impact of change in line with departmental culture.

This is a theme pursued by others in the discussion of academic work. Martin (1999) sees teamwork and team learning as vital to the conditions for the 'Learning University'. She illustrates her cases and relies heavily on Senge (1992) to apply the qualities of learning organisation to the university context. The five disciplines, or qualities, that Senge regards as essential for the staff of a learning organisation are:

1. *personal mastery*: developing a personal vision and having faith in one's own ability to make a difference within the organisation;
2. *mental models*: understanding the way oneself and one's colleagues think and reason;
3. *shared vision*: aligning one's own aims and ambitions with those of one's colleagues;
4. *team learning*: working with colleagues to go beyond one's own way of seeing;
5. *systems thinking*: seeing one's work unit as systems of a larger whole and understanding how what happens in one affects what goes on elsewhere.

The sharing of a purpose and a context for working should also therefore be extended into other contexts for professional learning. The emphasis is on the team's influence on the learning of the individual in context. Thomas and Willcoxson (1998) make a strong case for the role of junior academics to support each other in a grass-roots movement for change. The growth of teaching development against the grain of the organisational culture is achieved only by the peer group support at grass-roots level. They assert that the 'bottom-up' approach gave legitimacy to 'teaching experiments' and began to give rise to an emergent priority of excellence in teaching in their department (as opposed to a research-only focus).

> The junior academic enthusiast for change must be protected and supported by a group of others, junior or senior, who are able to act as 'sounding boards' and to share the enthusiasm, burden and credit ... for innovations. The creation of a common language and basis for communication within the initiating group is essential, and this language must then be used publicly to provide for dissemination of ideas beyond the initiating group. (p. 481)

Appropriate use of learning technologies is also crucial. Conception C, for example, understands learning technologies as a method for communicating with students at a distance. Many practice-based teachers of art, design and communication see their students face-to-face on a regular basis in the studio or workshop and this conception would suggest to them that the use of learning technologies would be inappropriate for them. By encouraging an awareness among teachers of their conceptions, appropriate use of technology can be understood and in ways that are beneficial to quality learning experiences for students.

12.5   Conclusion

Issues discussed in this chapter support the idea that there are relations between teachers' approaches to teaching and their perceptions of the teaching context. Research cited also confirms that relations have also been found between teachers' approaches to teaching and students' approaches to learning. The principle findings in this chapter are that many teachers in this context are adopting approaches to teaching which neglect aspects of student learning because their focus is on what the teacher does with the technology. Some teachers also reported being concerned with the students' use of the technology, but mainly as an instrumental focus and not concerned with learning aspects. The positive aspects of the findings are that many teachers of art, design and communication are adopting student focused approaches to teaching and conceive of learning technologies as one aspect of the context which is dependent more on appropriateness for student learning. It is this group of teachers who conceive of learning technologies with a learning focus who are more likely to conceive of teaching with a student focus.

The main recommendation is that teachers of this discipline should engage in course team-based development activities, primarily to increase awareness of their conceptions and approaches in learning and teaching, and within that context, to develop strategies for working with the appropriate use of learning technologies.

12.6   References

Forsyth, I. (1996) *Teaching and Learning Materials and the Internet*. London: Kogan Page.

Inglis, A., Ling, P. and Joosten, V. (1999) *Delivering Digitally: Managing the Transition to the Knowledge Media*. London: Kogan Page.

Gow, L. and Kember, D. (1993) Conceptions of teaching and their relationship to student learning, *British Journal of Educational Psychology* **63**: 20–33.

Kember, D. (1997) A reconceptualisation of the research into university academics' conceptions of teaching, *Learning and Instruction* **7**: 255–75.

Knight, P.T. and Trowler, P.R. (2000) Department-level cultures and the improvement of learning and teaching, *Studies in Higher Education* **25**: 69–83.

Littleton, A. and Stefani, L.A.J. (1999) Effective use of communication and information technology: bridging the skills gap, *ALT-J: Association for Learning Technology Journal* **7**(2).

Martin, E. (1999) *Changing Academic Work*. Buckingham: SRHE/Open University Press.

Martin, E. and Balla, M. (1991) Conceptions of teaching and implications for learning. In R. Ross (ed.), *Teaching for Effective Learning: Research and Development in Higher Education* **13**. Sydney: HERDSA.

Martin, E. and Milton, J. (1992) Role of the Computer in the Teaching of Design. *Educational Research and Development Unit Occasional Paper* (92.3). RMIT: Melbourne

Prosser, M. and Trigwell, K. (1997) Relations between perceptions of the teaching environment and approaches to teaching, *British Journal of Educational Psychology* **67**: 25–35.

Prosser, M. and Trigwell, K. (1999) *Understanding Learning and Teaching: The Experience in Higher Education*. Buckingham: Open University Press.

Ramsden, P. (1994) Using research on student learning to enhance educational quality, in G. Gibbs (ed.), *Improving Student Learning: Theory and Practice* (pp. 20–31). Oxford: Oxford Brookes University, Oxford Centre for Staff Development.

Samuelowicz, K. and Bain, J.D. (1992) Conceptions of teaching held by academic teachers, *Higher Education* **24**: 93–111.

Senge, P. (1992) *The Fifth Discipline: The Art and Practice of the Learning Organisation*. New York: Doubleday.

Thomas, J. and Willcoxson, L. (1998) Developing teaching and changing organisational culture through grass-roots leadership, *Higher Education* **36**: 471–85.

Trigwell, K. (2000) A phenomenographic interview on phenomenography. In J. Bowden and E. Walsh (eds), *Phenomenography*. Melbourne: RMIT Publishing.

Trigwell, K. and Prosser, M. (1996) Changing approaches to teaching: a relational perspective, *Studies in Higher Education* **21**: 275–84.

Trigwell, K., Prosser, M. and Taylor, P. (1994) Qualitative differences in approaches to teaching first year university science, *Higher Education* **27**: 75–84.

Trigwell, K., Prosser, M. and Waterhouse, F. (1999) Relations between teachers' approaches to teaching and students' approaches to learning, *Higher Education* **37**: 57–70.

Walker, P. and Entwistle, N. (1999) Conceptions of teaching and levels of understanding: emerging structures and shifting awareness. In C. Rust (ed.), *Improving Student Learning: Improving Student Learning Outcomes* (pp. 309–18). Oxford: Oxford Brookes University, Oxford Centre for Staff and Learning Development.

13 Towards the creation of institution wide support for improving Language for Study Skills for international postgraduate students: providing adequate learning infrastructures including learning technologies and student support

Sharon Waller, Sylvia Griffiths, Su Wu, Gina Wisker and Katalin Illes

Anglia Polytechnic University, UK

Keywords
action research; constructivist; international postgraduates; Language for Study Skills; learning environments; learning technologies; tertiary literacy

13.1 Overview

This chapter focuses on a year-long action research project funded by Anglia Polytechnic University's (APU) Learning and Teaching Fellowship scheme. The project was designed to improve the 'tertiary literacy' skills of international postgraduate business students by providing them with academic English language support via an interactive multimedia CD-ROM, *Excel at Academic English*, used as an integral part of workshops led by an experienced EFL (English as a Foreign Language) teacher. It soon became apparent that students considered the workshops an inconvenience rather than a welcome source of support. Despite efforts to find a formula that suited students' needs the workshops were terminated before the end of semester one. Nevertheless the project was successful in causing change within the university's business school's admission procedures for international postgraduates and was the impetus for the development and introduction of a new English language support module. The aim of this chapter is to offer an insight into the factors which influenced students' attitudes towards the workshops together with an examination of some of the issues which mitigated against the continuation of the project. The chapter begins by examining the methodology adopted and its implementation. This is followed by consideration of the practical problems encountered during the first semester and how these combined with the student's attitudes, values and beliefs to undermine the project's objectives. These findings will be used to inform future projects and hopefully guide the design of more effective integrated learning environments that incorporate the use of ICT (Information and Communications Technology) to support learning and teaching.

13.2 Introduction

Like many universities APU has seen a tremendous increase in the numbers of international students applying to study at both undergraduate and postgraduate level. To satisfy university entry requirements, international students are required to supply evidence of having attained a satisfactory level of English via a recognised examination such as the International English Language Testing System (IELTS). IELTS, and examinations like it, are designed to test reading, writing, listening and speaking skills. Each skill level is scored and an average of all four scores is calculated and awarded as the candidate's overall IELTS score which forms the basis for university admission. Despite having satisfied the required entry level (6.0–6.5), however, many international students perform badly, finding the application of their knowledge of English difficult in tertiary learning situations. For international students coping with the phenomena of 'culture shock'[1] feelings of anxiety and alienation are often compounded with a general frustration at their inability to express themselves in a foreign language with the level of sophistication expected from postgraduates. In other words they experience 'tertiary literacy' problems, unable to perform well in the epistemic tasks of *describing, explaining, predicting, arguing, critiquing, explicating* and *defining* – the cultural products of higher order learning (Ohlsson, 1995, p. 51) – although they understand the associated 'abstract concepts, ideas and principles'.

Following the award of a Learning and Teaching Fellowship the authors embarked on an action research project with the aim of ameliorating the 'tertiary literacy' dissonance experienced by international postgraduate business students. Despite best intentions, however, English support workshops were withdrawn before the end of semester one as they were not addressing students' needs. Nevertheless, as a result of the project's findings the Business School has revised its admissions procedures and approved the development of a new 'Advanced Postgraduate Business English' support module, compulsory with effect from September 2001 for all international postgraduates in need of additional English language support. All applicants accepting the offer of a place on the degree will receive a free copy of the CD-ROM *Excel at Academic English* to work on before the course starts. Those whose English level is considered inadequate will be required to attend the support module.

13.3 Methodology

Thirty-one students were recruited for the academic year 2000/01 of which 26 were international students. It was planned that the EFL lecturer, using the CD-ROM as the basis for workshops held in a computer room, would provide one hour's English language support once a week each for two groups of students for two 12-week semesters.

Students were advised that their English language skills would be tested before beginning the support programme to identify particular problem areas and again at the end to measure any progress made. It had been decided that the creation of a control group consisting of unsupported students for the purposes of comparing the progress made by those students receiving support would be unethical. It was therefore proposed that teaching staff be asked to compare the performance of this particular cohort with those of previous years' taking into account students' recorded English language levels on entry to the degree.

Students were invited to participate in three focus groups during the year to ascertain their: attitudes and approaches towards learning and being a Business postgraduate, feelings towards the support they were receiving, values, beliefs and preferred learning styles. The first two focus groups were held in weeks three and ten, respectively, of the first semester, and the final one in week 11 of semester two.

13.4 Preparing the students

Learners' expectations can influence their commitment to a course, particularly with regard to the extent to which the content 'will be interesting and/or relevant to his or her personal life', and can also 'influence the activities in which the learner engages, thereby determining the type and amount of material that is acquired' (Shuell, 1992, p. 32). To maximise conditions to foster 'meaningful learning' it was recognised that appropriate student expectations had to be established prior to the commencement of the programme, beginning with Induction, and maintained throughout the duration of the project via evaluation of their progress and relevant, timely feedback.

13.4.1   Induction week

The Course Tutor advised students that the Business School was concerned to ensure that *all* students should be enabled to perform to the best of their ability and that as the majority were non native speakers of English, some of whom were studying in England for the first time, academic English language classes were to be provided to support their learning. It was made clear that attendance of these classes was compulsory for all students until they could provide evidence that such classes were superfluous to their learning needs.

It was felt important that the British students should also attend the classes – indeed it was thought that some of them could also benefit from improved academic English skills – so that the whole cohort would begin to interact more quickly as a coherent unit identifying with and participating in a 'community of practice' bound by shared experiences and common aims (Lave and Wenger, 1991 in Greeno *et al.*, 1996, p. 26). It was believed that the international students would benefit simply from the presence of native English speakers who were encouraged to engage with and support their overseas companions. F. Smith (1988, cited in Greeno *et al.*, 1996, p. 26) observed that as it is generally believed we learn by and with the company we keep the design of learning environments should reflect that belief). There was also a concern that unless all students were required to attend the classes the international students might feel inferior or perhaps slighted as they too had been accepted on the basis of their existing qualifications. In other words there was an awareness that the provision of effective learning environments involves attending to the related needs of the whole person including possible affective and motivational factors likely to influence cognitive processes (Shuell, 1992, p. 27).

13.4.2   Testing

Twenty-three students were tested in listening, reading and writing skills using IELTS type tests. The remainder either did not attend or were admitted to the programme late. The results[2] were given to students in the first week of the programme when they had an opportunity to discuss them with the tutor. Many students (15/23, 65 per cent) achieved an average score below the required 6.5 for postgraduate entry and 39 per cent (9/23) achieved less than the 5.5 required for undergraduate entry. Worryingly, 26 per cent (6/23) scored less than 5.00 indicating that their level of English was scarcely sufficient to cope with a postgraduate degree taught in English. Interestingly, the average scores achieved by native speakers confirmed that British students would also benefit from additional English language support.

13.5   Support workshops

Workshops for the two groups took place, one after the other, on Wednesday afternoons. Originally the tutor had intended to work with a whole group on common problem areas using the CD-ROM as an anchor or point of reference to 'support thinking and learning activities' (Crews *et al.*, 1997, p. 143). In this way the CD-ROM was to be an integrated part of the learning environment. While it had been anticipated that students' problems would differ, requiring some small group work and individual tuition while the rest worked with the CD-ROM, the range of language abilities and cultural differences were so wide that this approach was quickly re-evaluated.

After three weeks each group was subdivided into two groups of similar abilities with one half working with the tutor for 20 minutes while the other half worked with the CD-ROM.

The groups then swapped over. This model derives from the Integrated Learning System (ILS) approach pioneered in the United States in the 1980s and piloted in UK schools in the early 1990s by the NCET (the National Council for Educational Technology[3]). While one half work with computer-based learning materials the teacher is freed to concentrate on specific rather than general problems as well as more creative and social activities with the other half (Sealey, 1994). This enables the smaller group to discuss problems related to their studies, exploring possible solutions with tutor support and actively participate in the construction of their knowledge within a meaningful social context. The aim was to create a balanced interactive learning environment designed to help learners construct their individual understanding by combining the two main conditions to achieve that state: opportunities for interactions with exercises and material on the CD-ROM together with social interactions with other learners. This framework corresponds to Greeno *et al.*'s interpretation of a constructivist learning environment (1996, p. 29).

In week five due to inconsistent attendance by students and practical difficulties resulting in their late arrival the students were given the option of working with the CD-ROM or engaging in tutor-led activities. At this time group sizes varied between two to seven students. By week nine, faced with the imminence of assignment submissions, no students were attending.

13.5.1   Semester Two

Under the rules for postgraduate courses students could choose one module from the undergraduate programme. The Course Team decided that in the second semester Business English or another foreign language would be the permitted option. One of the weakest students registered for Italian 'as English was rather too difficult'. Only four international students chose to take this module: one from Hong Kong (U), one from India (Q), two from France (M & W). They chose the time of their class and were taught by the same lecturer but separately from undergraduate students taking the module.

The Hong Kong student had tested out at IELTS 7.0 for writing and 6.0 for reading in the initial entry test. He lacked confidence in his English and chose to attend as he felt he needed to improve his English. He had not been able to attend more than two sessions of the English support classes in the first semester. During the second semester he attended almost all of the classes and achieved a 2:1 grade in the module assessment

The student from India confessed to choosing it 'as an easy option to counteract pressure from other subjects', her English level had tested out at near native competence (IELTS 7.0 for reading, 8.0 for writing) as the system of education for upper caste Indians is based on classical old-fashioned top English grammar schools and universities, she had a command of written and spoken English that was excellent. Her attendance was sporadic and her achievement in the oral part of the assessment very poor as she had not been present when the criteria were outlined (and failed to read the handout guidelines thus misunderstanding what was required). Overall, however, she achieved a low first as she had a good background from her first degree in business terminology, revised well from the textbook, had excellent aural comprehension and summary skills and a wide vocabulary.

The two French students were weak, both scoring below 6.0 in reading and writing for the initial entry test (they were fluent and articulate orally which may have boosted their official IELTS score). One was a mature student (W), previously a supermarket manager, who had emigrated to France from the Lebanon, who had the classic oral fluency and poor literacy skills of those in retailing and so found the amount of reading and writing required by the course a considerable challenge. He missed about a quarter of the sessions and found it difficult to complete any work suggested between seminars and thus failed the vocabulary and reading comprehension test at the end with a score of 26 per cent. His oral fluency and his listening competence, however, meant that overall he managed to achieve a pass of 40 per cent. Undergraduates taking the same module (but taught separately) achieved higher marks. This student's weakness in English may have led to his resorting to 'illegal collaboration' in his Marketing assignment. He attended a couple of the earlier classes of the semester one support programme but soon dropped out as it, and ensuing work for assignments, became increasingly difficult.

The other French student (M) made good progress through consistent attendance and a more conscientious application, completing work set for homework. She achieved a 2:2 in the overall assessment for the module. Her comments at the end of the course were that she felt she had improved her English considerably and had found the English support useful. She had been one of the fairly good attenders on the support programme and had worked through many of the CD-ROM exercises consistently albeit painfully.

13.5.2 Focus groups

Students were invited to attend three focus groups during the year. The aim was to try and establish students' preconceptions, expectations, attitudes, beliefs and values in relation to learning generally and their subject specifically and how these factors might affect their performance. We were particularly interested to learn of any mismatches with the pedagogical aims of their programme of study and how these might be realigned to produce more effective learning environments. The first two focus groups were structured around questions devised for a longitudinal interdisciplinary research project aimed at determining learning strategies common to good students regardless of their cultural background (see Wisker *et al.*, 2001). For the third focus group, questions, devised specifically for the international postgraduates were designed to determine whether their approaches to learning differed significantly from those of undergraduates, i.e. had they reached a higher plateau of intellectual development which would place them firmly on the path towards lifelong learning?

The first two focus groups revealed that the students' choice of postgraduate degree was driven by a strong vocational motivation – they were convinced it would increase their chances of employment in their respective countries. This being their primary driver they objected to the emphasis on theoretical business concepts claiming they had expected a more practical focus with greater reference to real-life case studies. In terms of learning opportunities they felt they spent too much time in a passive role, either listening or taking notes and would have liked to participate in more active learning activities such as giving presentations and practical work placements. Interestingly they all cited interaction with peers as being of vital importance to their learning.

The final focus group began with a thorough exploration of what it means to be a postgraduate. Students felt they needed to be more organized, more independent and more analytical. Whereas in their undergraduate courses students were given a problem and the tools to solve it, as postgraduates they had to find tools appropriate to the problem. *More supervision* was felt to be needed, with fewer gaps between modules and the final assessment, and these gaps should be filled with *tests* and *mock exams*. This would help the students who were used in their home country (France) to much greater external pressure (e.g. 36 hours of teaching per week), and who felt that 12 contact hours a week in the UK was an invitation to relax.

This need to be more independent and at the same time to have more supervision appears paradoxical. This puzzle is addressed by Sapochnik (1977, in Gibbs and Rust, 1997, p. 227) quoting Bion and Winnicott:

> Paradoxically, if the setting is not appropriate, a context aimed at facilitating independence will produce the opposite result ... Being a tutor is tapping into parenthood, and particularly motherhood, which are roles fraught with pitfalls. The completion of learning is achieved when the student brings the outcomes to the teacher and the teacher just confirms them to the student. Hence the request by students for staff to 'be there'. Once the tutor has been 'internalised', the student will carry the notion of the tutor, the real person can be left and parting can take place ... The mother substitute must be present as a supportive environment which can eventually be incorporated into the individual's inner world for independence to develop ...

The concept of self-motivated study was accepted in principle, but hard to practice.

Less theory would be appreciated, and much more *practical work*, especially focused on what they actually wanted to study, which was 'Marketing and Management', rather then generic skills which were less transferable than teachers seemed to imagine. They had learnt underlying theory at undergraduate level, and so did not expect to be confronted with it again as postgraduates. So theory should be replaced by relevant *business oriented practice* (and preferably with much more input from businessmen with a business background). They needed to know how and where to find information on trade fairs, websites and relevant demographics; hence the seminar they had on Internet addresses and websites was of more relevance and importance to them than abstract reflections on their own learning styles.

They also wished teachers to go slowly, clearly, and with self assurance, without comments such as '*I'm not sure. I don't know*', which were not helpful to them. Far from wanting to learn 'mindfully' from 'conditional' teaching approaches designed to engender flexible thinking by opening their minds to alternative solutions (Langer, 1997) the students preferred indisputable facts to uncertainty.

They felt questions about the supposed 'transition from undergraduate to postgraduate status', were misplaced, because they felt no transition. They were the same people, the same group, and could not suddenly change. They were simply studying more difficult things, and *still needed a lot of structure and support*.

Here again Sapochnik (1997, p. 226) has some illuminating comments:

> The environment does not make the individual, at best it allows the individual to realize potential. Learning is a transformational process requiring an environment where not-knowing, uncertainty and tentative exploration can be experienced and accepted as integral components of the learning experience ... Learning is not a mechanical process: there must be room for silence and not-knowing, even if the tutor will be reproached for what is not known ... At an early maturational stage the parent or substitute is blamed for the ... impossibility of immediate knowledge or growth. The student will inevitably have a dual, ambivalent and paradoxical attitude to learning, and at a fantasy level, the tutor must be the one who is deemed responsible for the difficulties of the learning, if the learning is to proceed.

Teachers were nice but the students felt they were just taking down and receiving information and not doing anything *active, not participating in practical projects*. This made them want to give up. Participatory modules in Business and Marketing would be more interesting and helpful. For example, 'International Business, Management, and Marketing' were practical and therefore 'good' modules. But abstract generic studies such as 'Working With Information' were not appreciated. On the Business specific rather than generic basis for critical thinking in business courses compare also Harris *et al.* (in Gibbs and Rust, 1997, pp. 277–87), who make a similar point.

They preferred exams and assignments. A half semester exam was needed. Exams would help them to see the point of the modules. Otherwise their activity curve was rock bottom, with a sudden sharp upward curve at the last moment. Teachers who gave examples from their own personal life experiences were valued, and helped students to do the same.

In summary, students expressed requirement for more:

- structured support;
- feedback;
- tests and exams;
- focus on practical participation in business life, less generic and theoretical material.

They also suggested *more social events*, organized early in the course, to which all students should be required to attend. Parties were good for networking and often for informally acquiring essential information unavailable by other means. More informal groups and visits for example to a Bank, the Treasury in London and the Cambridge Science Park etc., would be valuable.

13.6   Obstacles and barriers

13.6.1   Pragmatics

The one hour a week allotted to learning support for international students proved to be insufficient and the various factors which mitigated against learning, such as the class being held at some distance from the Business School, the tendency of the previous class to overrun, the excessive heat of the computer room, timetabling of the class at the end of the day, the fact that some students had spent the previous two hours working with computers etc. all meant that the learning experience was unsatisfactory. Moreover, as the course progressed, weaker students fell further behind as they struggled to do the required reading and started to work on assessed assignments. As the support programme was non-assessed and therefore regarded as unimportant they started dropping out. Attendance was intended to be compulsory for students needing it but this was not enforced.

13.6.2   Students' attitudes, values and beliefs

The project clearly illustrates how students' ability and willingness to learn are inextricably linked to and influenced by their attitudes to a learning activity, the value they place on it and their views of learning in general (Greeno *et al.*, 1996, p. 19). After the first two weeks it became clear that most of the students were hostile to the idea of an additional class which was non-credit bearing indicating a tendency to adopt performance rather then learning goals (ibid., p. 20). Moreover many did not feel that the class was relevant to their needs, as the CD-ROM based material was general rather than business specific. Previous research with international students on Business English modules (Griffiths, 1999), however, found that the main determinant of student success on academic courses was the level of English language proficiency on entry rather than specialist knowledge of business. Thus students, whose scores on the entry test were low, particularly for reading and writing, were disadvantaged in their postgraduate learning. Although they may have satisfied the entry level required for the degree, on re-testing this was not always found to be their current score and as entry was on an overall score students may have been weak in these skills but stronger in oral/aural skills.

Some students felt that their level of English was 'good enough to get through' even in the face of poor test results and did not want to *waste* free time on a non-credit bearing programme. For these students the desire to do well was tempered by their perceptions of the amount of effort required and how relevant the successful completion of the programme would be to their specific needs (Shuell, 1992, p. 27). In addition to these metacognitive factors the focus groups revealed that these students' attitudes appeared to be influenced by an apparently low level of intrinsic motivation. In the absence of any extrinsic motivators such as course requirements or credit-bearing assessments they were not prepared to invest the effort required to improve their performance.

Many students were offended at being compelled to attend what they saw as remedial classes and resented being tested after being accepted on the degree even though some acknowledged that their language deficiencies would hinder their performance. Students' resentment manifested itself variously by, for example, choosing to work on different units of the CD-ROM to those recommended by the tutor, changing groups each week, sullen responses and hostile body language, irregular or non-attendance. This general lack of willingness to actively participate in the learning process by adopting, instead, the passive role of subjects to whom teaching is 'being done' prevented the majority of students from investing in and assuming any responsibility for their learning suggesting that, culturally, many were used to and therefore more comfortable with being dependent on the external control of tutors (Hannafin and Land, 1997, p. 190). Learners, however, are not just at the centre of a technology-enhanced learning environment they are an integral part of it (ibid., p. 187), without their cooperation and collaboration therefore the learner-technology partnership is ineffective. Equally without their active participation in classroom practices the students were not contributing to the establishment of a learning community (Cobb and Bowers, 1999, p. 9). Given that few, if any, students valued the classes the development of such a community was thwarted from the beginning. The students were clearly not motivated to engage with the intended learning environment and as a consequence made little contribution to the development of shared values and practices which might have led, according to Lave and Wenger (1991) (cited in Greeno *et al.*, 1996, p. 26), to their identifying with the functioning of such a community within, initially, the context of the workshops. Ultimately this experience would have fed into and strengthened the learning community formed by virtue of their having chosen to undertake the same degree.

13.6.3   Reactions to the CD-ROM

Although the CD-ROM's generic academic content, and therefore the workshops' focus, had been cited as the main reason why the students did not want to attend this was not borne out by the majority of the evaluation forms.[4] Most of the students claimed that the content was relevant and individual exercises worthwhile:

The exercise was very meaningful and focus to the point of teaching. <??>

I think it's relevant and the exercise worthwhile because it learns us to study a text and show us if we understand quickly the main idea. (5.0)

Some students found working with the CD-ROM very tiring and preferred working with the tutor, whereas others were happier working on the computer. Other students' reactions seemed to be attributable to their learning styles, some appreciated being able to make mistakes in private and repeatedly redo exercises in their own time whereas others preferred the more traditional social interaction with a tutor and other students. Cultural differences also affected students' behaviour. The Scandinavian students' level of English was generally high and they did not appreciate having their learning mapped out for them. They were very aware of their weaknesses, which were mainly grammatical, and wanted a software package that concentrated solely on improving specific areas of grammar. Students who came from didactic educational cultures such as those of China, France, Spain and Greece were mostly content to work through the CD-ROM as planned.

13.7   Conclusion

The project findings illustrate that the implementation of effective technology-enhanced learning environments involves careful consideration of more than sound instructional design factors. The learners for whom the environment is intended must be adequately prepared for the proposed learning experiences in order to minimise possible mismatches between those experiences and their expectations. Nor is it enough to focus on supporting their cognitive processes, the possible effects of the affective and metacognitive aspects of learning must also be taken into consideration. If we are to understand how students perceive a particular learning activity we must adopt their viewpoint and try to see things the way they do, not simply observe their reactions to a situation (Cobb and Bowers, 1999, p. 10). 'Knowing your audience' therefore is more than being aware, for example, of their cultural differences it implies being able to diagnose students' characteristics, their range of knowledge and then accommodating these differences by providing a variety of learning opportunities and experiences (Shuell, 1992, p. 46).

The project also demonstrated that learners' attitude, values and beliefs exert greater influence on their reactions to a learning environment than anything else. In this particular case students' perceptions of the learning opportunities afforded by that environment were at odds with those of the authors' (Laurillard *et al.*, 2000, p. 3). Although the students were performance driven, as indicated by their desire for assessment and feedback, the project did not provide this form of extrinsic motivation and they were not helped to develop meaningful learning goals related to those of the project which would have helped them to succeed in the face of difficulties Greeno *et al.* (1996, p. 20). The challenge for the future therefore is to establish appropriate expectations in learners and enable them to take responsibility for their own learning thus eliminating the problem of trying to adapt learning activities to fit a diverse body of learners. By changing students' attitudes towards learning and their perceptions of themselves as 'knowing agents' (ibid., p. 26), we may be able to equip them to make learning opportunities more relevant to their own needs and to make learning material more meaningful to themselves (Langer, 1997, p. 75).

Notes

1. A 'temporary stress reaction where salient psychological and physical rewards are generally uncertain, and hence difficult to control or predict. Thus a person is anxious, confused and apparently apathetic until he or she has had time to develop a new set of cognitive constructs to understand and enact the appropriate behaviour' (Furnham, 1997, p. 15).

2. See Appendix 13.1.

3. Now known as BECTA – the British Educational Communications and Technology Agency. '

4. See Appendix 13.2.

13.8   References

Cobb, P. and Bowers, J. (1999) Cognitive and situated learning perspectives in theory and practice, *Educational Researcher* **28**(2): 4–5.

Crews, T., Biswas, G., Goldman, S. and Bransford, J. (1997) Anchored interactive learning environments, *International Journal of Artificial Intelligence in Education* **8**: 142–78.

Furnham, A., (1997) The experience of being an overseas student in D.McNamara and R. Harris (eds.) *Overseas Students in Higher Education Issues in Teaching and Learning*, (pp. 13-29). Routledge

Ferney, D. and Waller, S. (2000) Key factors in the design of an interactive multimedia CD-ROM for EAP learning. In P. Howarth and R. Herington (eds), *EAP Learning Technologies*. Leeds: Leeds University Press.

Ferney, D. and Waller, S. (2001) Reflections on multimedia design criteria for the international language learning community, *Computer Assisted Language Learning* **14**(2): 145–68.

Gibbs, G. and Rust, C. (eds) (1997) *Improving Student Leaning through Course Design*. The Oxford Centre for Staff and Learning Development, Oxford Brookes University.

Greeno, J.G., Collins, A.M. and Resnick, L.B. (1996) Cognition and learning. in D. Berliner and R. Calfee (eds), *Handbook of Educational Psychology* (pp. 15–46). New York: Simon & Schuster/Macmillan.

Griffiths, S.H. (1999) To what extent is proficiency in General English or knowledge of business in learners' first language a determinant of success rather than in prior knowledge of business in vocabulary acquisition and text comprehension? Unpublished.

Hannafin, M. and Land, S. (1997) The foundations and assumptions of technology-enhanced student centred learning environments, *Instructional Science* **25**(3): 167–202.

Langer, E.J. (1997) *The Power of Mindful Learning*, Addison-Wesley: Reading, MA.

Laurillard, D., Stratfold, M., Luckin, R., Plowman, L. and Taylo, J. (2000) Affordances for learning in a non-linear narrative medium, *Journal of Interactive Media in Education*. http://www-jime.open.ac.uk/00/2

Ohlsson, S. (1995) Learning to do and learning to understand: a lesson and a challenge for cognitive modelling. In P. Reimann and H. Spada (eds), *Learning in Humans and Machines: Towards an Interdisciplinary Learning Science* (pp. 37–62). London: Pergamon.

Sealey, M. (1994) Diplomatic illness, *Educational Computing and Technology*, Nov./Dec: 6–10.

Shuell, T. (1992) Designing instructional computing systems for meaningful learning. In M. Jones and P. Winne (eds), *Adaptive Learning Environments*. New York: Springer Verlag.

Wisker, G., Tiley, J., Watkins, M., Waller, S., Thomas, J. and Wisker, A. (2001) Discipline-based research into student learning in English, Law, Social Work, Computer Skills for Linguists, Women's Studies, Creative Writing: how can it inform our teaching?, *Innovations in Education and Teaching International* **28**(2).

Appendix 13.1 MA International Business/International Business Economics IELTS Assessment

	Names	Nationality	Listening	Reading	Writing
1	A	Mauritian	5.0	5.0	5.0
2	B	Danish	6.0	6.0 incomplete	6.0/5.5
3	C	French	4.0	3.0	did not do
4	D	Danish	7.0	7.0	8.0
5	E	French	6.0	5.0	5.0/5.5
6	F	Greek	6.0	7.0	6.0/6.5
7	G	Lithuanian	7.0	6.0	did not do
8	H	Chinese	6.0	6.0	6.6
9	I	Greek	4.0	3.0	did not do
10	J	Nigerian	5.0	5.0	7.0
11	K	British	6.0	5.0	7.5/8.0
12	L	British	8.0	8.0	7.5
13	M	French	4.0	5.0	4.5
14	N	French	4.0	5.0	5.0
15	O	French	5.0	5.0	5.0/5.5
16	P	British	7.0	7.0	6.0/6.5
17	Q	Indian	8.0	7.0	8.0
18	R	Danish	6.0	6.0	5.5
19	S	Greek	7.0	8.0	6.5
20	T	Chinese	5.0	5.0	6.0
21	U	Chinese	7.0	6.0	7.0
22	V	British	6.0	4.0	4.0
23	W	French	5.0	5.0	4.5/4.0

IELTS Levels

Band 9 – Expert User
Band 8 – Very Good User
Band 7 – Good User
Band 6 – Competent User
Band 5 – Modest User
Band 4 – Limited User
Band 3 – Extremely Limited User
Band 2 – Intermittent User
Band 1 – Non User

Appendix 13.2   EXcel at Academic English

Anglia Polytechnic University's CD-ROM for Academic English

To use 'Excel at Academic English':

1. Insert the CD-ROM disk in the CD-ROM drive, wait a few seconds for the computer to read it (you will see the CD-ROM drive light come on)

2. Click on the mortar board icon in the 'Excel at Academic English 2' program group on the Program Manager screen

3. Click on the INTRODUCTION button and select the 'How to Use this CD-ROM' option from the menu.

Please help us evaluate the CD-ROM's usefulness as a learning tool by filling in an evaluation form for each of the UNITS you complete.

Feel free to make any additional comments on the back of each form.

Please indicate your level of proficiency in the English language on the form and staple all your completed forms together before handing them back together with the CD-ROM to your lecturer.

> *NB. It would be most helpful to us if you work through and comment in detail on a complete UNIT rather than browsing quickly through the whole CD-ROM.*

The CD-ROM is divided as follows:

INTRODUCTION:	How to use this CD-ROM
	About Academic English Exams
	Thanks to … (Acknowledgements)
READING:	UNIT 1 – Identifying main and supporting points (5 exercises)
	UNIT 2 – Making notes and summarising (5 exercises)
WRITING:	UNIT 1 – Discursive compositions (5 exercises)
	UNIT 2 – Comparing and contrasting data (5 exercises)

LISTENING – 10 exercises

SPEAKING – 10 exercises

TEST YOURSELF READING – 3 exercises

TEST YOURSELF WRITING – 5 exercises

INTRODUCTION UNIT: ....

Screen Design e.g. How could it be improved? Is there too much text on the screen?

Content e.g. Is it relevant? Is it useful?

What did you BEST like about this unit?

What did you LEAST like about this unit?

Please indicate the EASE OF USE factor for this exercise on a scale of 1 to 5

1 - very easy to use   **2**   **3**   **4**   **5 - very difficult to use**

UNIT Name: .... Exercise Number: ....

Start Time .... Completion Time ....Screens skipped: ....

Instructions (Do you understand what you have to do?)

Screen Design e.g. How could it be improved? Is there too much text on the screen?

Content e.g. Is it relevant? Is the exercise worthwhile?

What did you BEST like about this exercise?

What did you LEAST like about this exercise?

Help facility e.g. Is the wording ambiguous? Does it really help you?

Please indicate the EASE OF USE factor for this exercise on a scale of 1 to 5

1 - very easy to use   2   3   4   **5 - very difficult to use**

14 Variation in ways of experiencing change in teaching, the development and use of learning technologies and the likely consequences for student learning

Jo McKenzie

Institute for Interactive Media and Learning, University of Technology, Sydney, Australia

Many different claims are made about learning technologies: that they are inherently student-centred or a threat to student-centredness, that they motivate students or isolate them and so on. Any of these could be the case, as learning technologies are simply tools which afford different kinds of use and outcomes. Whether learning technologies' potentials are realised depends on how teachers design and integrate them into the student learning environment (Alexander and McKenzie, 1998; Laurillard, 1993). Over the last three decades, an extensive body of research has developed on the relations between teachers' approaches to teaching and students' perceptions of their learning environment, approaches to learning and learning outcomes (Marton, Hounsell and Entwistle, 1997; Prosser and Trigwell, 1999; Ramsden, 1992). Teachers differ in the approaches they take to teaching. In classes where teachers report taking information transmission/teacher focused approaches, students are more likely to report taking surface approaches and less likely to report taking deep approaches. Where teachers report a conceptual change/student focused approach, students are less likely to report taking surface approaches (Prosser and Trigwell, 1999).

While these studies have been conducted largely in the context of face to face teaching, there is also evidence that differences in teachers' educational beliefs relate to differences in the focuses they take when designing and using computer-based learning (Bain and McNaught, 1996; Bain, McNaught, Mills and Lueckenhausen, 1998). Housego and Freeman (2000) use a series of easily recognisable case studies to illustrate differences in the use of web-based learning tools between teachers acting from more teacher-focused or more student-focused perspectives. Taking a relational perspective, Prosser and Trigwell (1999) argue that a teacher's approach to teaching in a particular situation is a relation between their prior experiences and their perceptions of their teaching situation. So we could say that when a teacher encounters a type of learning technology which could be used in teaching, the teacher's approach to developing or adopting that technology will be a relation between the technology, the teachers' prior experiences of teaching and similar innovations, and the teacher's perception of their teaching situation.

Much attention has been given to the adoption of information technologies in higher education, but most attention appears to focus on whether teachers will adopt technologies, and the skills and understandings necessary for them to do so. The most influential work on dissemination of innovations (Rogers, 1995) has identified five perceived attributes of an innovation which influence adoption decisions, of which two are: relative advantage, the degree to which an innovation is perceived as better than previous ideas or practices; and compatibility, the degree to which an innovation is perceived as being consistent with existing values, past experiences, and needs of potential adopters.

Taking Prosser and Trigwell's (1999) perspective, a teacher with prior experiences of teacher-focused approaches who perceives that their teaching situation affords teacher-focused approaches may perceive that an innovation which affords teacher-focused uses is compatible with their values and needs. A teacher with prior experiences of student-focused approaches who perceives that their teaching situation affords these approaches may perceive that an innovation which affords student-focused uses is more compatible. When an innovation affords both teacher-focused and student-focused uses, it is likely to be perceived and used differently by different teachers in different teaching situations.

This chapter makes links between three separate studies to suggest that teachers experience the change toward using information technologies in qualitatively different ways, which relate to differences in technology use and differences in students' perceptions and probable learning outcomes. According to Marton (Marton and Booth, 1997; Marton and Trigwell, 2000), variation is the key mechanism of learning. When teachers experience a change in their teaching, they discern particular patterns of variation in relation to their prior experiences and the perceived relevance structure of their teaching situations. Different patterns of variation relate to different ways of experiencing the change. So rather than focusing on whether teachers adopt learning technologies, this paper focuses on variation in *how* teachers adopt learning technologies and what they intend to achieve through using them. As adoption of a learning technology involves the teacher in making a change to some aspect of their teaching, the first study focuses on variation in ways of experiencing change in teaching.

14.1 Study 1: Variation in ways of experiencing change in teaching

This section of the chapter focuses on variation in university teachers' ways of experiencing change in teaching, based on a phenomenographic study in which 26 teachers were interviewed twice or three times over a two year period. Some of these teachers made changes involving learning technologies, others did not. Five categories of description were constituted, in which change in teaching was described as:

A changing the content which is taught
    A1 changing the selection of content included or excluded
    A2 changing the way the content is organised for teaching
B changing teaching strategies
C relating teaching more effectively to learning
D coming to experience teaching differently

These categories form a semi-inclusive hierarchy, where category D includes category C, which includes A1, A2 and B. The outcome space shown in Table 14.1 illustrates the relations between the different categories. The referential dimension of the outcome space shows differences in the primary meaning and focus of change, the structural dimension relates to the dimensions of teaching which are opened up for variation, reflecting the teacher's intention in making the change.

In categories A and B, changes are described as occurring for primarily teacher focused reasons. In category C, teachers describe making changes to either or both the content and teaching strategies, but with the primary focus on improving aspects of student's learning. In category D, the teacher's description focuses on variation in ways of experiencing teaching. Teachers describe themselves as becoming more student focused, and changes in teaching focus on realising these more student-focused intentions.

Structural ———————➔ Referential ↓	Teaching focus	Student learning focus – teaching in the background	Teacher learning and student learning focus
Content selection organisation	A1 A2		
Strategies	B		
Relating teaching to learning		C	
Experiencing teaching differently			D

Table 14.1 Outcome space for teachers' ways of experiencing change in teaching

Many individual teachers described experiences of change which related to more than one of these categories. Changes involving learning technologies were described in ways which primarily related to categories B and C.

14.1.1 Category B examples: using learning technologies to improve teaching

In changes related to category B, the teachers' accounts suggested a focus on technology as a teacher-focused strategy. Here is one example from a teacher I've called James, who in part of his interview describes the adoption of Powerpoint for lectures:

> I discovered a pedagogical aid called Powerpoint ... And I've found that that's a really good way of teaching. Not learning. I don't know how effective it is at learning, but it's a really good way to teach. It illustrates a subject well, it provides notes for the students so they don't have to write things down. They can concentrate, concentrate on the discourse. So the use of technology in teaching I thought was ... a significant occasion during my, my year.

> it certainly helps teaching because it organises my thoughts. When I sit here it takes me a day to organise an hour and a half lecture, right. But by the time I've finished, everything's in proper order. Everything makes sense. ... one of the responsibilities of a teacher is to be prepared and that assists me in this preparation. (James 2)

James' description shows aspects of both categories A2 and B. It suggests that he has adopted Powerpoint mostly as a teacher-focused strategy for improving his teaching presentation and his students' reactions to his teaching. Teaching appears to be in the foreground of his intention in making the change and the way that he judges its success, while student learning is in the background.

Shane's description also focuses on adopting information technology as a teacher-focused strategy. Shane was teaching large undergraduate classes and had seen how his colleague, John, was using a web-based learning tool in his subjects. He comments:

We've sort of put a lot more stuff on the net now too. We're sort of still not operating on the level that John is, but we're using it mainly at the moment just to distribute material to students. They can just download it and take it home. Save them coming to me, collecting a disc, copying it, bringing it back. Again, it's really just like an admin thing. ... I've really got to say that admin drives everything in terms of your approach to not only assessing the students but also the distribution and materials and the types of things that you teach them. I didn't really appreciate that until I did actually fully take over the course.

Shane also described gaining positive responses from students and using the web to automate a form of assessment and feedback:

Oh, it just provided a simple, and an alternative means of doing particular things I think. The assignment for instance ... previously they just wrote it down on a bit of paper and gave it to me. ... Now what I've got is a standard form on the Web. They can log in with their student name and number and they've just got to type the numbers in. And the program will tell them if they've met the criteria here and whether it adds up to 100% or whether they've got the minimum number of assets or not. And they enjoy it too. They sort of, I remember the first time, ... rather than just sort of handing out the outlines and reading it, I put the whole thing up on the screen and they just loved it. They, wow, they sort of think you're doing something really innovative. (Shane 3)

While Shane's colleague, John, was using the same web-based learning tool for student discussion, responding to students' questions and encouraging other students to respond, groupwork and self-managed quizzes, and not for distributing material, Shane chose to use the more teacher-focused aspects which assisted him with subject administration and saved him time. The focus of his description is primarily on efficiency for him and positive reactions from the students.

14.1.2 Category C example: improving the learning experience for students

By contrast, in descriptions related to category C, the teacher is focused more on their intentions for student learning and the ways of making learning possible. Lorraine, a teacher in health sciences who has developed a virtual clinic multimedia program, gave one example. The program enables students to interact with virtual patients, ask them questions, make tentative diagnoses and gain hints from a virtual professional guide. The change for her teaching was focused on enabling students to learn patient diagnosis in ways which were not possible without information technology.

I mean there are things like developing this virtual ... clinic which was unimaginable five years ago. ...
I know what I would like to do and I know what kind of patient I would like to drag in and show to the students and I know I can't do that and I know I would like to give them a patient to play with. They need some direction on how to play with the patient and so it's easy to design a program that just fulfils all the things that you would ideally like to do in a teaching situation but ethics and all sorts of things prevent it. And the students come in and say 'why can't we have patients to play with, right from like first year?'... so they are eager to do prac work, they are eager to do hands on stuff. (Lorraine3)

Making use of a learning technology enabled Lorraine to implement her intentions for student learning in a new way. Her focus was on improving the learning experience for her students and also responding to her students' desire for more practical work. At the time of this interview she was still in the planning stage of her innovation.

As is illustrated in part by the above quotes, descriptions related to categories B and C differed on two main dimensions of variation:

- the focus of the teacher's intention in making the change – primarily on improving teaching through improving strategies (B) or on improving student learning, with teaching in the background (C);

- the criteria for determining whether a change is successful or 'working' - teacher comfort or efficiency or student reaction (B) or students' engagement in learning (C).

In the next sections of this chapter, two further studies illustrate other aspects of variation in the focuses of teachers involved in developing and using learning technologies in teaching. The first study is a major Australian evaluation of IT projects for university learning (Alexander and McKenzie, 1998), which focuses on developers of IT projects and the second is a smaller scale study of the dissemination and adoption of a particular technology product in one institution (Freeman and McKenzie, 2000).

14.2 Study 2: Variation in intentions and reported outcomes for teachers who developed learning technology innovations

A major Australian evaluation of the effectiveness of information technologies for university learning (Alexander and McKenzie, 1998) focused on the experiences of 104 university teachers who developed funded IT projects. Most teachers in this study stated some intention to improve students' learning, and in fact the funding agency required that they describe how their project would improve learning. But the questionnaire responses from these teachers suggested a range of variation in focuses, with some similarities and some differences when compared with the findings from Study 1. Some interesting observations can be made from comparing descriptions of intended outcomes with reported achieved outcomes for students and staff. Table 14.2 summarises these, omitting the 20 per cent of

	For students		For staff	
	Intended outcomes	Reported outcomes	Intended outcomes	Reported outcomes
Improved quality of learning, or teaching related to learning	87	37	34	4
Improved efficiency or access to resources	39	12	40	25
Improved attitudes/motivation	16	63		
Teacher professional development			29	32

Table 14.2   Comparison of intended and reported outcomes of projects for students and staff

negative outcomes for staff which were reported. While efficiency and access to resources were seen as benefits for both students and staff, although sometimes differently, improved learning or teaching quality was seen as an intended outcome for students by most respondents but for staff by around one-third. Differences in reported outcomes were even starker.

Looking at sets of individual responses revealed what appear to be teacher-focused vs student-focused differences in intentions and reported outcomes. One group of responses focused on intentions to provide access to learning resources for students and availability of resources and efficiency for staff. Outcomes, where reported, focused on positive student reactions:

Intentions

For students: to provide them further opportunities for independent learning in order to improve their second language proficiency

For staff: to allow lecturers to spend time with students more efficiently. To give staff the opportunity to gain experience in the development of IT materials

Reported outcomes:

For students: Students enjoy the experience of computer-assisted language learning

For staff: Staff in my department are not interested. Only staff that have an interest in IT have shown an interest [Response 83]

By contrast, other responses focused more directly on the learning outcomes for students and described intentions for staff in terms of improving the design of the student learning experience. Benefits for staff and students were described in related rather than separate ways:

Intentions

For students: To help students take more control of their learning (pace and direction). To help them make sense of computer technology by integrating the complex concepts into their own semantic framework

For staff: To understand the problems facing students and to see how technology aspects could be better integrated into the learning process

Reported outcomes

For students: 'at last someone is looking seriously at our problems and trying to do something about it'

For staff: has meant a huge commitment to learning (a) the new technologies and (b) how best to integrate these into learning (Response 8)

Intentions

For students: Enhanced mathematical skills relevant to studies in [x], better appreciation of such skills, learning in a non-threatening and self-paced manner and a consistent form of assessment

For staff: Being able to use better teaching tools, consistent continuous feedback on teaching effectiveness, ability to monitor progress of course, timesaving on assessment

Reported outcomes:

For students: An improved understanding (learning) of the need for a mathematical approach. Better skills in analysis of practical problems. Better integration of applied knowledge

For staff: The ability to teach a difficult concept. An appreciation from students that staff are committed to improving student learning (Response 39)

The differences in focus of these and similar responses could be related to the two dimensions of variation outlined above and also to a third dimension of seeing the development of learning technologies as an end in itself (provision of resources or opportunities for independent learning) or as a means to the end of improved learning outcomes. As reported in Alexander and McKenzie (1998), teachers who focused on simply having the LT resources available were less likely to report successful learning outcomes than those who had clear learning designs and ways of integrating their LT projects into the learning and assessment environment of the course.

14.3 Study 3: Variation in teachers' intentions and uses of the same LT tool

Teachers who initiate and develop IT projects would usually be innovators (Rogers, 1995) and we might expect them to differ from the majority of teaching staff. Whereas study 2 focused on the developers of different IT projects, this example focuses on variation in what early-adopting teachers focused on in adopting the 'same' technology project. The project is called SPARK – for Self and Peer Assessment Resource Kit – and is a web-enabled system for self and peer assessment of teamwork (see Figure 14.1). SPARK enables students to rate confidentially their own and their peers' contributions to team tasks and team maintenance roles using a set of pre-defined criteria. The approach was adapted from a well-designed and evaluated paper-based peer assessment system in which students rated each other's contributions and the lecturer used the ratings to calculate adjustments to individual marks (Goldfinch, 1994). A prototype of the project was initially developed by an innovative teacher with several intentions: improving students' learning from team tasks, improving the fairness of group assessment, reducing the problems associated with unequal team contributions and improving the efficiency of the paper-based system (Freeman and McKenzie, 2000).

The initial stage of wider adoption of the system involved a team of teachers which had formed to develop a 'generic' version of the system which could be customised for different tasks. Team members were teachers who had a diversity of relevant forms of expertise, were

Figure 14.1   SPARK Welcome screen

interested in teaching and learning and were using group work in their subjects. In the first semester of development of the generic system, SPARK was used by team members in three subjects beyond the initial development context (Freeman and McKenzie, 2000) and in the second pilot semester a fourth teacher joined the group. Data on the pilot were gathered from minutes of meetings, interviews with the teachers, focus groups and questionnaires with students and teacher reports of students' learning outcomes.

Early evaluations and project team meetings revealed that the use of SPARK was perceived and implemented in different ways, which can be related to the two dimensions of variation described in the first study. The differences may be more subtle than those in the other two studies, as all teachers were essentially interested in learning and groupwork. But as far as using the SPARK tool was concerned, some teachers focused more on the control and administrative strategy aspects while others acknowledged these but focused more on the tool's learning benefits. In this example two contrasting cases are used to illustrate these differences.

14.3.1   Teacher A: SPARK as a tool for group management and efficiency

Teacher A had a reputation for good teaching, both within his discipline and across the university. He perceived learning benefits for students in doing groupwork, and had included teamwork related objectives in his subject. But his intentions in using SPARK focused mainly on its use as a tool for reducing student complaints about groupwork by controlling group free-riders and he described the system this way to his students. Students were given access to SPARK towards the end of their group task at the time when they needed to complete the self and peer ratings. The criteria for self and peer assessment were determined by the teacher but discussed with the students in class. In describing his initial interest he commented:

> I had always had an interest in groupwork and getting my students to really think as a team as well as individuals. However there always seemed to be a problem with free-riders, with certain individual students who didn't pull their weight and that caused aggro within the groups. So I thought this sounded an interesting project to look at that particular issue.
>
> I had a couple of intentions. One is, the particular area is a research assignment that they'd been doing individually ... as an individual student it can be quite time consuming to track down all the Australian materials and all the international materials. As groupwork that burden could be shared and so I felt I wanted to move to a group dynamic. ... But I was genuinely concerned with this free-rider problem and I found the software did work effectively and reduced the complaints, the whinges, the difficulties and I have to say as a by product it actually reduced the burden of marking for me and I feel, and I've been using a similar research project for 5 or 6 years, these were the best ones I'd ever seen. So I actually felt there was a slight raise in the quality of the end product.

Teacher A judged the success of SPARK primarily by positive student reactions and reductions in complaints with associated benefits for his workload, while acknowledging the improved research projects. His students also perceived it to be an effective tool for identifying free-riders, but about one-third of students also reported learning about teamwork through using it.

14.3.2 Teacher B: SPARK as a tool for improving students' engagement with group assessment

Teacher B had been interested in teaching and assessment for some time. Like Teacher A, he perceived benefits in groupwork and had relevant objectives in his subject. But unlike Teacher A, he focused on SPARK as a way of gaining greater student engagement in and ownership of the processes of assessment, particularly with respect to groupwork, as well as encouraging more equal participation. Assessment criteria were negotiated with students, who had access to the tool from the beginning of their project. He was aware of the efficiency and groupwork management aspects of SPARK, but they were not in the foreground of his perceptions of the system:

> My motivation for using SPARK, well let's take a middle stage, was actually to try and actually help students engage with project work because a lot of them were just switching off. They wouldn't engage with project work because they knew if they put more effort in they wouldn't get a result, a mark, for it. If they put less effort in they could get away with it. But that 'less or more' thing, that wasn't useful either. It was much more of a sense of how can I get students engaged in thinking about assessment as an important part of their learning experience. ... This project was learning about design history. There was a debate [online] where they would adopt a particular character or role as a team, and research that together and then have a debate with someone with an opposing view. ... So if they could see that that was something that was more interesting for them and that the assessment of that could also have more of their ownership then maybe they're going to engage more deeply.
>
> SPARK should be adopted across the whole university because it does solve a huge range of problems and it also gets the lecturers thinking about their design of the assessment process and that is the big plus, because they have to.

Teacher B judged the success of SPARK by students' ongoing engagement in the team assessment process, as well as by its success in resolving problems of unequal participation. His students perceived it to be a valuable tool for improving fairness and learning about teamwork. His perception that it forces lecturers to think about assessment design was certainly true for him but has not been true for all.

14.4 Implications from the three studies

Drawing together the findings from all three studies suggests that there are qualitative differences in how teachers experience the change towards using learning technologies. In studies 1 and 3, there were two main dimensions on which teachers' focuses differed:

- their intention in making the change – primarily as a strategy for improving aspects of teaching or on improving aspects of student learning with teaching in the background;

- the criteria for determining whether a change is successful or 'working' – teacher comfort or efficiency or student reaction, or students' engagement in learning or learning outcomes.

These dimensions were also present in study 2, but with the addition of another dimension related to the primary intentions of project developers:

- focusing on learning technologies primarily as an end in themselves – as resources or independent learning opportunities – or as a means to improve learning outcomes.

In all three of these dimensions, there is a distinction between more teacher-focused and more student-focused perspectives. Teachers who express more teacher-focused perspectives focus on learning technologies as tools in themselves or as strategies for improving their teaching comfort or efficiency or resources and their students' reactions. Teachers who express more student-focused views may also perceive these aspects of learning technologies but these aspects are in the background while their intentions for student learning are in the foreground. These differences in what teachers focus on when they change their teaching to use learning technologies may make the difference between expensive technological page-turners and innovative approaches which transform students' learning experiences.

In other aspects of the research reported in study 1, there was a relation between teachers' ways of describing change in teaching and their ways of experiencing teaching itself (McKenzie, 1999). Teachers who described change in teaching only in relation to content or strategies described more teacher-focused ways of experiencing teaching. Those who focused on relating teaching to learning or changing as a teacher described student-focused ways of experiencing teaching. Making connections between these findings and those of Trigwell, Prosser and Waterhouse (1999) and Prosser and Trigwell (1999), it seems reasonable to argue that differences in the focuses that teachers take when changing teaching with learning technologies are likely to relate to differences in their approaches to teaching and students' learning outcomes. Therefore it seems desirable to encourage and enable teachers to experience the adoption and use of learning technologies in more student-focused ways.

Research on variation and learning (Marton and Trigwell, 2000; Pong, 2000) suggests that in order for someone to change their way of experiencing something they need to become aware of variation in ways of experiencing and simultaneously and focally aware of the critical aspects of the new way of experiencing. In order to encourage all teachers to use learning technologies in ways which improve learning, we need to enable some to become aware of student-focused ways of using technologies and to discern how these differ from teacher-focused approaches. One way to do this may be to help teachers to experience differences between teacher-focused and student-focused ways of using the same learning technology tool, so that the tool aspect is held constant and teachers may become aware of the variation between teacher-focused and student-focused intentions.

14.5   References

Alexander, S. and McKenzie, J. with Geissinger, H. (1998) *An Evaluation of Information Technology Projects for University Learning. Canberra: Australian Government Publishing Service*

Bain, J.D. and McNaught, C. (1996) *Academics' educational conceptions and the design and impact of computer software in Higher Education*. Paper presented at the 3rd Interactive Multimedia Symposium, Perth WA, January 21–5.

Bain, J.D., McNaught, C., Mills, C. and Luekenhausen, G. (1998) *Understanding CFL practices in Higher Education in terms of academics' educational beliefs: enhancing Reeves' analysis.* Paper presented at the ASCILITE conference, Wollongong, December 14–16.

Freeman, M. and McKenzie, J. (2000) Self and peer assessment of student teamwork: designing, implementing and evaluating SPARK, a confidential, web based system. In *Flexible Learning for a Flexible Society*, Proceedings of ASET-HERDSA 2000 Conference. Toowoomba, Qld, 2–5 July. ASET and HERDSA. http://cleo.murdoch.edu.au/gen/aset/confs/aset-herdsa2000/procs/freeman.html

Goldfinch, J. (1994) Further developments in peer assessment of group projects, *Assessment and Evaluation in Higher Education* **19**(1): 29–35.

Housego, S. and Freeman, M. (2000) Case studies: integrating the use of web based learning systems into student learning, *Australian Journal of Educational Technology* **16** (3): 258–82.

Laurillard, D. (1993) *Rethinking University Teaching: A Framework for the Effective Use of Educational Technology.* London: Routledge.

Marton, F. and Booth, S. (1997) *Learning and Awareness.* Mahway, NJ: Lawrence Erlbaum Associates.

Marton, F., Hounsell, D. and Entwistle, N. (1997) *The Experience of Learning.* Edinburgh: Scottish Academic Press.

Marton, F. and Trigwell, K. (2000) Variatio est mater studiorum, *Higher Education Research and Development* **19**(3): 381–95.

Pong, W.Y. (2000) The space of variation. Paper presented at the Updating Phenomenography workshop. Hong Kong SAR China, 18–20 May.

Prosser, M. and Trigwell, K. (1999) *Understanding Teaching and Learning: The Experience in Higher Education.* Buckingham: Open University Press

Ramsden, P. (1992) *Learning to Teach in Higher Education.* London: Routledge.

Rogers, E. (1995) *Diffusion of Innovations* (4th edn). New York, NY: The Free Press.

15 Modelling aspects of institutional development: culture, infrastructure, expertise

Helen Beetham[a] and Grainne Conole[b]

a. Open University; b. University of Bristol, UK

15.1   Introduction

It is now widely recognised that the effective use of learning technologies (LTs) depends on a wide range of factors in the organisational environment. Once a concern of isolated enthusiasts, LTs now feature prominently in learning and teaching strategies, subject review documents and policy statements from the funding councils (e.g. HEFCE 00/44). Researchers have sought to describe the impact of LTs on institutional structures, processes and resources, both to further understanding of the overall trajectory of change and to provide institutions with tools for comparative and longitudinal monitoring. However, models that have been applied to date owe much to generic organisational development theory (Chandler, 1962; Leavitt and Bahrami, 1988). For example, tools for auditing institutional 'readiness for' LTs have been developed for use in the UK (e.g. BeCTA, 1998; TALENT, 1999) based on the work of the MIT90 group in the US, which defines readiness in terms of progress towards centralised budgets and administrative structures, top-down strategic decisions, clear divisions of labour and a focus on competitive advantage. There are a number of reasons why this approach may not translate well to UK HE, including its hybrid managerial culture (Hughes *et al.*, 1997) and the collaborative, project-based development that has characterised the sector's experience of LTs.

There is a more compelling reason to suspect models based on old concepts of the 'institution', however, and that is the revolutionary impact which LTs are having on the very nature of institutions, their core business and the way they relate to their staff and students – to the extent that the very 'idea of the university' is seen as under threat (Ford, 1996; Hanna, 1998). The impact of LTs on the academic institution can be traced in two apparently contradictory movements: the loss of control over the production and reproduction of knowledge, and the centralisation of information systems.

15.2   Knowledge dispersal and information integration

The convergence of telecommunications with digital computing applications has driven a massive expansion of digital networks, with an accelerating drop in the cost of bandwidth (Scott, 1998). As the cost of accessing information has fallen, so too have the costs of digitisation, electronic data storage and online publication. Higher education has played a determining role in the development of the global Internet and the accumulation of electronic resources, and remains the most significant owner, provider and user of electronic information (Brown and Duguid, 1998; JISC, 2000). Significantly, though, this status is now contested. The knowledge revolution, which began with university research communities, has undermined the university's privileged access to society's accumulated knowledge. The C&IT revolution has therefore contributed to a paradigm shift in the nature of knowledge, variously described as the *postmodern shift* (Newman and Johnson, 1999; Usher and Edwards, 1994), the shift from *mode 1* to *mode 2* knowledge (Gibbons, 1999) or more popularly the rise of the *knowledge society*. Universities have had to concern themselves more centrally with applied knowledge, for example by offering vocational degree courses, developing inter-disciplinary areas of study, and working in much closer alliance with the non-academic organisations which make use of their research efforts.

Now that the same networking opportunities are extending into learning and teaching activities, the physical structures and locations of academic life seem less and less central to the idea the university (Hanna, 1998). At the same time, the changing nature of work in the information economy increases both the demand and the opportunities for lifelong learning (DfEE, 1998a). As work patterns become more flexible and as work itself requires a wider range of knowledge-processing skills, universities are no longer providing apprenticeship to a knowledge elite but ongoing learning opportunities to an entire workforce in permanent information revolution. Theorists such as Landow have argued that the distributed nature of electronic information in itself 'challenges conventional assumptions about teachers, learners and the institutions they inhabit' (Landow, 1992).

The tendency for academic knowledge to become dispersed into multiple locations and networks undoubtedly presents a threat to the university of the nineteenth and twentieth centuries. At the same time, institutional systems have actually become more centralised and integrated as a result of the telecommunications revolution. Library systems, management information systems, student records, timetabling, computer and telephone networks, media services, email, shared electronic work spaces and of course managed learning environments are what define the modern academic institution, and they are increasingly subject to coordination from the centre (Agre, 1999). LTs themselves have developed from closed-box systems designed for access by individual students, or deployment by individual lecturers, to massive integrated architectures that demand wholesale re-ordering of institutional processes around their central services. The promise of these new learning environments is directed not at the student, nor even at the curriculum, but at the 'education infrastructure', the 'community', the 'mission' of the institution itself (see www.blackboard.com). Managed learning therefore serves to reinforce the ideal of a rational, bureaucratised and centralised academic institution.

15.3   Models of the learning/technology institution

What ideas are currently available for modelling institutional change in relation to the new LTs? Do they take adequate account of the two forces we have identified?

Hanna (1998) distinguishes seven organisational strategies for universities in the digital age. Of these, six offer some version of the 'virtual university' paradigm in which the learning and teaching activities of this university have dispersed entirely into the global Internet. 'Core' staff are no longer tenured academics with a strong research record – who become part of the flexibly employed periphery – but administrators and new professionals who facilitate the smooth running of the enterprise. The seventh model is of a traditional university extending its boundaries through the use of C&IT, with the nature of academic work less radically disrupted but a major redefinition of university business and strong central role for administrative services. Ford *et al.* (1996) offer perhaps the most crudely managerial model to date, analysing institutions in terms of the major 'business processes' undertaken. Student learning is one such process, taking subject-specific 'learning chunks' as its input, and providing (via a number of learning 'functions') 'motivated, qualified, employable students' as its output. The 'real' actors in this story are not learners, teachers and researchers but parcels of information.

Although business process models account well for the rational, centralising force of information technologies, they account poorly for the impact of decentralised knowledge on the life of academic institutions, and the attempts on the part of human players to reassert their identity. McNay's (1995) classification of institutions into (a) collegial, (b) bureaucratic, (c) corporation and (d) enterprise universities is perhaps more helpful. According to McNay, all institutions show elements of each of these models but the classic developmental trajectory is from (a) through to (d). We might therefore expect to find the Fordist university being superceded by a more enterprising, distributed institution with devolved leadership, flexible decision-making processes, and a focus on small project teams.

In fact neither Fordist nor enterprise universities are much in evidence in UK HE. In a 1999 survey, Henkel and Kogan (1999) found that universities have responded to pressures to adopt C&IT not through strong management or more flexible models of academic work but rather by reinforcing faculty structures and academic credibility. With the exception of some specialist distance learning organisations, UK HEIs have in the last couple of years moved away from ambitious plans for exploiting global markets and refocused on sustaining their existing markets in the UK (Kewell, Conole and Oliver, 1999), where student consumers seems to be putting their money on the face-to-face learning experience. There seems little doubt that the paradigmatic role of researcher-teacher is being challenged by new forms of knowledge-related practice (Hart, Ryan and Bagdon, 1999; Shneiderman *et al.*, 1998) but it is far from clear that these forms will fall naturally within the rational-cybernetic model of institutions preferred by Ford, or indeed within the corporate/enterprising model offered by McNay.

One reason to think this is that individuals with LT expertise, who are central to the project of technologising the institution's core activities, are not at all securely located within institutional structures and processes. LT specialists are often employed on short-term contracts and soft funding; they rarely have academic status; they work in units which are poorly defined and vulnerable to restructuring; and they usually sit tangentially to existing management structures. However, the distinction between 'real' academics and LT specialists are becoming blurred around practices such as LT secondments for academics, the evolution of LT units into research centres, and recognition of LT publications for the RAE. These are the boundary zones in which new meanings for academic work and the academic institution are being fought for. Modelling LT use in institutions, then, involves more than accounting for the business processes involved. It demands attention to the human, political, social and cultural forces at work (both within and acting on the institution), as well as to factors which can be accounted for within a rational, managerial framework.

McNaught and Kennedy (1998) identify three interrelated factors determining the effectiveness of institutional adoption of LTs: policy, culture and support. There are similarities here with Dearing's (NCIHE, 1997) intersecting areas of infrastructure, management and content. Both models are informed in their detail by the experience of LT innovators, and both suggest features of HE institutions that can usefully be evaluated and compared. Neither, however, takes the experience of learners or non-academic staff as central. Laurillard's (1998) *Conversational Framework for the Learning Organisation*, on the other hand, is derived explicitly from her conversational framework for understanding individual learning (Laurillard, 1993). This approach of understanding institutions from the perspective of student learning was an attractive one to the present authors and was taken as a model for the work reported here.

15.4 Modelling as shared practice

In this chapter, we outline three instances of institutional modelling which attempt to address some of the issues outlined above. All take account of the tensions that LTs impose on existing institutional structures and processes. These studies share a common set of underpinning premises, namely that the modelling process should:

- link theory, research and practice and provide an overt process of articulation among these three;

- be developmental, iterative and responsive to change: the tension between core and peripheral activities means that models need to be carefully contextualised;

- shared by stakeholders in the local environment: a co-constructive approach means involving change agents with both local expertise and an understanding of the modelling process.

The activity of modelling involves some degree of utopian thinking or, as Baker (2000) has it, 'abstraction from phenomena': as indicated, rather than beginning from an idealised management or information-processing system, we chose to begin with an idealised model of students learning with technology, and to ask what kind of institution would best support this learning scenario. Our choice of abstraction was not of course an innocent one but it was one which we hoped would appeal to the institutional change agents who were our stakeholders and collaborators in the studies (see Figure 15.1).

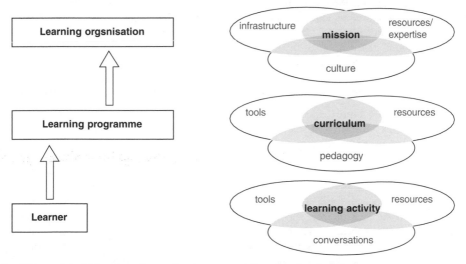

Fig. 15.1   Modelling learning technology use at three levels of analysis

Learning is assumed to involve purposeful *activity* that brings about some change (in knowledge, skill, awareness, personal identity etc) on the part of the learner. Learning activity is supported by *tools* (which may be generic, such as communication systems, or specific to the topic under study, such as instruments); *resources* (especially content resources relating to the topic understudy); and *conversations* (for example with a teacher, mentor or peer learner). These three aspects are represented as intersecting ellipses to show their intrinsic relationship, and the fact that each takes its meaning from the totality of the learning activity.

This same scenario can be viewed from the perspective of the learning programme, or perhaps the teacher when he/she is concerned not with an individual learner but with an entire cohort. From this perspective, the design and purpose of learning activities is largely given by the context of a *curriculum*. Learning *tools* and *resources* remain the same, but are brought into play according to the teacher or programme developer's perception of learners' needs in the context of the curriculum. Also from the teacher/developer's perspective, conversations with learners are understood from the perspective of a specific *pedagogy* (e.g. the aim may be scaffolding, instruction, encouragement, testing).

Taking the learning programme as the basic 'unit' of the learning and teaching process, the institution needs to employ staff to support each of the three aspects (tools, resources and pedagogy) and to deploy them in an integrated way to support student learning. The totality of learning activities and curricula are in some sense enabled by the institutional learning and teaching strategy or *mission*. The technical tools deployed in the course of realising that mission are enabled by the total institutional *infrastructure*, while *resources* are now seen in the wider sense of the entire knowledge resource of the institution including its human expertise. The various pedagogies and objectives that give purpose to learning interactions take place within the wider context of an institutional *culture*, including rules, roles and divisions of labour in the activities of learning and teaching. The 'roles' axis can then be extended to include institutional activities that do not have a direct bearing on learning programmes or learning interactions.

For each of the latter layers, matrices were drawn up which mapped the activities involved in using and embedding LTs against different academic roles within the institution at both programme and institutional level. These have been reported in more detail elsewhere (Beetham *et al.*, 2000). Having outlined a model for mapping LTs and roles across institutions, the next stage in the study was to analyse in more detail what types of LT activities were occurring and how these related to individual roles.

15.5   Case study I: The learning technologies scoping study

The first case study describes a model for understanding and auditing LT work in institutions. An audit tool was developed, comprising 58 separate activities involved in the development, embedding, use and support of LTs. This was complied from a number of sources including the EFFECTS learning outcomes; HERA categories of job function in UK HE and analysis of mission statements and job descriptions from LT-related units. The audit tool was administered to a total of 72 members of staff across 2 HEIs (one pre- and one post-1002). This gave a reasonable spread across subject locations and areas of work, including: technical support, library and learning resources, staff development, student (learning) skills support, specialist LT support, LT research and development, and educational research and development. Subjects indicated on a scale of 1 (not relevant) to 5 (central/crucial) how important each activity was in carrying out their current role. Using factor analysis, correlations were calculated between every possible pair of ratings and arranged in a matrix. The researcher then looked for 'clusters' or groups of ratings which correlated significantly with one another, and the activity clusters were taken to represent discrete roles in LT development, support or use.

A number of activities were scored at 4/5 (i.e. significant/crucial to their role) by over 50 per cent of the sample. These were taken to be 'core activities' for staff involved with LTs, and proved in the later factor analysis to form a robust cluster of their own. In descending order of frequency these are shown in Table 15.1.The factor analysis revealed 11 distinct roles, each with a characteristic range of activities. It should be noted, however, that

Activity	%
Actively seek to keep abreast of developments in LTs	70
Facilitate access to LT expertise and services	67
Liase & collaborate with other units in the university having related interests and objectives	61
Act as consultant, mentor or change agent for other staff	58
Advise and assist with introduction of new technology into learning & teaching programmes	58
Increase colleagues' awareness of best practice in LTs	58
Enable exchange of ideas and experience in technology-based learning and teaching	55
Facilitate & support access to computer-based learning resources	55
Consult with support staff on appropriate use of LTs	52
Identify needs and opportunities for development/deployment of LTs	52

Table 15.1   Activities scoring >3 for >50% of the sample

although these roles can be functionally separated, they do not correspond to actual divisions of labour among individuals. On average, respondents returned almost 20 (19.9) scores of either 4 or 5, indicating that just over a third (34.4 per cent) of all the activities were important or central to their role. These findings can be compared with the matrix of anticipated roles developed from the initial model in Figure 15.1 (see Table 15.2).

Expected role	Discovered role
Co-ordination/management - learning and teaching	Manager (projects)
Co-ordination/management - technical infrastructure	Manager (teams)
Co-ordination/management - learning resources	
Research/development – educational	Educational developer
	Educational researcher
Research/development - technical	Technical developer/ researcher
Research/development – resources	Resources/materials developer
Implementation	Academic innovator
Support – learning and teaching	Learning skills support
Support – resources	Learning resources support
Support – technical	Technical support
	Learning technologist – general

Table 15.2   A comparison of anticipated and discovered roles

From this it appears that the original model has some explanatory power in relation to LT roles in UK HE institutions. The most significant findings from this study, however, were the enormous range and variety of practices encompassed by the term 'LT work', even within a single institution; and the blurring of roles even across traditionally strong demarcations such as academic/support or technical/research staff.

15.6   Case Study II: Institutional audit

An institutional audit was carried out by key contacts at 25 UK HEIs over two months. The methodology for auditing was designed to ensure the involvement of stakeholders not only in the data collection process but also in interpreting and making sense of the overall findings. This relates back to the crucial importance of shared ownership and co-participation in modelling practice. As explained in the Notes for Auditors, our aim was

> to provide tools which are useful in raising the level of institutional debate about LT development, deployment and support, and about the staff who are involved in these processes... [to] be an intervention in the life of your institution as well as a data collection exercise.

The methodology and findings of the audit have been reported in detail elsewhere (Beetham *et al.*, 2000). Here we confine our discussion to the process of institutional modelling which gave rise to the audit tools, and feedback from auditors on their usefulness.

Candidate factors were selected from an existing matrix (TALENT, 1999); the outcomes of a national workshop for on embedding LTs strategically (EFFECTS, 2000); and a review of the literature on institutional embedding of LTs (Bates, 1997; Davis, 1997; Ford et al, 1996; Hart et al, 1999; Higher Education Quality Council, 1994; Lueddeke, 1998; McNaught, 2000; Taylor, 1998; Wright and O'Neil, 1995). These fitted well into the three broad areas of institutional focus identified in the model (culture, infrastructure and expertise). The consultation process with auditors was used to refine these factors and to arrive at a list of indicators which could be used to assess institutional status with respect to each factor. In the final audit tool, each indicator took the form of a positive statement about the institution, with which auditors indicated their agreement on a scale of one to five. The final version of the audit tool and findings of the audit are available at

http://sh.plym.ac.uk/eds/effects/jcalt-project/.

At post-audit focus groups, auditors were extremely positive about the impact of the audit process. A common response was that the audit had 'helped to clarify people's thinking', for example about the range of activities involved in effective use of LTs, or about the kinds of decision that need to be taken. Two auditors noted that the audit had helped the LTs unit become better integrated into, and more proactive within, the institution, while others found that it had helped bring people together in new ways, raise issues on relevant committees, or introduce new ideas for promoting change. The impact seemed to have been enhanced by the audit coming at the same time as the finalisation of learning and teaching strategies, which had led to an increased focus on institutional accountability.

On the other hand the actual data collection process had taken longer than anticipated and auditors expressed varying degrees of confidence in their results. The most confident had made use of existing institutional research such as the findings of staff surveys and believed their responses to be representative. Most of the rest believed that they had presented a reasonably accurate picture of their central service teams but that the situation in departments was 'complex and diverse'. Here it was 'impossible to do any kind of definitive survey' due to lack of information or indifference/hostility to 'anything which comes from the Centre'. Many auditors felt that the process revealed how little was known about LT related activities taking place in different parts of their institutions, and how poorly information was coordinated.

In addition to evaluating the key institutional indicators, auditors were asked to draw or describe the relationships among all the units, committees and institutional posts with responsibilities relating to LT use. On a separate matrix they were asked to indicate which person, committee, body or institutional process was responsible for decision-making in each of the key areas identified. The level of detail given by auditors was extremely variable, as were the precise management structures of their institutions, but this variability was difficult to interpret. No clear patterns emerged from the data such as would allow a classification of different institutional 'models' for strategic planning or coordination. Common features across many or all institutions are detailed in the full report, but include:

- the devolution of budgets to schools and faculties for learning-related issues;
- strategies determined centrally but interpreted locally;
- potential for conflict between central/priorities re: resource allocation;
- clearer responsibility for overall policy and strategy, than for planning, coordination and management of the same agendas;
- range of central services and committees with overlapping responsibilities for LTs;
- recent changes with the creation of new posts and committees to provide a single strategic vision for learning and teaching;
- new roles for academic staff in departments with remits for LTs;
- ongoing integration of technical networks and systems.

For a comparative analysis it was decided to consider features of managerial procedure and practice, as indicated in auditors' comments and descriptions, rather than models of institutional decision-making processes which were extremely difficult to classify. The five highest and five lowest scoring institutions according to the key indicators were compared, taking 'staff use of LTs' as the most representative overall measure – and noting that this measure was significantly correlated with scores on eight of the other measures. Auditors themselves identified these features as having a significant impact on their institution's ability to make effective use of LTs. Again, full details of the findings are given elsewhere, but it is important to note here that lower-scoring institutions did appear to have more collegial features (discipline based departments with considerable autonomy) while higher-scoring institutions had more enterprise features (McNay, 1995). This is clearly an issue which requires further investigation. Given the historical diversity of UK HEIs, however, it is quite possible that greater institutional use of LTs is associated with features of the 'enterprise university' without any direct causal relationship between the two.

15.7 Case study III: Toolkits for practitioners

The final case study describes a rather different modelling practice which address the needs of practitioners themselves at the middle/bottom layers of Figure 15.1.

LT has often been described as acting as a 'catalyst for change'. The very act of practitioners needing to consider the relevance and potential impact of LTs leads them to question their fundamental learning and teaching approach and philosophy. LTs have meant that practitioners need to gain new skills and competencies. One area where this has been particularly evident is the integration and evaluation of the impact of LTs. However, practitioners need guidance in carrying out these evaluations. The concepts of supportive frameworks and toolkits will be illustrated for these areas. The aspiration behind these frameworks and toolkits was that they should be easy to use and provide expert guidance. What has been particularly exciting about this work is that there is evidence that these kinds of structured 'models' do indeed support practitioners in their development of carrying structure expert plans, as well as provided a way of articulating practice. In a recent study we saw evidence that these toolkits allowed practitioners from different subject domains to develop a common shared understanding of their practice (Oliver, and Conole, 2002).

In essence frameworks and toolkits range from highly restrictive 'templates' or 'wizards' (which provide step-by-step guidance but little possibility of user-adaptation) through to 'theoretical frameworks' (which provide context and scope for the work but leave the user to devise their own strategy for implementation). Between these extremes lie a range of resources, including checklists, guidelines and step-by-step tutorials (Conole and Oliver, 2001).

Frameworks are open and flexible resources that scope out a defined area of underpinning research or provide guidelines according to a set of values or criteria. These help position, but not restrict the area of research. For example, a number of pedagogical frameworks have been developed to support LT. All develop from a particular theoretical viewpoint, aiming to encourage the application of good practice according to a particular pedagogical approach. Laurillard's conversational framework is adopted as a model for student-teacher interactions, allowing the framework to focus on educational interactions (Laurillard, 1993). Conole and Oliver (Conole and Oliver, 1998) have developed a framework for integrating LTs that builds on Laurillard's conversational framework. This provides a structured approach to integrating learning materials into courses: the user is led through the thought processes of re-engineering a course, beginning with an evaluation of the existing course. Different media types are then assessed, and in particular the different educational interactions they support is considered. A selection process then considers limiting factors, including resource issues and local constraints. The final part of the framework involves planning the new course.

Toolkits are decision-making systems based on expert models, positioned between wizards and conceptual frameworks (Oliver and Conole, 2000) in terms of support and restrictions. A toolkit is a model of a design or decision-making process, with tools provided at key points along the way. Each of these individual tools is designed to help the user access a knowledge base in order to make informed decisions. The format of toolkits means that they can be used in a standard, linear fashion, or can be 'dipped into' by users whose level of expertise is stronger in some areas of the design process than others.

The Evaluation Toolkit provides a structured resource to help practitioners to evaluate a range of learning resources and activities. (Conole, Crewe, Oliver and Harvey, 2001) It guides them through the scoping, planning, implementation, analysis and reporting of an evaluation. It assists the practitioner in designing progressively detailed evaluations over time, and allows users to access and share evaluation case studies. It consists of three sections: Planner, Advisor and Presenter, which guide the user through the evaluation process; from the initial scoping of the evaluation question(s) and associated stakeholders, through selection of data capture and analysis methods, and finally through the presentation of the findings.

Media Advisor is a toolkit which can be use to provide guidance on the appropriate integration of LTs into course redesign (Oliver and Conole, 2000). The Evaluation Toolkit guides the user through the evaluation process; from the initial scoping of the evaluation question(s) and associated stakeholders, through selection of data capture and analysis methods, and finally through the presentation of the findings (Conole, Crewe, Oliver, Harvey, 2001).

15.8   Conclusion

This chapter has compared traditional approaches to modelling institutions with a more flexible approach reported here. In particular the chapter has focused on the inadequacy of existing institutional models to account for new forms of organisational activity and academic work, which have arisen in part as a result of the impact of LTs. The examples given in the chapter demonstrate how different facets of this impact can be modelled effectively at institutional level. Typical findings from this co-constructive modelling approach include:

- the multi-competent nature of LT individuals;

- the lack of secure location, professional identity and academic status for their work;

- the role of LT practitioners as change agents, brokers and agents provocateurs, moving freely across organisational tribes;

- the blurring of boundaries between traditional 'academic' and 'learning support' roles;

- the crucial contribution made by LT specialists, as confirmed by institutional managers, but the relative difficulty of recruiting, developing, progressing and retaining these individuals;

- the lack of clear job specifications or career progression;

- the shigh degree of self-organisation by LT professionals across institutional boundaries, constituting a form of professional or research community with shared values (particularly in relation to student learning);

- the value across all levels of the institution of short-term, project-based work in collaborative, multi-role learning teams.

Academic institutions are at a turning point. LT work may become assimilated to more traditional forms of academic practice or may offer a model for a new kind of knowledge work in the post-enterprise, post-corporate university. There is clearly a role for models which can describe these changes, which are flexible in design and which can be used iteratively in conjunction with relevant expertise in the field. We believe that the models described in this chapter provide examples of this approach and its relevance to this field of work.

15.9   References

Agre P. (1999) Information technology in higher education: the 'global academic village' and intellectual standardization, *On the Horizon* **7**(5).

Baker, M.J. (2000) The roles of models in artificial intelligence and education research: a prospective view, *International Journal of Artificial Intelligence in Education* **11**.

Bates, A. (1997) Restructuring the University for Technological Change. Paper presented to the Carnegie Foundation for the Advancement of Teaching Symposium, *What Kind of University?*, London.

Beetham, H. *et al.* (2001) National Survey of Learning Technology Staff in UK HE, available online at: http://sh.plym.ac.uk/eds/effects/jcalt-project/

Brown, J.S. and Duguid, P. (2000) *The Social Life of Information*. Harvard Business School Press.

Chandler, A.D. (1962) *Strategy and Structure: Chapters in the History of the Industrial Enterprise*. MIT Press

Conole, G., Crewe, E., Oliver, M. and Harvey, J. (2001) A toolkit for supporting evaluation, *ALT-J* **9**(1): 38–49.

Conole, G. and Oliver, M. (1998) A pedagogical framework for embedding C&IT into the curriculum, *ALT-J* **6**(2): 4–16.

Conole, G. and Oliver, M. (2001) Embedding theory into practice, *International Conference on Advanced LTs*. Madison: IEEE Computer Society Press.

Davis, N. (1997) Strategies for staff and institutional development for IT in education: an integrated approach. In N. Davis (ed.), *Using Information Technology Effectively in Teaching And Learning: Studies in Pre-service and In-service Teacher Education*. London: Routledge, 255–68.

Department for Education and Employment (1998) *The Learning Age: A Renaissance for a New Britain*: http://www.lifelonglearning.co.uk/greenpaper/index.htm.

EFFECTS (2000) *End of Year Evaluation Report*; available from sh.plym.ac.uk/effects/publications/

Ford, P. *et al.* (1996) *Managing Change in Higher Education*. Milton Keynes: Open University Press.

Gibbons, M. (1999) Changing research practices. In Brennan *et al.* (eds), *What Kind of University?* Society for Research in Higher Education and Open University Press.

Hanna, D.E. (1998) Higher education in an era of digital competition: emerging organizational models, *JALN* **2**(20).

Hart, G., Ryan, Y. and Bagdon, K. (1999) Supporting organizational change: fostering a more flexible approach to course delivery, *The Association for Learning Technology Journal* **7**(1): 46–53.

Higher Education Quality Council (1994) *Choosing to Change*. London: HEQC.

Hughes, C., Blaxter, L. and Tight, M. (1998) Telling it how it is: accounts of academic life, *Higher Education Quarterly* **52**(3), July: 300–15.

Joint Information Systems Committee (2000) *Five Year Strategy: 2001–2006* (draft) http://www.jisc.ac.uk/curriss/general/#g1

Kewell, E., Oliver, M. and Conole, G. (1999) *Assessing the Organisational Capabilities of Embedding Learning Technologies into the Undergraduate Curriculum.* University of North London: ELT working papers #2.

Landow, G. (1992) *Hypertext: The Convergence of Contemporary Critical Theory and Technology.* Baltimore: John Hopkins University Press.

Laurillard, D. (1993) *Rethinking University Teaching – A Framework for the Effective Use of Educational Technology.* London: Routledge.

Leavitt, H. and Bahrami, H. (1988) *Managerial Psychology: Managing Behavior in Organizations.* Chicago: University of Chicago Press.

Lueddeke, G.R. (1998) The management of change towards an open learning framework: an higher education inquiry, *Open Learning* **13**(3): 3–17.

McNay, I. (1995). From the collegial academy to corporate enterprise: the changing culture of universities. In T. Schuller (ed.), *The Changing University?* Buckingham: The Society for Research into Higher Education & Open University Press.

McNaught, C. and Kennedy, P. (2000) Staff development at RMIT: bottom-up work serviced by top-down investment and policy, *The Association for Learning Technology Journal* **8**(1): 4–18.

National Committee of Inquiry into Higher Education (1997) *Higher Education in the Learning Society* ('the Dearing Report'), HMSO/NCIHE.

Newman, R. and Johnson, R. (1999) Sites for power and knowledge? towards a critique of the virtual university, *British Journal of Sociology of Education* **20**(1): 79–88.

Oliver, M. and Conole, G. (2000) Assessing and enhancing quality using toolkits, *Journal of Quality Assurance in Education* **8**(1):32–7.

Schneiderman, B. et al. (1998) Emergent patterns of teaching/learning in electronic classroom, *Educational Technology Research and Development* **46**(4): 23–42

Scott, P. (ed.) (1998) *The Globalisation of Higher Education.* SRHE/Open University Press.

Somekh, B., Whitty, G. and Coveney, R. (1997) IT and the politics of institutional change. In B. Somekh and N. Davis (eds), *Using Information Technology Effectively in Teaching and Learning.* London: Routledge, 187–209.

TALENT (1999) *The Book of TALENT:* http://www.le.ac.uk/TALENT/BoT/

Taylor, P.G. (1998) Institutional change in uncertain times: lone ranging is not enough, *Studies in Higher Education* **23**(3): 269–79.

Usher, R. and Edwards, R. (1994) *Postmodernism and Education.* London: Routledge.

Wright, Q. and O'Neil, C. (1995) Teaching improvement practices: successful strategies for HE. In Q. Wright et al. (eds), *Teaching Improvement Practices: International Perspectives.*Bolton: Anker Publishing.

16 Walking the electronic tightrope: questions surrounding infusion of IT into education subjects

Sandra Schuck

University of Technology Sydney, Australia

Keywords
computer-mediated learning; computers in education; ICT in education; infusion; teacher
    education

16.1   Overview:

This chapter outlines the questions that are faced by educators concerned with infusing Information and Communication Technologies (ICT) into their subjects. While many claims have been made about the value of computer-mediated education in developing new and powerful ways of learning, many of these claims need to be balanced against issues concerning access, individual learning styles, cost benefits and technical aspects of computer mediated learning.

In this chapter I will note some of the claims that are made about computer-mediated learning, suggest some questions critiquing these claims and then consider some of the ways in which these claims can be understood and achieved.

16.2   Introduction

Over the past decade the benefits of computer-mediated learning have appeared to be hovering just round the corner. Politicians, educators and higher education administrators seem confident that the promise and potential of the new technologies will be realised once computer usage is widespread. Consequently, academics in universities have been strongly encouraged to embrace the new technologies and infuse them into their subjects. However, a number of issues appear to be somewhat neglected in these discussions and some of these issues form the basis of this chapter.

The issues I discuss here are just a few of the issues impacting on staff in higher education institutions, with respect to computer technologies. They regard the claims and hyperbole surrounding the use of Information and Communication Technologies (ICT) in education. While many claims have been made about the value of computer-mediated education in developing new and powerful ways of learning, often these claims are untested. Windschitl (1998) suggests that the major part of the literature on computers, the Internet and learning, discusses activities and practices using these technologies but does not consider questions such as 'Are these practices helping students?' or 'Is the introduction of this technology changing pedagogy?' (Windschitl, 1998, p. 28). Further, many of the claims about ICT need to be balanced against issues concerning access, individual learning styles, cost benefits and technical aspects of computer-mediated learning.

Another area which gives possible cause for concern is the issue of who is driving technological developments. As universities and other higher education institutions find that funds for education are shrinking, administrators often turn to computer technologies in the hope that embracing these will save money. Further, universities are seeking to make themselves global institutions and attract students from distant countries. They wish to have smaller numbers of academic staff providing services for larger numbers of students. Online learning courses appear to be the obvious answer (Ryan, Scott, Freeman and Paxtel, 2000). The impact of such courses on learning, learners and teachers is likely to be great, with far-reaching effects. But are these effects all positive? Some developments have already occurred such as non-traditional institutions packaging courses in ways that enable the offering of courses at very cheap rates. Non-traditional institutions do not have the infrastructure of universities to subsidise and have commercial goals rather than social ones (NextEd, 2000). As a result, the nature of education is being challenged by newcomers to the educational market.

Carroll (2000) provides an analogy of the change from sailship to steamship to illustrate his suggestion that we need to reconceptualise learning and teaching in a technological age. Using this analogy he shows how minor modifications cannot tap the potential of the new technologies and he suggests we consider learning through a community of learners, in which the teacher is viewed as an expert learner (not the 'guide on the side', nor the 'sage on the stage' as in other learning theories) and the students are seen as interacting with the expert learner and each other and the community in a collaborative way. However, notions of communities of practice are not new (Lave and Wenger, 1991) nor are they restricted to electronic contexts.

So it seems that currently, education is being viewed as ripe for a major reconceptualisation, brought about by technological advances. But what is actually happening in practice? Are these visions of education as being revolutionised by technology actually realistic? Is the learning of all students being enhanced by the new technologies? Are certain people being left out of these visions? If so, who? And how are educators approaching these huge changes which seem to be required in their practice, beliefs and daily work?

In what follows, I shall consider a number of claims that have been made about computer-mediated learning, raise questions about those claims and propose some possible resolutions to the questions.

16.3 Questioning the claims

In the following discussion, I will identify some of the aspects of teaching and learning with, and through, ICT that are highlighted in the relevant literature. I will raise some of the questions that exist with respect to these areas.

Each of the following issues is based on a claim, or claims, made in the literature on ICT. Each of these issues will be discussed in detail following a listing of the claims and questions:

1. *Claim*: Computer mediated learning is underpinned by theories of social constructivism (Bonk and Wisher, 2000; Koschman, 1996).
   Question: Many teachers offering learning experiences using ICT merely repackage their existing learning offerings so that they are available in electronic form (Alexander and McKenzie, 1999). How do teachers who do not believe in the principles of social constructivism provide an online learning environment that is underpinned by such theories?

2. *Claim*: Using the new technologies will solve many of the problems arising in preparing teachers in teacher education programs (Blanton, Moorman and Trathen, 1998).
   Question: Most prospective primary school teachers have chosen this career because it offers opportunities for nurturing and care, in face to face situations, away from technologies (Foley and Schuck, 1998). How will increased use of new technologies satisfy their requirements as students?

3. *Claim*: Computer-mediated learning increases access to learning for non-traditional student groups (Burbules and Callister, 2000).
   Question: Lower socio-economic groups, rural groups and many minority groups do not have access to computers or feel confident in their use – how then does computer mediated learning increase access for these groups?

4. *Claim*: Efficiency and productivity in teaching and learning will increase if computers are used more in education (Cuban, 1993).
   Question: Teachers are spending more time and energy developing and coordinating computer mediated learning experiences than they did for traditional classes (Marchionini, 1995). How then does efficiency and productivity increase?

5. *Claim*: New ways of learning and teaching arise from the use of computers in education (Cuban, 1993).
   Question: Most students' main educational experiences have been of a passive nature, as recipients of knowledge (Akerlind and Trevitt, 1999). How do we prepare such students for new ways of learning?

Critical consideration of these claims and the accompanying questions is an essential step to ensure that the hyperbole surrounding computer use in education does not sweep educators into unthinking and uncritical practices. Rather we should be carefully analysing the use of computers in education to ensure such use is appropriate, valuable and adds to the educational quality of what we do.

16.3.1   The theoretical underpinnings of computer-mediated learning

The literature abounds with papers informing us that computer-mediated learning (CML) is underpinned by theories of social constructivism (Bonk and Wisher, 2000; Koschman, 1996). Ryan *et al.* (2000) suggest that computer-mediated learning moves away from the didactic model of teaching in which an expert delivers information to students who passively receive it. These authors offer a view of CML as having an emphasis on the learner and the role he or she plays in investigating, constructing understanding and mastering skills. CML is seen as being constructivist in nature (Ryan *et al.*, 2000, p. 33). These findings are supported by many other authors (for example, Hill and Smith, 1998; Means, 1994; Saye, 1997). Barker (1999) advocates the use of intranets as offering the potential to enhance the quality of students' experiences.

However, many teachers offering learning experiences using ICT merely repackage their existing learning offerings so that they are available in electronic form (Alexander and McKenzie, 1999). Collis (1996) believes that the teacher is a key figure in determining the nature of computer-mediated learning. She suggests that good teachers will achieve good results with CML and weak teachers will not. Means (1994) emphasises that teachers' views about learning are critical factors in curriculum reform and adoption of technologies that support reform.

The above research gives rise to a critical question: How do teachers who do not believe in the principles of social constructivism provide an online learning environment that is underpinned by such theories? Research by Becker and Riel (2000) considered the notion of 'professionally engaged teachers', whom they defined as those teachers who were involved in professional development of others. They found that

> the more extensively involved teachers were in professional activities, the more likely they were to (1) have teaching philosophies compatible with constructivist learning theory, (2) teach in ways consistent with a constructivist philosophy, and (3) use computers more and in exemplary ways. (Becker and Riel, 2000, p. 1)

They go on to suggest that if teachers who are professionally engaged are given access to computers they will not only use them in exemplary ways, but also help others to use them in similar ways. However, the research leads to the question of how to promote effective teaching with ICT for those teachers who do not engage professionally with their colleagues?

Collis (1996) suggests that to help teachers to integrate technologies into their teaching in appropriate ways, those who offer support should start with the teacher's classroom problems rather than with the technology. She advocates that the person offering support should work initially with the teacher to consider how to enhance the students' learning, and only then consider how the technology can further this process.

Research by Hayes, Schuck, Segal, Dwyer and McEwen (2001) supports Becker and Riel and makes recommendations that teachers are supported in their use of ICT by school-based colleagues who are enthusiasts and key players. They too suggest that good practice using ICT is intricately interwoven with teaching approaches, curriculum and teaching philosophies and that effective computer-based learning develops out of reform of the other factors mentioned here.

The discussion in this section suggests that it is inappropriate to assume that because teachers are using computers in their teaching that this computer usage is underpinned by constructivist thinking. Teachers who hold constructivist theories about learning will be likely to use computers according to these theories and teachers who hold other theories will use computers differently. However, with support and professional development which considers teaching and learning ideas rather than usage of computers, it appears possible to help teachers to use computers in ways that enhance the learning process.

16.3.2   Supporting teachers in teacher education programmes

Governments and researchers in the area of ICT suggest that the use of new technologies will solve many of the problems arising in preparing teachers in teacher education programmes (Blanton, Moorman and Trathen, 1998). For example, Blanton *et al.* suggest that these tools address the practice–theory divide by providing opportunities for prospective teachers to integrate knowledge about practical classroom teaching with theoretical knowledge acquired in university courses. Other studies (Oliver, 1994) show that prospective teachers who have been taught about ICT in ways that integrated ICT with their coursework subjects were more likely to teach in this way, than those who studied ICT in specific ICT subjects. The bulk of literature in this area appears to support infusion of technology into teacher education subjects. Furthermore, a study by Bennett, Hamill, Naylor and Pickford (1997) showed that when prospective teachers had the chance to work with children and computers, their concerns moved from computer hardware and software to the pedagogical issues that were arising from the technology use.

However, it appears that many prospective primary school teachers have chosen a teaching career because it offers opportunities for nurturing and care, in face-to-face situations, away from computer technologies (Foley and Schuck, 1998). How will increased use of new technologies satisfy their requirements as students? Further, the research heralding the integration of ICT into the usual classwork in teacher education programs is not conclusive. Other studies (Robertson, 1997; Sherry, 2000) do not show that computer skill acquisition is necessarily enhanced by integration, nor do students show awareness of how to integrate ICT into their teaching on practicum placements. Finally, many teacher educators are themselves uncomfortable with the use of ICT in their subjects, either because they do not see any value in using ICT with their students, or because they, themselves, lack skills in the area (Cuban, 1998). These studies raise questions about the ways in which prospective teachers are able to be supported by computer technologies.

Suggestions from change management literature (Scott, 1999) indicate that it is necessary to make the change fit the circumstances. Teacher educators who are supported in their development of appropriate uses of computer technologies, are more likely to use these in a sustained way (Collis and Carleer, 1992). Further, using methods of using new technologies which fit with teacher educators' personal theories of teaching and which show clear advantages pedagogically will encourage exploration of this usage (Collis, 1996). So a way forward in encouraging authentic use of computers by teachers and prospective teachers is to make a case for how this usage can improve their teaching. Computer technologies should not be used on occasions when face-to-face methods work equally well. It should be seen as a tool for allowing different kinds of teaching and learning to occur, rather than as a replacement for an activity which was effective without the new technology. And as well as examining this potential for enhanced teaching and learning, ongoing support for individual teachers to develop their skills is necessary.

16.3.3   Access to learning through computer-mediated tools

Through the characteristics of online and other computer technologies, it appears that learning in isolated places, or at unusual times, or from the comfort and convenience of your own home can now be offered without any difficulties. Computers afford learning in distant mode by providing possibilities for interaction through computer-mediated communication tools, increased access to information sources through the Internet and by facilitating access on a 24 hour a day, seven days a week basis. These affordances suggest that computers encourage access by non-traditional student groups (Burbules and Callister, 2000).

However, many studies show that the notion of a 'digital divide' is one with ever expanding dimensions. Originally, the digital divide was used to describe the chasm between two groups of people: Those who had access to computers, the Internet and software and those who did not. People who lack access to these tools are seen as being increasingly at a disadvantage. Discussion of this fact in the United States has led to a major goal by educators and policy developers there to reduce this digital divide as much as is possible (NTIA, 2000). However, studies show that in practice, state educational technology plans tend to privilege the innovative over social practices and discourses (Zhao and Conway, 2001). Further, Zhao and Conway suggest that in terms of educational goals, economic progress and productivity are valued over democratic equality in state policies regarding technology. The report *Falling through the Net* (NTIA, 2000) finds that Americans are becoming increasingly connected to the Internet, and gaining greater access to computers in all demographic groups and geographic locations. However, it also found that the digital divide is not only persisting but increasing. For example, in households with incomes above $75,000, computers are 20 times more likely to be available than for those at the lowest income levels and Whites are more likely to have access to the Internet from home than Blacks or Hispanics from any location. These facts are not surprising, given that socio-economic status has always been an indicator of educational opportunity.

Another kind of digital divide is also occurring which is not quite as obvious. For those people who do have access to the Internet, but are not represented by the content on the Internet, the impact can be on their ways of learning, entertaining themselves, getting jobs and other essential aspects of conducting a fruitful existence. The lack of culturally appropriate and relevant online content for lower-income people results in a loss of opportunity for these people regardless of whether they have access to the technology or not (Lazarus and Mora, 2000).

It is clear therefore, that to address the access and equity issue inherent in computer technologies, we must consider two different issues: one is the access to the computers and connections to the Internet. The other is the development of suitable and accessible content for those who are traditionally underserved. In Australia a project is underway called Vtown (www.vtown.com.au) which provides suitable material for a virtual community of people who have a desire to improve their education and who are traditionally among the underserved communities of this country. The project described by Lazarus and Mora (2000) is another such example.

16.3.4   Efficiency and productivity

Cuban (1993) suggested that use of computers should increase efficiency and productivity in both teaching and learning. This statement begs the question of what sort of use would lead to this efficiency and what sort of teaching and learning would occur. While the statement is probably true for some computer technologies, it is not possible to generalise about this usage and say that all such use would increase efficiency and productivity. Where such efficiency has occurred, it has often been accompanied by a loss in quality of the educational experience (Ryan *et al.*, 2000).

Most educators today see the value of computer technology as lying in the opportunities offered by the Internet. These opportunities are for greater information access and for greater possibilities in communication (Windschitl, 1998). If we consider these uses, it quickly becomes apparent that there are no gains in efficiency and productivity. Searching the huge expanse of information available on the Internet and using it critically will not take less time than other methods of finding information. Similarly, if we consider the use of computer-mediated tools, then it becomes quite apparent that the time needed for the teacher to coordinate, facilitate and moderate interactions is longer than the time needed to monitor similar interactions in a face-to-face environment. Teachers are spending more time and energy developing and coordinating computer-mediated learning experiences than they did for traditional classes (Marchionini, 1995).

Similarly, students have commented on the fact that it takes them longer to frame questions and responses on a computer mediated-discussion board than in a classroom. This phenomenon is due to the fact that committing oneself in writing is seen as much more permanent and knowing that your colleagues are reading your response leads to more thoughtful responses (Foley and Schuck, 1998). I would suggest that the increased reflection by students on their contributions to discussions is the benefit of the technology rather than the increased efficiency suggested by Cuban.

So perhaps the claim should not be for cost-effectiveness and efficiency but for more thoughtful learning experiences. The drive to be more cost-effective may disguise the benefits that arise from taking more time to be reflective.

16.3.5   New ways of learning and teaching

The suggestion that new ways of learning and teaching arise from the use of the new technologies is a pervasive one (Cuban, 1993; Pea, 1998). It is suggested that the 'what' of learning is changed as we have access to simulations, tools and techniques for understanding content differently. However, Pea (1998) goes further in this discussion and adds that the technology will not be the panacea on its own. All such tools are mediated by human goals, beliefs and activities. This point is supported by earlier discussion which highlighted the importance of the teacher as a key player in the way that technology is used. Once again, the point arises that without teachers in education institutions being committed to reform of general learning and teaching practices, and of curriculum, little change will occur in the actual teaching regardless of the tools or technologies being used. Teachers who use the tools to teach content that was formerly taught without computer technology will not be developing new ways of teaching and learning. Similarly, teachers who reflect constantly on their teaching and on how to enhance the learning of their students, will consider new content for their students and use that content which will achieve their aims.

From another perspective, students often come into higher education institutions with life experiences of being passive learners who have information fed to them (Akerlind and Trevitt, 1999). Therefore it becomes essential for teachers in higher education institutions to be able to challenge these views of learning and offer alternative models. However, it is also necessary to acknowledge that learners have different learning styles and that there are a diversity of teaching and learning experiences which are valuable and achieve the desired learning outcomes.

The most important question therefore, in working with new technologies, is not whether they allow new types of learning and teaching to occur, but whether they enhance the learning opportunities, experiences and outcomes of the students.

16.4   Conclusion

In this chapter I have raised a number of issues, considered the claims about what information and communication technologies can bring to the learning situation, and balanced those claims with research offering alternative perspectives. I argue that to ensure a more effective and appropriate use of ICT in learning and teaching, it is important to consider a variety of perspectives on them. I suggest that many of the claims for enhanced teaching experiences with new technologies should rather be claims about the effectiveness of teachers with different philosophies of learning and teaching. Computer technologies that support teachers who are implementing effective learning experiences will be effective themselves. Computer technologies which support less effective ways of teaching will be less effective.

I have made a case in this chapter for more considered use of computers and computer technologies. A more critical analysis of the use of ICT should lead to a closer approximation to many of the claims, that, at this point, remain largely unproven.

16.5   References

Akerlind, G. and Trevitt, A.C. (1999) Enhancing self-directed learning through educational technology: when students resist the change, *Innovations in Education and Training International* **36**(2): 96–105.

Alexander, S. and McKenzie, J. (1998) *An evaluation of Information Technology Projects for University Learning*. Canberra: Committee for University Teaching and Staff Development.

Barker, P. (1999) Using intranets to support teaching and learning, *Innovations in Education and Training International* **36**(1): 3–10.

Becker, H. and Riel, M. (2000) *Teacher Professional Engagement and Constructivist-Compatible Computer Use*. US: Center for Research on Information Technology and Organizations, University of California, Irvine and University of Minnesota.

Blanton, W.E., Moorman, G. and Trathen, W. (1998) Telecommunications and teacher education: a social constructivist review. In P.D. Pearson and A. Iran-Nejad (eds), *Review of Research in Education*, 235–75. Washington, DC: AERA.

Bonk, C.J. and Wisher, R.A. (2000) *Applying Collaborative and E-learning Tools to Military Distance Learning: A Research Framework*. (Technical Report #1107). Alexandria, VA: US Army Research Institute for the Behavioral and Social Sciences.

Burbules, N. and Callister, T. (2000) Universities in transition: the promise and the challenge of new technologies, *Teachers College Record* **102**(2): 271–93. http://www.tcrecord.org, ID Number: 10362.

Carroll, T.G. (2000) If we didn't have the schools we have today, would we create the schools we have today?, *Contemporary Issues in Technology and Teacher Education* (online serial), **1**(1): http://www.citejournal.org/vol1/iss1/currentissues/general/article1.htm

Collis, B.A. (1996) Computers in education. In *International Encyclopedia of Educational Technology* (2nd edn). Oxford: Elsevier Science Ltd.

Cuban, L. (1993) Computers meet classroom: classroom wins, *Teachers College Record* **95**(2): 185–210.

Cuban, L. (1998) High-tech schools and low-tech teaching: a commentary, *Journal of Computers in Teacher Education* **14**(2): 6–7.

Foley, G. and Schuck, S. (1998) Exploring the potential of a web-based conferencing tool in mathematics education, *Australian Journal of Educational Technology* **14**(2): 122–40.

Hayes, D., Schuck, S., Segal, G., Dwyer, J. and McEwen, C. (2001) *Net Gain? The Integration of Computer-based Learning in Six NSW Government Schools, 2000*. Report to the NSW Department of Education and Training. Sydney: UTS.

Hill, A. and Smith, H. (1998) Practice meets theory in technology education: a case of authentic learning in the high school setting, *Journal of Technology Education* **9**(2): 29–47.

Koschman, T. (1996) *Computer Supported Collaborative Learning: Theory and Practice of an Emerging Paradigm*. New Jersey: Lawrence Erlbaum.

Lave, J. and Wenger, E. (1991) *Situated Learning: Legitimate Peripheral Participation*. US: Cambridge University Press.

Lazarus, W. and Mora, F. (2000) *Online Content for Low Income and Underserved Americans: The Digital Divide's New Frontier*. CA: The Children's Partnership.

Marchionini, G. (1995) The costs of educational technology: a framework for assessing change. In H. Maurer (ed.), *Proceedings of Ed-Media 95*, World Conference of Educational Multimedia and Hypermedia, Graz, Austria, June.

Means, B. (ed.) (1994) *Technology and Education Reform: The Reality behind the Promise*. San Francisco: Jossey-Bass Inc.

NextEd (2001) Presentation UTS, Australia. Presentation to the eLearning Forum, UTS, Sydney, June.

National Telecommunications and Information Administration (NTIA) (2000) *Falling through the Net: Towards Digital Inclusion*. Washington: Department of Commerce.

Oliver, R. (1994) Information technology courses in teacher education: the need for integration, *Journal of Information Technology for Teacher Education* 3(2): 135, June 46.

Pea, R. (February 1998) *The Pros and Cons of Technology in the Classroom*. http://www.tappedin.org/info/teachers/debate (accessed 8/08/01).

Robertson, J. (1997) Does permeation work? promoting the use of information technology in teacher education, *Journal of Information Technology for Teacher Education* 6(2): 169–84.

Ryan, S., Scott, B., Freeman, H. and Patel, D. (2000) *The Virtual University: The Internet and Resource-Based Learning*. London: Kogan Page.

Saye, J. (1997) Technology and educational empowerment: students' perspectives, *ETR&D* 45(2): 5–25.

Scott, G. (1999) *Change Matters*. Sydney: Allen & Unwin.

Sherry, A.C. (2000) Expanding the view of preservice teachers – computer-literacy: implications from written and verbal data and metaphors as freehand drawings, *Journal of Technology and Teacher Education* 8(3): 187.

Windschitl, M. (1998) The WWW and classroom research: what path should we take?, *Educational Researcher* 27(1): 28–33.

Zhao, Y. and Conway, P. (2001) What's in, what's out – an analysis of state educational technology plans, *Teachers College Record*, http://www.tcrecord.org (ID Number: 10717, accessed: 6/08/01).

17 Researching and evaluating online learning

Glynis Cousin and Frances Deepwell

Centre for Higher Education Development, Coventry University, UK

17.1 Introduction

This chapter explores some of the methodological issues in the evaluation research of online learning. In support of this exploration, we offer an evaluative framework and some illustrative material based on our interim evaluation of online learning at Coventry University. We anticipate that our statement of the problem configuration as we have analysed it locally will be sufficiently replicated or matched elsewhere for generalisations to be drawn.

Evaluation theory has produced a bewildering number of models, often premised on different underpinning assumptions, methodological preferences or rhetorical styles (Scriven, 1981). In making our choice, we needed a model which could address three particular imperatives. First, we needed an evaluation study that could meet the information needs of a variety of audiences. At Coventry we have identified seven primary audiences with different information needs (see under Research Activity: http://www.coventry.ac.uk/ched). Secondly, we wanted to address what is often perceived to be the conflicting purposes of evaluation to satisfy an external audience on the one hand and to aid internal development on the other hand. Thirdly, we needed an evaluative framework that could handle institutional and local levels of data collection and analysis and the multiple sources and differential status of the data. As we elaborate below, the complexities implied by an engagement with these factors suggested to us the deployment of a hybrid model that drew on 'Stake's Countenance Model' and that of 'action-evaluation'. It also suggested that the evaluation be developed and presented online.

The Coventry online learning initiative has a number of features conducive to a sound evaluation. First, ready data was provided through the electronic learning environment offered for all of the modules in the University (WebCT). This enabled us to keep statistics of student use and to provide hard copy of bulletin board traffic and other postings or interactions. Numerical data was available in some detail and in a form permitting comparability between modules and courses although, as we discuss later, the statistical data on student use of online learning often needs to be carefully triangulated with qualitative data.

Secondly, Coventry University had, coterminous with the online initiative and functionally related to it, set up a Task Force in Teaching and Learning, made up of seconded university teachers with academic support from CHED (Beaty and Cousin, 2002). Task Force members were commissioned to progress individual projects within an overall scheme for developing learning and teaching and many did so in relation to online learning, using an action-research framework. This resulted in a number of developmental reports, many with a research or evaluation facet, but not under the control of an overall evaluation model.

Thirdly, since the Coventry online initiative represents a major investment by the university, there is a legitimate management interest in cost-benefit analysis capable of demonstrating describable enhanced learning at a calculated cost that has to be taken into account. Yet the comparative experimental model that appears most conducive to this demonstration was not operable, not least as the university allows tutors to implement WebCT to an extent individually determined, generating both minimalist and thoroughgoing versions of online learning. Although every module has a WebCT site, colleagues are not compelled to develop it. There is consequently no exact 'treatment', frozen or otherwise. In any event, in our view, flexible evolving innovations are not best seen as experimental 'treatments' but rather as organic and creative adaptive enterprises likely to be manoeuvring their way through myriad teething troubles capable of capture within a formative evaluation framework. Perhaps a defensible evaluation would have as its equivalent metaphor military intelligence rather than summative war history.

17.2   The Coventry choice: countenance evaluation with action evaluation

The evaluation model chosen initially to accommodate the kind of issues we have noted above was that of Stake's (1967) 'countenance model', a model originally applied to curriculum research. What we liked about this model was its ability to capture and compare intended and observed outcomes at varying layers of operation against the evidence of what is happening. First, the requirement of this model to present factual information in the light of declared intended outcomes satisfies audiences wanting to know what has been achieved across time. Secondly, either the congruence between what is intended and what is observed or the unintended outcomes logged provides the focus for formative evaluation (for a fuller account of Stake's model see the website noted above).

As we centred the reflective process on the results generated from the structure provided by Stake, we began to graft on to it a process of 'action-evaluation'. Action evaluation is a model of evaluation which is used in the area of conflict resolution and, as such, it is designed to handle differences of view and different levels of resistance. Like action-research, it is also committed to the view that contributors to the research are co-researchers rather than informants. In these respects, a weak element in Stake's model for our purposes concerned the 'outsider' posture it assumes for the evaluation research. We needed something that strengthened the participation of insider views and thus the reflexivity of the evaluation research. By incorporating into Stake's model principles of 'action-evaluation', we could give greater prominence to the formative function of the evaluation and to the many voices that needed to inform it.

A further distinctive feature of our evaluation is our use of the online medium for its dissemination. Because we have data of different kinds (e.g. qualitative and quantitative, descriptive and judgement, macro and micro levels) different audience needs and contributing researchers operating at different levels of analysis, we have deployed the versatility of the internet to structure our evaluation, using the hypertext facility to cross-reference and layer our data and analysis (see under Research Activity at http://www.coventry.ac.uk/ched). In this way the evaluation research output comprises an ongoing construction of a series of nested outputs which both stand alone and form part of our meta-analysis.

Having outlined the model of evaluation we have generated, we now turn to some of the methodological issues that have emerged in our handling of both the qualitative and quantitative data that sits within this model.

17.3   Qualitative evaluation and ethnographic case studies

In recent years there has been a proliferation of largely local research that attempts to explore the impact of online learning from within a qualitative framework. Much of this research has collected qualitative data to set alongside and assist in the interpretation of the readily available raw data from the cyber traffic generated by students and lecturers interacting (or not) on specific courses or modules. The views of what is eligible for collection as useful evaluation data have varied considerably in focus and scale. A number of cyber ethnographies have treated cyberspace as a field meant anthropologically. Much attention has been paid to the distinctiveness of cyber talk and virtual relations particularly in relation to their capacity to constitute virtual communities (Ho, 1997).

There are some conceptual difficulties in seeking to transfer the methods of ethnography to those of cyberspace in the absence of agreement as to the substance of virtual communities. Fieldwork in anthropological research is usually in a place where people are situated, typically a 'real' community (workplace, living area, kinship network etc.) with shared and negotiated mores. Eavesdropping on a cyber community while having no knowledge of contextual considerations involves a segmentation of the lives of its participants. The watcher will also be deprived of the many subtle and physical clues the ethnographer has at his/her disposal when in the real field. Silences, gestures, resistance, hostility etc. are much harder to capture in the analysis of online data. For the pedagogic researcher hoping to discover signs of a community of practice on the net these are pressing issues, suggesting that attempts to build up a 'thick description' of what is happening in virtual environments require that data is collected from more than one source. We do not think that enough can be read from the virtual field. In one study at Coventry, Turner (2000) combined a qualitative and quantitative analysis of contributions to the discussion forum with student reflections on the use of this facility. In the 'field' that was the discussion forum, Turner found contributions like the following:

> Shut it, chin boy, geography is a subject made up hundreds of sciences and specialist areas, but then you wouldn't know this as you cant seem to be able to see the wood for the trees. Geography rules and has done for many years before and will do for many years afterwards. However as I am actually doing a science and engineering based degree, I can understand why you are feeling a little bitter towards my gooood [sic] self ... go chew a few trees and come back later when you've calmed down..

> My dear D, being a Middlesborough supporter yourself means that you naturally know nothing about football

The mix of social and educational references in the first example and the banter of the second are common features of many discussion forums; the cyber ethnographer may be tempted to confine their analysis to contributions such as these because they offer interesting evidence of an emergent virtual student subculture. But in cross-referencing this evidence with students' evaluation of the discussion facility, we get a more problematic picture.

In generating students' evaluative comments, Turner concluded that some were deterred from using the discussion forum because contributions like the above were seen to be offensive or irrelevant, as one student put it:

> People have put some good ideas on the forum but instead of adding to them a few idiots would rather slag each other off. Speaking your mind is one thing but if it carries on being personal the forum might as well go.

In his research journal, Turner wrote:

> The feedback indicates that abusive or critical postings prevent some students from making postings. In a classroom situation I endeavour to create a 'safe' environment where students feel able to contribute; clearly such an environment was not being created here.

This observation suggests that we should avoid the temptation to celebrate the informality of bulletin board chat as an inclusive subversion of formal academic authority. In assessing the significance of 'irrelevant' traffic against the more educationally purposeful ones, Turner counted the number of overall contributions from students and provided a break-down of their functionality:

> Of around 370 postings, 19 different issues were discussed together with general postings. The organisation of group work has generated the most postings.

By coming at his analysis with three kinds of evidence, Turner was able to show that the generation of a learning community required more safety in the virtual environment. He also discovered that the discussion facility was used more for process issues than for substantive discussion. Finally, he learnt that a balance needs to be struck between allowing social use alongside educational use of the discussion forum. As we write, Turner is entering the second stage of his research in which he will repeat the data collection methods with a new cohort of students and with stronger moderation on his part. We will then have a comparative element to add to our analysis which can include a comparison of assessment results over the two cohorts. Such a comparison can only offer indicative evidence because, as we have suggested earlier, the conditions for experimental design are hard to generate. In any event, we think that it is more useful to generate rich case studies across and within programmes from which we can begin to make warranted assertions about the value of our practice (Stake, 1995) rather than to enter into a problematic quest for the truth.

17.4   Researching presence and absence

Another methodological issue concerns whether a learner's online postings offer *prima facie* evidence of learning either in terms of the quality of the posting or the quantity of them? Does, for instance, the evaluator have to interrogate these postings for other possible meanings such as signs of 'teacher-pleasing' (registering attendance, being a 'good' student' etc.) particularly if students know that their participation is tutor tracked? Similarly, what can be read into absences of participation and how can their nature be recorded and logged? And what is the 'reflective content' of those whose online presence is confined to lurking?

One learner in a module with a rich discussion forum was tracked by the software. Her contributions numbered only 10 (most active learners posted many more), however she 'read' all of the postings made online and her final assessed work was excellent. Similarly, in another module, learners were asked for feedback on the use of the online learning environment for the module from which the following comment is taken:

> I always read the molecular based ideas on the discussion forum although I seldom reply or contribute (more of a spectator!)

Similarly, in the module we discuss below in relation to online surveys, out of 48 students, 24 said that they checked messages on the discussion forum but did not leave any themselves.

Is this a question of learning style or of time management? Is watching/listening the first stage of using a discussion forum? Are some people more virtually gregarious than others? These kind of questions remain open and in need of investigation again with other methods if we are to avoid a positivist reading of contributions as 'facts'. What looks like easy snatch and grab data for the researcher, on closer inspection turns out to be problematic. We now turn to another source of data upon which we have drawn widely to throw further light on student motivations for different levels of participation, namely, the online survey.

17.5   Online surveys

Like any questionnaire research, most of the effort has to be invested into the design of the questions because collection and analysis are the relatively easy parts of the process. In our view, online surveys are very useful and we will support this claim by describing how a colleague lecturing in biology used the online survey facility of WebCT to evaluate innovative ways in which she was teaching mathematics for biologists on a particular module.

Again, like any questionnaire research a balance has to be struck between asking a sufficiency of questions and avoiding respondent fatigue. Our general principle with online surveys is that 'less is more'. The problem of respondent fatigue is lightened a little in online surveys because generally students can answer more quickly using a keyboard and mouse. In our case study, our colleague asked the following questions:

1. Question about the difficulty/ease of the unit (6 choices given).
2. With regards to the discussion forum, which of the following best applies to your use of this area (5 choices are given here)?
3. If WebCT has helped your learning, could you say how?
4. How often do you log onto the module (7 choices)?
5. Can you identify three good things about WebCT?
6. Can you identify three things to improve WebCT?

The technology enables the responses to be sorted and in the case of those questions offering numbered choices, frequency distributions are easily provided in graphic form. It is also possible to render anonymous the responses. Rates of response vary though typically, a tutor will press students to provide feedback during scheduled class time to maximise these (in this study we have 100 per cent returns). The feedback can also be uploaded easily into a qualitative software package for analysis (which is something that we have in the pipeline).

In terms of expressiveness, there seems to be at least an equivalence between what students will write manually and what they will type; at times, the latter medium is especially vivid. Take for instance, one response to a question about the 'good' in WebCT:

NO!!

Here is a strength of feeling which is conveyed by the ease of emphasis / repetition permitted by the keyboard. Here is another to the same question:

Lecture notes! Lecture notes! Lecture notes!

Besides the kind of online surveys we have conducted in this case, we have also used them to gather tutor experiences of their use and perceptions of online learning. We have been surprised by the richness of the material we have gathered in this way. In some cases, tutors themselves have provided an analysis of their evaluative data and we have been able to place this on our evaluation site; in other cases such as the above example of the biology lecturer, the data has been handed to us for our own use and cross-referencing with other data. We now turn to a discussion on our use of statistics in our evaluation.

17.6   Statistical analysis

The availability of so many statistics on hits offers an apparently attractive source for the quantitative researcher but these are not without their problems. A first research problem is an ethical one in that many of the hit statistics can be located behind the backs of lecturers and students and indeed can operate as a surveillance machine. A second problem concerns what we can read into hits and whether we can attribute hits to individuals or to machines. Without supplemental evidence, there is also no way of judging how many hits represent mistakes or fleeting encounters with the learning material. It is also important to avoid freezing the statistical picture at one point in time.

A survey of students during Induction Week (see Figure 17.1) presents a picture of happy students. The overwhelming majority praise the online system on first use. As the feedback continues to be gathered throughout the year, however, we have found that the tendency of students is to respond to the same survey with suggestions or complaints. Thus while the table below has can be put to some analytical and descriptive use for our evaluation, the findings it presents need to be tracked longitudinally.

Handling take-up numbers and reporting on patterns of adoption is fraught with difficulties but essential for the purposes of an evaluation. In our case study, we have sought to present evidence in the accepted divisions within our university, namely by module use within each school. The first issue here is fixing the number of taught modules, a number which varies over the year since some run termly, others by semester, some have multiple, simultaneous occurrences. The next issue is the discrepancy within the school that such a division obscures. For example, in the School of Mathematical and Information Sciences, the overall percentage figure for usage lies at 34 per cent whereas the usage recorded for one of the subject groups in the School (computer science) is nearer to 50 per cent and in another (maths, statistics and operational research) around 10 per cent. Even within these subject

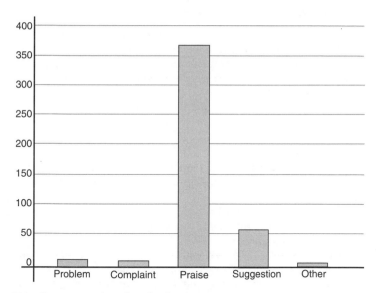

Figure 17.1: Categories of student feedback

groups, however, there is further distortion and we can report that two of the most active users of the online learning resource are in the low user subject group. And a final issue is the high usage of non-modular webs for online learning. There are a considerable number of these which have been set up to accommodate groups of learners who do not normally share a module, for instance those recruiting from a combination of modules or ones that have been organised for a specific purpose (e.g. year three placements).

Data retrievable from the server hosting the VLE differs from the data you obtain from within the individual web. For example, the number of hits on the homepage of an accounting module read from the server is 32,900. On the WebCT homepage for that module, the recorded hit count is 17,750. The discrepancy can in part be explained by the way that WebCT counts each hit as a session hit rather than repeatedly add up the hits during one session by a given learner. Moreover, WebCT does not track tutor accesses to the website. To discover the detail of learner access, to any significant measure it is necessary to enter each web and retrieve individual learner tracking. This then shows the number of pages accessed, discussion items read, posted and followed up, any glossary items viewed, when first and last accessed, total number of hits on the homepage, content, discussion and toolpages visited (including the assessment tool).

While you can only infer so much from statistics and it is important to consider threats to their validity, in our view they provide a powerful source of data. The presentation of statistical evidence renders some of the issues about adoption particularly vivid. So long as the one-dimensional character of some of the readings that might be made of quantitative evidence is acknowledged and so long as it is compared, where possible, with qualitative data, it is of much value to evaluation research.

17.7 Conclusion

We have sought to present a framework for evaluating online learning that allows for the capture of a complexity of research, presentation and developmental needs. By discussing methodological issues concerning cyber ethnography, survey research and statistical evidence, we have attempted to draw out issues of general relevance which we hope will prove to be useful for colleagues elsewhere.

The authors wish to thank Andrew Turner and Jan Coveney for allowing them to use their data.

17.8 References

Beaty, L. and Cousin, G. in Macdonald, R and Eggins (eds) (2002) *The Scholarship of Academic Development: An Action Research Approach to Strategic Development.* SRHE/Open University Press.

Geerz, C. (1983) *Local Knowledge.* Basic Books.

Ho, D. (ed.) (1997) *Virtual Politics : Identity and Community in Cyberspace.* Sage.

Scriven, M. (1981) *Evaluation Thesaurus.* Sage.

Stake, R.E. (1967) The countenance of educational evaluation, *Teachers College Record* 681.

Stake, R.E. (1995) *The Art of Case Study Research.* Thousand Oaks, Sage.

Turner, A. (2000) *Mickey Mouse and Football.* Unpublished paper, ELATE, April, 2001

18 Commenting electronically on students' reflective journals: how can we explore its effectiveness?

Elisabet Weedon and John Cowan

LEARN Reflective Practice Unit, University of the Highlands and Islands Millennium Institute (UHI), at Perth College, UK

18.1   Overview

This chapter reports on an ongoing action research project undertaken by two practitioners. The project aims to explore the impact, and ultimately, the effectiveness of comments made by tutors on students' reflective journals. It explains a set of categories developed for this analysis and it demonstrates how concepts based on social constructivist and constructivist theories of learning have provided a useful framework for this exploration.

18.2   Introduction

The main aim of this chapter is to explore comments on students' reflective journals and the potential impact that these comments may have on the development of their ability to reflect on their own capabilities. It reports on ongoing action research carried out by two tutors but does not attempt to provide answers. The main aim is to give an account of what we have found and, most importantly how the two of us have explored this topic so far. It also intends to identify a range of issues and questions that we hope will engage others in debate.

Social constructivist (or socio-cultural – the two are used interchangeably here) and constructivist perspectives are used. In particular we are interested in the concepts of Zone of Proximal Development and the related one of scaffolding from the social constructivist perspective (Bonk and King, 1998; Wertsch, 1985); and the Kolb cycle (Kolb, 1984) linking to the constructivist perspective.

The chapter:

- outlines the background to this action research and explains the setting;
- outlines the theoretical background and defines the conceptual tools;
- considers the specific impact of electronic commenting at a distance;
- describes and explains the methodology;
- reports on the data gathered to date;
- presents some analysis and a discussion of current data;
- concludes with some suggestions for next steps, for us and perhaps for others.

18.3   Background and setting

This project stems from our work on a 15 SCOTCAT credit module at level 3 on an ordinary BA Social Science degree within the University of the Highlands and Islands Millennium Institute (UHI). The module 'Enquiry Skills' encapsulates some of the teaching and learning aims of the UHI. These are to:

- apply constructivist and social constructivist learning theories;

- develop online learning opportunities that enable remote students to access education (UHIp Report of the LET working group, 1999);

- develop students' capabilities as well as content knowledge.

Our module reflects aspects of all three of these UHI aims in that it sets out to develop the students' enquiry skills through undertaking a small research project, and by reflecting on that process and on their own capabilities, with constructive intent. The UHIMI has developed its own framework for encouraging the development of capabilities within the curriculum that the students follow (Personal and Professional Capabilities at http://www.pdp.uhi.ac.uk); and the importance of development of capabilities is reflected within the teaching and learning activities, and also within the assessments.

18.4   The Enquiry Skills module

The Enquiry Skills module centres on a group enquiry project. It is a core Social Science module and an elective for Computing Science students. Reflective journals that encourage analytical and evaluative reflection are part of the learning experience and contribute to the summative assessments. This is novel to the students and a relatively new means of developing and assessing students within an HE setting, though the educational value of reflection is documented and draws on the literature of Schön, Habermas and Kolb (see e.g. Boud, 1985; Cowan, 1998; Moon, 1999). Our aim is to provide students with a 'mental tool' (Moon, ibid., p. 5) that allows them to explore and develop their own ability to input into specific aspects of the work of the module, both in relation to research and to working in a group. The students are required to submit ten journals in all; nine on a weekly basis each focusing on the development of a specific ability of their choice, and the tenth to summarise the learning and development throughout the semester. This use of reflection is novel to the students and it is unlikely to develop without guidance. The students are therefore provided with a structure for their journal, an illustrative set of 'already commented on' sample journals and a statement of criteria and standards which identify and amplify what we call a 'sound standard' for the journals (Cowan, http://www.ilt.ac.uk/redirectportal.asp?article).

An important, and certainly the most critical part of this journalling activity for the tutors, but also perhaps for the students, is the type of comments that the students receive on their weekly journals. The commenting is intended to develop students' abilities to improve their metacognitive grasp of what particular abilities entail for them, and how that could be developed through the application of their reflective abilities. It aims to encourage the student to pose valid and relevant questions and to seek answers to these through exploring a range of possible options. We have therefore developed a style of commenting which does not involve telling students what they should do but rather encourages them to explore, *while* writing rather than before writing, a set of possible options. We see this style of commenting as reflecting some of the principles of social constructivist learning theory in that we engage in a form of responsive dialogue with students, but aim to encourage their own further thinking rather than *telling* them how to carry out a particular task. Because of the novelty of these means of developing students' abilities and the demands on the students, we decided initially to evaluate the impact through a relevant course evaluation and also to embark on a small-scale action research project to inform our practice. It is worth noting that we have shared our students' experience by engaging in reflective journaling writing ourselves which have been commented upon by a colleague (Cowan *et al.*, 1999).

18.5   Commenting electronically – is it different?

There is a growing literature on the impact of the Internet and electronic communications (e.g. Collis, 1996; French *et al.*, 1999). Electronic submission was initially chosen partly because one of the commenters is at a distance from the campus; however, the main reason for using it is because it speeds up submission and feedback to the students. Subsequently and consequently, we have become increasingly aware of the potential impact both of asynchronous electronic submission and also, and perhaps more importantly, of the value of a commenter not being the person who is actually involved in teaching the students in the face to face setting. This has led us to consider issues about disclosures and understanding of comments. On the former, self-disclosure, a paper presented at British Psychological Society London Conference, December 2000, suggested that there is generally a greater willingness by people to disclose more in computer mediated dialogue than in face to face dialogue (Joinson, 2000); and also that there is a likelihood of greater self-disclosure when there is anonymity. Note that the disclosures we have in mind, and work with, are almost entirely directly related to the programme and demands of the module, and are only personal in the sense of being individual.

Commenting electronically also opens up greater opportunities for tutors to work collaboratively, which is an important feature of the UHI. This has led to the development where tutors within the UHI will comment on journals of students who are not enrolled in their own partner institution.

To summarise, commenting electronically is potentially different because of the way students and tutors respond to the remoteness of the electronic environment; but it is also different because it allows for separation of the role of commenter and tutor on the module. We will not pursue this issue further in this paper, but feel that it is an area for future exploration in relation to our teaching of this module.

18.6   Theoretical background and conceptual tools.

We are particularly interested in relating our commenting to Vygotsky's socio-cultural theory, especially in his concept of zone of proximal development (ZPD). This theory, primarily developed in order to explore children's cognitive development (e.g. Wertsch, 1985), is increasingly used in relation to exploring adult learning (e.g. Bonk and King, 1998). Vygotsky developed his concept for two specific areas within education; first, for the assessment of children's intellectual ability, and secondly, for the evaluation of instructional practice (Wertsch, 1985). The main use for us has been the second purpose – evaluation of instructional practice. The key emphasis of this concept is that it allows us to explore 'how a child can become what *s/he* not yet is' (Wertsch, 1985, p. 67; we have added the italics to emphasise that we need to include adults and both genders!). Vygotsky argued that teachers are better able to recognise intellectual ability through interacting with the child in dialogue. If this is translated into our setting, it describes how we use the comments on the reflective journals to create a dialogue with the student rather than simply to tell them what standard their thinking has reached. This concept of actively and deliberately setting out to draw out undeclared learning and understanding influenced later researchers such as Bruner (e.g. Wood *et al.*, 1976), who referred to it as 'scaffolding' – a term which has since been much used and misused. The research has tended to focus on children's development and often on development in relation to task related skills and not in relation to abstract thinking skills (e.g. Wood and Middleton, 1975). However, we are attempting here to test out these ideas in our own context, and in our categorisation of comments (below) we refer to scaffolding.

In addition, we felt that that the work of Kolb (1984), which focuses on how the individual develops metacognitive skills, could profitably be linked to the concepts of scaffolding and ZPD. It seemed to us that linking the development of critical thinking skills to the way that the student (and indeed we ourselves) need to engage with the different stages outlined in the Kolb cycle, provides us all with a mechanism for exploring both the individual's development and the development of the several dialogues that can potentially aid that development. It may also enable us, in future analyses, to consider the movement which some of our journallers can make from what Vygotsky referred to as the inter-mental (social) plane – thinking aided by dialogue with others – to the intra-mental (psychological) plane – thinking in dialogue with self. This is referred to as 'internalization' by Bonk and Cunningham, (1998, p. 38)

Other researchers have applied social constructivist concepts to education. Bonk and Cunningham (1998) developed a set of principles, based on social constructivist theory, that can be applied to online learning. Their set of principles, intended for use with complete learning environments, can be used as guidance when creating learning environments for students. We will use these principles in order to explore the extent to which our comments fit in with social constructivist principles developed by others; however it should be noted that in our case we are only exploring *one* aspect of the teaching and learning within a *single* module. Our comments would therefore not necessarily demonstrate inclusion of all these components which Bonk and Cunningham (1998) would expect to find in a *total* course experience.

The main aim of the present stage of our action research is to develop a robust means of categorising the comments that we make. The categorisation of the comments enables a number of potentially worthwhile activities on our part:

1. when we both comment on the same journal, we can compare the occasions which prompt comment, the purpose in commenting and the type of comments we make; and thus consider any possibility of the impact of differences in style;
2. we can explore the students' perceptions of the comment by asking them to classify the same comments;
3. we can link our comments to the social learning theory principles identified by Bonk and Cunningham (1998), to explore the extent to which our practice links to other researchers' interpretation and application of social constructivist theory;
4. we may be able, with the students' assistance, to trace the impact of particular type of comments on students' development throughout the module; and
5. we can further our aim to develop a more effective means of commenting in terms of greater understanding of the types of comments that are most likely to encourage purposeful reflection.

18.7 Methodology

18.7.1 Developing and using the categories

The starting point for both of us had been to carry out a Kelly Construct Analysis (see Weedon, 2000 for further explanation of this technique in relation to categorising feedback to students). Cowan refined a set of categories which were revised and extended after extensive dialogue with the co-tutor and other colleagues in an online mailbase. This led to the set of categories (in no hierarchical order) as shown in Table 18.1, which were used by both tutors to classify their comments.

Category of comment	Features looked for in comments
Tuition	'I explain something about the method which the student appears not to understand'
Facilitation	'I try to help the student to engage in reflection on practice and to apply it'
Contribution	'I offer ideas, information or suggestions which may enrich learning'
Judgement	'I tell how I rate what a student is doing or has done'
Scaffolding	'I help a student to draw out and display their full potential'

Table 18.1   Categories used to classify comments

The reflective journals were sent, each week, by the student to the tutor as an attachment to an email. The tutor added comments as footnotes and indicated the standard of the reflection by declaring a notional mark based on an amplified set of 'sound standard' criteria outlined to the student.

In addition, during session 2000–01, Tutor 1 considered the purpose of each comment before formulating the wording. Each comment was prefixed with a letter, indicating his purpose. He had no expectation that the students would pay much attention to these letters, except perhaps in the early stages when he made reference to the different types of comments, to assist the students to see the difference in particular between tuition regarding the method, and facilitation of the reflection. This potentially allows for him to:

- aggregate the figures for the full cohort, and display them week by week in graphical form, thus showing changes during the semester;

- do the same for individual students;

- compare the pattern of commenting with end of semester scores in the module, to which the abilities which featured in the journals should make direct and indirect contributions.

Tests with willing colleagues, on journals where the comment categories had been removed, suggested that colleagues generally categorised the comments as the commenter had originally done.

18.7.2   Data gathered to date

Tables 18.2a–c   Tutor 1: total number of comments and categories used

Figure in bold is Tutor 1's classification and figure in italic is Tutor 2's classification of the same comments. Please note that a single comment may contain two types of categories, e.g. a judgement (J) leading into a contribution (C)

Journal number	Tuition		Facilitation		Contribution		Judgement		Scaffolding	
4 (25 comments)	**4**	*5*	**16**	*12*	**5**	*4*	**0**	*7*	**0**	*1*
8 (16 comments)	**3**	*3*	**12**	*11*	**1**	*2*	**0**	*3*	**0**	*0*

Table 18.2a   Student A

Journal number	Tuition		Facilitation		Contribution		Judgement		Scaffolding	
4 (9 comments)	**2**	*1*	**6**	*6*	**0**	*1*	**1**	*3*	**0**	*0*
8 (8 comments)	**3**	*3*	**4**	*4*	**1**	*0*	**0**	*4*	**0**	*0*

Table 18.2b   Student B

Journal number	Tuition		Facilitation		Contribution		Judgement		Scaffolding	
4 (10 comments)	**0**	*1*	**10**	*6*	**0**	*2*	**0**	*4*	**0**	*0*
8 (11 comments)	**5**	*5*	**5**	*5*	**1**	*1*	**0**	*1*	**0**	*0*

Table 18.2c   Student C

Tables 18.2d-f   Tutor 1: total number of comments and categories used

Figure in bold is Tutor 1's classification and figure in italic is Tutor 2's classification of the same comments. Please note that a single comment may contain two types of categories, e.g. a judgement (J) leading into a contribution (C)

Journal number	Tuition		Facilitation		Contribution		Judgement		Scaffolding	
1 (10 comments)	**0**	*0*	**6**	*6*	**1**	*1*	**7**	*8*	**0**	*0*
3 (20 comments)	**2**	*3*	**10**	*11*	**4**	*3*	**6**	*7*	**2**	*0*

Table 18.2d   Student D

Journal number	Tuition		Facilitation		Contribution		Judgement		Scaffolding	
1 (7 comments)	**0**	*2*	**0**	*1*	**4**	*2*	**6**	*5*	**0**	*0*
3 (17 comments)	**2**	*0*	**12**	*16*	**2**	*0*	**3**	*5*	**0**	*0*

Table 18.2e   Student E

Journal number	Tuition		Facilitation		Contribution		Judgement		Scaffolding	
1 (12 comments)	**2**	*3*	**11**	*10*	**0**	*0*	**4**	*7*	**0**	*0*
3 (15 comments)	**2**	*3*	**11**	*12*	**0**	*0*	**1**	*8*	**0**	*0*

Table 18.2f   Student F

Table 18.3   A comparison of the number and classification of comments for each tutor

Figure in bold is Tutor 1's classification of the comments; figure in italics is Tutor 2's classification of the comments.

Tutor	Total no. of comments	Tuition		Facilitation		Contribution		Judgement		Scaffolding	
Tutor 1: Students A-C	72	**17**	*18*	**53**	*44*	**8**	*10*	**1**	*20*	**2**	*0*
Tutor 2: Students D-E	81	**8**	*11*	**50**	*57*	**11**	*8*	**27**	*41*	**0**	*0*

Each tutor analysed the comments made on six journals from three of her/his own students and then categorised, blind, the comments on the other tutor's journals. Thus a total of 12 journals from six students have been explored at this stage. Tutor 1 also engaged in an in depth analysis of one student's comments.

The data in Tables 18.2 and 18.3 suggest agreement between the commenters in terms of applying the categories. The main point of difference between the two tutors is in their use of the categories of 'judgement' and 'tuition'. Tutor 2 identified a number of comments as judgements that Tutor 1 had not identified as such on the journals that he commented on nor on the journals of Tutor 2. In relation to 'tuition' Tutor 2 used these comments less frequently than Tutor 1. A further, noteworthy point is that both tutors made very little use, in this module and with these students, ot he 'scaffolding' comments. This will be considered further in the discussion.

There was no noticeable trend in these examples of changes in the type of comments from the earlier to the later journal (but see later comment on this point). The main difference was in terms of 'tuition' for Student C and in 'facilitation' for Student E.

18.7.3   Ongoing analyses

1.   Analysis of changes in commenting over a semester. Tutor 1 explored the pattern of comments being made, for all of his students, as the semester progressed. This revealed interesting changes overall, though with marked individual variations. The (perceived) need to ask questions in order to prompt the journal writers to complete the descriptive record occurred much less frequently in some cases; the need to prompt the journal writers to dig deeper grew towards mid-semester, and then declined. The proportion of comments which echoed or extended the reflections of the journallers increased markedly in some cases. By late semester, some journallers probed their own thinking with follow-up questions. Tutor's comments thus began to contribute suggestions for associated or further thought, without that descending to the level of 'instruction'. Evidence on returned and retained journals showed that journal writers often reflected on the comments, and made their own notes upon them.

There were, however, noteworthy exceptions to this pattern because often a particular journaller was still struggling with the method, and needed tuition, and in other cases when a given journaller had had a difficult week, in that the reflection did not seem to gel.

This led Tutor 1 to heightened awareness of the effect of particular comments; and to a frank discussion about the type of comment which the student finds most and least helpful, and to the tutor's difficulties in commenting without immediate feedback – firing arrows of comments in the dark, without knowledge of their impact. This type of analysis is still ongoing and will be reported on at a later stage.

2.   Analysis of an individual student's perceptions. Tutor 1 engaged in a more detailed study with one student who was willing to assist. This student, shortly after the comments had been received, made notes of her reactions to them, which revealed how the comments had been interpreted by her. This was then compared with Tutor 1's notes of the intentions behind the comments, when made, which he had summarised separately. There were noteworthy and thought-provoking differences – in this case between commenter's intention and the journaller's reception.

Tutor and student together thus explored the potential of the classification as a basis for detailed joint enquiry into three linked questions:

(a) (Tutor) What was my purpose in writing this comment?
(b) (Student) What, if anything, did I take from this comment?
(c) (Both) Are these answers compatible?

The method was as follows:

- The tutor went over a recent journal and comments, and added notes to explain why the tutor chose to comment at that point, and what point the tutor hoped to make. For instance, the need to think about something could be an example of such a (facilitative) comment, and would leave the journal writer to do the further thinking.

- The student did likewise, making notes of reactions to the comments, and sometimes especially of the feelings they provoked.

- The tutor and the student analysed the commonalties and discrepancies both of which were in evidence. This in-depth analysis is going to form part of the next stage of the project for both tutors.

18.8   Discussion

The main aim of this chapter has been to explore possible ways that tutors can constructively review the way they comment on students' reflective journals, so that they can consider the impact that these comments may have on the development of the students' ability to reflect to good effect on their own capabilities. Our starting point for this was to try to develop a set of categories that allowed us to explore the type of comments we make. A further aim was to then link this to social constructivist and constructivist theories of learning, and to consider briefly the impact of technology.

18.8.1   Comments on the journals and the categories used

The categories used seem to be robust in that there was general agreement between the two tutors in applying them to the comments. This would suggest that we have a useful approach which, if developed, allows us to further explore and compare how we comment on the journals.

It was noted above that the 'scaffolding' category was not used to any extent. This could be interpreted in two ways:

1. the category is not a useful one;
2. 'scaffolding' comments appear only later in a developing commenting relationship.

The data gathered so far does not allow us to suggest which of these might be correct. If it is the latter, this might imply a kind of hierarchy where experience of, and response to tuition, facilitation, judgement and contribution is necessary before the scaffolding comments can be used. This does not fit in well with the suggestion that categories are not hierarchical.

The pattern so far on these journals does not suggest an overall trend with one type of comment being used less, as time progresses. It could be suggested that the only candidate for an 'early stages only' category might be 'tuition', as we would expect the student to require less and less of this kind of comment on the method being followed. This was not in evidence in this particular set of data since the noteworthy decline had tended to be in the early stages – over journals 1 to 3; however, it may be worth exploring this with a larger sample of journals over a longer period of time. Evidence contrary to this trend comes from one of the students (Student C) who was provided with a greater number of 'tuition' comments in the later journal. This impels consideration of the first suggestion that the scaffolding category is not a useful one. It may be that the 'scaffolding' category would be better considered as an overarching term which is applied to all the comments and that the nature of the scaffolding required can be explored in terms of the different types of comments that are provided by the commenting tutor.

On the other hand, some journal comments in the journalling in the subsequent semester (in a different module) were identified by the commenter as scaffolding, and as such, distinct from the other four types of comment. These comments evidenced active efforts to dig out 'buried' thinking which was there, but of which the journaller seemed unaware. The main distinction between facilitation and scaffolding would then be that facilitation provides questions that had been unasked and unanswered by the journaller, while scaffolding helps the journaller identify and make explicit and respond to questions whose answers may already be implicit in the journal. It is clear that this needs explored further. There may be a limited hierarchical relationship within the categories. It may be that that students have different commenting needs at different stages in their journalling. Notice, however, that our very attempts to categorise have led us to ask of ourselves deeper and more detailed questions about our activities as tutors.

In addition to looking at the comments on the individual journals and categorising them as we have done, we have a number of ways that we can extend this exploration of the comments. We could

- consider students' achievement in Journal 10 (the summative assessment of the reflective journals) and relate this to the type of comments used with a particular student; for example, does a student who receives a greater number of 'tuition' type comments in the early stages of journalling progress more than one who receives 'facilitation' and 'contribution' type comments?

- look more in depth at a change in the thrust and type of comments – this should allow us to consider the possibly hierarchical nature of the comments;

- engage in dialogue with individual students about the impact of the comments and tease out differences in apparent need in different types of students.

Such an extension should allow us to measure the impact we have on the students in a more effective manner. It may also allow us to provide useful guidance to tutors that are new to commenting on reflective journals.

18.8.2   Links to theoretical concepts

We have constantly considered our commenting in relation to both social constructivist and constructivist principles. We would suggest that the application of the set of categories to the comments above suggest clear links to social constructivist principles. In addition, it seems that we can comfortably fit our type of comments into the set of principles outlined by Bonk and Cunningham (1998) as illustrated in Table 18.4 opposite.

Our comments fit tidily within seven of these principles. But it may be that the way we have interpreted the comment of scaffolding is possibly slightly different from Bonk and Cunningham. They seem to suggest support in terms of *supplementing* what the student is doing; whilst our category stresses that it is about making the student *aware* of what s/he seems to be able to do, and encouraging them to act in their own strength. Social constructivist principles and concepts have thus provided us with a useful means of exploring our own practice.

18.8.3   Extending the Kolb cycle

As well as considering social constructivist theory we have found that an expanded Kolb cycle (Kolb, 1984), which shows how the other parties can interact with the person reflecting, provides us with an effective tool for exploring journal commenting. This applies irrespective of whether that reflecting person is a journalling student, or a developing commenter. This extension of Kolb potentially provides an interesting link between constructivist and social constructivist principles of learning. One, the social constructivist approach, allows us to consider the impact that 'others' have on an individual's learning, the other allows us to consider what happens for the individual, and the kind of different processes that s/he needs to engage with in order for learning to occur.

The way that we envisage this is shown in Figure 18.1.

We hope that in our commenting on students' journals we encouraged each student to follow the different stages of the Kolb cycle, with interventions as added to the basic diagram. The student thus started each week by identifying an experience of importance to him/her and was encouraged to reflect on this experience, by comments aimed to help the student generalise to other experience and to actively test out these generalisation. At all these stages there was potential for an input by the commenter. Students who had problems with identifying a relevant experience were engaged in dialogue about the value of exploring a question relevant to him/her, all students were, at least initially, provided with constructive comments in relation to the reflection, generalisations were enriched by further suggestions and the student was also encouraged to test out the ideas in other areas.

Principles of social constructivist theory based on Bonk and Cunningham	Example of comment from our analysis
Modelling – to illustrate performance standards and verbalise in visible processes	[In the use of the Sound Standard description]:'You have made a number of statements, noted * in the text, where you move to assertions or conclusions without seeming to have a reason for doing so'
Coaching – to observe and supervise students, thereby guiding them towards expert performance	
Scaffolding and fading – to support what learners cannot yet do and gradually removing the support as competence is displayed	
Questioning – to *request* a verbal response from learners while supporting them with mental functions they cannot produce alone	
Encouraging student articulation of their reasoning and problem-solving processes	'So subjects are going to learn to use a piece of software? That wasn't quite clear earlier, but maybe I've got it wrong.'
Pushing student exploration and application of their problem-solving skills	'On what basis? Will you try them out on someone, and get reactions and see how they behave before deciding?'
Fostering reflection and self-awareness through performance replays	'You seem to be setting yourself some clear and worthwhile goals here. Would it be worth considering how you are going to monitor the effectiveness of any of your inputs? Also might it be worth considering when you feel it is worth simply to listen ... and why this is the case? And when you decide to contribute ... if so what it is you contribute and how this is received?'
Providing cognitive task structuring by explaining and organising the task within students' ZPDs	'This seems to be a summary of thinking so far. A journal in which you are reflecting should be addressing a question for which you don't have an answer when you start, and for which you hope to have at least part of the answer when you finish. It should also focus on questions where the answer is likely to be of transferable use to you – in other words, not just this task, but in other tasks like this one. ...'
Managing instruction with performance feedback and positive reinforcement	'Some useful suggestions here ... but will you make different decisions for different situations? So are there several ways of doing the same thing depending on the final purpose of the exercise?'
Using direct instruction to provide clarity, needed content or missing information	'No, it didn't. It may have turned out that the non-interactive tuition was the more effective; but it also may have shown that one test was less searching than the other. All reasonable possibilities need to be considered.'

Table 18.4   Links between types of comments based on the categories that we have employed and Bonk and Cunningham's principles.

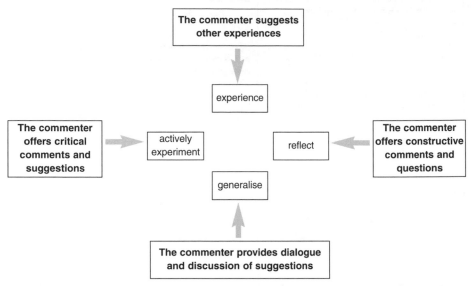

Figure 18.1   Kolb cycle extended to take into account the dialogue between reflecting person, and other

Similarly, however, we ourselves follow our own Kolb Cycle, through our own action research, the ability under development being that of commenting with useful effect on reflective learning journals. We started with a question about the value of commenting on journals, generalised after several iterations that the five categories described would enable us to explore our input to the journalling experience, actively experimented with these categories, testing them on colleagues. From here we considered specific instances of our experiences in commenting on journals and reflected on these drawing on the categories developed. In all of this we engaged in dialogue – with colleagues and with students.

For us, the linking of the Kolb cycle with the dialogue of the social constructivist perspective has proved a valuable way of exploring both our students' and our own development.

18.8.4   Concerns arising from this enquiry

Although we have categorised comments and explored the trends in our commenting we have not explored, except in one case, the students' perceptions of the comments. It is not certain that the student perceives a comment the way the tutor intended it. A good example of this can be seen in the case of a facilitative question ('How do you justify this conclusion from the points you have made?') which is intended to prompt reconsideration of the evidence and the conclusion which it may or may not justify, but is interpreted by the student as a judgement ('Your conclusion is not justified'). The impact of a comment on student learning should therefore not be judged by what the tutor intended but must be seen in terms of the message taken from the comment by the student to whom it is addressed.

In particular, one important area seems to be for us, the outcome of the making and receiving of comments that cause anger ('That's not what I meant at all; this tutor just does not understand!') – in circumstances where the tutor certainly did not set out either to misunderstand or to generate anger. Alternatively, there can be the reaction which begins from rejection or lack of understanding (perhaps accompanied by irritation), leads to revisiting of the negatively regarded comment during the ensuing day or so, and may eventually lead to a positive reaction, and to appreciation of some aspect of the comment.

These are clearly areas that require our further investigation. An intermediate attempt by one of us to obtain feedback from students at the end of semester 1 led to data which was insufficiently detailed to be of use. We are presently engaged in devising a more thorough method of enquiry, which is not over-demanding for learners in the midst of their studies.

18.9 Conclusion

We trust that this report has demonstrated the feasibility of developing a set of categories to analyse the type and patterns of commenting on reflective journals. It has shown reasonable concordance between two tutors involved thus demonstrating the value of such a set of categories. It has provided the two of us with considerably greater insights into our own commenting on reflective journals. We have used the concept of ZPD, and the related social constructivist and constructivist ones here, but we do not claim to have yet tested these concepts thoroughly with the evidence that we have provided here. However, we do feel that they have offered us a useful base for exploring our 'interventions' in a student's learning of a particular task. Our aim is to explore further the impact of our commenting, drawing on what we have developed so far.

18.10 References

Bonk, C.J. and Cunningham, D.J. (1998) Searching for learner-centred, constructivist and sociocultural components of collaborative educational learning tools. In C.J. Bonk and K.S. King, *Electronic Collaborators: Learner-Centred Technologies for Literacy, Apprenticeship and Discourse*. Hove: Lawrence Erlbaum.

Bonk, C.J. and King, K.S. (1998) *Electronic Collaborators: Learner-Centred Technologies for Literacy, Apprenticeship and Discourse*. Hove: Lawrence Erlbaum.

Boud, D., Keogh, R. and Walker, D. (1985) *Reflection: Turning Experience into Learning*. London: Kogan Page.

Collis, B. (1996) *Telelearning in a Digital World*. London: Thomson International Computer Press.

Cowan, J. (1998) *On Becoming an Innovative University Teacher*. Buckingham: The Society for Research into Higher Education and Open University.

Cowan, J. (2001) Plus/minus marking – a method of assessment worth considering? ILT Members' Resource Area [Internet] 27 April. York, Institute for Learning and Teaching in Higher Education. Available to ILT members from: http://www.ilt.ac.uk/redirectportal.asp?article=JCowan01a

Cowan, J., Joyce, J., MacPherson, D. and Weedon, E. (1999) Developing the ability to reflect – the role of others and self. Paper presented at the 4th Northumbria Assessment Conference, 1–3 September

French, D., Hale, C., Johnson, C. and Farr, G. (eds) (1999) *Internet Based Learning: An Introduction and Framework for Higher Education and Business*. London: Kogan Page.

Joinson, A. (2001) Self-disclosure in computer-mediated communication: the role of self-awareness and visual anonymity, *European Journal of Social Psychology* **31**: 177–92

Kirkley, S.E, Savery, J.R. and Grabner-Hagen, M.M. (1998) Electronic teaching: extending classroom dialogue and assistance through e-mail communication. In C.J. Bonk and K.S. King, *Electronic Collaborators: Learner-Centred Technologies for Literacy, Apprenticeship and Discourse.* Hove: Lawrence Erlbaum.

Kolb, D.A. (1984) *Experiential Learning: Experience as the Source of Learning and Development.* New Jersey: Prentice Hall.

Personal and Professional Capabilities at http://www.pdp.uhi.ac.uk

Savery, J.R. (1998) Fostering ownership for learning with computer-supported collaborative writing in an undergraduate business communication course. In C.J. Bonk and K.S. King, *Electronic Collaborators: Learner-Centred Technologies for Literacy, Apprenticeship and Discourse.* Hove: Lawrence Erlbaum.

Moon, J.A. (1999) *Reflection in Learning and Professional Development.* London: Kogan Page.

University of the Highlands and Islands Project (1999) *Towards a Learning Strategy for the University of the Highlands and Islands.* Report of the Learning Environments & Technology Working Group.

Weedon, E. (2000) Do you read this the way I read this?, *British Journal of Educational Technology* **31**: 3.

Wertsch, J. (1985) *Vygotsky and the Social Formation of Mind.* Massachusetts: Harvard University Press.

Wood, D.J. and Middleton, D.J. (1975) A study of assisted problem-solving, *British Journal of Psychology* **66**: 181–91.

Wood, D.J., Bruner, J. and Ross, G. (1976) The role of tutoring in problem-solving, *Journal of Child Psychology and Psychiatry* **17**: 89–100.

19 Integrating evaluation into the pedagogical process: a diary based strategy for illuminating the invisible and virtual

Rachel Johnson

School of Education, University of Nottingham, UK

19.1 Introduction

I use this chapter to assess the practical, pedagogical and evaluative success of an innovative approach to the evaluation of learning technologies. The evaluation under consideration aimed to investigate the student experiences of, and approaches to, a module that used a both face-to-face lecturer-directed contact and communications and information technology (C&IT) as pedagogical strategies. The explicit rationale for this mode of delivery of a 2nd year science module was to develop students' ability to learn both independently and co-operatively with peers. The module, that has been developed and taught over the past five years at the University of Nottingham ran this year as collaboration with the University of Hong Kong. As part of the assessed coursework, small groups comprising both Hong Kong and Nottingham students were required to use virtual communications technology in order to produce joint reports for web publication. The challenge of evaluating students' actions and reactions to pedagogy that is not classroom based – and the evaluator is in a different country – resulted in an evaluation design in which a reflective diary was used as primary method, and where other methods were implemented by colleagues in Hong Kong.

First, I outline the structure of the module. Secondly, I detail the evaluation design and schedule and use a review of research and literature concerning student learning with C&IT, and the evaluation of computer assisted learning and some practical considerations to justify this approach. Thirdly, I consider the practical demands and implications of collaborative implementation of evaluation. Fourthly, I assess how well the evaluation design succeeded in (a) supporting students' development as independent learners, and (b) producing illuminative data that had methodological validity and was of value to the academics who had designed and developed the module.

19.2 A brief outline of the module

The module is an optional, 10-week, 2nd year 'half' module offered jointly at and by the Universities of Nottingham of Hong Kong, with the Natural History Museum, under the auspices of the Universitas 21 consortium of universities. Assessment tasks are conducted throughout the course and comprise formative activities requiring students to work independently of lecturers on self- and group-managed projects. Assessment begins in week 5 with multiple-choice test based on the content of courseware provided through a dedicated interactive, multimedia learning environment known as 'The Scholar's Desktop'. The courseware is structured as a series of stand-alone units relating to particular issues, research and concepts in the subject. Each contains reading material with links that students 'click' to access further reading material (with additional links), and library and web-based references. In weeks 6 and 8, students are required to use courseware and material located in the library/ on the WWW to write a summary plan for two of four essay titles. At the end of the module, students produce a group report on a topic assigned to them by staff for publication on the local intranet. Students then complete a three-hour written exam approximately three weeks after the module's end. Students spend weeks one and two of the module in exercises and seminars that familiarise them with the module, the courseware and their UK/HK group partners. In weeks 3, 5 and 7 students attend 'guest' lecturers by external speakers and receive recognition for the quality of their questions to the speakers.

Technological and learning support is provided through regular access to the academic staff, an educational support officer and two technical assistants. On-line support and discussion is facilitated through a wide variety of web-based resources on the intranet of the Virtual School of Biodiversity. These resources include the module handbook, various references to further literature and resources, photo galleries, a helpdesk and discussion boards where students and staff email postings concerning issues such as the module, assessment tasks, and 'breaking news' relevant to the disciplinary field of the module.

19.3   Rationale for the evaluation design

The mix of methods used within the overall evaluation were designed and compiled at Nottingham by the independent evaluator in collaboration with academic colleagues in both the UK and HK schools offering the module. The design was informed by the following review of literature, and by some practical considerations that are detailed subsequently.

19.3.1   A review of the literature

Evaluation should not be a one-off snapshot (Draper *et al.*, 1996). Although summative measures of the impact of C&IT is understandable, given pressures on quality assurance and fundraising (Child, 1998), evaluators have begun to recommend a mixed methodology (Mulholland *et al.*, 1998a; Michaelson *et al.*, 2001), or note a general shift towards the use of qualitative, ethnographic approaches (Jones *et al.*, 1996; Mitra and Hullett, 1997). In criticising educational research into the use and value of learning technology for its lack of critical attention to the 'overly optimistic' claims of technology theorists, Selwyn (1997) argues that we should use longitudinal, ethnographic methods to examine the actual practices of students and teachers in the classroom. Such an approach would take into account the situated nature of learning, where the impact of C&IT on learning is mediated through, and influenced by a wide range of factors specific to the local context (Draper *et al.*, 1996; Jones *et al.*, 1996; Mitra and Hullett, 1997). Moreover, since evaluation should be systematic and specific to purpose (Draper *et al.*, 1996; Wills and McNaught 1996) and yet students' reactions to learning and opinions on their experience cannot be predicted in advance (Jones *et al.*, 1996), a flexible and open-ended enquiry methodology is more viable and valuable than experimental, scientific methods. While scientific factors attempt elimination of contextual and subjective influences on students' use of learning technology, a qualitative, illuminative approach appropriates and applies educational understanding and aims to evaluation (Draper *et al.*, 1996) and investigates inside the 'blackbox' (Spellman, 2000) of student learning to focus on how, and not what, students learn (Draper *et al.*, 1996). Illuminative approaches to evaluation take heed of the advice that it is the educational process that is of significance to, and should be taken into account in, the design of educational technology (Jones *et al.*, 1996). The shift towards qualitative, ethnographic methodologies thus represents a change in the purposes of evaluation of learning technologies, where the aim is now to study actual, contextualised instances of practice, and to take into account the multidimensional, complex nature of learning (Mulholland *et al.*, 1998a). This approach results in both improved sociological understanding of how learning technology makes education 'better', and aids the adaptation and integration of C&IT into the curriculum so that both technology and courses are relevant to the needs of identified teachers and students.

Essentially, the evaluation of learning technologies is a study of the use of a tool and not the tool itself (Mitra and Hullett, 1997). Because it is the student who participates in, and achieves the learning (Donald and Denison 1996), evaluations must centre on the student, allowing the student to evaluate on an on-going basis according to criteria students feel are important when using and learning through technology (Jones *et al.*, 1996), and taking into account the perceptual, social, spatial, temporal and engaged facets of the students' learning experience (Calvani *et al.*, 1997; Parlet and Hamilton, 1987). Furthermore, evaluations should take note of students pre-dispositions to IT and to learning using IT: students' predispositions will bear relation to the previous contexts and purposes for their uses of C&IT, and significantly affect their current approaches to, and feelings about learning using technology (Mitra and Hullett, 1997; Shaw and Marlow, 1999; Soong *et al.*, 2001). If the evaluation of educational technology fails to take the student perspective into account, and also fails to demonstrate educational and sociological implication, decisions taken on the basis of the evaluation outcomes are unlikely to lead to improvements in students learning experience and achievements (Weston *et al.*, 1997).

Shraw (1998) argues that students' academic success is closely related to their metacognitive abilities, or the organising and evaluative strategies the student employs to plan and structure their learning activity, to monitor the outcomes of this activity, and to assess their own progress. The incorporation of C&IT into the HE curriculum is often motivated by the aim of developing students' autonomy in learning and enabling them to study independently of teacher and classroom. It is hoped that this will lend students opportunity to shape the goals and processes of learning and make these personally relevant and appropriate (Dewhurst *et al.*, 2000; Sloane, 1997). Seaton (1993) notes that the use of C&IT enables distance, independent and autonomous learning, and yet these three forms of curriculum are conceptually and practically distinct. The educational goal of producing a student able to study on their own – autonomous learning – is contingent on the student's ability to apply critical thought to their activity and progress; critical thinking is, he argues a capacity that is built through an integrated, gradual programme of development. Similarly, research into group, collaborative and problem-based approaches to learning finds that metacognitive processes and autonomy are not necessarily enhanced just through engagement in tasks that draw actively on these capacities (Carswell *et al.*, 2000; Oliver and Omari, 2001). This again suggests it is essential that students are supported during learning activity by tasks that encourage them to focus and reflect on the processes and approaches they employ in study, in face-to-face and technology mediated communications, in group formation, and in group negotiation over the work process and task objectives (Brown, 1995; Calvani *et al.*, 1997; Carswell *et al.*, 2000; Curtis and Lawson, 2001; Hammond, 2000; Oliver and Omari, 2001; Wegereif, 1998). In particular, teaching strategies that reduce the role of the lecturer also diminish the influence of a teacher-centred culture of learning, and allow the student learning culture to predominate (McLoughlin, 1999). Thus if students' study habits are not compatible with the strategies demanded by computer-mediated autonomous study, the student should be supported and encouraged to recognise and adapt how they work (Ross and Schulz, 1999; Tait, 1998).

Many evaluators struggle to motivate students to participate in evaluation activities. This is unsurprising, given students' typical experience of the end of course questionnaire – an approach that for students, demonstrates only 'tokenistic' or 'bureaucratic' interests, and is of little benefit to them pedagogically or politically (Johnson, 2000). Thus while Draper *et al.* (1996) claim that evaluation can prompt students' reflection on their experience, the particular method chosen, and how it is introduced to students are of crucial significance. Breen *et al.* (2001) claim that a few well-constructed questions for students to answer in a diary-based evaluation are also satisfactory than questionnaires in obtaining information on IT related behaviour, both because the use of diary lends longitudinal insight into development and change in attitude and activity, and because an end-of-module questionnaire relies too heavily on memory. In some, mainly vocational areas of higher education, diaries are an established element of curriculum design, and are used both to promote active reflection on learning, and as research tool to interrogate students' learning strategies (cf. Badley, 1986; Bailey, 1990; Barclay, 1996; Halbach, 2000; Jorge, 1994; McDonough *et al.*, 1997; Porter *et al.*, 1990; Tuck, 1993).

The outcomes of this review of recent literature implied that the evaluation design needed to use methods that would generate qualitative, longitudinal detail of students' activity, provide contextual information and be of intrinsic benefit to students. The evaluator thought that students might value an approach that assisted their reflection on the process of learning. If students were assisted in this way, the evaluation might serve pedagogical purpose in developing students' self-evaluative and critical skills, and thus progress their autonomy and success as independent learners. The use of a student-centred reflective diary as one method of evaluation appeared potentially fruitful in addressing both pedagogical and evaluative concerns.

19.3.2   The local context

The initial aims of this evaluation were to find out what time students were devoting to which tasks, and when they studied. Given the above reading of research on technology assisted learning and its evaluation, the evaluator advised expansion of the evaluation aims to include an investigation of students experiences of, and approaches to the C&IT-mediated tasks. To support this investigation it was also agreed that we should gather factual information about the students' pre-dispositions to, skills in, and experiences of C&IT in education.

The factors constraining the design of the evaluation were that the evaluator and module team had limited time to devote to the investigation, and students were neither based in classrooms nor located in geographical proximity. Thus the evaluation methods had to be adaptable in three ways. First, the materials had to be suitable for students to use on an independent basis, because evaluators would be unable to spend great lengths of time in dialogue with or in observation of students. Secondly, the design had to be suited to, and implemented within, two contexts divergent in culture, semester structure, time and geographical location. Thirdly, the evaluation design and methods had to be acceptable to and accessible by the module team. Draper *et al.* (1996) stress the collaborative nature of evaluation and thus all parties: the evaluators the module team and the students had to understand and agree to participate in the evaluation, and support its implementation throughout. The eventual design used a mixed-methodology, where individual methods addressed a particular need or interest of the module team. The set of methods aimed to capture various perspectives on the student experience, and to produce different forms of data on multiple aspects of the context for learning in both countries. The outcomes of this approach are considered in the final section of this paper.

19.3.3   The evaluation design

The following lists and explains each method. Examples of the materials are given at the end of the chapter (see Appendix 19.1).

- A *Study Process Questionnaire* (Kember *et al.*, 1997; Wun *et al.*, 1999) [pre/post-module].

- A *'Starting Out' Questionnaire* in which students rated: previous experience of independent learning; previous use of C&IT in learning; their IT and web skills; the length of time they had used email; their written and reading proficiency in academic, scientific and other genres of English; whether they owned a PC/laptop, whether the PC/laptop was networked, where they used their laptop (if applicable) and whether they intended to sign-out a CD-ROM copy of the Scholar's Desktop courseware. This was appended to the front of the document containing diary/logbook (see next).

- A weekly *reflective diary* given to students with instructions, on floppy disk for completion on PC; the boxes in which students wrote their responses expanded automatically. The diary was structured by questions focusing on the current tasks at each week of the module. Each week, students responded to closed questions concerning their activity or feelings, and were then prompted to describe and appraise their learning activity, and offer potential resolutions for problems. Students then had the opportunity to give feed back about immediate concerns. Students retained their diaries until after all module tasks had been completed. Diaries were submitted to the evaluator by email from HK/UK, and presented as anonymous analysis to the course team.

- A *daily time log-book* appended to the back of the diary, in which students listed per weekday (as relevant) the amounts of time they spent on particular tasks and activities (e.g. searching literature; communicating with their group), and the time of day that they had worked).

- 3 x *student group discussions*. The UK evaluator and a member of the HK module team hosted discussions with students at three intervals. The methodology for the discussion was based around the Nominal Group Technique (Chapple and Murphy, 1996), in which students first work in small groups to discuss and summarise their responses to four questions. Group leaders then presented the results to the whole class with opportunities for whole class discussion. The discussions aimed to capture and interrogate competing views on the module (Hendershott and Wright, 1993). The notes and discussion were recorded for after analysis.

- 2 x student summative evaluation questionnaires (a) designed by the HK/UK module teams, and (b) adapted from the traditional questionnaire for the School (HK)/the mandatory university questionnaire (UK).

- The module team were also given a *reflective diary*. This was a template to structure notes on thoughts and experiences of running the course. Components were: running the show; teaching; students; module design; and the ICT element. Midway through the module staff summarised some of the main points in their diaries to inform the agenda for a group email discussion that was facilitated by an external discussant.

19.3.4   Evaluation schedule

(Approximate; slight divergence in actual timeline owing to HK/UK term structures).

Week 1   Evaluator introduces him/herself to the students and explains their role.
Completion of 1st SPQ
All module team commence reflective diary.
Week 2   Evaluators explain the evaluation process
1st student group discussion
Students receive the 'reflective diary'
Students complete 'Starting Out questionnaire' [appended to the front of the diary/logbook]
Students begin using the 'logbook'
Week 3   Students commence reflective diary
Week 6   2nd student group discussion.
First module team group email discussion
Week 10   Students complete 2nd SPQ
Students submit reflective diary and logbook to independent evaluator
3rd student group discussion
2 x Student summative evaluation questionnaires
Post module and initial analysis
2 x course team group discussions, with evaluators and external discussant.

Two further factors had lasting impact on the evaluation design and success. The first was a divergence between the evaluator's and module team's understanding of appropriate research methodology. While the evaluator preferred a qualitative approach, believing this to be better suited to the educational setting and the educational and motivational objectives of the evaluation, the scientists were greatly sceptical of non-experimental aims and methods. The second lay in a suspicion that the Hong Kong students would not adapt well to open-ended and discursive approaches. The mixed methodology felt like a compromise and risk to all, and this ambivalence generated problems in the implementation of the evaluation, and both students' and module team members' perceptions of its value. The reasons for this are discussed in the next section of this chapter.

19.4   Practical implications

Any evaluation is a collaborative activity conducted through the participation of those who request the evaluation, those who have responsibility for conducting the evaluation, and those who contribute to the evaluation, e.g. students. It follows that the predispositions of each set of actors will have influence on the evaluation at all its stages (Mulholland *et al.*,

1998b). Collaboration is contingent on consensus and co-operation in a team, and this in turn demands a set of shared aims and understandings across team members (Calvani *et al.*, 1997). Consensus and shared understandings proved crucial factor affecting the successful conduct and outcomes of the evaluation.

Draper *et al.* (1996) draw attention to the tension between the aims of scientific and educational research. The former are interested in measures of activity, and draw on scientific notions of validity and reliability in assessing the value of measures taken, and their implications for further research or decisions. Educational researchers tend to have interests and beliefs that encourage investigation of reflexive, subjective and contextual aspects of educational interventions that a scientific methodology would either exclude as biases or fail to capture. In this evaluation, the different research histories, traditions and experiences of evaluator and module team resulted in disagreements over the value and significance of the processes and outcomes of the evaluation. The issues raised and problems generated through conflict are however salient, in retrospect. They suggest that successful evaluation is contingent on consensus amongst collaborators throughout the evaluation. Consensus relies on, and enhances factors vital to the evaluation process: communication, conviction, coherent conduct; confidence and commitment.

19.4.1   Clarity of communication from the beginning

At first, the evaluator acted as consultant. It is likely that the evaluator did not spend sufficient time building relations with *both* UK and HK colleagues: the initial negotiation over the aims and objectives of the evaluation was progressed with the senior member of academic staff in the UK. At the start, the evaluator was unsure about what was communicated to the other colleagues, and what was their level of commitment and understanding. As the evaluation progressed it became clear that the module team had reservations about the endeavour per se, about its design and rationale and the appropriateness of the methods. The following comment is taken from a HK module team's diary notes:

> Running the evaluation and the course together has been a real pain. ... In a perfect world, I would have liked a year's trial and then the evaluation when we had the system running – as it is, the teething problems may influence the students' perception of the course and what it can achieve for them.

19.4.2   Conviction

The evaluation was beset with a further problem: the design had to be explained to colleagues in Hong Kong, and following adaptation of the materials to suit *all* students, the evaluation methods had then to be *implemented* by these colleagues. The process of explaining and negotiating the design was frustrated by the denuded forms of communication that are afforded by asynchronous media (e.g. email) and the time-lag. These initial communications took place at the same time as the evaluator got to know, tried to win the support of, progress dialogue with the HK team, and do this without the benefit to communication of sustained periods of contact, non-verbal cues and opportunities for immediate questioning and response. Actions and understandings were progressed best at the moments when the module team, or the module team and evaluator met face to face. Technical, structural, administrative and temporal problems (e.g. Chinese New Year, uploading software on to the HK network), arising from the practical experience of running the module in HK for the first time, and running the module on a joint basis for the first time, meant that the evaluation was perceived as source of confusion. Confusion led to loss of control by the evaluator in co-ordination of the evaluation process and materials. An example of this would be when a UK colleague flew to HK to launch the module to students on 29 January. On 2 February, the following email arrived to the module email list:

Dear all - please find attached comments from us re the evaluation (to try and ensure we are all doing the same thing!!) and also an amended Diary and Logbook (don't worry - only slightly) ... We are not sure about the meetings with students for 15 mins until we have talked to the colleague who will lead the discussions (who is away skiing as we speak!) - we hope to match the Nottingham ones as closely as possible. In these 15 mins sessions we understand ... that we will each use a similar set of questions. Is this correct and if so we assume you will supply the questions for the other weeks?

The module team's uncertainty about the evaluation was an ongoing problem, and was accentuated because it had to be taken into account at each stage of what was already a new, and unknown endeavour. This reduced the conviction of module team members about the evaluation, led to problems with its implementation; at times the evaluation was pointed to as the source of problems for staff and students in the module this year.

19.4.3   Coherent conduct

Both Breen *et al* (2001) and Draper *et al*. (1996) note that students have strictly limited tolerance for either IT-related or evaluation activities that are of no instrumental value to their own goals. It was crucial to the success of the evaluation that students did not develop a negative attitude and become reluctant to invest the 30 minutes time required. The intention was to explain the 'evaluation' to students as a pedagogic strategy of potential benefit to their learning and an integral (compulsory) part of the module. The evaluator made initial presentations that explained the nature and demands of independent learning and how students would be helped by their ability to identify, diagnose and adapt their learning strategies as necessary to achieve the module's learning tasks. The reflective diary was described as a means to stimulate reflection and critique, and lend opportunities for describing alternative solutions to problems. The time log-book was described as a tool to monitor the total time spent studying, and the time allocated to different tasks. The hope was that the students would accept these tasks and not see them as *additional* burden. It was necessary that the module team and evaluator were consistent and coherent in their references to the diary and log-book; the language used was important. However over the course of the module the language used by the module team, and picked up on by students was the term 'evaluation'. Indeed, the following text was placed on the Schools' website:

> *Evaluation*
> It may be of some comfort to you to know that evaluation returns and exam results over these last five years demonstrate both that this kind of learning is highly valued by most of our students, and that the performance profile of students taking the course is as full of achievement and diversity as that of any other. This year, we have asked professional evaluators in Nottingham and Hong Kong to help us probe a little more deeply into the challenges and rewards of this kind of teaching and learning from the student point of view. We hope you value it, and profit from this aspect of the course as well! Our thanks to all of you in advance for your help in this undertaking.

It may have been that students found the diary questions uninteresting and unhelpful, or that they were (reasonably) not as interested in thinking about learning as they were the subject content of the module and directing effort into tasks that were instrumental to completing the assessed work. Yet the lack of a coherent presentation of the 'evaluation' to students was potential factor in an increasingly ambivalent view amongst students. This chimed with the uncertainty of the module team and generated a fairly dim view of the diary and log book.

Q: Has using this diary helped you?
A: At first in helping me see the need for organisation, but after the first few weeks it became dull and pointless oops that was a bit blunt nevermind (UK, Week 9)

While data from the latter weeks of the students diaries and from the students' end of module questionnaires suggests that the 'evaluation' was of low concern relative to other aspects of the module, students were free to comment on the 'evaluation' activities within the diary and discussion sessions. Here, comments turned from sceptical to frustrated:

Q: What am I confused about right now?
A: Quite a bit of stuff actually. For one, how spending half an hour a week doing this will benefit me in the least. (Haven't you read the selfish gene?!) (UK, Week 3)

Q: List up to 5 negative comments about the module
A: The logbook and diary consumed a lot of time and did not help us to learn (HK, Week 9)

19.4.4   Confidence and commitment

The final practical implication of this evaluation was that the face-to-face activities with students had to be conducted in HK by a member of the module team (not involved in assessment) who was inexperienced in conducting qualitative research. The UK evaluator both described the method and purpose in detail at each stage in the evaluation, and debated the value of this method with the colleague during a visit to the UK. However discussion data produced from the three sessions in HK is limited in qualitative detail. It is possible students were encouraged to focus on producing summaries of their views. The aim of discursive techniques is to encourage divergence and debate of viewpoints in order to flesh out reasoning and experience. However a further possible reason may have been the students' lack of clarity or confidence in the methodology: the HK module team had warned that students would not understand or accept open-ended methods. If so, then this original concern should have been taken more seriously by the evaluator at the design stage. This latter 'cultural' analysis is supported by examination of the reflective diaries, which HK students have used to note summaries of their experience rather than to describe and reflect on their experiences. This latter issue is explored in more detail below.

19.4.5   Conclusion

The initial absence of consensus over the necessity for, and methodology of, evaluation, much of which lay in the problems encountered in communications proved vital factor in the subsequent unfolding of the evaluation. Had the evaluator spent more time in consultative activities, both building relationships and ensuring shared communication, the implementation of the evaluation may have proved more co-ordinated, collaborative and mutually supportive. Instead of this, a lack of coherence in understanding and application partially contributed to low levels of student commitment and concern among the module team over the value and utility of the data. The nature, status and value of the data is considered in the final section of the chapter.

19.5   The status and value of the evaluation outcomes

After initial consideration of the nature and status of the data produced, this final section assesses the success of the evaluation design in (a) supporting students' development as independent learners, and (b) producing illuminative data of value to the academics who had designed and developed the module.

19.5.1   The nature and status of data produced by each method

19.5.1.1   *The Study Process Questionnaire*

The Study Process Questionnaire was administered by, and of interest to the UK Educational Support Officer. Her analysis suggests that the module made little impact on the HK students but that the UK students appeared to have developed pre-dispositions more suited to a 'deep' approach to learning. She notes there are many criticisms of such generalisations. For instance: the SPQ provides only a snapshot of those students on particular days; that learning styles are not static; and, that changes over time could not be attributed to this module, because students were simultaneously studying five other modules.

19.5.1.2   *'Starting Out' Questionnaire*

The questionnaire produced statistical data that could be summarised to reveal differences between UK and HK students. Some of the results are of use when trying to understand these two groups' different attitudes to, and learning behaviour within, the module. These are discussed below.

19.5.1.3   *Students' reflective diary*

The data resulting from the diaries is in many ways disappointing, since both quantity and quality of written text is low. Students were using the diary to note and report their activity and immediate feelings. The comments read as if students were addressing an audience (the evaluator / the module team), rather than engaging in critical analysis of their views. There are also disparities between the UK and HK texts: the latter gave minimal contributions. The different qualities may reflect differences in students' commitment to the evaluation as well as different responses to reflective work. A further reason may have been the declining tolerance students had for the 'evaluation'. Yet although students claimed that the diary was a burden that took up a lot of time, the contributions are not substantial enough to support this.

19.5.1.4   **Daily time log book**

Students, particularly those in HK were honest in describing how they had often given false data. This could have been (a) because students found it tedious, or forgot to note their activity in the detailed and regular way demanded by the log-books; or (b) that students were keen to impress on the module their developing perception that the module workload was heavy. Both the evaluator and module team had reservations about what could be determined from this data aside from gross generalisations. If taken at face value the summary figures suggested that:

- each student spent about 50.95 hours on the module in total;
- each student spent the greatest amount of time in week 6 (8.13 hours);
- the least amount of time spent was in week 8 (5.38 hours);
- the courseware was allocated the maximum amount of time (16.01 hours) per student.

This implies that students were not studying for more time than they were supposed to according to university regulations for study-effort per module (75 hours contact + non contact time). This reduces concern over student allegations that they were spending more on this module than for others in which they were enrolled. This claim merely suggests that since the lecture-based approach does not require students to complete the background reading suggested, students are not devoting the full 75 hours of study to these modules. The larger sum of time that students claimed to have spent on courseware does echo the comments made about workload in group discussion, diaries and summative questionnaires.

19.5.1.5   3 x student group discussions

As noted above, the HK discussion data produced only a series of short bullet points. The UK discussion data was more expansive, and included divergent opinions across students. Three of the four questions that students were asked to address in discussion related to the study tasks in progress at the particular point in time. The fourth asked students to give more general views. The responses they gave tended to tally with, and expand on the comments they gave in their diaries. Some of the insights generated in analysis are discussed below.

19.5.1.6   Module team reflective diary and email discussion

Only a couple of the module team kept a reflective diary for more than one week, and none beyond week 5. Comments sent to the evaluator were sufficient to inform the agenda for group email discussion. However, course team interaction during the week allocated for contributions was minimal, and thus the discussion did not move beyond a brief explanation by each team member on their original input. Debate was most analytical and buoyant when the team met face-to-face. These meetings occurred on an ad-hoc basis, but there were two more formal meetings (mid and post module) that attempted reflection and action on the issues arising from the evaluation data. The post-module discussion of the evaluation data and its initial analysis generated a written document that gave details of (a) team members' opinions and (b) a set of recommendations.

19.5.1.7   Conclusion: different perspectives on the validity of the evaluation design

At the most general level, the validity of an evaluation can be assessed in terms of the fitness for purpose of methods for the evaluation aims and questions. The theoretical and empirical rationale for the design of this evaluation provides some justification for the partial integration of a combination of methods over a period of time.

The combination of three particular methods: the diary, the discussions and the summative questionnaire, each of which focuses on similar themes, provides for a limited triangulation. The responses of both HK and UK students reduce to a few common themes (albeit giving different views), and these themes reoccur in the data arising from each method. This effects validation of the data, despite disputes over the potential validity of the indivdual methods. Furthermore, when considered in combination with the contextual information generated through the starting-out questionnaire, the data arising from one method is coherent with, and serves to illuminate and explain, responses generated in another set of data. From an analytical point of view, the data generated by each method supports and extends the validity of other data. Without the mixed methodology assessments of the validity of the evaluation design would have continued to be sceptical. Moreover a design that produced data from one perspective, about one issue, or in a single form would not have provided the explanatory and illuminative insight necessary for developing understanding of the students' experience, activities and opinions.

Assessment of the validity of an evaluation design will also depend on the epistemological, ontological and disciplinary assumptions of the person who makes the assessment. Kvale (1996) supports the view that the validity of research is related to the practical utility of the findings. Practical utility depends on the relevance of the research conclusions to both the context for practice, and the particular problems of practice that research attempts to investigate. In this sense, the validity of the evaluation outcomes depended on the practical value of the outcomes. However, as discussed in section 19.4, the module team and the evaluator had divergent ideas of the value of qualitative data, and the module team were relatively inexperienced in both conducting qualitative research and making sense of the data. During post-module discussions of the data, its analysis and the implications of the findings, it became clear that this inexperience of the processes through which qualitative data can be collated, organised and presented meant that the module team were not able to draw inference and therefore value from the evidence that lay before them. This implied that the evaluation would have little practical value. At first, the evaluator attempted explanation of the principles of qualitative analysis. However this necessitated explanation of how the qualitative researcher does not 'stand behind' the data but stands fairly naked at the forefront of their analyses. The subjective nature of qualitative analysis did not satisfy the epistemological concerns of the scientist. The practical value of this evaluation will be maximised when analysis and presentation of data is made accessible, comprehensible and fit for both rigorous scrutiny and alternative interpretation by the module team. This job is yet to be completed.

19.5.2   The pedagogical value of the evaluation

During the final student discussion, time was given for the students to talk about the 'evaluation' with the module team. UK students admitted that the diary would have supported their learning, development of insight, and decision making had they used it as instructed.

If I had appreciated the importance of this diary as a time management tool, I'm sure it would have been more useful. I didn't use it from the beginning, so I didn't get into the habit of filling it out ... sorry.

So it could be that because students had not written discursive, reflective and self-critical contributions and only given short summary statements, they had not found the diary useful. It transpired in the second discussion session with UK students, and from final diary entries by HK students that the main problem they experienced was their limited ability and considerable lack of confidence in self-monitoring and evaluating whether they had 'done enough'. The diary had proved useful tool for some in keeping a record of the work completed, and being able to look back and see how far they had progressed:

I know my weaknesses better through answering questions in the diary (HK)

It produces a self-initiating work pressure (HK)

I can refer back to it and know that what're my problems and weaknesses (HK)

The diary and logbook help when filled in correctly: I remain aware of progress (UK)

There are also comments that suggest students are reluctant or resistant to reflect on their learning:

I feel it is unnecessary to continually assess what I'm doing, I prefer to just get on with things – nothing personal by the way (UK)

I already knew how I worked best and the problems connected with my method of working (UK)

It is not useful because it makes an extra work for me. Without this diary I can still do the tasks within my own planned period (HK)

The diary did not help me to learn. The diary only helped me to plan for the workload. (HK)

I can know my progress without signing the diary (HK)

It is salient to note that the diaries revealed that students were aware of the demands of independent learning. At the outset, there was a question that asked students to state what the module would require of them. Of 21 UK students, 11 reported self-motivation and self-discipline; 7 time-management; 4 organisation and planning ahead; 3 judgement about what it is necessary to do; and, 3 make more effective use of the resources provided. Of 36 HK students, 28 looked forward most to the freedoms associated with independent learning, but 24 were worried that they would have problems with time management. The UK students admitted later in the diaries that they were worried about their ability to manage their time and work (8 students); that they were having problems assessing whether they had done enough work (5) and juggling the workload (5); and that they found the experience of independent learning challenging because they were not coping with the self-discipline independent learning required (13). In the same week all 36 HK students mentioned that they were having problems with developing and putting into practice the learning skills required. This reading suggests that students require support in *adapting* their study habits to those *they realise* are necessary. The problem is less with a failure or lack of willingness to reflect than it is with the difficulties they have with changing their approach and coping with a non-directive, less structured approach to learning:

> My time management and organisation/planning skill will have to improve to get through this module with a reasonable grade. Which is a good thing but changing the way I work is very hard (I've been doing it or rather not doing it for 16 years) (UK week 3)

> I've thought a lot more about how to learn and manage myself, but I don't think I put it into practice enough during the module – perhaps this is my fault? (UK week 9)

> Q: *Do you think you met the learning objectives? Why?*
> A: No, because I am too lazy. *(HK, week 9)*
> A: *Most of the objectives but not the transferable skills* (HK, week 9)

Overall the pedagogical impact of the evaluation is difficult to assess. Examination results were similar to those in previous years, however this also is no test of the pedagogical value of the diary since any impact may only be realised by the students later in their studies.

19.5.3 The evaluative insights into students' experience of learning

The evaluation did provide insights into students' experience of the module tasks and the challenge of independent learning. Here I examine the comparative findings to illustrate the different forms and qualities of the data gained from the combination of diary, 'starting-out' questionnaire and discussion groups. The discussion highlights how the qualitative data is useful in conveying the tone and longitudinal changes in students' learning experience, and in particular their attitudes and habits.

19.5.3.1 IT

Comparative insights into the differences in attitude and skills were notable from analysis of the diary, discussion and Starting Out questionnaire. Hong Kong students were positive and confident in their IT skills and looked forward to developing these through the module. All Hong Kong students had lap tops and were able to work on the module when not on campus or in university IT facilities. In contrast whilst UK students claimed similar levels of skill and experience in using IT in learning, discussion reveals a higher degree of both negative and fearful attitudes towards 'evil' machines, and negative experience of using PCs that crashed and physical discomfort with 'staring at a screen' for hours in 'cold and smelly' laboratories.

19.5.3.2 Working in a group

Hong Kong students' assessments of the prospect of group work were hopeful, emphasising the possibilities of sharing and co-operating with their peers in both HK and the UK.

Q: What do I expect about group work?
'good chance to co-operate with and learn from both local and overseas students'; 'share different cultures'; 'work in harmony within a group'; 'strengthen friendship with UK students'; 'exchange ideas and solve problems with UK students. *(HK 1st discussion group)*

UK students were more hesitant, viewing the prospect with trepidation because it demanded a host of altruistic skills and attitudes:

Q: What do I expect about group work?
'co-operation'; 'patience and open-mindedness'; 'being nice'; 'tolerance'; 'compromise'; 'helping each other'; 'accepting other peoples' opinions' 'make efforts to tolerate and get on with my group members'; 'commitment – it's not just me I let down if I slack off'. (UK 1st discussion group).

UK students frequently internalised the problematic nature of their experiences; as noted above students tended to cite their deficiencies as reason for their lack of progress or failure to cope with the time and self-management required, as if in confirmation of innate inability rather than as a self-perception that was possible to change. In describing the same problems, HK students externalised the reasons for their problems, identifying the module structure, courseware or tasks as source of concern. In the preparatory documentation of their experience in the second discussion session 16 reported feeling under time pressures and 7 that they were 'falling behind'. 15 of these students cited lack of time management skills and 3 lack of organisational skills as reasons for these feelings. In contrast, the concerns of HK students were almost exclusively task focused (essay plans, test, group work, courseware and workload) with only three comments concerning time. Students admitted problems with managing their time, but cited *other modules* as reason for this: *'hard to manage time (too many other projects)'; 'not good in time management, difficult to handle the workload. Other subject is very demanding'.*

19.5.3.3 Motivations

When asked in the diary about what they were looking forward to achieving in the module, and what they were enjoying at the mid-point, 75 per cent of UK students made comments about learning more about the subject of the module, and enjoying researching widely and in-depth about issues that had caught their interest. The tone of HK diaries is far more instrumental and focused on achieving/completing the tasks.

19.5.3.4 Common problems

The experience of working in small groups using multimedia as means of communication was experienced as difficult, negative and frustrating by all students. The reasons for this appeared to support Calvani *et al.* (1997) and Carswell *et al.* (2000) who note that students need first to develop a sense of community, intersubjective understanding of the process and goals of task completion, and focus throughout on the process of working. Hammond (2000) notes that web-based communication implies social dimensions of communication similar to those of face-to-face communication. Without attending to the social dimensions of group work, task completion is frustrated. UK and HK students found the asynchronous nature of communication difficult because of the time-difference and because HK students were used to receiving immediate replies from peers who sat at their laptops on a regular basis. UK students tended to check their email accounts only once or twice a week; their different access to PCs meant that there was no student email culture. The two groups of students also set themselves different objectives: the Hong Kong students wanted to work on the group project throughout the module; the UK students were more caught up with attending to the immediate assessment task. HK diary entries and the summary comments of the first two discussion sessions invariably refer to communication with UK students and lack of progress with the group project. In contrast, UK students are preoccupied with the courseware, essay plan and test for the first six weeks of the module. By the time the UK students' attention turned to group work in week 7 their efforts had to be invested in pulling the work together rather than planning it:

Students found it difficult to resolve problems arising from their different habits and expectations; UK and HK students frequently complained in their diaries that group work would be easier to progress were they able to work face-to-face:

> if it was a group all based at Nottingham you could have proper discussions and exchange ideas properly.

> The time-lag means that we don't get emails at the correct time or at a convenient time. Also only two members of the group are in communication so we aren't quite sure what is being done by each subset.

> The timetable of the Hong Kong people is different to ours, so we may be waiting for a response whilst they are having to meet other coursework deadlines. The project will not proceed smoothly, but initially biased to what we have discussed here because of this wait.

> Communication is too slow and we have no way of motivating the rest of our group. We can't go up to them and say 'come on guys we need to get going'. We can only post a message and prey [*sic*] that they'll read it [Student 10]

Their learning activity in group work was more akin to frustrated, last minute co-operation, in which tasks were separated and worked on individually, than it was collaborative (cf. Curtis and Lawson, 2001).

19.6   Conclusion

The students' comments and statements in diaries and discussions lend useful insight into the culture and traditions of student learning. They indicate several problematic areas concerning module, materials and learning/IT skills. However the data lack the substance that would enable systematic analysis and thus bring rigour to the 'findings'. This evaluation has raised issues about assessment forms and timing, the centrality of group formation, and students experience of independent learning. However it has not been sufficiently successful for the module to identify *necessary* action in these areas. Doubts over the validity of the data, and the difficulty they experience in making meaning from the data, suggest that the evaluation findings are unlikely to transform or inform module teams' understanding of student learning to any great extent. Changes will be made but without greater certainty that improvements to the student experience of C&IT mediated independent learning will result.

19.7   References

Badley, G. (1986) Using a diary to evaluate a course or programme, *Journal of Further and Higher Education* **10**(3): 51–6.

Bailey, K.M. (1990) The use of diary studies in teacher education programs. In J.C. Richards and D. Nunan (eds), *Second Language Teacher Education*. Cambridge: Cambridge University Press, 215–26.

Barclay, J (1996) Learning from experience using learning logs, *Journal of Management Development* **15**(6): 28–43.

Breen, R., Lindsay, R., Jenkins, A. and Smith, P. (2001) The role of information and communication technologies in a university learning environment, *Studies in Higher Education* **26**(1): 95–114.

Brown, A. (1995) Evaluation of teaching and learning processes in a computer-supported mechanical engineering course, *Computers and Education* **25**(1–2): 59–65.

Calvani, A. Sorzio, P and Varisco, B.M. (1997) Inter-university co-operative learning: an exploratory study, *Journal of Computer Assisted Learning* **13**: 271–80.

Carswell, L., Thomas, P., Petre, M., Price, B. and Richards, M. (2000) Distance education via the Internet: the student experience. <??>

Chapple, M. and Murphy, R. (1996) The Nominal Group Technique: extending the evaluation of students' teaching and learning experiences, *Assessment and Evaluation in Higher Education* **21**(2): 147–59.

Child, J. (1998) Assessing the impact of Computer-Assisted Instruction (CAI) in undergraduate Latin American studies courses, *Computers and the Humanities* **31**: 389–407.

Curtis D.D. and Lawson, M.J. (2001) Exploring collaborative online learning, *JALN* **5**(1): 21–34.

Dewhurst, D.G., Macleod, H.A. and Norris, T.A.M. (2000) Independent student learning aided by computers: an acceptable alternative to lectures?, *Computers and Education* **35**: 223–41.

Donald J.G. and Denison D.B. (1996) Evaluating undergraduate education: the use of broad indicators, *Assessment and Evaluation in Higher Education* **(21)**(1): 23–39.

Draper, S.W., Brown, S., Henderson, F.P. and McAteer, E. (1996) Integrative evaluation: an emerging role for classroom studies of CAL, *Computers Educ.* **26**(1–3): 17–32.

Halbach A. (2000) Finding out about students' learning strategies by looking at their diaries: a case study, *System* B>**28**: **86–96.**

Hammond, M. (2000) Communication within on-line forums: the opportunities, the constraints and the value of a communicative approach, *Computers & Education* **35**: 251–62.

Hendershott, A. and Wright, S. (1993) Student focus groups and curriculum review, *Teaching Sociology* **21**(2): 154–9.

Johnson, R. (2000) *A Qualitative Study of Students' and Lecturers' Perceptions and Experiences of Student Feedback*. Unpublished thesis, Sheffield Hallam University/Sheffield University.

Jones, A., Scanlon, E., Tosunoglu, C., Ross, S., Butcher, P., Murphy, P. and Greenberg, J. (1996) Evaluating CAL at the Open University, *Computers Educ.* **26**: 5–15.

Jorge, J.R. (1994) Diary studies as illumination: case study of the Portuguese classroom, *Language Learning Journal* **10**: 64–6.

Kember, D. (1995) Learning approaches, study time and academic performance, *Higher Education* **29**(3): 329–43.

Kember, D. Charlesworth, M., Davies, H., McKay, J. and Stott, V. (1997) Evaluating the effectiveness of educational innovations: using the study process questionnaire to show that meaningful learning occurs, *Studies in Educational Evaluation* **23**(2): 141–57.

Kvale, S. (1996) *InterViews: An Introduction to Qualitative Research Interviewing*. London: Sage.

McDonough, J. (1994) A teacher looks at teachers' diaries, *ELT Journal* **49**: 57–65.

McLoughlin, C. (1999) Culturally responsive technology use: developing an on-line community of learners, *British Journal of Educational Technology* **30**(3): 231–43.

Michaelson, R., Helliar, C., Power, D. and Sinclair, D. (2001) Evaluating FINESSE: a case-study in group-based CAL, *Computers & Education* **37**(1): 67–80.

Mitra, A. and Hullett, C.R. (1997) Toward evaluating computer aided instruction: attitudes, demographics, context, *Evaluation and Program Planning* **20**(4): 379–91.

Mulholland, C., Au, W. and White, B (1998a) Courseware evaluation methodologies – strengths, weaknesses and future directions [http://www.cegsa.sa.edu.au/acec98/papers/p_mulh1.html].

Mulholland, C., Au, W. and White, B. (1998b) Identifying the evaluators of courseware – how agendas, assumptions and ideologies may impact upon evaluation [http://www.cegsa.sa.edu.au/acec98/papers/p_mulh2.html].

Oliver, R. and Omari, A. (2000) Student responses to collaborating and learning in a web-based environment, *Journal of Computer Assisted Learning* **17**: 34–47.

Parlett and Hamilton (1987) Evaluation as illumination: a new approach to the study of innovatory programmes. In R. Murphy and H. Torrance, *Evaluating Education: Issues and Methods*. London: Harper & Row.

Platzer, H., Snelling, J. and Blake, D. (1997) Promoting reflective practitioners in nursing: a review of theoretical models and research into the use of diaries and journals to facilitate reflection, *Teaching in Higher Education* **2**(2): 103–21.

Porter, P.A., Goldstein, L.M., Leatherman, J. and Conrad, S. (1990) The ongoing dialogue: learning logs for teacher preparation. In J.C. Richards and D. Nunan (eds), *Second Language Teacher Education*. Cambridge: Cambridge University Press, 227–41.

Ross, J. and Schulz, R. (1999) Can computer-aided instruction accommodate all learners equally?, *British Journal of Educational Technology* **30**(1): 5–24.

Schraw, G. (1998) Promoting general metacognitive awareness, *Instructional Science* **26**: 113–25.

Seaton, W.J. (1993) Computer-mediated communication and student self-directed learning, *Open Learning* **8**(2): 49–54.

Selwyn, N. (1997) The continuing weaknesses of educational computing research, *British Journal of Educational Technology* **28**(4): 305–7.

Shaw, G. and Marlow, N. (1999) The role of student learning styles, gender, attitudes and perceptions on information and communication technology assisted learning, *Computers & Education* **33**: 223–34.

Sloane, A. (1997) Learning with the web: experience of using the World Wide Web in a learning environment, *Computers Educ.* **28**(4): 207–12.

Soong, M.H., Chan, H.C., Chua, B.C. and Loh, K.F. (2001) Critical success factors for on-line course resources, *Computers & Education* **36**: 101–20.

Spellman, G (2000) Evaluation of CAL in Higher Education Geography, *Journal of Computer Assisted Learning* **16**: 72–82.

Tait, K. (1998) Replacing lectures with multimedia CBL: student attitudes and reactions, *Instructional Science* **26**: 409–38.

Tuck, R. (1993) The learning diary as a tool for reflective, self-directed learning, *NASD Journal* **29**: 28–30.

Wegereif, R. (1998) The social dimension of asynchronous learning networks, *JALN* **2**(1): 34–49.

Weston, C., Le Maistre, C., McAlpine, L. and Bordonardo, T (1997) The influence of participants in formative evaluation on the improvement of learning from written instructional materials, *Instructional Science* **25**: 369–86.

Wills, S. and McNaught, C (1996) Evaluation of computer-based learning in higher education, *Journal of Computing in Higher Education* **7**(2): 106–28.

Wun, Y.T., Chan, C.S.Y. and Dickinson, J.A. (1999) Does short-term problem-based learning change students' learning styles and preferences? In Proceedings of the 1st Asia-Pacific Conference on Problem-based Learning. [http://nt.media.hku.hk/pbl/book/SubProj12_WunY.pdf]

Appendix 19.1 Example of the diary and logbook

Week 4 Diary

Just describe what you have been thinking or feeling this week
Write as much as you need to give a full explanation (the boxes expand automatically!)
There are no 'right' or 'wrong' answers

Describe your experience of using courseware for the first time What was difficult? What was interesting?
Did you make notes when you were using courseware? If yes, give an example of the notes you took. What is helpful to you about these notes?
Did you keep a record of the 'marked words' or 'hot-spots' you clicked? What influenced your decision to click those 'marked words' or 'hot spots'?
Did you understand the learning objectives for the courseware?
What will you need to do to meet the learning objectives?
What are you worried about right now? What would help you?

End of diary for week 4

Appendix 19.1 contd

Logbook: Use this logbook sheet to record the time you spend working on the module this week. It is best to record your time immediately. You should use the log book each day that you work for this module

What I did in WEEK 9	Mon.	Tues.	Wed.	Thurs.	Fri.	Sat.	Sun.
Courseware							
Reading							
Writing							
Researching – online							
Researching – library							
Communication – online							
Communication – face to face							
Essay Plan							
Reading							
Writing							
Researching – online							
Researching – library							
Group Project							
Reading							
Writing							
Researching - online							
Researching - library							
Communicating - online							
Communicating - face to face							
Planning workload							
Compulsory course attendance							
Revision							
Troubleshooting							
Diary & log book							
Other [state what]:_____							
Other [state what]:_____							

Instructions:

Enter the time you spent in minutes against the activity you were working on.
State which time of day you were working by using the letters M, A, E, or N

Key:

M = Morning 08–13.00;
A = Afternoon 13.00–18.00;
E = Evening 18.00–23.00;
N = Night 23.00–08.00

Example: 90A indicates 90 minutes, in the afternoon, during the hours of 13.00 and 18.00

20 University teachers' attitudes to the impact of innovations in Information and Communication Technology on their practice

Holly Smith and Martin Oliver

Education and Professional Development, University College London, UK

20.1   Overview

Rapid developments in Information and Communication Technology (ICT) have led to a series of problematic discourses around the use of Learning Technologies. These complexities include costing (will economies of scale balance higher development costs?), access (does online learning create flexible opportunities or social exclusion?) and pedagogy (does ICT foster rich, interactive, collaborative learning or the transmission of textual content?).

In spite of the intractability of these problems, policies such as the Dearing Report have placed an increased emphasis on the use of ICT in teaching and learning. However, the extent to which ICT innovations are embedded depends upon the university teachers responsible for designing courses, assessments and learning activities. Although much has been done to investigate whether or not these academics have the skills required to embed ICT, their attitudes towards this remain unexplored, apart from the occasional account of fear or frustration.

If innovations in ICT are to be successful, a better understanding is required of the perspective of academics and of the extent to which they are aware of discourses around Learning Technology. Therefore, a study was carried out to identify the discursive repertoires used by university teachers in discussing the impact of ICT. A series of open-ended interviews was carried out with a small sample of newly appointed university teachers. These focused on their perceptions of the impact ICT would have on teaching and learning in universities over the next five years. The interviews were analysed using a form of Discourse Analysis adapted from Potter and Wetherell (1987). This permitted the identification of culturally available discourses that participants drew upon when discussing the topic.

The results of this study explore the complex congruence and divergence between the beliefs of ICT experts and those of university teachers, and emphasise the importance of contextual and disciplinary priorities on awareness. Although this research is clearly limited by its sample, it is important in a number of respects. First, it describes the discourses that ICT-based projects may encounter when working with academics. This is relevant to the design of professional development programmes in the use of ICT for university teachers; the implication of the present research is that such professional development programmes should emphasise engagement in critical debates over basic IT skills. Finally, it identifies the broader programme of research that is required if innovations in the use of ICT are to be effectively implemented in the academic mainstream.

20.2   Introduction

The use of ICT in HE is complex and widely debated. For example, there appear to be no simple answers about how best to use technology within courses (Conole and Oliver, 1998), what students do with it once it has been adopted (Jones, 1998), how much it costs (Bacsish and Ash, 2000), how one might go about evaluating its impact (Oliver, 2000), let alone whether or not it is effective. However, such discussions take place primarily within a community of researchers and specialist practitioners in learning technology; it remains open to question whether the conceptions and attitudes of other practitioners in HE contest the same issues.

All this poses particular problems for those involved in professional development in HE, since it means that there can be no definitive body of knowledge for those new to this topic. The implication of this is that it is necessary to engage with and challenge participants' conceptions and attitudes. However, such a dialogue requires detailed understanding of such attitudes. While several studies have identified students' attitudes towards technology, at least at the general level of enthusiasm or resistance (e.g. Åkerlind and Trevitt, 1999), the attitudes of staff remain relatively unexamined. The few papers that do address staff attitudes do so from the context of professional development, and such papers typically stress the need to overcome apathy or reluctance (e.g. Deepwell and Syson, 1999). Other studies also talk about general reluctance, but have gone on to mention a lack of confidence, an inability to see the benefits of ICT use and a lack of a basic understanding of electronic communication and electronic resources (e.g. Sosabowski *et al.*, 1998). For the most part, where attitudes are mentioned, it is within the context of the need to create a 'culture shift' within HE (e.g Haywood *et al.*, 2000).

While many of these papers discuss staff attitudes based on anecdotal reflections about practice, some researchers have actively sought data on this particular topic. Haywood *et al.* (2000), for example, carried out a survey of the attitudes of Scottish staff to technology as part of an evaluation of the Learning Technology Dissemination Initiative. This showed most respondents felt that technology was important in teaching their own subject. Interestingly, most respondents felt that they were above average in terms of experience of using technology, and that 'many [other] academic staff were hostile to learning technology or unwilling to use it' (ibid., p. 10). One explanation offered for this is that committed staff viewed a lack of action by their colleagues as antipathy, rather than as a difference of priorities. Haywood *et al.* also found that there was a generally positive attitude towards the value of ICT, although length of experience in HE and views about its potential were negatively correlated. Staff who rated themselves as 'experts', together with staff in support roles, held a more pessimistic view and felt that their colleagues were unwilling or hostile towards adopting ICT in their teaching. Many staff viewed technology as a means of enhancing or maintaining quality; everyone felt that there were opportunities for quality to be enhanced. Although some hoped that ICT use might lead to savings in staff time, it was widely felt that increased demands on time would be inevitable. Finally, the study identified a number of difficulties associated with ICT use in the comments of respondents, including a general lack of time once high priority tasks have been accounted for, the generally low status of teaching compared with research, a lack of ICT skills and problems with the local infrastructure or the availability of relevant software.

Haywood *et al.*, however, investigated attitude at a very broad, general level which may not be adequate for professional developers who wish to try and engage with these attitudes. An alternative approach is provided by classification schemes such as those of Fox and Herrmann (2000), who identify a number of 'archetypal stances', based on case studies, associated with technology adoption. These are Neutralitarians, who view technology as an unproblematic tool, Boosters, who see new technologies as all powerful, Oppositionals, who resist technology on the grounds that it rejects human values, Sceptics, who doubt the hyperbolic rhetoric that surrounds technology, and Transformationalists, who see the introduction of technology as broadly positive and consider their role as discovering, understanding and guiding this transformation. Fox and Herrmann go on to explain how these stances can be used in professional development, with participants being asked to ally themselves with particular stances, to debate their positions, and to reflect in order to become 'more aware, more critical users of technology' (ibid., p. 74). While the classification may well be valuable, the derivation and the epistemological status of the stances remain unclear. Moreover, they represent a sanitised and simplified account of the complexity that is present in the reported case studies. Consequently, although they may form an interesting focus for reflection, they remain difficult to use as a way of understanding the way people draw on culturally available discourses to construct their attitudes.

A more grounded approach is provided by Steel and Hudson (2001), who describe a study that involved interviewing 11 academics about their attitudes towards educational technology. The authors identified a number of themes that arose in analysis, including efficiency, enrichment, flexibility, enhanced communication and the shift to 'student-centred' learning. They also found issues such as the 'fragility' of technology, the sense of 'dislocation' from students, perceived management instrumentalism, the commodification of education and the threats that might be posed to lecturers' identity and job security. Interestingly, these interviews also touched upon the process of using ICT, including the notion of technology being part of everyday work experience, or as being something 'dabbled' with. One interesting feature of this study is the recognition of how such themes are used by groups. There was, for example, a perception that management used the rhetoric of student-centred learning to justify changes that would lead to cost-cutting. However, this particular study concentrates on providing 'a backdrop of information' (ibid., p. 107), and on the possibility that such discourses can be used illustratively as descriptions that typify the level of experience of particular academics. Whilst this is important, it does little to explain how various societal pressures (which are acknowledged as playing an important role in adoption) are constructed, and even used by, those involved in the various different aspects of ICT use.

To summarise, three problems have arisen from the studies described above. First, there is a paucity of literature that addresses the topic of staff attitudes to ICT use. Secondly, where research does exist, it remains very general and fairly simplistic. Finally, while a more grounded study of attitude generated a list of themes which do provide a more detailed account of attitudes, the approach that was adopted does not account for the relationship between these and issues of power or identity construction. This study attempts to address these issues by using Discourse Analysis to deconstruct a variety of statements about the possible impact of ICT on HE.

20.3 Methods

Discourse can be broadly defined as language in use and Discourse Analysis as trying to develop a theory of language in use. In a comprehensive introduction to the field Wetherell *et al.* (2001a) argue that researchers should be interested in language in use and meaning-making because the predominant intellectual movements of Western societies in recent years, poststructuralism and postmodernism, have focused attention on how knowledge is constituted through language. Wetherell describes how a 'turn to discourse' has taken place across the social sciences in the last decades of the twentieth century. This rejects the idea that language can simply describe reality or allow individuals to express inner states. Instead Discourse Analysis is a scientific method which seeks to discover and theorise patterns and order in the construction of identity, the process of making sense and the organisation of social relations. It is an entirely qualitative method but its rigour comes from the systematic and exhaustive way the text is approached.

The present study seeks to explore attitudes. However, the concept of 'attitude' has been subject to heavy criticism by social psychologists following Potter and Wetherell (1987). Traditional conceptions of attitudes have been beset with difficulties in defining attitudinal objects in a way that is universally recognised, and in producing measurable scales with a limited number of dimensions. They have also found inconsistency, contradiction and contextual variability in their attempts to define and measure attitudes, which threaten reliability and validity. Discursive psychologists have entirely rejected the idea that individuals hold 'attitudes' in their heads, which can be expressed through words or ticks in boxes marked 'agree' or 'strongly disagree'. Instead, they claim that people use language to create the objects of which they speak, to position themselves and others, and to make some ideas seem natural and right and others unthinkable. In doing so, no individual starts with a blank slate but uses the materials that are culturally available to them to construct their own account of reality. These materials are the discursive repertoires which the present study therefore seeks to identify in the interviews and texts which are analysed.

Although the field of discourse analysis is very young compared to other areas of social science there are different traditions and approaches. Wetherell *et al.* (2001b) identifies different traditions associated with Conversation Analysis, Sociolinguistics, Discursive Psychology, Critical Discourse Analysis and Foucauldian Discourse Analysis. The present study is perhaps most closely allied with discursive psychology in its focus on the discursive repertoires and rhetorical stances which people adopt in varying situations, but follows the procedures set out by Banister *et al.* (1994) which are influenced by Foucault's work and the poststructuralist tradition.

20.3.1   The selection of sources for analysis

In this study, two contrasting sources of data were selected, in order to allow comparisons to be drawn.

The first source was created specifically for this study. An email was sent to lecturers on the probationers' programme at UCL, who were just completing their first year of employment, explaining the purpose of the study and inviting them to take part. Six interviews were carried out. These were unstructured, taking the form of a conversation between the interviewer(s) and interviewee, although in practice the interviewees dominated the discussion. All the interviews commenced with the same question: 'How do you think that the use of information and communications technology will change teaching and learning in higher education over the next five years?' Unfortunately, environmental conditions such as excessive background noise meant that only four of these interviews could be transcribed in any level of detail. Of these four, two were selected as being particularly clear and interesting.

The second source of data consisted of material drawn from published sources which focused on predictions about the impact of technology in HE. These samples represented formal texts, as presented by influential people with relevant expertise. Two such sources were selected: an excerpt from the Dearing Report (NCIHE, 1997), and an introduction to a report by the Computers in Teaching Initiative (1992).

The Dearing Report was selected because of its wide influence on the sector. It is also a work that is widely associated with experts in this area, such as Diana Laurillard, whose book *Rethinking University Teaching* (1993) is one of the most widely cited texts in learning technology literature in the UK. For these reasons, the report represents an important expression of the opinions of influential people in the area. Its relevance for this study was further increased by the fact that it sets out to provide 'a vision for 20 years', something which clearly relates to the shorter-term visions discussed in the interviews. Since the report as a whole is far too extensive to analyse, a series of relevant excerpts was considered instead.

These were identified by searching an electronic version of the summary report for the use of the word 'technology' or the acronym 'C&IT'. All paragraphs and recommendations where either of these terms was used were included (paragraphs 20, 24, 34, 38, 65–8, 75 and 121 were included, as were recommendations 21, 41 and 46), along with the entire appendix on new approaches to teaching (Appendix 2).

The Computers in Teaching Initiative (CTI) report was produced after eight years of operation, to 'draw on the Initiative's experience to spell out the rationale for learning technology in higher education' (CTI, 1992, p. 5). The initiative was a HEFCE-funded national network that actively supported academics' use of ICT. The first section of the report is entitled, 'Previewing Higher Education in 2000'; much of this focused on how technology would affect teaching and learning. Importantly, the authorship of this section was unattributed, implying that it was subscribed to by the 39 contributors listed in the report, many of whom are still working and publishing on these topics. As such, it fulfilled the criteria of being close to the topic of the interviews and representing the voice of experts in the area.

The sources were then analysed, following Banister *et al.*'s method, collaboratively in order to ensure consistency and also to see whether our personal interpretations of the data were credible to each other.

20.4   Findings

In this section, the discourses identified through analysis of four different sources will be presented. Each source will be discussed in turn.

20.4.1   Source one

The first interview was with a probationary lecturer who taught a topic with an international focus, and who was away from the campus for a large proportion of each week. Of particular interest to him were the way in which technology allowed knowledge to be represented, and the practical pitfalls of being allowed to produce web-based 'portals' (see Belcher *et al.*, 2000) or CD-ROMS of materials. Analysis of the interview led to the following discourses being identified:

20.4.1.1   *The nature of knowledge*

Several different metaphors were used to describe knowledge:

- *Knowledge as a commodity.* The metaphor of knowledge as a commodity frequently recurs throughout the interview. The commodity is given or presented by the lecturer to the students in packages of raw materials or readings. It needs to be stored by the lecturer in a way that permits easy retrieval. The commodity can take different forms, such as books, journals, papers, CD-ROMS. The commodity is owned, by IPR, which prevents free distribution of the commodity, which must be paid for through subscriptions or CLA packs.

- *Knowledge as a terrain.* Knowledge has almost physical properties; it is arranged in areas, which are where people work, but these areas also contain important people. The people who work in these areas understand the local context, and can write guides for others (students) to follow. Without such a guide, students can get lost.

- *Knowledge as a hypertext* Knowledge (or knowledge artefacts such as papers) often has to be arranged along a single dimension, but its natural structure can be represented in three dimensions. Thus electronic representations of knowledge such as hypertexts are closer to this natural structure than traditional, linear papers, and web-based portals are better at managing these papers than filing cabinets. Both portals and filing cabinets are structured according to our personal understanding of the natural structure of knowledge.

20.4.1.2   The role of the intermediator

Lecturers know the relative value of pieces of knowledge. This enables the lecturer to filter information for students, who trust their judgement, and who would otherwise be unable to distinguish important things from marginal ones. Similarly, publishers can act as intermediators, providing quality control and validation in an era when anyone can publish anything. Trusting the recommendations of such intermediators saves students' time. This requires the acceptance of the knowledge as a commodity discourse and seems closely related to another metaphor of the lecturer as an interpreter for students.

20.4.1.3   The absent discourse of students

The voices of students are not represented anywhere, nor are they represented as agentic constructors of knowledge.

20.4.1.4   Networks

Networks are social structures, comprising of people who share common interests. Networks are international, and some are becoming 'virtual', in that communication is taking place via computers. Participating in a network is a learning process; this is a result of learning being a social process, of being a consequence of socialisation, which is an essential part of teaching. People (and, specifically, students) can be brought into your network by talking to them a lot.

20.4.2   Source two

The second interview was also with a probationary lecturer, working in science. Whilst she was clearly interested in technology, she was concerned about where the uses to which it was put and where responsibility for development work should lie. Analysis of the interview led to the following discourses being identified.

20.4.2.1   A new generation

The interviewee positioned herself as part of a new generation: a vanguard of younger lecturers and students who use technology to obtain information in the same way as they use books and papers and to do research. Thus technology should be integrated into the undergraduate study of their discipline. She contrasts this with an older generation of lecturers who do not use technology to do web searches or even word-processing themselves, possibly because they just don't like technology (even technology as homely as the microwave). She suggests they are incorrectly and ignorantly fearful of plagiarism of information made public through technology, and that they are unlikely to change their ways. This older generation of lecturers are presented as a problem that cause her frustration, who may be the majority in her department or may be leading the department. This frustration seems natural and understandable following her construction of the younger and older generations, and implies the only solution will be time, and the retirement of the older generation. She also establishes herself, as part of the new generation, as someone who has sought to correct the errors of the older generation.

20.4.2.2 The benefits of technology

A number of benefits are identified as being associated with technology. These include its use as a means of obtaining information, providing extras, such as very good illustrations, permitting interactive material so that students can prepare for assessments, providing publicity about courses to recruit good students, enabling differentiation (from remedial exercises to build confidence of weaker students to additional reading for advanced students) which is not permitted by lectures. Also, facilitating students' production of word-processed homework (which makes marking easier and quicker) and lecturers' production of word-processed tutorial questions which are free from spelling errors. In addition, technology in her own discipline is constructed as a valuable research method and as being related to a sought-after profession.

20.4.2.3 Job specification (is web authoring the new copy typing?)

The creation and maintenance of web pages is constructed as an additional burden on lecturers who can't or won't do it, and this burden should be relieved by a person, or by a new job specification for an administrator that takes on the creation, updating and maintenance of web pages. The presentation of who is qualified to do web authoring, maintenance, and updating is particularly interesting. Students can, but shouldn't be expected to, put aside their other work to do so. Administrators can do so as part of their job description as this is a valuable opportunity for them. There is some contradiction about whether lecturers might be able to, but the implication is that their time is too precious to burden them with this extra demand on their time. The only three references to 'someone' in the entire transcript are all in reference to 'someone' who must be paid to produce web pages.

20.4.3 Source three

The third source comprised excerpts from the Dearing report (NCIHE, 1997), which set forth a vision of the future of lifelong learning in the UK. These included an appendix on new approaches to teaching, much of which was concerned with costs, which lent a distinctive economic feel to some of the discourses that were identified through analysis.

20.4.3.1 The passivity of students

Apart from making an informed choice about which course to take (when given appropriate information), students are then 'developed' by HE.

20.4.3.2 The lecturer as materials developer

Traditional teaching methods cannot cope with expanded student numbers; the future will involve lecturers giving up teaching in order to concentrate on creating high-quality resources which will 'enshrine the core of their teaching'.

20.4.3.3 Education serves global competition

Society is competitive, nations compete, and in order to aid in this struggle, universities must compete.

20.4.3.4   Resource-based learning is the (expensive) future for HE

The expansion of student numbers renders most teaching methods ineffective; the only solution will be for institutions to collaborate to produce high quality (ICT) resources so that students can use these independently, without requiring additional time from lecturers.

20.4.3.5   Technology creates access to information

Information, which is a commodity, can be provided to students. Students need technology to have better access to information.

20.4.3.6   Education as the purchase of learning outcomes

Courses can be described in terms of their costs, and must be described in terms of their learning outcomes. Students make informed choices about courses, and are then developed by them.

20.4.3.7   The changing nature of HE

Student expansion with a decreasing resource per student is causing changes to HE. As numbers increase, existing methods of teaching become cost-ineffective. Groups sizes increase, diminishing the learning experience for students. In order to cope with this, managers take imaginative leaps to create strategies that cause change, and in doing so carry out experiments that might find solutions to these problems.

20.4.4   Source four

The fourth source was the introduction to the CTI report (1992), which previewed HE ten years from the time of writing. Analysis of this introduction revealed the following discourses:

20.4.4.1   The sceptical academic

Academics have a clear set of values, such as the link between research and teaching, and will not trust pre-prepared materials where they feel no sense of ownership.

20.4.4.2   A new era

This particular discourse contained two distinct components, which are related in the way that they contrast the current (or emerging) situation with what has gone before. These are:

- *A new generation.* Students and staff are different from how they were a decade ago. Students are increasingly diverse in some ways (such as age and background), but more uniform in others (such as computer ownership and literacy). Staff will be replaced as they retire by new teachers who will be open to a new academic culture, will be innovative and will use technology.

- *The changing sector.* HE has unified, expanded, and changed from elite to mass entry. This has altered its culture, so that teaching will be valued. The sector will also work in a more unified manner, with telecommunication across campuses, students transferring as a result of modular courses, and staff collaborating across institutions to produce courseware.

20.4.4.3   From individual to mass teaching

Changes in the sector have changed the type of teaching that can be carried out: individual, traditional forms (such as tutorials) will become impossible, and the collaborative, industrialised production of technology-based materials (particularly online materials) for widespread use will start to happen. This will make teaching more cost-effective.

20.4.4.4 *Teaching as a generic activity*

Although disciplines are the places where skills and knowledge are acquired, teaching cuts across this. Teaching happens in a range of contexts, and materials produced in one institution will be useable in others. The production of materials will involve standardised authoring tools and standardised delivery systems across consortia of institutions.

20.5   Conclusions

The analysis of the texts described above has led to the identification of a number of discourses that have been used to justify particular positions, characterise groups of people and establish relationships between these. Having reached this point, it is possible to examine the implications of the discourses and the ways in which they support or contradict each other, and how they create or reinforce particular power structures in society.

The recurrent discourse of a new generation, for example, is interesting in a number of respects. First, as used in source two, it is dependent on the idea that there are benefits to technology. However, it functions to protect this related discourse, putting it beyond the reach of criticism by identifying any critic as inherently being of the 'old' order. Similarly, in source four, it is used to naturalise the notion of the changing sector. A new generation will inevitably have different requirements to the old one; consequently, it is only reasonable to expect the sector to change in response to this.

Contradictions are also evident both between sources and within sources. For example, competition between universities is talked about within the Dearing Report (source three) as the inevitable competition of capitalism. However, this seems inconsistent with the suggestion that universities will have to co-operate by forming consortia in order to meet development costs for resource-based learning. What frames both accounts is the assumption that a rational analysis of economic costs is the only basis for decisions about HE.

The construction of the role of students and staff is central to any analysis. The Dearing Report's discourse of passivity of students operates to make HE accountable, because if once enrolled students have no possibility to influence their situation then institutions must be more responsible for what they do with students. The commodification of knowledge supports the transformation of students from learners to consumers, and ultimately purchasers of learning outcomes. This role of staff seems particularly rich in contrasts. While the Dearing Report characterises academic staff as material developers (a discursive move which supports its advocacy of resource-based learning), the job specification discourse in source two clearly rejects the notion that developing web-based resources is an appropriate task for an academic. The Dearing Report's depiction of academics as materials developers giving up contact with students as numbers expand also contrasts with the academic as intermediator, interpreting knowledge for students and drawing the students into their network in source one.

Such rhetorical tactics provide an important insight into the agendas of different groups with an interest in ICT. Doing this not only allows a better understanding both of academics' and experts' discursive repertoires, it has also permitted differences between these to be illustrated. This has a direct value for staff working with academics to support or encourage ICT use. By developing an awareness of the ways in which this may be constituted in talk, and understanding the stakes that are held and the ways that particular discourses are used to protect these, it becomes apparent that approaches which focus on skills development are likely to have only a limited impact. Instead, it becomes necessary to frame professional development as a critical debate, in which the interests of policy makers can be subjected to scrutiny, as can the interests of the academics and of the professional developers themselves.

Finally, it is worth noting that the analysis described in this chapter has, of necessity, remained relatively quiet on the mechanisms through which identities and power relationships are constructed. Also, little attempt has been made to frame these discourses in relation to a wider social and historical context. Whilst these are important issues, this chapter has laid the necessary groundwork by identifying a repertoire of discourses that can now be examined in greater depth. Such scrutiny forms an obvious next step in the development of this work, and promises a richer understanding of the discursive context of HE in which teaching, learning and ICT are constructed.

20.6   References

Åkerlind, G. and Trevitt, A. (1999) Enhancing self-directed learning through educational technology: when students resist the change, *Innovations in Education and Training International* **36**(2): 96–105.

Bacsish, P. and Ash, C. (2000) Costing the lifecycle of networked learning: documenting the costs from conception to evaluation, *ALT-J* **8**(1): 92–100.

Banister, P., Burman, E., Parker, I., Taylor, M. and Tindall, C. (1994) *Qualitative Methods in Psychology: A Research Guide*. Buckingham: Open University Press.

Belcher, M., Place, E. and Conole, G. (2000) Quality assurance in subject gateways: creating high quality portals on the Internet, *Quality Assurance in Education* **8**(1): 38–47.

CTI – Computers in Teaching Initiative (1992) *Computers in University Teaching: Core Tools for Core Activities*. CTISS: Oxford.

Conole, G. and Oliver, M. (1998) A pedagogical framework for embedding C&IT into the curriculum, *ALT-J* **6**(2): 4–16.

Deepwell, F. and Syson, A. (1999) Online learning at Coventry University: you can lead a horse to water ..., *Educational Technology & Society* **2**(4): 122–4.

Fox, R. and Herrmann, A. (2000) Changing media, changing times: coping with adopting new educational technologies. In T. Evans and D. Nation (2000) *Changing University Teaching: Reflections on Creating Educational Technologies*, 73–88. London: Kogan Page.

Jones, C. (1998) Evaluating a collaborative online learning environment, *Active Learning* **9**: 31–5.

Haywood, J., Anderson, C., Coyle, H., Day, K., Haywood, D. and MacLeod, H. (2000) Learning Technology in Scottish higher education – a survey of the views of senior managers, academic staff and 'experts', *ALT-J* **8**(2): 5–17.

Laurillard, D. (1993) *Rethinking University Teaching: a Framework for the Effective Use of Educational Technology*. London: Routledge.

National Committee of Inquiry into Higher Education (1997) *Higher Education in the Learning Society*. London: HMSO.

Oliver, M. (2000) An introduction to the Evaluation of Learning Technology, *Educational Technology & Society* **3**(4): 20–30.

Potter, J. and Wetherell, M. (1987) *Discourse and Social Psychology: Beyond Attitudes and Behaviour*. London: Sage.

Sosabowski, M., Herson, K. and Lloyd, A. (1998) Identifying and overcoming staff resistance to computer based learning and teaching methods: shedding millstones to achieve milestones, *Active Learning* **9**: 26–30.

Steel, J. and Hudson, A. (2001) Educational technology in learning and teaching: the perceptions and experience of teaching staff, *Innovations in Education and Training International* **38**(2): 103–11.

Wetherell, M., Taylor, S. and Yates, S.J. (eds) (2001a) *Discourse Theory and Practice: A Reader*. London: OU/Sage.

Wetherell, M., Taylor, S. and Yates, S.J. (eds) (2001b) *Discourse as Data: A Guide for Analysis*. London: OU/Sage.

21 The distance learning task as a pedagogical context for learning technologies: are students' and tutors' perceptions similar?

Wendy Garner, Lin S. Norton, Simon Asquith, Audrey Beaumont and Steven Caldecott

Liverpool Hope, UK

Keywords
  B.Ed students; distance learning; Ideal Distance Learning Task Inventory; tutors' and students' perceptions

21.1   Overview

A hundred 4th year B.Ed (Bachelor of Education) students and their tutors took part in a research study to ascertain how similar their perceptions were of the characteristics of a distance learning task. An adaptation of the Ideal Self Inventory (ISI) (Norton, Morgan and Thomas 1995; Tilley and Norton, 1998) was given to 14 tutors who generated 90 characteristics describing their view of an 'ideal distance learning task'. Subsequent content analysis yielded a 6-item version of the 'ideal distance learning task' representing the tutors' composite views which was then given to students to rate according to their own experiences of having undertaken distance learning tasks during the course of their B.Ed degree. The research findings will be discussed in the framework of researching pedagogical issues of distance learning. Readers will be invited to explore the ISI methodology relating to their own use of learning technologies and distance learning tasks.

21.2   Theoretical background

Using learning technologies to improve student learning should mean focusing on the pedagogical philosophies and then using the technology to fit those philosophies rather than starting the other way round (Forsyth, 1998). A similar point is made by Laurillard (1993) who writes:

> Educational technologies, especially new ones, attract effort and ingenuity to the design and development of materials, but rarely to the embedding of those materials in their educational niche. (p. 210).

The purpose of this chapter is to look at one such educational niche – how the 'ideal distance learning task' is conceptualised by both tutors and students. Currently there appears to have been little quality research carried out on distance education but Richardson (2000) makes a convincing case for applying mainstream pedagogical issues to distance learning. One of the robust findings to come out of the mainstream research has been the effect of the teaching context on how students learn. Applying this to the use of learning technologies in distance tasks means that teachers should ensure that the demands of the task are compatible with their pedagogic intentions. One way of doing this is to establish whether or not students' and tutors' perceptions of the task will be similar.

21.3   Methodology

21.3.1   Stage 1: eliciting tutors' views of the ideal distance learning task

During a residential staff development weekend, tutors from the Education Deanery at a college of higher education in the North West of England were asked to complete an adapted version of the Ideal Self Inventory (ISI) with a view to eliciting their view of the characteristics of an ideal/non-ideal distance learning task. To do this the original inventory was renamed the Ideal Distance Learning Inventory (IDLTI) and Wedemeyer's (1971) definition of distance learning was given:

> providing learners with opportunities to continue learning in their own environments, and of developing in all learners the capacity to carry on self-directed learning.

The tutors were made aware of the purpose of completing the IDLTI, by the researchers and were told that their responses would inform the subsequent stages of the study. Tutors were asked to read the instructions carefully. These read as follows:

1.   Using the definition and thinking about distance learning tasks that you have had experience of, list six characteristics that would describe your ideal distance learning task. On each line list their opposites to describe your not ideal distance learning task. These descriptions can be words or short phrases. Please note that the opposites do not have to be literal opposites, it's how you choose to describe them that is important.
2.   Now put these characteristics into rank order by deciding which characteristic is the most important and assigning a 1 to it in the column headed 'Rank', and continue until you reach the least important characteristic and label that 6. See the example in Figure 21.1

Example IDLTI

Rank	An ideal distance learning task	A not ideal distance learning task
6	Is clearly related to overall aim of module	Is one that you can't see the point of
3	Has been clearly explained by the tutor	Has been given to occupy students and free tutors' time

Your IDLTI

Rank	An ideal distance learning task	A not ideal distance learning task

Figure 21.1

Tutors were asked to complete the IDLTI in their own time; 14 responses were collected from tutors during the following few days. No difficulties in completing the IDLTI were reported.

21.3.2   Stage 2: content analysis of tutor responses

The 14 completed tutor IDLTIs were then content analysed by the first author and by a research assistant. This process involved creating categories in which similar responses could be grouped and then assigning each tutor characteristic into one of the categories. Through a process of iteration, merging and deleting categories, a final version of the IDLTI was produced which represented the 'composite' tutor's view of an ideal distance learning task. See Figure 21.2

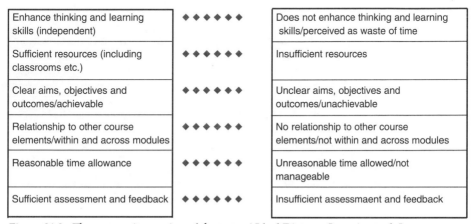

Figure 21.2   The composite version of the tutors' Ideal Distance Learning task Inventory

21.3.3   Stage 3: student responses

During a core Year 4 Education lecture, a class of final year B.Ed students were asked to complete the composite tutors' IDLTI with a view to eliciting the degree of match between their experience of distance learning tasks during the course of their study and their tutors' perception of ideal distance learning tasks. The order of the 'ideal' and 'not ideal' dimensions of the characteristics was changed in the version given to the students to avoid response set (i.e. in both the left hand and right hand columns there was a mix of 'ideal and 'not ideal' dimensions, unlike Figure 21.2 which shows all the 'ideal' in the left hand column and all the 'not ideal' in the right hand column). The students' version also contained the Wedemeyer definition and the following instructions:

1.   Below is a list of characteristics that represent your tutors' collective view of the characteristics of a distance learning task.
2.   Looking at each characteristic, please circle the point which you think most closely matches your experience of distance learning tasks.

The students were made aware of the purpose of completing the IDLTI and the way in which their responses would inform the subsequent stages of the project. The role of research data in course evaluation was also discussed. Examples of distance learning tasks administered by tutors during the B.Ed course were presented so that students had a shared understanding of the term 'distance learning task'. Students were asked to carefully read the instructions on the IDLTI regarding its completion. 100 responses were collected from students at the end of the lecture. No difficulties in completing the IDLTI were reported.

21.3.4   Stage 4: comparing tutors' and students' perceptions

The final stage of this study was to ask the 14 tutors also to complete their own composite inventory of that given to the students. This was intended to ascertain the degree of match between tutors' perceptions of the student experience and the students' perceptions of their own experiences. These findings are currently being prepared for publication elsewhere.

21.4   Results

The students' completed IDLTI's were then scored for each tutor-defined characteristic on a scale of 5 to 1 where 5 signified the point closest to the 'ideal dimension' of the characteristic and 1 signified the point closest to the 'not ideal' dimension. In this way each completed IDLTI yielded individual scores for each characteristic plus an overall range of scores from 30 to 6, where the higher the score the more students would perceive their experience of having done distance learning tasks to match their lecturers' conception of an ideal task.

21.4.1   Overall ratings of the IDLTI

Looking first at the students' overall ratings, this produced a mean of 18.24 (sd 3.32), with a minimum score of 11 and a maximum score of 26. For a distribution of students' overall scores, see Figure 21.3.

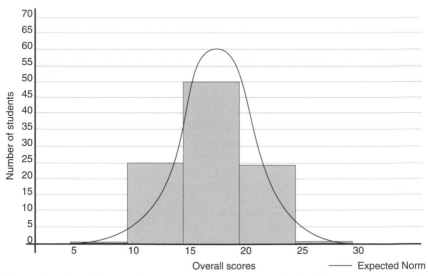

Figure 21.3   Distribution of students' overall scores on the Ideal Distance Learning Task Inventory

In terms of percentages this meant:

- 25 per cent of the students rated the distance learning tasks they had experienced as very positive overall (scored 21 or over)

- 50 per cent of the students rated the distance learning tasks they had experienced as fairly positive overall (scored between 15 and 20)

- 25 per cent of the students rated the distance learning tasks they had experienced as slightly negative overall (scored between 10 and 15)

- None of the students rated the distance learning tasks they had experienced as very negative overall (scored less than 10).

These findings suggest that the final year B.Ed students who participated in this study were positive in general about distance learning tasks they had experienced. To tease out further, where their perceptions differed and where they were less positive, each of the six tutor-defined characteristics were then examined individually. The results of these separate analyses will now be presented in turn.

21.4.1.1 Enhances thinking and learning skills versus does not enhance thinking and learning skills/perceived as a waste of time

Analysing students' ratings of this characteristic produced a mean of 3.12 (sd 1.09), with a minimum score of 1 and a maximum score of 5. For a distribution of students' overall scores, see Figure 21.4.

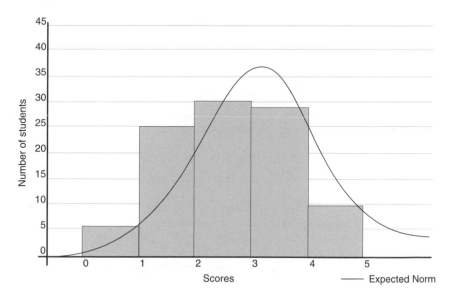

Figure 21.4 Distribution of students' scores on the thinking and learning skills characteristic

In terms of percentages, 39 per cent thought their experiences of a distance learning task definitely enhanced thinking and learning skills (scored 4 or above); 30 per cent were not very sure (scored 3) and, 31 per cent thought their experience of a distance learning task did not enhance learning thinking skills and was perceived as a waste of time (scored 2 or below).

Clearly, these findings showed quite a strong difference of opinion with the majority of students expressing some reservations about the usefulness of such tasks in enhancing their thinking and learning skills.

21.4.1.2 *Sufficient resources including classrooms/computer suites etc. versus insufficient resources*

Analysing students' ratings of this characteristic produced a mean of 2.64 (sd 0.85), with a minimum score of 1 and a maximum score of 4. For a distribution of students' overall scores, see Figure 21.5.

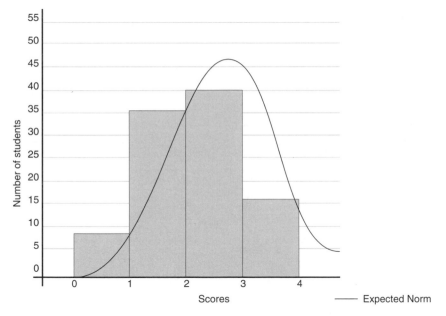

Figure 21.5 Distribution of students' scores on the resources characteristic

In terms of percentages, only 16 per cent of students thought there were sufficient resources for the distance learning tasks they had experienced (scored 4), and in fact no student rated this as 5; 40 per cent weren't sure (scored 3) and, 44 per cent thought there were insufficient resources for the distance learning tasks they had experienced (scored 2 or below).

On the issue of resources, then, most of the students thought the distance learning tasks they had experienced were insufficiently resourced.

21.4.1.3 Clear aims, objectives and outcomes versus unclear aims, objectives and outcomes

Analysing students' ratings of this characteristic produced a mean of 3.33 (sd 1.04), with a minimum score of 1 and a maximum score of 5. For a distribution of students' overall scores, see Figure 21.6.

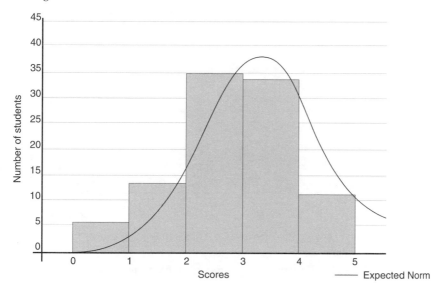

Figure 21.6   Distribution of students' scores on the aims, objectives and outcomes characteristic

In terms of percentages, 46 per cent thought the aims, objectives and outcomes of distance learning tasks they had experienced were clear (scored 4 or above); 35 per cent weren't sure (scored 3) and, 19 per cent thought the aims, objectives and outcomes of distance learning tasks they had experienced were unclear (scored 2 or below).

As far as this characteristic was concerned, the ratings were more positive, although just over a third were not sure.

21.4.1.4 Relationship to other course elements/modules versus no relationship to other course elements/modules

Analysing students' ratings of this characteristic produced a mean of 3.02 (sd 0.92), with a minimum score of 1 and a maximum score of 5. For a distribution of students' overall scores, see Figure 21.7.

In terms of percentages, 33 per cent thought the distance learning tasks they had experienced were related to other course elements/modules (scored 4 or above); 37 per cent weren't sure (scored 3) and, 30 per cent thought the distance learning tasks they had experienced were not related to other course elements/modules (scored 2 or below).

These results show an almost equal split into thirds between positive, negative and not sure.

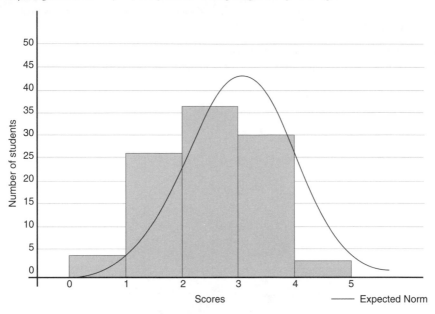

Figure 21.7   Distribution of students' scores on therelationship to other course
elements/modules characteristic

21.4.1.5   *Reasonable time allowance versus unreasonable time allowance*

Analysing students' ratings of this characteristic produced a mean of 3.76 (sd 1.06), with a
minimum score of 1 and a maximum score of 5. For a distribution of students' overall scores,
see Figure 21.8.

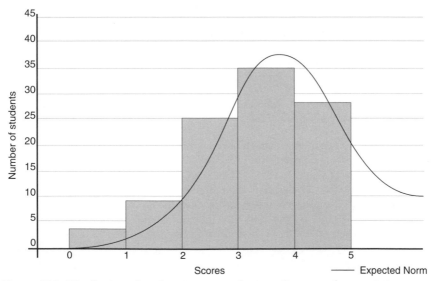

Figure .21.8 Distribution of students' scores on thetime allowance characteristic

In terms of percentages, 63 per cent thought that there was a reasonable time allowance for the distance learning tasks they had experienced (scored 4 or above); 25 per cent weren't sure (scored 3) and, 12 per cent thought there was an unreasonable time allowance for the distance learning tasks they had experienced (scored 2 or below).

Of all the individual characteristics of the IDLTI, this one on time allowance was viewed the most positively by the students.

21.4.1.6 *Sufficient assessment and feedback versus insufficient assessment and feedback*

Analysing students' ratings of this characteristic produced a mean of 2.32 (sd 1.17), with a minimum score of 1 and a maximum score of 5. For a distribution of students' overall scores, see Figure 21.9.

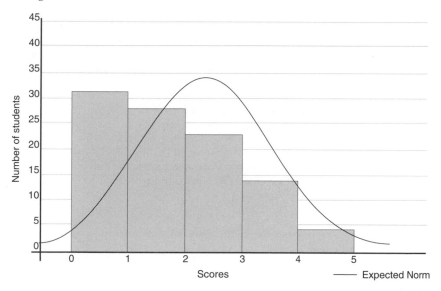

Figure 21.9   Distribution of students' scores on the assessment and feedback characteristic

In terms of percentages, only 18 per cent thought there was sufficient assessment and feedback on the distance learning tasks they had experienced (scored 4 or above); 23 per cent weren't sure (scored 3) and, 59 per cent thought there was insufficient assessment and feedback on the distance learning tasks they had experienced (scored 2 or below).

Clearly this finding shows that this is the characteristic of the distance learning task that students see as the most unsatisfactory, in terms of their own experience.

21.5   Conclusions

The main conclusion of this study is that the distance learning tasks experienced by these students need to be reviewed. Although the overall ratings of the IDLTI were positive, the breakdown analysis showed two areas, in particular, that need attention. Specifically, these results suggest that resource implications of such tasks and assessment and feedback relating to such tasks need to be considered critically by tutors on this programme. Since the other four characteristics were perceived more positively, this might suggest that there is a distinction between task documentation and task execution. The characteristics which might usually be defined within the task documentation/ explanation, such as timescale, aims and objectives, development of thinking skills, and relation to other course components were generally perceived as reasonably satisfactory, whereas the characteristics relating to subsequent stages of the task – execution (using resources) and assessment – were generally perceived as unsatisfactory. In reality, the latter two characteristics are often the most time consuming aspects of task-setting for tutors and therefore it would be worth exploring the extent to which resource auditing, assessment and feedback are effectively undertaken with regard to such tasks.

21.5.1   Implications

Distance learning tasks, some of which will require the use learning technologies (web-based learning for example), need to be firmly rooted in pedagogic philosophy and clearly defined learning intentions. This study implies that for these intentions to be fully realised, sufficient and appropriate resources and feedback (in addition to other important characteristics of effective teaching and learning contexts), are essential for student satisfaction and recognition of their own learning.

21.5.2   The Ideal Self Inventory as a research tool

This inventory has been used in a number of different applications including pedagogical research such as the study described here. It is now called the Ideal *** Inventory (Norton, 2001) and colleagues who would like to use it in their own research or find out more about its potential applications are invited to contact Lin Norton (nortonl@hope.ac.uk)

Acknowledgements

The authors gratefully acknowledge the contribution of Sandra Ardley who acted as research assistant on this research project.

21.6   References

Forsyth, I. (1998) *Teaching and Learning Materials and the Internet*, 2nd edn. London: Kogan Page

Laurillard, D. (1993) *Rethinking University Teaching: A Framework for the Effective Use of Technology*. London: Routledge.

Norton, LS (2001) The Ideal *** Inventory. A useful tool for pedagogical research in higher education. Electronic paper produced for the ILT Members' Resource Area.

Norton, L.S., Morgan, K. and Thomas, S. (1995) The Ideal Self Inventory: a new measure of self esteem', *Counselling Psychology Quarterly* **8**(4): 305–10.

Richardson, J.T.E. (2000) *Researching Student Learning: Approaches to Studying in Campus-based and Distance Education*. Buckingham: The Society of Research into Higher Education and Open University Press.

Tilley, A. and Norton, L.S. (1998) Psychology lecturers' conceptions of the ideal student using the Ideal Self Inventory (ISI)., *Psychology Teaching Review* **7**(1): 14–23.

22 Building a European Internet School: the OTIS experience of collaborative learning

Sharon Green,[a] Gillian Armitt,[b] Martin Beer,[b] Andrew Sixsmith,[c] Johanna van Bruggen,[d] Ramon Daniels,[d] Ludo Ghyselen,[e] and Jan Sandqvist[f]

a. Department of Occupational Therapy, University of Liverpool; b. Department of Computer Science, University of Liverpool; c. Department of Primary Care, University of Liverpool; d. Department of Occupational Therapy, Hogeschool van Amsterdam, Amsterdam, Netherlands; e. Department of Occupational Therapy, Hogeschool West-Vlaanderen, Belgium; f. Department of Occupational Therapy, Linköpings Universitet, Linköping, Sweden

Keywords

case studies; e-learning; occupational therapy; problem-solving approach

22.1   Overview

In common with other health professionals, occupational therapists are required to work collaboratively in addressing client needs. Resolution of such needs may sometimes be facilitated by high-level assistive technology, the application of which varies widely across Europe. The new exploratory Occupational Therapy Internet School (OTIS) united these major themes, as it supported a European collaborative approach to assistive technology learning for occupational therapists and students in Belgium, the Netherlands, Sweden and the UK. OTIS adopted a problem-based learning style, in which students communicated online with tutors, their peers, patients and experts, in order to propose solutions to carefully designed case studies. The supporting Internet environment is based on the Virtual Campus metaphor and has been specifically developed to promote collaboration and a problem-solving approach. Student and tutor evaluations plus assessment results show that some students performed very well, despite language barriers, while others struggled to understand both the concept and content of the course. The SOLO technique revealed the development of deep learning during the course. A number of practical issues have been encountered in developing and running the OTIS pilot course within an international context, for example, collaborative management, language, and the need to comply with a diverse pattern of term dates and working hours.

22.2   Introduction

The OTIS project was a feasibility study for setting up a virtual Internet School across collaborating institutions. Partners in four European countries collaborated in the design, delivery and evaluation of a course that promoted a high degree of interaction between students in the different countries. The OTIS pilot course, entitled *High Level Assistive Technology in European Occupational Therapy*, was undertaken by occupational therapy students and postgraduates in West-Vlaanderen in Belgium, Amsterdam in the Netherlands, Linköping in Sweden and Liverpool in the UK.

Prior research (HEART, 1995) has indicated that technology awareness among health professionals needs to be improved. The same HEART report recommends:

> A European curriculum with similarities between the European countries, is of great importance for the development of assistive technology, for addressing the needs of the elderly and disabled and to form a single market in this field. (HEART, 1995, p. 18)

European research funding via the TENTelecom programme has enabled the OTIS project to address the HEART Report's recommendations in an innovative way within the occupational therapy domain. It is helpful for occupational therapists to be familiar with different approaches in use in other European countries. Many students each year, as in other disciplines, now take up a module that is taught in another country, where the curriculum is recognised to be comparable. Ultimately too there is transferability in the workplace. For example an occupational therapist who qualifies in the UK becomes a member of the World Federation of Occupational Therapists, and can then practise in any European country or in many other countries further afield.

Specifically the TENTelecom funding supported the following collaborative work:

- development of course materials;
- running and comprehensive evaluation of a full pilot course addressing high level assistive technology;
- design of a business plan with a view to introducing further courses.

This chapter describes the stages in the process of course design and delivery and the evaluation results obtained.

22.3 Collaborative course design

There was unanimous agreement that the OTIS course must be stimulating and must promote the deep learning essential for today's health professionals. Educators suggest that students who are personally involved in learning from real life situations are the ones who are most likely to experience deep learning. McAllister *et al.* (1997) suggest that

> deep approaches to learning are found in students who are affectively involved in searching for personal meaning and understanding (their own personal practical knowledge), seeing the whole picture or person – not just the isolated features or disembodied problems – drawing on their personal experience to make sense of new ideas and experiences and relating evidence to conclusion. These deep learning approaches are in marked contrast to surface approaches exhibited by students who seek only to memorise and reproduce information or skills, see only the discrete 'bits', expect the educator to be in control of their learning, and are largely motivated by the external imperative to pass an assignment or gain their qualification.

It is important for all health professionals to experience deep learning in their professional training programmes. This not only ensures quality learning but it is also a safeguard for the future, in that such health professionals are most likely to display a holistic approach to their clients, with emphasis on quality of care. Clinical education has been shown to be effective in facilitating deep learning (Coles, 1989; 1990) and for students in the academic environment, realistic case studies explored via a stimulating problem-solving approach, can form a close approximation to learning from real life.

There was agreement too that problem-based learning was an appropriate method of learning for the OTIS students, but there was not unanimous agreement as to whether an Internet environment facilitated this approach in its entirety. The course team recognised the background and benefits. 'Problem based learning has now been in use for more than 25 years and brings many real benefits to health professions' education' (Davis and Harden, 1999). Some of the recognised benefits are:

- integration of knowledge is encouraged, so that the whole patient in his environment is studied, rather than a list of signs and symptoms;

- essential core skills are fostered, such as problem solving, communication and team working;

- a deeper approach to learning is encouraged; not merely the learning of taught facts, memorised in order to pass an examination.

The starting point for learning 'should be a problem, query or puzzle that the learner wishes to solve' (Boud, 1988). Medical courses which use a formal problem based learning (PBL) approach are systematic in the way the cases are presented; study is conducted via small groups, each facilitated by a tutor, and face to face feedback sessions are held regularly. It was recognised that while OTIS students would benefit from the use of a PBL approach, an Internet based course cannot meet the formal structure of problem based learning groups. Instead, the course design team aimed to develop essential professional skills by designing materials which could be addressed via the use of a problem-solving model (Hagedorn, 1992).

Hagedorn's comments are particularly pertinent to the OTIS course objectives:

> The problem solving approach is a conscious attempt to avoid the assumptions and blinkered thinking which may be inherent in other models, and to view the patient holistically and objectively before deciding on the nature of the problem and how (or if) to treat it ... One of the features ... is that it may highlight that the 'problem' does not lie with the patient, but with her physical or social environment. (Hagedorn, 1992, p. 30)

In terms of adult learning, idealism provoked course designers to employ autonomy as a pedagogical principle. However results and feedback from the pre-pilot testing caused the course team to modify this principle a little and to add further structure to the course, in order to ensure that the students could complete the course in the allocated time.

Practical issues such as timing the course in the academic calendar and scheduling the sessions to fit in with other ongoing curriculum commitments were initially deemed as straightforward and needing little discussion time. In the event considerable negotiation was needed before a common time slot could be allocated for the regular Tuesday morning tutorial. European partners preferred an early 9.30–10.30 am tutorial, meaning that UK students needed to be logged on and ready to begin at 8.30 am. Structuring the ten weekly sessions to fit in with four differing academic calendars, each with their own fixed patterns of clinical work, assessment and vacation periods, also proved to be a less than easy task. In the planning stage too a decision was made to hold a weekly virtual staff meeting, to follow each tutorial.

22.4 Establishing a core curriculum

Intense periods of collaborative debate preceded the landmark stages to course introduction:

- establishing core course content;

- agreeing assessment strategies and assignments;

- accreditation.

It was recognised as essential that the core curriculum with its aims, outcomes and methods of assessment was acceptable to all parties and this was achieved. The course was accredited to carry 10 credit accumulation transfer (CATs) points or three European credit transfer (ECTs) points for all students who successfully completed the course. Liverpool University due to local quality assurance measures, retained the need for an approved external examiner to validate the marks of students registered only in Liverpool. Although in this instance it presented no problems, such an Institute policy could be seen as a drawback to full European equality and collaboration in terms of course delivery.

The resulting course comprised a carefully designed, educationally driven module which:

- ran for 10 weeks comprising 80 hours of study between January and March 2001;

- focused on enabling technologies for occupational therapy clients;

- was based on a problem-solving case-study approach with students working in international tutorial groups which met on-line on Tuesday mornings

- enrolled 21 students with approximately equal numbers from all partnership institutions. Of note here is that recruitment was more difficult when English was an additional consideration. For Belgian students for instance, English was a third language.

Three assessments were designed to complement the course objectives and learning style. They comprised a completed case study, a peer review of a fellow student's case study from another country, and a reflective learning account of course participation. All assessments were marked by two tutors from different countries in order to ensure parity of standards.

22.5 Designing the learning environment

A key requirement in achieving learning of the core curriculum was full support from the online learning environment for a problem-solving case study approach, as follows:

- defining the problem;

- identifying the desired outcome;

- developing possible solutions and selecting strategies;

- data gathering – assessment and info gathering;
- developing action plan;
- evaluating the outcome.

Essential features of the learning environment supporting this requirement were the 'library' of learning resources and facilities for real-time (synchronous) communication sessions:

- weekly tutorials in concurrent groups;
- peer meetings, to be organised by the students;
- meetings with 'patients' and health care professionals;
- meetings with representatives from companies marketing healthcare products.

The learning environment was based on a 'virtual campus' metaphor as illustrated in Figures 22.1 (main map) and 22.2 (courtyard), and is described in detail in Armitt *et al.* (2001).

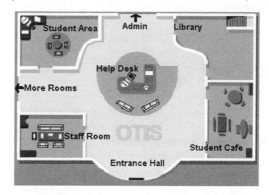

Figure 22.1   Main OTIS map

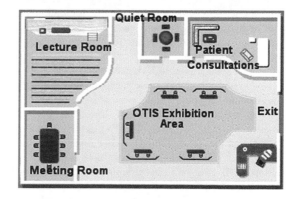

Figure 22.2   The Courtyard

It was designed to be as user-friendly as possible. Not all students were experienced users of computers, and it was important that the learning environment should be as intuitive as possible. The eighty hour course is too short for students to spend time learning complicated software. The Help Desk (see Figure 22.1) could be used by students when they had technical queries. FAQs (frequently asked questions) provided some instant solutions here; personal queries could also be dealt with via email.

The learning resources comprised four complete case studies with illustrations, a CD-ROM containing audio and video clips, an online library and a full set of course administration documents. The library contained resources such as links to websites, search engines, scanned documents such as book extracts and company brochures showing assistive technology devices, and sundry documents in Word or PDF format. Resource compilation was time-consuming and at all times needed to be fully compliant with data protection and copyright requirements.

Figure 22.3 portrays online communication underway during the OTIS course.

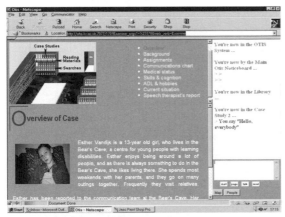

Figure 22.3   On-line communication underway

Students and staff communicate using a form of Internet Chat, in which the user types his/her message in the small box on the right hand side of the screen. The user then clicks on the 'Talk' button to send the message to everyone located in the same virtual room as the user, or on the 'Page' button to select specific recipients in any room in the virtual campus. The large area on the right hand side of the screen shows all incoming and outgoing messages addressed to/from the student, as well as confirming the current location (virtual room) of the student.

Technological resources were at the heart of the OTIS project, both in the design phase and in the weekly conduct of the course. The project highlighted a number of shortcomings in the management of IT resources within and between the colleges, notably the fragility of the links to each other across the Internet. Much time was lost in the weekly synchronous tutorial sessions, due to communication bottlenecks, breaks in network cables, maintenance work on Internet routers and sundry other problems. These problems were dispiriting for students and staff alike. When a technical hitch occurred on a Tuesday morning for example this could mean that one or more students missed some or all of the weekly tutorial. On such occasions the facility to copy the recorded transcript of the tutorial to tutees was invaluable. The same facility also assisted students who struggled a little, working in English as a foreign language in the online tutorials.

22.6   Evaluation

The course ran as timetabled. Students initially needed considerable support, much as in a non-virtual environment when first encountering higher education. They generally found the course stimulating and hard work; 18 of the 21 original students remained registered with the course throughout. Tutors had found the weekly staff meetings important in effecting speedy and consistent management of course-related issues; such extra meetings did however constitute an additional demand on staff time.

Structured evaluation comprised the following strategies:

- interviews and questionnaires with students;

- study of the assessment results;

- use of the SOLO technique to assess deep learning.

22.6.1

Student comments

Researcher-led interviews were conducted with the students during the course. At its close, each tutor led a focus group with the students on site. Questionnaires were completed by all students, both before and after the course.

The interviews initially revealed interest, a general awareness that computer learning was 'a good thing', anticipation of flexibility in regard to study site and time of learning and pleasant anticipation in meeting and discussing with European counterparts. A little later during the course there were general concerns about amounts of work and how to fit this in with other courses, clinical practice etc., questions about how to meet the course deadlines and some frustrations when the technicalities had not worked perfectly and students felt learning time had 'been lost'. Tutors each led a focus group on course completion. Predominant comments here were 'interesting, stimulating, knowledge-enhancing and hard work'.

The questionnaires. Generally student opinion remained constant in supporting the principle of on-line learning for part of a degree course and in appreciating the comprehensive materials that could be studied at a time which was convenient for the individual. Before the course, students placed high hopes on meeting international colleagues online and they looked forward to ongoing discussions. Due perhaps to the small number of students on the course, it proved unlikely that ad hoc discussions would happen as student log-on times varied greatly; this was a disappointment to some students. The organised peer meetings were however more successful (see SOLO evaluation to follow). Student comments on the final questionnaire revealed the following points:

- Overall, the responses of students were quite mixed on most questions. This may reflect that OTIS was not a positive experience for all and/or that e-learning in general may not suit every student. There were language problems for some students

- 71 per cent felt that e-learning was an exciting way of taking courses, but 50 per cent experienced feelings of isolation.

- 75 per cent felt Internet course provision in higher education to be a good idea, a useful addition to traditional courses.

- Over 65 per cent felt they could achieve a good standard of work when 'working at a distance'. On the same theme, 30 per cent felt that e-learning caused them problems and they could not achieve good standards.

- In terms of personal preferences, only 16 per cent felt that e-learning did not suit their personal circumstances, but most (78 per cent) still preferred traditional courses.

22.6.2

Assessment results

Even before submission of the first assignment, tutors were aware that some students were struggling to understand both the principles of remote, independent study and the non-standard assessment formats. Many supportive email exchanges took place to help the weaker students with the result that most students were enabled to complete and submit most of the assignments. The results are shown in Figures 22.4 and 22.5.

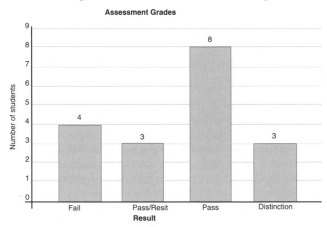

Figure 22.4   Assessment results I

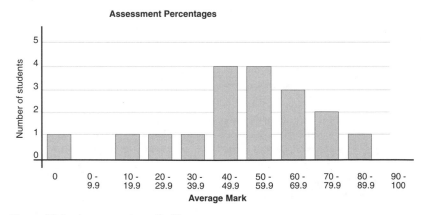

Figure 22.5   Assessment results II

It is interesting to note from these figures that a few students performed exceptionally well, while a similar small number performed very poorly. It was clear that students who entered the course with strong motivation for independent study, coupled with effective time management strategies, plus some experience of complex problem-solving were able to demonstrate their new knowledge in an impressive manner. It was equally clear that students who lacked these same skills could quickly fall behind with the course work and worryingly for tutors, such students could effectively 'disappear' until deadlines were passed. In a face-to-face learning environment tutors are better able to monitor and assist those students who fall behind with work but who do not actively seek help. It was, however, encouraging to note that the weaker students who failed at first attempt, were mostly able to succeed when they resubmitted their work. The reflective learning accounts also provided qualitative support for the learning that had taken place as the following examples show:

> I also looked for info about the assistive technology on the websites at the library. I looked on xxx That is really interesting!! It will be hard to found out what is the best for Mr. Jones!

> When we were working with assignment three we had the opportunity to speak to an expert ... a good chance to be able to ask questions to a well-informed person.

> If you would ask me if I have achieved my personal learning goals during this course, I would have to say that I have done that because I now have more knowledge about how AT aids like computers, could help to prevent people from isolation and to be more independent.

22.6.3   Use of SOLO technique to assess deep learning

As section 22.3 of this chapter indicates, deep learning is essential for today's health professionals. It was therefore important to the course team to examine whether this objective was achieved during the running of the OTIS course.

The SOLO taxonomy is a well-established technique for ascertaining the presence of deep learning, and is becoming widely used in education, including:

- allocating a cognitive level to individual course objectives helping students analyse their own work and see how to improve it;
- explanation of assignment grades;
- assessment (Hoddinott, 1998);
- predictor of potential (Crowley and Tall, 2001);
- research into education (Anderson and Walker, 1997).

Briefly the SOLO technique measures the complexity of thought processes in the utterances, based on a classification into prestructural, unistructural, multistructural, relational and extended abstract, where extended abstract is the most complex. Utterances are expected to show a continuum of learning from initial recognition to reflection and complex understanding (Hewson and Hughes, 1998). Students had provided signed agreement before the beginning of the course that their personal data could be studied for research purposes. Accordingly the course team was able to examine transcripts of the on-line tutorial sessions for evidences of learning (see Figure 22.6 for the results).

SOLO Level Weeks:	2	3	4	5	6	7
Prestructural	-	-	-	-	-	-
Unistructural	8	34	-	34	4	1
Multistructural	3	19	1	12	18	3
Relational	-	11	-	27	24	7
Extended Abstract	-	-	-	-	1	2

Figure 22.6   SOLO levels, weeks 2–7

Of interest in Figure 22.6 is the overall general increase in the more complex exchanges that took place as the course progressed. It should be noted that first and last course weeks are not shown as tutorials were used mainly for administrative matters at these time. An example of a relational exchange that took place in week 5 is given below; the names have been changed to protect confidentiality:

> Ingrid asks 'there are some amazing things you can do to adapt the pc, for example running it with infrared light so you just have to be able to move your head slightly etc, have you tried that?'
> Dirk says, 'i did once'
> Gerhard asks, 'me neither, is it easy to do so regarding to Esthers problem?'
> Ingrid says 'I don't hink the infrared is a solution for Esther since she might have some problems in focusing and keep the balance with her head, maybe scanning would be something for her, or pointng as she do now'
> Dirk says, 'that is why i asked to mr vandyk [Esther's father] how she can use her head, he answerd that it s difficult when she is tyred, and i don't know if that is very good for the spastic patern '
> Dirk says, 'i agree with that ingrid'

In the above exchange none of the three students has English as a first language, but they are nevertheless making themselves clearly understood and are coping well with both the course content and its problem-solving approach.

22.7   Summary and recommendations

Results highlight that:

active learning is fostered by:

- peer exchange;
- synchronous discussion;
- student motivation to work independently;
- prior development of the skills of enquiry and autonomous learning.

active learning may be hampered by:

- students allocating insufficient time to the course, due to
  - (a) personal undeveloped time management skills; or
  - (b) unresolved conflict in academic timetabling, such as the course clashing with clinical practice sessions;
- technical problems that deny student access to the virtual environment at a pre-scheduled time;
- student feelings of de-motivation when a course demands a high degree of independent study.

Recommendations in developing future courses of a similar nature are as follows:

1. *For the course team*:

- adequate preparation time; quality collaborative courses demand much time at the design phase;
- close and ongoing collaboration during course delivery to ensure tutorial consistency and clear delineation of tasks;
- ongoing attention to detail. In a European course, such a small point as the time zone for a tutorial not being specified can mean students can miss a tutorial!;
- rigorous attempt to create a sizeable student community so that students have maximum opportunities to meet and exchange ideas with international peers;

2. *For future students*:

- appreciation of the style of the course and its time commitment;
- prior practical experience of using a problem-solving approach;
- a good working grasp of the course's language of delivery.

22.8   Conclusions

Recent evaluations of both a qualitative and quantitative nature were undertaken during the OTIS pilot course. The data gathered indicate that the course and its associated technologies has provoked some strong reactions. For some students their active learning has been facilitated and learning objectives achieved. Other students, however, have struggled to understand and achieve the necessary course outcomes. Students who are not self-directed learners at course commencement appear to experience the greatest difficulties. Additional areas are also revealed as worthy of further exploration. These include a number of practical problems which can hinder the learning process within an international context. For example students can quickly fall behind if confronted with additional hurdles such as language misunderstandings, timetabling complexities across time zones and term dates which are out of line with local arrangements.

Despite the difficulties which must be addressed in realising courses such as OTIS, e-learning provides a means of bringing together geographically separated students to work towards a common purpose. As such, e-learning is a powerful adjunct to traditional course delivery whenever there is a learning imperative for students to experience direct international discussion and exchange of ideas concerning best practice.

Acknowledgements

The OTIS project is funded by the European Union through the TENTelecom programme.

Thanks to Dr Frances Slack of Sheffield Hallam University for her assistance with the use of the SOLO technique.

22.9 References

Anderson, D. and Walker, R. (1997) Quality of learning outcomes amongst teacher education students, *Refereed Proceedings of the 27th Annual Conference of the Australian Teacher Education Association (ATEA)*, Yeppoon, Queensland, Australia, July 1997 [online] http://atea.cqu.edu.au/content/soc_base/anderson.html

Armitt, G., Green, S. and Beer, M. (2001) Building a European Internet School: developing the OTIS learning environment, *European Perspectives on Computer-Supported Collaborative Learning, Proceedings of the First European Conference on Computer-Supported Collaborative Learning*, March, Maastricht, Netherlands, pp 67–74, Maastricht McLuhan Institute.

Boud, D. (1988) *Developing Student Autonomy in Learning*, 2nd edn. London: Kogan Page.

Coles, C. (1989) The role of context in elaborated learning. In J. Balla, M. Gibson and A. Chang (eds), *Learning in Medical School: A Model for the Clinical Professions. Hong Kong: Hong Kong University Press.*

Coles, C. (1990) Elaborated learning in undergraduate medical education, *Medical Education* **24**, 14–22.

Crowley, L. and Tall, D. (2001) Attainment and Potential: Procedures, Cognitive Kit-Bags and Cognitive Units, submitted to PME25, July 2001 [on-line] http://www.uky.edu/LCC/MATH/Crowley/papers/PME25.pdf

Davis, M. and Harden, R. (1999) AMEE Medical Education Guide No. 15: Problem-based learning: a practical guide, *Medical Teacher* **21**(2:) 130–9.

Hagedorn, R. (1992) *Occupational Therapy: Foundations for Practice*. Edinburgh: Churchill Livingstone.

HEART (Horizontal European Activities in Rehabilitation Technology) (1995) *Horizontal European Activities in Rehabilitation Technology: Condensed Report*. Brussels: European Commission, DGXIII.

Hewson, L. and Hughes, C. (1998) Templates for online teaching, *ASCILITE'98*, 329–38 [online] http://cedir.uow.edu.au/ASCILITE98/asc98-pdf/hewsonhughes.pdf

Hoddinott, J. (1998) Constructive alignment: a pedagogical model applied to a plant physiological ecology subject delivered over the World Wide Web, *ASCILITE'98* Proceedings Supplement 21–2 [online] http://cedir.uow.edu.au/ASCILITE98/abw_09c.html

McAllister L., Lincoln, M., McLeod, S. and Maloney, D. (eds) (1997) *Facilitating Learning in Clinical Settings*. Stanley Thornes: Cheltenham.

23 Improving student learning via online assessment

Meg O'Reilly

Teaching and Learning Centre, Southern Cross University, Lismore, Australia

Keywords

online assessment; online learning; peer-directed assessment; student-directed; teacher-directed

23.1 Overview

It has long been understood, particularly in the domain of distance education, that from the students' perspective the processes of assessment represent 'the de facto curriculum' (Rowntree, 1977). This has been reinforced and broadened to the higher education context as a whole by Ramsden (1992) in his statement that 'assessment defines the curriculum'.

In the current context of rapidly increasing use of networked computer technology within higher education, recent Australian research (Alexander and McKenzie, 1998) highlights the disjunction between expectations of students and staff, and their actual experiences with technology. The significantly improved attitudes of students to their learning, was sadly not matched by improved quality of learning. The enthusiastic expectations of students and staff to the new opportunities promised by online connection were not fulfilled. On closer analysis the single major cause of this shortfall was that assessment processes were not changed to better suit, or indeed take account of, the unique context of learning as supported by networked computer technology.

This chapter examines new approaches to online assessment through five case studies – three examples from the author's university and two from European universities. An online assessment framework is presented which shows the benefits to students and staff in teacher-directed, student-directed or peer-directed assessment activities carried out online. New types of learning to be assessed in the online medium are highlighted and issues arising from online learning and assessment are considered.

23.2 Introduction

With the increased adoption of networked technologies into mainstream approaches to teaching and learning, both on-campus and off-campus learners have seen an emergence of techniques for assessment which are capable of offering both the flexibility and openness of distance education, as well as the interactivity and immediacy of on-campus learning. Capabilities of the online environment promise educators many innovative and enhanced strategies for assessing our students, but are these promises being realised?

This chapter presents some case studies of assessment practices tailored for the online environment and suggests a framework detailing the benefits of online assessment to both students and staff. Discussion draws out features of assessment practices online, innovative aspects and benefits to teaching and learning.

23.3   Assessment: the key to learning

It has long been understood, particularly in the domain of distance education, that as far as the students' perspective goes, the processes of assessment represent 'the de facto curriculum' (Rowntree, 1977) and the driver of students' approaches to study (Morgan, 1993). This has been reinforced and broadened to the higher education context as a whole by Ramsden (1992) in his statement that 'from our students' perspective, assessment defines the curriculum'.

Regardless of the mode of study, we know that assignments assist the learning process through the aid of practice and feedback (formative), and measure achievement of learning outcomes (summative). Assessment processes therefore provide learners with opportunities to discover whether they understand, are able to perform competently and demonstrate what they have learnt. Furthermore, the feedback and grades which assessors communicate to students serve to both teach and motivate (Thorpe, 1998).

Self- and peer-assessment approaches also develop students' capabilities for self-diagnosis, stimulate personal insight and empowerment. Whether assessing students online or offline, the basic qualities of good assessment need to be evident.

23.4   Features of good assessment practices

Principles of good practice for assessing students have been described by several authors. The following draws upon the works of Brown, Race and Smith (1996); Biggs (1999), the American Association for Higher Education (n.d.) and the summary in Morgan and O'Reilly (1999). In general, assessment needs to be:

- *a vehicle for educational improvement* – through effective formative feedback and summative assessment processes, we can measure what we most value in students' learning; a complex integration of strategies for supporting motivation, competence and insight must be monitored and seen in performance over time;

- *explicit in values, aims, criteria and standards* – primarily assessment should be for the students, however, clear goals are useful not only for students but also for assessors, the faculty and institution; the implementation and communication of any shared goals of assessment also ensures a fuller range of needs are served;

- *concerned with both process and outcomes* – an effective alignment of course objectives, learning activities and assessment tasks enhances learning under structured conditions; assessment is best as ongoing and developmental rather than being episodic; feedback should always be given (formative and summative);

- *inclusive of the greater learning context and responsibilities* – students are a diverse group, who commonly study several subjects at one time; our awareness of this broader context ensures support from the broader educational community; our responsibility to professional and vocational stakeholders is to improve student learning, thus our commitment to continuous improvement needs to be reflected through assessment processes which are both inclusive and collaborative, as well as being reliable, valid and consistent;

- *relevant, authentic and holistic* – assessment should reflect evidence of learning which matters to students, and ultimately is useful in applied settings such as the academic programme as a whole, and in the external context of industry or professional practice. When students see the relevance of their learning embedded within assessment tasks, their motivation and level of achievement are enhanced.

Angelo (1999) claims that 'it's time to put the highest priority on doing assessment as if learning matters most'. This applies in the online context just as in all other teaching and learning contexts. What is required to facilitate assessment online are the same two dimensions which Angelo (1999) urges us to utilise to enliven our assessment practices – an explicit valuing of collaborative learning in communities, and a cultural change insofar as academic cultures needing to 'value self-examination, reflection and continuous improvement' (p. 2). These are suggested as elements of a transformative model of 'assessment-as-culture-change', vital for online teaching and learning.

23.5   Online learning

If we consider the online environment as a new space for teaching and learning with its specific affordances and constraints, it is clear that it is not the technology per se which improves learning. Many would agree with Alexander and Boud (2001) who say 'most of what we know about teaching and learning is applicable in all learning environments, including online' (p. 4).

Recent Australian research (Alexander and McKenzie, 1998) highlights the disjunction between expectations of students and staff, and actual experiences with technology. The significantly improved attitudes of students to their learning (16 per cent intended improvement; 62.7 per cent actual improvement), was sadly not matched by improved quality of learning (87 per cent intended improvement; 37 per cent actual improvement). This shows that the enthusiastic expectations of students and staff to the new opportunities promised by online connection were not fulfilled. On closer analysis the single major cause of this shortfall was that assessment processes were not changed to better suit or take account of, the unique context of learning online.

As with Angelo's (1999) transformative model of 'assessment-as-culture-change', Alexander and McKenzie (1998) clearly illustrate that attention to assessment can determine the effectiveness of our teaching and learning online, just as it has been shown to determine effectiveness of learning outcomes in general.

23.6   Online assessment

To improve learning online, the constructive alignment model (Biggs, 1999) would see us place assessment considerations at the forefront of our design concerns. By designing relevant assessment tasks and ensuring we are assessing the achievement of learning objectives made explicit to students, we can maintain standards while also realising the potentials of the online environment. Good assessment practices will motivate students to learn whether online or not, enable them to learn by doing, facilitate their learning through prompt feedback, and to make sense through ongoing reflections on their learning in a safe and predictable context (Race, 1993). Assessment strategies can also be depicted in three categories according to their intentions as to whether they allow for direction by teacher, student or by a group of student peers.

Opportunities to explore new assessment methods and styles are also now afforded online, for example, auto-graded MCQs, timed online exams, group-based innovations and publishing projects, international collaboration, peer- and self-assessment for distributed learners (O'Reilly, in press; O'Reilly and Morgan, 1999). The online learning environment has also extended the range of skills to be assessed, for example, it is now possible to assess collaboration between remote students, blend cohorts for 'mutual assist', support development of information literacy skills, co-generatively examine emerging models of online group processes, and assess online publishing and web-design in their value to end-users, future students and staff.

The Online Assessment Framework, shown as Table 23.1, illustrates how assessment designed for either teacher-directed, student-directed or self-directed implementation can

1. Teacher -directed

Assessment types	Benefits to students
• Group discussion for individual and group assignment preparation • Research, critical review of resources • Formal/informal debate • Email games • MCQ, short answer quiz • Open book timed online exams • Design in web environment	• Rapid detailed feedback • Easy links to 'real' data • Online 'expert' available • Collaborative learning support • Online submissions allow more time for preparation (submit @ 12 m.n.) • One question viewable at a time, reduces exam anxiety • Can be authentic workspace

2. Student -directed

Assessment types	Benefits to students
• Digital portfolios • Collaboration on common project or presentation • Reflective journal • Task and criteria negotiated, 'Learning contract' • Adjust variables in simulation or role-play • Self-review quiz • Design and present in web environment by negotiation	• Student choice eg 2 from 5 submissions for marking • Self-assessment via reflection for personal and profession development • Authentic tasks add meaning and allow immediate application • Support knowledge testing, reduce cheating

3. Peer -directed

Assessment types	Benefits to students
• Peer review of publishing, presentation, project, role play • Mutual aid in problem solving • Critical debate of disciplinary literature • Combine with reflective journal, activity log • Student-designed MCQs • Student generated assessment criteria	• Email transactions (anon, known, individual, collective) • Others involved e.g. mentors, workplace peers, moderators, colleagues • Relevant, authentic tasks • Students learn via assessing • 'Ownership' embeds criteria for improved performance • Complete archives

each have a range of benefits. The framework has been informally and collaboratively developed as a summary aid to designing assessment for the online context. In reality, assessment types are rather more fluid than this framework suggests, particularly where efforts are made to design assessment to address learning outcomes required in professional practice or applied contexts. The categories in this framework should therefore not be seen as a concrete delineation of assessment types, but rather serve as focal areas when considering the learning outcomes critical to one's discipline area, subject, and target group of learners. Nightingale *et al.*'s (1996) eight categories of learning outcomes have been listed in the right hand column to indicate their relevance across the spectrum of online assessment methods.

Benefits to teachers	Learning Outcomes
• Archives of all interactions • Better submissions for quality reusable resources • Shared criteria for markers • Randomising assessment to contain workload of marker and for later re-use of tasks • Automatic marking, track usage/ performance, rapid response, reduce human error	1. Thinking critically, making judgements 2. Solving problems, developing plans 3. Performing procedures and demonstrating techniques 4. Managing and developing oneself 5. Accessing, managing information 6. Demonstrating knowledge, understanding 7. Designing, creating, performing 8. Communicating

Benefits to teachers	Learning Outcomes
• Manageable workload via sampling • Reinforcement of industry and/or vocational relevance • High student motivation to achieve standards, mastery core skills • Formative feedback readily sent to individuals, groups	1. Thinking critically, making judgements 2. Solving problems, developing plans 4. Managing and developing oneself 5. Accessing, managing information 6. Demonstrating knowledge and understanding 8. Communicating *Possibly also (by negotiation):* 3. Performing procedures and demonstrating techniques 7. Designing, creating, performing

Benefits to teachers	Learning Outcomes
• Marking workload shared with students = enhanced quality/quantity of f'back • Student generated assessment criteria = deeper understanding • Assessing is used as learning process – students find where/how to improve • Best early in course, develop skills in self/peer assessment	1. Thinking critically, making judgements 2. Solving problems, developing plans 3. Performing procedures, demonstrating techniques 4. Managing and developing oneself 5. Accessing, managing information 6. Demonstrating knowledge and understanding 7. Designing, creating,performing(peer review) 8. Communicating

Table 23.1   Online assessment framework (developed from O'Reilly, Freeman and Donald, 2001; with reference to Race, 1993; Eight Categories of Learning Outcomes from Nightingale et al., 1996)

23.7   Case studies

Let's now turn to some examples of online assessment practices and their effectiveness in improving student learning. This collection of current creative online teaching and assessment practices includes three cases from Southern Cross University and two cases provided by colleagues from Europe. They have been collected in the process of educational design practices and professional associations over the past 12 months.

These particular cases have been included to illustrate exemplary practices in reconceptualising pedagogy for online assessment across disciplinary boundaries, irrespective of modes of study. These examples show that online assessment can enhance the experience of human–human interaction and not simply human–computer interaction. The case studies also report on student feedback obtained through either formal or informal evaluations and thus offer a somewhat more informed perspective on improvements to student learning.

23.7.1   Case study 1: Teacher-directed assessment – International Management (Southern Cross University, Australia)

This third-year subject in the Bachelor of Business programme aims to familiarise students with global changes in the business world and to prepare them for engaging with the dilemmas of human resource strategy, ethics, trade and the political forces upon domestic management operations within an international context. Enrolments are around 35 students, both on-campus and off-campus. All are required to pass two assignments and an exam to satisfactorily complete the unit. Assignments are submitted online and in the case of Assignment 2, are accessed via discussion archives.

The first assignment (20 per cent of total) occurs over the entire semester, requiring students to submit five fortnightly case studies, of which the best four are counted towards the final grade. Students are alphabetically assigned to their five case studies from among the ten case studies provided.

The second assignment (30 per cent of total) involves topic tracking whereby each student selects an article from their choice of business publications. A total of five articles are required for submission and interactive commentary over a nine week period. Each article is to be critically analysed according to the theories discussed within the study materials and supplementary resources. Applications of theories in workplace settings as presented in the published articles thus become the source for discussion online. Whether a student is the first to post critical commentary on an article or whether they post comments which extend emerging discussion on the same article, either way students are considered to be engaging critically with the issues and their relevance to the theoretical or professional literature. Through interaction with their student peers and, where possible, reflections upon workplace experiences, this assignment directly reflects the objectives of the unit, that of identifying the major factors in international management and critically analysing management activities as evidenced in practice.

Feedback from students reveals that their capacity to build upon each others' points of view results in a sense of engaging with the literature collaboratively rather than competitively. The focus on critical analysis of the literature of choice means that students are purposefully engaged in their 'general reading' of the subject. The pace of weekly submissions throughout semester is perceived as motivating to some students, but seems quite onerous to others. Lecturers indicate that the design provides excellent support for off-campus students in particular. In future, development of discussion threads can be taken further by lecturers through more consistent, strategic input to discussion, while avoiding interference in student expressions of mutual support.

23.7.2 Case study 2: Teacher-directed assessment – Information Resources Management (Southern Cross University, Australia)

Within the Bachelor of Information Technology, this is a core first-year subject and has enrolments of 100 –150 students per semester. Assessment tasks include three assignments and a final exam.

The first assignment introduces students to the online environment by allocating a small proportion of marks (3 per cent) to the development of a personal page within the university's online environment, accessible only by students enrolled in this subject. Development of personal pages enables this large blended cohort of on-campus and off-campus students to identify each other as they proceed to be organised into small work groups and to go about the following activities throughout the semester.

The second assignment is worth 20 per cent. Groups of three students (irrespective of mode of study) are required to work consistently through the semester to answer three types of questions according to a complex matrix of tasks. Roles for group members are specified including: information recorder, presenter to class online or offline, responder to questions, activities submitter online. There are five separate activities that each group must perform each week. Review Questions, Discussion Questions and Internet Exercises must be completed. Students are also required to ask questions of three other groups, and to support general group discussion on their own topic.

For the Internet Exercise questions, students summarise the actions they took (including the websites visited) and their findings. For the Discussion Questions, a stimulus post is made on Thursday prior to the following week when discussion is to occur and be facilitated by the assigned group. Each week, a different sample of groups is selected by the lecturer to be graded for this assignment. This serves to both sustain interest and commitment of students, while containing markers' workloads.

The third assignment is an independent learning contract undertaken by pairs of students who have not yet worked together. Students investigate, research and report on an issue closely aligned to at least one of the topics in the unit. Topics must have prior approval from the lecturer and must not have already been chosen by another group. Additional information from websites must be attached in the form of Appendices. All collaborative activities are carried out online. The 3,000–4,000 word report forms 20 per cent of final marks.

Initial feedback from students indicates that for ease of interaction between the full group on-campus and off-campus, a fortnightly turnaround might be easier to manage than weekly submissions. Although lecturers did not use the synchronous chat area for facilitating discussion, it was found that students made use of this to work within time constraints. Online interaction was valued by students as an aid to managing a complex series of activities and staying connected with a large number of peers in the blended cohort. Much was achieved within a tight timeframe.

23.7.3 Case study 3: Teacher-directed assessment – The Holocaust and Other Massacres (University of West England, UK)

This case from the Faculty of Economics and Social Science is a trimester-long subject from the Sociology major, taken by either 2nd or 3rd year students. Online conferencing environment is the FirstClass system and students are offered the opportunity of having 30 minutes initial training in its use.

The assessment process requires that students work in groups throughout the study period. Self-selected groups of up to four students are required to engage in ongoing online discussion and cooperate on the development of ideas around a topic which is provided each week. The learning outcomes which are explicitly assessed include the extent to which students demonstrate: the clarification of definitions and behavioural demarcation issues; discussion of key facts; discussion of problems associated with obtaining relevant information to support emerging viewpoints of the group; and a critical engagement with appropriate theoretical frameworks. This component of assessment including the assigned written work deriving from discussions is worth 50 per cent of total marks, with the balance being obtained through final examination.

With approximately 60–90 students undertaking this subject in each cohort, the workload of handling numerous small group discussions online remains manageable due to both the absence of a moderator and the provision of comprehensive and clear instructions from the outset. For example, students are advised that their contributions must be made consistently throughout semester, that simply 'dumping' messages to the group conference is unsatisfactory, and that copying and pasting from the Internet for the substance of one's contributions needs to be supplemented by original comments of a critical nature. Students are also forewarned that the subject matter is of a distressing nature and are asked to be prepared for handling their own reaction and, to some extent, the reactions of others in their small group.

Initial evaluations of effectiveness of this online strategy show that 'students performed better on average' than they did on other courses (Stein, 2000). Suggested reasons for this are that the conferencing medium provided novelty and supported social engagement, collaboration and learner autonomy, where significant impact was experienced not only in one's cognitive understanding but also in affective responses.

23.7.4 Case study 4: Student-directed assessment – Group Processes (Southern Cross University, Australia)

The core subject Group Processes is found within the Bachelor of Social Science programme, as part of the Human Relations and Communications major and can be taken in any year of study. Traditionally taught both on-campus and off-campus, with the on-campus version based on much more interactive processes than the off-campus version, in 1999 this subject was redesigned for flexible delivery utilising print-based readings, structured and moderated online interaction activities and self-reflection.

It is recommended that students pace themselves on a weekly basis in order to have the opportunity to experience the formation, development and, where possible, the winding up of a group. Previously this meant the application of theories and principles to the classroom situation, or in the case of off-campus learners, through their experience within a community, workplace or personal interest group. With the addition of the online environment, students are required to choose early in semester whether they will use involvement with their online peers for the purpose of observing and recording group processes. Students choose the mode for participant observation, i.e. online, in class, or in the community, with online activities more closely resembling the original on-campus version of this subject. Size of the online class is limited to 20 to optimise the experience, small groups of 4–5 are formed, and the full class participates in plenary sessions.

The full list of assessment tasks includes:

(a) an observation report where students select a specific group event to observe and provide comment on their observations in relation to theories of group processes;
(b) a reflective journal in which students record their ongoing reflections upon critical experiences in the group with a view to heightening their own awareness, critical thinking and communication skills, as well as considering their role in the group;
(c) an essay in which students evaluate the effectiveness of the group as a whole relative to the criteria for effectiveness found in the literature.

Feedback from students reveals that their experiences with online groups can successfully be the focus of observation and analysis. A greater sense of belonging and trust was seen to be supported and facilitated by the availability of full text-based archives. Specific questions for further exploration in the online context include: group formation and group identity in a faceless environment; participation and commitment to one's unseen peers; forms and styles of communication and leadership; establishment of roles and approaches to conflict. These questions can be informed by existing theories in traditional group process contexts, as well as in turn informing the emergent awareness of the nature of online communication. Outcomes of reflections, including those captured from online students, are indeed serving as formative contributions to the building of knowledge and theory in the area of online group processes (Fisher, Phelps and Ellis, 2000).

27.3.5 Case study 5: Peer-directed assessment – Telematics Applications in Education and Training (University of Twente, NL)

This subject is structured with an appropriate balance between the 'Participation, and Acquisition Models' of learning (Sfard, 1998 in Collis and Moonen, 2001) for later year students in the Faculty of Educational Science and Technology.

Assessment tasks include:

- a group project, where each group is responsible for developing a report of resources and supplementary information for the assigned topic; drafts of reports are posted on the website for peer review and assessor's feedback; final reports are also posted to the Web for critical comments from peers; links are created between reports and used by the next cohort of students who supplement these;

- students submit a portfolio of new resources and innovative uses of technology to support flexible learning.

Feedback on this subject over the years indicates that the developing resource base of technological and multimedia innovations for use in educational contexts, is valued by both students and staff. The nature of assessment tasks is considered highly authentic and of practical relevance, as students utilise the work of previous students to critique, modify and improve on, while progressing towards their own learning goals.

23.8   Discussion

As assessment is so critical to the process of learning, our course development activities must prioritise the constructive alignment of course objectives and learning activities with the assessment tasks. This is even more critical in the online environment where in some instances there has been a tendency to deliver content with an expectation of improved outcomes. But it is now clear that learning outcomes cannot improve without changing assessment to better suit, or indeed take account of, the unique context of learning as supported by networked computer technology.

Implicit in the case studies provided are several important issues for design of online assessment including how to:

- encourage a good level of student engagement in learning activities;
- support the inherent motivation for 'mutual assist' within a safe context;
- support and manage equitably, a blended cohort of diverse students;
- develop online learning skills by students and staff, and where relevant the assessment of these extended literacy, publishing, design and interaction skills;
- sustain a manageable workload for staff both in the facilitation of discussion and in the marking of a range of online activities.

It is evident from both the framework provided and the case study examples that advantages of online assessment are afforded to both students and staff. In particular, improvements to staff work practices cover a broad range of advantages and those illustrated include:

- the ability to save archives of all discussion activities, randomise sample marking and sustain manageable workloads (Case study 2);
- the quality of submissions improve with the increased experience of participation in critical discussion and technical expertise over time, thus providing excellent resources for re-use by staff with future cohorts (Case studies 1 and 5);
- student choice in participation fosters a high level of motivation for staff to work with, new group processes online enable staff and students to generate and reflect on new knowledge (Case study 4);
- mutual assist processes in unmoderated discussion provide opportunities for broad based peer support in both the cognitive and affective domains (Case study 3), thus relieving teachers from exclusive responsibility for these extended roles.

Improvement to student learning via online assessment was evident through the case studies as follows:

- authentic, applied activities increase student motivation and processes of situated learning (Case studies 4 and 5);

- opportunities for student choice can be increased through the use of (a) online archives, (b) private areas for small workgroups, (c) modes of study to suit learning styles (Case studies 1, 2 and 4) and (d) expanded range of resources available to students (Case studies 1 and 5);

- safe environment for self-reflection within a group context, archives kept for dispute resolution (Case study 3);

- learning by continuous engagement in iterative assessment tasks (Case study 1);

- participation in graded discussions helps to reduce the sense of isolation often experienced by off-campus students and encourages an atmosphere of collaboration rather than competition (Case studies 1, 2, 3, 4 and 5).

23.9   Conclusion

There are many ways in which student learning can potentially be improved via online assessment. Although the broad capabilities of the online environment promise educators innovative and enhanced strategies for assessing students, it is the long established principles of good assessment practices which continue to require our application if we are to truly improve students' learning. Online, where for the past few years content delivery and strategic marketing have led to high expectations of enhancements to education, the principles of good assessment practices are now more important than ever, not only to attract and retain our students but to effectively teach and support their learning. This chapter argues that through constructive alignment of course objectives, learning activities and assessment tasks which are embedded in the design of the learning experience from the outset (Biggs, 1999), we have the possibility for addressing the prime factors described by Race (1993). Good assessment practices online can serve to motivate our students to learn, enable them to learn by doing, facilitate their learning through feedback, and to make sense through their ongoing reflections on learning in a safe and predictable context online.

The framework provided indicates benefits of online assessment for student-directed, teacher-directed and peer-directed learning activities and relates these benefits to learning outcomes as detailed in the literature. A few examples of assessment practices tailored for the online environment were provided as illustrations of current practices in two continents, and as a whole they detail the benefits of collaborative and reflective online assessment for continuous improvement by both students and staff.

Acknowledgements

Sincere thanks to Mark Christensen, Julian Dimbleby, Stuart Stein, Kath Fisher and Betty Collis for kindly allowing access to assessment details and evaluations which were available at the time of writing, plus comments on early drafts.

23.10   References

Alexander, S. and McKenzie, J. (1998) *An Evaluation of Information Technology Projects for University Learning.* Canberra: AGPS, CUTSD.

Alexander, S and Boud, D. (2001) Learners still learn from experience when online. In J. Stephenson (ed.), *Teaching and Learning Online.* London: Kogan Page.

Angelo, T. (1999) Doing assessment as if learning matters most, *AAHE Bulletin*, May, available from http://www.aahe.org/Bulletin/angelomay99.htm

Biggs, J. (1999) What the student does, *Higher Education Research & Development* **18**(1): 57–75.

Brown, S., Race, P. and Smith, B. (1996) An assessment manifesto. In *500 Tips on Assessment*. London: Kogan Page, http://www.lgu.ac.uk/deliberations/assessment/manifest.html

Collis, B. and Moonen, J. (2001) *Flexible Learning in a Digital World*. London: Kogan Page.

Fisher, K., Phelps, R. and Ellis, A. (2000) Group processes online: teaching collaboration through collaborative processes, *Educational Technology & Society* **3**(3) http://ifets.ieee.org/periodical/vol_3_2000/f06.html

Morgan, A. (1993) *Improving Your Students' Learning: Reflections on the Experience of Study*. London: Kogan Page.

Morgan, C. and O'Reilly, M. (1999) *Assessing Open and Distance Learners*. London: Kogan Page.

O'Reilly, M. (in press) Orchestrating distributed communities of learners via online assessment. In G. Shaw *et al.* (eds), *Tertiary Teaching: Doing It Differently, Doing It Better*. Darwin: NTU Press.

O'Reilly, M., Freeman, M. and Donald, C. (2001) Online learning and assessment. Notes for National Teaching Forum, Canberra, Dec. 2000; ASCILITE workshop, Coffs Harbour 2000; Learning Technologies workshop, UNITEC New Zealand, May 2001.

O'Reilly, M. and Morgan, C. (1999) Chapter 16– online assessment: creating communities and opportunities. In S. Brown, P. Race and J. Bull (eds), *Computer Assisted Assessment in Higher Education*. London: Kogan Page/SEDA, pp. 149–61.

Race, P. (1993) Quality of Assessment. SEDA paper 80. Available http://www.lgu.ac.uk/deliberations/seda-pubs/Race.html

Ramsden, P. (1992) *Learning to Teach in Higher Education*. London: Routledge.

Rowntree, D, (1977) *Assessing Students: How Shall We Know Them?* London: Kogan Page.

Stein, S. (2000) Facilitating learning via computer conferencing: aspirations, requirements and hard facts. In J. Bourdeau and R. Heller (eds), *Proceedings of EdMedia 2000*, Montreal, Canada: Association for the Advancement of Computing in Education, 1049–54.

Thorpe, M. (1998) Assessment and 'third generation' distance education, *Distance Education* **19**(2): 265–86.

24 Generating puzzlement: constructing a space for learning

Kate Patrick and Sue Johnston
RMIT University[1], Australia

24.1 Overview

How can technology promote transformative learning? How can it help students engage with key aspects of curriculum and come to see their experience differently?

This chapter addresses these questions in the context of a staff development project focused on designing learning activities for electronic simulations. It argues that a space for learning opens when students encounter a gap between what they expect and what they observe. In terms of variation theory, this implies that students' expectations contribute to the variation they experience. The variation needs to be challenging and important, and students need time, opportunity and a language to work it through.

24.2 Introduction

The starting point of this chapter was a staff development project concerned with the transformational use of electronic simulations. This chapter explores how we used variation theory in this project to construct spaces for learning. We describe the thinking which led us to a design model incorporating variation, and report on our work with academic staff at RMIT University, using the model to design learning activities for use with simulations.

24.3 Background

The work reported in this chapter was undertaken as part of a nationally funded staff development project. Our aim was to develop an approach to bringing interactive electronic simulations into use with students. The project was conceived as a way of addressing two significant and related issues. First, we noted that disappointingly few academics actually use any of the expensive multimedia resources which have been funded by Australian university teaching grants (Alexander and McKenzie, 1998). Secondly, effective use of these resources requires careful investigation and reflection (Hedberg et al., 1998). Bain and his colleagues, researching the use of multimedia in university teaching, found that without support teachers were likely to use new resources in ways which were consistent with their existing practices; they report instances where simulations and other multimedia resources have been used didactically and with a focus on procedural knowledge (Bain et al., 1998).

We concluded that it would be useful to provide support which would extend the experience of using electronic media beyond the circle of innovators and 'early adopters' involved in the development process. Participants in the project, nominated by their programme leaders, were expected to have identified an electronic simulation which was ready to use, so that their work in the project could focus on bringing the simulation into use.

Guidelines for the choice of simulation provided that the simulation should be interactive, providing intrinsic feedback; engaging; relevant; and theoretically sound. We expected that the project would support staff in taking advantage of some of the particular advantages for learning which are provided by electronic simulations: they can

- respond quickly;

- provide multiple representations;

- access invisible or inaccessible features of a phenomenon;

- support repetition, providing the same outcomes for the same input (cf Laurillard *et al.*, 1991).

We focused on developing tasks which would challenge students' assumptions, and enable them to gain insights that they might not achieve merely by playing with the simulations.

Underpinning the project was a theoretical framework which developed from the doctoral research of one of the authors (Patrick 1990, 1992, 1998). Patrick argued that what students learn is intimately related to the content and design of the learning situation in which they participate – the focus of the tasks which are set and the frame of reference in which they are presented. Marton and Booth (1997) propose variation theory as a way of analysing and understanding these critical features of a particular learning situation. According to variation theory, the learning afforded by the learning situation is constituted by what the teacher focuses on, what s/he holds constant and what s/he varies (cf. also Runesson and Marton, 2000). Variation theory provides a strategy for analysing learning activities in relation to intended learning outcomes.

However, as Prosser and Trigwell (1999) point out, there is often a gap between the learning afforded by the design of a learning situation and the outcomes which students actually achieve. Chinn and Brewer (1993) identify a range of ways in which people respond to unexpected variation: we may use our observations to re-evaluate our expectations, or we may alternatively resist, deny, segregate, re-interpret or fail to notice the variation. Bereiter and Scardamalia (1993) distinguish between students who focus on what is familiar in a novel situation and those who focus on aspects of the situation which are inconsistent with their expectations. They argue that it is when students focus on what is unfamiliar or unexpected that their learning is expert-like, or as we would say transformative.

We inferred that students' expectations of the content and of the learning process also constitute part of the variation in the learning situation. Bringing these propositions together, we proposed that for a space for transformative learning to open up, students must encounter and engage with variation between what they expect and what they observe. We think of this engagement as productive puzzlement; hence our name for the project, 'Generating Puzzlement'. We aimed to work with fundamental and difficult concepts and relationships, where productive puzzlement would be most useful.

Based on this thinking, we developed a framework for designing learning activities which we called the Puz model. This consists of three phases:

REFLECT/PREDICT   What do you expect ... or: What do you predict?
    The aim is to disengage students from espoused theory and help them surface and explain their tacit expectations.

OBSERVE / EXPERIENCE   What do you notice? An activity and accompanying questions focus students' attention on a significant and unexpected key idea, so that they discern variation between their expectations and their experience.

REFLECT   How do you evaluate what you have experienced? What questions does it suggest? Students work with the variation which they have observed.

The Puz model differs significantly from the classical Predict, Observe, Explain model, where students are typically asked what theory leads them to predict. We focus on helping students to articulate tacit knowledge rather than getting them to recall espoused theory. This chapter reports on a series of staff development workshops working with this model. The 'key idea' embedded in these workshops was the concept of challenging tacit knowledge: while the Puz model provided a strategy for surfacing and challenging tacit knowledge, we anticipated that this approach would be unfamiliar to participants in the project. We hoped that the workshops would assist our participants to articulate their own tacit knowledge of their topic and students' difficulties with it, and to identify points where students' expectations needed to be challenged.

How did this work, and what change was visible in the approaches adopted by participants in our workshops?

24.4   Methodology

To date we have run two series of workshops involving 17 participants in five or six two-hour workshops, with additional one-to-one meetings and individual activity. The participants were RMIT staff, including teachers of vocational courses, undergraduates, and postgraduates, in a range of discipline areas – engineering, physics, chemistry, social science, nursing, geospatial science, psychology, biology. Nominations required details of the simulation to be used, responses to a checklist of criteria, as described above, and a statement indicating what students were expected to gain from working with the simulation. Time release for the participants was negotiated and funded and participants undertook to report their work to their colleagues via papers and presentations. A website was established for online discussions between participants; this is being transformed into a publicly accessible project archive (www.puz.rmit.edu.au).

We used the Puz model as a framework both for designing learning activities, and for the workshops themselves:

- Our initial *reflective questions* focused on what students would gain from using each simulation. This was included on the project application form; it was also the topic of discussion at the first workshop in each series, and explored with several participants in one on one sessions.

- In the *experiential* phase, each participant was asked to devise a three-step activity using the model and trial it with the rest of the group. Acting as quasi-students, the rest of us reported what we had discerned as the key idea and what we had discovered about it, and what we had found difficult. Discussions were conducted in pairs and participants' responses shared in the group and via the online discussion site. The aim here was to help participants attend to unexpected responses to the learning activities they were constructing, and hence to reflect on the perspectives students might bring.

- In the final *reflection* phase, participants were asked to revisit their key idea and review the activity they had designed in the light of feedback from other participants.

The workshops provided a forum where trial activities were discussed in terms of the insights they afforded. Variation in relation to each trial activity was provided by the questions and comments of participants, including us as facilitators. The general tone was described by one participant as 'really good in open, honest and frank discussion of issues in teaching and learning – very good in that respect'. At the end of the first round of workshops most participants reported that they had developed activities to the point where they could be trialled with students. Difficult aspects of the workshop process including trying to limit the number of 'key ideas' and seeing what could be gained from responding to other participants' simulations. In the second round of workshops, we added discussion of readings on learning (this gave us a common language and examples to refer to) and an additional task: we insisted that participants reflect on how they could apply their experience of someone else's simulation to their own work.

Documentation of the workshops was collected via the project website and a formative and summative evaluation process. Participants contributed reports and reflections on their experiences and initial and revised versions of the learning activities they designed. Additionally, in all the workshops, participants were asked to record some of their responses electronically using threaded discussion. Before and after documentation was provided by the participants' initial proposal forms and their concluding reports.

24.5   Results

By mid-2001 15 of the 17 participants had provided reports on their implementation plans. They indicated that:

- activities had been planned, trialled and mostly implemented;
- planned activities focused on key underlying principles;
- evaluations of activities conducted suggest reasonable effectiveness;
- dissemination to colleagues was being undertaken via presentations within departments; an internal RMIT forum; and at least one conference paper was in preparation.

From our perspective, a key outcome was that participants' formulations of their key ideas were clearer and more student-focused. Initially, they described the learning they wanted for their students in terms of fairly broad topic statements. By the time of the final report, their proposed objectives had been reworked to focus much more tightly on critical concepts or relationships.

For example, see Table 24.1

Name[1] & field	Topic	Initial statement[2]	Final report[3]
Alan **Genetics**	Breeding fruit flies	Teaching genetics really requires some real exposure to patterns of Mendelian inheritance. It is all very well to talk about Mendel's ratios, but seeing them occur is better... For the newcomer, merely seeing the monohybrid, dihybrid crosses and sex linkage in action will probably be enough. For others I want the ideas of a test cross and some of the more 'interesting' variation to Mendel's 'rules' to be where they explore.	To get students to think about inheritance patterns and to determine ways of assessing what form of inheritance is being seen in a particular breeding program.
Karen **Social science**	Mediating disputes	I want students to learn about power imbalances in mediation and how to address those power imbalances by mediating online. Online role-plays give the students the opportunity to consult relevant literature during the role-play. This generally cannot occur in face-to-face role-plays.	Increase students' awareness of personal biases that may affect their ability to be a 'neutral' mediator.
Tony **Nursing**	Washing hands	Infection control in relation to issues of hand washing.	Awareness that the required procedure is different from normal handwashing practice.
Nicholas **Engineering**	Retaining wall design	Geotechnical engineering principles - users are involved in the solution . process	The effects of varying the ground water table, behind or in front of the wall, and backfill soil physical and strength properties on the stability of a retaining wall or on the factor of safety.
Lindsay **Engineering**	Using n statistics to control production	An understanding of the ongoing and dynamic nature of Statistical Process Control.	The key idea for me was dealing with variation in the statistical . sense. The simulation was a machine making parts, after it was set working the machine was programmed to change its own parameters so that it produced parts of different sizes. The statistics to identify what goes wrong and when... The better students did well and found it useful. Most students, it went over their heads... The key idea may be a bit too sophisticated. Maybe I'll have to break it into smaller tasks in preparation, with the real key idea coming at the end

Table 24.1   Sample participant outcome statements

Name[1] & field	Topic	Initial statement[2]	Final repor
Paul **Physics**	Harmonic oscillator	My simulation is a basic harmonic oscillator (a mass on a spring with . friction and a driving force) in which students can vary the parameters and see the effect of this on the time-dependent oscillations. We already have an experiment about the mechanical oscillator, and want to teach similar concepts to those taught in the experiment: natural frequency, resonance, transient behaviour and steady-state behaviour	How does the graph relate to a real oscillator such as a mass on a spring? How do the parameters such as mass, spring stiffness and friction affect the oscillations?
Tim **Chemistry**	Using a polarographic instrument	Using this simulation, students will learn about the capabilities of a polarographic instrument, how to collect, analyse and critique polarographic data, and how to create an effective experiment.	Key ideas that this engaged students with were: • The diffusion current is proportional to the concentration of the electro-active species • The diffusion current and the shape of the wave is dependent on the number of electrons involved in the redox process • The half-wave potential (position of the wave) varies as the identity of the electro-active species is changed.

Notes
1. All names are pseudonyms.
2. Statements are verbatim quotations from the participant's initial submission or from his/her introductory contribution to the web discussion board.
3. Statements are verbatim quotations from participants' concluding messages or final report.

Table 24.1 (continued)   Sample participant outcome statements

These sets of statements indicate a substantial shift of perspective, from a focus on a topic or theme to a focus on insights which students were to achieve. Over time, most participants came to express their key idea from the student's perspective, describing what they wanted students to do and the insights they wanted students to achieve. Two participants did not complete their project reports, indicating that they had not had time to follow through the work on their simulation.

Some sample comments from the concluding evaluation workshop:

Paul   At the beginning, I just changed a couple of parameters – start simple, calculate natural frequency, check with the simulation, go on to another key idea. almost a copy of the original lab. Now I ask them what they expect, and leave the calculations to later ... The fact that there has to be a key idea in each part of the lab isn't obvious at first. I know that you should structure it – otherwise they get lost – I found it a useful design principle. It makes you focus, gives you a fulcrum, otherwise it's easy to wander off the point. If you don't focus on the key idea you can't conduct the simulation properly, you have to keep in mind what the key concept is, what is the main purpose. If you can sum it up in a single question you're doing okay.

Nicholas   If you don't think about it in advance you might talk about lots of interesting points but the key idea which is behind what is happening is missing. You have to concentrate and force the students to think about it.

Paul   It's a very structured way of approaching it. You can only do it when you have got control of what they do. If you leave it to chance without guidance they will just aimlessly explore.

Nicholas   When I showed the Retaining Wall to Kate – I found that if I changed the sequence it worked better. You have to think about where to start the process and where to continue ...

Lindsay   You can just end up showing it to the students. You need to find a mechanism to hook the students ... The approach is valuable, it exposes the students' misconceptions, what they understand and don't understand. With traditional teaching, the students can mask their misconceptions and do reasonably well ... Every student in the class did better than with the traditional approach.

The variation machine was an enormous benefit to the students. Learning comes from resolving contradictions. You try to reconcile things that seem opposing, that leads to active learning, making things work, looking at things from different perspectives. So there is enormous value in working like this. Then if you bring them into the puz moment at the end all the students got more benefit. They didn't like it much, they felt a bit threatened, but the work they presented was good ... they had the beginnings of an understanding what the subject was about and they could begin to relate the subject to reality.

We turn now to a discussion of the struggles involved in this project and the insights we gained from them.

24.6   Discussion

Participants in this project encountered both variation which arose from the character of the group, and variation which was constituted by exchanges between participants.

A key issue in the first round of workshops was the variation in the group. Several participants were engineers and physicists, others were from social science, nursing and humanities. The mathematics of the science-based exercises were difficult for some, the language of design was difficult for others. As a group, we directly experienced puzzlement as a potential space for learning. We puzzled over the intentions of the exercises, tried to second-guess what to do with the fruitfly breeding based on dim recollections of school biology classes. As in the heat transfer exercise trialled in the presentation of this paper at the ISL conference, there was real difference in the expertise of the participants and it was genuinely useful to discuss what we knew and what we expected. The result was that we were able both to explore jointly what students might make of the subject at hand and to experience the value of our joint and diverse explorations.

More profoundly, we encountered differences which arose from the expectations we variously brought to the workshop. An example is our struggle over the concept of the key idea. In the workshops, there were difficult discrepancies between the participants' initial formulations of their key idea, and the questions we were asking as facilitators. The variation which opened up in this discussion can also be seen as constituting a space for transformative learning.

As shown in Table 24.1, the initial statements were framed in terms of a topic or theme, something contained in or offered by the curriculum. Discussion in the workshops also expressed the notion of offering material to students, as can be seen in the following exchange on the threaded discussion site:

Nicholas   The simulation lends itself to numerous learning outcomes but difficulty was
experienced in determining a key idea because the simulation can be learnt with students at
different stages of learning about beams ...
Tim   I am in the same situation ... a single key idea becomes so decontextualised that it
appears almost banal and unproblematic. I will want to use the simulation for students to work
through a series of exercises, each of which will have a key idea or two ...
Alan   I agree that identifying 'the' key idea is problematic. in addition to the idea in its context,
another is the competency students bring with them – I would think that the challenging key idea
will occur at different stages for different students.

In these comments, students are positioned in relation to something made available by the simulation. Nicholas says that the simulation can be learnt; Tim says that each exercise will have a key idea or two; Alan says that the challenging key idea 'will occur at different stages'. While these comments focus on the role of the simulation in the encounter between the student and the simulation, there is some variation in how the participants express it. Alan is moving towards the idea of the student's perspective on the encounter ('the competency students bring with them'). The next section of the discussion took forward this perspective:

Kate   ... The 'key ideas' which I think are worth getting students to focus on are the ones where
the actually come with some misconception which it's important to disturb!
Karen   Is it then a good idea to identify the key misconception. In my case ... the key
misconception is that gender does not affect negotiation because women of today are not
affected by the issues of gender. Many students believe there is equality. The literature would
suggest otherwise.

By the time of her final report, Karen had moved from an initial formulation focusing on the theoretical issue of power and gender to a key idea which incorporated the issue of self-awareness which she identified in this discussion.

Another aspect of variation in the project was the different ways of using simulations which emerged from the work of different participants. Some simulations (the fruit fly breeding, the harmonic oscillator, the polarographic instrument) were built on mathematical models. In some cases these simulations provided an opportunity to see what the theory meant – because the results were predictable, it was possible to devise situations with graphic and unexpected outcomes (such as the introduction of a lethal gene). Other simulations, like the engineering production simulator, were randomised so that the bolts dropping on to the production line varied across and beyond fixed tolerance dimensions – these simulations provided a virtual experience. And yet other simulations – such as the electronic role play of a mediation – enabled students to experience actual negotiation in the context of a simulated scenario. And some participants were interested in getting students to develop their own simulations, engaging with and critiquing the underlying theory.

In the first round of workshops, the differences of discourse and type of simulation were in fact somewhat of a difficulty for participants. Several of them commented that it was hard to see what could be gained from participating in discourses and activities which were so unfamiliar. In effect, they did not perceive the differences as constituting variation, but rather as distinctly different phenomena (cf. Patrick, 2001). In the second round of workshops, we focused more explicitly on the structure of the learning situation: we provided readings about learning and the role of variation (Bereiter and Scardamalia, 1993; Marton and Booth, 1997); we used examples from Runesson's work (Runesson and Marton,

2000) to generate discussion of the significance of the exact way an activity is framed. As already mentioned, we got participants to reflect explicitly on what they could learn from their experience of each other's simulations.

The level of engagement in the second round of workshops was noticeably higher, and more of the participants commented in their closing evaluation that they had gained insights into students' learning generally. Although the numbers are too small to demonstrate this quantitatively, it is our view that the detail of the workshop design had a significant effect. In the first round of workshops, it was the Puz model that constituted the shared discourse of the group and enabled us to discuss strategies for challenging students' expectations. In the second round, we collaborated in developing connections between the readings and different instantiations of the Puz model. Our shared discourse was more effectively theorised, and provided a clearer framework for engaging with all the various simulations which members of the group were working on, so that the variation between them was experienced as useful rather than irrelevant. The result was that more participants commented on their insights into the design of learning activities – such as the participant in the final evaluation workshop who commented that 'it's a useful programme for the individual lecturer to improve their teaching style as well as the students' learning'.

In this project, we focused explicitly on generating puzzlement – surfacing discrepancies between expectations and experience – and we explored as a group how a learning activity which generates puzzlement can be designed to help students achieve important insights. We believe that this approach provided the workshop participants with a space in which transformative learning was possible. Unlike the users of multimedia reported by Bain *et al*. (1998), the Puz participants developed and implemented new approaches to their teaching. They report that their students are positive about the experience, and several of them have commented that they can see how the approach can be applied beyond the context of the electronic simulation. As Paul put it, 'I think of it as a model that I'm going to keep at the back of my mind when I design any learning experience'.

Acknowledgement

This project was supported by an Institutional Staff Development Grant from the Australian Committee for University Teaching and Staff Development.

Notes

1. Address for correspondence: Dr Kate Patrick, Quality Unit, RMIT University, GPO Box 2476V, Melbourne 3001, Victoria, Australia; kate.patrick@rmit.edu.au

24.7   References

Alexander, S. and McKenzie, J. (1998) *An Evaluation of Information Technology Projects for University Learning*. Canberra: AGPS.

Bain, J.D., McNaught, C., Mills, C. and Lueckenhausen, G. (1998) Describing computer-facilitated learning environments in higher education, *Learning Environments Research* **1**: 163–80.

Ball, J. and Patrick, K. (1999) 'Oh I see!' Learning about heat transfer. Paper presented to the Annual Frontiers in Education Conference, Puerto Rico, November.

Bereiter, C. and Scardamalia, M. (1993) *Surpassing Ourselves*. Peru, Illinois: Open Court.

Chinn, C.A. and Brewer, W.F. (1993) The role of anomalous data in knowledge acquisition: a theoretical framework and implications for science instruction, *Review of Educational Research* **63**(1): 1–49.

Hedberg, J., Harper, B., Lockyer, L., Ferry, B., Brown. C. and Wright, R. (1998) Supporting learners to solve ill-structured problems. Paper presented at the 15th Annual Conference of ASCILITE, Wollongong, December.

Laurillard, D., Lindstr$oumlaut;m, B., Marton, F. and Ottosson, T. (1991) *Computer Simulation as a Tool for Developing Intuitive and Conceptual Understanding*. Department of Education and Educational Research, University of G$oumlaut;teborg.

Marton, F. and Booth, S. (1997) *Learning and Awareness*. Mahwah, NJ: Lawrence Erlbaum Associates.

Marton, F. and Ramsden, P. (1988) What does it take to improve learning? In P. Ramsden (ed.), *Improving Learning: New Perspectives*. London: Kogan Page.

Patrick, K. (1990) Teaching and learning at year 12: differences in teachers' conceptions of history. Paper delivered at the Annual Conference of the Australian Association for Research in Education, Sydney, November–December.

Patrick, K. (1992) Teaching and learning physics: the construction of an object of study. Paper delivered at the joint AARE and NZARE conference, December. Geelong: Deakin University.

Patrick, K. (1998) Teaching and Learning: The Construction of an Object of Study. Unpublished PhD dissertation, University of Melbourne.

Patrick, K. (1999) Playing with hypotheses: simulation as a tool for learning. Paper presented at the Annual Conference of HERDSA, Melbourne, July.

Patrick, K. (2001) Constructing a space for learning. Paper presented at the Conference of the European Association for Research in Learning and Instruction, Fribourg, 28 August–1 September.

Patrick, K. and Johnston, S. (1997) Why don't penguins' feet stick to the ice? A multi-use, multi-disciplinary multi-media project. Paper presented at the 14th Annual Conference of ASCILITE, Perth, December.

Prosser, M. and Trigwell, K. (1999) *Understanding Learning and Teaching: The Experience in Higher Education*. Buckingham: Open University Press.

Runesson, U. and Marton, F. (2000) The space of learning. Paper presented at New Phenomenography workshop, Hong Kong, June.

25 From distance education to online learning: challenges and opportunities

J. Lynley Hutton

The Open Polytechnic of New Zealand

25.1 Overview

The convergence of distance education with traditional face-to-face education prompted by the increased use of technology in the form of the Internet for course delivery and student support creates challenges and opportunities for educational institutions, regardless of their previous methods of delivery (Tait, 1999). These challenges and opportunities have been cited as the impetus for change predicted to revolutionise education, for example Garrison (1989), Romiszowski (1997), Peters (2000). In some respects institutions dedicated to distance education, or with a history of dual delivery may initially have had an advantage, processes already being established for the design of courses to be offered at a distance using other technologies for delivery, such as paper-based materials, audio and video tapes. Despite these apparent advantages, challenges exist as distance education institutions adjust to the use of technology for such purposes as communicating with students and facilitating student-to-student interaction, requiring the development of strategies and skills more commonly associated with face-to-face classrooms (Oliver, 1999).

One such distance education institution facing the challenge of being a paper-based provider shifting to online delivery and student support is The Open Polytechnic of New Zealand, a provider of tertiary distance education for nearly 60 years with over 33,000 students. The Open Polytechnic has instigated a number of ventures into online learning over the past four years, including the trialling of the delivery of materials in electronic format, the formation of an online campus offering student support services, and the use of online forums as part of course delivery and support. Research conducted on the various projects associated with these developments highlighted the needs of students and tutors in relation to online communication. Arising from this a training course to be delivered via an intranet was developed to train tutors in effective practices in online facilitation (Hutton, 2000a). The latest online project, initially offering over 20 courses online in 2001, is now underway with an associated research project to monitor and evaluate the project.

This chapter outlines the projects against a literature framework drawing on, educational psychology, distance education and communication. The main focus will be on the evolution of distance education theory and practice in view of technological advances (Garrison, 2000; Peters, 2000). In particular issues of supporting learners in the online environment, considering such aspects as learning styles and cognitive development, will be addressed (Hutton, 1995; 1998; 2000b).

25.2   The way we were

In the not too distant past, distance education was defined as study that was not under the continuous supervision of tutors who were physically present with their students, the emphasis being on the physical distance between the student and the tutor (Holmberg, 1995; Naidu, 1994). Other definitions of distance education described the communication process as being the characteristic distinguishing it from other traditional forms of education. For example Cropley and Kahl (1983, p. 28) described it as 'a kind of education based on communications procedures which permit the establishment of teaching/learning processes even where no face-to-face contact between teacher and learner exists'.

The terms *distance education* and *open learning* were frequently used interchangeably (Rowntree, 1992). The standard criteria for determining openness were the grounds of flexibility in regard to entry, time, place, and pace; criteria which could also be used in evaluating or discussing distance education. Some theorists went so far as to argue that distance education was a subset of open learning on the basis that open learning could take place in a lecture room or at a distance, whereas distance education must, by definition, be at a distance (Race, 1994).

The practice of distance education tended to follow a standard pattern of students enrolling, being sent a package of mass-produced course materials which they work on independently, then sending in work for assessment by a teacher. Course materials were often heavily reliant on the printed word, sometimes supplemented by audio and video tapes. Most communication between teacher and student was written and restricted to the assessment process, with some students making use of the telephone to contact their teachers. Many courses had compulsory start and finish dates. Some included a block course at which students attended face to face sessions of a lecture or tutorial nature. Increasing technology options meant that some courses had other means of communication, such as audio and video conferencing.

This was the way we were. Many predictions were made by writers and researchers from both face to face and distance education backgrounds, that the changing nature of education, particularly due to technology developments, would see distance education converge with traditional education in the future, for example Florini (1990) and Garrison (1989). Now, with the rapid growth of the World Wide Web and the facilities available to use from it due to technological advances, distance education has entered a stage of evolution that has been heralded as reconceptualising teaching and learning (Ely, 1999). While the future of distance education is assured, the underlying practices and theory are in a state of flux, as advances in technology open up new possibilities for learning. Both face to face institutions and distance education institutions must respond to the challenges and opportunities confronting them as a result of these possibilities, focusing on the needs of learners rather than being driven by the technology. This requires constant evaluation and reflection on the lessons learnt, and developing a coherent theoretical base from which practice can evolve.

25.3 Online developments at The Open Polytechnic of New Zealand

One distance education institution rising to the challenge of changing its mode of delivery from paper-based to online delivery, learning from the pilot projects instigated along the way, is The Open Polytechnic of New Zealand. The Open Polytechnic of New Zealand is the leading provider of tertiary distance education in New Zealand with over 33,000 students enrolled in more than 400 courses offered by traditional distance education methods of delivery. Like other educational institutions, The Open Polytechnic has followed a path of pioneering activities where online activities were undertaken by enthusiastic individuals on an ad hoc basis, followed by an initiation phase where strategic decisions were made and projects instigated to test online capabilities and student satisfaction, before institutionalising some of the initiatives (Collis and Moonen, 2001). Current activities include implementing full course delivery of selected courses (see Table 25.1).

Time-line	Developments
Pre-1998	• Adhoc use of list-servers to support technology related courses • Some limited use of web resources to support technology related courses
1998 **Online Course Delivery Project**	• Three courses delivered via the Internet. • Project Aim: to trial the development and implementation of online learning resources and student support.
1999 **Online Campus Pilot Project**	• Establishment of the Online Campus • Project Aim: Determine usage patterns and satisfaction of students accessing Online Campus • Evaluate experiences of staff members
2000 **Online Campus**	• Use of Online Campus institutionalised • On-line tutor training course
2001 **Discovery Project**	• Launching of 'Open Mind Online' • Project Aim: to implement an integrated system for delivery of courses on-line

Table 25.1   Online Developments at The Open Polytechnic of New Zealand

25.4.1   Lessons learnt

The obvious, and expected, lesson of the Online Delivery Project was the need for courses to be designed for online delivery rather than being electronic copies of course materials designed for paper delivery. This has been a criticism of online courses (Oliver, 1999) but was done for pragmatic reasons in the project rather than with the intention of continuing doing so as normal practice. What stood out as a valuable lesson was students' attitudes to the possibilities of an online environment, which were very positive particularly in regard to the communication opportunities, student expectations being of interest for further developments (Brace-Govan and Clulow, 2000).

The Online Campus Pilot project explored other possibilities of the online environment, especially the communication potential. The main lesson of note with this project was the need for strategies to encourage interaction in online forums. Interaction doesn't happen of its own volition: it requires some facilitation. Providing a virtual space for students to converse without structure or meaning will not in itself encourage them to use the facility, as has been discovered in other research projects (Gillham, Buckner and Butt, 1999). It is evident that there is much value in using forums for student interaction, three commonly sited advantages computer conferencing has over face to face discussions are that it can support discussion, debates, and collaborative efforts for people in different locations; that learners are able to reflect on their ideas and other participants, before making a response; and that different types of thinking can be scaffolded (Jonassen, 1999). However, the value of participating in a forum needs to be perceived by students, rather than seen as an add-on adding more busy work than meaning (Vrasidas and McIsaac, 1999).

Both projects highlighted the need for staff development. Regardless of what environment the tutor has previously taught in recognising changes arising from the use of technology for new methods of delivery can be daunting (Pincas, 2000). Aside from hands on use of hardware and software that may be a formidable task for the less technologically adept, roles for online tutors include subject expert, coach, and assessor (Shepherd, 2000). Although these tutoring roles may have parallels in both face-to-face teaching and distance education, the focus can change in an online learning environment, with staff being challenged to develop skills in areas outside their comfort zone. For instance, while tutors still need to have subject expertise, and thus skills in presenting, demonstrating and referring to resources, an online environment may require a modification or extension of existing skills. Consequently new strategies for the tutor as coach, mentor or counsellor may need to be developed. An online course was created for academic staff to address this need (Hutton, 2000a).

The Discovery Project is currently underway, with courses being offered on the Internet from the beginning of 2001 to test systems for developing and supporting online courses. Fourteen courses are operational, with more to be added to the Open Mind Online site. Evaluation of the courses is underway, however results are unavailable as yet. A theoretical framework and practical issues relating to student support have been considered from which to make the evaluation.

25.5   Evolution of distance education theory

Evaluation is essential to continuing growth and development of online learning, however it must be on a solid foundation. Pedagogical questions have to be raised as to what we do, why we do it, and how can we do it better in a digital learning environment, with the pedagogy driving the use of the technology, not vice versa (Freeman and Capper, 1999). As with any educational programme, evaluation is essential to ensure educational standards are met and maintained, and that goals of continuous improvement aspired to by some educational organisations are achieved (Lines, 2000). Developing a framework for evaluating online learning environments is critical to the evolution of teaching and learning practices within the environment (Robson, 2000).

As an emerging field, the evolution of theory to use as a framework for research and practice is not without its problems, and is burgeoning in a somewhat haphazard fashion with viewpoints reflecting the educational background of the theorist and researcher. From a distance education perspective, changes in theory and practices required from using the Internet for course delivery and support are akin to progressing from an industrial era to a post-industrial era. The focus is no longer on the structural constraints determined by geographical distance but is dominated by transactional issues of teaching and learning (Garrison, 2000). Other perspectives are gained from looking at various research disciplines for a theoretical base including pedagogical theories from educational research, media effect theories, group interaction/social influence theories to render a theoretical framework (Hiltz, 2000). Some research frameworks proposed for exploring online education would appear to have little in the way of theory underpinning them, yet it is well known that theory is needed for understanding and communicating aspects of a field of practice such as its goals, purpose and methods (Garrison, 2000).

Online learning is a comparatively new field of education, therefore it is fair to ask whether it is mature enough to render guidance on what are the best methods or practice (Jones, Asensio and Goodyear, 2000). A plethora of advice is available on what to do and what not to do, a natural bias arising from whichever side of the educational continuum the authors reside, for example White and Weight (1999) suggest methodologies based on a face to face classroom model. However, much of what is written is in the handy tips category arising from what is essentially an action research methodology of reflecting on practice, such as Cooper (2000) and Harrison and Bergen (2000). One consistent theme is the use of communication facilities to foster a learning community (Harrison and Bergen, 2000), advocates for the use of particular strategies and online facilities engaging in healthy debates over the applicability and benefits of different online facilities, for example the use of synchronous or asynchronous communication (Shotsberger, 2000). These offerings and debates do not amount to a solid theoretical base. Furthermore studies need to address other issues of learner support in online environments, as well as looking at individual variables such as learning styles and cognitive development.

25.6   Learner support in an online environment

Challenges faced by students studying in an online environment are similar to those faced by distance education students in the past. With students having the choice of when and where to study, and at what pace they want to study (within the confines of their own personal circumstances as well as the deadlines set by the course), they have more freedom of choice than students studying in a face-to-face environment (Race, 1994). While in some respects this freedom is an advantage, it can create more problems than could be experienced by learners in a face-to-face environment. All learners potentially face problems of a similar nature, however distance may create additional problems for learners studying in that mode (Moore, 1989), for example the lack of immediate access to a tutor may create problems, or the only place available to study may not be suitable for the learner's needs. Some challenges can be ameliorated by the instructional design strategies included in courses, while others can be dealt with by the student support systems used by the institution.

Mills (1982) claims that student support services to meet individual needs form an integral complement to the mass-produced materials of a distance teaching system. This must also apply to online teaching systems. Student support can take many forms, such as counselling services, induction courses, learning skills development workshops, and pre-enrolment advice. Tutors also provide support by guiding and directing students to achieve their learning goals, the use of email and forums enabling more support than was possible in the past. Learning materials can provide support by structuring information in a way which also helps guide and direct students, not merely in the achievement of goals directly related to the content of a particular course, but also in processes which empower students by giving them knowledge and insights enabling them to have more control over their learning strategies. Online learning materials can utilize a greater range of media in one package, with the student having more control over learning pathways. Well-designed materials can be assist students in developing skills to give them greater independence as learners, a characteristic that is deemed to be important for success in a distance education learning environment (Paul, 1990).

Kasworm and Yao point out that 'each learner brings to the learning experience varied psychological and cultural factors, such as individual learning styles, the goals for involvement in learning, expectations and motivations, educational history and beliefs of learning, and maturity' (1992, p. 78). Furthermore they argue that certain characteristics are necessary in distance education, such as internal motivation. Atman (1988) emphasises the importance of self-management as a skill that is critical for the success of individuals engaged in distance education, enabling them to structure things, including time and space. As students do not have a class timetable or teacher to structure their learning times, they must be motivated to do it themselves. For some students the physical absence of a teacher can create a barrier to learning which is demotivating (Myer, Fletcher and Gill, 1992), and distance learners in the past did not usually have access to fellow students who could aid motivation by giving support and encouragement.

A characteristic often referred to as a requirement for distance education students is that of being 'self-directed', or of being 'independent', terms which are at times used interchangeably. Paul (1990, p. 83) describes the concept of an independent learner as

> not an absolute one, but a notion that graduates should be more 'self-sufficient' learners than they were at the point of entry. It involves changes in personal values (openness to new ideas and to rethinking current beliefs) and attitudes (self-motivation), as well as the development of new skills (time management, study skills, problem conceptualisation, critical and lateral thinking, and research and library skills). A quest never completely fulfilled, it is a process central to the concepts of open learning and lifelong education.

Candy (1991) makes links between independent learning and self-directed learning, claiming that they are both catchall phrases for 'educational practices having some bearing on the notion of learner-control' (p. 11). When learners are in 'new, unfamiliar situations where they have no experience with the subject area' or where 'they have low self-esteem, related to their personal lives or to the instructional situations or they have never experienced self-directed learning', adult learners will be dependent according to Cranton (1989, p. 202). Discussing issues such as dependency Cranton refers to instructional design based on the characteristics of the learner as a solution, with particular reference to addressing learning styles.

Examining different characteristics which could have an effect on student success, Powell, Conway and Ross state that 'The question of why some students successfully study through distance education and others do not is becoming increasingly important as distance education moves from a marginal to an integral role in the provision of post-secondary education' (1990, p. 5). This question is just as relevant today, if not more so given the increasing use of the Internet to deliver distance education, thereby creating a potentially different learning environment which may provide new challenges for learners.

25.6.1   Learner differences

No matter what the learning environment, learning starts with the learner. Their age, gender, education level, previous experiences, background knowledge and individual style of learning can all impact on their ability to learn in any given learning environment. Hence instructional design and learner support should be developed on the basis of awareness of these variables, for example:

- Learning styles have been interpreted in many ways, with various definitions used and a range of models available. One model defines learning style as 'comprised of the conditions under which each person begins to concentrate on, absorb, process, and retain new or difficult information and skills' (Dunn, 1986, p.3). Various factors can be included within a learning style model, including cognitive style, sensory modalities, social preferences for studying, and environmental influences, various learning environments supporting these factors to varying degrees.

Potentially the Internet, by enabling the use of a range of media, could provide an environment supporting a wider variety of learning styles. The question has to be asked whether that is useful for learners. A study undertaken at The Open Polytechnic of New Zealand found no relationship between sensory modalities and success in distance education courses. From that study however, it was discovered that very few students in that study had a high preference for visual learning (3 per cent), while a significant proportion (30 per cent) had a high preference for auditory learning (Hutton, 1998). Some supporters of online course delivery cite the multi-sensory learning environment as a benefit of the medium, yet this may not be appropriate for all learners, too much sensory stimulation possibly being more of a distraction than a learning aid. This view was supported by some learners in research undertaken at The Open Polytechnic, who did not want a lot of the features which could be included in online courses, such as video and graphic simulations, as they found them to be a diversion which didn't help their learning (Hutton, 1999).

As aspects of learning styles can change over time in response to developmental stages and the learning environment, the preferences of learners could change in the future. Increasing exposure from an early age to the sensory stimulation provided by television and computer games may encourage the development of styles which are attuned to a technology-created multimedia environment. Whatever the definition of learning styles or whatever the learning environment, an awareness of the possible impact of individual differences can help us create courses which better meet individual needs. With the options available using the Internet for course delivery and support we may be in a better position to do so. However, simply creating a replica of what has been before – either in a face-to-face learning environment, or in an open learning environment – is not likely to make a great deal of difference to learners. It is the needs of the individual which must guide developments, not the need to use the technology. As Romiszowski (1993, p. 64) points out:

> There may be whole areas of human thinking that are not only dependent on the analysis, organization and manipulation of knowledge but are also highly dependent on personality and emotional traits that may be well beyond the capabilities of replication within computer software.

However incorporating an awareness of the pedagogical needs of various learning styles can enhance the design of, for example, multimedia software, as shown in a study by Montgomery (1995).

- Age is another variable which may impact on a students preferences for how and where they learn. In the past, ages in traditional face to face classrooms were often homogenous, tertiary institutions reflecting this with the majority of students attending straight from secondary school. Today age distinctions are becoming increasingly blurred particularly in open and distance learning which draws on a wide age population. The life stage and experiences of students can vary hugely across a course as a result of age differences, influencing not only the depth and breadth of prior knowledge, their social relationships and living arrangements, health status and many other aspects relevant to a modern formal learning environment.

- Educational levels can influence success in learning, some research studies have found a relationship between previous educational levels in distance learners and exam success, the higher the level the more likelihood of success (Bajtelsmit, 1990, Cookson, 1989). Bajtelsmit suggests that 'students at lower educational levels may benefit considerably from highly structured study methods and be debilitated when left to their own devices in the context of independent study'. These points need to be considered when designing courses for other non-traditional educational environments, such as the Internet.

- Gender differences may impact on the learning choices made, not only in types of courses chosen, but also in the type of learning environment. For example, research shows that gender differences in the use of computers exist with computers being viewed as a male domain, attitudes and computer literacy in gender comparisons reflecting this. Experience with computers has been found to ameliorate these differences (Fletcher-Flinn and Suddendorf, 1996). Nevertheless, when designing a learning environment involving computer use such as is needed with online courses, awareness of potential differences in terms of previous experience and attitudes from a gender perspective need to be taken into account (Corley, 1994).

25.7   Learning environments for tomorrow's world

As learning environments become increasingly complex with the use of technology creating other dimensions previously not explored or utilised to the same degree in formal learning situations, the instructional design of courses must reflect this to maximise the benefits of the environment for students. Theories of learning need to recognise the complexity as well as integrate it with knowledge of the differences in learners that can influence their responses to the learning environment.

An integrated learning model acknowledges the learner as central to learning, recognising that each learner has their own learning styles preferences which they bring to bear on the environment. Other facets of the learner influencing their ability to function successfully within a particular environment include their prior knowledge, learning skills and strategies. The micro learning environment, as found in a particular situation such as a formal course, is part of the macro environment of a dynamic, multi-dimensional world, incorporates information and appropriate technologies. Regardless of what or where the learning environment is, it exists within the social-cultural framework of the learner, thus directly impacting on the learner and the environment. Communicating on a one to one, or one to many basis within the micro and macro learning environments assists the learner to construct their knowledge beyond their existing learning parameters. Consideration of all of these factors must be integrated into the design and evaluation of courses.

Rather than the traditional environments of education where stability was the norm, today's environment is one of change with a new educational climate being created by the Internet (Healey, 2000). Although some views and ventures into online learning appear to be driven more by administrative or political (Cookson, 2000; Gillham, Buckner and Butt, 1999), others are pragmatically based on the realities of the workplace with the expectation that 'people will look to tertiary education providers to train them in a manner that will serve them best on entering a workplace' (Healey, p. 63, 2000).

Online delivery and support is applicable to all areas of education, not just business. There is no doubt, as Fox states, that 'Society expects graduates to emerge from their university experience with appropriate digital technology skills and abilities irrespective of the level of importance of such technology within individual disciplines' (1999, p. 1). This has far reaching implications for anyone involved in education. Peters (2000) comments we now have a 'cumulation, compression and intensification of presentation that has never been seen before because it was never before possible' (p. 4) as well as new means of facilitating communication and interaction to meet students needs (Solloway and Harris, 1999), making the future one of exciting possibilities.

25.8   Conclusion

The challenges posed by an educational innovation, such as the Internet, force us to reconsider established theory in light of the changes necessary for the innovation to gain acceptance. By viewing the innovation from all possible angles, developing theories which have the power to better explain how it works in practice, evaluating how the innovation works in practice on that basis, and learning from that evaluation, we increase our chances of getting it right – of making the innovation work so that it adds value to the education process.

The starting point for any learning theory, for educational research and evaluation must be the learners who are central to the process, not the technology: technology is only the tool, its how we use it that can make a difference to learners. Integrating all the knowledge we have of the learner, their learning environment, and other surrounding variables can help us create courses which achieve this.

25.9   References

Atman, K.S. (1988) Psychological type elements and goal accomplishment style: implications for distance education, *American Journal of Distance Education* 2(3): 36–44.

Borthwick, R.A. and Jones, D.R. (2000) The motivation for collaborative discovery learning online and its application in an information systems assurance course, *Issues in Accounting Education* 15(2): 181–210.

Brace-Govan, J. and Clulow, V. (2000) Varying expectations of online students and implications for teachers: findings from a journal study, *Distance Education* 21(1): 118–35.

Candy, P.C. (1991) *Self-Direction for Lifelong Learning: A Comprehensive Guide to Theory and Practice.* San Francisco: Jossey-Bass.

Collis, B. and Moonen, J. (2001) *Flexible Learning in a Digital World: Experiences and Expectations.* London: Kogan Page.

Cookson, P.S. (2000) Implications of Internet technologies for higher education: North American perspectives, *Open Learning* 15(1): 71–80.

Cooper, L. (2000) On-line course: tips for making them work, *Journal of Instructional Science and Technology* 3(3). http://www.usq.edu.au/electpub/e-jist/vol3no3/index.htm

Cranton, P. A. (1989) *Planning Instruction for Adult Learners*. Toronto: Walls and Thompson.

Dunn, R. (1986) Learning styles: link between individual differences and effective instruction, *North Carolina Educational Leadership* 2(1): 3–16.

Ely, D. (1999) Toward a philosophy of instructional technology: thirty years on, *British Journal of Educational Technology* 30(4): 305–10.

Florini, B.M. (1990) Communications technology in adult education and learning. In M. Galbraith (ed.), *Adult Learning Methods: A Guide for Effective Instruction*, 367–89. Krieger: Malabar.

Freeman, M. and Capper, J. (1999) Exploiting the web for education: an anonymous asynchronous role simulation, *Australian Journal of Educational Technology* 15(1): 95–117.

Garrison, D.R. (1989) *Understanding Distance Education: A Framework for the Future*. London: Routledge.

Garrison, R. (2000) Theoretical challenges for distance education in the 21st century: a shift from structural to transactional issues, *International Review of Research in Open and Distance Learning* 1(1). http://www.irrodl.org/iuicode?149.1.1.2

Gillham, M., Buckner, K. and Butt, R. (1999) The cautious student – a user-centred evaluation of web-supported learning, *Innovations in Education and Training International* 36(4): 327–33.

Harrison, N. and Bergen, C. (2000) Some design strategies for developing an online course, *Educational Technology*, January–February, 57–60.

Healey, N. (2000) Online education: why businesses are moving skills training online, Internet.au, February, 59–61.

Hiltz, R. (2000) Measuring the importance of collaborative learning for the effectiveness of ALN: a multi-measure, multi-method approach, *Journal of Asynchronous Learning Networks*. http://www.aln.org/alnweb/journal/Vol4_issue2/le/hiltz/le-hiltz.htm

Holmberg, B. (1995) *Distance Education* (2nd edn). London: Routledge.

Hutton, J.L. (1995) Learning to think: implications for course design in distance education. In Nouwens, F. (ed.) *Distance education: crossing frontiers: papers for the 12th Biennial Forum of the Open and Distance Learning Association of Australia, Vanuatu, September 1995*. (pp. 171–4). Australia: Central Queensland University Distance Education Centre.

Hutton, J.L. (1998) What's the difference?, *Open Praxis*, April, 19–21.

Hutton, J.L. (1999) *Courses on the Internet: Students' Strategies, Satisfaction and Styles, and the Implications of Academic Staff*. Unpublished report for The Open Polytechnic of New Zealand.

Hutton, J.L. (2000a) Online course delivery and student support: past, present, and future possibilities. Accounting Educators Forum, Sydney, 30 Nov.–1 Dec. (paper presented – proceedings to be published).

Hutton, J.L. (2000b) Supporting learners in a brave new world. In G. Hart (ed.), *Readings and Resources in Global Online Education*. Melbourne: Whirligig Press, 54–60.

Jonassen, D.H., Peck, K.L. and Wilson, B.G. (1999) *Learning with Technology: A Constructivist Perspective*. Prentice Hall: Upper Saddle River.

Kasworm, C.E. and Yao, B. (1992) The development of adult learner autonomy and self-directedness in distance education. In B. Scriven (ed.), *Distance Education for the Twenty-First Century*. Selected papers from the 16th World Conference of the International Council for Distance Education, Thailand, November.

Mills, A.R. (1982) Student support services in continuing education. In J.S. Daniel (ed.), *Learning at a Distance: A World Perspective*. Edmonton: Athabasca University.

Montgomery, S.M. (1995) Addressing diverse learning styles through the use of multimedia. http://fre.www.een.purdue.edu/fre/asee/fie95/3a2/3a22/3a22.htm

Moore, M.G. (1989) Recruiting and retaining adult students in distance education, *New Directions in Continuing Education* **41**, 89–98.

Myers, C.I., Fletcher, M.D. and Gill, P.L. (1992) Learner-centred distance education: strategies and evaluation. In B. Scriven (ed.), *Distance Education for the Twenty-first Century. Selected Papers from the 16th World Conference of the International Council for Distance Education* (pp. 279–82). Queensland: Queensland University of Technology.

Naidu, S. (1994) Applying learning and instructional strategies in open and distance learning, *Distance Education* **15**(1): 23–41.

Oliver, R. (1999) Exploring strategies for online teaching and learning, *Distance Education* **20**(2): 240–54.

The Open Polytechnic of New Zealand (1994) *Charter*. Lower Hutt: The Open Polytechnic of New Zealand.

Paul, R.H. (1990) *Open Learning and Open Management: Leadership and Integrity in Distance Education*. London: Kogan Page.

Peters, O. (2000) Digital learning environments: new possibilities and opportunities, *International Review of Research in Open and Distance Learning* **1**(1). http://www.irrodl.org/iuicod?149.1.1.7

Pincas, A. (2000) New literacies and future educational culture, *Association for Learning Technology Journal* **8**(2): 69–80.

Powell, R., Conway, C. and Ross, L. (1990) Effects of student predisposing characteristics on student success, *Journal of Distance Education* **5**(1): 5–19.

Race, P. (1994) *The Open Learning Handbook* (2nd edn). New Jersey: Kogan Page.

Robson, J. (2000) Evaluating on-line teaching, *Open Learning* **15**(2): 151–72.

Romiszowski, A.J. (1993) Developing interactive multimedia courseware and networks: some current issues. In C. Latchem, J. Williamson and L. Henderson-Lancett (eds), *Interactive Multimedia: Practice and Promise* (pp. 57–78), London: Kogan Page.

Romiszowski, A.J. (1997) Web-based distance learning and teaching: revolutionary invention or reaction to necessity? In B.H. Khan (ed.), *Web-Based Instruction* (pp. 41–6). New Jersey: Educational Technology Publications.

Rowntree, D. (1992) *Exploring Open and Distance Learning*. London: Kogan Page.

Shepherd, C. (2000) Online tutoring skills, *Open Learning Today*, July: 34–7.

Shotsberger, P.G. (2000) The human touch: synchronous communication in web-based learning, *Educational Technology*, Jan. –Feb., 53–6.

Solloway, S.G. and Harris, E.L. (1999) Creating community online. negotiating students' needs and desires in cyberspace, *Edcom Review* **34**(2): 8–13. http://www.educause.edu/ir/library/html/erm99021.htm

Tait, A. (1999) The convergence of distance and conventional education: some implications for policy. In A.N. Tait and R. Mills (eds.), *The Convergence of Distance and Conventional Education: Patterns of Flexibility for the Individual Learner* (pp. 141–9). London: Routledge.

Vrasidas, C. and McIsaac, M.S. (1999) Factors influencing interaction in an online course, *The American Journal of Distance Education* **13**(2): 22–36.

Wegner, S.B. (1999) The effects of Internet-based instruction on student learning, *Journal of Asynchronous Learning Networks*. http://www.aln.org/alnweb/journal/Vol3_issue2/Wegner.htm

White, K.W. and Weight, B.H. (1999) *The Online Teaching Guide: A Handbook of Attitudes, Strategies, and Techniques for the Virtual Classroom*. Allyn & Bacon: Needham Heights, MA.

26 What makes a good skills website? Optimising the impact of study skills advice using web-based delivery

Janet Macdonald, Clive Barrett, Vicki Goodwin, Marion Phillips

Open University, UK

Keywords
keyskills; learning skills; ; resources; student support; web-based

26.1   Overview

The delivery of study skills advice to students in Higher Education, using either print-based media or face-to-face sessions, is familiar territory for educational developers, and by and large we know the message which we wish to convey. With the options for web-based delivery now available, it is important to assess how the use of this medium can improve on existing methods of student support, or increase motivation, or provide more effective feedback.

The question of context is particularly of relevance when considering web-based skills support. Most of the literature in this field is concerned with the design of online environments for *courses*, which have a fixed start and finish, a cohesive group of students, an assessment strategy which serves to motivate and provide opportunities for feedback, and an allowance in staff time to guide students and mark their assignments. On the other hand, for web-based *resources* with no assessment strategy and where staff intervention is probably strictly limited, there are new challenges.

This chapter engages in some reflective practice on what constitutes effective practice in this field, and in this medium. It describes experiences at the UK Open University in developing skills development material for a web-based environment, and then goes on to discuss the lessons which can be drawn from an examination of other web-based resources on learning skills development.

26.2   Introduction

The use of the Web for teaching and learning online offers a variety of ways of presenting or structuring learning opportunities which were not previously available. Probably the most important of these is the opportunity for students to interact and communicate with others, either in real time or more importantly asynchronously, allowing flexibility in the time and space when the system can be used. Secondly, online systems 'extend the reach of content' (Good, 2001, p. 167) in the sense that students have the opportunity to access further resources, whether on the Web or from fellow students.

However, the evidence for 'what works' in web-based instruction is bewildering, and the literature in this area is growing at an alarming rate. Hypertext environments can be used not only to help learners acquire and construct knowledge (see e.g. Carver *et al.*, 1992) but also to give them an overview of the semantic structure of a knowledge domain (Jonassen and Wang, 1992). On the other hand the use of hypertext environments may lead to disorientation (being 'lost in hyperspace') and distraction (Marchionini, 1988), in fact, far from helping users construct knowledge, hypertext can undermine comprehension (Plowman, 1996).

The characteristics of hypermedia users have been described by a variety of colourful names, including feature explorers, cyber cartographers, resource junkies, video hoppers, apathetic hypertext users or disenchanted volunteers (Barab, Bowdish and Lawless, 1997; Lawless and Kulikowich, 1996), illustrating a wide variability in enthusiasm, ability or motivation. Martinez (2001) stresses the significance of affective issues in web-based learning environments. Similar variations are described by MacGregor (1999), who found that some students were highly dependent on pre-structured lists, while others were able to construct their own navigation routes in more individual and purposeful ways. Some work (Britt *et al.*, 1996; Weyer, 1982) observes that students tend to rely on familiar tools and the use of slower and safer conservative search and navigation strategies, while others prefer to turn to a table of contents rather than relying on hypertext links.

Indeed the success of searching and making sense of information in hypertext environments appears to be influenced by a complex mix of factors, and Hill and Hannafin (1997) suggest that these should include metacognitive knowledge; perceived orientation (getting one's bearings); perceived self efficacy (self confidence); system knowledge and prior subject knowledge.

In common with learning in any face-to-face, or text-based situation Alexander and Boud (2001) stress the importance of designing opportunities for students to maximise their learning from experience, by including activities which allow them to build on what they already know and to make sense of new information by reflective interaction with their peers. In a similar vein, Collis and Moonen (2001) maintain that students should be encouraged to become active learners, by contributing to course resources, and becoming part of a course community. They advocate a focus on learner activities, the chance to participate and contribute, and a move away from pre-structured learning materials. Again, the emphasis is on design for flexibility and adaptability, and active learning.

An environment for active learning needs to provide a focus for students, so that their learning is channelled appropriately. Laurillard *et al.* (2000) maintain that the designer should start with a consideration of what learning activities are needed to understand a topic. They can then create affordances, or opportunities for these activities to take place within the environment.

However, the fact is that all this useful research is difficult to apply constructively if we ignore the context in which the system is to be used (Jackson and Anagnostopoulou, 2001). The context will include not only the design of the online environment, but also the learning situation and constraints of the individual student, and the attitudes and aspirations of the teacher. In other words, it is impossible to predict the effectiveness of any system for all learners, for all learning situations. The lesson is that the technology should be flexible enough to accommodate a variety of different teaching and learning approaches, or its uptake will be limited.

This question of context is particularly of relevance when considering web-based skills support. Most of the literature is concerned with the design of online environments for *courses*, which have a fixed start and finish, a cohesive group of students, an assessment strategy which serves to motivate and provide opportunities for feedback, and an allowance in staff time to guide students and mark their assignments. On the other hand, for web-based *resources* with no assessment strategy and where staff intervention is probably strictly limited, there are new challenges. For example, it becomes problematic to define who the potential students are, in terms of what level they might be studying, from what course, when they might wish to access the site, and why they might want to in the first place. The site must be flexible enough to offer guidance and support to students studying a wide variety of different courses, at different levels, accessing materials at unpredictable times, and studying under different working constraints. Is this an impossible task? How should such sites be designed for effective learning? These are the generic problems to be addressed in the provision of effective web-based skills advice.

The experience of developing skills development material for a web-based environment and our plans for integrating these resources into a web-based portal for our students has led us to engage in some reflective practice on what constitutes effective student support in this field, using this medium. This chapter describes our experiences at the Open University, and then goes on to discuss the lessons which we have learnt, and inspiration we have drawn, from an examination of other web-based resources on learning skills development.

26.3   Developments at the Open University

When we started to consider how we might offer skills advice on the Web we were particularly mindful of the learning context of our students. Our students come to us from a very wide variety of backgrounds in terms of their educational qualifications and life experiences. Because we are an open-access institution, students may enter their programme of undergraduate studies with the Open University at any level, and many students with previous experience or qualifications in HE choose to start at second or third level. During their course of study they may move more freely between disciplines than the traditional undergraduate, which can mean that they are meeting requirements for different academic learning skills around every corner, and need to adapt their skills. In addition, students do not always make the most appropriate choices of entry point and discover during their studies that they lack the study skills required.

Open University students are offered support for study skills in a variety of ways. Some opportunities are formally built into course materials and activities, whilst others are generic. Some are assessed and lead to the award of CATs points, others are not. Skills support is provided at a variety of levels, in a wide variety of presentation media, whether in voluntary face-to-face tutorials, workshops or residential schools, in electronic form or through specific publications.

We have published a series of nine Student Toolkits in the form of A4 booklets of 30–40 pages, to provide generic guidance on particular skills. They are designed to encourage a reflective and active approach to study, are stand-alone, in other words not related to a particular course, and are free to registered students who need them. It was intended that all nine of these toolkits would be reversioned for presentation on the Internet, but this proved over-ambitious and only two of the web toolkits are currently available.

The online student toolkits have been housed within the learning skills development section of a website known as *The Learner's Guide to the Open University* (www.open.ac.uk/learners-guide). This website provides an online learner service offering support for learning and educational advice and guidance for students and prospective students of the Open University. The service includes support for activities such as choosing and planning a study programme, careers guidance, organising study, thinking about study needs (including facilities for disabled students), developing learning skills and monitoring progress. A major aim of this service is to help students become autonomous, so support for learning is an important aspect of the service. In terms of support, students may need help to 'learn how to learn', to learn study skills or to learn how to plan for their development.

Reversioning was not simply a matter of putting the text of the paper-based toolkits online, but rather of adapting the material so that it made best use of the opportunities afforded by the medium. Our conviction was that to support learning we needed to engage the student in *active* learning by offering activities that would allow them to reflect on their concerns. Such activities not only help users engage with the advice, and provide feedback, but also help to make the exercise more meaningful for each individual.

We were also convinced that a generic site should allow individuals the choice to duck and weave their way around helpful materials and activities. It was important to offer a variety of ways in which students might access support material 'at time of need' and to allow them choice and flexibility in as many ways as possible. Through strategies, or through reflective activities or alternatively practical exercises, a student can link into further sites relevant to their particular needs. Hopefully the student will come back to various sites as they progress in their studies, not working through material in a sequential way but rather in an individual-specific way which both meets their needs but also alerts them to other learning skills possibilities which they had not considered.

26.4   Lessons from existing web-based resources on learning skills development

One of the best ways of articulating what might constitute effective student support is to look at the ways in which other organisations have approached the problem, and then to identify features they have used which may be of relevance to your own situation. The following account is a distillation of the ideas which we have gleaned from a study of a variety of web-based learning skills resources from other universities.

26.4.1   Flexibility

The need to tailor resource content to the market, for example whether undergraduate or postgraduate, which subject discipline, at which level. Given the openness of generic skills support, it is probably important to provide a variety of routes into the resources in order to cater for a wide range of interests and levels. While some support may be applicable to a wide spectrum of subjects, other areas may need to be tailored for a particular discipline. Some learning skills advice is most effective when it can be contextualised within the subject of study. (See for example the Resource Discovery Network Virtual Training Suite, RDN VTS, http://www.sosig.ac.uk/vts/education which provides subject discipline routes into resources on the use of the Internet for education.)

- *Flexibility of access* While some students prefer to work exclusively online, others appreciate the flexibility to work at least part of the time away from a computer. Therefore downloadable files are probably a sensible option. In this way students have a choice of online or offline study. (See for example Plymouth University learning skills leaflets, which they provide in addition to an online tutorial program http://home.plymouth.ac.uk/services/help-advice/studyguides.html).

- *Flexibility in pedagogic approach* The structure of the website must reflect in a recognisable way the needs and problems which students bring to it, or they are unlikely to return. By definition these needs are likely to be diverse, and so the planning of a learning skills site might need to include a variety of types of resource, including structured online tutorials (see for example Internet Detective http://www.sosig.ac.uk/desire/internet-detective.html); a file of FAQs or a concise 'quick tip' (see UniS 'Tip of the Week' http://www.surrey.ac.uk/Skills/Pack/).

- Students may arrive at the resource with problems which are not expressed in the language of conventional study skills. One approach could be to start with the problems and use them as an index to the resource (see for example the OU Revision & Examinations site http://www.open.ac.uk/learners-guide/learning-skills/revision/index.htm where the *strategy list*, or *key concerns* gives students the opportunity to follow up advice related to a particular area). Alternatively students could be encouraged to identify their concerns, perhaps in an activity, before looking for information. For example Surrey University's Skills Pack offer opportunities for diagnostic testing, in their skills self-assessment audit (http://www.surrey.ac.uk/Skills/Pack/audit.html).

26.4.2   Ease of use and attractiveness

- *Optimising opportunities for non-linear study* One of the challenging aspects of hyperlinked information is that it can be, and often is, studied in a non-linear way. Attractive resources are easily navigable, and usable from a variety of entry points. The reader should be able to jump to a relevant section if required, and bookmark it for future reference (the RDN VTS has a useful 'links basket' idea for bookmarking). Signposting from the home page should also be visually appealing and easy to follow, and pictorial representations of alternative routes have been used to great effect (see for example the first page in the downloadable Skills Shop program from Plymouth University http://home.plymouth.ac.uk/services/help-advice/skillsshop.html, or the UCL Key Skills grid http://www.ucl.ac.uk/keyskills/grid.html).

- *Volume of information per page*   This is related to the issue of flexibility of access. If a resource is designed to be studied online, the consensus is that screen-based information takes up to 20 per cent longer to read than print-based, and therefore large chunks of text need to be broken up with headings and images. It is worth comparing the different approaches adopted by the University of Surrey site, (http://www.surrey.ac.uk/Skills/Pack/essay.html) with that of the RDN VTS (http://www.sosig.ac.uk/vts/education). For online users who may be looking for a particularly 'quick fix', there is an argument for even more stringent restrictions on the amount of information to be presented per page (see the Student UK site http://www.studentuk.com/advice/academic/). Other users may prefer to have greater detail in a more traditional downloadable leaflet.

- *Use of feedback and activities*   It is well established practice to include some form of feedback and activity where students are following an online tutorial, as this helps to engage them and can make learning more effective. Many activities are enhanced by building in some response to the students' efforts. In this way, the program has more of an interactive 'feel', and even a short comment which the student reaches from a hotlink can act as an encouragement to complete the activity. This builds added benefit on conventional paper and pencil activities, and the response can give students a sense of dialogue. Feedback may offer students the opportunity to compare their own work with an official response, or alternatively they can be given a questionnaire to complete, and then invited to compare their responses with a grid of advice, or links to further reading. For more protracted feedback and debate, a link can be included to a computer conference with peers or staff, see for example UNISA online workshops http://www.unisanet.unisa.edu.au/learningconnection/wkshpol/general.htm.

Activities often require time and reflection, and therefore some students may wish to complete them offline. Some skills websites offer activities as downloadable files if the activities are likely to be particularly time consuming (see the University of Surrey downloadable exercises http://www.surrey.ac.uk/Skills/Pack/download.html). As an alternative, students can be encouraged to log off, whilst keeping the relevant screen on their browser, and then to log on after completing the exercise.

- *Simulations/examples*   Lastly, illustrations and examples can help where abstract advice fails to communicate. See for example the use of case studies in the RDN VTS (http://www.sosig.ac.uk/vts/education/), or the illustrative use of students' comments on successful strategies on the OU Revision & Examinations site: (http://www.open.ac.uk/learners-guide/learning-skills/revision/index.htm)

26.4.3   Message first, then medium

- *Integration of resources*   Students who reach the website will be looking for *any* help and advice on their particular problem. It follows that web-based advice and activities can be greatly enhanced if they are integrated with other categories of resource. A home page might include links to the following elements:

  - learning skills topics for study online or in downloadable files;

  - an index to particular problems, with links to relevant parts of the information resources online;

  - a noticeboard advertising face-to-face sessions;

  - an online problem page/agony aunt; very often students appreciate the opportunity to discuss what they have read, or advice they have encountered elsewhere; it is also an opportunity to feed back queries on areas which students find of interest, but which are not covered by the information presented on the website;

  - help: email to relevant staff; alternatively, help could be dealt with in an online conference;

  - links to subject specific advice;

  - links to further reading, websites and programs such as electronic concept maps; often students themselves are a ready source of information on interesting web sites, and so this information could be fed back from an online conference;

- news, FAQs, links to further help, notices of meetings, quick fix, bite sized chunks of information;

- this strategy has been implemented to great effect at the 'Learning Connection', University of South Australia (http://www.unisanet.unisa.edu.au/learningconnection/learnres/index.htm).

26.5 Conclusion

What makes a good skills site? Well, we are probably no nearer a definitive answer to this question than we were at the start. It will always be a challenge to design a generic resource which will effectively meet the needs of a significant proportion of an unknown and potentially highly diverse group of students. That is the task of a learning skills website.

Our own experiences with skills site development, together with our trawl of similar sites in other universities, has raised some issues, and provided some useful examples of solutions. Clearly, the resource must cater for diversity, in terms of providing flexibility in subject linkage, access to resources and a variety of pedagogical approaches.

Since the resource is not assessed, there must be a recognition that the motivation and enthusiasm of students to use it could wane readily. It is therefore crucial that the website should be engaging, attractive and easy to follow.

Lastly, there is much to be gained from conceptualising the learning skills website as an integral part of a range of resources which could be appropriate to a particular need. The aim might be a single site for all learning needs. After all, the student simply wants an answer. The medium should be immaterial.

26.6 References

Alexander, S. and Boud, D. (2001) Learners still learn from experience when online. In J. Stephenson (ed.), *Teaching and Learning Online: Pedagogies for New Technologies*. London: Kogan Page.

Barab, S.A., Bowdish, B.E. and Lawless, K.A. (1997) Hypermedia navigation: profiles of hypermedia users, *Educational Technology Research and Development* **45**(3): 23–41.

Britt, M.A., Rouet, J.-F. and Perfetti, C.A. (1996) Using hypertext to study and reason about historical evidence. In J-F. Rouet, J.J. Levonen, A. Dillon and R.J. Sprio (eds), *Hypertext and Cognition* pp. 43–72. Mahwa, NJ: Lawrence Erlbaum Associates.

Carver, S.M., Lehrer, R., Connell, R. and Erickson, J. (1992) Learning by hypermedia design: issues of assessment and implementation, *Educational Psychologist* **7**(3): 385–404.

Collis, B. and Moonen, J. (2001) *Flexible Learning in a Digital World*. London: Kogan Page.

Good, M. (2001) On the way to online pedagogy. In *Teaching and Learning Online: Pedagogies for New Technologies*. London: Kogan Page.

Hill, J. and Hannafin, M. (1997) Cognitive strategies and learning from the World Wide Web, *Educational Technology Research & Development* **45**(4): 37–64.

Jackson, B. and Anagnostopoulou, K. (2001) Making the right connections: improving quality in online learning. In J. Stephenson (ed.), *Teaching and Learning Online: Pedagogies for New Technologies*. London: Kogan Page.

Jonassen, D. and Wang, S. (1993) Acquiring structural knowledge from semantically structured hypertext, *Journal of Computer Based Instruction* **20**(1): 1–8.

Laurillard, D., Stratfold, M., Luckin, R., Plowman, L. and Taylor, J. (2000) Affordances for learning in a non-linear narrative medium, *Journal of Interactive Media in Education* **2**.

Lawless, K.A. and Kulikovich, J.M. (1996) Understanding hypertext navigation through cluster analysis, *Journal of Education Computing Research* **14**(4): 385–99.

Macgregor, S.K. (1999) Hypermedia navigation profiles: cognitive characteristics and information processing strategies, *Journal of Educational Computing Research* **20**(2): 189–206.

Marchionini, G. (1988) Hypermedia and learning: freedom and chaos, *Educational Technology* Nov., 8–12.

Martinez, M. (2001) Key design considerations for personalized learning on the Web, *Educational Technology and Society* **4**(1).

Plowman, L. (1996) Narrative, linearity and interactivity: making sense of interactive multimedia, *British Journal of Educational Technology* **27**(2) 92–105.

Stanton, N., Correia, A.P. and Dias, P. (<??>) Efficacy of a map on search, orientation and access behaviour in a hypermedia system, *Computers and Education* **35**(4): 263–79.

Strivens, J. and Grant, S. (2000) Integrated web-based support for learning employability skills, *Educational Technology and Society* **3**(1).

Weyer, S.A. (1982) The design of a dynamic book for information search, *International Journal of Man-Machine Studies* **17**: 87–107.

27 Assessment of experimental skills and creativity using a modified OSCE-method: a summative performance-based examination in chemical engineering

Thomas Olsson

Lund Institute of Technology, Lund University, Sweden

27.1 Introduction

Assessment is probably the single most important aspect of student learning in higher education. There is compelling argument presented in the literature that the method of assessment has a major influence on the way students accomplish their studies (e.g. Biggs, 1999; Prosser and Trigwell, 1999; Ramsden, 1992).

27.1.1 Background

Within the chemical engineering curriculum (Bachelor of Science level) at Lund University we have introduced carefully prepared and formulated educational objectives – *knowledge, skill and attitude* – at all levels within the curriculum. An important and serious problem is that the assessment is still too much focused on knowledge. Learning is a complex holistic process involving many aspects besides knowledge. The assessment should stimulate a deep oriented, holistic learning and focus on all educational objectives of the curriculum.

Most courses in a chemical engineering curriculum include practical experimental parts. These parts are normally assessed formatively in the laboratory. Students hand in reports and demonstrate their assignments and they get immediate feedback. This is very important and commendable. However, summative assessments of practical engineering skills are of rare occurrence in engineering curricula. An individual summative assessment could be of major importance to influence students to focus on the skill objective of the curriculum.

27.1.2 Overview of the project

What do chemical engineering students think about laboratory teaching? Which are the most important aspects? Section 27.2 presents an outline of student views of laboratory teaching.

Medical education all over the world uses a summative performance-based examination called *Objective Structured Clinical Examination*, OSCE (Harden *et al.*, 1975). Can these ideas of assessment be used in a chemical engineering curriculum? Section 27.3 presents a summative performance-based assessment of experimental skills and creativity.

Qualitative studies using a modified *Course Experience Questionnaire* (Ramsden, 1991) and different *Focus Groups* are presented in section 27.4. Assessment of skills, attitudes and intellectual development (Perry, 1970), approaches to learning and learning technologies are discussed in relation to laboratory work.

Evaluation tools used in this project are the SOLO taxonomy (Biggs and Collis, 1982) and Perry's scheme of ethical and intellectual development (Perry, 1970). The SOLO (Structure of the Observed Learning Outcome) taxonomy is a model for qualitative evaluation of teaching and assessing. It consists of five levels of increasing structural complexity. Perry's scheme of ethical and intellectual development is used to characterise students' intellectual development from dualism through multiplicity to relativism and commitment.

27.2 Student views of laboratory teaching

27.2.1 Methodology

Which are the most important student views on laboratory teaching in chemical engineering? We should know more about this question for many reasons. Teaching in the laboratory is by far the most resource demanding part of an educational programme and it is very important that we reach adequate educational objectives in the laboratory.

The Metaplan Technique (Metaplan GmbH, 2001) is a tool used to make group discussions more effective. It comprises visualisation techniques, interaction techniques and dramaturgical planning techniques. This study uses a modification of an interaction technique called the 'card question technique'.

The method gives a survey of ideas and priorities of a group of people on a given question. It is an illustrative and quick method and the opinion of each group member is accounted for. The modified technique used in this project is described below.

Each participant receives five pieces of paper.

Each person writes five statements that he/she thinks are especially important regarding the question discussed. All pieces of paper are collected, the statements are read to the group and categorised (clusters of similar statements are created and given titles decided by the participants) and finally pinned to a white-board.

Each person now gets 8 marks (self-sticking dots) to distribute among the categories. The more important you think a category is the more marks you give it. A maximum of 4 marks can be given to a single category.

All participants mark the categories (at the same time to make sure that the decisions are made independently from each other) and the marks are counted. The result is a measure of the importance of the different categories among a group of people. Figure 27.1 shows what the results might look like.

27.2.2 Findings

The question that the students were asked to answer was:

> Which are the most important aspects of laboratory teaching?

They were told that the question had no restrictions and that they could write down anything they think is important about laboratory teaching. No other information was given at this point.

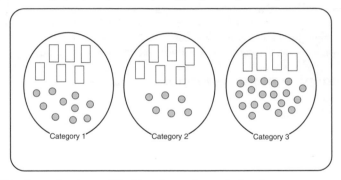

Figure 27.1   Example of a modified 'card question technique'

The investigation was repeated independently with three different groups of students. The students in two of the groups were in their second year of the chemical engineering curriculum and one group in their third and final year. Each group had 6–8 participants.

Five categories of statements emerged. It is very interesting to observe that the same categories emerged in all three groups of students and that they were given approximately the same relative importance. The categories were:

- Category 1:   *'Connections between theory and reality'* 37 % of the marks (by all participating students)
- Category 2:   *'Opportunities to think, plan and design independently'* 28 %
- Category 3:   *'Instructions and planning'* 20 %
- Category 4:   *'Educational objectives and future profession'* 9 %
- Category 5:   *'Reports and assessment'* 6 %

Figure 27.2 gives a pie chart that shows the different categories and their relative importance for all participating students. Figure 27.3 gives pie charts that show the different categories and their relative importance for the three groups of students independently. As can be seen from this figure there are only minor differences between the groups.

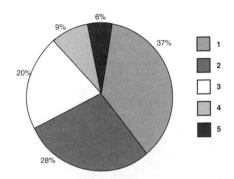

Figure 27.2   Different categories and their relative importance for all participating students

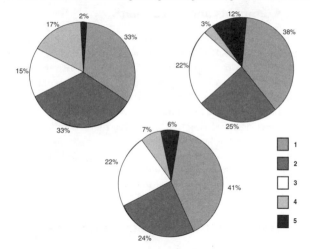

Figure 27.3   Different categories and their relative importance for the three groups of students

Some representative examples of statements given in the different categories are shown below. The total number of statements was 93. The distribution was 30, 19, 30, 10, 2 and 2 statements for category 1, 2, 3, 4 and 5 respectively.

Category 1: Connections between theory and reality

'An opportunity to apply theory in real situations'
'Increase the understanding of theory'
'Connection with reality'
'Discussions. Why? What happens?'
'When you have left the laboratory you should be able to answer questions about the theory that you did not understand before'

Category 2: Opportunities to think, plan and design independently

'I have always wanted to plan and perform experiments without instructions or any other kind of help'
'Give opportunities to think independently'
'... where you must think for yourself'
'Find out how to perform an experiment'

Category 3: Instructions and planning

'Clear instructions'
'Discuss the theory in advance'
'Learn to plan an experiment – time schedule'

Category 4: Educational objectives and future profession

'Knowledge and skills used in the professional life'

Category 5: Reports and assessment

'Clear instructions about the report'
' Increase report writing skills'

27.2.3 Comments and discussion

The Metaplan technique with its different visualisation, interaction and planning techniques is very useful in research as well as in evaluation of teaching and learning.

In smaller groups (8–10 persons) it is possible to use the 'card question technique' as a starting point for further investigations using other Metaplan techniques (Metaplan GmbH, 2001). This procedure makes it possible to find out more about the categories that receive the highest number of marks. Combinations with focus group interviews can also be useful.

It would be very interesting to use the Metaplan Technique as an alternative to traditional evaluations of undergraduate courses.

The results from the present investigation of aspects of laboratory teaching are interesting since the same categories emerged with the same relative importance in all three groups of students. However, the results should not be interpreted quantitatively only as a qualitative measure of student views on the subject.

27.3 Assessment of experimental skills and creativity

27.3.1 Modified OSCE method

The aim of the OSCE (Objective Structured Clinical Examination) method (Harden *et al.*, 1975) is to test students' clinical and communication skills in a planned and structured way. The examination consists of several stations each presenting a scenario. At each station an examiner is observing the student's performance. The result is decided by judging how well the performance meets a number of stated criteria.

The original OSCE-method takes considerable resources. This chapter presents a study of an assessment of experimental skills and creativity in chemical engineering using a modified OSCE-method. The main modifications include:

- presenting tasks at different levels of performance – at some stations students only present ideas of performance or constructions of equipment while at other stations a complete performance must be demonstrated;

- stations where groups of students are assessed as well as stations where students demonstrate their abilities individually;

- the use of learning technologies (video/audio recordings and computerised collection of results) to observe student performance.

A typical examination will last for 3–4 hours and consists of 6–8 different stations. More than 25 different tasks have so far been constructed. They test students' experimental skills, planning of experimental work, critical and reflective thinking and creativity and they are constructed so that they will require students to combine knowledge and skill to perform a task. It is important that most of the tasks are open-ended to allow students to show different qualitative approaches (Biggs and Collis, 1982). Students will be asked to discuss and explain ideas and procedures, formulate and test hypotheses, design experiments etc. – students must perform their understanding. Some of the ideas behind the different tasks originate from practical problems developed at the Department of Chemical Engineering, Centre for Chemistry and Chemical Engineering at Lund University (Axelsson, 1995; Olsson, 2000).

27.3.2 Examination tasks

27.3.2.1 *Determine experimentally the power consumption of a microwave oven*

Besides a microwave oven different equipment and materials can be provided to the students. However, the degree of difficulty of the task depends very much on what equipment and materials are provided. A thermometer, a beaker, water, a balance and a stopwatch are needed to solve the task.

This problem will test many abilities. Students must realise that the energy delivered by the microwave oven can be determined by measuring the absorption of the microwaves in a substance (e.g. water) that is placed in the oven. If you know the amount of water (weight), the heat capacity of the water (physical constant) and the increase in temperature of the water you can calculate the amount of energy transferred to the water. Then students must know the difference between energy and power. The energy determined is the energy transferred during the time the microwave oven is turned on. This time must be measured if the power is to be calculated.

The highest level of performance of this examination task is of course a situation where only the microwave oven is provided. If you put a thermometer, a balance, water etc. beside the oven the problem becomes much easier to solve.

Discussions of the reliability of the experimentally determined power consumption should also be required. A discussion of different sources of errors is fundamental in any experimental investigation.

Other substances than water can of course also be used. Do you get different increases in temperature for different substances? Why? What happens if more than one substance is heated at the same time? What physical mechanism explains why a substance is heated? Is it easier to heat liquid water than ice? Many discussions can easily be generated and it is possible for students to demonstrate qualitative learning at high SOLO levels. Discussions at the relational and even extended abstract levels are common.

27.3.2.2 *Determine experimentally the power required to make coffee in a coffee machine*

Figure 27.4 shows in principle how a coffee machine works. Water (A) flows through a tube and is heated with a heating coil (B). After the heater the flow in the tube consists of both liquid water and steam. It is a two-phase flow where the steam lifts the water upwards and into the filter where the coffee is brewed.

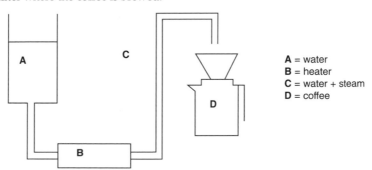

Figure 27.4 A coffee machine

This problem is similar to that of the microwave oven but more difficult because energy is needed both to heat the water to the boiling point and to vaporise some of the water to steam. Not all of the water (A) will end up as coffee (D) and the measurements must take this into account.

The coffee machine problem also initiates discussions about heat of vaporisation, two-phase flow, mammoth pumps etc. Such discussions often reach high SOLO levels.

27.3.2.3   Construct a plate heat exchanger

This problem is different from the two problems just described since no measurements are performed. A plate heat exchanger consists of different kinds of plates (Figure 27.5). The plates, usually corrugated, are supported in a frame. Hot fluid passes between alternate pairs of plates exchanging heat with the cold fluid flowing between adjacent pairs of plates. Students receive a number of plates each marked with a number. The task is to build a plate heat exchanger, in working order, according to given specifications and to tell where the hot and cold streams enter and leave the apparatus.

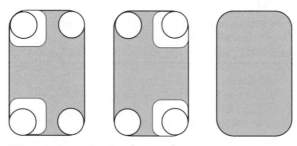

Figure 27.5   Some different plates of a plate heat exchanger

The solution of the problem is easily presented since all that students have to show is a correct series of numbers.

27.3.2.4   Construct a plate and frame filter press

This problem is similar to the plate heat exchanger problem. A filter press consists of plates, frames and washing plates. The task is to build a filter press, in working order, according to given specifications.

27.3.2.5   Some other examples of examination tasks:

- experimental estimation of the viscosity of a fluid
- experimental determination of the characteristic curve of a centrifugal pump;
- experimental estimation of the risk of cavitation of a centrifugal pump;
- experimental determination of the friction factor of a pipe-line;
- experimental determination of the loss coefficient of a globe valve;
- experimental determination of the heat conductivity of a solid;
- measurements of temperature in an oven;

- experimental determination of overall heat transfer coefficient of a heat exchanger;

- experimental determination of the plate efficiency of a bubble-cap distillation column;

- experimental determination of the apparent overall heat transfer coefficient of an LTV evaporator.

Several other problems have been developed and they all show the same general structure as the problems described above.

27.3.3 Comments and discussion

All problems developed can be solved at different levels of performance. Students can be assessed individually or in groups of students. This flexibility makes the proposed modified OSCE method an appealing assessment method used as a summative performance-based examination in the laboratory.

Discussions of the problems with teachers enable students to demonstrate learning at high SOLO levels. The occasion of the examination becomes an occasion for learning.

27.4 Qualitative research – design and findings

The methodology employs the use of a modified Course Experience Questionnaire (Ramsden, 1991) and different Focus Groups (e.g. Morgan and Krueger, 1997). These tools are used to investigate attitudes, intellectual development (Perry, 1970) and approaches to learning. The total number of students participating in the investigations is between 20 and 30 and the obtained data should *only* be *used qualitatively*. All investigations are focused on laboratory teaching and especially performance-based assessment.

27.4.1 Modified 'Course Experience Questionnaire'

The Course Experience Questionnaire (CEQ) is a quantitative research and evaluation method that consists of about 40 statements covering good teaching, clear goals, appropriate workload, appropriate assessment, student independence and approaches to learning.

In this project new statements about assessment and intellectual development have been constructed. These new statements are all added to the CEQ and mixed with the original statements of the questionnaire. All students answered the complete modified CEQ but only items relevant for this study were used in the evaluation of the results.

When a 'course' is referred to in the statements the students were asked to think about 'laboratory teaching'. Students responded to the statements on a scale from 1 to 5 where:

1 = definitely not
2 = hardly
3 = maybe / maybe not
4 = agree
5 = exactly

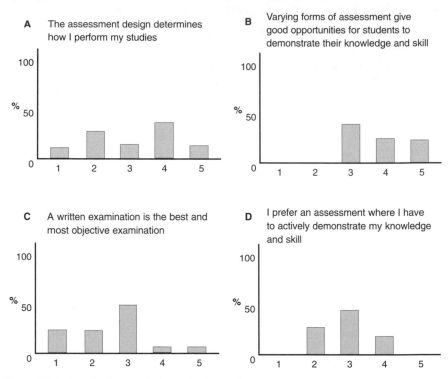

Figure 27.6   Results from questionnaire items about assessment

27.4.1.1   Assessment of skills

Figure 27.6 gives four new statements (A–D) about assessment and the corresponding results.

The students do think that varying forms of assessment are positive and increase their abilities to demonstrate knowledge and skills and they do not think that a written examination is the most objective examination. However, perhaps all students do not quite realise the impact of assessment on how they perform their studies (statement A).

27.4.1.2   Intellectual development

Five new statements about intellectual development have been added to the CEQ. These statements are connected to the different stages in Perry's scheme of ethical and intellectual development (Perry, 1970). Perry argues that all students follow a development from dualism through multiplicity to relativism and commitment.

Figure 27.7 gives the statements and the results. Statements A and B deal with duality, C with multiplicity, D with relativism and finally D deals with commitment.

It is interesting to discuss these kind of questions but the results are difficult to interpret. At a first glance the results of A and B seem quite inconsistent. However, many students probably understand statement A as roughly 'a teacher must be a skilful communicator'.

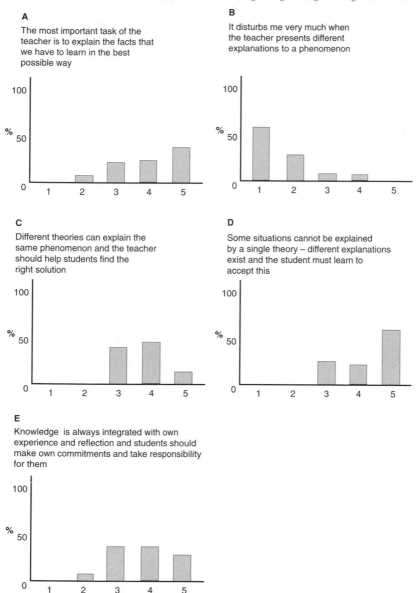

A

The most important task of the teacher is to explain the facts that we have to learn in the best possible way

B

It disturbs me very much when the teacher presents different explanations to a phenomenon

C

Different theories can explain the same phenomenon and the teacher should help students find the right solution

D

Some situations cannot be explained by a single theory – different explanations exist and the student must learn to accept this

E

Knowledge is always integrated with own experience and reflection and students should make own commitments and take responsibility for them

Figure 27.7   Results from questionnaire items about intellectual development

If statement A is disregarded the result shows that the students' intellectual development is well on its way towards the higher levels of Perry's scheme. More discussions about intellectual development and connections to laboratory teaching follow in section 27.4.2.2.

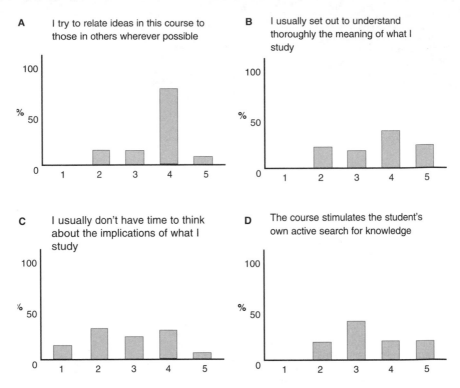

Figure 27.8   Results from questionnaire items about approaches to learning

27.4.1.3   Approaches to learning

Figure 27.8 gives the statements and the result. The statements about approaches to learning are from the original CEQ (A, B and C). A new statement (D) is also added.

The result shows that the students have an acceptable deep approach to learning. Statement C, indicating a surface approach, is disturbing but probably more a manifestation of an overall heavy workload than a surface approach attitude. Discussions with students indicate this.

27.4.1.4   General questions and overall quality

Figure 27.9 gives statements and results for some general questions about workload, goals and future professional life. All statements are considered in connection with laboratory teaching.

27.4.2   Focus groups

Focus groups are group interviews where a small group of people discusses a topic decided by a moderator (Morgan and Krueger, 1997). Focus groups are a qualitative research method where the interactions between the participants, guided by the moderator, generate a rich understanding of experiences, views and beliefs of the participants. The data from focus groups are what the participants say during the interviews.

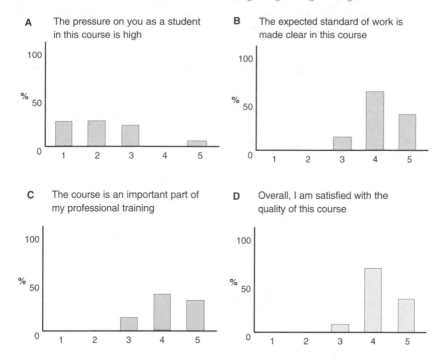

Figure 27.9 Results from questionnaire items about general questions and overall quality

In this study three different focus group interviews, each with 6–8 students, were carried out. The topics discussed were assessment of skills, intellectual development and learning technologies. All topics were focused on laboratory teaching. Each focus group interview lasted for about one hour and the entire interview was audiotaped.

27.4.2.1 Assessment of skills

The discussions about assessment were lively and instructive. A general view is that performance is not properly assessed today and most students would welcome a summative assessment. Some of the most important and representative comments are listed below:

'The report is assessed - not how the work is done'
'Emphasise planning and performance'
'Laboratory work should be a part of the examination'
'The assessment should be individual – even if the laboratory work is done in groups'
'Clear instructions are important but they must not be too detailed'
'... now we are ready with this report – get on with the next one – and the next .... an examination at the end of the course prevents this'

27.4.2.2 Intellectual development

The students are surprisingly aware of their intellectual development. These discussions were mature and showed interesting views of the matter. Students especially demand a much better follow-up of intellectual development with individual interviews, group discussions and more individual responses to students from teachers during their years at the university. Some representative comments:

'Discussions at the laboratory make you realise that there are different ways to reach the same goal'

'It is at the laboratory you realise that theory does not provide you with one single solution to a problem'

'In school you learn that things are right or wrong. Suddenly this is not so. It is frustrating. Discussions with other students and teachers help you overcome this. But it is a process of maturity. It is complex. The more you learn the more you understand about this. Especially the laboratory work helps you realise what it is all about ...'

'Emphasise the role of an engineer'

'More responses from teachers to individual students'

27.4.2.3   *Learning technologies*

These discussions focused on video and audio recordings. Most students are positive and the main argument is that then all students must demonstrate their abilities. Important comments from the focus group interviews are listed below:

'All students must be active'

'It is good – nobody can wangle'

'Interesting – you can see how students think and it is easier to correct any faults that occur'

'Good method – but it can have a restraining effect on shy students'

'Time-consuming – but instructive'

'If it is really good – broadcast it as a "docusoap" called "a jolly good time at the lab ..."'

27.4.3   **Comments and discussion**

It is important that varying examination methods are used within an engineering curriculum. Laboratory work should be a part of the assessment and a summative performance-based examination has many benefits.

Students develop intellectually during their education at the university. Teaching and assessing at the laboratory influence this development positively. However, the ethical and intellectual development should be discussed more between students and teachers.

27.5   Final conclusions and reflections

A summative performance-based assessment influences the way students accomplish their studies

- students must focus on all educational objectives;

- students must demonstrate different abilities;

- students qualitative level of learning is increased – higher SOLO levels are reached;

- students must focus on a deep approach to learning;

- students intellectual development is favoured.

Learning technologies

- provide better feedback on student performance;
- can facilitate the assessment;
- ensure that everyone is seen (important and common student view).

Finally, and most important, the assessment becomes an opportunity for learning – not just testing.

Acknowledgements

The study presented in this chapter is part of a larger project, 'Qualitative Assessment in the Chemical Engineering Curriculum', financed by the Swedish Council for the Renewal of Higher Education. More information about this project can be found at: http://hgur.hsv.se/activities/projects/financed_projects/k-s/olsson_thomas_99.htm

27.6 References

Axelsson, A. (1995) Solving practical problems – an alternative in the chemical engineering laboratory. In *Proceedings at the Conference on Teaching Science for Technology at Tertiary Level, 7–9 June 1994, Stockholm.*

Biggs, J.B. (1999) *Teaching for Quality Learning at University.* Society for Research into Higher Education & Open University Press.

Biggs, J.B. and Collis, K.F. (1982) *Evaluating the Quality of Learning. The SOLO Taxonomy (Structure of the Observed Learning Outcome).* Academic Press.

Harden, R.M., Stevenson, M., Wilson Downie, W. and Wilson, G.M. (1975) Assessment of clinical competence using objective structured examination, *British Journal of Medical Education* 1: 447–51.

Metaplan GmbH (2001) *Primer for the Metaplan Technique.* http://www.metaplan.com

Morgan, D.L. and Krueger, R.A. (1997) *The Focus Group Kit. Vol. 1: The Focus Group Guidebook. Vol. 2: Planning Focus Groups. Vol. 3: Developing Questions for Focus Groups. Vol. 4: Moderating Focus Groups. Vol. 5: Involving Community Members in Focus Groups. Vol. 6: Analyzing & Reporting Focus Group Results,* SAGE Publications.

Olsson, T. (2000) Qualitative aspects of teaching and assessing in the chemical engineering curriculum – applications of the SOLO taxonomy. In C. Rust (ed.), *Proceedings of the 7th International Improving Student Learning Symposium, University of York, 1999. Improving Student Learning Through the Disciplines,* pp. 304–24, Oxford Centre for Staff and Learning Development.

Perry, W.G., Jr (1970) *Forms of Ethical and Intellectual Development in the College Years: A Scheme.* Holt, Rinehart & Winston.

Prosser, M. and Trigwell, K. (1999) *Understanding Learning and Teaching: The Experience in Higher Education.* Society for Research into Higher Education & Open University Press.

Ramsden, P. (1991) A performance indicator of teaching quality in higher education: the course experience questionnaire, *Studies in Higher Education* 16(2).

Ramsden, P. (1992) *Learning to Teach in Higher Education.* London: Routledge.

28 Technology and student attitudes in large lecture classes

Lisa M. Coutu,[a] Mark Alway[b] and Nana Lowell

University of Washington, Seattle, USA: a. Department of Speech Communication; b. Educational Technology Development Group; c. Office of Educational Assessment

Keywords
large lecture classes; technology; student attitudes

28.1 Overview

An introductory large-lecture course in human communication was revamped to include a technology component in order to increase students' opportunities for active learning. We examined two research questions in order to understand more fully the relationship between student attitudes toward technology and (1) their performance on technology-based exercises and (2) their attitude toward the course and instructor.

We found no significant relationships between students' attitudes towards technology and their performance on technology aspects of the course at the beginning of the course, but did find a significant positive correlation between their attitudes towards technology and their performance at the end of the course. Student assessments of the course and instructor were significantly different for the two groups studied, with the technologically enhanced course students assessing the course and instructor more positively in 16 categories and more negatively in one category than the traditionally taught course students.

28.2 Introduction

Institutions, instructors, and students are increasingly experimenting with technology's role in teaching and learning. Universities are establishing centres for learning and technology (e.g. University of Washington's Catalyst initiative and Center for Teaching, Learning and Technology from the Office of Educational Partnerships and Learning Technologies). Pennsylvania State University's Commonwealth College created the Royer Center for Learning and Academic Technologies to 'lead and support a change from heavy reliance on lecture-based instruction to a rich learning environment characterized by active, cooperative learning, supported by technology' (Deden, 1998, p. 58). In addition to university specific centres, faculty in many institutions attend workshops to increase their understanding and use of web-based technologies in the classroom (e.g. Wetzel et al., 1998).

Instructors are adopting online learning technologies in response to both institutional and pedagogical demands. Mayer and Coleman (2000) enumerate questions that educators should ask when including technology in the classroom, particularly in larger lecture courses:

What do students think about the technology? How do they assess the effectiveness of technology as an aid to learning? How do their behaviors and assessments depend on different instructors and teaching strategies? Does the use of technology affect the content, presentation, and organisation of lectures and other course materials? How does it help – or hinder – a teacher's ability to provide effective instruction? (p. 598)

Students' sense of their learning in relation to technology is an important venue for understanding how technology impacts education.

Oliver, Omari, and Herrington (1998) relied on constructivist theories of education to frame their employment and study of technologies in the classroom. That is, they focused on how students engage with material in ways that are effective and meaningful to the students. One way to think about students' sense of their learning experience in relation to technology is to focus on constructivist notions of technology and education.

Constructivist theory, according to Krajcik *et al.* (1994), 'assign[s] primary importance to the way in which learners attempt to make sense of what they are learning rather than to the way they receive information [and] . . . pictures students as actively constructing their knowledge by working with and using ideas' (p. 485). Krajcik *et al.* delineate the following tenets of constructivism:

- 'the need for students to learn by addressing authentic problems' (p. 486);
- 'the need for students to construct multiple representations and to apply information' (pp. 487–8);
- 'the role of a learning community in creating understanding' (p. 488);
- a focus on the ways in which learners may develop cognitively through the use of learning tools.

In a constructivist learning environment, the key is to have knowledge 'constructed by an intellectually active learner striving to build a meaningful personal representation of experience' (Gallus, Yarger and Herzmann, 2000, p. 2205). In other words, it is not sufficient for teachers to present material; students must also engage the material meaningfully.

28.3   Research questions

Our goal was not only to implement technological learning tools in the classroom, but also to study their effect on students' perceptions of their learning experience, especially their comfort with technology and their perceptions of the course and instructor. To begin to understand the impact of technology on students' experience, we posed the following questions:

1. What is the relationship between student attitudes towards technology and their performance in the technology aspects of the course?
2. How does the use of technology in the course classroom affect student attitudes about the course and instructor?

28.4   Methods

28.4.1   Course modification

An existing lower-division course at a Research-I university[1] provided an opportunity to investigate the research questions identified above. *Speech, the Individual, and Society (Sp Cmu 102)* focuses on human communication, with topics ranging from ancient rhetoric to intercultural communication. Due to fiscal constraints, the course historically has been taught as a large lecture (250–300 students) class, with five 50-minute class meetings each week. This format inherently limits one-to-one communication among the students and between students and instructor.

In Autumn 2000, Sp Cmu 102 was redesigned to incorporate technology-based learning tools to improve communication and to increase active learning in the classroom. Pence (1993) remarked that to assess truly the effectiveness of technology, comparison to a course taught without the technology would be ideal. In the current study we have a baseline course taught by the same instructor without any technology components, to which we compared the revised technologically enhanced course.

Revisions to the Autumn 2000 course conformed to suggestions outlined by Chizmar and Walbert (1999) in their description of 'web-based learning environments guided by principles of good teaching'. Specifically, a course website[2] was created forming students into virtual quiz sections and including links to online exercises and asynchronous discussions related to course content. The number of weekly lectures was reduced from five to four, and course grades, previously based only on course exams and (to a small extent) extra credit activities, now took into account student participation and performance on the online course components. To isolate the effects of these instructional changes, all other aspects of the course such as lecture and exam content and schedule remained the same. The principles and corresponding instructional strategies are summarised in Table 28.1.

Autumn 1999 (Group A). During this term, the course was taught by an experienced instructor who had delivered the course in the same, traditional format several times previously. The approach taken in this course was representative of the way in which the course historically had been taught, and information gathered during this academic term provides a point of comparison for the modified course.

Students attended a 50-minute lecture five days per week for ten weeks. They were administered three multiple-choice exams, the third of which was a two-hour cumulative exam. Aside from two relatively minor extra credit opportunities, the students' grades were based solely on their exam scores. The only instructional technology utilised in the course was email correspondence between the students, the instructor and the single teaching assistant. The teaching assistant was responsible for writing exam questions, making multiple versions of the exam, holding office hours and maintaining the grade sheets. Exams were multiple-choice and were scored mechanically.

Autumn 2000 (Group B). Although the content and structure of the course remained the same in the experimental class, several changes were made to the learning environment utilising various instructional technologies.[3] The goal of the introduction of technology was to engage students more actively in the course, with the hope of positively influencing their perceptions of and performance in their learning experience.

Our revised course included a course website in which students were divided into eight virtual quiz sections of 40 students each. Online discussions and exercises replaced one day of

Instructional Principle	Instructional Strategies and Technological Tools (tool names in parentheses where applicable)
1. Encourage contact between students and faculty	We facilitated communication between the students and the instructor and teaching assistants using: • email • asynchronous discussion boards (EPost)
2. Use active learning techniques	Students defined and explained concepts in their own words, and applied them to novel situations • online course exercises (WebQ) Students discussed course material in light of larger social contexts. • asynchronous discussion boards (EPost)
3. Develop reciprocity and cooperation among students	We created virtual quiz sections in which students discussed issues, formed study groups, and worked together to master course material • asynchronous discussion boards (EPost)
4. Give prompt feedback	Instructor posted model responses to online course exercises on the website the same day exercise was completed • course website
5. Emphasize time on task	We extended learning outside the classroom • online course exercises (WebQ) • asynchronous discussion boards (EPost)
6. Communicate high expectations	In addition to general criteria for student performance, we posted specific criteria before each online activity • course website
7. Respect diverse talents and ways of learning	We included a more diverse array of learning and teaching opportunities • course website • email • asynchronous discussion boards (EPost) • online course exercises (WebQ)

*Chizmar & Walbert (1999)

Table 28.1. Instructional elements corresponding to principles of good teaching *

lecture each week, and were designed to provide students with an opportunity to explain and apply course concepts to novel situations. Participation in discussions was graded as credit/no credit, based on students' informed contributions. Exercises were graded on a five-point scale based on students' ability to work appropriately with the course concepts. Students were administered three multiple-choice exams matched in their content and structure to those administered to Group A. Course grades were determined by exam scores and extra credit opportunities as in the previous term, with the addition of scores from the online discussions and exercises. The course was taught by the instructor who had taught the comparison course, assisted by four teaching assistants[4] who carried out the same duties as the single teaching assistant in the previous term, as well as grading online exercises.

28.4.2 Participants

Two groups of students were included in this study. Group A consisted of all students (N = 261) enrolled in Sp Cmu 102 during Autumn 1999. Group B consisted of all students (N = 221) enrolled in Sp Cmu 102 during Autumn 2000.

28.4.3 Data sources

Several types of data were gathered to address our research questions.

28.4.3.1 Student learning

Scores on course exams provided the most direct measure of student learning. Two mid-term exams comprised of 42 multiple-choice questions were given each term, along with a 72-item multiple-choice final. Exams were scored as a straight percentage correct, with no adjustment of the class curve. Students could choose two questions not to answer. The content and structure of the exams were strictly parallel for Groups A and B in order to optimise between-group comparisons, and additional performance data were available on Group B only. Scores on participation in online discussions and online exercises helped to clarify the relationship between utilisation of online resources and student learning.

28.4.3.2 Student attitudes

Two end-of-course surveys obtained student assessment of the course and perceptions of their own learning. Standard course evaluation forms[5] included rating-scale items about various aspects of the course as well as open-ended questions. Responses to scaled items were collected on machine-readable forms.[6] Twenty-two six-point items asked about course quality (0 = *very poor*; 5 = *excellent*); five seven-point items compared the present course to other college courses taken (0 = *much lower*; 6 = *much higher*). Four items asked about hours spent on the course and expected grade. Open-ended questions were presented separately, with room allowed for write-in responses.[7] Course evaluation forms were completed by students in both Groups A and B.

A second end-of-course survey was conducted for students in Group B only. This survey was conducted online and included six five-point rating scales, three multiple-choice, and four open-ended items. The survey addressed specific aspects of student experience with the modified course, and also asked students to give specific permission to include their course grades in this study.

28.4.3.3 Technology use

A large amount of information relative to Group B use of the online tools was available from the *Catalyst* web access logs and master database. Of particular interest was the volume and pattern of student use of the online discussion tool. Student access to the online activity tool was examined in the third week of the ten-week quarter, and access to the discussion tool was examined in week six.

28.5   Results

Data from each of the sources described above are reported and summarised below as they pertain to each of the research questions.

RQ1: What is the relationship between student attitude toward technology and performance in the technology aspects of the course specifically?

Attitudes towards technology among Group B students were assessed using an end-of-term online survey. The questions asked and summarised student responses are shown in Table 28.2. Students felt more comfortable at the end of the course with the technologies used than they did at the beginning ($t = 12.96$, $df = 224$, sig. $= .000$). If they needed help with the course, they most commonly asked another student or a teaching assistant. The online discussions were rated as most useful in helping to students to *understand different points of view* and *understand the course material better*, while the online exercises helped them to *better understand concepts* and *apply terms and concepts to new situations*.

Students rated the technologies used in the class as significantly more interactive than attending a large lecture five days a week. They also rated the technologies as significantly more productive to their learning than either a large class lecture five days a week or a small class session of 30 students (see Table 28.3).

Grades on course discussions (DISCUSS) and the online exercises (ASSIGN) were uncorrelated with students' ratings of their comfort with technology *before* the course, but positively correlated with students' grades at the end of the course. There were also significant positive correlations between students' grades on the online discussions and their belief that the technologies (1) helped them put their ideas into words, (2) helped them apply terms and concepts to new situations, and (3) helped them know how well they were doing in the class. In addition, there were significant positive correlations between students' grades on the online exercises and their perceptions that the exercises (1) created a forum where they felt comfortable sharing, (2) helped them better understand concepts, (3) helped them know how well they were doing in the class, and (4) helped them evaluate their own progress and understanding (see Table 28.3).

RQ2: How does the use of technology in the course affect student attitudes about the course and instructor?

Attitudes towards the course and the instructor were collected using a single-page machine-readable questionnaire that was part of the standard course evaluation system at the university. Significant differences were found on 17 (63.0 percent) of the 27 scaled items (see Table 28.4).

QUES1	At the beginning of the quarter how comfortable did you feel with the technologies that you were going to be using? (1 being not at all comfortable and 5 being very comfortable) **Mean** = 3.58 N = 221
QUES2	At the end of the quarter how comfortable do you feel with the technologies that you used in this course? (1 being not at all comfortable and 5 being very comfortable) **Mean** = 4.52 N = 221
QUES3	When you needed help with a technology, where did you go for assistance? N=214 43.0% Other students 34.1% Teaching Assistants 7.9% Professor 9.3% Other 5.6% UWired staff
QUES4	Discussing class concepts in the EPost discussion board: (N=221) 71.0% Helped me understand different points of view 63.3% Helped me understand the course material better 57.9% Helped me put my ideas into words 50.2% Helped me go more in-depth with concepts 48.9% Helped me feel like an active member of the class 38.9% Created a forum where I felt comfortable sharing 13.6% Provided greater access to TAs and instructor 7.7% Other
QUES5	The WebQ exercises helped me: (N=221) 78.3% Better understand concepts 77.4% Apply terms and concepts to new situations 71.5% Better define terms used in class 66.5% Learn which concepts I needed to study 56.1% Evaluate my own progress and understanding 33.5% Know how well I am doing in the course 3.6% Other
QUES6	In comparison to attending a large lecture five days a week with 280-300 of my peers, the technologies used in class (email, EPost discussion boards, WebQ exercises) were: (1 being much less interactive and 5 being much more interactive) **Mean** = 4.01 N = 219
QUES7	In comparison to attending a class section one day a week with 30 of my peers, the technologies used in class (email, EPost discussion boards, WebQ exercises) were: (1 being much less interactive and 5 being much more interactive) **Mean** = 3.23 N = 209
QUES8	In comparison to attending a large lecture five days a week with 280-300 of my peers, the learning I experienced using the technologies (email, EPost discussion boards, WebQ exercises) in class was: (1 being much less productive and 5 being much more productive) **Mean** = 3.68 N = 221
QUES9	In comparison to attending a class section one day a week with 30 of my peers, the learning I experienced using the technologies (email, EPost discussion boards, WebQ exercises) in class was: (1 being much less productive and 5 being much more productive) **Mean** = 3.41 N = 210

Table 28.2.   Group B response to end-of-term online survey

	DISCUSS			ASSIGN		
	r	sig.	N	r	sig.	N
At the beginning of the quarter how comfortable did you feel with the technologies that you were going to be using?	.092	.174	219	.082	.226	219
At the end of the quarter how comfortable do you feel with the technologies that you used in this course?	.294 **	.000	219	.248 **	.000	219
The online discussions:						
Helped me understand different points of view	-.073	.283	219	-.041	.550	219
Helped me put my ideas into words	.164 *	.015	219	.065	.339	219
Helped me understand the course material	.119	.078	219	.112	.098	219
Helped me go more in-depth with concepts	.099	.145	219	.117	.085	219
Helped me feel like an active member of the class	.108	.111	219	.017	.800	219
Created a forum where I felt comfortable sharing	.122	.072	219	.151 *	.026	219
Provided greater access to TAs and instructor	.036	.600	219	.067	.320	219
The online exercises helped me:						
Better define terms used in class	.070	.304	219	.121	.075	219
Better understand concepts	.089	.189	219	.142 *	.036	219
Apply terms and concepts to new situations	.152 *	.024	219	.069	.308	219
Know how well I am doing in the course	.173 *	.010	219	.203 **	.003	219
Evaluate my own progress and understanding	.124	.066	219	.174 **	.010	219
Learn which concepts I needed to study	.000	.995	219	-.017	.797	219
In comparison to attending a large lecture five days a week with 280-300 of my peers, the technologies used in class were [much less] [much more] interactive.	.227 **	.001	217	.278 **	.000	217
In comparison to attending a class section one day a week with 30 of my peers, the technologies used in class were [much less] [much more] interactive.	.054	.444	207	.106	.127	207
In comparison to attending a large lecture five days a week with 280-300 of my peers, the learning I experienced using the technologies in class was [much less] [much more] productive.	.199 **	.003	219	.144 *	.033	219
In comparison to attending a class section one day a week with 30 of my peers, the learning I experienced using the technologies in class was [much less] [much more] productive	.174 *	.012	208	1.49 *	.032	208

Table 28.3.   Relationship between online discussion and exercise grades and attitudes toward technologies used

scale:	0= very poor, 1=poor; 2=fair; 3=good; 4=very good; 5=excellent	Group A	Group B	
Item		Mean	Mean	
ITEM1	The course as a whole was:	3.98	4.23	**
ITEM2	The course content was:	3.76	4.05	**
ITEM3	The instructor's contribution to the course was:	4.35	4.57	**
ITEM4	The instructor's effectiveness in teaching the subject matter was:	4.25	4.49	**
ITEM7	Explanations by instructor were:	4.20	4.40	**
ITEM8	Instructor's ability to present alternative explanations when needed was:	4.10	4.41	***
ITEM9	Instructor's use of examples and illustrations was:	4.32	4.56	**
ITEM10	Instructor's enhancement of student interest in the material was:	3.91	4.35	***
ITEM11	Student confidence in instructor's knowledge was:	4.37	4.54	*
ITEM14	Interest level of class sessions was:	3.54	4.05	***
ITEM15	Availability of extra help when needed was:	3.81	4.10	**
ITEM17	Instructor's interest in whether students learned was:	4.15	4.44	***
ITEM19	Relevance and usefulness of course content were:	3.78	4.05	*
ITEM21	Reasonableness of assigned work was:	4.14	3.84	**
	Relative to other college courses you have taken:			
	scale: 0=much lower; 3=average; 6=much higher			
ITEM25	The amount of effort you put into this course was:	3.49	3.98	***
ITEM26	The amount of effort to succeed in this course was:	3.69	4.02	*
ITEM27	Your involvement in course (assignments, attendance, etc.) was:	3.99	4.39	**

* $p < .05$; ** $p < .01$; *** $p < .001$

Table 28.4. Course evaluation item means by group (significant items only)

28.6   Discussion

We found that students' attitudes towards and comfort with technology were not significantly correlated with their performance on the technological aspects of the course at the beginning of the quarter, but were at the end. We found this heartening because students who were not comfortable with technology were not disadvantaged in the course with the addition of the technological components of the course. However, as students became more comfortable with the technology during the quarter, their grades were positively correlated with their comfort with the learning tools. Students found the technologically enhanced course to be more interactive and productive than a large lecture class on its own and, surprisingly, more productive than a small discussion section used in conjunction with a large course. This finding added credence to our theory that adding an appropriate technology component to a course can improve students' perceived learning in a large lecture class. Further research is needed to investigate the role the type of technology plays in students' assessment of and performance with technological learning experiences.

The present study also begins to formulate responses to Mayer and Coleman's (2000) questions regarding students' assessment of technology. A comparison of instructor and course evaluations from Group A and Group B showed significant differences in 17 areas. All but one of the items evidenced a positive change. The one item that went down was Item 21, reasonableness of assigned work. Given this feedback, the number of technology-based activities in subsequent courses was reduced.

We found significant positive changes in the course ratings between Group A and Group B in regard to students' sense of the course as a whole, the course content, the interest level of the class, and others. We also found significant positive changes in the instructor ratings between Group A and Group B in regard to the instructor's contribution to the course, effectiveness, enhancement of student interest, interest in whether students learned, among others. In response to Mayer and Coleman's (2000) questions, the students in Group B found that a technologically enhanced course was correlated with a more positive sense of their learning experience in the course and their sense that the instructor was invested in their learning. It should be noted that course evaluations were high in both Group A and Group B, indicating that an already good course was made better, in the assessment of the students, by the introduction of technology.

Notes

1. The University of Washington, located in Seattle, Washington has a student enrollment of approximately 30,000 and is the top-ranked recipient of federal research grants among public post-secondary institutions in the United States.

2. See http://courses.washington.edu/coutu102/index.html.

3. Course modifications were supported by a grant from the Office of Undergraduate Education at the University of Washington (UW). The instructor was assisted by the UW Center for Teaching, Learning and Technology (CTLT) and the Instructional Resources Center of the UW Department of Speech Communication in developing a course website (http://courses.washington.edu/coutu102) and a set of online learning experiences. The specific software used was drawn from *Catalyst*, an instructional support database with online user interface developed by the UW Ed-Tech Development Group and maintained at the CTLT.

Catalyst resources used were (a) WebQ (an online questionnaire development tool used to create online learning exercises), and (b) EPost (supporting asynchronous online discussions).

4. The four teaching assistants were integral to the implementation of the revised course. Lisa Coutu would like to thank Cynthia L. King, Jody Koenig, Scott Ku, and Larry M. Massey for their support, hard work, and professionalism in the course.

5. The *Instructional Assessment System (IAS)* provides a variety of machine-readable rating forms to gather student evaluation of post-secondary instruction. Standard printed reports are produced, and data can be downloaded for specialised analysis or archiving. The IAS was developed by, and is available through, the Office of Educational Assessment at the University of Washington, Seattle, WA.

6. IAS Form B, see http://www.washington.edu/oea/iasformb.htm.

7. *Student Comments*, see http://www.washington.edu/oea/iascmmt.htm.

References

Chizmar, J.F. and Walbert, M.S. (1999) Web-based learning environments guided by principles of good teaching practice, *Journal of Economic Education* **30**(3): 248–64.

Deden, A. (1998) Computers and systemic change in higher education, *Communications of the ACM* **41**(1): 58–63.

Gallus, W.A. Jr, Yarger, D.N. and Herzmann, D.E. (2000) An interactive severe weather activity to motivate student learning, *Bulletin of the American Meteorological Society* **81**: 2205–12.

Krajcik, J.S., Blumenfeld, P.C., Marx, R.W. and Soloway, E. (1994) A collaborative model for helping middle grade science teachers learn project-based instruction, *Elementary School Journal* **94**(5): 483–97.

Mayer, K.R. and Coleman, J.J. (2000) Student attitudes toward instructional technology in the large introductory U.S. Government course, *PS, Political Science and Politics* **33**: 597–604.

Oliver, R., Omari, A. and Herrington, J. (1998) Investigating implementation strategies for WWW-based learning environments, *International Journal of Instructional Media* **25**(2): 121–38.

Pence, H.E. (1993) Combining cooperative learning and multimedia in general chemistry, *Education* **113**(3): 375–80.

Wetzel, M., Dempsey, D., Nilsson, S., Ramamurthy, M., Koch, S., Moody, J., Knight, D., Murphy, C., Fulker, D., Marlino, M., Morgan, M., Yarger, D., Vietor, D. and Cor, G. (1998) Faculty workshop on using instructional technologies and satellite data for college-level education in the atmospheric and earth sciences, *Bulletin of the American Meteorological Society* **79**: 2153–60.

Vivien Hodgson[a] and David McConnell[b]

a. Management Learning, Lancaster University; b. Department of Educational Studies, School of Education, University of Sheffield, UK

Many higher education institutions are currently implementing some form of networked learning – or e-learning – with a view to using the technologies of the Internet and the Web, and other associated information and communication technologies, to provide courses.

Although research in this field is growing rapidly, researchers often face new challenges in designing research which can illuminate, among other things, the benefits of learning and teaching via ICTs. Indeed, in researching the improvement of learning using learning technologies such as the Internet and the Web, we are often faced with having to conduct research via the technology itself. This new medium for conducting research into learning brings advantages and disadvantages. Internet research generally is a new, and likely to be expanding, field.

The aim of this symposium was to explore a variety of methods for researching networked learning in higher education, and to critically discuss the issues we face in carrying out that research and in making use of the research outcomes.

The symposium brought together a wide range of expertise, interests and perspectives which we hope provided the basis for a critical and lively discussion of methods for researching networked learning.

29 Researching networked learning

Vivien Hodgson, Philip Watland and Mireia Asensio
Lancaster University

Keywords
collaborative learning; management education; management learning; networked learning;
    research methodology

29.1   Overview

The purpose of this chapter is to review the different methodologies and methods that are used for researching learning within ICT supported learning environments. The chapter focuses particularly on networked learning environments. We assume networked learning to refer to those learning situations and contexts which, through the use of ICT, allow learners to be connected with, in particular, other people (learners, teachers/tutors, mentors, librarians, technical assistants etc.) as well as to learning resources and information of various kinds and types. In practice we looked at studies that focused primarily on CMC (computer mediated communication) based courses through to resource rich Web courses that emphasised collaboration and interaction.

It is frequently stated that more research is needed to understand the issues and potential benefits for education and learning that are offered by LT. It is our view that much of the research that has or is being done has been of a rather dispersed and fragmented nature, using a range of different approaches and methods. In this chapter we will first review what has been done, methods that have been used and the kind of results obtained etc. Then we focus specifically on research in the field of management education and learning as an area that is increasingly using networked learning and one that represents well the general pattern and approaches to research into networked learning

29.2   General background on research into networked learning.

Ehrmann (1995) argues in research about technology for teaching and learning we have not asked the right questions. He claims that too much research has attempted to see if learning is better achieved by using technology than not. In addition it seems to us that a lot of the current work is actually often descriptions of case studies and evaluations of case studies and not about research into key issues and processes important for developing a theory of networked learning

In a recent article in JCAL, M. Anderson & D. Jackson (2000) surveyed the progress in the use of computer support for networked-based learning – their focus was on computer software and hardware solutions that have been proposed and implemented. Our own emphasis is rather more on the pedagogical and learning design issues plus the learners experience when using networked learning. Their review is none the less valuable and is indicative of much of the dominant approaches that we have also identified in the management education and learning literature

They point out that typically much of the research performed on distance learning systems are studies into the use of CMC as a medium for delivery of material to distance learners and as a means of facilitating communication among students and tutors. This research has tended to focus on the benefits of introducing CMC in terms of learner satisfaction or perceived benefits and effect on learning and/or results.

Anderson and Jackson summarise the main lessons that have been learnt from research of both distributed and distance learning systems using computer support for networked-based learning as

- the value of a uniform interface to any courseware which is derived/used;
- improved communications support, particularly in overcoming issues of temporal and/or spatial barriers;
- potential for depersonalisation

More relevant to this chapter they summarise some of the main findings associated with models of distance learning that place enormous emphasis on collaboration, co-operation and communication and which makes the availability of software tools to support such models vital. They point to some of the peculiar difficulties that have been identified for these forms of distance learning:

- domination of discussions by a small group of individuals;
- frequently requires regular, structured and sustained activity at the computer;
- time and effort required creating and administering courses of this kind.

Anderson and Jackson's article is a review article and methodological approaches adopted in the various studies are not detailed. However, for the most part the methods that are commonly adopted in the kinds of studies reviewed by them are likely to be similar to those used by Oliver and Omari (2001) in a recent paper on Web-based learning.

In this article Oliver and Omari give more information about the approach taken and methods used in a study intended to explore both students' learning strategies and successes in a web-based learning environment designed to support collaborative problem-based learning. Oliver and Omari explain that their approach was an action research one. The methods adopted in the study included, feedback on the success of weekly activities based on scores achieved each week, interviews with a small sample of the 240 students, and an online questionnaire towards the end of the course asking students to provide feedback on their feelings and impressions. Oliver and Omari report on both how the different student groups organised themselves in order to complete the weekly problem set them and how students responded on a Likert scale response to questions on feelings about problem based learning, student centred learning, group activities, and learning with technology. Finally they examine to what extent the students' problem-solving skills apparently improved during the course as reflected in the weekly scores for solutions submitted. Oliver and Omari's study thus uses a range of methods and measures commonly adopted by other researchers for investigating web-based courses and learning

Other methods are also used for researching networked learning and it is interesting to look at Holt *et al.* (1997) which demonstrates some of the ways that using different approaches and methods affect the kind of results and understandings obtained. We would consequently like to describe this paper in some detail to show how methods can potentially effect how we think about networked learning and what we know about it from research.

The paper describes an initiative that involves/uses online environments as the medium for 'public deliberation' of the kind practised in National Issues Forums in the USA. Public deliberation here refers to the processes involved whereby through group conversations people move from a position of personally held opinions to public judgement (they refer to the work and ideas of e.g. Farland and Henry, 1992; and Mathews, 1997). Mathews (1997) defined deliberation as a slow-moving process that changes people by changing their opinion of other people's opinions. Public deliberation is a dynamic group process to determine what action is in the best interest of the public – including those not represented in the group. And Farland and Henry comment that 'Real public deliberation ... [is about] more than just talk. It is a way of moving beyond facts, and acquiring an understanding of what facts mean to others' (Farland and Henry, 1992). Thus public deliberation is a process that has recognisable similarities to network learning and collaborative learning in particular.

What is interesting about the paper is that over a period of three years the researchers used different research methods in an attempt both to assess online deliberation and to establish if deliberation can occur online. At the beginning of the project short online summative evaluation and longer offline evaluations were carried out and analysed and moderator's journals notes examined. This gave some interesting indications about how the participants experienced using an online forum and indicated that age and national diversity were both important dimensions. It did not, however, it seems, provide evidence about whether public deliberation was occurring online. Consequently, in the second year discourse analysis of the online forum was also used and this led to information on the nature and kind of online interactions that were taking place. Critical discourse analysis allowed them to see that macro norms and patterns of discourse reproduce themselves in cyberspace. In addition it allowed them to identify/confirm that 'democratic' interaction is contingent upon the interactants choosing to respond rather than on their capacity to speak. Finally it revealed greater interactant-to-interactant response patterns when in the listserv forum used for the first and second year and greater interactant-to-moderator response patterns for the web forum used in the third year.

They comment that discourse analysis proved extraordinarily fruitful for examining the importance and effectiveness of the moderator. Results, they say, suggested that the actions of a moderator are peripheral instead of central and interventions should aim at facilitating and supporting interactant-to-interactant transactions.

In the third year of the study two further methods were used which give again different insights and understandings about online deliberation. Student journals for recording their private deliberations or opinions were used and protocol analysis was used to assess the level or stage of public deliberation attained in the online forum against a Six-Step Model of Public Deliberation.

Again some interesting results were obtained. Analysis of student journals revealed little evidence of private deliberation but instead a great deal was said about how individuals responded to the group dynamic of the web conference and the extent they felt themselves to be part of or different to the group. With regard to the six-step model of public deliberation the protocol analysis revealed that most responses during the 6 weeks of the online forum remained below level 4 of the model and did not reach steps 5 and 6 of Coming to a Public Judgement and taking Deliberative Action or proposing an agenda for action.

Arguably in this study the researchers progressively moved from using methods that focused on student satisfaction to methods that looked closer at the process and experiences of online interactions in order to investigate more specifically the extent public deliberation and dialogue occurred online.

The main research methods and approaches used and the main findings or results of each for this study can be summarised as:

- Summative evaluation; based on questionnaires and moderators journals:
    - indicated the importance of being responded to in online discussions;
    - indicated that age and national diversity / differences were important dimensions.
- Discourse analysis; focusing on online interactions and the macro norms and patterns of online discourse:
    - demonstrated that democratic interaction is contingent on interactants choosing to respond;
    - demonstrated macro norms and patterns of discourse reproduce themselves in cyberspace;
    - revealed a greater interactant-to-interactant response patterns when in the listserv forum and greater interactant-to-moderator response patterns for a web forum;
- Student journals:
    - emphasised group dynamic of the web conference and the extent students felt themselves to be part of or different to the group;
- Protocol analysis:
    - provided information on the extent that public deliberation occurred online in the web based online forum.

Holt *et al.* reflect on the appropriateness of using methods developed for analysing face to face interaction for analysing virtual interactions. They comment that:

> In the case of National Issues Forums conducted in cyberspace, a macro structure emerges which appears to be very similar to face-to-face discourse. The consequence, however, is that cyberspace interaction is being normed by specific cultural, social, and political discourse practices. This is significant in that the same communicative action which privileges some and not others in face-to-face interaction is reproduced in cyberspace. Factors which inhibit communication across cultural, social, and political differences are thriving and in-play in cyberspace forums. The reproduction of face-to-face norms in cyberspace, however, gives credence to adapting face-to-face discourse analysis methodologies for investigations of cyberspace talk, in particular, National Issues Forum.

In the study just discussed the researchers progressively changed and developed the methods they used to better fit their original research question. They do, however, assume that it was acceptable to adapt face to face discourse analysis methodologies for investigations of interactions or talk online. Not all researches have taken this view. Benigno and Trentin (2000) for example point out that new distance education models based on online collaborative learning strategies have a particularly strong impact on approaches to research and evaluation of such courses. They explain that when it comes to deciding the criteria for online courses most people adopt the same ones used for analysing computer conferencing because the key element in online courses is participant interaction. Indeed in relation to their own work they comment that:

> It is taken for granted that satisfactory participation (accurately demonstrated by the participant's regular productions and contributions to online activity) will in any case lead to individual learning of course topics. (p. 263)

Benigno and Trentin go on to say that in their opinion it is not possible to analyse computer conferencing messages using the same criteria adopted for other forms of texts. They say that each message in a conference bears a particular meaning, both as an individual contribution and in relationship to those of other participants.

They refer to the work of Henri (1992) and de Vries *et al.* (1995) who have devised particular methods for message analysis. Henri, for example, proposes a method based on three key elements:

- a framework defining the dimensions of the analysis – of which there are 5, participative, social, interactive, cognitive and metacognitive;
- an analytical model corresponding to each of these dimensions;
- a technique of analysis of message content.

Henri's approach remains poplar among researchers. Barrett and Lally (1999), for example, use Henri's framework and categories, among other methods, to look at gender differences in online learning environments. Barrett and Lally found that that men and women take distinctively different roles in online processes and that, although the cognitive and metacognitive content of seminar contributions for men and women were similar, the social and interactive online behaviour of male and female students were significantly different. This finding was in addition to identifying a difference in the number and length of contributions for men as opposed to women. They found that while men made more 'social' messages women made more 'interactive' messages.

That Barrett and Lally chose to focus on gender in their study is itself interesting. Few studies of networked learning look at specific issues such as gender, indeed gender appears to be one of the few issues chosen for specific attention. Yates (2001) reviews the research and methods employed that have generally been used to look at the role of gender in educational CMC interactions. She claims that such research has tended to either focus on the communicative practices present in interactions or on users' perceptions and uses. According to Yates research that has focused on content and communicative practices has generally highlighted the problems and inequalities of online discourse from a gender perspective (e.g. Herring, 1993; Barrett and Lally, 1999). The studies of perceptions and outcomes on the other hand have tended to highlight the educational and social benefits of using CMC that are frequently experienced by women users (e.g. Yates, 1993).

Yates argues that both these approaches are relevant and give different but equally valid insights into the issue of how gender differences manifest themselves in online interactions and environments.

29.3 Summary on research into networked learning

In general most research associated with networked learning has been based on the study of case study courses using a variety of methods. The dominant methods appear to seek to make use of surveys of student satisfaction and perceptions and examination of learning outcomes. Observations and analysis of process are also quite common. It appears that most research is intended to gauge, from the learner's perspective, the delivery of material to distance learners and their satisfaction with this method, their learning strategy, and the benefits and/or effect on their learning. There is a further focus on computer software and hardware solutions that emphasise collaboration, co-operation, and communications between learners and tutors. There are differing opinions on the methods used for investigating interactions between learners using network learning. Increasingly researchers have focused on online communicative practices. Methods for doing this range from existing methods of discourse analysis to ones specifically developed to look at online discussions. Studies of online communicative practices have tended to focus on gender issues but have also looked at other online dynamics and experiences. There is limited research conducted on specific issues, and when done, gender issues appears to be the topic of choice perhaps because of the apparent ease of comparing communication practices and content in a network learning environment.

Very few studies appear to be taking a phenomenographic approach of the kind described in a recent article by Jones and Asensio (2001) which, as they explain, can provide useful information on specific aspects of the learners' experience which could be used to inform the design of networked learning.

29.4 Research on networked learning in the field of management education and learning

We decided to look more closely at studies in the management education and management learning field within the period of 1999–2001. We choose to focus our search specifically on two journals, the American *Journal of Management Education* and the UK journal of *Management Learning*. In fact within this period there were only two articles published in *Management Learning*, Arbaugh (2000a) and Salmon (2000).

In the same period there were, however, 14 articles published in the *Journal of Management Education* which discussed the use of technology in management education. Sixteen editions of the journal were surveyed. The December 1999 Special Issue covered the topic of management education in the information age. Of these 14 articles, eight were discussion articles that explored the use of technology in management education. The remaining six articles were reports on research that explored the use of technology in management education, typically a case study (see Table 29.1).

Management Education Articles that reported on research	6
Management Education Discussion articles	8
Total Management Education Articles referencing technology	14

Table 29.1   Summary of survey

The general themes of the articles were:

- Student satisfaction

The examination of student satisfaction with technology although receiving less attention than other themes seems to reflect a view that satisfaction with technology impacts satisfaction with distance education of management education (Arbaugh, 2000c).

- Distance versus classroom based learning

The examination of distance versus classroom based learning is an area that is receiving a lot of attention; however, there is a shift from advantages versus disadvantages to a balanced examination of the capabilities and appropriateness of technology and distance education (Arbaugh, 2000b; Bigelow, 1999; Chen and Lippert, 1999; Human *et al.*, 1999; Meisle and Marx, 1999).

- Experiences with technology in management education

The use of technological capabilities to facilitate new learning opportunities (and to some extent improve existing support systems) is receiving the most attention. This relates primarily to the inherent time and spatial independence of distance education as well as technological capabilities such as storage, access and speed of disseminating information. (Berger, 1999; Brindle and Levesque, 2000; Chappel and Schermerhorn, 1999; Fornaciari and Roca, 1999; Mundell and Pennarola, 1999; Shrivastava, 1999).

- Influences of technology on the management education sector

The influence and pressure that technology has applied on management education is also receiving attention as it relates to changing business requirements of graduates' competencies with technology and the effect on the competitive/business aspects of higher education. (Fornaciari *et al.*, 1999; Watson and Temkin, 2000).

Of the two articles published in *Management Learning* during the same period the one by Salmon (2000) looks at experiences with technology in management education. In the case of this article a range of methods were used to study both the tutors' and the learners' response to and experience of using CMC on an MBA programme. The focus in this study is towards the communication, co-operation and collaborative aspects of online working.

The paper by Arbaugh (2000a) is a study intended to examine the gender effects on an Internet-based MBA programme. In the study Arbaugh seeks to establish whether the collaborative design and Internet based discussions used in a course on strategic management favours women participants. The study, however, is based on a small sample and a series of statistical tests and analysis of the data collected fails to show any significant differences between men and women

This is the only study of those we looked at in the management education and learning literature that explicitly focused on the issue of gender. In terms of other studies looking at gender it is closest to those described by Yates (2001) as studies of perceptions and outcomes. It takes an essentially quantitative and objectivist approach. Arbaugh measured course participants learning by administrating a pre-test and post-test 50 MCQ exam. In addition each student's comments during the six modules were counted and perceptions of interaction difficulty on the course were measured using a three-item instrument that asked whether interaction on the Internet course was more or less difficult than in other MBA classes.

29.5   Methodological perspectives and approaches

In order to look more closely at methodology we decided to make use of the framework developed by Morgan and Smircich (1980) because of its focus on the assumptions regarding the nature of knowledge and human nature that are embodied in different research paradigms and methodologies. We chose this article because it was an early contribution in the organisational and management literature to the subjective versus objective approaches or paradigms of research. The article is interesting in several regards not least because it does not automatically assume that the key differences in methodology are explained in terms of qualitative versus quantitative methods. Indeed Morgan and Smircich make the point that a preoccupation with methods alone obscures the link between assumptions the researcher holds and the overall research effort. They equally point out that techniques may be used to serve research requirements consistent with many different positions along the subjective–objective continuum.

In their paper Morgan and Smircich present the key differences in basic assumptions when looking at research approaches in terms of subjectivist and objectivist assumptions as in Table 29.2.

The six research studies in *JME* and the two articles in *ML* were each further analysed using the following headings in an attempt to map their methodological approaches:

Research question or focus of each article;
Methodological approach;
Methods used;
Findings and results.

The research question or focus of each article was used to determine if the article related to network learning as defined above. The use of film, for example, as part of a classroom-based course was not considered for this review.

Findings and results were reviewed to consider further each article's relationship to our definition of network learning.

Of most interest for this paper, however, was the methodological approach and methods used. In each of the eight studies the methodological perspective was generally not stated explicitly which leaves the methodological perspective left to interpretation. This perspective is critical in understanding the paradigm used by the researchers. As Morgan and Smircich state:

> The development of organisational theory, like other social disciplines would be better severed if researchers were more explicit about the nature of the beliefs they bring to their subject of study. (p. 499).

Compounding the effort to determine methodologies the reliance of methods does not offer definitive connection to the methodologies used as Morgan and Smircich further state:

Subjectivist approaches to Social Science → Objectivist approaches to Social Science

	Reality as a projection of human imagination	reality as a social construction	reality as a realm of symbolic discourse	reality as a contextual field of information	reality as a concrete process	reality as a concrete structure
Core Ontological Assumptions	Reality as a projection of human imagination	reality as a social construction	reality as a realm of symbolic discourse	reality as a contextual field of information	reality as a concrete process	reality as a concrete structure
Assumptions About Human Nature	'Man' as pure spirit, consciousness being	'man' as a social constructor, the symbol creator	'man' as an actor; the symbol user	'man' as an information processor	'man' as an adapter	'man' as a responder
Basic Epistemological Stance	To obtain phenomenological insight, revelation	to understand how social reality is created	to understand patterns of symbolic discourse	to map contexts	to study systems, process, change	to construct a positivist science
Some Favored Metaphors	Transcendental	language game, accomplishment, text	theater, culture	cybernetic	organism	machine
Research Methods	Exploration of pure subjectivity	hermeneutics	symbol analysis	contextual analysis of Gestalten	historical analysis	lab experiments, survey

Source: taken from Morgan and Smircich (1980).

Table 29.2

A preoccupation with methods on their own account obscures the link between and overall research effort, giving the illusion that it is the methods themselves, rather than the orientations of the human researcher, that generate particular forms of knowledge. (p. 499)

Having stated these limitations we felt that it was possible to place the themes and research studies previously identified along Morgan and Smircich's subjective–objective continuum. By focusing on the themes of the studies as well as the methods used we believed that this supported Morgan and Smircich's idea of a continuum rather then classifications of different methods.

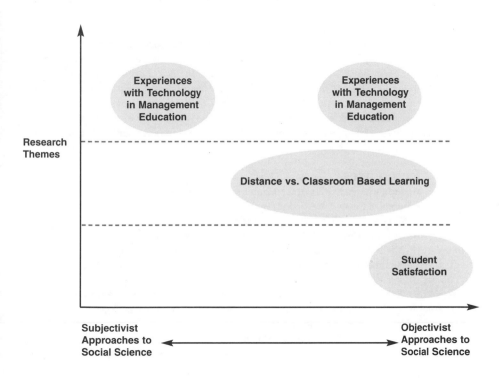

Table 29.3   Research themes on Morgan and Smircich's subjective–objective continuum

29.6   Discussion and conclusions

It did appear to us that studies in the management education and learning literature were mostly towards the objective end of the methodological perspective continuum. While researchers frequently used a range of qualitative methods their assumptions about 'human' nature seemed to reflect Morgan and Smircich adapter or information processor assumptions and rarely did they appear to assume an ontology based on actors involved in the social construction of reality. Most studies were case study based and frequently used questionnaires plus observation of discussions to evaluate 'effectiveness'. There is a tendency to do comparisons between technology and classroom based approaches based on exam results/measures. While several studies did use interviews there was apparently no use of discourse analysis and very little focus on specific research topics or issues.

It would seem that in general there is a question about whether the methods that are being used to research networked learning are consistent with the supposedly constructionist and collaborative approaches claimed for the courses themselves. It also seems that few studies are focusing on specific issues that might be considered important for learning through the use of learning technologies. This is particularly true for the studies examined in the management education and learning literature where one study looking at gender was found. There are many other issues that research into networked learning could consider including, for example, experiences of the group dynamic, development of online identity, discourse and power, design for learning etc. But these would, we assume, require a different range of methods to those that are currently most frequently adopted.

We believe that to support the development of networking learning theory and build on research published in journals, there is a benefit in stating the theoretical perspective of the researcher. As we have seen, research methods do not necessarily correlate to methodologies, and different methods yield different results even with the same research topic, setting and researchers. Overall we found that research reviewed within the management education and learning field supported the wider body of research in network learning but in general it appears that the core issues of epistemology and pedagogy remain largely uninvestigated.

29.7   References

Anderson, M. and Jackson, D. (2000) Computer systems for distributed and distance learning, *Journal of Computer Assisted Learning* **16**(3): 213–28.

Arbaugh, J.B.(2000a) An exploratory study of the effects of gender on student learning and class participation in an Internet-based MBA course, *Management Learning* **31**(4): 503–19.

Arbaugh, J.B. (2000b) Virtual classroom versus physical classroom: an exploratory study of class discussion patters and student learning in an asynchronous Internet-based MBA course, *Journal of Management Education* **24**(2): 213–33.

Arbaugh, J.B. (2000c) Virtual classroom characteristics and student satisfaction with Internet-based MBA courses, *Journal of Management Education* **24**(1): 32–54.

Barrett, E. and Lally, V. (1999) Gender differences in an on-line learning environment, *Journal of Computer Assisted Learning* **15**(3): 48–60.

Benigono and Trentin, G. (2000) The evaluation of online courses, *Journal of Computer Assisted Learning* **16**(3): 259–70.

Berger, N.S. (1999) Pioneering experiences in distance learning: lessons learned, *Journal of Management Education* **23**(6): 684–90.

Bigelow, J.D. (1999) The Web as an organizational behavior learning medium, *Journal of Management Education* **23**(6): 635–50.

Brindle, M. and Levesque, L. (2000) Bridging the gap: challenges and prescriptions for interactive distance education, *Journal of Management Education* **24**(4): 445–57.

Chappel, D.S. and Schermerhorn, J.R. Jr (1999) Using electronic student portfolios in management education: a stakeholder perspective, *Journal of Management Education* **23**(6): 651–62.

Chen, D.J. and Lippert, S.K. (1999) The lure of technology: panacea or pariah?, *Journal of Management Education* **23**(6): 743–6.

De Vries, L., Naidu, S., Jegede, O. and Collis, B. (1995) On-line professional staff development: an evaluation study, *Distance Education* 16(1): 157–73.

Ehrmann, S.C. (1995) Asking the right questions: what does research tell us about technology in higher education? *Change*, March/April, 20–7.

Farland, M. and Henry, S.M. (1992) *Politics and the 21st Century: What Should Be Done on Campus?* Dubuque, IA: Kendall/Hunt Publishing.

Fornaciari, C.J., Forte, M. and Mathews, C.S. (1999) Distance education as strategy: how can your school compete?, *Journal of Management Education* 23(6): 703–18.

Fornaciari, C. and Roca, M.F.L. (1999) The age of clutter: conducting effective research using the Internet, *Journal of Management Education* 23(6): 732–42.

Henri, F. (1992) Computer conferencing and content analysis. In A.E. Kaye (ed.), *Collaborative Learning Through Computer Conferencing*, 117–36, Springer-Verlag, Berlin.

Herring, S. (1993) Gender and democracy in computer mediated communication, *Electronic Journal of Communication* 3(2).

Holt, M.E., Rees, F., Swenson, J.D. and Kleiber, P.B. (1997) Evolution of evaluations for critical, reflective and deliberative discourse: national issues forums on-line. Presented at *New Assessment Methods: 'Comparing and Contrasting Styles and Outcomes*, for the Special Interest Group on Assessment and Evaluation of the European Association on Learning and Instruction Conference, Athens, Greece, August 1997.

Human, S.E., Kilbourne, L.M., Clark, T.D., Shriberg, A. and Cunningham, B. (1999) Using web-enhanced instruction in an interpersonal skills course, *Journal of Management Education* 23(5): 584–606.

Jones, C. and Asensio, M. (2001) Experiences of assessment: using phenomenography for evaluation, *Journal of Computer Assisted Learning* 17(3): 314–21.

Mathews, D. (1997) Deliberation makes democracy work, *The National Voter (The League of Women Voters)*, March/April, 15–16.

Meisle, S. and Marx, B. (1999) Screen to screen versus face to face: experiencing the differences in management education, *Journal of Management Education* 23(6): 703–18.

Morgan, G. and Smircich, L. (1980) The case for qualitative research, *Academy of Management Review* 5(4): 491–500.

Mundell, B. and Pennarola, F. (1999) Shifting paradigms in management education: what happens when we take groups seriously?, *Journal of Management Education* 23(6): 663–83.

Oliver, R. and Omari, A. (2001) Student responses to collaborating and learning in a web-based environment, *Journal of Computer Assisted Learning* 17(1): 34–47.

Salmon, G. (2000) Computer mediated conferencing for management learning at the Open University, *Management Learning* 31(4): 491–502.

Shrivastava, P. (1999) Management classes as online leaning communities, *Journal of Management Education* 23(6): 691–702.

Watson, C. and Temkin, S. (2000) Just-in-time teaching: balancing the competing demands of corporate America and academe in the delivery of management education, *Journal of Management Education* 24(6): 763–78.

Yates, S. (1993) Gender and computers and communication: the use of computer-mediated communication on an adult distance education course, *International Journal of Computers in Adult Education and Training* 3(2): 21–40.

Yates, S. (2001) Gender, language and CMC for education, *Learning and Instruction* 11(1): 21–34.

30   What ethnography sees: networked learning as a context for action

Christopher. R. Jones

Lancaster University, UK

30.1   Overview

This chapter explores the use of ethnography as a tool for the study of networked learning environments. The chapter looks at the limited role ethnography has played in the study of networked learning and contrasts this with the more developed body of work that has emerged in the related field of Computer Supported Co-operative Work (CSCW). Drawing on observations from two pieces of empirical research the chapter argues that ethnography can be a useful means to make visible certain aspects of the educational process that become imperceptible or which are placed in the background by other research approaches and methods of analysis. The first piece of research concerns the use of transcripts as a source of evidence that naturally occurs as the record of a computer conference. The second looks at the role of assessment and accreditation as they are experienced in the day-to-day interactions of students with each other and the course tutor.

Traditionally ethnography has conducted research in the field and has claimed to be able to provide an insider's view. Some of the basic techniques and practices of ethnography are reviewed in the context of virtual or networked environments. The chapter goes on to examine the idea of virtual ethnography and touches on how ethnographic techniques may need to be adapted to make them more applicable in networked environments. Finally the chapter provides an ethnographic view of the situation in relation to learning as an example of how the method can be used to cast light on key aspects of education. It draws attention to the argument for a 'post-disciplinary' approach to empirical research and the place of ethnography in that approach.

30.2   Ethnography

The standpoint of this chapter is that ethnography can provide a useful research approach for the study of networked learning. This is not meant to imply that ethnography is uniquely suited to this task and no claim is made that ethnography is either the best or sole method for this type of research. Rather a case is made for the use of ethnographic methods to obtain particular insights, in other words a recommendation is made on the grounds that ethnography is fit for certain purposes. Ethnography has relied on field workers immersing themselves in a setting, often defined geographically with setting implying a physical place or 'field'. Originally developed to report on the peoples encountered through exploration and colonisation, ethnography has been adapted, most notably by the Chicago School, for use in sociology. The aim has been to understand a setting from the point of view of those involved in it.

Ethnography is fundamentally a descriptive task that relies on first-hand accounts of experience from the point of view of those who live and work in the setting being observed. Data collection can be a messy and unstructured process, which can involve observation, interviews, transcription of gossip etc. These accounts can be recorded in a variety of ways that include field notes, collection of documents and artefacts and audio and video recording. Ethnography starts from the proposition that human activities are socially organised and as a result focuses on understanding and interaction between people and collaborative patterns of behaviour. Traditionally the methods used are 'naturalistic' in the sense that they rely on the study of people and their activities in their natural environment (Fetterman 1998; Hammersley and Atkinson 1995).

Within education the ethnographic tradition has a long and distinguished history. Martyn Hammersley is a prolific example of this tradition, writing about education from an ethnographic standpoint (1983, 1985, 1986) and about the methods of ethnography themselves (Hammersley and Atkinson, 1995; Hammersley, 1992). Ethnography has also emerged as a key methodological insight in the developing field of Computer Supported Cooperative Work (CSCW). CSCW is an interdisciplinary field, including a range of human sciences alongside computer technical disciplines. A concern with the social properties of the work setting has suggested the appropriateness of ethnographic methods in this field (Hughes *et al.*, 1993; Randall *et al.*, 1996). Some of the limits of ethnography when used for the study of work organisation have been well documented (Forsythe, 1999; Harper *et al.*, 2000; Randall *et al.*, 1992; 1995). They concern the generally small-scale nature of research contexts, which tend to be well defined and often sequestered settings such as control rooms that are well suited to close observation by a fieldworker. Faced with large organisations with distributed systems and unclear boundaries ethnography can present problems in obtaining adequate knowledge of the domain. A further problem for ethnography when used as an applied research method arises from the long duration of classic ethnographic research. Time constraints can mean that ethnographers conducting applied research have to adopt 'quick and dirty' approaches to data gathering.

Outside of the commercial contexts within which CSCW research has taken place similar concerns have been raised. Organisational studies are often prescriptive and there has been some concern that educational research is similarly prescriptive and that a method derived from anthropology has been applied incorrectly and out of context (Zaharlick, 1992). Advocates of 'critical' ethnography have claimed that when ethnography has been incorporated into academic and governmental research it has been at the expense of its critical edge (Jordan and Yeomans, 1995). The claim made here is that ethnography can be used in applied research in education even when this entails explicitly evaluative purposes (Jones, 1998). Ethnographic research has proved useful in educational evaluation by providing the users perspective and by providing descriptions of in situ programmes (Fetterman, 1984; Hammersley, 1986). The natural field for ethnographic evaluation is in 'illuminative' evaluation but a case has also been made for an iterative design process using ethnography and 'nth phase' evaluation (Hughes *et al.*, 1996; Oliver, 1997). The claims made here are modest. Ethnography can by its unintrusive style illuminate areas obscured by other methods.

30.3   Ethnographic research in networked learning

Ethnography has been applied to networked learning environments but it has not been as fully developed in the area of Computer Supported Collaborative (Cooperative) Learning (CSCL) as it has been in CSCW (Bruckman, 1998; Eastmond, 1995; Jones, 1998, 1999, 2000).

Dan Eastmond has conducted ethnographic research in distance education from the perspective of a committed participant. He commented that he had a 'vested interest' in making sure the computer conferencing courses he developed were successful (Eastmond, 1995, p. viii). In contrast the research conducted by this author was undertaken from an explicitly 'indifferent' stance (Jones, 1998, 1999, 2000). Both Jones and Eastmond questioned the technological determinist stance that assumed interactivity, collaboration and reflection were unproblematic outcomes from the use of the technology. Eastmond and Jones also both indicated that the promise and potential of computer conferencing depended upon contingent factors in particular the tutor's approach to teaching (Jones 2000).

30.4   Virtual ethnography

Since the mid-1990s the most significant development of networks has been in the rapid expansion of the Internet and in particular web-based access to services using the Internet. It has become commonplace to think in terms of a Network Society with the implication that social forms are being reconstituted as new technologies are deployed (Castells, 1996). In higher education the idea of virtual or networked learning has grown in parallel and higher education is seen as a prime site for the emergent networked society (Jones and Steeples, 2001). As educational applications make use of the facilities of web-based systems it will be important to develop a proper understanding of research approaches as they transfer to the new environment. In ethnography there has been a growing interest in 'virtual' or 'online' ethnography (Hine, 1998, 2000; Mason, 1999; Paccagnela, 1997; Wittel 2000). More generally a literature has grown up that has begun to set out research approaches in relation to the Internet (Mann and Stewart, 2000).

In her book entitled *Virtual Ethnography*, Hine (2000) sets out ten principles on which she bases her experimental ethnography. She notes that the notion of a site for interaction is called into question by the way in which virtual or Cyberspace is thought to be distinct from 'real life' and face-to-face interaction. Hine notes that networked technologies show 'a high degree of interpretive flexibility' (p. 64). She argues that his flexibility derives from the way the technology is dependent upon different contexts and the way that the technology has to be 'acquired, learnt, interpreted and incorporated into context' (p. 64). These comments point to at least two significant factors. Networked technologies increasingly allow for connection at any time and any place. This means that the context in which networked interactions take place constantly vary for the user. Secondly it points to the way technologies do not do things alone. Computers and networks are mobilised by their users in distinctly different ways. Hine also notes the temporal dislocation of a virtual setting such that 'immersion' can only take place intermittently. The temporal and spatial dislocations amount to an ethnography that cannot aspire to be 'holistic' and ethnographic accounts derived from it will naturally be conditioned by considerations of purpose. Nonetheless Hine's conclusion is that:

> Virtual ethnography is adequate for the practical purpose of exploring the relations of mediated interaction, even if not quite the real thing in methodologically purist terms. (p. 65)

Andreas Wittel has also explored the move 'From Field to Net to Internet' and has suggested a move from field work to an ethnography of networks (2000).

Networks are still strongly related to geographical space – like field. Unlike field, a network is an open structure, able to expand almost without limits and highly dynamic. And even more important: A network does not merely consist of a set of nodes but also a set of connections between nodes. As such, networks contain as much movement and flow as they contain residence and localities. An ethnography of networks would contain the examination of nodes of a net and the examination of the connections and flows (money, objects, people, ideas etc) between these nodes. [5]

Wittel's formulation, by continuing to place an emphasis on the node within a network, has the advantage over Hine's of retaining some aspects of the idea of location alongside flow and connectivity.

The move towards networked learning and increasingly distant and virtual relationships in education should not rule out the use of ethnography reshaped in the form of a virtual ethnography. This term as Hine has pointed out is useful as it emphasises the current use of the term virtual but it also implies that this form of ethnography is not quite the same as the classical form. There are in fact reasons why participant observation might be more necessary in virtual environments. Mann and Stewart note that:

> Perhaps even more than in FTF conversation, CMC loses part of its sense and meaning when reread afterwards by those who had not been involved. (2000, p. 87)

The examples below draw on research conducted in networked learning environments in campus-based and distance universities. They provide two short examples that illustrate the uses for ethnography and how the issues of virtual ethnography present themselves in research contexts.

30.5   What ethnography 'sees'

As an illustration of what sorts of results can be obtained by study and evaluation using ethnographic techniques I have included research that illuminates two major issues concerning the use of groupware systems in higher education. The first of these concerns the use of transcripts as a source of evidence that naturally occurs as the record of a computer conference. The second looks at the role of assessment and accreditation as they are experienced in the day to day interactions of students with each other and the course tutor.

Research conducted on campus raised questions about the limits that might need to be placed upon the interpretation of the transcripts of computer conferences (Jones and Cawood, 1998). The research concluded that the transcript was at best a partial record and one that was contrived to be for public display. It was partial because students' engagement with the networked course was only intermittent and their contacts were not restricted to the technology deployed on the course. The authors also concluded that transcribed conference interactions had some of the features of ordinary conversation but lacked others. In particular they pointed to the inability in a computer mediated environment of ensuring the attention of the 'listener'. The example chosen from this research is a single interaction that presented a problem of interpretation for the researcher.

30.5.1   Transcript: Flaming abuse!?

This example illustrates how the researcher made use of observation and the transcribed record of a computer conference to make sense of a short incident of flaming that occurred after the sending of an abusive rap in a message that was later removed from the conference. The message formed one part of an exchange online which, with the exception of this one message, remained in the transcript. The offensive rap was posted during the second module of a campus based course in February 1996. I had not been present on the day when the string of messages began. The transcript records a mildly abusive exchange between students discussing a birthday. The messages showed a disregard for the public nature of a computer conference and they showed some of the characteristics of private talk between friends. I found making sense of the message and its content difficult. To try and clarify the issue I emailed the student who had written the rap but he was less than forthcoming. He replied that much as he would like to help he had given the tutor his word not to repeat the abuse and that 'the message ... is best not mentioned again' (personal mail, 13/2/96).

In an email message not directly connected to the incident a student from the previous cohort of students brought to my attention that another student not directly implicated in the flaming may have had some involvement. Re-reading the transcript with this advice it was apparent that he had been messaging in the computer lab at the same time and with some marginal involvement in the exchange. The student who had given me the information had developed the idea from:

> Just something he said to me about making the suggestion to who ever it was who started the 'stripper thread'. I think he just feels a bit of an outsider because no one wants to work with him. (personal message VS to CJ, 11/2/96)

Without this chance remark the transcript may well have remained opaque, yet the information was there and available to me once 'sensitised' to the issue. The event is underdetermined in the sense that no one reading is 'right', rather information about the conference and available to the participants, makes some readings more likely than others. In this case the transcript alone did not give me a good 'picture' of what went on. My attempts to reconstruct events were largely unsuccessful but when pointed in a particular direction the transcript contained information supporting a suggestion derived from a 'chance' remark that had been made offline about events during online activities that were themselves not available in the transcript. The transcript informed a reading of events originating elsewhere, it provided missing context to messages otherwise thought insignificant, the messages read in the new context 'confirmed' an otherwise unsubstantiated assertion.

This example is one of many that may be familiar to tutors of online courses. Participants in a networked learning environment constitute meaning from a large number of available sources. A number of points can be made using this example to illustrate the potential use of virtual ethnography. The transcript alone did not contain sufficient information to allow a satisfactory understanding of the exchange between students. The additional information about context was obtained from an informant known from participation in the setting but with no direct involvement in events. The relationship depended upon participation in the online course, not on meeting together or co-location, though we had met on many occasions. The information from this source was obtained in an email. Even though her knowledge came from a face-to-face meeting, it did not depend on face-to-face contact. She could just as easily have been told about the events in an email or using some other remote technology such as a telephone.

In this case the online course was on-campus and students met for other courses and in the computer labs. In a distance course where all participants were remote from each other the only resource for understanding would be remote technologies. These might not be restricted to the course itself indeed we might expect students to explore private channels of communication outside the public space of an online course. The question can be asked whether networked environments alone can provide sufficient resources for the application of ethnographic methods. The example above relied on offline contact but much of the work was done remotely. I was not present for the original exchange and my questions were sent by email. What 'really' happened is not available to any one participant. All participants and observers have to make sense of the interactions using a range of available resources. This example illustrates that in so far as university courses can be run in a virtual environment then so can the same means be used to investigate those courses. If the means of communication are sufficient to allow participants to understand each other then an ethnographic observer could use the same means.

30.5.2   Assessment: misunderstandings

This example provides a number of insights both into the uses of ethnographic research and the way in which it might be translated into a networked environment. This work reinforced earlier work that had identified assessment and accreditation as features that pervaded the interactions of students and tutors on an online course (Jones, 1999). This was an example of the way in which ethnographic research can make visible features of a setting that can become invisible when viewed from a theorised perspective. It is common to view educational activity as learning and to ignore the institutional constraints that the requirement to grade students has on the day-to-day activities within universities. Recently Brown and Duguid (2000) have suggested that under the pressure of new technologies universities could reorganise themselves as Degree Granting Bodies, that is they identify the core function of universities as the provision of credentials. This view is supported by the findings of ethnographic research that shows the detailed and day-to-day influence of assessment and accreditation on the activity of participants in networked learning environments.

The research that is reported in this example was part of a larger study that was informed by phenomenographic methods. This particular case study was unusual in the context of the research in that I participated as the local course tutor for the course. A fuller description of the research can be found in Jones and Asensio (2001). The findings reported how assessment criteria were understood by students on a distance learning course taught using networked learning technologies. The course had a clear and published approach to assessment that used assignments to motivate students to adopt new patterns of learning while still covering course content. For this aim to be achieved students needed a clear and commonly held understanding of the assessment's intentions. The following example illustrates what may be a fundamental problem with the way that students' experiences vary in what may be unpredictable ways.

The task and marking scheme for the final project assignment, was given in a separate 12-page booklet providing detailed instructions. The booklet contained sections on the aims of the group project, the activity to be undertaken, report structure, mark allocation and advice on establishing group working. The mark allocation is shown in Table 30.1.

Group element	(total 30%)
Report Summary	10%
Themes discussion in conference	10%
Report conclusion	10%
Individual element	**(total 70%)**
General structure and coherence of argument	30%
Use of supporting evidence and course materials	20%
Contribution to group tasks and discussion in conference	20%

Table 30.1

The students when interviewed expressed their interpretation of the aims of the assessment differently. These contrasting interpretations are illustrated in the following quotations (interviewer in italics):

> *What did you conceive that task to be?*
> I would assume that it was more to continue the computer mediated conferencing as an exercise in itself for people to work together to sort of exchange ideas and irrespective of what the particular project was to work on. (Daniel)
> *What do you think the emphasis was?*
> Your personal individual um your personal big 500 words or whatever
> *So the individual submission was ...*
> Was more important than the group work
> *And how about content and process if we split it that way?*
> Content
> *Rather than process ...*
> Rather than process and yet it's, I would argue the process probably took as much time as writing the content if not more (Lillian)

The two students were co-operating in the same group to produce a joint project yet they had different views of the task they had been set. This occurred despite the extensive documentary guidance provided in the assessment booklet. When prompted to re-read the booklet, Daniel, who had identified the task as being to conduct group work, revised his view and conceded that content may have been more important.

Among the other students it was Daniel's initial view that was most common. The view expressed by Lillian was clearly instrumental and she worked to the assessment guidance. Daniel was less focused on the assessment criteria. There were two other reasons offered by students in the group that shed light on why the group process dominated over the intention of the assessment criteria. First the group process was novel and pervasive:

> I couldn't just approach it on my own, it's a TMA (Tutor Marked Assignment) that's impossible to approach as an individual (Wayne)

Students used the conferencing throughout the course but were only expected to work collaboratively using the system for two assessments. The project was only the second occasion that students had used FirstClass for collaborative work, it was unusual even within the individual course structure.

Secondly the ability to communicate was a valued and novel element within the overall experience:

> it's the isolation I think when you're doing a course like this ... That's the main thing for me – it takes away that little bit of isolation. (Frank)

Computer conferencing was experienced as important because it offered an unusual level of communication for distance students. Both of these reasons point to influences outside of the assessment document, which was interpreted by students in a wider context that was not in the course design team's control. The course documentation was interpreted by students who had many external factors influencing their reading of standard materials.

This example points to the increased potential for misunderstanding in distance environments. This supports the arguments of Mann and Stewart (2000) in relation to the reasons why participant observation might be more important in virtual environments. The participant has an increased level of understanding of communications within the network that otherwise might be difficult to interpret and lead to significant misunderstanding. In this case the example also illustrates that participation is no guarantee of understanding. Understanding in a distance setting cannot be ensured by improved documentation and must rely on a narrow set of resources. The same resources can be available to a participant observer and our understanding of the experience of networked learning can only be enhanced by ethnographic research that makes use of the same resources as the participants to make sense of the networked learning environment.

The example also illustrates the different degrees of distance that we might encounter in networked learning. The students were distance students and conducted most of their activity from home or in some cases from work. When I visited the students I visited them where they usually did their university work. In one case this was in their workplace, all others were at home. The settings were significantly different. One student had two small children and an open-plan ground floor. The computer and desk were situated under the stairs and work could only have been done without distraction when the children were asleep as the student worked during the day. By contrast other students worked in well-equipped dedicated study rooms. This variety of environments illustrates the ways in which networked learning is likely to increase the variety of contexts in which learning is achieved. In this way the students display the characteristics of a 'virtual' or networked setting. On the other hand they were encouraged to attend local tutorial groups which met on six occasions over the nine month duration of the course. Not all students attended all, or in some cases any, of the tutorials. Contact with the tutor and other students was maintained using the phone and standard email as well as the course conference. Networked environments are likely to display a range of contact with more or less distance between participants. The way ethnographic methods are applied will need to reflect that variety. There is not likely to be one virtual ethnography, it is more probable that a range of techniques and styles will be generated to meet the range of contexts generated online.

30.6   Conclusions: a post-disciplinary approach to virtual ethnography

The claims that ethnography has made have been traditionally based on an idea of the ethnographer as instrument. The individual ethnographer has travelled to distant places and by their participation in normal everyday events they have become immersed in the culture and better able to understand the setting from the point of view of the participants. The translation of ethnography from a face-to-face setting to a networked environment questions a number of fundamental assumptions because ethnographic research is highly dependent upon the credibility of the account given by an ethnographer. A virtual ethnography will need to develop a revised description of its own methods to sustain that credibility.

The account of ethnography given by Hammersley and Atkinson (1995) relies upon participation. The ethnographer doesn't simply observe rather they interact with other participants, asking questions, trying to gain insight into a way of life that involves intentional activity and is more than simply observation of a scene. The Internet is a limited medium that places limits on the opportunities for direct experience and interaction. However all the participants in a networked environment experience this same limitation. The ethnographer is in a similar position to the students and tutors in a networked learning environment and can indeed participate as one of the students or the tutor. The potential bonus to be gained from virtual ethnography is that the participant observer can gain an understanding of the experience of what it is like to be part of a networked setting. This can then help inform an understanding of the account of networked interactions recorded in the transcripts. The vulnerability of networked exchanges to misunderstanding may make participant observation more necessary in networked environments because of the limitations of the medium. In this reworking of ethnography it becomes a valuable experiential way of coming to know and understand that may be particularly appropriate for the study of the experience of being a student or tutor in a networked learning environment. The virtual and the real are not so distinct as to make them different in kind. The way we decide what is real under normal circumstances is repeated in the more impoverished environment online. The virtual in that sense is no less real than face-to-face environments but it is another type of reality and as such it demands a review of current practices in research.

Writing from a CSCW perspective a recent discussion of organisational change in retail finance has advocated what they describe as a post-disciplinary approach to ethnography (Harper *et al.*, 2000). This approach is situated neither in a critical theoretical nor in a prescriptive approach to design. The approach is interested:

> in the kind of social science which engages with the question of how to provide grounds for decision-making about change rather than specifying the changes to take place. (p. 153)

Ethnography can usefully inform the design of networked learning and the decisions of policy-makers about networked learning. The emergence of networked technologies is not a hindrance to that project, indeed a virtual ethnography will be a necessary aid in the design and successful deployment of networked learning.

30.7   References

Brown, J.S. and Duguid, P. (2000) *The Social Life of Information*. Boston MA: Harvard Business School Press.

Bruckman, A. (1998) Community support for constructionist learning, *Computer Supported Cooperative Work* 7(1–2): 47–86.

Castells, M. (1996) *The Information Age: Economy, Society and Culture Volume 1. The Rise of the Network Society*. Oxford: Blackwell.

Eastmond, D.V. (1995) *Alone But Together: Adult Distance Study Through Computer Conferencing*. Cresskill, NJ: Hampton Press, Inc.

Fetterman, D.M. (1984) *Ethnography in Educational Evaluation*. Beverly Hills, CA: Sage.

Fetterman, D.M. (1998) *Ethnography Step by Step*, 2nd edn. Newbury Park: Sage.

Forsythe, D.E. (1999) 'It's just a matter of common sense': ethnography as invisible work, *Computer Supported Cooperative Work* 8: 127–45.

Hammersley, M. (ed.) (1983) *The Ethnography of Schooling*. Driffield: Nafferton.

Hammersley, M. (1985) From ethnography to theory: a programme and paradigm for case study research in the sociology of education, *Sociology* 19(2): 244–59.

Hammersley, M. (ed.) (1986) *Case Studies in Classroom Research*. Milton Keynes: Open University Press.

Hammersley, M. (1992) *What's Wrong with Ethnography?* London: Routledge.

Hammersley, M. and Atkinson, P. (1995) *Ethnography: Principles in Practice*, 2nd edn. London: Routledge.

Harper, R., Randall, D. and Rouncefield, M. (2000) *Organisational Change and Retail Finance: An Ethnographic Perspective*. London: Routledge.

Hine, C. (1998) Virtual ethnography. IRISS '98 conference paper. International Conference 25–27 March 1998. Bristol. Available at:
http://www.sosig.ac.uk/iriss/papers/proceed.html

Hine, C. (2000) *Virtual Ethnography*. London: Sage.

Hughes, J.A., Somerville, I., Bentley, R. and Randall, D. (1993) Designing with ethnography: making work visible, *Interacting with Computers* 5(2): 239–53.

Hughes, J., O'Brien, J., Rouncefield, M. and Rodden, T. (1996) 'They're supposed to be fixing it': requirements and system re-design. In P. Thomas (eds), *CSCW Requirements and Evaluation*. London: Springer-Verlag.

Jones, C. (1998) Evaluation using ethnography: context, content and collaboration. In M. Oliver (ed.), *Innovation in the Evaluation of Learning Technology*. LaTID, University of North London, 87–100.

Jones, C. (1999) Co-operating to collaborate: course delivery using computer conferencing in higher education. In A. Eurlings *et al.* (eds), Integrating Information and Communication Technology in Higher Education. *Kluwer, Deventer, pp 271–89*.

Jones, C. (2000) From the sage on the stage to what exactly? Description and the place of the moderator in cooperative and collaborative learning. In D. Squires, G. Jacobs and G. Conole, *The Changing Face of Learning Technology – Selected Papers from ALT-J*. University of Wales Press, Cardiff.

Jones, C. and Asensio, M (2001) Experiences of assessment: using phenomenography for evaluation, *Journal of Computer Assisted Learning* 17(3): 314–21.

Jones, C. and Cawood, J. (1998) The unreliable transcript: contingent technology and informal practice in asynchronous learning networks. In *Networked Lifelong Learning; Innovative Approaches to Education and training through the Internet*. Proceedings of the 1998 International Conference. University of Sheffield, Division of Adult Continuing Education, 1.9–1.14

Jones, C. and Steeples, C. (2001) Perspectives and issues in networked learning. In C. Steeples and C. Jones, *Networked Learning: Perspectives and Issues*. London: Springer-Verlag.

Mann, C. and Stewart, F. (2000) *Internet Communication and Qualitative Research: A Handbook for Researching Online*. London: Sage.

Mason, B. (1999) Issues in virtual ethnography. In K. Buckner (ed.), *Esprit P Workshop on Ethnographic Studies in Real and Virtual Environments: Inhabited Information Spaces and Connected Communities*. Queen Margaret College, Edinburgh.

Oliver, M. (1997) *A framework for evaluating the use of educational technology.* BP ELT Report no. 1, University of North London.

Paccagnella, L. (1997) Getting the seat of your pants dirty: strategies for ethnographic research on virtual communities, *Journal of Computer-Mediated Communities* [Online journal], **3**(1). Available at:

http://www.ascusc.org/jcmc/vol3/issue1/paccagnella.html

Randall, D. Hughes, J.A. and Shapiro, D. (1992) Using ethnography to inform systems design, *Journal of Intelligent Systems* **4**(1–2): 9–28.

Randall, D., Rouncefield, M. and Hughes, J. (1995) Chalk and cheese: BPR and ethnomethodologically informed ethnography in CSCW. In *Proceedings E-CSCW 1995*, Stockholm: ACM Press.

Randall, D., Twidale, M. and Bentley, R. (1996) Dealing with uncertainty – perspectives on the evaluation process. In P. Thomas (ed.), *CSCW Requirements and Evaluation*. London: Springer-Verlag.

Wittel, A. (2000) Ethnography on the move: from field to net to Internet [23 paragraphs], *Forum Qualitative Sozialforschung/Forum: Qualitative Research* [Online Journal], **1**(1). Available at: http://qualitative-research.net/fqs

Zaharlick, A. (1992) Ethnography in anthropology and its value for education, *Theory into Practice* **31**(2): 116–25.

31 Researching networked learning: issues arising from the use of a variety of different research methods

David McConnell
University of Sheffield, UK

31.1 Overview

This chapter examines several different approaches to researching networked learning. I draw on recent research projects and present the approach adopted in each as a case study in networked learning research. The approaches span traditional ones used in face-to-face settings, and innovative ones carried out virtually, using the technology of the Internet.

Four case studies are presented which illustrate the following broad approaches:

1. synchronous and asynchronous online research, using email, chat forums and electronic concept mapping;
2. transcripts from networked learning events analysed using a grounded theory approach;
3. a collaborative, reflective-critique approach to understanding networked learning, involving face-to-face group sessions in which course participants and tutors read transcripts of their online discussions/work, with a view to recalling, discussing and analysing the online experience;
4. e-questionnaires used to evaluate EU-based Internet courses.

In this chapter I present examples of the use of each approach and critically discuss and analyse each approach with the following in mind:

- the insights into the experience of learning which each approach offers;

- the usefulness of each approach for understanding networked learning;

- the practicality of employing the different approaches;

- the outcomes and usability of the research.

31.2 Introduction

Learning via the Internet and the Web is a topical issue at the moment. Practitioners and organisations are experimenting with 'virtual' learning environments. Governments are invoking e-universities as the saviour of higher education.

Researching the social processes of the Internet, and researching learning that takes place via the Internet and the Web – what is often called networked learning (or e-learning) – is also very topical (Asension *et al.*, 2000; Jones, 1999).

This chapter examines several different approaches for researching networked learning. I draw on recent research projects and present the approach adopted in each as a case study in networked learning research. The approaches span traditional ones used in face-to-face settings, and innovative ones carried out virtually, using the technology of the Internet.

Four case studies are presented which illustrate the following broad approaches:

1. synchronous and asynchronous online research, using email, chat forums and electronic concept mapping;
2. transcripts from networked learning events analysed using a grounded theory approach;
3. a collaborative, reflective-critique approach to understanding networked learning, involving face-to-face group sessions in which course participants and tutors read transcripts of their online discussions/work, with a view to recalling, discussing and analysing the online experience;
4. e-questionnaires used to evaluate EU-based Internet courses.

In the chapter I present examples of the use of each approach and critically discuss and analyse each approach with the following in mind:

*   insights into the experience of learning which each approach offers;
*   the usefulness of each approach for understanding networked learning;
*   the practicality of employing the different approaches;
*   the outcomes and usability of the research.

It is not my intention to be exhaustive, or comprehensive, but to indicate how each method was used and what the benefits or outcomes of the research were for understanding networked, or 'e', learning.

31.3   Four methods for researching networked learning

31.3.1   Synchronous and asynchronous online research, using email, chat forums and electronic concept mapping

The focus here is on using synchronous and asynchronous communications systems, and electronic concept maps, to elicit teachers' conceptions of learning and teaching in networked learning environments, and to explore the relevance and effectiveness of online methodologies for carrying out this kind of research (Noakes, 2000).

This researcher used the Web as the vehicle for conducting his research for two reasons:

*   He lives in Hong Kong and the research participants lived in the UK and South Africa. Travel to meet them to carry out his research would have been prohibitively expensive.
*   He felt that he should use an online medium so as to explore its potential for carrying out educational research.

Data collection methods included various combinations of synchronous and asynchronous interviews with the completion of concept maps asynchronously or synchronously.

The author proposes a number of advantages of computer mediated communications (CMC) in carrying out educational research (Noakes, 2000, p. 45) which revolve round time, space, the absence of physical presence and the potential for anonymity. These are:

- extending access to participants: CMC can break down time and space barriers which might limit face-to-face research;

- cost and time savings: travel, venue hire and other costs are reduced or eliminated;

- eliminating transcript bias: CMC transcripts provide content and context, and are immediately available for analysis (*but they may be less rich than traditional face-to-face interview transcripts*);

- easier handling of data: electronic handling of data and data processing are easier (*transcribing can be easier and data can be submitted immediately to qualitative computer analysis software*);

- the participants' perspective: participants' can choose which medium to use (email; chat rooms etc.); CMC is conducive to dialogue and participants usually feel easy using it; they are often more open in this informal context; participants may feel 'safer' using this medium, and can participate anonymously if they wish.

The author cites various challenges to carrying out qualitative educational research via CMC:

- computer literacy: both researcher and participants need to be fully computer literate; they need to feel comfortable using web and concept mapping technologies; researchers require advanced skill in facilitating the interviews or other research processes;

- making contact and recruitment: issues of where to find your participants, how to recruit them once found have to be considered;

- ensuring and sustaining cooperation: as with all research, maintaining contact with participants and sustaining their involvement in the research process is difficult online: participants can 'disappear' and ignore your emails;

- interactive skills online: keyboard skills may hamper interaction, especially in synchronous interviews; skill in communicating and expressing yourself via text is required – there are no physical cues to help the communication process;

- losing access: some participants may lose their CMC connection due to moving on or leaving their place of learning/work;

- Internet access and usage: users of the Internet are predominantly white and middle class. This has implications for sampling and access to particular groups, though this is rapidly changing.

He concludes that online concept mapping is not a trivial exercise, and concept mapping may not suit those who are not visual learners. The skill required to present ideas via this medium may be unrealistically high. Generally, he suggests that educational research conducted via the Web should seek to reduce the technical issues; ensure participants can easily take part within their existing commitments; and provide training for researchers wishing to interview online.

Other studies using related or similar methods (Mann and Stewart, 2000).

31.3.2 Transcripts from networked learning events analysed using a grounded theory approach

The use of transcripts of online discussions as a source of research data is a widely employed method of researching networked learning (see e.g. Lally, 2001). Often the transcripts are subjected to some kind of content analysis, which involves the use of existing categories or theories, which are mapped on to the data.

The grounded theory approach has a different purpose: the researcher examines the transcripts in order to develop categories and build theory.

In this case study (McConnell, in press (a)) which focuses on an examination of students' experiences of networked collaborative assessment two sets of data were used: the first set consists of transcripts of the communications and work of an e-learning group, easily available from the electronic communication system (in this case Web-CT). The second set consists of data from face-to-face in-depth interviews between the researcher and course participants. Both sets of data were analysed using a grounded theory approach (Glaser and Strauss, 1968; Strauss and Corbin, 1998).

Grounded theory is a well-established qualitative research method which helps researchers apply a set of procedures to interpret and organise data:

> These usually consist of conceptualizing and reducing data, elaborating categories in terms of their properties and dimensions, and relating through a series of prepositional statements. Conceptualizing, reducing, elaborating, and relating often are referred to as coding. (Stauss and Corbin, 1998, p. 12)

This qualitative research approach allows the emergence of sensitising concepts, which are:

> less specific suggestive ideas about what might be potentially fruitful to examine and consider, an emergent meaningful vocabulary that alerts the researcher to promising avenues of investigation. (Clarke, 1997)

rather than the generation of definitive concepts from data abstracted from their social milieus. The purpose is to remain close to the natural world being researched, and be sensitive to the words and actions of the people who are the focus of the research (Strauss and Corbin, 1998).

In the case under study here, the author started by reading the e-learning transcripts and making annotations in the margins indicating different features of the group's work. This approach is rather like that of an ethnographer. In adopting a grounded theory approach, the researcher is not bringing existing theory to the analysis of data, but rather developing theory inductively from the data itself. The theory must grow out of the data and be grounded in the data (Moustakis, 1994). It is of course appreciated that the interplay of data and the researcher's meaning-making is a creative one in which 'interpretations are the researcher's abstractions of what is in the data' (Strauss and Corbin, 1998, p. 294). No researcher enters into the process with a completely blank mind. So in this case, the researcher immersed himself in the data, reading it in detail and trying to understand what was going on in the e-learning groups, and why. In doing this, he was attempting to unravel the elements of experience and their interrelationships and develop theory that helped him, and hopefully others, understand the experience of this group of learners (Moustakis, 1994).

This approach to analysis is both scientific and creative:

> Analysis is the interplay between researchers and data. It is both science and art. It is science in the sense of maintaining a certain degree of rigor and by grounding analysis in data. Creativity manifests itself in the ability of researchers to aptly name categories, ask stimulating questions, make comparisons, and extract an innovative, integrated, realistic scheme from masses of unorganised raw data. It is a balance between science and creativity that we strive for in doing research. (Strauss and Corbin, 1998, p. 13)

This first reading of the transcripts allowed the researcher to 'get a feel' for the group's work and to immerse himself in the data. By a process of progressive focusing (Parlett, 1981) issues of relevance and potential importance concerning the nature of e-learning group work became apparent. For example, some of the issues that emerged in the early analysis included such things as shared ideas, disclosure, planning for chat sessions, summaries of chat sessions, the production of documents, discussions of the documents, joking, sharing professional practice, sharing resources, the production of timetables of planned work and reference to stakeholders. The notes accompanying the analysis amounted to some 20 pages of handwritten text with detailed notes on each issue. As part of the procedure he also made analytical notes to himself, highlighting possible interesting issues for investigation and analysis.

All the issues represent potential categories. As a category emerged from the analysis, he would make a note of it and proceed with the analysis of the transcript trying to find evidence that might support or refute each category being included in the final set of categories. He would then look in depth at these emerging categories, re-read the margin annotations and notes to himself, moving back and forward from the text of the transcripts to his notes. A new set of notes was made on the particular category, clarifying for example who said what or who did what, how others reacted to that, and how the group worked with member's ideas and suggestions. Typically, he would then proceed to engage in a new round of analysis in order to illuminate the category in some more detail (Parlett, 1991).

In this way, categories were reworked and re-conceptualised on the basis of re-readings and analysis of the transcripts in an effort to produce the final explanatory categories. Sometimes new categories emerged as he reduced the data and merged categories. The rigour of this approach is a measure of the 'trustworthiness' (Lincoln and Guba, 1985, p. 290) or validity of this kind of research. The development of the categories and emergent theory are *grounded* in rigorous analysis of the data (Dey, 1993).

Three broad categories concerning the experience of collaborative e-assessment were developed from this grounded theory-approach (McConnell, in press (a)):

31.3.2.1 *Appropriateness of collaborative assessment*

- The role of the tutor

- Appropriateness of the medium

31.3.2.2 *Collaborative assessment as a learning event*

- From unilateral to collaborative assessment

- Enjoyment, frankness, anxiety and tensions

- Responsibility to others

- The development of collaborative assessment skills

- Access to others' learning

- Motivation to learn

- Intrinsic vs extrinsic validation of learning

The focus for assessment

- Should participation be assessed?

- Assessing participation by sharing perceptions of participation

This grounded theory-approach to researching networked learning contributed to the literature on self and peer-assessment by providing rich insights into students' experiences of collaborative e-assessment. It also validated the use of collaborative assessment in e-learning environments. It showed that the purpose of collaborative assessment is to foster a learning approach to assessment and to develop a shared power relationship with students. The research shows that a positive social climate is necessary in developing and sustaining collaborative assessment and that this form of assessment helps students reduce dependence on lecturers as the only or major source of judgement about the quality of learning. Students develop skill and know-how about self and peer assessment and see themselves as competent in making judgements about their own and each other's work, which are surely good lifelong learning skills.

31.3.3   A collaborative, reflective-critique approach to understanding networked learning

The method used here involved a group of students and tutors who had worked together online meeting face-to-face to research their group work collaboratively. They wanted to understand how they worked together in a networked learning environment, and how to go about improving their performance and productivity as a group.

They read through their asynchronous discussion transcript, as a group of actors might read through a play. Each person read their own entries and stopped when they wanted to discuss what was happening to them at that point in the e-discussion. The transcript was therefore used as a basis to help recall what was happening at the time when they made their entries online, why they made the entry and what they now had to say about the online events. This allowed issues of importance to each individual and issues of interest to the group to emerge during the discussion (McConnell, in progress).

This free-ranging discussion was audio recorded and later transcribed. The final analysis was carried out by the author (who was one of the tutors) and involved working with both the transcript of e-discussions and the transcript of the face-to-face discussion, which were read and analysed together.

The focus is on the groups' defined purposes within the e-discussions and their experience of working collaboratively online. The study is concerned with developing an understanding of the ways in which groups 'function' in networked learning environments, from the perspective of the participants' in the groups. This is essentially a phenomenological approach aimed at being open to the concerns, constructs, assumptions and logic of the participants in the groups. The cooperative research design allows the matching of the groups' defined purposes with their own analysis of their functions, processes and longitudinal development. In addition participants and tutors alike are in a position to develop an understanding of the process of learning as it occurs online.

From this collaborative, reflective-critique approach to researching networked learning several categories which helped explain the way in which the members of the group worked online emerged:

- problems of working cooperatively and making collective decisions;

- the cooperative learning contract: implicit or explicit?

- roles online: formalised and non-formalised;

- highs and lows of interaction;

- problems of asynchronous communication and responding while online;

- barriers to group work and cooperation online;

- working in ways 'not natural';

- concerns for others and group processes;

- tutors;

- self disclosure online;

- the group 'product'.

Several beneficial outcomes of this collaborative research process were described, including:

- sharing of meanings and constructions of group work online: the complexity of e-groups and the ways in which individuals' participate can be discussed and different viewpoints examined and explained;

- developing an awareness of what is avoided in the groups: there is often little time to discuss how the group is working as it works online; this research approach allows members' time to reflect on their processes and develop an awareness of the barriers to their e-group work;

- addressing issues of power and control in the learning process: reflective analysis of this kind allows those involved time to examine the dynamics of the group and the ways in which power is shared and controlled between participants themselves, and between participants and the tutors;

- a way of collaboratively designing and evaluating the learning event: this research approach allows tutors and participants the opportunity to understand how the course design works for and against them, and how they could change it;

- exposing the tutor to critique by participants: participants are freed-up to challenge tutor interventions and participation. They often become aware of how the tutor functions online as they read the transcript and can raise for discussion difficult issues, which they felt unable to address online.

The author concludes:

> The particular context, purpose and dynamic of each group, the trust that people have in each other, and the way the discussions are facilitated, may well determine what is discussed and what is avoided in e-groups. The medium itself is not intrinsically unsupportive of confrontation or argument.

> This 'reflective critique' approach to researching CPD based networked learning has helped both tutors and participants understand the nature and processes they are involved in during their online work. The experience of working online has become observable. This approach to learning has allowed tutors and participants to make changes to the design of the Masters programme on the basis of their collective experiences. Participants and tutors have become more observant of their relations online.

31.3.4   E-questionnaires used to evaluate EU-based Internet courses

Questionnaires are a highly used method for carrying out educational research, but their use in Internet-based research, and in networked learning research specifically, is a relatively untested area.

The method used in this study involved collecting students' and tutors' perceptions of two e-courses, offered across Europe, by questionnaires sent to them via email (McConnell, 2000).

The students were sent three questionnaires, one at the beginning, middle and end of each course.

- The pre-course questionnaire focused on the students' professional development backgrounds, their purposes for taking an Internet-based course and their familiarity with the technology.

- The mid-course questionnaire covered the time they spent studying on the course, their use of resources, their participation in the online collaborative learning processes and their experiences of studying via ICT.

- The post-course questionnaire considered their general enjoyment of studying in this mode, the effectiveness of the course and their comparison with other modes of learning.

The tutors were sent one email questionnaire. It asked about their background, the aims and objectives of the course they were offering, their experience of being an online tutor, their perceptions of the experiences of their students, problems and success, the time spent working on the course and their views about online teaching and learning.

The author cites a list of research outcomes from this study:

The students' experience

- Students say that, on the whole, these courses provided a very positive learning experience and they would be willing to take similar courses in the future.

- These forms of Internet courses offer flexibility for learners in pacing their studies and in deciding when to study.

- Some students did not complete one of the courses. We cannot be sure about why this happened, though we do know that several students took the course for experience only, and did not intend to work towards certification of any kind.

- Many, but not all, the students who took the courses were fairly familiar with the technology involved, and had good access to it in order to participate. They were, in many cases, self selected and so in this respect the trials have been somewhat 'skewed'.

- Many students found it hard to organise their studies – mainly because time was at a premium as they were all full time workers.

- The perceptions of the effectiveness of this form of open and distance learning varied from course to course. On the whole, most students thought that, as examples of open learning, these courses were 'effective'. Most described them as being just as effective as any other course they had taken by traditional methods.

The tutors' experience

- All tutors reported that the courses provided a very positive learning experience and that they would be very willing to teach in this way again.

- With one exception, all tutors had previous experience of teaching via the Internet.

- This form of course provision allows for flexibility in the time of day, and day of week for teaching.

- Tutor views of their online roles differed from course to course, and at times even within the same course. This might be a function of the differing purposes of each course, and the associated teaching and learning processes. More research is required to understand the relationship between course aims and objectives, and associated tutor roles.

- From the tutor perspective, the *advantages* of this form of learning are:

    - easier access for students;
    - independence of time and distance;
    - flexibility of time and place;
    - ability of participants to take part who would otherwise not be able to;
    - access to online references and resources, and a wider community of practice;
    - excitement and challenge of online learning;
    - the possibility to do some things 'better' online (compared with traditional distance learning);
    - construction of interactive sessions in lessons;
    - ability to communicate fast via computer-mediated communications, e.g. for asking questions and giving answers; for facilitating discussions and group work;
    - ability to use hyperlinks to an 'ocean' of relevant information on the Internet;
    - ability to have group discussions and collaborative work online.

- the *disadvantages* are:

  - the slow pace of asynchronous exchanges;

  - attenuated sense of presence in a largely text-based environment;

  - more preparation work for the teacher.

Several issues limited the use of this research method:

1.	In course one the questionnaires were distributed by two means: as a Word.rtf file attachment to an email. The formatted questionnaire opened on the participant's PC for them to complete and return. We also sent the questionnaire in the form of ASCII text within the body of an email. The latter type was not of course formatted, but did have the attraction of being simple and easy to open, complete and return. In the second course the questionnaires were distributed via Lotus Notes emails within the body of the email itself. When they were opened they were presented as fully formatted rich text, and also returned in this way.

We considered providing the questionnaire on the Web itself, for online completion, but were not able to implement this fully within the time-span of the evaluation. It is, however, possible that respondents may not in any case have been inclined to take the trouble to visit the web site in order to complete the questionnaire. But this method would have been interesting to try out.

In all cases, each email was prefaced with a courteous message explaining the purpose of the survey and offering to discuss with respondents any queries they might have about the evaluation of the courses. Introductory messages are considered an important factor in attaining good response rates to electronic surveys (Witmer *et al.*, 1999).

Reminder emails were sent to those not returning their questionnaires.

2.	Past experience of evaluating these kind of courses suggested that respondents were not very tolerant of having to complete long or complicated questionnaires. The questionnaire had to be easy to complete – especially for those whose first language was not English. This suggested a largely self-completion format, with fixed questions and some opportunity for respondents to elaborate on answers where necessary, or where they wished. In drawing up the student questionnaire, it soon became apparent that the number of issues we wished to cover was too much for one questionnaire alone. We therefore decided to design three shorter questionnaires, one distributed prior to the course, one during the course and the third after the course. There was only one tutor questionnaire.

Problems experienced with this research method:

- Low returns of some student questionnaires: in the first course there were low response rates, ranging from 14 per cent to 29 per cent (for the different questionnaires) of all those enrolled. The reasons for this are not clear. Some students did not complete one of the courses, and some courses had 'occasional' participants who were not registered, or who did not wish to fully participate, and so perhaps did not feel inclined to complete the questionnaires. It is not clear if the method of distribution of the questionnaires proved too difficult for respondents to relate to. Although we emailed those who did not return questionnaires, most of them did not respond. So our results do not fully take into account the views of all students, and may only reflect the views of those who set out to complete the course (53 per cent of those completing this course did return the post-course questionnaire). Other researchers also report low response rates to online surveys, sometimes as low as 10 per cent, and indicate the potential pitfalls of data collection via emails generally (e.g. Witmer *et al.*, 1999). To what extent conventional snail mail survey techniques (and other research techniques generally) translate to email questionnaire surveys is an interesting research question for those of us involved in conducting course evaluations via the Internet.

- The standardised questionnaires did not always compliment the different purposes and designs of each course. This is perhaps inevitable in this kind of research method. Follow up interviews via the Internet might have offered an opportunity for respondents to expand on their answers, but there was no time to do this.

- Restricted responses: it is not possible to know the extent to which those responding actually understood the questions asked. This is possibly the case with those whose first language is not English. There is some indication in the replies that some respondents did not really understand what some of the questions were asking, or that their understanding of terms and words used had different and unique local and cultural meanings.

- Interpreting written responses: there were occasions when it was difficult to interpret some of the written (typed) responses. We sometimes wanted to ask respondents exactly what they meant, especially those replying whose first language was not English. However, this was not possible.

31.4   Conclusions

Methods for researching networked learning are in many ways no different to the general spectrum of methods used in educational research. We have seen that methods such as grounded theory, stimulated recall, ethnography, interviews and questionnaires are all effective in researching networked learning.

But the networked learning environment itself affords new opportunities to explore the learning that takes place. The technology of the Internet affords a new environment in which to conduct our research. This is a novel, and as yet not very well understood medium for conducting the process of educational research, and its potential is worthy in itself of being the focus of our research.

What can we conclude about methods for researching networked learning, and the issues that have arisen from the use of these different research methods?

31.4.1   Using the technology itself to conduct research

When the technology is used in a communication (CMC) mode, bringing researcher and participant together, it works well and the research process can be effective and acceptable in terms of the processes involved and the research results. Participants seem to be motivated to take part in the research due to the person-to-person contact involved. A social relationship is developed which helps sustain the research process.

When the technology is used to distribute a research tool, such as an electronic questionnaire or concept map, then it seems that the willingness of people to participate diminishes. The lack of a personal, social dimension to the research process may be an important limiting factor.

31.4.2 Using networked learning transcripts

Electronic transcripts of networked learning are easy to obtain and lend themselves to a variety of analytical techniques. When used by students and tutors in face-to-face meetings as a form of stimulated recall, they can provide a rich source of data for reviewing and assessing their networked learning group work. By reading the transcripts, they can recall what they were doing during the group work and reflect on the effectiveness of that for sustaining group processes and promoting their learning.

31.4.3 Grounded theory and ethnography

Transcripts of networked learning events can also be submitted to analysis by a variety of methods. We have seen that two methods - grounded theory and ethnography – offer particularly rich ways of using transcripts, which in turn provide interesting and useful insights into the networked learning process.

31.5 References

Asensio, M., Foster, J., Hodgson, V., McConnell, D. (2000) *Networked Learning 2000: Innovative Approaches to Lifelong Learning and Higher Education Through the Internet.* Sheffield: University of Sheffield.

Glaser, B. and Strauss, A. (1968) *The Discovery of Grounded Theory.* London: Weidenfield & Nicolson.

Jones, S. (ed.) (1999) *Doing Internet Research.* Thousand Oaks: Sage,.

Mann, C. and Stewart, F. (2000) *Internet Communication and Qualitative Research: A Handbook for Researching Online.* London: Sage.

McConnell, D (1999) Examining a collaborative assessment process in networked lifelong learning. *Journal of Computer Assisted Learning* 15, Sept.: 232–43

McConnell, D (2000) *Implementing Computer Supported Cooperative Learning,* 2nd edn. London: Kogan Page.

McConnell, D. (2002) Complexity, harmony and diversity of learning in collaborative e-learning continuing professional development groups. published in: Stahl, G. (Editor) (2002) *Proceedings of CSCL Conference, Boulder, USA.* Distributed by Lawrence Erlbaum associates, Inc., Hillside, New Jersey, USA (pages 265–274).

McConnell, D. (2002) The experience of collaborative assessment in e-learning, *Studies in Continuing Education, 24(1), 73–92.*

McConnell, D. (2002) Action research and distributed problem based learning in continuing professional education, *Distance Education,* 23(1), 59–83.

McConnell, D. (in progress) *Understanding Group-work in E-learning: A Collaborative, Reflective-Critique Approach.*

Noakes, N. (2000) *Online Educational Research On-the-line.* M.Ed. dissertation, Sheffield: University of Sheffield.

Strauss, A. and Corbin, J. (1990) *Basics of Qualitative Research: Grounded Theory Procedures and Techniques.* London: Sage.

Witmer, D.F., Colman, R.W. and Katzman, S.L. (1999) From paper-and pencil to screen-and-keyboard: toward a methodology for survey research on the Internet. In S. Jones (ed.), *Doing Internet Research: Critical Issues and Methods for Examining the Net.* Thousand Oaks: Sage.

Alan Staley
University of Central England in Birmingham, UK

The next two chapters (32 and 33) are based on two papers that originally formed part of a symposium on computer supported experiential learning and which arose from a four-year research project entitled Computer Supported Experiential Learning, at the University of Central England in Birmingham, UK. This project has explored the 'mapping' of a variety of learning technologies on to a well-established curriculum model — experiential learning (Kolb, 1984). The project has focused on trying to improve the quality of student learning through the use of learning technology as opposed to increasing student numbers via distance learning or tying to gain cost benefits through economies of scale.

The project has actually comprised many small projects that have considered the use of learning technologies in different disciplines and very different contexts. Chapters 32 and 33 are case studies that illustrate this diversity. The 'Problems at Crumpton' case study in Chapter 32 concerns the use of an online spoof university for an academic staff development programme. In particular this case study focuses upon multimedia representations of practice as a means of promoting reflective practice, and also the impact of assessment upon the use of learning technologies. The case study in Chapter 33 describes the experiential learning cycle and considers the application of technology to each stage of the cycle in the context of foreign languages and intercultural studies.

The evaluation of the student learning experience across all of the projects was conducted by the Centre for Research into Quality (CRQ) at the University of Central England. The broad aim of this research was to try and establish:

- What does learning technology do better?
- What works where?
- What is transferable?

In addition, CRQ interviewed all academic staff involved in the CSEL projects to identify institutional and cultural issues that affected the implementation of ICT. These findings, together with all the case studies, can be found in Alan Staley and Niall MacKenzie (eds), *Computer Supported Experiential Learning*, Learning Methods Unit, University of Central England in Birmingham.

32 Problems at Crumpton: case study

Niall MacKenzie
University of Central England in Birmingham

32.1 Introduction

This chapter discusses the 'Problems at Crumpton' project, which was just one of a number of projects included in the four-year Computer Supported Experiential Learning (CSEL) project at the University of Central England. Crumpton is an online spoof university which is having problems because of poorly designed curricula. Academic staff, in this case staff enrolled on the Postgraduate Certificate in Education and Professional Development (PGCEPD), can access the Crumpton website and discover the problems by examining fictitious course documentation from the degree in Socio-Historical Studies and also by watching a series of short video clips that vividly represent practice at Crumpton University. The video clips are situated in real world contexts and attempt to portray problems in a non-threatening and humorous way, enabling staff freely to discuss otherwise difficult issues. After a structured study programme, staff collaboratively discuss ways of tackling the Problems at Crumpton using an asynchronous online conference. It is an analysis of the contributions to the conference that this chapter focuses on and explores ideas of internalisation and self-reflection, which are enabled by the 'safe distance' of virtual representations of real life. Where successful, this promotes very deep learning and perhaps even a shift in values.

32.2 Project background

32.2.1 Website

The CSEL project looked at pilot projects that had used Kolb's cycle as a basis for their approach to experiential learning. There were three scenarios where the experiencing stage of the cycle could be placed; real world, artificial or virtual. Problems at Crumpton represents the third scenario – virtual experiences in a 'real world' context. The home page is shown in Figure 32.1.

An attempt has been made with Problems at Crumpton to set a concrete context for learning by using the technology offered by the Web. A series of short video clips helps to 'bring alive' the academic life at the fictitious Crumpton University. These include: Critical Incidents at Validation; Teaching Team in Action; Mutiny in the Common Room, Employer's Comments, and The Students Rebel.

Once staff have familiarised themselves with the background and problems at Crumpton, there is a highly structured study programme to follow. Each study period comprises six learning components; *Learning Outcomes, Resources, The Key Concept Map* (which adapts the idea of mind maps [Buzan, 1989]), *Frequently Asked Questions, Self Assessment* and the *Conference*.

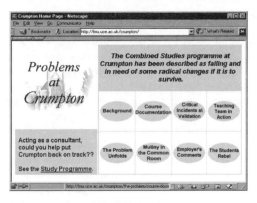

Figure 32.1 Setting the context for the problems at Crumpton

Conferencing is perhaps the most important of the learning components. It provides a communication tool for the learner, their peers, the lecturer and anyone else who is invited to take part in online discussions. The lecturer can structure task-orientated work and feedback that is visible to the whole group can help learners feel that they are far from isolated during their periods of independent study. Used effectively, conferencing can support collaborative learning, reflective practice, and also address some of the higher order learning outcomes.

There is a notion that deep learning occurs when learners are active rather than passive (Biggs, 1999). Ahmet and Fellows (1999) agree, 'There is little doubt that student motivation is greatly enhanced when the learning is active, relevant and resulting from the individual's experience.' (p. 7). They go on, 'Where students see the relevance and can make the connections between theory and the "real world" the level of interest and enthusiasm improves dramatically' (p. 10).

White (1999) suggests that, 'Probably the highest level of interactivity is achieved by incorporating dialogue into the learning process' (p. 153). White sees conferencing at the active end of a learning scale that also places static web pages at the passive end.

In Crumpton, the conference component is where some of the learning activities are structured and feedback gained.

In particular, the conference is where staff discuss the issues involved at Crumpton, identify problems, and suggest tentative solutions. Staff then go on to consider their own experiences in the conference area. For those staff studying the PGCEPD, the contributions in the conference were assessed against comprehensive criteria shown in Table 32.1 to form part of the summative assessment.

(a)	Contribution to the conference in response to the tutor's tasks within each study period that relate to the student's own experience of curriculum design, teaching or learning.
(b)	Replying constructively to another student's contribution in the dialogue. Being supportive and inviting further dialogue.
(c)	Contributions to the conference in response to the tutor's tasks within each study period that relate to the problems at 'Crumpton'. Diagnosis of problems and tentative solutions.
(d)	Raising an issue germane to the problems at 'Crumpton' or the subject content of that study period, that has not been previously raised by the tutor or another student.
(e)	Bringing to the class's attention an item of relevant Web material not already indicated in the study programme.

Table 32.1 Assessment criteria for conference contributions

32.2.2 The case study conference

Quotes from the conference: in most cases the contributions are taken verbatim from the WebBoard conferences, although anonymity has been protected. Where the sense would have been completely lost by typing errors, some very minor adjustments have been made, however all grammatical errors have been left as typed.

The Problems at Crumpton case study was set as an assignment for university lecturers studying a module entitled 'Designing Courses to Support Self Study' as part of the PGCEPD. This represented a portion of independent study in between traditional face-to-face teaching sessions. The module was taken by 32 academic staff (19 female, 13 male). For most of these staff the course was compulsory due to limited teaching experience, although a small number of very experienced staff volunteered to take the course. There was a mixture of full-time and part-time staff, and a diverse range of ICT skills within the group.

Initial topics for discussion were divided between issues at Crumpton and issues that related to the lecturers' own experience. This structuring of the conference for study period one is illustrated in Figure 32.2.

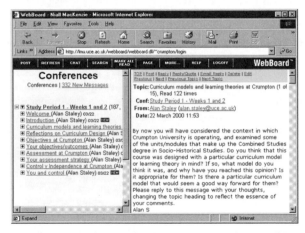

Figure 32.2 Initial topics for discussion in study period one

Points could be gained for contributions to each type of topic, but there was sufficient flexibility in the marking scheme to allow staff not to contribute to particular topics if they did not want too. Staff could also gain points for raising new issues, replying to each other, and posting details of relevant online resources.

Each week the contributions were scored against each of the five assessment criteria previously shown in Table 32.1.

A weekly deadline for contributions was set at midnight Sunday. The tutor could award up to five points against each of the assessment criteria (irrespective of the number of contributions made), making it possible to gain 25 points per week. No more than 25 points could be scored in any week thereby encouraging regular contributions.

WebBoard was used as the conferencing software and the conference went 'live' on 23 November 1999 and the last contribution was posted on 31 May 2000. The assessed part of the conference did not start until week 18, after a period of social interaction and other general and structured tasks.

It was assumed that none of the participants had ever used WebBoard and so introductory sessions in the use of WebBoard were provided. This approach to introducing new technology to all participants, regardless of skill level, is advocated by Hiemstra (1998). Some guidance was also given on using asynchronous conferences as a learning tool and support was available for all participants throughout the early use of the conference.

32.3   Analysis of contributions

Figure 32.3 shows the number of contributions to the conference over the 26 week period. The histograms also show which area of the conference the contributions were posted to. The straight line shows the percentage of the group who were contributing.

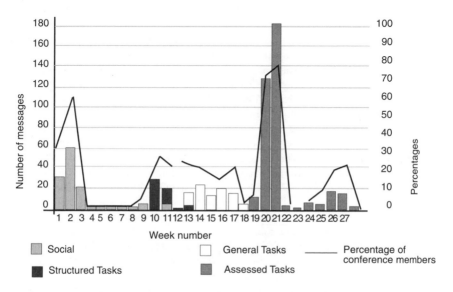

Figure 32.3   A graphical representation of the online contributions

As suggested by many studies (e.g. Hiltz, 1994) the conference began with an area for social interaction. Participants were asked to introduce themselves briefly and informally, stating their area of teaching and some biographical details. They were then asked to reply to two other introductions. In the initial three weeks, leading up to the Christmas vacation, the 'Social' area had well over 100 messages posted to it and in the second week almost two-thirds of the 32 academic staff had contributed. Some technical difficulties had prevented one or two from logging on but as the break for Christmas and New Year approached all but four staff had logged on and posted at least one message.

Only a handful of messages were added to the Social conference when staff returned in January. In week 9 some 'General Tasks' were introduced as a new and separate conference. The tasks were based around work being done in the face-to-face sessions on the PGCEPD course and were voluntary and very open-ended. In a four-week period, which included a reading week between semesters (week 11) when there were no student lectures, just over 50 messages were posted in the 'General Tasks' area. More significant was the number of staff generating these messages that never reached double figures in any of the four weeks.

Less than one-third of staff contributed to the conference and over half of the messages were posted by just four members of staff. Although the study is using a very small sample this confirms the findings of previous studies (Hiltz and Turoff, 1978; Wells, 1995) that 10 per cent of participants can often account for up to 50 per cent of the messages.

However, it was determined from the logfiles that over half of the participants had been reading conference contributions without necessarily posting anything themselves. The familiar conference phenomenon of 'lurking' (reading without posting) accounted for ten participants during this phase, which is slightly higher than the 25 per cent recorded in the studies mentioned above.

During weeks 12–17 'Structured Tasks' with very clear and explicit instructions were introduced to the conference and this generated 83 messages. The tasks were again voluntary but participants were organised into learning sets where experienced and inexperienced technology users were grouped together. The pattern of contribution was very similar to that seen during the 'General Tasks' phase. Less than a third of the group were actively contributing and the participants tended to be those who had contributed in the previous 11 weeks. The voluntary phases seemed to concur with the findings of Mason (1995) that approximately one-third participated, another third lurked and the remainder did neither. Although Mason's study dealt with distance learners and the final third dropped out of the course the comparison and similarity was interesting to note.

Towards the end of week 18 the assessment was introduced. Unsurprisingly the levels of contribution rose dramatically and in the two weeks before the Easter vacation over 300 contributions were posted to the conference. In both of those weeks, about three quarters of the group contributed with just five participants failing to contribute in either week before the Easter break. The nature of the assessment had enabled most contributors to score enough points to pass the assignment within the first two weeks and this was reflected in the participation levels in the following weeks of assessment. Only about 50 more messages were posted to the conference, the majority coming from members of staff who were still to gain the necessary number of points to pass the module. However, there were still participants who contributed long after they had scored the required number of points. These tended to be the staff that had contributed during the voluntary phases of the conference.

The participation patterns of each group member were analysed and some of these are represented below. They revealed some very different approaches to conference contribution and may be a strong indicator of some of the participants' learning styles. However, contributions alone do not reveal the full picture of an individual's learning style and more detailed analysis of time spent logged on to the conference was also gained by looking at the WebBoard log file in detail. By careful examination of login times and the activities recorded in the log file, periods of continuous conference activity could be recorded for each individual. Periods of inactivity for an hour or more were deemed to be separate sessions. Where an individual had logged off and back on again within an hour they were also regarded as separate sessions.

Figure 32.4 shows the log-on pattern for one individual and highlights exactly why some consider asynchronous conferences to be 'any time, any place, anywhere' learning. The lines show the periods this individual was logged on to the conference – the length of the line indicating the length of time online. Log on times are spread throughout the day, from morning until midnight and the effect of assessment did not seem to affect the frequency of logging on but clearly did affect the length of time the individual was using WebBoard (indicated by the length of line).

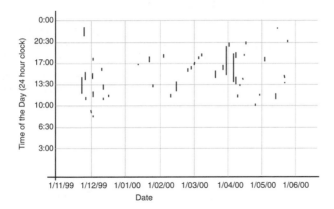

Figure 32.4   Time spent by a learner on WebBoard

32.4   The effect of assessment

32.4.1   Assessment as a motivating factor

Contributions to the conference were analysed and counted to see how much of a motivating factor assessment had been on the quantity of contributions to the conference. Figure 32.3 has already shown the effect of assessment on the group as a whole but contribution patterns were broken down for each individual.

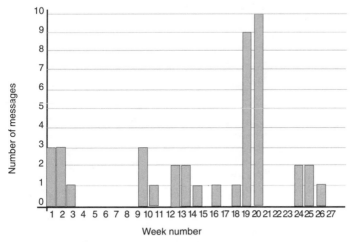

Figure 32.5   Contribution Pattern 1

The pattern shown in Figure 32.5 was remarkably close to the pattern of the whole group shown in Figure 32.3. Steady contributions in the voluntary phases of the conference suddenly rose dramatically when assessment was introduced. This learner showed that assessment increased extrinsic motivation, although a good level of intrinsic motivation clearly already existed.

32.4.2   Assessment promoting strategic learning

The contribution pattern of the individual shown in Figure 32.6 appeared to exhibit a very strategic approach to learning as contributions were only posted when necessary. The learner appeared to be contributing to the conference in order to fulfil the assessment criteria successfully. However, the quality of this individual's contributions were very high and it subsequently emerged that although this individual had not contributed during the voluntary phases they had been an enthusiastic 'lurker'.

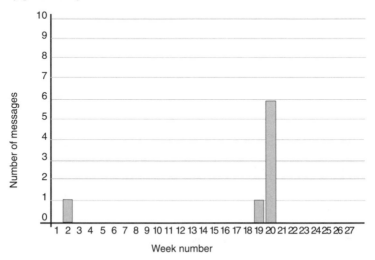

Figure 32.6   Contribution Pattern 2

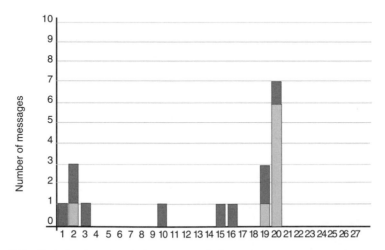

Figure 32.7   Contribution Pattern 2 (Logins added)

In Figure 32.7, the areas added to the contribution pattern in Figure 32.6, show the days when the contributor had logged on to the conference and read messages without necessarily contributing. The effect of assessment is still clear to see and the learner may still be exhibiting the signs of taking a strategic approach; however, 'lurking' can hide the amount of learning an individual is actually undertaking.

The difficulty in assessing this style of learning is clearly problematic as discovering the depth of learning of an individual by simply analysing their online behaviour is difficult. Lurking is a valuable conference learning process but what assessment criteria could capture it?

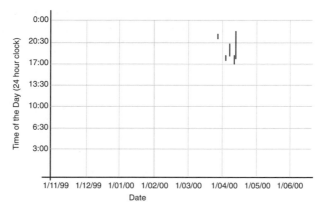

Figure 32.8   Time spent by a learner on WebBoard

Figure 32.8 represents an even clearer example of a learner who only contributed or logged on to the conference when assessment required them to do so. However, this can be misleading. This individual's contributions were very well thought out and clearly showed evidence of deep learning. What the figures and log files don't reveal is the amount of preparation put in by this learner before they contributed. They had studied the Problems at Crumpton long and hard (online and offline) before entering the conference.

32.4.3   Assessment having little effect

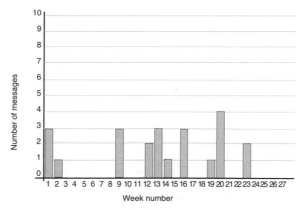

Figure 32.9   Contribution Pattern 3

Pattern 3 in Figure 32.9 shows a learner who appears not to be motivated by assessment at all, with their contribution level constant throughout the conference. Although some learners must obviously acknowledge and pass the assessment criteria, it has very little effect on their patterns of study.

32.5   Days of contribution

The effect of assessment on which days contributions to the conference were made was noticeable. If we take Friday as an example, the contribution pattern is fairly consistent throughout the 26 week period. As Figure 32.10 shows, the number of contributions made during the assessment period is not significantly higher than peaks throughout the conference.

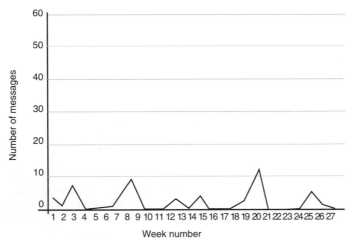

Figure 32.10 Contributions made on Friday

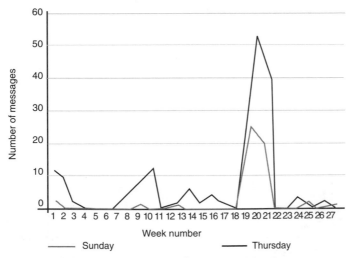

Figure 32.11 Contributions made on Thursday and Sunday

However, as Figure 32.11 shows, if Thursday and Sunday contributions are analysed then the effect of assessment is marked, with significantly more contributions on both Thursday and Sunday during the assessment period. The face-to-face sessions for this group of learners occurred on Friday and perhaps peer learning acted as a motivating factor, ensuring that staff wanted to go to the face to face sessions well-prepared. This became heightened during the assessment phase.

The Sunday contributions were almost negligible (never higher than two per week) for the entire 26 week period apart from the assessment period when contributions rose to 25 and 20 respectively. As stated earlier, the contribution deadline was midnight on Sunday and staff appeared to be motivated by that assessment deadline.

32.6   Contribution analysis

32.6.1   Safe distance

Did the 'safe distance' provided by using virtual representations encourage public discussion? It appeared so. Some staff responded very strongly to the video clips as indicated by this contribution:

> I think that the teaching staff we saw in the video clips are the dregs of our profession. They are the lazy, self-centred and unfortunately unsackable elements who needed to be given a reason to exist by virtue of their tenure.

This contribution perfectly emphasises the ability for conference participants to use the 'safe distance' provided by virtual scenarios to make some extremely provocative statements. Imagine if this contributor was referring to teaching staff at his/her own institution? The contributor was being deliberately provocative, as they admitted later in the discussion but nevertheless, the video clips of Crumpton lecturers had provided a neutral platform from which such comments could be made.

32.6.2   Virtual vs real experience

Making personal attacks on the fictitious characters seemed to make it easier for staff to then reflect upon their own teaching with a great deal of honesty:

> Correspondingly have we not all had times in our career when perhaps we did not represent the epitome of our profession (I certainly have). Thank goodness I wasn't sacked on the spot but encouraged to reflect and learn from what were (or are) usually difficult circumstances at the time. I'd like to know I'm not the only one who isn't perfect all the time.

The same contributor went on to make a further courageous disclosure later on, that was also startling in its honesty.

> An example, I think I had my first student fall asleep in a session this afternoon. Is that a reflection on me or her or neither?

This illustrates the differences between contributions that discussed the issues being portrayed at 'Crumpton' and those that asked staff to reflect upon their own experiences.

Would these candid remarks have been made without the 'trigger' of Crumpton? Making revealing contributions in front of the whole group can be difficult enough face-to-face; doing so in writing given the permanence of a conference can be sufficiently threatening to deter contributors (Hardy *et al.*, 1991) or lead to disappointingly trite contributions.

32.6.3   Critical reflections

The next quote reveals just how powerful Crumpton had been in helping staff reflect upon their own experiences:

> Although I am out of the 'game' [this member of staff no longer needed to contribute for assessment purposes] I had some thoughts on Barrie the Brummie. I did my degree as a mature student and had the usual financial concerns plus three children to think about and I think that I got through for two reasons firstly the obvious self motivation, I wanted to complete the degree but more importantly some although not all of my tutors were sufficiently motivated and more importantly were 'good teachers'. the interesting thing is that the lecturers I had who were good had all done some form of PGCE and those that were bad had just gone straight through from undergrad to post-grad to lecturer with no real time to think or learn about the process of learning.

32.6.4   Internalisation

Staff were able to relate the scenarios presented at Crumpton to their own specific courses and then project the arguments in a more abstract way. The following contribution raised the issue of entrance routes at Crumpton, and made the link to progression rates considering his/her own course. This generated 20 replies in what became a very lively discussion.

> On our course we have a wide range of students. Over the years student progression has been monitored in relation to students' entrance qualifications. The results have shown 90 per cent success for A level students and less than 50 per cent success for Access course students.

> I would be interested to hear other people's experiences particularly in relation to professional courses.

> There are clearly a range of entrance routes at Crumpton and this is probably true of all our courses. Widening access to higher education is clearly important but it presents many challenges to teaching.

32.6.5   Shift in values

Alternating between reflecting upon carefully contrived virtual representation of practice and real experience appears to promote very deep learning, perhaps even a shift in values.

The power of the debate became further strengthened when the ideas being put forward were actually put into practice. Staff acknowledged that they had digested and reflected upon the discussions and in some cases changed their thinking and practices. Obviously it would be a bold claim to attribute this to the conferences alone, as they formed only a small part of the PGCEPD course, but some staff did make this link implicit.

The first example of this shows a member of staff realising what it is like to be a student again, and subsequently changing their practice.

> I used to berate my students for leaving their courseworks until the last possible moment on the basis that they had a timetable for coursework submissions and plenty of time between the launch of a coursework and its submission. All that was required was good time management. I am leaving the PG Cert Ed submissions [conference contributions] until the last possible moment because there are so many other activities to be accommodated. So, I'm no longer merely criticising students, but offering assistance as to how they spend their time in a very productive manner. Of course, I am being hypocritical because I know that I behaved in exactly the same way when I was a student. Is it a case of do as I say, not as I did?

Another contribution takes this a stage further and reveals that Crumpton has had a sufficiently powerful effect to cause a change in values concerning the educational system. This is a good example to illustrate the highest order outcome in the affective domain of Bloom's taxonomy of objectives (Krathwohl, 1964). This example is also interesting in that the member of staff refers directly to the 'habit' of conferencing despite already passing the assessment for the conference 'game'.

> This week I was in the middle of a chalk and talk lecture (wearing my expert hat) when I began to feel very uncomfortable. Looking out at a sea of faces that were rapidly glazing over I almost came to a complete halt. I tried convincing myself that this was one of the topics areas that had to be approached in this way. The students needed to know about children's developmental phonological processes, a topic which is like anatomy, one of those unavoidable term-laden subjects that professional needs dictate they learn. I told myself that this was not an area that could be approached from a 'problem-based' learning strategy. However, after watching the Crumpton 'elite' I am not sure whether I can justify my claim, I am beginning to feel that the whole system of education we currently rely on has its roots in a 20 century ideology that stems from the 'gatekeeping' of an intellectual elite. I think that there has to be a better way of teaching my subject which consists of far too many formal lectures, and a great deal of surface learning by the students. Yes they pass the exams but they find it hard to use that knowledge when they go out on placement.

Some comments were made away from the conference which revealed very different reactions to the online conferencing. One is fairly negative about the whole experience.

32.6.6   Conferencing as a prohibitive factor in learning

> One of the commendable things about the PGCE so far is that I have found it very stressless and unthreatening [many more complimentary points are then made about the PGCEPD course] ... Crumpton differs from all the above. It has caused stress – I am already planning when I am going to go online for week 3 of the conference. I am not worried that I'm going to fail but I do not feel I am benefiting much from doing the exercises and am taking a very strategic – almost devious – approach to completing the exercise...

As a result of this feedback and other comments, the second time Problems at Crumpton was used on the PGCEPD the assessment criteria were modified. Rather than the assessment of online contributions, which proved to be stressful for the conference contributors and the online tutor, staff would submit a written submission that cited online contributions. Deadlines for contributions were set but this was to act purely as an extrinsic motivator. It was not as rigidly imposed as the previous year's deadlines.

It is also vital to point out that from the point of view of the tutor, assessment of online contributions is an extremely time consuming activity. Figure 32.12 shows the amount of time the tutor was logged on during the 26 week period and the vast amount of time needed to assess all contributions during the assessment period.

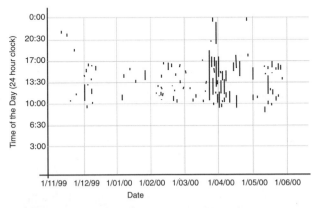

Figure 32.12 Time spent by the tutor on WebBoard

32.7   Conclusion

In introducing conferencing to the PGCEPD, strategies to provoke and encourage participation were deliberately employed. As identified by Wells' (1995) criteria, assessment and careful intervention by the facilitator can all affect participation rates. The online conference generated considerable participation, and while the assessment necessitated this, the tutors considered the contributions to be of a high quality and not simply an indication of a strategic approach to the assignment. Many contributions were of a deeply reflective nature revealing self-analysis, commitment to changing practice, and a great deal of honesty. Crumpton and the virtual representations of practice within it, appeared to act as an 'ice breaker' provoking discussion and enabling staff to comment without the feeling of being in a threatening environment. It was clear that connections were being made to the courses and characters at Crumpton and this subsequently made staff think deeply about their own practice, courses, and indeed institution. Therefore reflecting upon virtual experiences can be a valuable step in promoting discussion in an online environment, and can ease the process of critical self-reflection in the context of teaching in higher education. Whether any or all of the above would have been possible without the introduction of assessment is open to debate. The evidence points to assessment providing the necessary extrinsic motivation to enhance the intrinsic motivation of learners online.

Problems at Crumpton can be found at http://www.ssdd.uce.ac.uk/crumpton

32.8 References

Ahmet, K. and Fellows, S. (1999) Experiential learning through practicals. In K. Ahmet and S. Fellows (eds), *Inspiring Students: Case Studies in Motivating the Learner*. London: Kogan Page.

Biggs, J.B. (1999) What the student does: teaching for enhanced learning, *Higher Education Research & Development* **18**(1).

Boud, D., Keogh, R. and Walker, D. (1985) *Reflection: Turning Experience into Learning*. London: Kogan Page.

Buzan, T. (1989) *Use Your Head*, 3rd edn. London: BBC Books.

Elton, L. (1996) Strategies to enhance learner motivation: a conceptual analysis, *Studies in Higher Education* **21**(1): 57–68.

Hardy, G. *et al.* (1991) *Computer Mediated Communication for Management Training and Development: A Research Report*. Lancaster: CSML, Lancaster University.

Hiemstra, R. (1998) Computerised distance education: the role of facilitators, *MPAEA Journal of Adult Education* **22**(2): 11–23.

Hiltz, S.R. and Turoff, M. (1978) *The Network National: Human Communication via Computer*. Reading, Massachusetts: Addison-Wesley.

Hiltz, S.R. (1994) *The Virtual Classroom*. Norwood, NJ: Ablex.

Kolb, D. (1984) *Experiential Learning: Experience as the Source of Learning and Development*. New Jersey: Prentice Hall.

Krathwohl, N. (ed.) (1964) *Taxonomy of Educational Objectives: Handbook II – The Affective Domain*. Longman.

Mason, R. (1995) Scalability of on-line courses. Conference paper delivered at ALT-C (Association for Learning Technology Conference), The Open University, Milton Keynes, 11–13 September.

Wells, R. (1995) *Computer-Mediated Communication for Distance Education: An International Review of Design, Teaching and Institutional Issues*. ACSDE Research Monography No 6. University Park, Pennsylvania: Pennsylvania State University

White, S. (1999) Using information technology for teaching and learning. In H. Fry, S. Ketteridge and S. Marshall, *A Handbook for Teaching and Learning in Higher Education*. London: Kogan Page.

33 Computer-supported experiential learning for intercultural studies and foreign languages

David A Green and Kirsten Söntgens

University of Central England in Birmingham, UK

33.1 Introduction

The Computer-Supported Experiential Learning project (CSEL) was launched at the University of Central England (UCE) in March 1997 by the University's Learning Methods Unit (LMU). It aims to investigate and evaluate the appropriate use of information and communication technology (ICT) to improve the quality of student learning. Various projects in different faculties and subject areas have been carried out since the inception of the CSEL project. The Centre for Research into Quality (CRQ), an independent research unit based at UCE, was commissioned to undertake an analysis of the use of information technology for learning and teaching. This analysis was complemented by independent research by a PhD student who evaluated our websites as a tool for learning and teaching. This chapter thus describes the development of interactive websites for intercultural and language learning and will provide examples of good practice.

In 1999 we started to develop a Divisional Website (http://bsstudents.uce.ac.uk/dlib) as well as a module website for 'Cultural Diversity' (http://bsstudents.uce.ac.uk/cd) to facilitate the teaching and learning of languages and intercultural studies at UCE Business School. The websites are based on the well-established curriculum model of Kolb's experiential learning (Kolb, 1984), recognising that a sound pedagogical basis is needed for any educational development, including the use of technology (Figure 33.1).

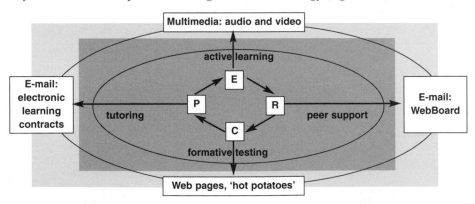

Key: P = Planning; E = Experience; R = Reflection; C = Conceptualization

Figure 33.1   Interpretation of Kolb's Experiential Learning Cycle using ICT

33.2 Developments in language modules

Planning for experience is essential in increasing the awareness of the learning experience. This stage is concerned with methods for preparing learners prior to experiences so that they make most of those experiences (Kolb, 1984). Methods used here include guided questions, observation checklists and assessment criteria devised by students themselves (Gibbs, 1988).

The extension of Kolb's cycle to include technology can be achieved through the use of email whereby students plan ways of applying theory to practice with a tutor by private email communication (Staley and Eastcott, 1999) and via electronic learning contracts to encourage the setting of learning objectives, and monitoring and evaluating progress.

This process led the Division of Languages and International Business to introduce a portfolio of independent learning for post-A Level students in German, French and Spanish. This forms part of the nationwide TransLang project which explicitly seeks to facilitate the development of transferable skills through language learning.

Students are actively involved in planning their learning, monitoring their own progress and evaluating learning outcomes as outlined in Kolb's experiential learning model (stages of planning and reflection). This is achieved via an electronic learning contract which can be accessed on the website (Figure 33.2).

1. Save this document onto disk. 2. Complete only the white boxes. Make sure that you write full answers. 3. Save your completed document. 4. E-mail your completed document AS AN ATTACHMENT to your language tutor.		
First name		Last name
Degree course		
Learning task		
Which language skills or general skills are you hoping to develop, and why?	How will you go about these tasks? Which resources will you use?	Evaluate how well you think you performed. What would you do differently next time?

Figure 33.2   Learning Contract
   (http://bsstudents.uce.ac.uk/dlib/langs/port/pfcontract.doc)

It has been found that the use of an online learning contract encourages students actively to engage in a dialogue with the tutor, as email facilitates a faster, as well as a more private, means of communication with the tutor. After a skills analysis, students are required to priorotise three skill areas they wish to develop during the semester. The learning contract aims to make them think about why they have chosen a particular skills area, which subskills it consists of and how these skills can be transferred to other areas of their learning. The identification of resources will then lead learners to the development of strategies to complete a chosen task. Finally, students will evaluate how well they feel they have done and make suggestions as to how they could improve further. An example of how a student has been guided through the compilation of a learning contract is provided in Figure 33.3.

The student's comments are in plain text, with subsequent advice from the tutor in bold. A sample of completed work will routinely be displayed in the 'Student Zone' of the website, encouraging ownership of the site and motivating students to evaluate each other's work, thus facilitating collaborative reflection according to Kolb's model.

Learning task	EXPLORING WEBSITES	
Which language skills or general skills are you hoping to develop, and why?	**How will you go about these tasks? Which resources will you use?**	**Evaluate how well you think you performed. What would you do differently next time?**
I hope to improve my IT skills and my Research skills through searching for specific information using the Internet. **Which IT skills? Keyboard skills …? Can skills developed searching the Internet be transferred to other 'research' skills (i.e. paper based)?**	I will use the Internet. **HOW exactly did you use it? Did you look at the specified sites only? What do you do if a site no longer exists? Did you try out any other links? Did you do a search etc? Did you get lost at all? What strategies for using the Internet have you developed for future use in German and other subjects?**	I now know where to find Information for languages on the Internet **(are you happy with how you completed the task? Did you spend more or less time on the task than anticipated? How will completing this task help you for other language tasks in the future?)** and have subsequently joined the Tandem Learning Network to improve my language learning. **GUTE IDEE! Explain why you joined and what you are hoping to get out of it (which language and other skills you might be able to develop).**

Figure 33.3   Example Learning Contract with tutor's comments

Reflecting on the learning process has often been achieved through the use of logbooks to record and discuss previous learning experiences. The introduction of ICT has made collaborative reflection possible through the use of asynchronous facilities, such as discussion lists and email public folders. These facilities promote discussion, reflection and collaborative learning between tutor and students or between peers. We have favoured the use of the WebBoard conferencing program because it provides a very structured means of reflection, as discussion threads can be followed easily. Moderation and assessment of contributions is made easy through extensive tracking facilities. Assessment criteria have been drawn up to encourage students to show initiative and support one another in the discussions. In languages, WebBoard has also been used to support students on their residence abroad, as part of the discussion of current topics and as a focus on language forms.

The experience stage in Kolb's original model was concerned with ways of providing classroom-based experiences as substitutes for work or other personal experience (Kolb, 1984). Staley and MacKenzie (1999) have developed the model further in considering different kinds of experience and their value in the learning process. Real-world experiences such as work-based learning are seen as providing the best opportunities where theories can be tested and concepts applied to real situations. However, as real-life experiences are not normally available to foreign language students in this country, learners need to be provided with 'substitute artificial experiences' that closely mirror tasks they will encounter in real life and develop skills needed in future professional roles. In this model, tutors need to design learning activities which promote 'learning by doing'.

We have made audio and video clips available online in the German language, to provide realistic scenarios and to simulate real-life interactions. Some of the video clips have been recorded on site in Germany, thus providing opportunities for both intercultural reflection and language use. Tasks involve group discussions of cultural differences, based on the content of the clips, and strategies employed by native speakers in terms of expression in the language. Open-ended situations require the students to 'take part' in language learning activities. Tasks can be carried out individually or by groups of students via the website, on campus or at home at a time convenient to them. An example of a successfully completed task can be seen in the 'Student Zone' of the website. For this task, students had to respond to a voicemail from a conference organiser requiring them to register for that conference. This involved scanning a photograph as well as recording a voicemail for registration purposes. The addition of technology has made the task 'come alive' and has produced increased motivation and a better standard of work.

The conceptualisation stage is concerned with how a problem-based curriculum would encourage learners actively to seek appropriate and relevant knowledge to solve a problem. Adding technology at this stage of the cycle also means providing self-assessment opportunities for learners so that they can receive immediate feedback. Software packages such as 'Question Mark', 'CASTLE' or 'Hot Potatoes' provide these opportunities but put the onus on to the tutor to create exercise banks. In languages we have been experimenting with giving students control of this aspect, in other words, students develop the exercises themselves and monitor 'their' exercises after they have been checked by tutors. Examples of this can also be viewed in the 'Student Zone' of the website.

33.3   Developments in intercultural studies

In Cultural Diversity, technology has been used selectively to address particular aspects of the Experiential Learning cycle. The module, which is taken by second-year undergraduates on an International Business Management degree, has two key emphases: theories of culture and encouraging awareness of diversity within cultures. It is supported by a purpose-built website, with links updated each week to ensure that students are not too daunted by the site at the outset. Web pages for each week of class are linked directly from the homepage, as are the five main areas of the site: module information, assessment, study aids, resources, and online conferences. All other pages on the site have direct links to each of these five areas, and back to the home page to ease navigation (see Figure 33.4).

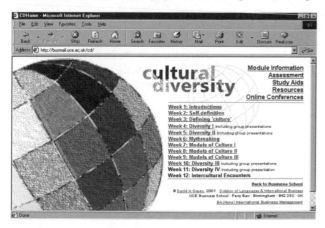

Figure 33.4   Cultural Diversity homepage (http://bsstudents.uce.ac.uk/cd)

Conceptualisation: Students were required to read specific chapters of the set text for the module *before* coming to class so that class time can be used productively to resolve outstanding questions, rather than covering material which the students had understood more readily. Online self-assessment tests (using 'CASTLE' software) were devised for each chapter so that the students could check their level of comprehension before class.

Planning: Having read the chapter and completed the self-assessment tests, students come to class where they are presented with a list of the key aspects of each chapter. Students then vote to decide which to discuss in greater depth with the tutor: usually two aspects are then covered. This gives students greater control over the content of the classes, encourages them to complete their reading on time and carry out the self-assessments, and will hopefully lead to more constructive classes.

Experience: These 19–20-year-old students often lack a breadth of experience to which they could apply some elements of the cultural theories examined in the module, and using examples from real life may demand too much historical and socio-political knowledge from business students at this stage in their learning, so an alternative vehicle has been found. A professional storyteller comes to one class and tells a collection of tales from different cultures, without mentioning the stories' origins. Using the terms of McDrury and Alterio (2000), the storytelling session has a formal setting, multiple listeners and predetermined stories; in other words, the class is carefully structured, delivered to the entire group and uses selected stories, rather than allowing for spontaneous stories from the group or the teller. The stories are agreed by the tutor and storyteller in advance to ensure their suitability for the cultural theories at the heart of the module. As part of the class, the storyteller also engages the students in activities which will aid their ability to recall information and to summarise succinctly.

Reflection: In class, after discussing the aspects of each chapter they voted for, the students then *apply* the cultural theories from that chapter to a specific story they heard. This enables them to see how these concepts may work in practice, and allows plenty of scope for debate. Outside the class, the students can then use online conferencing to discuss the theories and stories further if they wish. Stories are used again at the end of the module, when one of the tales, in an expanded and altered form, becomes the examination paper, to which the students must apply the various models of culture they have learned.

In four of the twelve weeks for this module, the focus shifts from theories of culture to diversity within cultures. In these weeks, students give group presentations on specific aspects of diversity which lead on to assessed online discussion of these issues in greater depth. Some of these discussions are on sensitive issues which it may be difficult to discuss face to face, without time to reflect and consider responses carefully (for example: gender, sexuality, race, religion, class). Online conferencing allows students the distance to think before posting messages, and can be undertaken at any time, not just in normal class hours. Conferencing can also encourage students who are generally quiet in class to express themselves (Rimmershaw, 1999), as the medium is neutral and less likely to be dominated by individuals. As with work in foreign languages, these contributions are assessed using clear criteria set out at the start of the module: critical and reflective approach; collaboration and support; demonstrating initiative and relating theory to practice; enhancing research skills.

33.4   Evaluation

This evaluation is based on questionnaires and focus groups conducted by a PhD student from another university who is researching the use of information and communication technology in learning and teaching in Higher Education. She evaluated the responses from students studying German and Cultural Diversity.

33.4.1   German

For German, all students accessed the Web from both university and home. Students generally had no problems accessing the site, although access from home could be slow. Students thought that the web site was easy and straightforward to use, though one suggested that the address should be easier (the site is on a local intranet with off-campus access). The home page also made navigation easy.

Due to time factors, students did not tend to browse the website. On average they accessed the site once a week and mainly used the specific aspects they required. Students thought that having web-based resources was most useful as a backup to paper-based versions in class; links to other sites were also highlighted as a main advantage. However, while students found the site 'useful', not all of them necessarily 'enjoyed' using it. Nevertheless, all felt that the use of the web did fit in well with the rest of the subject, confirming that the website was well integrated into the learning, teaching and assessment for this module. Students also confirmed a general enthusiasm for the use of the internet in learning and teaching in HE thus making the transferability of learning tasks and activities to other subject areas more realistic.

A significant difference in the usage and perception of WebBoard was found between final year students and first and second year students. Final year students seemed to access the site for shorter periods (0–20 minutes on average), hinting at the fact that they responded to the discussions online, while only one final year student prepared contributions offline. Students in years one and two tended to read the contributions and then prepare their response offline. They found discussing with other students quite difficult, though not purely for linguistic reasons: students often responded just before the deadline, leaving little or no time for others to reply to their messages. A lack of instant feedback was identified as a problem for a number of students, though they did not state whether they meant feedback from other students or from the tutor. Having limited vocabulary and trying to lead an argument on a topic of interest was also felt to make it difficult to discuss the topics in depth, though the asynchronous nature of the discussions was perceived as an advantage when students were later asked what was good about using the web and what they had learned:

> Formulate a structured argument rather than speaking an argument, which is sometimes not thought out.
> How to have in-depth discussions through the use of the Internet.
> How to express myself in terms of 'heated topics', even if a bit directly!

First and second year students were not concerned about posting messages that could be seen by everyone else in the group, though they did not want students from other groups, or native speakers, involved in the discussions: they clearly felt more comfortable with their group alone. Generally students felt that the discussion was quite impersonal, as if they were writing just to the computer, with one student citing the lack of the spontaneity and eye contact found in face-to-face discussions as a key difficulty. They had mixed feelings about whether the contributions should be assessed, but felt that it was a good way to improve their writing skills gradually. They also claimed that they would contribute regardless of assessment.

Final year students did not feel that using web-based resources made the course 'impersonal.' However, the following comment reveals that final year students felt that they would have benefited from more interaction with native speakers:

> I thought the WebBoard would offer the opportunity to discuss heated topics with people from all over the world, but not many people were interested.

Unfortunately only one German native speaker could be motivated to join the discussions. It is certainly the case that students who have already spent some time abroad would benefit linguistically from the contributions of native speakers who would also bring in an added dimension in terms of intercultural understanding. Even so, the students did feel their awareness of German culture had improved through using the Internet in general for the module and that they could locate information on Germany more easily through increased research skills.

33.4.2   Cultural Diversity

For the 25 respondents for Cultural Diversity, 68 per cent used only university facilities to access the site, while 32 per cent also accessed it from home, which, as with the languages site, was sometimes slow. Navigation – both from the homepage and in general around the site – was considered straightforward. The site was also used more intensively than for German, with 80 per cent of students spending more than three hours per week on it. Although we had expected that students would access the site more often during assessed weeks for online discussions, in fact this was only the case for 20 per cent of the students. This appears to support the views of students in German who claimed assessment would not affect their level of contribution online. These findings contradict those of Mason (1991), who found that students' online behaviour was dictated by assessment towards a final grade.

80 per cent of students said they enjoyed using the website and that it fitted in well with the rest of the module, again indicating that it was well embedded in the overall structure and design of the module. Though the students were generally enthusiastic about using ICT in learning, it should be noted that there was a greater spread of responses here than for German (see Figure 33.5). This may in part be related to the greater level of participation and contribution demanded in this module.

Student comments on online contributions are again rather different to those for German. 40 per cent of them felt it was good to discuss issues of diversity online rather than face to face because it helped them to consider their opinions and prepare responses. 24 per cent believed the use of WebBoard encouraged them to think and reflect per se, and also to learn about other students' opinions. One student reported feeling hurt by some comments on WebBoard, while another felt misinterpreted by classmates: some of this may be due to poor written English skills (only a third of the students were native English speakers), while the sensitive nature of the discussions themselves may also be partly responsible. While students are given guidance and tips on the use of non-confrontational language, inevitably this is not always heeded and can result in 'flaming' (Rice and Steinfield, 1992). More encouragingly, though, one student commented: 'I hope I have lost some of my prejudices. I could say it has matured me.'

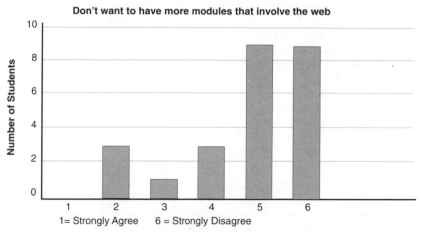

Figure 33.5   Student responses for Cultural Diversity

In general, the students did not find using the website led to an impersonal module, perhaps because the class continued to meet each week, as well as there being work to carry out online (Figure 33.6 below). The vast majority of students felt that the ICT element of the module had no negative impact on getting to know one another or getting to know the module tutor.

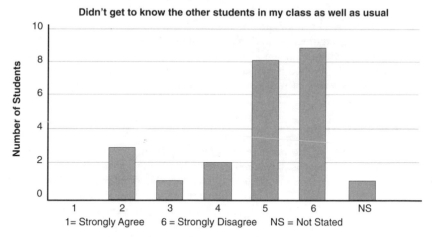

Figure 33.6   Student responses for Cultural Diversity

In fact, it is clear from students' comments that the technology helped increase the rapport across the group and aided collaboration:

> I learned where everyone else comes from and a little more about their backgrounds than what people told in class.
> It's better to learn from experiences other people made than only getting information from the teacher.

This supports Pincas's findings that conferencing can enable students to form 'their own knowledge structures through collaborative work' (1995). Bringing together an international group of students and encouraging them to find out more about one another was one of the main aims of the module, and in some instances, it has clearly succeeded. When asked 'What do you think you have learned that you hoped to learn from this course?' responses included the following:

> Understand more why people do some things we cannot relate to or understand and therefore ignore or dislike them.
> New things about foreign cultures, feelings, reactions, thinking.
> To accept other people's beliefs, and it helps not to feel you're being badly treated.

However, responses were not entirely positive. One student made many more contributions on WebBoard than her peers, and felt there was a lack of interaction as a result. She also suffered from eye strain after spending so long at the computer, and requested greater use of green on the site to ease the eyes. Conversely, other students found there was too much information on WebBoard, and became confused. This can partially be resolved by closing discussions altogether, rather than allowing them to continue until the end of the semester. While this means some interesting and productive discussions may end abruptly, which could demotivate, students should not feel as overwhelmed: this will be a difficult balancing act in future.

Some students also wanted more feedback from the tutor on WebBoard. It was the intentional policy of the tutor not to contribute to the discussions unless there were any problematic postings or arguments: our previous experience with online conferencing has shown us that students will moderate one another's comments, often ignore the tutor's advice to temper their arguments, and end up making the exact contribution the tutor would have made, provided they are given a little longer to think about their responses (Green and Staley, 2000). While this may aid independent learning for some students, it is perceived by others as a lack of responsiveness which we will have to address in future iterations of the module.

33.5   Conclusions

The students' comments on the potential benefits of including the web in learning and teaching seem to justify its use as they correspond to the aims envisaged by the tutors, such as the development of independent learning, intercultural learning and transferable skills. We believe the key to successful outcomes on these modules has been the careful embedding of ICT as an integral element with a clear purpose. By making this explicit at the beginning of the modules, students are aware of the educational arguments in favour of using ICT, and many of them appear to seek to demonstrate that they have taken this on board and are making the most of the experience.

In both languages and intercultural studies, ICT is being used selectively and is tailored to the specific subject to ensure coherence in modules with mixed modes of delivery. Again, this pays dividends by enhancing the scope of the modules and creating new opportunities for students to learn and develop.

There are clearly still difficulties to be overcome, though in the examples provided in this chapter, these are not substantial or insurmountable. The level of online feedback is an issue which may in part be resolved by changing students' expectations in advance, and by encouraging greater autonomy and peer review. Planned changes to assessment criteria for online discussions are intended to remedy the perceived problem of inadequate debate: requiring students to post messages on two non-consecutive days each week (with a clear cut-off date for each discussion) provides greater opportunity for students to find messages to which they feel they can respond, and can expect a reply in turn, thereby raising not only the level of debate, but hopefully also student motivation since their messages are far more likely to be read by others. This will be the subject of future research using discourse analysis to compare contributions from different student cohorts under different assessment schemes.

ICT can be used effectively as part of an experiential learning model, whether it is applied to part of the cycle or to all four stages. Tutors must ensure that rather than employing all available aspects of ICT, they choose each element to fulfil a specific aim in order to maximise the potential to improve student learning.

33.6   References

Gibbs, G. (1988). The Seminar. *The New Academic* Summer 1992: 4–5.

Green, D.A. and Staley, A. (2000). Using Information Technology in Traditionally "Soft" Subjects. *International Conference Proceedings. International Conference on Learning with Technology 2000.* Temple University, Philadelphia, USA.
<http://www.temple.edu/iclt/>

Kolb, D. (1984). *Experiential Learning: Experience as the Source of Learning and Development.* New Jersey: Prentice Hall.

Mason, R. (1991). 'Refining the Use of Computer Conferencing in Distance Education' In *Computers and Learning.* Eds O Boyd-Barrett and E Scanlon. Wokingham: Addison Wesley.

McDrury, J. and Alterio, M. (2000). Achieving Reflective Learning Using Storytelling Pathways. *IETI* 38/1: 63-73.

Pincas, A. (1995). Analysis of Face to Face and Computer Conferencing Interactions in University Teaching. In *Empowering Teachers and Learners Through Technology.* Ed. C O'Hagan. Birmingham, UK: SEDA.

Rice, R. E. and Steinfield, C. (1992). Experiences with New Forms of Organizational Communication via Electronic Mail and Voice Messaging. In *Telematics and Work.* Eds J H Andriessen and R Roe. New Jersey: Lawrence Erlbaum. 109–37.

Rimmershaw, R. (1999). Supporting a Culture of Collaborative Study: Collaborative Study in Undergraduate Courses Using a Computer-Based Conferencing System. *Networked Lifelong Learning: Innovative Approaches to Education and Training Through the Internet.* Sheffield: University of Sheffield, UK. 48-54.

Staley, A. and Eastcott, D. (1999). Computer-Supported Experiential Learning (Phase One: Staff Development). *ALT-J* 7(1): 39–45.

Staley, A and MacKenzie, N. (1999). Using Technology to Link Theory and Practice in the Future Information Society. *International Conference Proceedings. RUFIS '99: The Virtual University.* Northern Arizona University, Flagstaff, USA.

Evaluating EFFECTS – what did we learn, and what have we changed?

Martin Oliver,[a] Jen Harvey,[b], Helen Beetham[c] and Adam Warren[d]

a. Education and Professional Development, University College London; b. Learning & Teaching Centre, Dublin Institute of Technology; c. The Open University and The University of Bristol; d. Centre for Learning and Teaching, University of Southampton

During the last decade there have been an impressive number of centrally funded initiatives in learning technology development in UK HE, along with a great diversity of projects in departments and institutions (Reinhardt, 1995; Schank, 1994; Somekh, 1998). In fact, the Dearing Report noted that the UK was already a world leader in this field (NCIHE, 1997), and HEFCE has estimated that around 70 per cent of all UK HEIs are involved in an externally funded learning technology programme of some kind (cited in Kewell *et al.*, 1999). Nevertheless, the current JISC five-year plan reports continuing failure to embed the outcomes of development projects into mainstream learning and teaching practice. This concern is not confined to the UK: the latest Campus Computing Survey from the United States (Green, 1999) documents a widespread failure 'to make effective use of new technologies in ways that support teaching, learning, instruction and scholarship'.

Like many TLTP projects, EFFECTS set out with the ambitious intention of embedding ICT in mainstream courses across UK higher education. What made EFFECTS distinctive was that it concentrated on co-ordinated bottom-up change rather than on centrally managed resources or services. Individual innovators were supported through the creation of institutional staff development programmes, which aimed to provide the support and skills required to embed ICT appropriately, encourage dissemination and create a forum for critical debate about improving student learning. By providing a set of generic learning outcomes, developed in light of national policies but shaped through wide consultation with practitioners, the project enabled these institutional initiatives to co-ordinate their development and activity, sharing lessons and resources. But what has the impact of this been? How successful was EFFECTS in supporting innovation in and dissemination of the use of learning technologies?

The decision to consider three layers in the EFFECTS evaluation strategy – its impact on participants, on partner institutions and nationally – is reflected in the structure of the symposium which formed the basis for the three papers from which the following three chapters (34, 35 and 36) originate. Each of the three chapters considers one level of the evaluation. In addition, Chapter 34 introduces the EFFECTS project and the evaluation framework that it adopted, and provides reflections on its efficacy as a way of researching student learning.

34 Evaluating the impact of EFFECTS on academic staff

Jen Harvey[a] and Martin Oliver[b]

a. Learning & Teaching Centre, Dublin Institute of Technology;
b. Education and Professional Development, University College London

34.1   Introduction

34.1.1   The problem of impact

Many projects in higher education are expected to demonstrate their impact through evaluation. However, it can be extremely hard to demonstrate a causal link between a project and any signs of change (Patton, 1997). Moreover, education is a complex process, and the introduction of technology only serves to complicate this situation further. Consequently, it can be difficult to know where to look for impact, to recognise it, or to know why it happened.

To illustrate ways in which such impact can be evaluated, this chapter will draw on the experiences of the Effective Framework for Embedding C&IT through Targeted Support (EFFECTS) project. EFFECTS was expected to have an impact at the level of individual academics' practice, at an institutional level, and at a national level. This chapter will focus on the impact on participants, but will also consider the relationship between the participants and their institution.

34.1.2   Impact on staff

While it is possible to consider impact on learning within the context of assessed programmes (several EFFECTS courses fell into this category), areas such as skills and attitudes are much more commonly investigated. In most cases, it is considered adequate simply to ask participants about their attitudes, for example through an interview or survey. However, attitudinal changes tend to be viewed as a relatively weak form of impact.

Instead, the relatively small number of staff registering for courses means that greater attention can be paid to more subtle, but perhaps more important, signs of change. One simple approach that is unlikely to be viable when considering institutional impact is observation. For example, with technology-related developments, there is likely to be a tangible difference in the type of resources used – evidence for this may be available from sources such as the units who maintain and support the software.

An additional important type of impact for academics concerns their role and their conceptions of teaching and learning. While observation might provide some evidence of this, documentary analysis of outputs such as research reports or course descriptions, or discourse analysis of discussions of teaching and learning issues, may well indicate a shift in attitudes towards (say) student-centred learning. More broadly, their perception of themselves in relation to their discipline may alter – the development of a new area of research interest, for example, might be evidenced by a conference or journal submission. Investigation of personal perceptions would be equally relevant for students, but due to the time-intensive nature of the analysis involved would be unlikely to be practical.

In the next section, the EFFECTS project is introduced. This gives a particular context in which some of the issues of impact were addressed, and will provide a necessary context for the study that follows.

34.2   Background

34.2.1   The EFFECTS Project

In 1997, the professional development of academics had become a major issue for debate within the UK. Preliminary work towards the Booth Report (CVCP, 1998), for example, coincided with the planning of EFFECTS, and national discussions about the establishment of the Institute for Learning and Teaching (ILT) followed soon after. At this time, several disparate centres for staff development within UK Higher Education Institutions (HEIs) were considering how best to support staff who were starting to engage with the problem of embedding communication and information technology (C&IT) into learning and teaching. Through discussions at conferences and exploratory messages to mailbase lists, the project manager identified a range of institutions who were willing to undertake a project to address this topic, and who, between them, represented a complementary range of institutional profiles and expertise: Plymouth, Oxford Brookes, North London, Southampton and UMIST (Ducker, 1998). This consortium proposed, consulted upon and then trialled a set of generic learning outcomes which, it was argued, would allow institutions to establish programmes of staff development in the use of C&IT which would eventually be accredited at a national level. The initial set of outcomes is given in Table 34.1 (Phelps *et al.*, 1999).

Generic outcome
1. Analysed and reviewed opportunities and constraints in using C&IT
2. Selected appropriate C&IT with an understanding of the underlying educational processes
3. Designed and planned strategy for integrating appropriate C&IT
4. Managed and implemented a developed strategy
5. Evaluated impact of the interventions
6. Disseminated the findings of the evaluation
7. Reviewed, planned and undertaken appropriate actions related to own Career Development Plan

Table 34.1   Generic outcomes and sample level descriptors of the EFFECTS framework

34.2.2   The format of EFFECTS courses

The diverse group of institutions participating in EFFECTS meant that different staff needs and institutional contexts had to be taken into account by the programmes of professional development that were created. Consequently, a varied array of courses was developed around the shared learning outcomes. However, as the project progressed, there was evidence of convergence in format, with all courses eventually describable as different points along one continuum (Smith and Oliver, 2000). All accredited EFFECTS courses shared an action research component, which was framed as an embedding project and assessed by portfolio. In addition, all provided 'consultancy' support for participants, as will be discussed below. The difference between the courses lay in the degree of formal training that also accompanied the courses. At one extreme, a series of scheduled workshops on pre-defined topics (for example, one on each of the outcomes) was provided to train staff in the basic skills they required. At the other, training was provided on demand, with the content and timing negotiated with participants. However, all courses provided some degree of training.

34.2.3   The internal evaluation of EFFECTS

Evaluation was on the project's agenda from the outset, and one of the first reports produced laid out an ambitious evaluation plan that was integrated with the project's management strategy and which would help steer progress and communicate experiences within the project team (Oliver *et al.*, 1998). This involved a systematic analysis of the project's structure and aims, starting with a discussion of the identity and role of stakeholders in its activities, and recommending the implementation of an hierarchy of evaluation wherein each level drew upon and synthesised the conclusions of disparate studies carried out at the level below, as illustrated in Figure 34.1. In addition, lessons about the process of creating and implementing EFFECTS courses were to be shared by the project team's nominated evaluator, who would monitor the management reports the team members were required to produce for incidents or observations with wider relevance, as illustrated in Figure 34.2. This model would also allow longitudinal institutional case studies and national 'snap shot' studies to be constructed. This design was intended to minimise the additional burden placed on the project team by the evaluation by making maximum use of the data required by the National Co-ordination Team (NCT).

34.2.4   The external evaluation of EFFECTS

In addition to the ongoing, internal formative evaluation outlined above, in the final year, this was complemented by formative and summative data collection as part an external evaluation study. This comprised several types of data, including:

- questionnaires from Partner Institution course developers and participants, EFFECTS contacts and national bodies;
- interviews with project team members;
- a focus group with representatives from partner institutions;
- a review of relevant project literature, including web sites, participants' case studies, project reports and published papers.

These data were analysed using a range of qualitative and quantitative methods, and the results presented to the project as a consolidated report, structured around the original aim and outcomes of the project, and also around a number of supplementary questions that had be raised by the project team (Harvey and Oliver, 2001). The findings that follow have been drawn from this report.

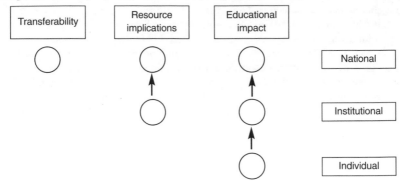

Figure 34.1   The impact evaluation model

	Site 1	Site 2	Site 3	Site 4	
Month 6	x	x	x	x	
Month 5	x	x	x	●	"Model of good practice"
Month 4	x	x	x	x	
Month 3	x	x	x	x	"Snapshot"
Month 2	x	x	x	x	
Month 1	x	x	●	x	
		"Case study"			

Figure 34.2   An illustration of the intended method of evaluation processes within EFFECTS

34.3   Findings: the impact of EFFECTS

The external evaluation of EFFECTS identified a number of areas of impact; however, this chapter will concentrate on the participants in the project, and their relationship with their institution. A selection of examples of impact relating to these topics is presented here. Quotes are taken from the interviews and focus groups with project staff and participants, and the tables summarise responses to surveys.

34.3.1   Clear indicators of impact

One aim of EFFECTS was to embed C&IT into 70 teaching modules across the five institutions. As noted, the relatively modest numbers of staff participating in EFFECTS meant that evidence towards this outcome could be directly observed and recorded by project staff.

By July 2001, at least 57 courses had embedded C&IT, with more likely to be embedded at a later stage. Importantly, observation allowed the project team to identify participants who were only experimenting with technology; this figure represents those staff who were actively using C&IT as part of teaching.

Assessing participants provided other direct indicators of impact. Also by July, 36 case studies and 19 portfolios had been completed, with further examples of each still under development.

34.3.2   Patterns of support provision

For EFFECTS programmes to support academics in embedding C&IT, various institutional issues had to be addressed, including strategies for the provision of pedagogic as well as technical support. One important question was how to maximise the impact of the small number of support staff that were available.

A number of methods were used to provide support, including seminars, workshops, presentations and newsletters. Some were open to everyone, in spite of the fact that they were linked in to EFFECTS programme outcomes. Others, however, were arranged exclusively for participants. Project teams needed to initiate timely but appropriate courses in order to address a range of different needs and requirements.

> There are two things, we have a course and we have a local support network, and I think not everybody in the local support network wants to do the course but everyone who wants to do the course necessarily needs the local support network.

Seminars, workshops and special interest groups also functioned as a way to recruit staff to EFFECTS programmes and, more significantly, created mutual support structures by linking people interested in similar uses of C&IT.

> Separate workshops were run to support common topics (e.g. WebCT), and a users' group for this was set up.

Generally, the way in which the staff supported the programmes was felt to be adequate (the highest rating offered), and for some was their reason for registering for the programme (Table 34.2). In some cases, participants spontaneously added in an extra category of 'very adequate' or 'more than adequate' as an indicator for their feelings.

	UNL		SOTON		UMIST		OLY		OBU	
Adequacy	**A**	**NA**	**A**	**NA**	**A**	**NA**	**A**	**NA**	**A**	**NA**
EFFECTS staff	96	4	88	0	100	0	100	0	100	0
resources	39	61	13	50	44	44	29	57	83	17
time	26	74	0	75	33	56	14	71	83	17
colleagues in own institution	61	39	25	50	67	11	29	57	100	0
external.support	0	100	0	38	22	11	0	57	33	17

Table 34.2   Percentages of staff perceiving support to be adequate or inadequate at each institution

The nature of the tutor support varied between institutions. There was a heavy dependence on some tutors to carry out technical tasks, while others worked solely as facilitators so that groups of participants would learn how undertake such tasks by themselves. In some EFFECTS programmes, participants were recommended to find a mentor within their own subject discipline or were allocated to a group in order to provide additional support.

Closely related to the issue of tutor support was the feeling of most project teams that internal 'consultancy work' on participants' projects took up a larger proportion of their time than the development of materials or running workshops. Such consultations built upon the discussions that took place between participants and tutors, involving face-to-face support as required by participants' project work. However, although this was an important element of the targeted support offered within the project, the details of how this consultancy service operated remain somewhat unclear. The teams did comment, though, that most of their participants only got in touch if they had technical difficulties, problems with practical issues, or clarification about assessment criteria rather than for pedagogical reasons.

> Participants appeared to get in touch with their tutors for 'specific technical advice' – never pedagogic advice.

34.3.3   The changing relationship between participants and support units

Many participants' projects required staff from across the institutions to become involved in the implementation process. In some instances this was the first time such collaborations had occurred. Precedents were set, so that in some institutions C&IT training and academic development were perceived as being inter-related for the first time.

> The issues about implementing Perception across the institution has brought together a group of people from registry, management information services, faculty administrators, lecturers, computing services, network services, application teams, you know it has stretched across every single area, it's hard to find an area that hasn't been impacted really.

This change in the relationship between different support units led to their roles, functions and in some cases interactions with participants being renegotiated, which prompted a series of questions to be asked of participants:

- Would academic staff approach for help/advice/training within and outwith each of the institutions?

- At what point would academic staff feel able to undertake C&IT related activities and when would they expect central and/or EFFECTS staff to become involved?

- Did the EFFECTS programme train staff to be self-sufficient or to know when/how to ask support staff for assistance?

Answers to these questions are summarised in Table 34.3.

In some cases, where participants wanted to find out more about technology, they did not feel like undertaking a full course. For these people it was more appropriate to discuss their needs with one of the centrally provided services than the tutors of an EFFECTS course. However, it is notable that forging a link with academics through delivery of a course created expectations of ongoing support that may not be sustainable.

Sources of C&IT						
UNL	**Self**	**EFFECTS**	**Cent.**	**Dept**	**Ext.**	**Unsure**
WWW pages	11	61	7	14	0	4
Integrating C&IT	18	57	0	7	0	11
CAA	14	39	0	7	0	32
CAL info	18	36	0	11	4	18
Online course	18	54	0	11	0	7
SOTON						
WWW pages	11	61	7	14	0	4
Integrating C&IT	18	57	0	7	0	11
CAA	14	39	0	7	0	32
CAL info	18	36	0	11	4	18
Online course	18	54	0	11	0	7
UMIST						
WWW pages	11	61	7	14	0	4
Integrating C&IT	18	57	0	7	0	11
CAA	14	39	0	7	0	32
CAL info	18	36	0	11	4	18
Online course	18	54	0	11	0	7
PLY						
WWW pages	11	61	7	14	0	4
Integrating C&IT	18	57	0	7	0	11
CAA	14	39	0	7	0	32
CAL info	18	36	0	11	4	18
Online course	18	54	0	11	0	7
OBU						
WWW pages	11	61	7	14	0	4
Integrating C&IT	18	57	0	7	0	11
CAA	14	39	0	7	0	32
CAL info	18	36	0	11	4	18
Online course	18	54	0	11	0	7

Table 34.3   Sources of help likely to be approached (%)

One question that arose was whether or not this dependency arose equally for people who had been involved in a series of workshops as for those that had been supported on accredited programmes. In order to investigate this issue, a comparison was made between two samples of participants at one institution: those who were involved in undertaking an EFFECTS programme through a series of workshops and another group who were undertaking the module as part of a certificate programme. The second group (see Table 34.4) appeared more likely to approach central services and colleagues than EFFECTS staff for help when undertaking C&IT related activities, suggesting a more sustainable approach in terms of EFFECTS staff workloads (especially given that these appointments were mainly fixed-term). This difference was most pronounced when considering the development of web pages and the integration of C&IT into a course. However, a few of the first group were willing to undertake some of the activities themselves, and others remained unsure of who to approach, whereas none of the second group responded in either of those ways.

	Self	EFFECTS	Cent.	Dept	Ext.	Unsure
WWW pages	9	47	18	18	0	9
Int LT	14	57	11	7	0	11
CAA	14	38	3	7	3	34
CAL info	13	33	10	13	3	27
Online course	16	47	9	13	0	16
	Self	EFFECTS	Cent.	Dept	Ext.	Unsure
WWW pages	0	0	60	40	0	
Int LT	0	38	38	25	0	
CAA	0	29	43	29	0	
CAL info	0	33	44	22	4	
Online course	0	43	29	29	0	

Table 34.4   Comparison between percentages of two sample groups of participants indicating who they would approach for help with C&IT related activities

34.3.4   Problems for implementation

In spite of the considerable efforts put into supporting participants, problems remained which limited their success at implementing C&IT.

While many of the issues raised are course-related, a number also have a bearing on issues of implementation, such as technical problems. However, the other common problem that was encountered was, unsurprisingly, a lack of time.

Participants were also asked directly what areas of the course they had found to be difficult. The results of this question are summarised in Table 34.5.

Further investigation of this issue showed that financial resources, institutional support and time release from other activities were considered to be lacking by the majority of respondents. It was emphasised that if institutions were serious about encouraging the use of technology, they would have to provide appropriate resources.

> Time was the only missing resource, the university needs to budget for this if it is to take training seriously.

Any parts of the course where you had difficulties					
UNL	None	7	**PLY**	none	2
	WebCT/tech probs	6		time	3
	time/finish	4		portfolio	1
	course content	3			
	diff skills in groups	2			
	misc	2			
UMIST	none	3	**SOTON**	no	1
	portfolio	2		webCT/tech probs	1
	evaluating approaches	1		more flexible outcomes	1
	Technology related	1		lack of course continuity	1
OBU	none	3			
	technical	2			
	time				

Table 34.5   Difficulties encountered by EFFECTS participants

34.3.5   The problem of evaluation

Even when staff were able to implement C&IT successfully, their evaluation remained limited. In later stages of the project, new strategies and examples were integrated into several of the EFFECTS programmes in order to encourage participants to try different approaches to evaluation and to make more appropriate use of evaluation tools.

When this problem was investigated, it was found that participants used (or even considered using) a very limited range of approaches to evaluate the effectiveness of their use of C&IT. Of those who felt that they had reached the stage of undertaking an evaluation, 31 per cent relied on informal feedback from students and 26 per cent depended on the existing module feedback forms.

34.3.6   Assessment of participants

The assessment of participants was central to the project, and thus was subjected to considerable scrutiny. As already noted, certain aspects of the assessment were seen as irrelevant by some of the participants, most notably implementation (which was the lynchpin of the assessment process) and evaluation. As such, there was little opportunity (and still less incentive) for these people to complete their assessment.

> Yes ... evaluation, reflection and writing up case studies appeared to be universally difficult.

Moreover, the format of portfolios was unfamiliar to many participants. Even the project team agreed that this represented a fairly arduous form of assessment.

> On the one hand I'm saying this [a portfolio] is what you should be doing; on the other I'm not doing it myself because I actually find it difficult to do.

Another troublesome outcome, as indicated by the above quote, was the production of case studies. This had been committed to as part of the original EFFECTS objectives, and was intended as a way of disseminating good practice. However, some participants felt that their time could be spent more productively undertaking activities more clearly linked to rewards or personal priorities:

> A portfolio is nice to have rather than an essential thing. I think publishing in a refereed journal would be more valuable to the average member of academic staff than the portfolio or the qualification really.

This raises an important challenge, which is beyond the scope of the project to tackle: while accrediting courses may be laudable, it may be of little benefit if the individuals or institutions do not value the certificate that is awarded.

Although portfolios were difficult to engage with, participants who completed one did acknowledge its benefits as a means of encouraging review and reflection, and as a way of demonstrating what they had achieved. Project team members found it particularly helpful having completed a portfolio prior to tutoring on an EFFECTS programme and supporting participants through the same process. Moreover, the consensus of the project team was that portfolio-based assessment remains necessary in order to validly assess participants' use of C&IT – which lies at the heart of the project's aims. Unless new developments are properly integrated into participants' teaching, the EFFECTS programmes will only be able to provide technical skills training, rather than the more scholarly and reflective processes valued by the project. Making the assessment easier to complete would have increased project 'outputs', but at the expense of project values.

In addition to these issues, there were cases when the structure of the assessment conflicted with the structure of the courses. Some participants expressed concern about the perceived continuity of programmes that relied on a series of self-contained workshops, particularly on programmes that did not require an action research project plan. Ironically, however, those participants who enrolled on the course precisely because they already had a clear project in mind found that the assessment requirements sometimes conflicted with their development plans.

> I found the structure frustrating... the 7 outcomes were a nightmare...
> The courses ... seemed to be largely constrained by the need to fulfil the requirements of the EFFECTS course.

For such participants, it was the support that was offered – not the accreditation – that was of primary importance. As such, completion of the assessment was an unwanted burden that interfered with their work.

34.3.7   Issues of participant diversity

EFFECTS was developed to support academics who wish to embed C&IT into their teaching; its open approach was reflected in the fact that no minimum levels of technical competence were set as a pre-requisite for participation. Consequently, participants registering for the course ranged for those with no technical skills nor clear idea of what they wanted to achieve, to those with high levels of expertise and a specific project in mind.

> They were people who didn't feel they knew much at all and they got up to quite a reasonable level in one big injection, whereas I knew a reasonable amount already but I had very definite goals because I knew this course was looming over the horizon.

Such diversity can cause difficulties when providing appropriate levels of support, especially within workshops or programmes with structured outcomes. Some participants registered on short programmes commented on the different skills levels of other participants. They also worried about the possibility of a new skills gap developing between themselves and other members of their department.

> What concerns me is really not where I'm going to find the time to do the things I'm committed to but it's the fact that most of my colleagues are already committed to developing distance learning courses and that they 1) haven't been on the EFFECTS course and 2) they're way, way, way behind me.

Another problem that arose was that some participants felt that particular sections 'dragged a bit' as a result of people with low IT skills being there. Different strategies were suggested in order to address these issues, some of which might even be interpreted as being contradictory, such as mixing ability groups or using 'sets' of similar ability.

> Having some slightly more experienced people pulled the whole thing along a bit, and that felt that there was a bit of learning from each other, but it also created more of a dynamic, you know, it rolled along pretty well. If everybody had come in at the level that I was at then it could have been done a bit faster.

> Put staff members into different groups according to their learning needs.

Clearly, there is no easy way of resolving this problem.

34.3.8 Changes in roles

As a result of their involvement with EFFECTS, some participants reported that their role within their departments had changed. Others had changed jobs.

> I've become increasingly involved with colleagues regarding the development of online materials for their areas.

> Became a member of university PCLI steering group, have now been able to raise funding for a new project.

Although the majority of respondents did not report a change in their jobs ('only less time to carry out the work'), some talked about other people's change in perception of their roles now that they had completed the course.

> I'm now considered the dept. expert in LT.

> Yes I've fallen behind in my research (so my status has been lowered if anything.

> I have become increasingly involved in discussions with other colleagues regarding the development of online materials for their areas.

34.3.9 Sustainability of the project's impact

Due to the complexity of EFFECTS, different aspects of its sustainability must be considered separately. For the individuals concerned, the skills and values that were developed will clearly have a longer-term impact, and can be sustained through their involvement in a community of like-minded practitioners. The technical skills training that formed a part of EFFECTS courses may well become obsolete with time; however, the more scholarly, process-oriented skills and practices are likely to have considerably longer currency.

For the courses and the institutions, the situation is more complex. One of the aims of the project was to embed C&IT into 70 teaching modules across the five institutions. As noted earlier, 57 courses had embedded C&IT as a result of EFFECTS. Initially, it might be assumed that such outcomes will be easy to sustain, now that they are embedded in institutional structures. However, the ongoing process of course replacement and revalidation means that such developments should be viewed as a recurrent activity, not just as a one-off event. Thus if these are to be truly sustainable, staff will need to incorporate appropriate maintenance and updating into their regular round of curriculum development activities. Whether such a long-term cultural shift will take place is beyond the scope of the project to investigate.

An important motivation for EFFECTS was the idea that pump-priming projects might be an efficient way to promote piloting activities, but may not be sustainable in the longer term. In part, this reflected the concerns of the project team who were often approached about development work by academics who had received funding but did not have staff in place to carry out the work within their own department. Such situations meant that demand on central services became erratic, making it difficult to appoint staff with the skills required to meet such demands.

As noted above, however, participation in an EFFECTS course does not necessarily lead to the steady and appropriate use of central resources. In some cases, the staff involved in supporting participants were happy to carry out certain pieces of work for them, meaning that there was no requirement to learn the relevant IT skills – only what to ask for. Whilst this resulted in short-term savings in academic staff time, in the long term it may lead to an unsustainable culture of dependency, with requests for routine tasks coming from a steadily growing group of ex-participants. It is important to recognise that even when project staff worked alongside participants on the development work, their speed and efficiency meant that the participants were not able to understand (let alone acquire) the technical skills that were being used.

Short courses or consultancy services alone do not necessarily develop staff to a level where they are able to work independently or feel confident enough to provide support for others wishing to use C&IT. Completion of a full portfolio, however, was intended to be a demonstration that the participant has developed a full complement of the skills involved in embedding C&IT. This suggests that the initial conception of EFFECTS may indeed allow staff to develop as independent users of C&IT, but that the reality of EFFECTS, which involves many participants who engage with it simply to raise their awareness, is unlikely to avoid the issues of sustainability outlined above.

34.4   Conclusions

The complexity of EFFECTS provides a useful example with which to illustrate the difficulties of demonstrating that a project has had an impact. Some of its aims and objectives were only fully understood as the project developed, and others remain contested. In such a situation, deciding what to evaluate – let alone how the necessary data should be gathered – is inherently problematic.

However, the structured model of internal evaluation provided systematic evidence of progress and enabled a number of important questions to be identified, even though some aspects of it, such as the full participation of all partners in the evaluation process, remained difficult to achieve (Oliver *et al.*, 1999). The triangulation of complementary evaluation methods in the external evaluation then allowed these questions to be investigated, resulting in the findings presented above. These approaches, and the types of impact that they measure, may provide a useful starting point for the design of evaluation strategies for other projects involving collaborative research into cultural change.

In this specific case, several indicators of the project's impact on academic staff were identified. Perhaps most importantly for the participants involved, their roles altered (or were perceived by others to have altered) as a result of their involvement. In some cases, this allowed greater input into decision-making; in others, the experience was less positive, with staff in their department depending on them for support and guidance on the use of C&IT.

For the participants, their own ability to call for support was changed too, with an increased tendency to turn to the staff and tutors with whom they had built up a working relationship. As a result, whilst some participants developed into autonomous practitioners, others became dependent on central support for what might be considered to be routine activities. This has implications for the sustainability of the impact of the project. However, more positively, the various central services that could provide support have been encouraged to work together in order to meet the needs of participants – a change which will have long-term benefits for all users of these services.

It was also clear that the development of academics' abilities was not even across all of the learning outcomes. As a result of the time-consuming nature of some of the work, the differences in motivation for engaging with the programme, and participants' lack of familiarity with portfolio-based assessment, outcomes such as implementation and evaluation were sometimes neglected. However, changes in emphasis within the programmes have gone some way to addressing this issue. What remains harder to resolve is the best way of coping with the wide range of abilities within the cohorts taking part in the courses.

Thus the impact of EFFECTS has proved to be demonstrable, but mixed. This approach to evaluation has shown that roles and culture have changed, but the changes have not been straightforward. Participation has proved effective and beneficial, especially for those who engaged fully with the programmes and with the assessment. However, it has also been demanding, and has raised colleagues' expectations. Perhaps most importantly, the partial participation of those seeking to raise their awareness or develop specific skills has, in some cases, increased the level of dependency on central services. This suggests that EFFECTS represents a valuable approach to supporting academics, but that it may highlight (rather than diminish) other problems within an institution, such as central support. While EFFECTS can clearly make an important contribution to creating a culture of appropriate and even scholarly use of C&IT, it cannot overcome ingrained problems such as under-resourcing or the relatively low value attached to such curriculum development activities.

34.5   References

CVCP (1998) *Accreditation and Teaching in Higher Education*. Final Report (the Booth Report).

Ducker, P. (1998) Origins and development of the bid. Unpublished project report: NCT project visit.

Harvey, J. and Oliver, M. (2001) *EFFECTS External Evaluation*. EFFECTS Project report, Dublin Institute of Technology.

Oliver, M., Conole, G., Phelps, J., Maier, P., Wilkinson, D. and Bailey, P. (1998) *The EFFECTS Evaluation Framework: A Transferable Model for Collaborative Projects*. EFFECTS Report no. 1, University of North London.

Oliver, M., Phelps, J., Beetham, H., Bailey, P. and Conole, G. (1999) *Evaluating EFFECTS: Identifying Issues and Assessing the Evaluation Framework*. EFFECTS Report no. 3, University of North London.

Patton, M. (1997) *Utilization-Focused Evaluation*. London: Sage.

Phelps, J., Oliver, M., Bailey, P. and Jenkins, A. (1999) *The Development of a Generic Framework for Accrediting Professional Development in C&IT*. EFFECTS Report no. 1, University of North London.

Smith, J. and Oliver, M. (2000) Academic development: a framework for embedding learning technology, *International Journal of Academic Development* 5(2): 129–37.

35 ALTO and the EFFECTS evaluation strategy

Adam Warren

Centre for Learning and Teaching, University of Southampton, UK

35.1   Introduction

Most UK HE institutions are currently introducing or expanding their use of virtual learning environments such as Blackboard or WebCT, and are typically seeing an exponential growth in that use (Watson, Boardman and Pavey, 2000). This chapter describes ALTO (Active Learning and Teaching Online), a model of staff development that aims to provide the advice, training and support needed to help academics implement effective online learning. It explores the factors that promote innovation within a 'culture of resistance' (Atkins 1998) and shows how the EFFECTS project evaluation strategy was used to meet the needs of a range of stakeholders. Finally, it draws on the experience gained and suggests further developments to the model.

EFFECTS was a TLTP Phase 3 project that developed a framework for staff development programmes intended to ensure the effective integration of learning technologies into HE curricula (Bailey *et al.*, 2001). Members of the project consortium adopted differing programme models according to the needs of their institution. However all these models were based on the framework and this allowed useful comparisons to be drawn between the diverse programmes.

ALTO was the EFFECTS programme developed and implemented at the University of Southampton, and was intended to help a small group of academics develop and manage networked learning materials and activities using the WebCT virtual learning environment. It was piloted by the CLT in Spring and Summer 2000 and used a mix of self-study online resources, discussion groups, short workshops and individual support. Notable features included flexible delivery, content and workload to fit the participants' needs and the use of a small amount of funding to assist the development of individual projects. It aimed to provide practical training in the use of WebCT as well as assisting the development of online resources and activities based on sound pedagogy and good practice.

To place ALTO in context, the University of Southampton is part of the 'Russell Group' of UK universities which consider themselves to be 'research-led' and pride themselves that their research-active academic staff are well placed to deliver high-quality teaching. However, the reality of the situation is that each academic's career is determined by their research record and that innovation in teaching is not rewarded. The common view is that time spent on novel curriculum developments would be better spent on research. Atkins (1998) identified this 'culture of resistance' in relation to the need to change attitudes to the use of C&IT.

The reasons for this resistance are explored in detail by Littlejohn and Sclater (1999) and Warburton (1999) but include lack of institutional support, a focus on research activity, lack of time for curriculum development, lack of suitable skills and knowledge, fears about increased workloads, lack of recognition for innovation and cynicism about the educational effectiveness of learning technologies. The solutions they suggest involve an strategic approach by the institution supported by a change management process based on staff development, and it is only fair to say that Southampton is now starting to develop this approach.

35.2   ALTO: a flexible and authentic programme

During the initial planning of ALTO in early 2000, a review was conducted of the literature available about professional development aimed at helping academic staff make use of learning technologies, especially in higher education in the UK. Although many of the sources found focused on promoting the use of distance-learning or computer-moderated communication, they often contained useful and relevant ideas.

A common theme throughout many of the sources was the need for a flexible programme that enables individual participants to customise their own learning experience. For example, Milligan (1999) suggests that professional development should be 'tailored, personalised and relevant', a point echoed by Tickner (2000) in her description of the principles underpinning the Glasgow University Initiative in Distance Education (GUIDE):

> As an institution-wide service set up to support distance education and promote its development, a core part of GUIDE's work is in assisting staff who are new to the concepts, processes and methods involved in setting up an running their distance education programmes. We consequently strive to identify the specific knowledge and skills these staff will need when they embark on the design and development of such a course for the first time. This includes the skills required for networked learning. This information then directs our staff development programmes.

Bowskill (2000) points out that any programme will have to cater for a complex range of skills that reflects the diversity of needs of the participants, while Tickner (2000) and Wills (1998) both identify a combination of fixed workshops and self-study resources as an inadequate alternative to one-to-one support. Bowskill also states that one-to-one support will need to be provided by people with both technical and pedagogical skills.

Another aspect of flexibility is the timing of the programme and its activities, so that participants are able to undertake development when they have time (Milligan 1999). Similarly, Wills (1998) suggests that participants are offered relevant sessions at convenient times and are invited to join groups in targeted one-off online activities.

Participants who choose to take part in non-accredited voluntary programmes such as ALTO are likely to start with strong intrinsic motivation. Thompson (1997) lists 'run with staff who are keen and motivated' as one way that institutions can 'achieve more with less' when introducing learning technologies. She goes on to suggest that motivation could be strengthened by using modularised courses in the context of a staff-driven programme that has specific relevance to its participants. Wills (1998) also emphasises the power of programmes that are centred on the participants' own practice and that lead to specific outcomes for them, while Tickner (2000) makes the point that learning through 'real-world' tasks fosters engagement.

It was these sources that informed the two key ideas which underpinned the ALTO programme:

Authenticity

All participants were required to plan and implement the use of online resources and activities in one of their courses. This enhanced their motivation to participate by ensuring the relevance of their work, a factor noted by Surry and Land (2000), and Littlejohn and Sclater (1999). It also ensured that the effort and cost of the programme would produce real, measurable outcomes for the university.

Flexibility

As far as possible, the programme used a combination of online resources, short workshops and face-to-face support that were closely aligned to the participants' actual needs and availability. Finding mutually convenient times for workshops was often a problem which had no easy solutions. One of ALTO's aims was to investigate the relative merits and costs of these methods in order to develop future programmes that could support more participants at an acceptable cost. This was clearly an important outcome given the increasing use of virtual learning environments within the university.

A significant challenge faced by ALTO was the recruitment of academic participants who were willing to invest their own time in these projects in spite of the barriers arising from a 'culture of resistance'. An important part of the ALTO evaluation was an exploration of the factors that motivated their participation in order to improve the appeal of future programmes. In particular, I was keen to recruit ordinary academics who were not already known innovators.

One of the ways in which recruitment was encouraged was the availability of small grants, which participants could use to 'buy out' some of their time or pay for a research assistant. It was hoped that these grants would also provide a degree of recognition and reward for the academic's innovation and work. These grants were tied to the production of case study documents by each participant that could be used to disseminate their experiences to the rest of the institution.

Most accredited EFFECTS programmes were based around assessed portfolios, the production of which was often problematic. Given ALTO's non-accredited status it was decided that only a short case study document around four pages in length was required, on the basis that a simple evaluation was better than none at all. An additional benefit was that these brief case studies were much more likely to be read by other academics than lengthy and complex portfolios.

35.3 Findings from the project's evaluation

Despite university-wide advertising, only 14 individuals drawn from a wide range of disciplines attended the introductory sessions and of those only nine played an active part in the programme. Feedback suggested that ALTO would be more effective if it was based in a faculty so that the participants had more in common.

Each participant had to submit a project proposal for approval before they could join the programme, providing an opportunity to review their plans and suggest appropriate changes. The production of these proposals also ensured that the participants thought carefully about what they hoped to achieve at an early stage, a process that the evaluation revealed as helping them to clarify and develop their ideas.

Although the participants stated that the grants were not a major motivational factor, it was noted that those who used the funds to pay for two weeks help from a research assistant made significantly better progress with their projects than those who used them in a less focused way. This led to a decision that funding would only be used to pay for research assistants in later instances of ALTO.

The ready availability of support proved to be both the primary motivational factor for taking part in ALTO and the most valued aspect of the programme. In most cases the level of individual on-demand support required was only two or three hours in total per project; the crucial aspect was that the support was available quickly when needed. Participants could use phone or email and to get a rapid response, and brief face-to-face sessions were often possible the same day if required. This timeliness meant that their projects could make good progress whenever the participants had the time available to work on them.

Experience showed that the case studies did not arrive until a year or more after the end of the programme. In most cases this was because the case study could not be written until a cohort of students had experienced the innovation and submitted their end-of-year course evaluation questionnaires. Even then, production of the case studies was seen as a low-priority task by the participants despite its linkage to the funding and proved to need a good deal of personal encouragement. The latest instance of ALTO has some funding for a research assistant based in the CLT who will assist the participants produce a timely case study of the quality required.

Evaluation skills (or more properly the lack of them) has proved to be one of the most difficult issues for the various EFFECTS programmes. Academic staff also have little motivation to develop these skills while there is no recognition or reward for outputs such as papers in educational journals. ALTO now includes a workshop to develop the participants' awareness of evaluation techniques.

35.4   ALTO and the EFFECTS evaluation framework

The EFFECTS evaluation design (Oliver and Conole, 1999) is intended to be 'participative and flexible' (Parry-Crooke and Croft-White, 1998) by using an action research model that encourages participants to improve their practice relating to the use of learning technologies. In ALTO, this was implemented by requiring each participant to produce a case study based on a simplified version of the EFFECTS learning outcomes that encouraged a planned approach to evaluation. This simplification was needed because feedback from earlier EFFECTS programmes at Southampton and elsewhere (Harvey and Oliver, 2001) showed that participants were unwilling or unable to create substantial portfolios for assessment. Flexibility was ensured since each participant was free to choose the evaluation methods that best suited their project, guided by advice from colleagues and staff at the CLT.

The EFFECTS evaluation strategy is based around the idea that the evaluation should be geared towards 'intended use by intended users' (Patton, 1997) and that these users should be specific individuals rather than generic audiences. Three groups of stakeholders were identified at Southampton – the participants, the Centre for Learning and Teaching and the University – and the evaluation activities were designed to met their needs.

The *participants* needed to be guided through a simple evaluation process which did not impose a heavy workload. Most previous innovations in the use of learning technology at Southampton had not been properly evaluated for reasons identified by Oliver (2000) as the low priority attached to evaluation combined with a lack of expertise and prior experience in educational research. ALTO attempted to address the 'low priority' issue by tying the provision of funds to the production of case studies, although this was not as successful as hoped.

The *Centre for Learning and Teaching* needed evaluation which could be used to improve the delivery, efficiency and efficacy of the programme, as well as measuring its costs. A range of tools were used to evaluate ALTO, ranging from interviews and questionnaires to the analysis of web access logs and email records. One of the reasons for this approach was to gain experience in their use and see which ones yielded the most valuable data. In addition, multiple data sources would support the use of triangulation to increase the reliability of any findings. Later instances of ALTO would have less time and effort available for evaluation and so it was also important to identify the most effective tools.

Another key issue in the choice of evaluation tools was the effort and time they required from the participants. Given the voluntary nature of the programme it was essential that the impact of the evaluation activities on the participants was minimised.

Paper-based questionnaires proved to be a useful means of gathering basic information quickly and were used for an initial survey of skills and interests as well as a final survey of their experiences and views. Online questionnaires were tried but it was found that the overall time taken to process and analyse them was greater than that needed to enter the data manually from paper forms for the small number of participants involved.

Semi-structured interviews were used halfway through the programme to investigate the participants' experiences with ALTO. These were difficult to schedule and time-consuming to write up. The data gathered was very useful but could have been more easily gathered by asking the participants to reply to the same set of questions by email. Interesting responses could have been followed up by further emails or phone calls. Another less costly alternative would have been a single group discussion involving all the participants.

The analysis of the web logs and email messages was less useful and revealed little apart from a predictable pattern of use and an estimate of the average time needed to support each participant. It was clear that the participants did not use the online discussion list to explore issues or share experience in spite of my efforts to facilitate such use. When questioned, the participants cited lack of time as the overriding reason.

The *university* needed evaluation which could guide its policies on the development of networked learning and disseminate good practice within the institution. The key questions were therefore 'did ALTO support innovation and dissemination?' and 'what has been the impact at an institutional level?'

Looking at the first of these, 'did ALTO support innovation and dissemination?', the answer is a qualified 'yes'. All nine participants produced networked learning resources and activities, although two of them were not embedded in their taught units due to the time pressures from other commitments. The evaluation found that the ALTO programme provided the support required by the participants while the projects acted as a focus for their learning and innovation. The case studies are available as part of a 'case studies database' maintained by the CLT and available online within the University. However, this is a passive form of dissemination and more active uses of these case studies in professional development sessions and policy-making activities are currently the focus of further research by the CLT.

The second question, 'what has been the impact at an institutional level?' is much harder to answer, since Southampton is still in the process of developing its Learning Resources and Learning and Teaching Strategies, particularly those aspects that relate to eLearning. In terms of the proportion of staff who have participated in ALTO, the institutional effect is obviously negligible, but the experience gained through ALTO about the type and level of support required to support innovation is much more valuable and forms one of the inputs to the committees developing the strategies.

35.5 Conclusions

In addition to its practical role in supporting educational innovations by a small group of academics, ALTO explored the level and type of support required as well as the motivational factors that persuaded the academics to participate.

Although the total individual support needed by each individual was an average of two or three hours, that typically comprised around ten support requests. Some could be dealt with by email or phone while others required face-to-face assistance. The critical factor was not the total support provided, but the timeliness that meant it was rapidly available when needed. This would indicate that a 'help desk' approach might be an appropriate solution for institutions wishing to promote the use of educational technologies.

The availability of this type of support was the major factor that persuaded the academics to participate. The small amount of funding available assisted the implementation of the projects, especially when its use to employ a research assistant provided a concrete deadline and focus for the work. The major problem expressed by the participants was the lack of time which they felt able to commit to their projects, and was the sole reason that two of the projects failed to become embedded by the end of the programme. Time release for academics wishing to develop their use of learning technologies is clearly a key issue that must be addressed at an institutional level if the 'culture of resistance' is to be overcome.

The EFFECTS evaluation framework was an effective mechanism for meeting the needs of the ALTO programme's stakeholders, while its outputs continue to guide future improvements to its implementation. For example, it is clear that the participants need training and assistance to help them overcome the lack of time and skills needed to evaluate their own projects effectively. Evaluating the institutional impact of ALTO is problematic since strategy and policy are influenced by a wide range of inputs. However, it should be noted that the university has continued to fund further instances of ALTO that develop further and extend that model of staff development.

One criticism of the ALTO pilot is that it perpetuates a culture in which eLearning is only adopted by isolated enthusiasts. Further funding was obtained by ALTO in 2001 from the university's 'Learning and Teaching Development Grant' scheme to assist a group of academics from the Faculty of Social Science to make use of computer-assisted assessment (CAA) in their units. This collegial and more focused approach was suggested by the evaluation of the ALTO pilot, with the intention of developing a core of expertise within a faculty in order to catalyse further innovation. It is still too early to tell if this will work as planned, although initial findings suggest that the diversity within a faculty is still too great and that a departmental basis might be needed to promote effective peer support.

35.6   References

Atkins (1998) *An Evaluation of the Computers in Teaching Initiative and Teaching and Learning Technology Support Network.* HEFCE.

Bailey *et al.* (2001). TLTP3/89 EFFECTS Project Final Report (available online at http://www.sh.plymouth.ac.uk/eds/effects/).

Bowskill, N., Foster, J. *et al.* (2000) Networked Professional Development: Issues for Recipients and Providers. Networked Learning 2000, Lancaster (available online at http://collaborate.shef.ac.uk/nlpapers/bowskill-p.htm).

Drysdale, J. and Creanor, L. (1998) Leading new teachers to learning technology, *LTDI: Evaluation Studies* 13–18 (available online at http://www.icbl.hw.ac.uk/ltdi/evalstudies/esleading.pdf).

Harvey, J. and Oliver, M. (2001) *EFFECTS external evaluation.* Project report for the TLTP3 EFFECTS project.

Littlejohn, A. and Sclater, N. (1999) *Developing the Millenium Teacher, FOCUS. 2000* (available online at http://www.focus.ac.uk/).

Littlejohn, A. and Sclater, N. (1999) *Overcoming Conceptual Barriers to the Use of Internet Technology in University Education*, Centre for Academic Practice, University of Strathclyde, 2000 (available online at http://www.strath.ac.uk/Departments/CAP/allison/papers/webnet/skills.html).

Milligan, C. (1999) *Delivering Staff and Professional Development Using Virtual Learning Environments*, Heriot-Watt University (available online at http://www.jtap.ac.uk/reports/htm/jtap-044.html).

Oliver, M. (2000) An introduction to the evaluation of learning technology, *Educational Technology and Society* 3(4): 20–30.

Oliver, M., Conole, G. et al. (1999) *The EFFECTS Evaluation Framework*. London, University of North London (available online at http://sh.plym.ac.uk/eds/effects/downloads/evalarticle.PDF).

Parry-Crooke, G. and Croft-White, C. (1998) User participation: does it make a difference? In *UK Evaluation Society Conference*. London.

Patton, M. (1997) *Utilization-Focused Evaluation*. London: Sage.

Surry, D.W. and Land, S.M. (2000) Strategies for motivating higher education faculty to use technology, *Innovations in Education and Training International* 37(2): 145–53.

Thompson, L. (1997) Professional Development for Online Learning. NET*Working 97: *Shaping the Online Learning Environment*, Adelaide (available online at http://www.nw97.edu.au/public/papers/thompson.html).

Tickner, S. (2000) Staff Development for Networked Distance Education. Networked Learning 2000, Lancaster (available online at http://collaborate.shef.ac.uk/nlpapers/tickner-p.html).

Warburton, S. (1999) Factors affecting changes in the use of educational technology within HE establishments: Working document, TELRI project, 1999 (available online at http://www.warwick.ac.uk/ETS/TELRI/change1.pdf).

Watson, B., Boardman, K. and Pavey, H. (2000) duo: Durham University Online Presentation at 'Successful Implementation of a Learning Environment', University of Durham, December 2000.

Wills, S. (1998) Teaching Academics About Flexible Delivery. Invited panel speech for RIBIE98, Brasilia (available online at http://cedir.uow.edu.au/CEDIR/flexible/resources/wills3.html).

36 Developing learning technology networks through shared representations of practice

Helen Beetham

The Open University and the University of Bristol, UK

36.1 Introduction

Why have often excellent learning technology initiatives failed to have the desired impact? One problem may be with the notion of 'dissemination', which implies that changing learning and teaching practice is a matter of information flow: once staff are fully apprised of the latest innovations they will naturally embrace them. That this does not happen indicates the way the learning technology revolution challenges fundamental paradigms, cultures and divisions of labour (Goodyear, 1997; Kewell *et al.*, 1999; Schank, 1994; Somekh, 1998).

Two projects funded under the TLTP3 programme have taken a fundamentally different approach. The EFFECTS project (http://maris.ilrt.bristol.ac.uk/effects) was premised on the belief that learning and teaching staff need to be empowered in relation to new challenges, not simply with new technical tools but with new concepts of learning, new skills in curriculum development and new modes of collaborating with colleagues. Inevitably, this process also involves articulating personal values and identities in relation to the new learning environment. Development, not dissemination, was the overarching rationale. EFFECTS therefore offered a framework for the educational development of academic and related staff, via structured programmes of action research or supported curriculum development. The focus was on developing high level skills such as information management, needs analysis, project planning, collaborative development, evaluation and educational design (Beetham and Bailey, 2001), while assuming a high degree of proficiency in discipline pedagogy.

A series of project evaluations (Beetham *et al.*, 1999; 2000; Harvey and Oliver, 2001) has shown that the EFFECTS learning outcomes, sample evidence and interactive documents represent a useful framework for understanding and supporting learning technology work, even without the benefits of a structured programme. At most of the participating institutions, for example, a 'lite' version of EFFECTS was offered – as part of a general learning and teaching certificate course for new lecturers, as a one-off workshop, or to support staff with small-scale learning technology development projects – with some success. The Evaluation Report notes that partner institutions were eager to adopt the framework because

> In addition to providing a structure for staff development and assessment, it enabled support to be allocated to each step in the embedding process in a far more systematic way than was previously possible. Moreover, such a structure can be viewed as a 'road

map', helping practitioners to embed C&IT more effectively and appropriately, with sensitivity to issues such as student learning... (Harvey and Oliver, 2001)

The same report found that the experience of developing and refining the framework had been extremely valuable for the personal and professional development of the project team. This suggests that the EFFECTS framework functioned as a 'shareable representation of practice' (Goodyear and Steeples, 1997), and that as such it offered a powerful means of developing practice both among peer collaborators and in more formal mentor–mentee situations.

Secondly, the SoURCE project (http://www.source.ac.uk) set out to develop a national library of educational software, along with the case studies, guidance notes and other contextual materials that would help practitioners to adopt and adapt the software into their own learning and teaching practice. Once again, the assumption was that software alone would be insufficient to engender change. The project was interested to discover what kinds of representation of practice, and what kinds of interaction with others, would allow new software tools to be effectively adopted into the curriculum.

A separately funded study (Beetham *et al.*, 2001) found that people already proficient in the skills of embedding learning technologies had not acquired those skills through formal development. The typical learning technology specialist or enthusiast is highly information literate and has a range of strategies for locating online and offline resources. Perhaps thanks to the plethora of centrally funded initiatives in this area, or perhaps due to the collaborative approach required by complex technologies, learning technology staff are also used to working in multi-role development teams. Their favoured approach to acquiring new skills is 'peer supported experimentation'. This suggests that individuals involved with learning technologies have the potential to behave as communities of practice – to develop and share understandings of their practice across institutional, project, discipline and professional role boundaries – in ways which are open to few other groups of people.

This chapter reports on a recent research project into representations of practice, their potential uses in the learning technology community, and other factors influencing the degree to which such representations can be used to support changes in practice. The research was carried out by the author on behalf of the SoURCE and RESULTs projects in the period April–July 2001. The aim was to decide on the feasibility of a national resource of case studies, staff development materials and other documents relating to learning technology practice.

36.2 Theoretical background

Lave and Wenger are the authors most closely identified with the idea of community of practice, which they describe as 'a set of relationships among persons, activity and world, over time, and in relation with other tangential and overlapping CoPs'. This term has become so widely used, however, that it has little analytical power as it stands. A useful distinction is made by Seely Brown and Duguid (2000): between communities of practice and networks of practice, where CoPs are 'people working together on the same or similar tasks'; 'usually face to face communities that continually negotiate with, communicate with, and coordinate with each other directly in the course of work'. In contrast, networks of practice are more loosely coupled groupings of people who 'have practice and knowledge in common' but nay never communicate with one another directly or work on common projects. Hildreth *et al* (2000) distinguish between networks of individuals who are 'motivated to a particular pattern of work' as against teams of people who are 'directed' to a particular task of work. Networks are valuable for their reach, which is greatly extended by information technology, while communities are valuable for their reciprocity. Networks are efficient at sharing information about practice while communities are effective at producing new forms of knowledge and practice through collective action. Learning technology specialists would seem to constitute a network, though through collaborative projects such as EFFECTS or SoURCE they can clearly take on characteristics of a community. In fact, one way of strengthening a network may well be to set about consciously producing new forms of practice knowledge through shared authoring of and commentary on communally-owned documents. *Participation* in Lave and Wenger's work is a term limited to collective activities in which all members have a shared goal and a shared understanding of its significance.

The CoP model of individual learning as enculturation fails to the address the question of how communities develop their collective modes of practice and understanding, an issue which is of crucial importance in relation to learning technology work. It also sheds little light on how shared artefacts can contribute to the migration of knowledge about practice, whether within local communities or across a broader network. Leaving aside the issue of how practice is judged to be 'good' and therefore worth sharing, how should any complex practice such as learning technology use be represented so as to be useful to other practitioners? For these issues it is interesting to consider some insights from knowledge management and knowledge modelling. Knowledge modelling aims to capture the procedural and tacit knowledge deployed in expert practice among different communities of expertise (Stefik, 1995), but it is well recognised that the process of modelling can 'miss' those aspects of practice that are most salient to practical learning and professional development. There may even be resistance to the process of modelling (McKinlay, 2000) if it is seen as compromising effective local practice through over-generalisation, or seeking to replace human experts with databases and standardised procedures. General resistance to the adoption of learning technologies on the part of the academic community may in part entail resistance to the codification and modelling of practice.

Appropriate forms of representation – i.e. those that can be used to mediate future practice – must therefore be developed with sympathy for the community's needs, values, goals, cultures and existing forms of practice (Bowker and Star, 2000). The very broad spectrum of roles and affiliations among learning technology practitioners, however, means they should be regarded as a series of interlinked communities or networks, with their own sometimes differing needs, values and forms of practice. Software developers and academics, for example, have been shown in studies to apply completely different assumptions to the common task of developing usable learning systems (Davidson, Schofield and Stocks, 2001). Learning technology as an academic discipline has different procedures, rules and cultural assumptions from learning technology as a professional practice. It will be important, therefore, to value the separate communities and networks of learning technology work while allowing a broad knowledge base to develop through our common interest in student learning mediated by technology.

Haye and Walsham (2000), in a five-year study of groupware in knowledge-based companies, found that even when the technologies and vocabularies for knowledge sharing exist, the dominant culture or reward structure of a company can make it unprofitable for individuals to actually engage in it. This is clearly the case in the academic community where the valued modes of knowledge production are research, publication and peer review. The traditional modes of knowledge representation which arise from these practices – theories, models, academic articles, classifications, methodologies – are not obviously useful for representing learning and teaching practice. Educational developers, for example, tend to rely on forms such as action research reports, learning diaries and case studies for the transmission of information about practice, while placing the greatest emphasis on face-to-face dialogue with mentors and structured participation such as teaching observations. Software developers use graphical representations of educational interactions to 'paper prototype' learning systems, along with standard protocols for user testing (Baxter, 2000). Academics themselves look for 'tips and tricks' on how to use specific technical tools in the classroom. However valuable they may be to end-users, these modes of representation are accorded a low intellectual status and are therefore relatively unrewarding for individuals to produce.

Knowledge modelling in academic communities is also strongly biased towards subject knowledge and traditional modes of pedagogical practice in the different disciplines. The ASTER project, for example, has found that the term 'seminar' stands in for a completely different set of pedagogical practices in a psychology undergraduate classroom from an equivalent classroom in the humanities (http://www.aster.ac.uk). The phrase 'embedding learning technologies' (into the curriculum), which has now displaced the phrase 'disseminating good practice' in UK HE, encapsulates this awareness: that new learning tools, techniques and activities cannot be used 'off the shelf', but must be adapted, translated and integrated into new disciplinary and institutional contexts. The process skills involved are complex, and not even very rich representations of practice can substitute for a learning and professional development experience such as an EFFECTS programme.

A related issue is that in using learning technologies, academic staff and students are required to undertake major changes to their existing practice, in ways that may challenge some fundamental beliefs and expectations. This positive stance towards change must be reflected in the chosen forms of representation and in the forums for community debate. In other communities of practice facing supercomplexity (Barnet, 1999) and continuous change, there has been a move away from topographical forms such as benchmarks and matrices, which map stable domains of practice from one instance to another, towards narrative forms which tell stories about successful processes of change and can be applied in a metaphorical rather than a linear fashion (Orr 1996; Otala, 1995). One outcome of the final EFFECTS evaluation forum (June 2001) was a consensus that our insistence on standardised case studies had been a mistake. Some of the most successful disseminations of EFFECTS projects had taken the form of lunchtime seminars to colleagues. Here the 'real story' of the development process could be told, colleagues could ask questions and make sense of the project from their own perspectives, there were opportunities to explore the local technical, political, cultural and educational context, and new meanings could be negotiated for the project and its outcomes.

Finally, learning technology development and use do not constitute stable practices, carried out by a clearly defined community in a commonly understood context. In fact the proliferation of ICT in the learning environment has contributed to a diversification of roles and identities among staff, and ongoing contestation over the nature of academic teaching practice. These changes have been accompanied by a general paradigm shift in ideas about university learning, in which the transmission of information via lectures and set texts has given way (rhetorically at least) to a model of active, constructive learners, supported by peers and learning professionals (Goodyear *et al.*, 2000). Individual academic responsibility for pedagogical practice is giving way to corporate responsibility and new collaborations in curriculum development. The ICT revolution has certainly helped to bring about this realignment (Bates 1997). Therefore any attempt to understand, represent and transform learning technology practice must be sensitive to the variety of identities and roles with which practitioners are working, the ways in which professional identity is negotiated –

including through emergent practices – and the new forms of collaboration that are being engendered.

A modified version of the activity system triangles, taken from Engestrom (1999) is used here to illustrate the process of sharing practice across a practitioner network (see Figure 36.1).

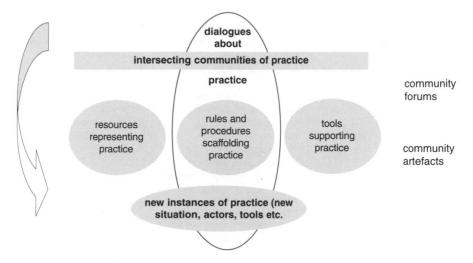

Figure 36.1   Migrating examples of practice in communities of practice

36.3   What kinds of network? What kinds of representation?

The research reported in this chapter took the form of an online survey (n > 120) of learning technology practitioners, a series of structured interviews and four national focus groups, aimed at uncovering ways in which learning technology practice is actually developed through networks and through sharing representations of practice.

A review of library, gateway and portal projects relating to learning and teaching in HE was used to produce a list of artefacts currently in use by the UK HE community for sharing knowledge about learning and teaching practice. The list was subsequently been developed into a taxonomy according to the intended end user and intended end use of the resource (i.e. the activity mediated rather than, for example, the medium used, in accordance with the overall focus on practice). Intended end users were divided into four broad categories: learners, teachers, technical developers and educational developers, where developers were not directly involved in the learning and teaching interaction. Ways in which artefacts might be used to mediate practice are described along a continuum from tools supporting practice to texts describing practice (see Figure 36.2). The full taxonomy and a discussion of the text-tool continuum are available from the author.

From this matrix the list of resource types given in Figure 36.3 was derived for use in the study.

Perspective of user Type of Artefact	1. Learner	2. Teacher, learning facilitator	
Tool supporting practice (enabling or constraining of practice, focus on activity/production, inherently interactive)	Learning environment and components (tools for taking part in learning transactions: administration, resource and time management, assessment etc) Authoring/design tool. Data analysis tool. Tools for drafting, developing, commenting, discussion, argumentation. Subject-specific tool or instrument (Artefacts designed to structure and support learning – may be more or less subject specific)	<- all of column 1 (to structure and support teaching objectives) Learning environment and components (tools for design and facilitation of learning transactions: administration, resource and time management, assessment etc) (Artefacts designed to structure and support teaching and lesson planning)	
Framework or protocol scaffolding practice (prescriptive of practice, focus on sequence and structure, designed to be used interactively)	Hypertexts, web pages, learning activities, courseware. Guidelines, interactive documents, assessment tasks	Frameworks, toolkits, models, guidelines, 'tips and tricks'. matrices, interactive documents (Interactive representations of L&T practice, more or less structured/prescriptive as to future practice)	
Resource or texts describing practice (descriptive of practice, focus on content and outcomes, not inherently interactive)	Learning resource (Material offering specific learning content)	Pedagogical theory, hypothesis, model. Report, case study, teaching observation. Video recording, audio recording Interview, structured dialogue etc. (Account of learning and teaching practice – generic or subject specific, structured or freestyle)	

Figure 36.2   Typology of artefacts used to support learning and teaching practice from different perspectives of use

A literature review was then used as the basis for a typology of *interaction types*, i.e. practices or activities engaged with by potential users in relation to the resources or representations of practice offered. Although independently developed, this typology might be compared with Oliver and Conole's (2001) classification of information-related behaviours (gathering, using, communicating, evaluating) and with Whittington and

3. Resource developer (educational artefacts e.g. systems, software, materials)	4. Educational developer (individual educational practice)	5. Strategic developer (collective/organisational practice)
Authoring and design tools, programming tools and languages, builder environments, publishing tools		
Design protocols, process frameworks and models, guidelines, interactive documents. (Interactive representations of design/development practice, more or less structured/prescriptive as to future practice)	Protocols, process frameworks, guidelines, models etc relating to professional development. (Interactive representations of development practice, more or less structured/prescriptive as to future practice) <- all of these as frameworks to support the practice of others	Protocols, process frameworks, guidelines, models etc relating to organisational development.. (Interactive representations of development practice, more or less structured/prescriptive as to future practice)
<- all of column 1 as examples or components for new artefacts Instructional design theory, hypothesis, model. Case study, report, account etc of design practice	<- all of columns 1 and 2 as examples for new learning and teaching practices. Educational development theory, hypothesis, model. Developmental case study, report, account of practice	Organisational development theory, hypothesis, model. Developmental case study, report, account of practice. Examples of strategies, policies etc from other organisations.

Figure 36.2 (cont.)

Dewar's (2000) spectrum of user behaviours in a digital environment (presentation, collection, practice, interaction, production). The activities can be arranged in progressive order with the later activities generally requiring greater confidence and expertise (as per Whittington and Dewar). Again, there is a close match with Dwyer *et al.*'s (1990) five-stage model of the transformation of teaching practice in ICT classrooms: their additional stage is 'appropriation', which in the present model is seen as a feature of both 'adoption' and

a.	**Review**: overview/evaluation of a specific technology or technology-based resource from a practitioner perspective
b.	**Guidelines**: how-to' advice relating to a specific learning technology, a specific practice or approach
c.	**Staff development material**: hand-outs, exercises or tutorials relating to specific uses of learning technology (more reflective than guidelines)
d.	**Case study (curriculum)**: account of the use of ICT in a specific curriculum (i.e. learning and teaching) context
e.	**Case study (strategic)**: account of supporting/embedding learning technology in a dept. or institutional context – focusing on staff or organisational development
f.	**Framework/toolkit (curriculum)**: model, template, interactive document etc. to aid learning technology use in the curriculum, e.g. student needs analysis, decision-making tool
g.	**Framework/toolkit (strategic)**: model, template etc to aid development of learning technology strategy or support, e.g. audit tool, staff skills matrix
h.	**Article/report**: any structured account of learning technology use, e.g. chapter, conference paper, journal article, project report, strategy document
i.	**Software: learning tool**: generic application e.g. assessment software, communications tool, authoring tool, VLE, specifically for use in learning and teaching
j.	**Software: activity shell**: structured courseware or courseware component which may be customised by adding new content
k.	**Software: learning object**: multimedia content for re-use in new contexts, e.g. text, image, animation, simulation, a/v clip, dataset
l.	**Information resource**: annotated link to alternative learning technology resource, e.g. database, portal, journal, image bank or web site
m.	**Project/service**: annotated link to learning technology project, service or contact

Figure 36.3   Resource types or 'representations of practice' included in the study

'adaptation'. However, as experts do not stop engaging in earlier activities once they have progressed, the activities might better be presented as a cycle in the manner of Oliver and Conole. A second column was added to illustrate relevant collaborative activities involving the same representations of practice (see Figure 36.4).

This matrix was simplified to give four solo and two collaborative options, available as multiple (i.e. non-exclusive) selections for each resource type (see Figure 36.5).

The final questionnaire was available online over a period of six weeks in June–July 2001, and was returned by over 120 respondents. As anticipated from the sampling strategy this was a relatively experienced group (mode and median = 'proficient' users of educational software), with 28 per cent describing themselves as academics, 22 per cent as educational developers, 18 per cent as learning technologists, and 32 per cent as belonging to one of the other roles. A series of structured interviews and focus groups was also carried out during this period.

36.4   Findings on representations of practice

The most informative resources were found to be (in descending order): articles, reviews, curriculum case studies and information from projects. The resources most adopted in practice were found to be (in descending order): software learning environments and tools, staff development materials, guidelines and curriculum frameworks. Overall, therefore, the relationship between the *inform* and *adopt* responses seemed to reflect the distinction

	Interactions with resources	Interactions with others (involving resources)
Information seeking	**Using heuristics and tools for information retrieval (e.g. search tools and indexes)** Usingmethodologies for data collection	Asking, interviewing Negotiation of information needs, goals and priorities. Developing/choosing methodologies for data collection. Developing/choosing heuristics for information retrieval and recognition
Application	Applying models, frameworks, hypotheses to own practice. Using toolkits, guidelines, tips and tricks Deploying learning tools and artefacts in a specific learning context Selecting relevant aspects of information resource	Formal teaching, mentoring, staff and educational development (deploying resources to support practice of others) Apprenticeship,guided practice
Adaptation	Customisation and redesign of resources. Change of practice (new forms of application)	Commenting on resources (and contexts of use). Discussion, elaboration, annotation, re-presentation Collective adaptation (changes of cultural artefacts, documents, procedures, rules of thumb).
Creation	Creation of new representations of practice	Collaborative development of new representations of practice

Figure 36.4   Typology of knowledge-based interactions*
* A more carefully elaborated version of this matrix is available in H. Beetham (2001) Designing representations of practice for knowledge practitioners. Paper to International Conference on Advanced Learning Technologies, Madison, Wisconsin, August 2001

I would use this to **inform** myself about learning and teaching practice	I would **adopt** (ideas from) this for use in my own practice	I would **adapt** or customise this to suit my own needs	I would **create** my own resources of this type	I would **guide** or facilitate others' use of this to support their practice	I would **comment** on or evaluate this in light of my own experience

Figure 36.5   Knowledge based interactions included in the survey

between texts about and tools for practice offered in Figure 36.2, with articles, reviews, case studies and information resources being closer to the text end of the spectrum, frameworks and guidelines being at the middle end of the spectrum, and the highly adoptable software being at the tool end of the spectrum.

Following this line of reasoning, 'text' and 'tool' types were amalgamated as indicated above and tested against the total number of responses as indicated in Figure 36.6. Chi square tests were carried out against each possible combination of data and the four null hypotheses were all found to be significant at $p < 0.001$:

	Inform	Adopt
Texts	497	202
Tools	406	336

Figure 36.6   Total responses for 'text' and 'tool' resource types against 'inform' and 'adopt'

All resource types were significantly more likely to be used for information than adopted for use in practice. However, texts were significantly more likely to be used for information than tools, and tools were significantly more likely to be adopted than texts. As compared with other resource types, software tools showed a much smaller differential between 'inform' and 'adopt': in other words, participants who expected to encounter software objects in the course of thinking about their practice expected to adopt them relatively frequently.

When asked to express a preference, academic respondents wanted access to (in descending order): staff development materials (possibly for self study?), software tools/environments, and case studies in curriculum development. Non-academics wanted access to: staff development materials (possibly for re-use in the support of other staff?), information resources, reviews and guidelines. As compared with academics, these staff appear to be more focused on re-usable and adaptable resources for guiding the practice of others.

Respondents in the study reported that they were actually creating staff development materials and guidelines (around 40 per cent); and to a lesser extent curriculum development frameworks, articles and information resources (around 30 per cent). Very few were creating software environments or tools, strategic frameworks for practice, or project-based resources, all of which were regarded as very useful. There were fewer contributors than users in every category of resource, though the greatest differential came with the 'text' type resources: reviews, articles and case studies. Although they were regarded as the most informative (ca. 90 per cent) there were relatively far fewer people actually creating and sharing them (ca. 30 per cent).

There were few significant differences among types of respondent in their use and creation of objects, except in the important category of staff development materials, which were both used and created significantly more by non-academic staff. Since the predominant categories of these staff were educational developers and learning technology support staff, this is a fairly trivial finding. However, these materials were also extremely popular among academic staff, indicating that they are both highly usable and highly available for facilitating change of practice. No significant differences were detected across the different roles in terms of practices engage in, including the practice of 'guiding' other staff in their use of resources. This suggests that participants who identified themselves as academics were nevertheless taking considerable responsibility for the development of others – a finding borne out in interviews.

Overall these findings indicate that frameworks such as EFFECTS, along with interactive documents, matrices, toolkits, guidelines and other representations that can be applied directly in practice, are regarded as highly usable both by specialist learning technology staff and by academics with an interest in learning technologies. Staff development materials in general make excellent candidates for sharing representations of practice as they are both readily available and highly usable in practice: the SeSDL project in Scotland has already pursued this approach. Case studies, articles, evaluation reports and longer descriptive texts are highly informative but poorly used except by staff already fairly specialist in the field. These findings have been used by the SoURCE project to underpin the development of a metadata-driven database of materials relating to the use of learning technologies in higher education. In order for these materials to be effectively deployed in practice, however, it is understood that they must be fully integrated into the practice of specialist developers who are actively intervening in the lives of academic teachers in institutions of higher education.

36.5   Findings on networks of practice

Most academic staff interviewed in this study had become proficient in the use of learning technologies with the support of specialist staff from a learning technologies unit, educational development unit or similar. Particularly as less enthusiastic and technically confident members of staff become involved with learning technology use, it must be anticipated that the demand for support will increase, whether this is provided by structured programmes such as EFFECTS or by less formal staff development opportunities and mentoring.

The most effective dialogues for developing day-to-day practice proved to be those that took place naturally in the course of collaboration. Participants were often members of: working parties, committees, regional collaborations ('it's the ability to physically network as well as conduct things viritually'), professional networks and 'self help groups', or had strong personal links with people in similar positions at nearby institutions. New kinds of dialogical forum were evolving: institutional learning and teaching forums, 'change agent' networks, research seminars or reading and discussion groups in which practitioner-researchers talked with educational developers and academics in educational studies. While participants in this study were enthusiastic networkers at all levels, there was a sense that the time and effort involved was difficult to negotiate in the context of existing demands:

> At the moment I feel just swamped with initiatives while trying to do my day to day job... there is a tension between increasing your network while still trying to manage things locally.

Among educational developers, collaborative development and delivery of courses across universities was surprisingly common, with a willingness to share materials, course development and even facilities. 'Each institution would host [a workshop] once or twice a year. Whoever was coordinating would collect all the materials together from the presenters and that material was given out to all the staff developers at all the participating universities'. It is interesting to note that the funding model as well as the ethos of academic staff development promotes a sharing of educational ideas and materials across institutions, while the funding model for student learning encourages competition. Learning technology staff have at least this advantage over the LTSN networks: that participants are likely to come from a centrally-funded and collaboratively-minded sector of HE staff.

Given the nature of dialogues identified as enabling development, it is perhaps not surprising that the preferred medium was overwhelmingly face to face, especially with hands-on access to the learning technology itself:

> I tend to find relating to somebody personal, being able to have the personal experience and empathy ... Also some sense of what they're trying to do. You can't decontextualise it. I'd say that face to face is essential to get the ball rolling, but for them to be able to go away and reflect individually using electronic resources.
> Before you start using any sort of software you need to sit down with somebody and talk through the theory behind it, what you really want to do with it and why.

Failing this, participants would turn to the telephone, email, or possibly videoconferencing to communicate with someone already known to them:

because we know each other very well we're often in communication by email or
videoconferencing
my experience with things like using VC in a working environment ... it doesn't usually
work too well until you've had a physical meeting.

More experienced users would turn to discussion lists first if they were not sure who to ask
about a specific issue: one commented that for academic discourse email had the advantage of
a written record for reflection and slightly more formal expression of ideas. However, these
users were already confident with both pedagogical and technical issues, and tended to be
seeking specific information rather than general practical support or educational discourse.
Asynchronous media introduced an element of discrimination between 'active' and 'passive'
participants in the dialogue and perhaps therefore between expert and novice users:

At the moment I'm passive in my use of [a particular discussion forum] – I will log on,
have a read through, see if there's anything appropriate to the stuff I'm doing, take it on
board, look up any references that they may quote. What I'd like to do is get into the
position where I can actually start to be a bit more active there.

While research has pointed up the value of legitimate peripheral participation (Wenger,
1999) in enculturating novices to general discourses and forms of practice, it is less clear that
online participation can substitute for more directive, scaffolded support when practitioners
actually have to get to grips with new tools. As the survey findings showed, there can be a
steep learning curve between being 'informed by' and 'adopting' new ideas in learning and
teaching practice. An important role learning technology networks will therefore be to
support those people who are supporting others – helping them to reach new
understandings of their own transformative practice, and new ways of thinking about the
local dialogues and interventions in which they are engaged. This is work which has already
been begun by the NetCulture regional forums in Scotland. It is interesting that these forums
have focused on the development of shared practice frameworks.

There was strong support for networking from all participants:

There are people like me at every university in the country and we could all be working
separately to get this kind of information together.
You need information from outside the system. You can't work in a closed system

However, academic staff generally regarded their subject-specific LTSN as the network they
were most likely to encounter in the course of everyday reflection on their practice. This
suggests that a network of learning technology specialists may need to be developed,
outside the subject area perspective of most academic staff. The purpose would be to
enhance the practice of these more experienced users, especially those in a position to
support more novice members of staff. Rather than delivering materials directly to academic
staff, the aim would be to develop an economy of shared resources that can be adapted,
adopted and reused in the context of development work; in other words which can be
cascaded to others via the various institutional and departmental interventions of the
specialist members of staff.

36.6 Development opportunities

As a result of this research it is possible to identify some very specific opportunities for continuing the work of SoURCE, EFFECTS and other funded learning technology projects. Since early 2000, the two projects have collaborated with a number of other TLTP3 projects to review ways in which project outcomes can be embedded into the practice of the learning and teaching community in a more lasting way. A common goal has been to create a resource base in the form of project outcomes, case studies, (action) research reports, guidelines, reviews, generic software tools, 'toolkits' and resources for reflection/study/professional development. These should be described according to common metadata and controlled vocabularies for keyword and resource type (an IMS compliant schema has now been developed) to enable cross searching by different user communities. This opened up the possibility of sharing representations of practice beyond the original target users of the projects.

As a result of the current study and the various evaluation studies reported on in this symposium, there is little evidence of academic teaching staff accessing resources of this kind for their own use, however well evaluated and described they may be. Instead the projects have turned their attention to how representations of practice can be situated within developing communities of practice, both contributing to and benefiting from the shared resource. The artefacts that support and formalise practice are secondary to the actual community with its aims and agenda, rules of engagement, values, philosophies, theories-in-use and divisions of labour. In their continuation phase, therefore, the EFFECTS and SoURCE projects are working to develop a network of regional learning technology groups, which will both contribute to and make use of the shared resources. The aim is for the networks and resources to become mutually supporting over time, with materials being adapted, inserted into programmes of staff development, commented upon and collaboratively re-developed. A pressing need identified in this study and throughout the SoURCE and EFFECTS projects is for a programme of research committed to overall analysis of the outcomes of learning and teaching innovation. With a research programme of this kind in place to complement the regional networks and resource base, there is every hope that an ongoing community of practice can emerge with the resources constantly to re-evaluate and reinterpret its own understanding of learning technologies for the benefit of all staff working in the sector.

36.7 References

Barnet, R. (1999) *Realizing the University in an Age of Supercomplexity*. Oxford: Oxford University Press.

Bates, A. (1997) *Restructuring the university for technological change*. Paper presented to The Carnegie Foundation for the Advancement of Teaching symposium, What Kind of University? London, 18–20 June.

Baxter, L.F. (2000) Bugged: the Software Development Process. In C. Prichard *et al.* (eds) *Managing Knowledge: Critical Investigations of Work and Learning*. London: MacMillan Press.

Beetham, H. and Bailey, B. (2001) Enabling organisational change through continuing professional development. In J. Wisdom and R. MacDonald, *Evaluating Learning Technologies*. SEDA/SRHE.

Beetham, H. et al. (1999) *EFFECTS Evaluation Report, Year One*. Available from the author.

Beetham, H. et al. (2000) *EFFECTS Evaluation Report, Year Two*. Available from the author.

Bowker, G. and Star, L.S. (2000) *Sorting Things Out.* University of MIT Press.

Davidson A.L, Schofield J. and Stocks J. (2001) "Professional Cultures and Collaborative Efforts; a Case Study of Technologists and Educators Working for Change", *The Information Society* **17**: 21–32.

Dwyer, D.C., Ringstaff, C. and Sandholtz, J.H. (1990) *Teacher Beliefs and Practices: Patterns of Change in the Evolution of Teachers' Instructional Beliefs and Practices in High-Access-to-Technology Classrooms: First–Fourth Year Findings.* Cupertino, Apple Computer Inc.

Engestrom, Y. (1999) Activity theory and individual and social transformation. In Y. Engestrom, R. Miettinen and R-L. Punamaki (eds) *Perspectives on Activity Theory.* Cambridge: Cambridge University Press.

Goodyear, P. and Steeples, C. (1997) "Shareable Representations of practice", *ALT-J* **6**(3)

Goodyear P. et al. (2000) *Effective Networked Learning in Higher Education: Notes and Guidelines.* Centre for Studies in Advanced Learning Technology, Lancaster University.

Harvey, J. and Oliver, M. (2001) *Evaluation Report: the EFFECTS project.* Available from http://sh.plym.ac.uk/eds/effects/.

Hayes N. and Walsham G. (2000) Safe Enclaves, Political Enclaves and Knowledge Working. In C. Prichard *et al.* (eds) *Managing Knowledge: Critical Investigations of Work and Learning.* London: MacMillan Press.

Hildreth, P., Kimble, C. and Wright, P. (2000) "Communities of practice in the distributed international environment", *Journal of Knowledge Management* **4**(1): 27–38.

Kewell, E., Oliver, M. and Conole, G. (1999) *Assessing the Organisational Capabilities of Embedding Learning Technologies into the Undergraduate Curriculum. University of North London: ELT working papers #2.*

McKinlay, A. (2000) The Bearable Lightness of Control: Organisational Reflexivity and the Politics of Knowledge Management. In C. Prichard *et al.* (eds) *Managing Knowledge: Critical Investigations of Work and Learning.* London: MacMillan Press.

Otala, M. (1995) "The learning organization: theory and practice", *Industry in Higher Education,* June.

Orr, J. (1996) *Talking About Machines: an ethnography of a modern job,* Ithaca: IRL press

Oliver, M. and Conole, G. (2001) *Using Toolkits to embed theory into practice.* Paper to International Conference on Advanced Learning Technologies. 6-8 August, Madison, USA.

Schank, R.C. (1994) Active learning through multimedia, *IEE Multimedia* **1**(1): 69–79.

Seely Brown, J. and Duguid, P. (2000) *The Social Life of Information.* Harvard: Harvard Business School Press.

Somekh, B. (1998) Designing software to maximise learning, *A LT- J* **4**(3): 4–14

Stefik, M. (1995) *Introduction to Knowledge Systems.* San Francisco: Morgan Kaufmann

Wenger, E. (1999) *Communities of Practice: Learning, Meaning, and Identity.* Cambridge: Cambridge University Press.

Whittington, D. and Dewar, T. (2000) "Online Learners and their Learning Strategies", *Journal of Educational Computing Research* **23** (4): 385–403

Eileen Tuimaleali'ifano
University of the South Pacific (USP), Suva, Fiji

Introduction

In discussing the broad topic *Multimodal course delivery and support at the University of the South Pacific (USP)*, we first examine some of the experiences by the USP in the use of technology to deliver teaching and learning to distance students dispersed throughout the region of the university. Combining these experiences with some recent research data, we discuss challenges that currently prevail, many unique to our university but some having global relevance, as well as challenges that we anticipate will arise for us in the future. Such information is essential in providing the platform for effective planning by the university in flexible teaching and learning with the ultimate aim of removing the distinctions between distance and on-campus delivery.

USPNet 2000

The opportunities for multi-modal delivery became available with the upgrade and expansion of the university's satellite-based communications network called USPNet 2000. The system, which is wholly owned and operated by the university, provides

- fully interactive video and audio conferences;
- full data, email, Internet, intranet, and similar services;
- one-way video broadcasts; and
- pending telephony and fax services.

The USPNet experience

Our symposium consists of three presentations: the first paper (Chapter 37) is a summary report of a research project which monitored the emergency use of the upgraded and much expanded USPNet, in the second half of 2000 to deliver courses to full-time students grounded in their home countries at the height of the political crisis in Fiji. The research treated this emergency use of the facilities as a trial of the effectiveness of the technology for the USP and its region, and sought to identify conditions and factors conducive to this effectiveness. The second presentation (Chapter 38) examines and discusses the university's past and current use of audioconferencing facilities to provide interactive learning support for distance students studying mainly through print-based course packages. This chapter also provides a brief historical description of the university's initial involvement with technological delivery in the early 1970s via a limited USPNet. In the third paper (Chapter 39) the experiences of tutors teaching in the pre-degree (pre-tertiary) programme of the USP, as users of USPNet facilities, are discussed. In light of these experiences and the results of the research project in the first presentation, future plans for continued and extended use of USPNet facilities to deliver and enhance the delivery of courses in the pre-degree studies programme are presented.

USPNet in the context of USP

Some important facts about the USP and the region that it serves, are necessary to provide the context, and the dynamics within this context that will impact on how effective USP can be in the use of technology to deliver its programmes of study:

- The USP has the unique feature of being a *regional university* owned and operated by 12 island nations in the Pacific.

- These countries are spread over 33 million square kilometres of ocean, making the USP region one of *vast physical distances.*

- As a result of the 180th meridian passing through the Region, USP has to contend with *five time zones.*

- The total population of the USP Region now stands at about 1.5 million people belonging to many different ethnic, culture and language groups both indigenous and migrant making it a region of *vast socio-cultural diversity.*

- Students bring a *wide-range of formal educational backgrounds* to their studies as a consequence of the region's colonial past, continued links with metropolitan countries and current moves towards national curricula.

- The current *disparities in economic development,I> among the various countries of the region are reflected in the differences in need and demand for education and training across the region.*

- Communication and information technology *are still beyond the financial reach of the majority of the region's population.*

In the second semester of 2000, USP registered 12,601 enrolments in its distance courses, which represent 46 per cent of FTES. In moving towards flexible course delivery via technology, USP is challenged on a number of broad fronts, specifically:

- general unfamiliarity of the people of the region with modern communication and information technology;

- the need to provide appropriate infrastructure; and

- the need to design and develop teaching and learning opportunities responsive to the diverse circumstances and conditions of its distance students.

37 Jumping right in: a report on the University of the South Pacific Semester 2, 2000 video broadcast experience

Melissa Gold and Eileen Tuimaleali'ifano
University of the South Pacific (USP), Suva, Fiji

37.1 Overview

Due to political events outside of its control, the University of the South Pacific (USP) accelerated its move towards multi-modal delivery of courses to remote off-campus students by offering 24 video broadcast courses to students in the Cook Islands, Kiribati, Samoa and Tonga who chose not to come back to the main campus in Fiji for semester 2, 2000. This report looks at the impact of the University's decision to jump right in to large-scale use of its newly inaugurated USPNet satellite communications system on the effectiveness of its teaching and learning mission. Not surprisingly, issues such as lack of knowledge, time, planning and coordination all were found to have a negative impact. However, many of the main issues did not seem to be related to the technology itself but rather other factors that could be improved.

37.2 Introduction

As a result of the civilian coup in Fiji on 19 May 2000, the schedule and delivery of programmes of study by the University of the South Pacific (USP) at its Laucala Campus in Suva were seriously threatened. Many of the on-campus students of the University had returned soon after the coup to their home countries in the Region or to the various parts of Fiji where they lived. These students sat for final examinations for their first semester courses at USP Centres throughout the Region rather than in Suva. By the eve of the second semester, many regional governments were still hesitant about returning their students to Fiji because of the continuing political unrest. Seven countries finally did; of the remaining five, the Solomon Islands withdrew its students from their studies in the second semester as a result of the simultaneous political problems within their country, and Cook Islands, Kiribati, Tonga and Samoa retained some or most of their scholarship students.

The University was faced with the problem of delivering second semester courses to these students. It found part of its solution in the facilities of its newly upgraded (March 2000) satellite-based USPNet communication system. With its 24-hour voice and data communication link across the 12 member countries of the USP Region, the system provided opportunities for video broadcast delivery of courses and various forms of student support, enabling these full-time, normally on-campus students to study from their home countries.

Thirty-four courses were originally identified for video broadcast delivery to remote full-time students in the region, but only 24 of these attracted enrolments in the countries in question. Lectures for these courses were delivered on the Suva Campus and then sent either live or delayed to the students at the USP Centres in the four countries via the USPNet Satellite. The lectures were supplemented by a combination of audio, print and online support.

This chapter describes a research project undertaken to monitor this experimental use of the USPNet facilities, particularly with a view to finding out how effective the technology was in the provision of learning opportunities to students at a distance.

37.3   USP's experience in the global context

It is clear from the literature that there is now a strong and growing global move towards flexible delivery of teaching and learning made possible by the increasingly widespread availability of communication and information technologies (Bates, 1991; Dekkers and Andrews, 2000; Fischer, 1996; Heydenrych, 2001; Luke, 1999; Potashnik and Capper, 1998; Tait and Mills, 1999). At its essence, this move is fuelled by the desire to make education and training as widely available as possible, particularly in recognition of the increasing number of adult learners now seeking access to higher education but constrained by work and family commitments.

USP, too, recognises the advantages that technology can bring to its distance education programmes. It recently upgraded its satellite communications network (USPNet) to enable it to become more flexible in the delivery of its teaching and learning mission to remote students. The University's aspirations for USPNet are clearly articulated throughout the current USP Strategic Plan (1998); for example, the plan states that 'USPNet ... holds great potential for providing more flexible approaches to study for extension students in the region' (p. 28) and that 'the [USPNet] project ... will ensure that the University reclaims its leadership in the technological aspects of distance education' (p. 37). By adding video, voice and data transmission and Internet access to the print mode currently available to remote students, USPNet technology is referred to in University terminology as 'multi-modal'.

However, the literature cautions against using learning technologies based largely on perceptions of their power or on the argument that successful case studies have global applications (Bates, 1991; Clark, 1994; Forsyth, 1991). Bates also raises a concern, quite common in the literature, that a fixation on technology can lead to the loss of the 'educational experience' present in learning materials that have been professionally designed for learners who need more support or who have poor home study conditions.

37.4   The research project

The researchers on this project were looking at USP's rapid move, based on political events outside of the University's control, to the use of USPNet to deliver multi-modal learning opportunities for remote students. Specifically, the researchers were looking for factors that influence the effectiveness of teaching and learning using USPNet. They aimed to collect data related to the following four categories.

- lecturer and student preparedness and attitudes towards the technology;
- capacity of the technology to delivery teaching and learning;
- operational issues;
- administrative issues.

37.5   Methodology

The main method of data collection was via questionnaires developed for lecturers assigned to deliver courses using video broadcast during the semester and for students receiving such courses in the USP regional Centres in the Cook Islands, Kiribati, Samoa and Tonga. Questions were focused on and designed for feedback on the four specific dimensions above. Questionnaire data was supplemented by a limited number of interviews conducted among a selection of staff and students to add a qualitative dimension to the questionnaire data.

In addition, to investigate the technical and administrative aspects of the project, data was collected from technical and other staff involved in facilitating video broadcast/conference delivery and audio conferencing via their technical and scheduling records.

37.6   Data analysis

Of the 24 on-campus courses taught via video broadcast, 16 lecturers representing 15 of these courses returned questionnaires, and 7 were interviewed.

In addition, 17 students enrolled in 13 courses returned 20 questionnaires (students were asked to fill in questionnaires by course). This was out of a total of 132 enrolments by 90 students in the 24 courses. As Table 37.1 shows, this was a disappointingly low return particularly in the larger Centres of Samoa and Tonga.

Centre	No. enrolments	No. students	No. returned questionnaires
Cook Islands	3	2	3
Kiribati	5	5	3
Samoa	78	52	10
Tonga	46	31	4

Table 37.1   Number of enrolments, students and returned student questionnaires, by centre

In addition to the questionnaires, five Samoan students were interviewed about their participation in the video broadcast courses.

A frequency analysis of questionnaire responses was undertaken to provide a general profile of the video broadcast experience from both lecturer and student perspectives. Specific features of this profile were then examined in greater detail using answers to open-ended questions in the questionnaires and interview data from both lecturers and students.

Results of the analysis are discussed within the four broad areas of investigation in this research project, in the following section.

37.7   Lecturer and student preparedness and attitudes towards the technology

37.7.1   Lecturer

In this project preparedness was measured in two ways. The first was by familiarity with the technology in terms of extent, frequency and purpose of prior use. The second was by type, level and duration of training received before the start of the semester. Both of these are good indicators of whether or not a lecturer is familiar with the strengths of the technology in delivering pedagogy and also with the protocols associated with effective and efficient use of particular media.

Table 37.2 is a summary of responses by lecturers to questions about their past experience with and training in the various technologies that were available to them during the semester.

	Technology						
	Video broadcast*	Video conferencing	Video tape	Audio conferencing	Audio graphics	Audio tape	Online
Experience	2	0	1	4	0	0	1
Training	1	0	1	1	0	0	0

* This includes both live and delayed video broadcast

Table 37.2   Number of lecturers with technological experience and training with various
technologies

Of the eight people who indicated some past experience, this was mostly for the purpose of teaching on a regular basis. For instance, the four lecturers with audio conferencing experience used the facility in support of their distance teaching.

With regard to prior training, the people with video training indicated that it had been very limited, and the person with audio conferencing training indicated that this had been on-the-job training in the use of radio.

Clearly then, for this cohort of lecturers, there was very little or no experience or training before they embarked on video broadcast course delivery with multi-modal support.

Although the courses studied during this project were known as video broadcast courses, they were actually delivered to the students in three different ways: through live broadcast, delayed broadcast, or on videotape. In addition, lecturers had a variety of support media available to them, including video and audio conferencing and email.

The questionnaire asked the lecturers to indicate which technologies they were using in their courses. Their responses are summarised in Table 37.3.

	Video broadcast	Delayed video broadcast	Video tape	Video conferencing	Audio conferencing	Online
Number	11	4	9	2	4	4[b]

Table 37.3   Number of lecturers indicating use of various technologies[a]

a. No lecturer indicated use of audio graphics or audio tape, so these were omitted from the table.
b. While only 4 out of 16 lecturers circled 'online' as a mode they use in their course, 14 indicated that they used email either daily or weekly to communicate with their students.

Interestingly, not all of the lecturers indicated that their course was being delivered by video broadcast or by videotape. However, records kept by the USPNet technicians indicate that every one of these courses was broadcast as well as videotaped. The mismatch indicates a lack of understanding on the part of the lecturers as to how they were reaching their students. The comments of one lecturer indicate this point well: 'I honestly don't know which mode is being used for [my course]'.

In terms of their enthusiasm towards using the technology, the lecturers were asked to rate their level of excitement and/or distress at being asked to teach in the various modes.

In spite of their lack of experience and training, of the 11 lecturers who indicated a use of video broadcast for teaching, about half (5) indicated that initially they felt excited and comfortable about their involvement. The rest were not so comfortable and even unhappy. The split in feelings was roughly the same for the other media, with slightly more people expressing initial feelings of distress at using the technology. The exception was the online mode, where three out of four lecturers expressed initial excitement about using the technology.

When asked to rate their feelings after a couple of months of using the technology, the lecturers tended to remain or become negative, as shown in Table 37.4 below. This was especially true in their use of video broadcast and videotape. It is also interesting to note that not one respondent started out negative and then became positive as a result of his/her experience.

The people who remained or became most negative admitted that their courses were never designed for remote delivery and that they found it difficult to try to balance the needs of on-campus and remote students in one lecture. Also mentioned as significant was the lack of training, which rendered the exercise one of 'flying blind'. This did not appear to improve with experience. Other problems expressed were mainly to do with logistics involving late delivery of materials to students and lack of proper communication to them of schedules and study requirements in preparation for lectures. There were also concerns expressed about access by students to the technology, and quality and/or lack of transmission.

With regard to the more positive responses, a few sounded as if the issue of whether the students were learning or not was not a matter of relevance. What was more important was the fact that they were required to use the technology and they were responding to this call; e.g. this was just 'normal teaching, nothing fantastic'; and 'I am just doing my job'. One lecturer even described the presence of video cameras in his lecture room as 'only a minor intrusion on lecture delivery'. Perhaps through a combination of this attitude and lack of experience, many lecturers were not making effective use of the technology.

Mode	Change in feelings				
	No change: Pos.	Neg. to Pos.	No change: Neg.	Pos. to Neg.	Total responses
Video broadcast	3	0	4	1	8
Videotape	2	0	3	3	8
Video conference	2	0	0	1	3
Audio conference	1	0	1	1	3
Online	2	0	1	1	4
Total responses	9	0	8	8	26

Table 37.4　Mid-semester lecturer views in comparison with initial feelings

37.7.2 Students

Feedback from students shows that their situation was similar to that of the lecturers in many respects. All but four of the students had no prior experience with learning technologies. None of the students had training in any of the technologies. Also, interestingly, when asked the purpose of the technology in their courses, the large majority of the students responded that it was for receiving lectures and learning materials instead of stimulating student participation and interaction.

It was therefore encouraging to see the students' responses with regard to their initial feelings about using the technology. Nine out of 17 responses indicated initial excitement and comfort with the idea of video broadcast delivery. Likewise, three out of five respondents expressed satisfaction with the idea of receiving material on videotape, and all four students who were to participate in video conferencing did not have any problems with this mode of delivery. By far the most comfortable medium with students was audio conferencing, where eight out of nine students indicated satisfaction with their upcoming participation.

However, some of these feelings changed over the course of the semester. Table 37.5 represents a summary of responses by students comparing their initial reaction to the various technologies to their feelings at least two months in to the semester.

	Change in feelings				
Mode	No change: Pos.	Neg. to Pos.	No change: Neg.	Pos. to Neg.	Total responses
Video broadcast	3	1	5	4	13
Videotape	2	1	0	3	6
Video conference	2	0	0	1	3
Audio conference	5	0	0	1	6
Printed materials	1	0	0	0	0
Total responses	13	2	5	9	28

Table 37.5   Mid-semester student views in comparison with initial feelings

The data in the table encouragingly indicates a large number of respondents who stayed with their initial positive reaction to the various technologies. It also shows two responses that changed from negative initially to positive later on. These students indicated that they found the opportunity provided by the technology to be satisfactory.

On the other hand, Table 37.5 also indicates negative feelings. These are particularly noticeable with the video broadcast mode, where five students started out and remained negative, and four changed from positive to negative. This data represented nine out of 13 respondents, a percentage that is especially significant given that video broadcast was the main mode of all of these courses.

The most common reasons given for negative feelings about video broadcasts were poor quality, or becoming discouraged as a result of lectures being cancelled due to power cuts, equipment breakdown, or other reasons (as a result, these students indicated a preference for the videotape). Mid-semester, students in this group described themselves as 'disappointed' or even 'upset, lost and hopeless'.

37.8 Capacity of the technology to delivery teaching and learning

Factors considered in relation to the capacity of the technology to deliver teaching and learning include lecturer use of support materials outside of the technology, and lecturer and student perceptions of the effectiveness of multi-modal teaching in comparison with face-to-face.

37.8.1 Use of support materials

As was shown in Table 37.3, a few lecturers supported their video broadcast or videotape delivery of lectures with two-way video conferencing or audio conferencing, and most (see footnote in table) used either daily or weekly email support. However, in spite of all of this use of the technology, almost all of the lecturers (15 out of 16) found the need to provide printed materials to their students. Most print materials were sent out weekly through the University's dispatch system.

37.8.2 Lecturer views on effectiveness

In the questionnaire, lecturers were asked to assess their multi-modal teaching experience by rating the effectiveness with which they were able to present content, engage students and assess student progress in comparison to face-to-face teaching. Table 37.6 summarises the responses.

Teaching function	Ability to perform function			
	Effectively	**Satisfactorily**	**With some difficulty**	**With great difficulty**
Present content	3	2	7	4
Engage students	1	3	4	8
Assess progress	0	5	3	8
Total	4	10	14	20

Table 37.6   Number of lecturers indicating ability to perform functions multi-modally by comparison to face-to-face teaching

The data shows that the majority of lecturers found some or great difficulty carrying out all three of the teaching functions during the semester.

Those that answered more negatively seemed mostly to be commenting on video broadcasting. Here are the most common and significant pedagogical difficulties they mentioned, in order of frequency of response:

- *Limited or no opportunity for physical and verbal interaction and feedback*   The medium of video broadcast is one-way, so the opportunity to interact with remote students did not exist at all during lectures. Several lecturers also commented that restriction of movement placed on them because of the need to stay within camera range also greatly inhibited and reduced their ability to choose appropriate techniques for interacting with students within the classroom.

- *Inappropriate course design*   Some lecturers commented that their current classroom strategies did not work for video broadcast delivery of teaching and learning and felt that to be effective, they needed to be repackaged for remote students. As one lecturer phrased it, 'I use an interactive teaching approach that is not conducive to video broadcast.'

- *Required changing assessment strategies to types more suitable to this non-interactive, non-participatory mode*   Lecturers whose courses typically involve group participation, class exercises, and individual and/or group presentations as an important part of assessment found themselves severely handicapped. While these lecturers rewrote the assessment requirements for their remote students, using options such as tests and reports that were more suitable, they saw this as a compromise of course standards.

From the students' perspective, only 1 out of 19 respondents preferred their video broadcast course experience to on-campus studies, although more students (10 out of 14 respondents) preferred it to extension (text-based) studies. For the majority of the latter, the main benefit mentioned was the opportunity for interaction with course lecturers via the support structures of email and audio conferencing.

Students preferred on-campus study because it gave them opportunities for and immediacy of study support and interaction. On the other hand, on the positive side of the experience, one student commented that the lack of available information and resources forced her to be 'more active'.

37.9   Operational issues

Data for operational issues was gathered from lecturer and student comments.

For lecturers, it appears that the main operational difficulties were protocols required by the various media. For instance, many lecturers found the need to restrict their movement to camera range for their live broadcast inhibiting in delivering their pedagogy. There were complaints that media studios were not conducive learning environments because there were students who were camera-shy or found the bright camera lights off-putting.

There were also problems related to equipment and access. Internet sources became ineffective because of limited or no student access to computers with Internet links. Use of fax machines as another means of distributing materials to the Centres had to be limited or abandoned because of poor quality copies.

A concern at the broader level was the need to reschedule lectures because of power cuts in Suva, or to relocate because of equipment breakdown or failure. This often affected the ability of students to receive the broadcast in the region and even caused them to miss lectures. As one lecturer complained: 'expectations have been held out to students that I will repeat classes that could not be transmitted ... when I have indicated that it was logistically impossible to do so'.

In this way and others, operational problems affected the students more than they did lecturers. For those students who remained or became negative about their experience, much of their feeling had to do with operational issues. Power cuts, for instance, were a common and frustrating problem for the Samoan students. In addition, compressed video was for most people distorting and distracting; this coupled with poor transmission quality could lead to more serious learning issues such as the word 'not' giving the sentence a negative meaning, being lost in cyber transit (point made by one interview student)!

Many students complained, too, that the camera did not dwell long enough on lecture notes before shifting back to the lecturer.

Table 37.7 summarises feedback from the students on operational problems they encountered with each of the media they used.

Delivery mode	Operational problems						
	Poor quality			Other issues			
	Picture	Sound	Overheads	Compression	Power cuts	Equipment failure	Not available
Video broadcast	9	9	2	2	2	3	2
Video conference		1				1	
Videotape	1	3	1				
Audio conference		1					

Table 37.7   Number of students indicating operational problems with different modes of learning

37.10   Administrative issues

Various aspects of the video broadcast project were taken care of by different sections of the University. For instance, responsibility for sending out course texts, references and other printed materials rested with the Library. The Media Centre made copies of videotaped lectures and sent these out to the relevant Centres. University Extension (UE) administered student enrolment and provided dispatch services for materials going out to the Centres and for students.

Of the 13 lecturers who responded to the question about facilities for providing supplementary material to remote students, nine indicated displeasure with the services they received. There seemed to be confusion among them about who was responsible for what both at the main campus and at the Centres and a general lack of communication among the various sections involved. Core and supplementary print materials required in conjunction with the video lectures were distributed by various means to students – via the Library, via UE Despatch, by email attachments and by fax. A number of lecturers complained that these did not reach students on time. In one case, a course text reached students five weeks late; in another, course printed materials finally made it to students in the seventh week of study after materials were first misplaced, found in the sixth week and made available to the students involved one week later! This meant that progress through the course was varied among the different groups of students and lecturers had to make adjustments in dealing with their students taking this into account.

This was substantiated by students who indicated problems with receiving hard copies, video materials and email attachments in time to be relevant and useful at the right time. Often, this delay meant students were going back in their schedule to accommodate the material, while lectures scheduled for that time were a fair way in advance.

Another significant cause of administrative difficulties was the lack of responsiveness by Centres to email from Laucala campus. Important queries were not answered even if tagged as urgent, and some lecturers found that print materials sent to Centres by email attachment were not printed and distributed to students. As indicated earlier, the fax option was not effective as copies were often too poor to be reproduced.

Some lecturers did not receive class or student distribution lists until many weeks into the semester and these students did not received materials and/or support from the lecturers until their existence was known. From the student perspective, materials were received in lots and had to be dealt with under pressure.

37.11   Discussion

In semester 2, 2000, USP took a leap forward towards its goal of using USPNet technologies to reach regional students in different ways. However, this leap was precipitated and accelerated by a political crisis outside of the control of the University, rather than by deliberate planning. This research project was able to look at some of the consequences of this rapid change from conventional to multi-modal teaching and learning.

The results show that pressure to deliver courses, lack of time to plan them, lack of coordination both within the main campus and with the Centres and lack of know-how about the technology had a negative impact on USP's attempt to accommodate its full-time students in their remote locations using multimedia means. The factors which led to this impact need to be taken into account in future attempts by the institution to become flexible, in order to make the exercise a viable one for both students and lecturers.

In the following paragraphs, results of data analysis are interpreted and discussed as significant points, in light of the goal of the research to find out how effective the technology was in the provision of learning opportunities to students at a distance.

- For the majority of staff and students, while the experience was an opportunity to continue teaching and learning in difficult times, this opportunity was marred by the problems that characterised it throughout the semester. At best the novelty of the experience was appealing to many, some of whom continued to enjoy it while others became disillusioned. At worst, many realised from the start that this was a form of teaching and learning that needed careful planning and pedagogical expertise as prerequisites to its success.

- Thus many lecturers indicated that video broadcast and multi-modal teaching had to be specifically designed as such to be effective. Teaching and learning opportunities in the classroom such as group discussions and spontaneous class/teacher interactions are not readily transferable via live broadcast, and particularly so when the broadcast is limited to a single camera. Alternative strategies need to be thought out beforehand using both live and delayed possibilities, to achieve the same end. This included assignments specifically designed to be undertaken via appropriate media, keeping as closely as possible to assignment objectives within the course.

- A major shortcoming of the project was the lack of sufficient/satisfactory opportunity for interaction between lecturer and students and among the students themselves. This was articulated by both staff and students as an advantage the latter would have had as on-campus students and a disadvantage as extension students. However, on the positive side, the failure to provide this opportunity was not so much a shortcoming of the technology as it was lack of proper training, preplanning and coordination of the various components of the course during the semester, and also of shortcomings in the provision of and access to the technology.

For example, those lecturers and students who had email contact indicated that this was used to great advantage. Similarly, the main reason that audio conferencing was the most effective technology for both students and teachers was the opportunity it afforded for two-way communication during which such classroom functions as feedback to students, answers to queries and clarifications of points made in the lectures were enabled.

- Coordination is a key ingredient in ensuring that all the parts in a multi-modal experience come together at the right time and the right place. In this respect, constant and regular communication among lecturers, students and administrators is crucial. There was much complaint that messages and queries were not responded to on time or at all. Instructions about who was in charge, scheduling information and procedures for the distribution and collection of materials were often not clear or sometimes not provided. Sometimes crucial information was inaccurate and one consequence of this was the delay in materials reaching Centres and students on time.

Acknowledgements

The authors would like to thank Alanieta Lesuma and Georgina Veilaveyaki for their research assistance, as well as lecturers and students who returned questionnaires and participated in interviews, which provided crucial data for this research project. Thanks are also extended to staff at the four USP Centres who assisted with data collection, and also to technical staff at the University Media Centre for their records of student attendance and for information on the technical aspects of the project. This report is the result of our combined efforts.

37.12   References

Bates, A.W. (1991) Third generation distance education: the challenge of new technology, *Research in Distance Education*, April: 10–15.

Chandra, R. (2000) From dual-mode to multi-mode, flexible teaching and learning: distance education at the University of the South Pacific. Keynote paper presented to the Conference on Distance Education in Small States, The University of the West Indies, Ocho Rios, Jamaica, 27–28 July 2000.

Clark, R.E. (1994) Media will never influence learning, *Educational Technology Research and Development* **42**(2).

Dekkers, J. and Andrews, T. (2000) A meta-analysis of flexible delivery in selected Australian tertiary institutions: how flexible is flexible delivery? Paper published in the ASET/HERDSA International Conference Proceedings, *Flexible Learning for a Flexible Society*. Toowoomba, 3–4 July 2000.

Fischer, M.J. (1996) Integrated learning systems: an application linking technology with human factors and pedagogical principles, *Educational Technology Research and Development* **44**(3).

Forsyth, I. (1991) Never mind the quality: feel the technology, *Aspesa Papers* **11**, Dec.

Heydenrych, J. (2001) Computer mediated communication and WWW: delivery modes and implementation variables: the case of the University of South Africa, *TechKnowLogia*, July/Aug.

Luke, R. (1999) The virtual classroom, *New Outlook*. University of South Australia, June.

Potashnik and Capper (1998) Distance education: growth and diversity, *Finance and Development*. March, 42–5

Tait, A. and Mills, R. (1999) The convergence of distance and conventional education: patterns of flexibility for the individual learner. In *The Convergence of Distance and Conventional Education: Patterns of Flexibility for the Individual Learner*. London and New York: Routledge.

University of the South Pacific (1998) *USP Strategic Plan: Planning for the 4th Decade*. Suva: Fiji: The University of the South Pacific.

38 Exploring the use of multi-modal delivery in the pre-tertiary distance programmes of the University of the South Pacific

Emily Moala

Co-ordinator Pre-Degree Studies Unit, University of the South Pacific, Suva, Fiji

38.1 Introduction

The Pre-Degree Studies Unit (PDSU) at the University of the South Pacific focuses on the preparation of students for tertiary studies. It offers a study programme at the Preliminary and Foundation level, which is equivalent to the last two years of high school in the USP region (years 12 and 13). The programme consists of 22 courses, in science and social science subjects, all offered by distance mode in the 12 member countries of the University.

The 11 academic staff of PDSU are responsible for course writing, course development and the co-ordination of delivery processes in the regional countries. In course writing and course development, the academic staff of PDSU are linked with a designated team of course developers and instructional designers in the Distance Education Unit within the University Extension division of the University.

With the launching of the USPNet 2000, the staff of the PDSU were required to be trained in the use of the latest technology and to be prepared to make use of this provision in the delivery of its courses in the region. The training included the use of video-broadcast, video-conferencing, audiographics and WebCT.

The type of students enrolled in PDSU programmes of study are basically in two broad categories: the school leavers and the mature students. The latter are normally people who have completed secondary schooling and taken up employment for some years. They find that they need to upgrade themselves for various reasons through some formal education therefore taking up Foundation studies. They not only find that getting back to formal education is a challenge at this stage but they are also confronted with the use of new technologies and studying in a distance mode.

Based on the findings of research conducted by University Extension staff on the use of the USPNet technology in the provision of learning opportunities and on the use of audio teleconferencing at the University of the South Pacific (Evans, 2001; Gold and Tuimaleali'ifano, 2001), this chapter is an attempt to find effective means of course delivery and teaching by the distance mode at pre-degree level. The great challenge that is facing providers of pre-degree study materials is to find out what, where and when can the 'new' technology be most effectively used. Up till now the mode of delivery has mostly relied on print materials with some audio and video materials and supported by audio teleconferencing, local tutors and tutorial visits. Where any of the new technologies can be found more effective, one needs to decide whether the existing print based materials can be completely discarded and design print material to support the new modes or continue with the existing printed materials and support them with new technologies.

As the USPNet technology can be found new and unfamiliar to a high percentage of distance learners in the USP region, various questions of credibility and reliability need to be looked into. Are the learners and teachers prepared to use the new technologies? What will be the impact of continuous power failures and maintenance shortfalls on the learners? How does the question of access and equity affect the learners?

38.2   The reality of USP situations

The population of the South Pacific region represents a number of diverse cultures and races, including Micronesians, Melanesians, Polynesians, some 300,000 Indo-Fijians, groups of Chinese as well as part Europeans and others. The use of distance education in the University imposes a 'western' model of tertiary/university education on these cultures. This has brought a lot of stress and problems to learners.

Although the University's distance education services has shown great success throughout the years, it must bear in mind the continuing pressures and the kind of problems arising from this ethnic diversity. Course writers and instructional designers must bear in mind that the students at the other end are required to adapt to a new learning style and cognitive approach to knowledge. There must be a more sensitive approach to resolve the problem of cultural dissonance. There is no easy answer but whatever is done should be able to present 'western' values and others to students in an impartial way giving them a chance to make up their own mind.

With the unique diversity of the USP region and the scattered nature of its geographical locations, the provision of study programmes by distance education has been accepted as a cost-effective means of reaching out to isolated and rural learners. The cost of studying overseas at tertiary and university level is out of reach for the average family in the South Pacific. The cultural implications for young people, especially girls, to leave home and travel to strange and distant countries have made distance education most appropriate. The competition for scholarship and sponsorship to complete studies at a specified time has dominated a lot of educational goals in the Pacific communities.

Studying at home is a preference. However, there still remains the conflicting view of whether studying from home is as academically recognised as studying on campus at a University institution. The mixed feeling of accepting distance education as a means of academic education still dominates the use of the distance mode. There is a predominant social influence in students organising and budgeting their time in order to handle social obligations at home as well as find time to study. The part-time workers are also greatly affected by finding time between work and family duties to do their studies. The responsibilities of a distant learner may be found demanding and can make learning stressful.

There are limited places where students can turn for study. Homes are often small with inadequate space. They are places for social meetings where relatives and neighbours visit at their own time. It is not a place that is conducive to learning. The distant learner remains a part of the social unit at home and in the village. The concept of having education brought to the village is still one that students ponder about. The sense of isolation from the educational medium is made worse if students live on remote islands with poor transport links and no means of electronic communication.

The provision of audio-cassettes allows students to keep in touch with the voice of the teacher. Further to that, the study materials ought to be written in a style that is both conversational and encouraging. Students should be exposed to texts that are motivational. The feedback on assignments should be kept comprehensive and positively helpful. The marker's response needs to reflect personal interest in each student as an individual. The closest personal contact in the islands are the learning support centre staff. They must be aware that they are the link between the University and the students. The exposure of USP headquarter's staff to life experiences in remote areas in the region would promote understanding and sympathy.

38.3   Coping with new technologies

The use of new technologies in distance learning in the USP regional countries has been taken in different ways. There are those who are embracing it with a strong will to adapt and those who accept it with a lot of reservation. People are at different levels of education and therefore pose a variety of reactions to the proposed change. The supporters are too enthusiastic to cope with the reality of the system and the consequential effect. They expect actions and results that are not envisioned in the study materials. The unexpected results and shortfalls in the use of the technology may result in disillusionment.

The antagonistic reaction and reservation may erode the confidence in the course and study materials even before delivery. Reasons for reservations may be due to 'economic constraints or fear of the 'new' (Forsyth, Jolliffe and Stevens, 1999). However, those who readily accept the changes may take change itself as a goal. If change is to result in improving the level of the learner and study opportunities then it is fine. Most of the restructures in educational provisions have occurred because of structural and systematic changes. Another feature of change is 'enforced'. Changes are happening as new technology impacts on education and development.

The competency-based learning approach indicates that learners need to develop a sense of purpose in their education therefore adopting the use of technology in learning. The use of the Internet as a delivery tool allows students to have access to more and a variety of information. Students are faced with the challenge of making the information meaningful to learning. Technology is a tool and not the solution. The use of technology in delivery will not alone assure the quality of education and training.

The initial use of audio-conferencing was to support distance learners who are disadvantaged in terms of isolation and lack of support. However, the quality in an educational system is not enhanced by the application of technologies as such: it is how they are used that matters (Kirkwood, 1998). The full potential of the technology has not been exploited especially with the expected improvement in interaction between tutor and students and among the students themselves. Another identified feature in the actual use of audio conferencing is the low rate of student attendance. Not only that students are still remote from the teaching support centre but it accounts for other administrative structures. Either students are not informed, the timing is unsuitable to students or the experience is not worthwhile (Evans, 1998). Audio conferencing on the whole generally plays an important role in bringing the 'distance' closer by the provision of 'immediate feedback' and dialogue between tutor and student.

38.4   Learner preparedness

There have been many incorrect assumptions made about learning. Often, educational providers and course writers assume that the learner is ready to accept without question any kind of materials and any strategy to deliver those materials. According to the survey carried out by Gold and Tuimaleali'ifano (2001), with the lecturers forced by the situation in the coup to offer courses by distance mode, there was 'very little or no experience or training before they embarked on multimedia course delivery and support' (p. 5). The lecturers were not ready to write courses for multimedia delivery due to the ad hoc nature of the demand.

Apart from the question of student access, quality and lack of transmission, the issue of student preparedness has come out to be a constraint in the use of the new technology. The issue of whether the students were learning or not seemed to be irrelevant. It was more important for lecturers to feel that they were using the technology required to be used for the purpose of delivery. Equally, students showed similar situations with lecturers. There was no prior experience of learning technology and learning through it. Many used technology for the main purpose of receiving lectures and learning materials rather than to participate in learning interaction. The majority of the students preferred face-to-face lectures mainly because of the interaction and immediate support and feedback.

The novelty of the experience in the use of new technology can be appealing to some at the beginning but the reality of the learning outcome may result in disillusionment. Students need to have confidence and be knowledgeable about the learning technologies. Spontaneous interaction is not readily transferable via live broadcasting. Using multimedia as a form of teaching and learning needs careful planning and pedagogical expertise.

38.5   Learning conception

Various studies have identified factors affecting the outcome of formal learning: how students affect learning tasks; conception of learning and conditions of learning. Of the three factors, students learning conceptions tend to adversely affect learning by distance. Students have been brought up in a secondary education system where it is highly teacher directed and teacher dependent. The teacher gives what to learn and how to learn. The students heavily rely on the teacher. Students hold mainly reproduction learning conceptions leading to surface approaches to learning (Mugler and Landbeck, 1997). In a distance education delivery where students depend entirely on the course package, the course providers should facilitate deep understanding and culturally appropriate approaches.

The condition of learning by distance is quite different. Interaction is restricted between staff and students despite the use of telephone, satellite and electronic mail. Support centres in the region often call for the use of summer schools and tutorial visits from lecturers. The access to learning resources such as libraries, multimedia and computing facilities is also limited. The development of telecommunication facilities and Internet compensated for this but this is only true where telecom facilities are good and reliable.

The heavy dependence of students on the printed material they receive results in students failing to become critical, independent thinkers (Garrison, 1993; Ratuva, 1996). For students to be critical and independent thinkers, dialogue with staff and fellow students in learning communities is essential. The materials that are designed to be 'stand alone' and require no other reading and interaction may discourage independent learning. The structure of the materials and its context should be linked to the study strategies. The 'missing teacher' is a feature of extension studies that needs to be compensated within the study package.

38.6 Learning strategies

A study of extension students at USP identified two strategies predominantly used by students. These are the 'pragmatic' strategy and the 'sequential' strategy. Whatever strategy students use in learning, are found to be assessment-driven. A majority of the students learn through a pragmatic strategy where they only concentrate on what is required for the assignments, tests and exams. They therefore would only read the relevant texts. They normally claim that they have no time to read others. Those who learn through a sequential strategy follow the guide step by step but are sometimes forced to be pragmatic because of 'deadlines'.

The materials need to be culturally appropriate and to generate culturally sensitive pedagogy. The content should contain the concepts of the course designed in a way that students can relate to through their cultural experience and be developed in a sequence with some aid to help the students relate to them.

According to Landbeck and Mugler, the secondary school system in the South Pacific is very teacher dominated and described by students as consisting of 'spoonfeeding'. The curriculum is 'examination driven' and the effect on the learners have carried through to higher education. The survey found no significant changes in learning style across cohort of student in different years at University (Landbeck and Mugler, 1995).

The students' experience of secondary education plays an important role in determining their conceptions of learning and their approaches to studying. Given the reality of learners in the USP region, the effective integrating of new technologies into the learning environment is challenging. The lack and inequity of student access to the different levels of technologies and the different level of technological experience within the group of course writers are serious issues of concern. A recommended step to take is to separate the technology of development and delivery. There is also a need to develop the multimedia component using a familiar development environment rather than the specialised expensive and unfamiliar software. The training time may be kept to a minimum and the writers can remain focused on pedagogy. Overall, there should be collaboration among the diverse and multi-cultural team of experts in subject matter, distance education and media.

In a study of 'distance education in the South Pacific', students viewed education as a privilege rather than a right ... such positive attitude should be turned to distance education (Robert, 1993). Because of its cost effectiveness, distance education has been used as a method of expanding formal education.

South Pacific countries often experience problems in the supply of electricity and its reliability. This is seen as a major constraint in the use of technology and the print medium has been the core learning resource, supplemented with face-to-face contact and the occasional use of radio, audio-cassettes and satellite. It has also been claimed that one reason for the traditional teacher-centred schooling in the South Pacific is the limited resources. Students largely depend on the teacher to interpret the text which they in turn memorise for the tests and examinations. The emphasis is upon learning factual information for regurgitation rather than using facts to advance arguments.

The extension students must make a quick transition from this learning dependent environment to one in which they must become independent learners. When this is difficult, students are left behind and feel a failure. It can be a devastating and discouraging experience to suddenly become isolated and separated in time and space from teachers and the classroom. Becoming an independent learner takes time and determination. The provision of distance learning must take this into consideration and facilitate the pedagogical approach through the most effective medium.

The lack of books and reading materials in the homes and the learning environment and the difficulty in acquiring reading materials in schools have led to the 'talk and chalk' approach. The one way communication in big classes results in children learning to rely on listening and there is little opportunity to develop independent learning skills. The emphasis on the print medium in distance learning may be found daunting. Students need to acquire the skills of extracting what is important to learn. Lacking this skill may relate to a situation where there is a tendency to emphasise rote-learning rather than interacting with the text to get the meaning.

At pre-degree level, the challenge would be to find a strategy to counteract the learning problems that originate from the schooling system students undertake before entry to USP. The staff should be made aware of the problems and to be sympathetic with students. The teaching staff must facilitate learning methods geared to the learning needs of students at Pre-degree level and quickly 'remove' students from their dependent learning techniques. The students need to be orientated and taken through a learning system that will permeate the ability to think and work independently. Additionally, the study materials should be intended to be 'user friendly' in its presentation and to give direction using the various techniques of effective instructional design. The learning approach should attempt to address the problem by ensuring that the students are 'weaned' from the schooling approach and allow students to decide what they will study. There should be careful monitoring of all study materials in order to achieve the transition from dependent to independent learning. The material needs a sequential development of the subject content rather than handling them as discrete units. Sequences of subjects must be treated holistically so that the pedagogical processes of change are well developed as the subject content.

38.7 Language problems

Students entering university studies are often assumed to be equipped with sufficient standard of English. Failure to acquire the expected competence often result in withdrawal or failure.

Because of the diversity of language found in the university region, the problem in the use of English language as a medium of teaching has persisted and no real solution has been able to minimise its effect on student learning. This is worse in situations of distance learners as they are left to translate the study materials themselves without the presence of a lecturer. The use of technical and foreign concepts in the study materials can make learning rather difficult and depressing. Learning in a language which is not their mother tongue are intensified by their isolation from the teaching staff. Students who are not readily accessible to electricity, phones and the support centres rely heavily on the material. A lot of time therefore is taken in reading and re-reading the texts again and again.

Apart from the question of language competence, readability of the study materials is often a problem. When students are confronted with readability problems, they can only save themselves in the process through rote-learning. This cannot be solved by instructional designers alone. Furthermore, the use of audio-technologies makes it worse as lecturers normally do not elaborate or explain definitions that are expected to have been understood by students without the situation of interaction.

38.8   Challenges in the use of technologies

The use of technologies in teaching and learning has been an educational advancement with invaluable benefits. Without technology, higher learning would be restricted to few learners and small range or resources. The learning environment is bursting its previous bounds with more people gaining access to a wider range of people and things. The duration and pace of interaction has changed (Ehrmann, 1999). Technology has allowed interaction between students and students, students with experts and students with academic resources.

All changes have disadvantages and advantages. Similarly, the challenges in the use of technology will cause harm as well as good. Information on the Web is seen to be disorganised and of questionable validity. Learners need to gather, organise and critique information in order to learn. They need to learn the various associated skills especially to master the new genres of electronic communication. In making use of the opportunities, they should acquire the desire and ability to take more responsibility for their own learning, individually and collectively. They should be more conscious of how they learn and be able to assess their own learning and be able to take joy in learning.

According to Ehrmann, technology provides for information literacy and proficiency at intercultural communication having the exposure to different learners from different cultural backgrounds and learning interests. Interpersonal interaction is usually an ingredient for helping students learn. They become role models for one another and they learn to possess personal skills. Interpersonal interaction teaches students how to deal with other people especially preparing them for admittance into communities of enquiry and professional practice. Students who worry about making the incorrect response in a face-to-face situation feels protected by 'facelessness'. However, it is my greatest fear that if the ingredients for student learning is not pounded well to be digested by the regional students then the outcome of academic constipation will be found more detrimental than intellectual starvation.

38.9   Recommendations

1. The use of a multi-modal and flexible learning strategy may cater for the diversity in cultural, social, economic, language and academic levels.
2. There should be more research to assess the pros and cons of open learning and face-to-face in the context of the rapid use of technologies in the Pacific.
3. The 'technology of development' should be carefully integrated into the 'technology of delivery' with a pedagogical approach that is appropriate and effective to the cultural context of diversified learning styles and learning situations.
4. From the above recommendations, those responsible for the provision of distance education should:

- the social, political, economic and cultural contexts in the region;

- develop culturally appropriate curriculum and approaches appropriate to students' learning style;

- concentrate on developing multi-modal delivery strategies to accommodate the multi-flexible learning contexts;

- be aware of the diversified learning need of the students;

- ensure that study materials are pedagogically designed to accommodate the need of students and their learning styles;

- be aware of the difficulties arising from the application of 'western' model approaches to other cultures with great diversity;

- appreciate that the philosophy of distance education may take a long time for people in the Pacific region to accept let alone the use of 'new' technology;

- appreciate the flexibility in integrating technology into the development and delivery of learning materials.

38.10   References

Ehrman S.C. (1999a) Access and/or quality? redefining choices in the third revolution. <??>

Ehrman, S.C. (1999b) Grand challenges raised by technology: will this revolution be a good one? <??>

Ehrman, S.C. (2000) Technology and education revolution: ending the cycle of failure, *Liberal Education*, Fall: 40–9.

Evans, J. (1999) Audio teleconferencing at the University of the South Pacific: the case of 'satellite' tutorials. Paper for 19th ICDE World Conference, Vienna, June.

Forsyth I., Jolliffee, A. and Stevens, D. (1999) *Delivering a Course: Practical Strategies for Teachers, Lecturers and Trainers*, 2nd edn. London: Kogan Page.

Gold, M. and Tuimaleali'ifano, E. (2001) Jumping right in: a report on the USP video broadcast experience. Paper for 9th ISL Symposium, Edinburgh, Sept.

Kirkwood, A. (1998) New media mania: can information and communication technologies enhance the quality of open and distance learning, *Distance Education* 19(2): 228–41.

Landbeck R. and Mugler, F. (2000) Distance learners of the South Pacific: study strategies, learning conditions, and consequences for course design, *Journal of Distance Education* 15(1).

Laurillard D. (1998) *Rethinking University Teaching: A Framework for the Effective Use of Educational Technology*. London: Routledge.

McMechan P. (1995) *A Commonwealoth Asia/Pacific Distance Education Network*. University of the South Pacific, Suva.

Matthewson, C. and Va'a, R. (1999) The South Pacific: kakai mei tahi. In K. Harry (ed.), *Higher Education through Open and Distance Learning*. London: Routledge.

Northwott, P., Hamilton, B., Inglis, A., Kelly, M. and Livington, K. (1981) Pedagogical reports: the Lund studies in correspondence education. <??>

Richardson, J.T.E., Roger, L. and Francis, M. (1995) *Approaches to Studying in Higher Education: A Comparative Study in the South Pacific*. Carfax Publishing Ltd.

Robert, D. (1997) *Distance Education in the South Pacific: Some Reflections for the Future...* University of Tasmania, Tasmania.

Tremewan T. and Koroi, T. (1998) How far can one language reach? English in distance education at the University of the South Pacific. <??>

Tuimaleali'ifano, E. (1997) *Coping with Diversity Education at the University of the South Pacific: A Discussion of Selected Approaches and Initiatives*. University of New England.

Williams, E.B. (2001) Crossing borders: women and ICTs in open and distance learning in the South Pacific. <??>

39 Learning from our experiences? Audio and audiographic tutorials at the University of the South Pacific

Jennifer Evans

University of the South Pacific, Suva, Fiji

39.1 Regional challenges and distance education

In 1971, just two years after the establishment of the University of the South Pacific (USP), it began offering distance education courses. Only one year later it was able to use audio teleconferencing via satellite to support those courses. As Matthewson and Va'a (1999) point out: 'Distance education in the Pacific "small states" is notable ... for the use of a particular technology: satellite for teaching support. From 1972 ... USP pioneered the sustained use of satellite technology for educational delivery' (p. 283).

It is not remarkable that USP moved so quickly into distance education and boldly declared itself to be a dual mode university well before many universities scarcely knew the meaning of the term. The regional nature of the university with its 12 small island country members (Cook Is., Fiji, Kiribati, Marshall Is., Nauru, Niue, Solomon Is., Tokelau, Tonga, Tuvalu, Vanuatu and Samoa) and its mission to deliver higher education to their citizens have dominated USP's concerns about access and equity. It was clear that there were very real challenges of distance and traditional face-to-face teaching was never going to be adequate for USP's needs. Small populations scattered over millions of kilometres of Pacific Ocean, and relatively low incomes, meant that from its beginnings USP was faced with isolated students who were unable to afford to come to study on a university campus located far from their home countries. As a regional institution, the university had to be cognisant of the fact that 'member governments applying precious resources to a university thousands of miles away expected it to reach their communities, have a strong in-country presence and contribute to their ongoing development as newly independent states' (Matthewson and Va'a, 1999, p. 279).

There are now three USP campuses; the main campus in Suva, Fiji's capital city, and smaller campuses in Vanuatu (School of Law) and Samoa (School of Agriculture). There are also 12 national USP Centres and a number of sub-centres. Despite regional commitments, not surprisingly given Fiji's relatively large population compared with other USP member countries, 75 per cent of all USP students are located in Fiji (4350 out of 5792 FTES in the year 2000). Even among the Extension students, Fiji Islanders constitute the vast majority (70.5 per cent or 1541 out of 2187 FTES) (USP, 2001, p. 1.6).

It is perhaps more surprising that in a region with limited financial resources, difficult and expensive telecommunications, and a relatively low level of technology uptake we should find the early adoption of a sophisticated educational technology such as audio teleconferencing via satellite. However, technological innovations in this area have largely been enabled and driven by international aid, combined with the obviously very attractive and useful prospect of being able to communicate effectively across the huge distances of the USP region. Audio teleconferencing has had many uses over the years. It has enabled valuable administrative links between USP's campuses and Centres; allowed discussion between teaching staff (mostly centrally based in Suva) and tutors in remote locations; and provided the opportunity of a forum for regional associations (without expensive and difficult travel arrangements). Most importantly from an educational point of view, it has made tutorials possible for distance students who may be especially disadvantaged in terms of isolation and lack of learner support.

39.2   Satellite history

USP first became part of the PEACESAT (Pan Pacific Education and Communication Experiment by Satellite) network using ATS-1 (Applications Technology Satellite) in 1972. This was a demonstration project involving the University of Hawaii with the objective of studying 'the benefits arising from direct conference communications between groups with like interests in widely separated countries of the Pacific' (Apted and Livingston, 1981, p. 17). In 1974, USP was invited by NASA to establish its own network on ATS-1 and this was the beginning of the USPNet, USP's own telecommunications system. The capacity of this early system was limited and did not connect to all USP Centres. Some countries were linked by UHF radio but the quality of transmission was unstable and often inadequate for conducting tutorials. By the late 1990s only six USP Centres were effectively linked with Suva.

It was not until the launch of the upgraded USPNet in the year 2000 that USP was able to connect to all 12 of its nations via satellite. The new system, a dedicated VSAT telecommunications network entirely owned and operated by USP, was constructed at a cost of about US$7 million dollars and with estimated annual recurrent costs of about $US500,000 (Va'a, 2000, p. 62). This has largely been funded by Japan, New Zealand and Australia, with some assistance from the USP member countries. The technological possibilities provided by the upgraded USPNet, including video conferencing, video broadcasting, computer conferencing and Internet access, are allowing even the remotest USP Centres to sample the delights of the information age. However, given constraints such as limited computer access for students, narrow bandwidths and the restriction of video conferencing to Suva linking with only one other country at a time, audio teleconferencing is likely to remain a core technology for USP for the near future. The data transfer capacity of USPNet has also made audiographics possible and this offers potential to improve the delivery options in audio teleconferencing tutorials.

39.3   Modes of delivery

The majority of distance courses at USP have been, and still are, essentially standalone print-based courses with some multimedia components, such as audio and video tapes. This is influenced by resources and capacity, but is also a reflection of a prevailing institutional philosophy that is concerned with serving all students in the USP region; i.e. even if students are located on small remote islands without access to a USP Centre or tutor, poor communications, and even without electricity, they should still be able to complete a USP Extension course without undue disadvantage.

39.3.1   The correspondence model and on-line learning

Recent experiments with more flexible, multi-modal, multi-media approaches, and even online components, are moving away from catering for worst case scenarios of student location and resources. The majority of USP's students are not in such circumstances and to be fair to the majority and their needs USP has to be forward looking and innovative in its approach to learning technologies. However, as a developing country university, it is most definitely on the wrong side of the global digital divide, and the route on to the information superhighway has to be plotted extremely cautiously.

We also have to remember that the correspondence model of distance education, based on printed educational materials, is very suitable in the USP context and has served it very well over the years. Beginning with just six courses and 150 students in 1971, the extramural arm of USP, 'University Extension', has grown over 30 years to be a relatively large and complex organisation. As the opening of last year's *Review of Distance and Flexible Learning at USP* rather grandly put it:

> Its accomplishments this year, in providing approximately 100,000 pieces of course material to over 10,000 distance learners in twelve countries and across 33 million square kilometres of Pacific Ocean, is a tremendous achievement and one we fully acknowledge. (Lockwood *et al.*, 2000, p. iii)

In speaking of distance education worldwide, Sir John Daniel points out, 'correspondence education is a robust and effective form of instruction' that has proven its 'longevity and reliability' (1999, pp. 51, 56). Interestingly he also draws attention to the fact that its tradition, focused on individual learning and asynchronous communication, most closely resembles the emerging pedagogy of online education: 'With the rise of on-line teaching the correspondence tradition is now much the dominant mode of distance learning around the world' (Daniel, 1999, p. xviii). With its strong print-based distance education foundation, USP is probably well placed in terms of skill and pedagogical understanding to enter on-line education. But it must certainly take care not to throw out a very valuable, healthy baby with the bath water in embracing online learning with its many hazardous teething problems. In this sense USP has the advantage of not being an early adopter and should be able to gain from studying the sometimes costly experience of other institutions and emerging principles of good practice in this relatively new form of educational delivery.

39.3.2   Extending the synchronous classroom

A different institutional profile is presented in relation to the synchronous communication of remote classroom teaching, the other major approach to distance education. USP was an early adopter of the telecommunications developments in the 1970s that made for the more effective linking of groups in locations distant from each other. As already mentioned, it ranks among the pioneers of educational satellite technology.

Apted and Livingston (1981) mention two experimental vocational short courses in the 1970s that were principally delivered through audio teleconferencing, but otherwise it appears that USP's educational use of satellite technology has predominantly been used as a support mechanism for its print-based courses. Audio teleconferencing sessions, or 'satellite' tutorials as they are called colloquially at USP, are offered at the discretion of the course tutor. The number of tutorials for each course varies considerably with some offering weekly or fortnightly sessions and others only one or two sessions over a complete semester (18 weeks).

Attendance at 'satellite' tutorials is optional for students and is not related to assessment. The reasons for this are again tied to the perceived inequality of offering a service to only some students of the region. Students can be excluded either because their local centre cannot be connected to the network (in the past because there were no connections to some centres or now because of occasional technical problems); or because it is not feasible to attend a centre because of distance, a lack of transport, incompatibility with work or family commitments or other difficulties. There is no compulsion, little expectation, reward or incentive for those involved in 'satellite' tutorials. It is a great credit to the commitment of USP staff that so much activity does take place in this area of distance education at USP. Table 39.1 indicates the number of courses that are supported in this way.

Year/semester	Total no. courses offered by extension	No. of courses with audio tutorial support	Percentage of courses supported over whole year
1998 s1	98	42	
1998 s2	76	43	
1998 total	**174**	**85**	**49 per cent**
1999 s1	90	47	
1999 s2	100	50	
1999 total	**190**	**97**	**51 per cent**
2000 s1	102	72	
2000 s2	160	89	
2000 total*	**262**	**161**	**61 per cent**

* The sudden increase in courses offered and supported in 2000 is related to the need to cope with the disruptions to the normal running of on campus courses due to the attempted coup and subsequent civil unrest.
Source: Evans (1999); Veilaveyaki et al. (2001)

Table 39.1   Courses offered by distance education and audio teleconferencing tutorial support

39.4   Learning our lessons

39.4.1   Research and practice

It is difficult to trace fully the history of USP satellite use as much of it is contained in USP internal documents that have not been comprehensively stored or archived. This is possibly a reflection on the relative lack of an institutional research culture in regards to distance education until the last few years, although it has certainly been raised as an issue in the past and some individuals have produced a notable body of work.

The need to build up evidence from more institutional research in order to inform practice was considered crucial in the USP *Review* by Lockwood *et al.* (2000). They saw a need for all USP staff to be:

encouraged to research and evaluate ... using USPNet and USP's flexible learning models so that the experiences can be documented, codified and fed back into the institutional memory and policy making system. USPNet and the distance teaching operation generally are expensive technologies. It will be important to evaluate their utilisation systematically if they are to be efficiently and effectively used to serve the Pacific student community. (p. 107)

In 1981, Maurice Apted (the Satellite Programme Officer) and Kevin Livingston (the Co-ordinator of Extension Studies) produced a very interesting report on USP's first ten years (1971–81) of teleconferencing via satellite in distance education. In their summary of that paper they pointed to the needs for planning and organisation before the audio teleconferencing process, and for preparing staff and students for their contributions and participation in the active process of the audio teleconferencing sessions. They also urged the need for a 'post-active' phase where 'the experience of distance educators and the teleconference organisers merge' in an 'evaluation process' (p. 39). They were drawing attention to the need for analysis and documentation, in short the kind of systematic institutional research that Lockwood *et al.* are prescribing for the newer dimensions of educational technology at USP and USPNet. It seems that Apted and Livingston's recommendations were not acted on.

Apted also wrote guideline booklets for staff and students on the use of the satellite for tutorials. Williams and Gillard (1986) commented on the good advice given in these booklets, but concluded: 'Unfortunately, due to staff changes and in particular the loss of the communications manager position, such guidelines have not been disseminated for a number of years' (p. 264). In 2001, Williams's statement is still pertinent. No written guidelines are currently available for staff or students involved in audio teleconferencing sessions, although these would certainly be useful.

Williams and Gillard's 1986 paper was based on research carried out in 1983–84 because of a concern about the quality and effectiveness of audio teleconferencing. Their observations revealed 'less participation than is desirable in satellite tutorials' (p. 261). Student attendance was generally low, many tutors used the tutorials for 'lecturing', and there were few attempts to use techniques to encourage student participation. The authors' interventions to improve the tutorials in terms of achieving 'optimal interactivity' through advice and workshops with tutors led them to conclude fairly optimistically that 'there are indications that desirable changes are taking place' (p. 261).

Ten years later, in 1996, I began working at USP and was impressed by the satellite technology used in University Extension. I was also struck by how much audio teleconferencing was taken for granted. It was just something that USP did and received relatively little special attention. I carried out some research on the audio tutorials that took place over 1998 and questioned the staff who conducted them. My results echoed many of Williams and Gillard's 1986 perceptions. Most noticeable were low student attendance (average attendance no more than 15 per cent of enrolled students) and tutor dissatisfaction with the level of interaction. While almost all tutors acknowledged the interactive potential of audio teleconferencing and the obvious importance of providing student/tutor and peer interaction and feedback for distance students, they also found this extremely difficult to achieve. Of the 42 tutors who took tutorials 35 answered my questionnaire. Of these 91 per cent (32) admitted that they ended up doing nearly all the talking and 'lectured' rather than facilitated a tutorial, with 60 per cent (21) indicating that this was almost always the case

(Evans, 1999). What was going on in satellite tutorials was obviously not satisfactory to the majority of participants especially if their major purpose was seen as interaction, and perhaps if it was not, then audio teleconferencing was not the most appropriate technology. Audio teleconferencing has been identified as *not* being an effective medium for delivering lectures (Bates, 1995, p. 165; Robinson, 1984, p. 129).

It may be that the perception of audio teleconferencing as an extension or imitation of the face-to-face classroom can lead institutions and tutors to assume that no particular techniques or pedagogy apply. While USP satellite operators can offer tutors technical assistance on the working of equipment, no special training is offered on the application of audio teleconferencing as an effective teaching and learning tool. It appears that to a large extent the institution has provided the technology and let the pedagogy take care of itself. Nevertheless many writers, including those referring specifically to USP such as Apted, Williams and Gillard, have clearly indicated the need to recognise the distinct requirements of audio teleconferencing as a medium:

> appropriate planning and instructional development must take place, as with any educational exercise. It must not be assumed either that the medium is perfectly transparent, nor that it is some other medium, such as contiguous teaching, or a telephone. It must be dealt with in its own right. (Williams and Gillard, 1986, p. 274)

Tuimaleali'ifano (1993) drew attention to the 'ad hoc' and 'reactive' nature of the USP satellite tutorial support programme and the need for 'research and user training' to direct the technology 'more realistically towards the diversity of students of the USP region' (p. 291). One of the difficulties in developing a more structured, organised and consistent approach to the educational use of audio teleconferencing has been that overall responsibility for the quality and effectiveness of 'satellite' tutorials has not clearly been the concern of any one section within the institution. University Extension staff are informally involved in staff development and training through the course development process. Content specialists from the faculty who are unfamiliar with distance education philosophy and conventions become oriented to these in the active process of working with a team to produce a course in the distance mode. 'Satellite' tutorials are an optional extra and not an integrated part of this process and what a tutor should choose to do at the point of course delivery, such as in an audio teleconferencing session, is not part of the University Extension staff remit. More formal staff development and training have come under the University's Centre for Enhancement of Learning and Teaching (CELT), but their focus has been more on campus and face-to-face teaching. However, with USP's move into a greater diversity of educational technologies and the possibilities of the USPNet, University Extension staff are being given more diverse responsibilities in staff development and training, and there should be greater possibilities for collaboration with CELT. The move into audiographics is receiving attention and the increased profile of USPNet is creating a situation of greater accountability for the use of its resources.

39.4.2 Institutional amnesia, laissez faire policy and the learning organisation

USP's early involvement in using audio teleconferencing by satellite to tutor the remote student has not given it an institutional lead in this field. After 30 years' experience, the level of practitioner expertise appears patchy and issues that were raised more than 20 years ago are still unresolved. All too often the University's institutional memory seems to rely on knowledge that is stored in the heads of one or two individuals, or information that exists only in the realms of oral tradition. It suffers from an institutional amnesia that makes it very difficult to establish practices, procedures and sound policies based on the learned lessons of past experiences and achievements.

In relation to the question of establishing policies and practices, USP is influenced by its regional situation. In being owned by 12 different countries it must satisfy 12 ministers and ministries of education. In terms of policy it is also operating in an extremely fluid situation at the regional and national level. This 'laissez-faire higher education policy' was the first key point the Lockwood *et al. Review* (2000) raised in the analysis of the USP context: 'The lack of a clear policy framework may have resulted in a degree of duplication, unfocused programming and a lack of integrated provision – so vital if scarce resources are to be used efficiently for higher education in the region' (p. 1).

Having to operate without a clearly given policy framework is particularly challenging for an organisation of USP's complexity and it does have an impact at many levels of the University's activities.

The situation of institutional difficulty in learning from experience however is not particularly related to the uniqueness of USP's situation. Rather it should be seen in the context of the conservatism of institutions of education in general. Most universities and schools have until relatively recently largely been free from financial accountability in terms of profits and competition. This is a blessing because they can be driven by higher ideals than the dollar, but a handicap in leaving them prone to be inefficient conservative organisations that are not easily open to change or innovation:

> Most schools, and for that matter the traditional distance education institutions, are not learning communities. They are simply closed organized structures designed to turn uneducated individuals into educated ones. They do themselves, as social entities, not learn and are not designed to do so. (Visser, 1997, p. 3)

By contrast, businesses are often complex adaptive systems that learn and change to survive. If USP were a commercial enterprise audio teleconferencing would have probably been evaluated and disposed of years ago, along with all attempts to provide education for the smaller countries of the region, as being unnecessary and unprofitable. Fortunately, this is not the case.

39.5 An appropriate technology?

Audio teleconferencing as a learning technology has clearly had its pitfalls and weaknesses at USP, but are these outbalanced by its strengths and potential? Time for audio teleconferencing at the Suva studio is heavily booked, with 70 out of 111 courses offering audio tutorial support in the first semester of 2001. This suggests that USP staff consider it worth persisting with its use. Is it really an appropriate educational technology? There are many reasons to believe that the answer is 'yes'.

39.5.1 Doing the possible

Circumstances outside of the control of distance educators at USP have brought about the provision of telecommunications satellite technology. The equipment for audio teleconferencing exists. It can reach all of the countries of the USP region, and despite some of the shortcomings discussed in this chapter, it is a technology with which the institution has some experience and familiarity. Until there are greater advances in computer access and provision, or greater bandwidths and bridging possibilities for video conferencing, audio teleconferencing is likely to be able to support more students and more courses than other available educational technologies at the present time. As a technology it is also affordable because USP now owns the satellite. It's there, so it would seem sensible to make the best of it. If the satellite capacity is not fully used then in effect resources are wasted.

39.5.2 Serving student needs

USP has made a positive commitment in its *Strategic Plan* to 'more flexible teaching and learning' (1999, p. 8) and is aware of global developments in higher education and the convergence of distance and conventional education. However, for the foreseeable future at USP there will be genuinely distant students in the region with little local support. There may be additional problems of second or third language use, inadequate study conditions at home, difficult access to any information resources apart from course materials, no local library, and a lack of familiarity with tertiary level study. Students facing such obstacles can benefit from having the social interaction of the synchronous classroom extended to them, and audio teleconferencing is a means of doing this.

Discussion, collaboration, group learning are important parts of the educational process. It is possible to generate social exchange and learning communities asynchronously online, but technical and resource constraints mean this can only be an option for a small proportion of USP courses. The print-based correspondence model that must serve the majority can offer activities within the text, perhaps at best an interactive CD-ROM, but the social element of learning is missing. Audio teleconferencing is a feasible way to break the loneliness of the long-distance learner.

39.5.3 Independent learning, pedagogy and culture

Distance students may be expected to be independent learners but few of USP's students will have been prepared for this role by their schooling: 'Throughout the South Pacific the schooling provided is, usually by Western standards, authoritarian and traditionally teacher-centred' (Roberts, 1993, p. 266). On the whole, students are used to being told what to do, when to do it, and learning by rote. They are not used to taking the initiative, questioning the teacher, or carrying out independent research as is often expected at university level. USP has an obligation to provide forms of student support to help students make the transition to forms of study and learning that may be unfamiliar and appear to be at odds with cultural norms and traditional ways of showing respect for status and hierarchy.

The oral synchronous nature of audio teleconferencing as a technology gives it an advantage in terms of its cultural appropriateness:

> That higher education solutions in Commonwealth 'small states' should lie in asynchronous, electronic delivery undertaken virtually alone is culturally questionable. Pacific providers expand their human contact and synchronous communication networks for reasons other than technology unfriendly conditions. (Matthewson and Va'a, 1999, p. 288)

If the sage is going to be pushed off the stage in the Pacific it will have to be done in a culturally sensitive way. Audio teleconferencing, used imaginatively and interactively, could be used as a tool to help students break away from passive expectations of the one-way transmission of knowledge and on to an understanding and enjoyment of a more active constructivist role in the creation of their own learning. As Young and Marks-Maran say, 'The challenge of distance learning is creatively establishing learning-support structures to enable students to engage with each other, through the activities in the package, and with the teacher, to allow the learning to be interactive and co-constructive' (1999, p. 182).

39.5.4   Audio and audiographic learning

While online asynchronous learning is the main focus of global attention in education technology, distance education programmes are still making quite extensive use of the synchronous medium of audio and audiographic learning. In the USA for example the University of Wisconsin, which like USP began using audio teleconferencing in the 1970s, now runs 'WisView' an audiographics network that operates in 25 cities (UW-Extension, 2000). Over the years there have been many favourable reports on the use of audio teleconferencing as a viable and effective learning technology (e.g. Garrison, 1990; Hardy and Alcott, 1995; Robinson, 1994). Burge and Roberts describe the interactive techniques of audio and audiographic learning as the 'cornerstone of the information highway' (1998, p. 71). In Australia, results of a study by McLoughlin and Oliver (1998) 'affirm that audiographics environments can be designed to foster higher order thinking, and both the audio channel and the visual channel can contribute to a communicative setting where learner dialogue and exchange of ideas are fostered' (p. 262).

Audiographics only became possible late in 2000 so experience of using this technology has been limited. In 2001, 21 tutors are making use of this facility in some way. Initial interviews with these staff are indicating that this may be a very positive development in making 'satellite' tutorials work more successfully. 'Graphics' are sometimes text, but are often prepared attractively in colour using Powerpoint, and are adding greater interest to the sessions. Photographs of the relevant tutor are shown at the beginning of the tutorial, so adding an important personal touch. Also, after the tutorial, the audiographics may be accessed by students in their own time on computerised archives. After only five sessions, one particularly enthusiastic tutor said that she had 'hated' the audio only sessions but was now feeling that she and her students are getting much more satisfaction from their meetings.

Of course, this is not to say that audiographic learning is the magic bullet, but new moves mean that there is opportunity to take a fresh look. Interestingly, audio teleconferencing emerged quite positively from the research of Gold and Tuimaleali'ifano (2001) on multimedia experiments at USP as a 'comfortable medium' for students and one that was valued for the communication opportunities that it afforded.

Content specialists and tutors, distance educators, administrators, technical staff and students all need to cooperate and communicate to create appropriate teaching and learning strategies and policies for the South Pacific context. Audio teleconferencing does have the potential to support distance education more effectively at USP if the obvious needs for planning, research, evaluation and training are seriously revisited.

39.6   References

Apted, M. and Livingston, K. (1981) Teleconferencing via satellite in a distance education programme: the USP experience 1971–1981. Paper for the Australian & South Pacific External Studies Association 5th Forum, Suva.

Bates, A.W. (1995) *Technology, Open Learning and Distance Education*. London: Routledge.

Burge, E.J. and Roberts, J.M. (1998) *Classrooms with a Difference* Montreal: McGraw-Hill.

Daniel, J.S. (1999) *Mega-Universities and Knowledge Media: Technology Strategies for Higher Education*, rev. edn. London: Kogan Page.

Evans, J. (1999) Audio teleconferencing at the University of the South Pacific: the case of 'satellite' tutorials. Paper for the 19th ICDE World Conference, Vienna, June.

Garrison, D.R. (1990) An analysis and evaluation of audio teleconferencing to facilitate education at a distance, *American Journal of Distance Education* 4(3): 13–26.

Gold, M. and Tuimaleali'ifano, E. (2001) Jumping right in: a report on the USP video broadcast experience. Paper for the 9th ISL Symposium, Edinburgh, Sept.

Hardy, D.W. and Olcott, D. Jr (1995) Audio teleconferencing and the adult learner: strategies for effective practice, *American Journal of Distance* 9(1): 44–59.

Lockwood, F., Smith, A. and Yates, C. (2000) *Review of Distance and Flexible Learning at the University of the South Pacific*, Aug.

McGoughlin, C. and Oliver, R. (1998) Planning a telelearning environment to foster higher order thinking, *Distance Education* 19(2): 242–64.

Matthewson, C. and Va'a, R. (1999) The South Pacific: kakai mei tahi. In K. Harry (ed.), *Higher Education through Open and Distance Learning*. London: Routledge, 277–91.

Roberts, D. (1993) Distance education in the South Pacific: some reflections for the future .... In T. Nunan (ed.), *Distance Education Futures*. Adelaide: University of South Australia, 241–60.

Robinson, B. (1984) Telephone teaching. In A.W. Bates (ed.), *The Role of Technology in Distance Education*. London: Croom Helm.

Tuimaleali'ifano, E. (1993) Coping with diversity in distance education at the University of the South Pacific. In T. Nunan (ed.), *Distance Education Futures*. Adelaide: University of South Australia, 279–96.

USP (1999) *USP Strategic Plan*. Suva: University of the South Pacific.

USP (2001) *USP Statistics*. Suva: University of the South Pacific, Planning & Development Office.

Va'a, R. (2000) *Appropriate Telecommunication and Learning Technology for Distance Education in the South Pacific*. Suva: Pacific Islands Regional Assoc. for Distance Education.

Veilaveyaki, G., Usuramo, J. and Va'a, R. (2001) Facilitating student support via audio conferencing: adaptations and innovations in the use of educational technology. Paper for the 15th ODLAA Forum, Sydney, Sept.

Visser, J., 1997, "Elements for a vision of where the world of learning is going", paper for the 18th ICDE World Conference, Pennsylvania State University, June. <http://www.unesco.org/education/educprog/lwf>

Williams, I. & Gillard, G., (1986) Improving satellite tutorials at the University of the South Pacific, *Distance Education*, 7(2), 261–274.

University of Wisconsin-Extension, 2000, WisView Audiographics, <http://www.uwex.edu/ics/wisview>

Young, G. & Marks-Maran, D., (1999) A case study of convergence between conventional and distance education: using constructivism and postmodernism as a framework to unconverge the mind in Tait, A. & Mills, R. (Eds.) *The convergence of distance and conventional learning*, 1999, London: Routledge, 175-187.

John Hedberg,[a] Geraldine Lefoe,[a] Cathy Gunn,[b] Lori Lockyer,[a] John Patterson,[a] and Bronwyn Stuckey[a]

a. Faculty of Education, University of Wollongong; b. University of Auckland

This symposium draws together the research of three different studies of professional communities that are supported by learning technologies. The learning community is a powerful approach to teaching and learning and a potent strategy for change and improvement. Key features of effective communities include: the collegial and facilitative participation of a champion who invites input in decision-making; a shared vision that is developed from members' commitment to their own development and their students' learning; and application of professional development to solutions that address student needs.

Some outcomes that have been realised by professional teaching communities:

- reduction of isolation of teachers;

- increased commitment to the agreed mission and goals;

- powerful learning that defines good teaching and classroom practice and that creates new knowledge and beliefs about teaching and learning;

- new understanding of the expertise and role of teachers;

- commitment to change.

The value of a community of learners or a community of practice has been highly regarded in education and training. The three research papers on which the following three chapters are based clarify the role of learning technologies in building and maintaining communities.

The studies investigate the concept of community from a face-to-face environment supported with learning technologies through to a wholly virtual or online environment. The first study (Chapter 40) takes an institutional model and examines the role of the technology in creating a distributed learning environment which can be seen as innovative by members of staff and which can also help to change the curriculum and pedagogy of a whole undergraduate programme.

The second study (Chapter 41) examines the links between student teachers and their profession as they seek to establish and manage a professional support structure, which can draw teachers in current professional practice into a range of support activities, and to ensure professional relevance into the preparation of new teachers. The third study (Chapter 42) describes a community built around the implementation of an innovative computer-based tool and how the staff development of teachers may occur through the roles and resources offered to them in an electronic network. This study examined issues related to the creation and maintenance of a motivating environment for a specialised community in a discipline area not usually known for high computer skill levels.

The symposium focused on key factors for community success, the importance of research and evaluation in developing and sustaining the community, outcomes associated with participant involvement and lessons for effective implementation.

40 Forming learning communities in a distributed learning environment: what role can technology play?

Geraldine Lefoe,[a] John Hedberg,[a] and Cathy Gunn[b]

a. University of Wollongong, Australia; b. University of Auckland, New Zealand

Keywords
community of practice; distributed learning environment; evaluation; learning community

40.1   Overview

An evaluation of a distributed learning environment of a regional NSW university provided the context to examine how a community of practice formed in its first year of operation. The distance from the main campus made communication difficult for the tutors, lecturers and students and the use of information and communication technologies (ICT), at times, added to the challenge. This chapter identifies ways that ICT can support the development of a community of practice in new learning environments.

40.2   Introduction

An evaluation of the inaugural year of an interdisciplinary Arts degree examined the perceptions of the students, tutors and lecturers in order to capture the experience of teaching and learning in a new distributed learning environment. It also aimed to identify how academic staff could be supported during the implementation phase and the implications this has for academic staff development within the institutional context. The evaluation did not seek specifically to examine the notion of learning communities, however the analysis of the data identified this as a theme and highlighted the importance of being part of a learning community for those involved.

Although the literature on learning communities has been around since 1927, there has been a resurgence of interest in the last ten years as universities face the challenge of providing quality teaching and learning in an era of social, political and economic reforms. Building and sustaining learning communities is a challenge in any university setting (Angelo, 2000; Gabelnick *et al.*, 1990). For centres remote from the original campus, it may provide much needed support for students and tutors in the first year of a new venture.

This chapter examines the learning community created at one of the centres through the perceptions of the students, tutors, and lecturers. Rather than focusing on the learner–teacher relationship, the chapter focuses on how the tutors created a community of practice to inform their teaching practice and their social relationships with other members of the institution. It also examines the perceived challenges to using communication technology to support the new development with a view to expanding the learning community within and across the centres. Finally, it offers recommendations for future research on how learning technology can be better utilised to support the development of learning communities, specifically in a distributed learning environment.

40.3   Background

Since the 1990s institutions of higher education in Australia and overseas were undergoing a period of rapid change. This is influenced by many of the social, economic, political and technological reforms that are pushing universities to be more businesslike in their management and to provide a better service to their client base, the student. Institutions are competing for students at a national and international level, student expectations with regard to a quality education are higher and politicians are placing unprecedented demands on higher education to do more with less as the public purse tightens in all areas of spending. (AV-CC, 1996; Daniel, 1996).

The major discourses identified in the literature as having significant impact on the changing face of higher education in Australia include: reduced funding by government bodies (NCIHE, 1997); competition between institutions (Yetton, 1997); the globalisation of education (Cunningham *et al.*, 1998); the emergence of the need for lifelong learning with the consequent changing student profile (Candy *et al.*, 1994); the changing role of the academic (Scott, 1999; Taylor, 1999) and the impact of emerging technologies on the provision of quality teaching and learning (Biggs, 1999; Ramsden, 1992). The impact these issues had on the University of Wollongong led to expansion to a regional campus and access centres in order to increase access for students and to increase funding allocation. It also led to the development of an interdisciplinary Arts degree, which moved beyond traditional methods of teaching and learning to incorporate new technologies including videoconferencing and web-based teaching and learning.

The University of Wollongong is a regional institution located on the South Coast of NSW, Australia. A new campus and two new access centres on the South Coast of NSW are sufficiently distant from the University of Wollongong campus to require a rethinking of current teaching and learning practice. The combination of distance with limited funding after seed funding has provided opportunities to rethink teaching and learning strategies. Competition from traditional distance education providers in the area meant that, strategically, Wollongong had to 'think differently'. An early decision was made by the University and government funding body that teaching and learning would be supported through technology that included using, for example, videoconference and computer facilitated learning environments, as well as local tutor support (University of Wollongong, 1996). As Steve Ehrmann pointed out in the keynote address to the ISL conference, one of the key factors in using technology was to reach out to learners who would not otherwise be able to access tertiary education. Evaluation strategies are in place to ensure that these learners receive a quality education (Ehrmann, 2001).

40.4   The degree and teaching methods

The first year of an interdisciplinary Bachelor of Arts (Community and Environment) is the focus of this research. This new degree, developed over four years, is one of several degrees the University of Wollongong offers to students studying at the Shoalhaven Campus and at access centres in Bega and Batemans Bay. The degree has been designed to utilise a flexible learning approach in this distributed learning environment. Lecturers for the subjects were based at the Wollongong campus and local tutors were located at each of the centres. Students were required to attend tutorial sessions either once per week or once per fortnight for each subject. Their learning was supported through such things as paper-based materials, video, videoconferencing and web-based content and/or communication.

An interdisciplinary degree suggests the blurring of the disciplinary boundaries, drawing from the approaches of a number of disciplines, with the focus on issues and themes. This approach would for example use readings from a number of different disciplines, e.g. history, literature, philosophy (Rinn and Weir, 1984). When the degree was developed in 1998 there were only a couple of other degree specialisations within the faculty that were not firmly based in single humanities or social science disciplines (Lefoe, Albury, Littler, and Trivett, 2001). The development of an interdisciplinary degree required several years of planning and organisation as the members of the faculty challenged their beliefs about interdisciplinary degrees (Lefoe *et al.*, 2001). They also had to think differently about how they would teach in a new distributed learning environment.

Distributed learning is a model of teaching and learning which blurs the boundary of campus-based and distance education. It is focused on learner needs, and provides opportunity for faculty and students to enter the learning environment at different times from different locations, 'enabling both synchronous and asynchronous interaction through the integration of pedagogically appropriate technologies' (University of British Columbia, 1995). Oblinger and Maruyama (1996) argue that for universities to create such an environment they 'must address both human and technological issues through planning, institutional support, and technology architecture' (Oblinger, 1996, p. 6). The University of British Columbia states that this approach 'gives instructors the flexibility to customise learning environments to meet the needs of diverse student populations, while aiming to provide both high quality and cost-effective learning opportunities' (University of British Columbia, 1995).

The new degree required flexible teaching and learning methods to be incorporated in the subject design because of the distance to the new campus and access centres and the perception that technology could support teaching and learning in this new learning environment.

40.5 Research methodology

This study examined a distributed learning initiative which provided the focus for a naturalistic evaluation (Guba and Lincoln, 1981) and was undertaken using a case study methodology (Merriam, 1998; Stake, 1995). Data was collected through focus groups, interviews and surveys and analysed to identify major themes (Creswell, 1998). While a review of the literature identified a number of national and international studies in the area, little could be generalised to this study in this specific context (Chalmers, 1999; Collis and De Boer, 1999; Fowler and Branch, 2000). Perceptions of participants in this case were quite different to perceptions of those in other cases, due to the difference in context. The focus was on the process of implementation that was unique to a particular institution, thus the implementation was viewed through the eyes of those involved, in order to understand their experience.

The results were designed to improve institutional processes for creating distributed learning opportunities and to support further development of the Arts programme in particular. An additional concern was the identification of academic staff development needs to underpin like projects. Therefore, the study does not attempt to generalise the understandings to other contexts, though recommendations for more formal research were generated as a result of the study.

In order to protect the anonymity of those interviewed, the specific centre for this study is identified as The Centre. The tutors, students and lecturers are identified by their role only and specific subjects are not identified.

40.6   Participants' profile

There were a small number of students enrolled in Bachelor of Arts at the Centre, including part-time and full-time students, with an age range from 19 to 60. The students were predominantly mature-age students. Seven subjects were offered within the Arts degree and an elective could be chosen from within the Faculty of Commerce degree, which was also on offer at the Centre. There were six local tutors and one tutor, who was based at another centre. This tutor used technology and some face to face visits to support the tutorials. The majority of the tutors did not have teaching experience in tertiary education, though some had experience in vocational and secondary education areas, or in running workshops for community activities and groups. The lecturers or subject coordinators were all based on the main campus, an eight-hour return journey by road from the Centre. Two of the subject developers were on study leave, which meant their subjects were coordinated by experienced academics who had not been involved in the subject development. One of the other coordinators was a part-time lecturer and was not at work and contactable on the day the tutorials were held in the centres. Six of the lecturers/coordinators were experienced tertiary educators, though not necessarily in flexible teaching methods.

40.7   Researcher's role

While conducting activities for the evaluation, the researcher was a lecturer in the Centre for Educational Development and Interactive Resources (CEDIR). In this support role the researcher had been a member of design teams for the subjects and continued to work with subject developers and tutors in the areas of subject design and in a staff development role. The researcher was also the chair of the evaluation committee charged with the task of reviewing and monitoring the initiative.

40.8   The Centre

This small rural community is approximately four hours from a major city. Although the resident town population is 4,200 the region had a population of 29,400 in 1996 (Australian Bureau of Statistics, 1996). Analysis of the age ranges in the area indicate that many 18–24 year olds leave the area to further their education, and do not return. The access centre was built to meet the needs of post-secondary students who did not or could not leave the area for financial reasons, and for mature age students to improve their employability (Illawarra Regional Information Service, 1996). A report on the viability of the education initiative indicated that this town was the best place for the access centre because of 'its remoteness, but also because of the demonstrated high level of interest in participating in post-school education and because it displays the drive and community initiative that will need to be harnessed in support of such an enterprise' (IRIS, 1996, p. 108).

The access centre opened in 2000. It is a new red brick building, located in a residential area opposite the local high school. Inside the centre are two small tutorial rooms (seating for about ten), a computer laboratory, with seating for about 30, a larger teaching space, with seating for about 25 and another computer laboratory with external access for the high school. There is an office for the coordinator, a small kitchen and shared amenities. Between the tutorial rooms and the main laboratory is an open space with casual seating where people congregate for coffee and food. In the kitchen there is a sign indicating who has contributed to the communal tea and coffee, which includes names of staff and students. Library resources are located a block or two away in the community library.

40.9 The nature of the community

The Centre is situated in a small, isolated rural town. Many of the tutors knew each other prior to the opening of the university centre through their involvement in protecting the environment, in political groups and in other educational contexts in their local community. The opening of a new tertiary education centre provided an opportunity for employment, for a support network for some for their postgraduate studies and for their obvious commitment to their local community. They were keen to make a success of the Centre and were aware of the need for this if the Centre was to survive beyond the initial funding. At a tutor workshop they attended, prior to the opening, they identified 'strong relationships and personal support' as key factors in the success of the Centre. They also identified that the Centre should be 'alive, vibrant and interesting' and that it should have an 'awareness of a sense of belonging to the [main] campus'.

The development of community would seem integral to achieving these goals but led to a number of questions for the researcher. What kind of community developed? How did it inform teaching practice? Who were the members? How can this membership be expanded? What role did technology play (if at all) in supporting the community?

Community in tertiary institutions is described variously in the literature as learning communities (Kellog, 1999), professional learning communities (Hord, 1997) and communities of practice (Wenger, 1998). If we add the educational technology literature we also have virtual communities (Rheingold, 1993) and networked communities (Harasim *et al.*, 1995). The word community itself seems to defy an agreed definition – there are many varied ideas of what a community entails. Palloff and Pratt (1999, p. 21) state, 'people seeking commonality and shared interests formed groups and communities in order to pursue the interests that distinguish them from other groups'. Kim (2000, p. 28) asserts that 'a community is a group of people with shared interest, purpose or goal, who gets to know each other better over time'. Both studies support the notion that people want to feel a sense of belonging and to connect for a greater purpose as lifestyle changes bring changes to the way they perceive family, neighbourhoods and towns. Community can also be described as a 'dynamic whole' that emerges when a group of people share common practices, are interdependent, make decisions jointly, identify with something larger than the sum of their individual relationships, and make long-term commitments to the well-being of themselves, another and the group (Palloff, 1999; Shaffer, 1993). When people make a conscious commitment to a community, beyond that of location or family and religious connections, there is an emphasis on 'member's needs for personal growth and transformation, as well as the social and survival aspects of the community' (Palloff and Pratt, 1999, p. 26). The notion of community, in this sense, is not new to the tutors at the Centre. However the development of a learning community in a new centre was something they had not been involved in before, and the incorporation of technology to support the community was also outside their experience.

The term 'learning community' can be used to mean; extending the classroom into the community, bringing community members into the classroom, and simultaneously engaging students, teachers and administrators in learning (Hord, 1997). Its basis lies in the notion of a community that learns, and it is fundamental to tertiary institutions (Taylor, 1999). It is also tied to the notion of learning organisation (Senge, 1992), as used in the business world and emphasises the importance of social relationships in changing practice. Community of practice is the term which probably best describes this kind of learning community.

A community of practice involves people who share their expertise and experience, in this case for teaching, and regularly interact to enhance their learning in this area (Wenger, 2000). 'Communities of Practice' is a term coined by Lave and Wenger (1991) to describe how people share their understandings of work, responsibility, and knowledge within the workplace. Wenger later identified that for this to happen three essential characteristics must be in place: mutual engagement, shared repertoire, and joint enterprise (Wenger, 1998; Rogers, 2000). Mutual engagement implies that the members of the community are involved in shared activities, while maintaining their identity through developing social relationships, and providing reciprocal and overlapping capabilities to the group. The boundaries and ideas about practice can be extended through joint enterprise as the members share a common purpose. A community negotiates meaning through its shared repertoire. This refers to the 'pool of resources that members not only share but contribute to and therefore renew' (Rogers, 2000, p. 388).

40.10   Evidence of a community of practice

The tutors and the centre coordinator at this Centre formed a community of practice as they developed knowledge and understandings of the larger organisation of which they were a part. The opening of new centres required new policies and procedures be put in place at the University. Despite several years of planning, there were many issues to be addressed in the first twelve months involving administration, technology, pedagogy and student support (Lefoe, Hedberg and Gunn 2001). While espoused administrative and pedagogical practice at the main campus appeared to work well, the actual practices, when used in distributed environments, did not. New knowledge, understandings and procedures are required for such initiatives and the tacit knowledge of those in Wollongong of how the system worked was not readily available to those at the new Centre. Consequently the ties between the members of this particular centre were strengthened through their isolation and their ability to support each other in the first few months after the Centre opened. A community of practice developed out of a need, a need to belong in a new learning environment, a need for a shared understanding of the practices at the distant campus so members could access knowledge and support as they required it, and a need for professional development to improve their teaching practice.

The tutors described their developing relationships in the face-to-face environment, and the level of trust that was developing:

> I went through finding my own feet in it. I didn't quite know what was expected and I was thinking 'Oh, this is because I actually haven't done an Arts degree – I've done a science degree' and so I talked a lot with [tutor] and [tutor] (Tutor 1).

> [Tutor] and I have chatted over heaps – we felt we moved from tutoring to teaching, and we felt we had to move fast into that. The first few weeks, we thought we were in the role of tutors, and very quickly that wasn't enough. We had to actually teach (Tutor 2).

> So it was really left up to the tutors, and I ended up, just because I really wanted to do the right thing by the students and I wasn't sure whether I was being to harsh or too generous, I spoke to a tutor from the first session who looked over some of the work, and we talked about what marks she would have given them (Tutor 3).

> Just, for staff development, I think that, for particularly for new tutors, with our training we didn't actually look at what we do on that first day. I mean, I worked it out by talking to other tutors and sort of did myself a kind of, a plan (Tutor 1).

> We just had this theorem on the board, we had half the commerce students in here trying to do it as well, and we still couldn't get the same answer as the computer. So fortunately [tutor] arrived, so I sort of, drawing on all the university resources available in [the Centre] and he came in and found our simple error in one column and away we went (Tutor 41).

As they developed relationships within the Centre, they were able to develop their understanding and ability as teachers. The ties with the other centres were not as strong however:

> We really haven't had a lot of contact, actually. I'd rung both other tutors, but they've not rung me. [Tutor] rang me back after I rang her, but they haven't really been pro-active. I tried to get a WebCT thing happening where our students met on line at a certain time, and they couldn't really join in through circumstance. I really think it needs to be a closer team between the tutors and between all of the students (Tutor 1).

> I spoke to another...the tutor from [other centre] for the same subject and she read a couple of the essays to compare them with her students so that was a bit of process which I had to work out ...we had to work out ourselves, there wasn't any sort of centralised comparative exercise going on (Tutor 2).

Ties between the tutors at the Centre and the lecturers/subject coordinators were not very strong either. One tutor, when talking about the relationship with the lecturer stated:

> A relationship where, if something was more solid in a relationship, say if it was you, I'd already kind of developed a friendship with you that I could have just said look 'I'm a bit lost, I don't know what's required here' but when you can't even come up with a question ... do you know what I'm getting at?

Another tutor commented:

> Not very regular contact – at the beginning we were sending email and we had a couple of phone conversations just to talk about the first tute and what he would like covered in that first tute, but I mean, my main contact with (name) has been just reading his responses to students on the bulletin board.

The tutors realised that there were other issues that impacted on those in Wollongong and were relieved that they were far enough away not to be involved:

> There's a fabulous 'little community' feel in that place – that feels great. And, you know, we'd even comment about how busy and stressed that all seemed up there (in Wollongong), whereas while we were busy and a different kind of stress, it wasn't that pressure stress, that 'unsettling' locally. Yeah – so in a way we felt, yes, there are a few loose ends, but to me it felt like we've got such a much better atmosphere here, we feel like the privileged ones from my perspective. I hope further down the track, with [the Centre], it's a success and continues and strengthens, and I hope that work never impinges really.

There were some obviously strong ties developing with the tutors at the Centre, not surprising given that the Centre is small and isolated. Ties, albeit weaker ties also exist with tutors at the other centres and with the institution and its members, as identified by the broken lines in Figure 40.1.

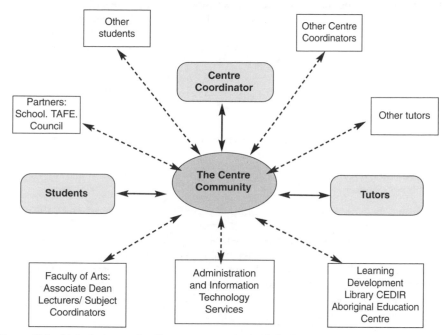

Figure 40.1 Links between the Centre community and the institution

The development of a community of practice follows five stages: potential, coalescing, active, dispersed and memorable (Wenger and Snyder, 2000). At this stage the community are starting to come together and recognise their potential as they explore their connectedness, define their joint enterprise and negotiate community (Wenger, 1998). By strengthening the links identified, particularly between the tutors and those at the other centres, and between the lecturers and the tutors, the community has the potential to expand so that the members participate further in their professional development through their membership. What insights can this context provide to nurture this community of practice? Can we use technology to expand the membership of the group?

40.11   Expanding the community membership – how can technology help?

The tutors at this centre showed their willingness to include others in their community. However, many were still novices at using the available technology and described their difficulties with using it in their teaching. Their skills improved greatly over the year of the study, so in future they could start to make more use of both videoconferencing and web-based systems to develop their community of practice (further skills workshops were be held to support this development after this study concluded). As the community grows, the members need to take the lead to instigate further communication with other tutors and with the lecturers. 'Out of sight, out of mind' was a problem one lecturer identified. Increased numbers of students on the main campus, an increased workload and a requirement to research and publish has meant that lecturers have other constant and competing demands on their time. They may need frequent reminders and invitations to participate as a member of the community; occasional videoconferencing with the tutors could develop the social relationships and build the trust needed between the groups. The tutors themselves may benefit from a shared web space where they can talk about their teaching in a safe environment and share teaching materials. Stuckey, Hedberg and Lockyer (2001 identify the hallmarks of communities of practice as

- a clear focus driven by the members;
- employment of appropriate technologies and styles of communication;
- membership of a social network where their expertise, leadership, content and contributions are valued; and
- providing ongoing discussion, sharing of, and collaboration on, commonly valued things (Stuckey *et al* , 2001).

It is clear that the development of this community of practice has been driven by the needs of the members who value each other's contributions and their ability to share their knowledge and expertise. While they are able to share and collaborate at the local level, they would like to expand their community to include members from other centres and the Wollongong institution. Relationship building in a distributed learning environment requires greater effort on the part of all of those involved. Leadership and planning by the members is required to encourage this development. The use of appropriate technologies for communication and sharing artefacts such as material on shared marking procedures could benefit the expansion of the community.

Technology can be used to strengthen the links between tutors and lecturers through such things as videoconference meetings to encourage the development of trust. Increased communication between tutors/lecturers through email, listservers could also serve to enhance this development. Finally a website could provide a place for community members to discuss teaching and learning strategies and to access information about teaching.

40.12 Conclusion

The Centre members have begun to develop a community of practice. If the institution can nurture and expand this enthusiasm through developing skills in using appropriate information and communication technologies, it will not only support the professional development of the community members but also highlight the role technology can play in their teaching and communication. A distributed learning environment requires people to change their practice. A community of practice may well provide an avenue to support people through this change by providing stronger links between all of those involved in teaching and supporting the teaching and learning activities. Further research on how learning technologies can be better used to support the growth of effective learning communities should identify useful strategies and also support innovation and change specifically in distributed learning environments.

40.13 References

Angelo, T. (2000). Doing academic development as though we value learning most: transformative guidelines from research and practice, *Research and Development in Higher Education* **22** (Cornerstones of Higher Education), 111–22 (available: http://www.herdsa.org,au/vic/cornerstones).

Australian Bureau of Statistics (1996) *ERP and Components of Change* (Cat No 3208.1). Canberra

AV-CC (1996) Exploiting information technology in higher education: an issues paper. Australian Vice-Chancellors' Committee (available: http:// www.avcc.edu.au/avcc/pubs/eitihe.htm [21/8/97]).

Biggs, J. (1999) *Teaching for Quality Learning at University: What the Student Does.* Buckingham: Society for Research into Higher Education and Open University Press.

Candy, P.C., Crebert, G. and O'Leary, J. (1994) *Developing Lifelong Learners through Undergraduate Education* (Commissioned report No. 28). Canberra: National Board of Employment, Education and Training, Australian Government Publishing Service.

Chalmers, D. (1999) A strategic university-wide initiative to introduce programs of study using flexible delivery methods, *Interactive Learning Environments* 7 (2–3): 249–68.

Collis, B. and De Boer, W. (1999) Scaling up from the pioneers: the TeleTOP method at the University of Twente, *Interactive Learning Environments* 7(2–3): 93–111.

RHEFP (1998) *Learning for Life: Final Report of the Review of Higher Education Financing and Policy.* Committee chaired by Roderick West. Canberra, AGPS: Department of Employment, Education, Training and Youth Affairs. http://www.deetya.gov.au/divisions/hed/hereview

Creswell, J.W. (1998) *Qualitative Inquiry and Research Design: Choosing among Five Traditions.* Thousand Oaks, Calif.: Sage.

Cunningham, S., Tapsall, S., Ryan, Y., Bagdon, K. and Flew, T. (1998) *New Media and Borderless Education: A Review of the Convergence between Global Media Networks and Higher Education Provision.* Canberra: DETYA.

Daniel, J. (1996) New kids on the box: distance education enters its third generation. Paper presented at the 3rd Interactive Multimedia Symposium, Perth, Western Australia.

Ehrmann, S. (2001) Fallacies of common sense: a counter intuitive route to transforming higher learning with technology. Keynote address presented at the *Improving Student Learning using Learning Technologies* conference, Edinburgh.

Fowler, J. and Branch, S. (2000) Supporting students and staff in flexible learning environment: a case study. Paper presented at the ASET/HERDSA Joint Conference: *Flexible Learning for a Flexible Society,* Toowoomba, Queensland.

Gabelnick, F., MacGregor, J., Matthews, R.S. and Smith, B. L. (1990) *Learning Communities: Creating Connections among Students, Faculty, and Disciplines.* San Francisco: Jossey-Bass.

Guba, E.G. and Lincoln, Y.S. (1981) *Effective Evaluation.* San Francisco: Jossey-Bass.

Guba, E.G. and Lincoln, Y.S. (1989) *Fourth Generation Evaluation.* Newbury Park, Calif.: Sage.

Harasim, L., Hiltz, S.R., Teles, L. and Turoff, M. (1995) *Learning Networks: A Field Guide to Teaching and Learning Online.* Cambridge, Massachusetts: The MIT Press.

Hord, S. (1997) Professional learning communities: what are they and why are they important?, *Issues ... about Change* 6(1) (available: http://www.sedl.org/change/issues/issues61.html; accessed 16/08/01).

Illawarra Regional Information Service (1996) Post-compulsory education curriculum options for the South Coast of N.S.W. (unpublished). Wollongong.

Kellog, K. (1999) *Learning Communities* (ERIC-HE Digest Series EDO-HE-1999-1). Washington: The George Washington University. http://www.eriche.org/digests/99-1.pdf

Kim, A. J. (2000) *Community Building on the Web.* Berkeley, CA: Peachpit Press.

Lave, J. and Wenger, E. (1991) *Situated Learning: Legitimate Peripheral Participation.* Cambridge: Cambridge University Press.

Lefoe, G., Albury, R., Littler, C. and Trivett, N. (2001) Collaborative partnerships: changing roles for academic and support staff in new learning environments. In J.G. Hedberg (ed.), *On-line Learning Environments: Research and Teaching.* RILE Monograph. Wollongong: Faculty of Education, University of Wollongong.

Lefoe, G., Hedberg, J. and Gunn, C. (2001) Evaluating the first year in a distributed learning environment: the students' perspective. In T.A. Kamali, J.R. Metzner and L.L. Bornstein (eds). Paper presented at the *e-ducation Without Borders* Conference, Abu Dhabi.

Merriam, S.B. (1998) *Qualitative Research and Case Study Applications in Education.* San Francisco: Jossey-Bass.

NCIHE (1997) *Higher Education in the Learning Society.* Committee chaired by Ronald Dearing (London HMSO). London: Report of the National Committee of Inquiry into Higher Education, HMSO. http://wwwd2.leeds.ac.uk/niche

Oblinger, D.G. and Marayama, M.K. (1996) *Distributed Learning.* Boulder, Colorado: CAUSE.

Palloff, R.M.P.K. (1999) *Building Learning Communities in Cyberspace: Effective Strategies for the On-line Classroom.* San Francisco, CA: Jossey-Bass.

Ramsden, P. (1992) *Learning to Teach in Higher Education.* London: Routledge.

Rheingold, H. (1993) *The Virtual Community.* Reading, MA: Addison Wesley.

Rinn, F. J. and Weir, S.B. (1984) Yea, team, *Improving College and University Teaching* 2(1): 5-10.

Rogers, J. (2000) Communities of Practice: a framework for fostering coherence in virtual learning communities, *Educational Technology & Society* 3(3). (available: http://ifets.ieee.org/periodical/vol_3_2000/e01.pdf).

Scott, G. (1999) *Change Matters: Making a Difference in Education and Training.* St Leonards, Australia: Allen & Unwin.

Senge, P.M. (1992) *The Fifth Discipline.* Sydney: Random House Australia Pty Ltd.

Shaffer, C. and Anundsen, K. (1993) *Creating Community Anywhere.* New York: Jeremy P. Tarcher/Perigee Books.

Stake, R.E. (1995) *The Art of Case Study Research.* Thousand Oaks: Sage Publications.

Stuckey, B., Hedberg, J. and Lockyer, L. (2001) Professional development on-line – doing IT pedagogically. Paper presented at the ODLAA Conference, Sydney.

Taylor, P.G. (1999) *Making Sense of Academic Life: Academics, Universities, and Change.* Philadelphia, PA: Open University Press.

University of British Columbia. (1995) *Post-Secondary Policy Forum on Distributed Learning Environments* (Report): University of British Columbia. http://www.ctt.bc.ca/edtech/policy/toc.html (accessed 10-04-00).

University of Wollongong. (1996) Submission to the Commonwealth/ State Working Party on Higher Education Provision on the South Coast of New South Wales (unpublished report). University of Wollongong.

Wenger, E. (1998) *Communities of Practice: Learning, Meaning, and Identity.* Cambridge: Cambridge University Press.

Wenger, E. and Snyder, W. (2000) *Learning in Communities.* LINE Zine, 1. http://www.linezine.com/1/features/ewwsic.htm (accessed 20/08/01).

Yetton, P. (1997). *Managing the Introduction of Technology in the Delivery and Administration of Higher Education* (EIP 97/3): Department of Education, Training and Youth Affairs http://www.detya.gov.au/highered/eippubs/eip97_3 (accessed 01/06/98).

41 Learning technologies and professional development: enhancing a community of physical and health educators

Lori Lockyer and John Patterson

University of Wollongong, Australia

Keywords

community of practice; health education; information and communication technologies; learning technologies; physical education; professional development

41.1 Overview

Educational literature is replete with examples of learning communities which take on various forms and focus. Regardless of design or concentration, learning communities are considered powerful because of their 'ability to take advantage of, and in some cases invent a process for exchanging ideas and learning collectively' (Schwier, 1999, p. 282). Historically, the campus-based and outreach programmes of pre-service teaching institutions have actively facilitated the initiation and maintenance of educators into the community of practice. The changing educational environment has necessitated exploration of innovative approaches to teacher education and professional development. This chapter describes a project that seeks to effectively utilise learning technologies to enhance this community of physical and health educators based in New South Wales, Australia.

41.2 Background

Within the professional community of physical and health educators, key members include teacher educators (i.e. university-based academics) and pre-service teachers (i.e. students enrolled in education faculty undergraduate and graduate certificate teacher training programs) and practicing teachers (Figure 41.1).

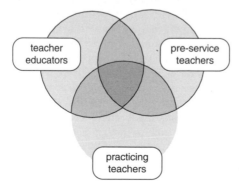

Figure 41.1 Key members of the teaching community of practice.

41.3 Context

The Faculty of Education at the University of Wollongong located in New South Wales (NSW) Australia has prepared secondary school physical and health education teachers since 1965. This institution has actively supported this community of practice through the various stages of teachers' career from initiation through continuing education to facilitation of teachers' involvement in strategically positioning the discipline and development of pedagogical practices. Members of this existing community of practice (i.e. faculty, students and teachers) have formally and informally participated in the evolution of the profession. Participants have traditionally fostered successful processes for the exchange of ideas and mentoring newcomers into the community of practice. In this context this has been exemplified through involvement in policy and syllabus consultation; curriculum and resource development; practice teaching experiences; and professional and continuing education activities.

41.4 Challenges for the community

Challenges for this community of practice exist in their day-to-day working environment and within their profession generally. As such, the effectiveness of traditional implementations of the partnership model has been the discussion of recent debate and calls for reform in an era of social, fiscal and time constraints (Ministerial Advisory Council on the Quality of Teaching, 1998; Ramsey, 2000).

For teacher educators, the ratio of face-to-face teaching allocations have increased along with demands for participation in administrative activities. Thus, limited time remains for curriculum innovation and involvement in outreach activities. Opportunities for practical experience placements of pre-service teachers continue to become difficult to identify and teacher educators are increasingly unable to make themselves available for a level of supervision and mentoring that might be required or advantageous.

For practising teachers, while student numbers within schools are increasing, full-time staff in physical and health education departments are declining. The need for professional development is being emphasised by education systems during discussion of teacher registration and / or changing syllabus structure or curriculum evolution. Yet school budget lines devoted to professional development rarely cover basic fees for either in-service or external programmes much less provide for costs of employing casual teachers to cover out-of-class time for permanent staff.

Another important factor for individual teachers' participation in the community is related to their stage in the career cycle. Fessler (1985) puts forward a model that considers the interaction of teacher career stage with personal and organisational environment. As teachers move from their early 'induction' stage through 'competency building' and into an 'enthusiastic and growing' they are eager to develop skills, support their peers, investigate and implement new practices and innovations. It is at this competency and enthusiasm stages where teachers often effectively participate in developing the community of practice actively seeking professional development opportunities, sitting on committees to influence organisational curriculum focus, creating and sharing teaching resources, supervising pre-service teachers during practice placements and / or acting has executive member of professional associations.

However, as teachers' organisational environment and personal situations move them to career 'frustration' through 'stability' and on to a 'wind-down stage' involvement in the community of practice may plateau, diminish, or, in the worst cases, be detrimental to the community. It has been noted that a supportive and nurturing organisational environment helps to sustain enthusiasm and facilitate teachers towards a positive wind-down and exit stage (Wood and Lynn, 2001). The negative organisational environment provides for movement into the 'frustration' or burn-out stage. It is important for the community to identify opportunities to support their members through such phases and find vehicles for revitalising involvement.

While organisational challenges mentioned above may be a factor in moving teachers in this region to the less active phases of their career, the demography of this particular community may also be a factor. Like their counterparts in other countries such as the USA and Canada, the majority of the teachers within the physical and health education community in New South Wales are moving toward retirement or next career outlook. It is in the best interest of the community to find opportunities to tap into the wealth of experience and knowledge base of these members prior to their departure from the group.

41.5   Professional development needs

Practising teachers are under continuing pressure to stay in touch with current knowledge in physical and health education, demonstrate the use of information technology in their teaching as well as provide their students with opportunities for the development of information technology skills.

A needs analysis conducted with teachers within the local professional organisations indicated the greatest need for resources lay in the identification of specific physical and health education websites, lesson ideas, assessment tasks, online learning activities, and teaching support sites. Teachers require access to relevant sources and do not wish to spend an inordinate amount of time searching or being presented with resources that are not going to value-add to the learning experience.

Professional development literature is validated by the discussions with these local teachers in highlighting the wish to collaborate and share experiences and resource development rather than work in isolation. The bulk of literature supports the view that continued growth through the career cycle requires support and encouragement with teachers working together on activities such as collaborative projects or peer mentoring relationships (Butt *et al.*, 1990; Hargreaves and Fullan, 1992; Little, 1986).

41.6   Potential of learning technologies

To address the challenge of sustainability and revitalisation for this community, investigation into the utilisation of information and communication technologies was undertaken. The focus, therefore was on how ICTs could be used to enhance and strengthen an existing community which enjoyed a history of collaboration (see Figure 41.2 and related articles for this symposium).

The literature provides both commentary and empirical evidence for the benefits of information and communication technologies (ICTs) in facilitating the roles and responsibilities of the physical and health educator (Committee on Enhancing the Internet for Health Applications, 2000; Lockyer and Kerr, 2000; Lockyer, Patterson and Harper, 1999; Milio, 1996). ICTs may facilitate time and place independent access to resources, instructors and other learners; provide of tools for development and presentation of ideas and concepts; and communication vehicles that may allow for in-depth exploration of controversial or difficult to manage issues.

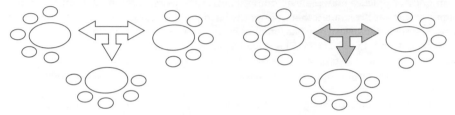

Figure 41.2   Technology used to enhance existing community (Stuckey, Hedberg and
    Lockyer 2001)

41.7   *ActiveHealth* – web technologies to enhance community

The *ActiveHealth* web environment (http://www.activehealth.uow.edu.au) (see Figure 41.3) was created to facilitate access to the Physical and Health Education undergraduate and postgraduate programs including online practice teaching forums; support continuing professional development activities; and act as a repository for information and teaching resources.

Figure 41.3   *ActiveHealth* homepage

The development of the web environment was undertaken as a collaborative endeavour to provide opportunity for all members of the community to propose and contribute to activities thereby addressing the suggested attributes of a professional learning community including: supportive and shared leadership; collective creativity; shared values and vision; supportive conditions; and shared personal practice (Hord, 1997).

Through their participation in the development of the web-supported community, university-based academics (i.e. teacher educators) enhance their understanding of the use of ICT for teaching and learning within the discipline. This translates into the integration of such concepts into the curriculum of the programme. Students propose projects that will add to the resource base of the community and allow them to gain credit toward their teaching degree. Projects involve collaboration with lecturers, other students and/or practising teachers and promotes, as Bruffee (1993) suggests the opportunity to speak the language of their profession and thus, 'speaking the language fluently defines membership in the community' (p. 130).

To respond to the aforementioned need for relevant teaching and learning resources in the area of physical and health education a process and technological solution became a priority for the professional development initiatives undertaken. The result (see Figure 41.4) ensures members of the community have opportunity to create and/or suggest specific resources be added to the site and participate in reviewing those suggestions. The *ActiveHealth* resource database has been developed with WebObjects' technologies to ensure system stability and ease of use for this contribution, reviewing, maintenance and accessing process (see Rowland, Lockyer and Patterson, 2001).

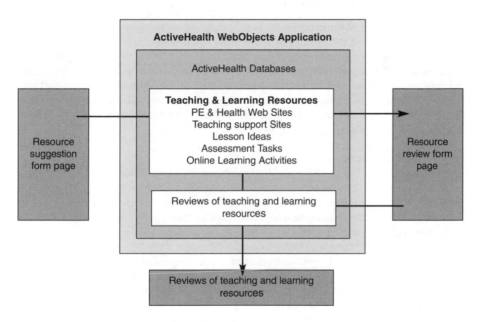

Figure 41.4   ActiveHealth resource contribution, review and view process from Rowland, Lockyer and Patterson (2001)

While the *ActiveHealth* website supports storage, reviewing and sharing of resources and ideas, development of such resources has been focused on teachers' traditional tendency toward face-to-face continuing education settings.

Working with local schools, professional associations, technology companies, and the state government education authority the University of Wollongong has engaged in outreach activities to support the professional development of the community focusing on collaborative teaching resource design and production and technology skill development. Collaborative activities have focused on:

- design of online learning activities for a senior secondary school personal development and health curriculum;

- exploration of the use of physical and health education websites for classroom activities;

- evaluation of online learning activities created by pre-service teachers;

- development of lesson plans that utilise online resources.

Products developed through these workshops are reviewed by members of the community and are shared through the *ActiveHealth* resource database.

41.8   Future developments

Preliminary evaluation of the experiences of participating community members, quality of developed resources and the vehicle for share those resources suggest that technology use has provided a level of enhanced activity for this community at the very early stages of its introduction. Certainly engaging in only face-to-face collaborative activities limits the number of members that can be involved at any one time and the number of events that can occur over the course of an academic term or session. Future activities for this community might explore how online communication and collaborative tools might further enhance and address professional development needs.

41.9   References

Bruce, B.C. and Easley, J.A., Jr. (2000) Emerging communities of practice: Collaboration and communication in action research, *Educational Action Research* 8(2): 243–59.

Bruffee, K.A. (1993) *Collaborative Learning: Higher Education, Interdependence, and the Authority of Knowledge.* Baltimore: The Johns Hopkins University Press.

Butt, R., Townsend, D. and Raymond, D. (1990) Bringing reform to life: teachers' stories and professional development, *Cambridge Journal of Education* 20(3): 255–68.

Hargreaves, A. and Fullan, M. (1992) Introduction. In A. Hargreaves and M. Fullan (eds), *Understanding Teacher Development.* New York: Teachers College Press.

Hord, S. (1997) Professional learning communities: what are they and why are they important?, *Issues ... about Change* 6(1).

Fessler, R. (1985) A model for teacher professional growth and development. In P.J. Burke and R.G. Heideman (eds), *Career-long Teacher Education* (pp. 181–93). Springfield, IL: Charles G. Thomas.

Kim, A.J. (2000) *Community Building on the Web: Secret Strategies for Successful On-line Communities.* Berkeley, CA: Peachpit Press.

Little, J.W. (1986) Seductive images and organisational realities in professional development. In A. Lieberman (ed.), *Re-Thinking School Improvement.* New York: Teachers College Press,

Lockyer, L. and Kerr, Y. (2000) Learner as designer-producer: physical and health education students experience web-based learning resource development. In *Proceedings of ED-MEDIA2000 World Conference on Educational Multimedia, Hypermedia and Telecommunications* (pp 591–5). Charlottesville, VA: Association for the Advancement of Computing in Education.

Lockyer, L., Patterson, J. and Harper, B. (1999) Measuring effectiveness of health education in a web-based learning environment: a preliminary report, *Higher Education Research & Development, Special Issue: Learning-Centred Evaluation of Innovation in Higher Education* **18**(2): 233–46.

Lockyer, L., Patterson, J. and Harper, B. (2001) ICT in higher education: evaluating outcomes for health education, *Journal of Computer Assisted Learning* **17**(3): 275–83.

Ministerial Advisory Council on the Quality of Teaching (1998) *Towards Greater Professionalism: Teacher Educators, Teaching and the Curriculum.* Sydney: Department of Education and Training New South Wales.

Ramsey, G. (2000) *Quality Matters: Revitalising Teaching: Critical Times Critical Choices; Report on the Review of Teacher Education.* NSW.

Rowland, G., Lockyer, L. and Patterson, J. (2001) Exploring on-line communities: supporting physical and health education professional development opportunities. In N. Smythe (ed.), *Proceedings of Apple University Consortium Conference* (pp 22-1–22-7). Sydney: Apple Computer Australia.

Schwier, R.A. (1999) Turning learning environments into learning communities: expanding the notion of interaction in multimedia. In *Proceedings of ED-MEDIA99 World Conference on Educational Multimedia, Hypermedia and Telecommunications* (vol. 1, pp. 282–6). Charlottesville, VA: Association for the Advancement of Computing in Education.

Stuckey, B. Hedberg, J. and Lockyer, L. (2001) Growing an on-line community of practice: community development to support in-service teachers in their adoption of innovation. In C. Rust (ed), *Proceedings of the 2001 9th International Symposium, Oxford Centre for Staff and Learning Development. Improving Student Learning Using Learning Technology.* OCSLD Oxford

Woods, A.M. and Lynn, S.K. (2001) Through the years: a longitudinal study of physical education teachers from a research-based preparation program, *Research Quarterly for Exercise and Sport* **72**(3): 219–31.

42 Growing an on-line community of practice: community development to support in-service teachers in their adoption of innovation

Bronwyn Stuckey, John Hedberg, Lori Lockyer

Faculty of Education, University of Wollongong, Australia

Keywords
community of practice; creative and performing arts; diffusion of technology; in-service education and training; online community; professional development; teacher education

42.1   Overview

This chapter reports some early findings of an action research programme in which in-service teachers were offered professional development through a network that was created and supported on-line. The study examined the classroom practices of teachers of the performing arts and their adoption of a CD-ROM based knowledge construction tool (Hedberg, 1997) StageStruck developed by the partnership of the University of Wollongong's emLab and Australia's National Institute for the Dramatic Arts (NIDA). The ongoing focus of the study is to identify the emerging issues in relation to the affordances of the technological and social connections formed through an Internet-based community of practice. The full study will report on the extent to which a community of practice can be facilitated and sustained through activities and resources in an online network and quantify the effectiveness of that online community in providing professional development for adoption of an innovation.

42.2   Background

Australia on CD was an Australian Government funded cultural programme entitled Creative Nation (http://www.acn.net.au/articles/1998/05/ozcd.htm) initiated in 1995. Over $A6 million was committed to produce 10 CD-ROMs designed to bring Australian culture to the public through new media technologies. This programme was essentially a cultural promotion, the results of which were CD-ROMs for use in educational settings. Sadly it was never intended that there be any professional development or support for teachers in the use of each or any of these products.

StageStruck, produced by the University of Wollongong and National Institute for Dramatic Art (NIDA), was one of those 10 CD-ROMs. It was launched on 29 January 1999. Copies were distributed to every school in the country in the first semester of 1999. *StageStruck* the product is recognised as a teaching innovation and as a multimedia technology for creative arts teaching and learning. More importantly it has been recognised as a pedagogical innovation because of its constructivist underpinnings and design realisations as a highly effective knowledge construction tool (Hedberg, 1997).

Despite widespread distribution and acclaim and having won several prestigious Australian and International multimedia awards (AMIA, 1999; BAFTA and EMMA, 1998) there has been only very moderate uptake of the tool's use. Discussions with educators indicate that many, perhaps most, were unaware of *StageStruck*'s existence and were yet to explore its educational benefit. There had been little or no discernable promotion of the product to teachers by the funding agencies. There has been no organised professional development to support the teachers in their use. Website material related to this educational software had been limited to descriptive material on the developer website and some downloadable files of teaching notes and lessons on the NSW Department of Education and Training website.

Ever dwindling budgets and explicit curriculum priorities in educational systems have restricted the number of curriculum areas supported at any one time by the education systems. Professional development still has to occur for all learning areas but with vastly reduce funds for those non-target areas in the current priorities. Communication and multimedia technologies are being proffered as cost effective and efficient training and development solutions to this declining traditional professional development budget with the added bonus that online technology may also overcome the tyranny of distance and the isolation of many rural Australian classrooms. There is ample evidence that such online professional development is enthusiastically received by teachers across a large system: in early 1999 the NSW Department of Education and Training advertised online delivery of an information skills course for teachers; it netted replies from one in two schools in the state.

Exploration of the literature in the critical areas of professional development, learning theory, technology affordances and technology diffusion raised some often-repeated issues. For instance, many writers criticise the effectiveness of the past practices in professional development. Practices such as the decontextualised, out of workplace singular event or one-day workshop have had little effect in promoting change or adoption of new technologies. Current best practice in professional development (Novick, 1996; Pennell and Firestone, 1998) indicates that networks or communities where teachers have the opportunity to take control of their personal professional development will best serve their needs and promote knowledge sharing and change. Support for the effectiveness of networks can be found in the theories of social constructivism where learning is viewed a social process, a process of acculturation into an established community of practice (Vygotsky, 1978). The environment and the dynamics, the people and their interconnections affect learning. The work of Jonassen and Mayes (1992) among others, ties in the role of online environment to this community potential, as it explains that novices to the Internet are able to collaborate with their peers and work alongside experts, to share and to explore and learn as part of a network.

The question is raised then if networking with peers is as an effective strategy for professional development how can this best be achieved in today's financial climate? The complementary and somewhat converging learning theories of Social Constructivism (Duffy and Cunningham, 1996; Vygotsky, 1978), Cognitive Flexibility (Spiro *et al.*, 1991), Cognitive Apprenticeship (Collins Brown and Newman, 1989), Situated Learning (Brown Collins and Duguid, 1989), Situated Cognition (Clancey; 1997; Lave, 1991) all implicitly support high expectations for the affordances of the Internet and hypermedia in learning.

With these bodies of knowledge as the foundation, this study originally set out to ask what part could be played by well-researched and designed online activities in shaping the future of, and meeting the needs for, teacher professional development. It also sought to investigate how such professional development might support the implementation of educational reforms and innovation. Over time and through extensive research of the literature and investigation of cases the community of practice (Lave and Wenger, 1991) emerged as a complex yet attractive vehicle for the foci of the research. The community of practice concept informed the design and development of the fledgling web-mediated community reported on in this chapter and in advancing the goal of implementation of innovation.

A preliminary investigation led to an extensive exploration of communities and community building and associated web design over the year 2000. The resultant *StageStruck* Professional Development Community (http://www.stagestruck.uow.edu.au) design was built on the best practice distilled from that exploration and a needs analysis of teachers of performing arts in the K-12 school environment in Australia. The prototype *StageStruck* Professional Development Community was launched in November 2000 at the Apple Innovative Technology Schools Conference. At the time of presentation of this paper, the web interface had been in operation for some months. The bounded history of the site development and the network establishment forms the body of this chapter. The research will go on to produce qualitative case study data derived from the cases built over the 2002 period. Quantitative data included web logs and data is being collected through instruments adapted for this study from the Concerns Based Adoption Methodology CBAM (Hall, Wallace and Dosset, 1973). This data will be used to describe the effectiveness of the on-line environment in supporting the adoption of innovation.

Over the initial establishment phase of this community (mid 2001) the research question changed to 'How does a web-based network become a community and how can this community support the professional needs of its individual members?' Thus the study evolved to explore the roster of issues arising as the communities of practice theory was applied to the case of on-line teacher professional development.

42.3   Defining the community solution in this case

Stuckey and Hedberg (2000) offer from the literature a diversity of definitions of community in an effort to demonstrate the difficulty that the humanities, other fields of endeavour and now educators have faced in settling on a single definition of community. They chose to examine recognisable hallmarks to describe the nature of community rather than be diverted into a semantic debate for which there might be no resolution. The terms community and online or virtual community are used synonymously and this definitional problem does require some attention. The person who coined the term 'virtual community' Howard Rheingold was moved recently in an online conference to describe the business communities that he is called to consult on as 'online social networks' rather than communities. The term has become so marketable and widely and blindly used that it means vastly different things to so many people. The cautionary tale is perhaps best articulated by Grossman and Wineburg (2000, p. 6):

> The word community is at risk of losing its meaning. From the prevalence of terms such as 'communities of learners', 'discourse communities', and 'learning communities' to 'school community', 'teacher community', or 'community of practice', it is clear that community has become an obligatory appendage to every educational innovation. Yet aside from linguistic kinship, it is not clear what features, if any are shared across terms. This confusion is most pronounced in the ubiquitous 'virtual community', where, by paying a fee or typing a password, anyone who visits a Web site automatically becomes a 'member' of a community.

It is also clear that not all groups meeting online are communities and that the term 'virtual community' is a misnomer. The community exists in its own right it is not virtual. It is the technologies that support the interface and communication of the community that exist only online or provide the virtual not the community itself. Since proposing this chapter and with

Researcher	Attributes of community
Figallo (1998)	• Member feels part of a social whole • Interwoven Web of relationships between members • Ongoing exchange between members of commonly valued things • Relationships between members last through time
Etzioni (1988)	• Bonding, not one to one, but a group of people to each other • Shared set of values and culture – much more than interest
Mueller (1999)	• Frequent, multilateral and for a certain period durable communication contacts • Commonly shared norms, values and collective practices • Defined boundaries between inside and outside, and development of common identity
CLN On-line (1999)	• Promotes discussion, sharing, and active collaboration • Provides responsive resource for those seeking assistance and information • Is driven by the participants, as a real grassroots initiative
Hagel and Armstrong (1997)	• Distinctive focus • Integration of content and communications • Openness to competitive information/access • Commercial orientation • Valuing of member generated content
Preece (2000)	• Clear purpose for the community • Help to create social policies that guide not stifle • Support social interaction • Sociability built through trust, collaboration and appropriate styles of communication
Kahn (1998)	• Content in context • Creativity in communicating knowledge • Collaboration for building communities of learners
Galston (1999)	• Limited membership • Shared norms • Affective ties • Sense of mutual obligation

Table 42.1   Community attributes proposed by community developers and researchers (Stuckey and Hedberg, 2000)

the hindsight from further research, the title should more correctly read, 'Growing a community of practice with on-line technology support'.

The refocused study set out to determine the perceived benefits of community as a professional development vehicle, to define the true nature of community as it is afforded by Internet technologies and synthesise the features that are shared across these various communities and how these might be supported online.

The range of attributes of community is described in Table 42.1. From this pool Stuckey and Hedberg distilled four key hallmarks for recognising community. Community is achieved when:

- a clear and shared focus is driven by the members;

- appropriate technologies and styles of communication are employed;

- the members feel part of a social network where their expertise, leadership, and content contribution and requests are all valued;

- there is ongoing discussion, sharing of, and collaboration on, commonly valued things.

42.4 Pedagogy, professional development and online environment

Joyce and Showers (1992) reported that the most effective teacher professional development activities are those that combine theory, modelling, practice, feedback and coaching for application, particularly peer coaching. Novices in a community may collaborate with peers, work alongside experts, share, explore and learn as part of a network. Learners can be given opportunities through the community for 'reciprocal teaching' (Vygotsky, 1978). Teachers teaching teachers and teachers as learners are both concepts integral to this idea of reciprocal teaching and reform in professional development. Learning can be supported in a 'zone of proximal development' (ZPD) established through the community of novices and experts and enabled by appropriate Internet-based activities, resources, opportunities and practices, beyond the physicality of being together in the same place at the same time. There is a body of practical work to indicate that the Internet does have more than just the potential to effectively facilitate teacher professional development. One example is an international online project EdNet@UMass (Reilly, 1999) which has shown evidence of the value of educational Internet communities. EdNet@UMass involves educators from the USA and 29 other countries in what is described as a forum for 'promising practices' and exploring possibilities.

42.5 The relevance of the community of practice in online educational contexts

Much has been touted in recent years about the creation of online communities and what can be achieved through them. The sceptics ask how a website can deliver professional development that is meaningful, relevant and empowering. The pundits propose community solutions to address a vast array of knowledge management and communication issues, from globalisation to team building. What are the implications of all this discussion for education?

True communities are much more than just websites or groups of people. Communities require member participation and contribution, ownership, quality support and facilitation, shared direction, goals and projects (Kim, 2000; Palloff and Pratt, 1999; Wellman and Gulia, 1997). They are an investment in time and nurturing. That old adage of 'if you build it they will come' certainly does not apply to developing community, for it is the members who create the community not the website developers or facilitators.

What remains unclear is whether community is required in all of the situations that we see it applied. Whether another form of connectedness may better serve the needs, the context, the return on investment and the time. It also remains to be seen whether a 'true' community can be established through a wholly web-based structure and what that structure might look like in various educational contexts. Four online structures are related to community and three of these may serve as stages in or components of the development of community, but they are not communities. Table 42.2 defines the differences in resources, roles, success factors and maintenance tasks for each of these online structures.

	Portal/hub	Network	Interest group	Community
Development resources	Database programming Automated updating Administrator controlled	Database and leader to user communication Administrator controlled	Database and users to users communication Administrator controlled	Database and programmed . structures for move to member contribution, authoring and administration
Roles for users	Consumers	Receivers Contributors	Users Contributors Leaders Facilitators	Facilitators Moderators Leaders Mentors Reviewers Team members Producers
Success factors	Measured in numbers of hits on the Web site	Measured in x numbers of members	Measured in numbers of contributions or postings Measured in numbers and types of issues and responses/ ratings	Role adoption Engagement Initiated ideas Teams Development Trends Group Tasks F2F activity
Main tasks maintenance & support	Database management	Database and listserv management	Database and listserv managementt Ongoing Facilitator/ leader (part-time ad-hoc)	Database and listserv management Ongoing Facilitator Offline coordination and motivation of members

Table 42.2   Investment required for interactive web structures (Stuckey, Lockyer and Hedberg, 2001)

42.6   Technology and the ties of community

> Educators are 'islands of excellence' with no ferry service to connect them to each other or to groups of their peers. (Reilly, 1999, p. 60)

Reilly's statement describes the problem that exists for in-service education where practising teachers find themselves operating in isolation once the door to the classroom closes. The 'ferry service' Reilly speaks of can be delivered for widely distributed individuals through a network or community supported by online technologies.

Much of the literature about communities of practice, whether face-to-face or on-line describes the activity of an already existing group or the ways that the group became distributed to draw in remote nodes. The group being formed at the centre of this research, if indeed it becomes a community remains to be seen, did not exist before people were attracted to become members online. Participants are each members of other communities and may have ties through these communities to some other members but no one community already exists to tie all the anticipated teacher groups (primary, secondary, drama, dance, design, creative arts, English) for the *StageStruck* community. As such this community is creating ties between distributed and for most previously unconnected individuals. The strength of those ties over time will serve to show whether the *StageStruck* Online Community operates as a group, a network or a community.

The *StageStruck* community is therefore unique in attempting to create new ties between wholly distributed individuals. This creation of ties and the role of technology are worth further exploration, for the technology and the ways it can be used in connecting people vary from extending and enhancing an existing community through to establishing a new community.

The following three models describe the roles of online technology used in the three research papers presented in this symposium.

Extending — extending the small community, with strong internal ties to include members and groups of the larger organisation (Lefoe *et al.*, Chapter 40, this volume).

The smaller tightly knit community of a new satellite campus where people have banded together now seeks to embrace members and groups in the larger main campus community

Figure 42.1

Enhancing — strengthening the value and relevance of existing ties between communities. (Lockyer *et al.*, Chapter 41, this volume). An existing community of teachers, teacher educators and pre-service teachers are exploring the online environment to strengthen and enhance the ties between them (see Figure 42.2).

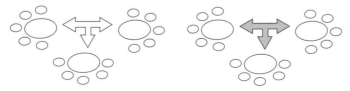

Figure 42.2

Establishing — building the ties to connect distributed individuals where no single inclusive set of ties previously existed. The *StageStruck* Professional Development Community seeks to, in managed phases, bring distributed individuals together through a network and eventually a community (see Figure 42.3).

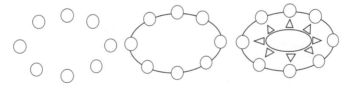

Figure 42.3

The website will serve as the meeting place of the group and the online tools offered there will serve to build first a loosely tied network and finally, through collaborative activity and development of a value system and shared purpose, a community of practice.

42.7   The plan and progress of the research

Etienne Wenger (1998) has described five stages as part of the natural development community.

1.   POTENTIAL – formation of a loose network with similar issues and needs
2.   COALESCING – people come together an find value in engaging in activities
3.   MATURING – members are engaging in joint activities and developing commitment and relationship
4.   ACTIVE – the community is established and goes through cycles of activities
5.   DISPERSING – the community has outlived its usefulness and people move on

These stage have been adopted in order to create the development plan for the StageStruck Professional Development Community seen in Table 42.3. The researchers cannot develop the community but can create opportunities throughout the development stages to assist the members to build a sense of community. It is recognised that such development requires time for uptake by the members and the plan therefore is to follow the activity over the following two years.

Established by	Task	Focus	Stage (Wenger 1998)
Organisation	ANALYSISE	• Needs	
	DESIGN	• On-line Environment	
* September 2001	ESTABLISH	• Group • Network	1st stage Potential
Members 2002+	BUILD	• Community	2nd stage Coalescing
	EVALUATE	• Roles And Activity	3rd stage Maturing

Table 42.3   The development process for StageStruck Professional Development Community

> Community is clearly something that can be facilitated and supported, but not created or controlled. It's a process that leaders can't mandate but can impede or prevent. (Cothrel and Williams, 1998, p. 24)

NEEDS ANALYSIS
1999/2000

DESIGN ON-LINE ENVIRONMENT
2000

CREATE A NETWORK
2001

BUILD A COMMUNITY
2002

Figure 42.4   The development timeline for StageStruck Professional Development Community

42.8   The online environment

Figure 42.5   http://www.stagestruck.uow.edu.au

To date the site has been registered and fax promotions were delivered to NSW state schools (primary and secondary). Formal educational organisations have been informed of the professional development nature of the site and curriculum leaders have been informed of the site's existence and the possibilities for involvement.

This has netted some 160 registrations from various members of the educational community. Teachers, lecturers, curriculum officers, professional development companies and students have registered as members on the site. However contributions to the site have not been forthcoming. Teachers have visited the site areas and downloaded tutorials and resources but made little addition to the discussion and sharing areas of the site. The site remained largely as it was for the first six months' existence in mid to latter 2001.

While registrations have grown steadily overt involvement has not. It has taken a very personal face-to-face and one-to-one approach to elicit the initial teacher contributions. Teachers registered on the site were each approached by email and asked their experience level with *StageStruck* and their interest in being a contributor. Teachers were asked to describe themselves as either 'newbie', 'experimenter' or 'expert' with using *StageStruck*. Most of those who replied described themselves as newbies with a few more experienced users describing themselves as experimenters. These experimenters were then encouraged to explore ideas for contribution to the site. Email communication was still not working as the way to communicate and encourage these members. So meetings and phone calls were scheduled where time and geography allowed. It was also decided to tap into some of the existing communities that these teachers belong to and to attend functions and workshops of these groups to promote involvement in the network. This is the stage that the research is currently working through, seeking out teacher communities and working through these existing networks with personal communications to build the membership but more importantly to build the interest in active involvement and contribution. It is the contribution and collaboration of a critical mass of members that is vital to establish a community. Community will not develop if consumption of resources made centrally available by the organisers is the sole member purpose.

This need for personal communication is borne out by the research findings of Cothrel and Williams (1999, p. 23) when they studied 15 different online communities. They state as part of their findings:

> Often community managers would place phone calls to the individuals who they wished
> to participate in the community. One organization created a 'social weaver' role,
> responsible for initiating a small number of members into the OLC. Such roles may be the
> key to bringing (and keeping) people on-line [...] In some OLCs the start-up phase involved
> active, one-on-one recruitment of members. Often OLC managers personally solicited
> participation from individuals who they thought could offer value to the community.

This personal approach and face-to-face activity seems even more critical when the community has no existing ties or relationships to rely on.

We have begun to research and investigate within the university the possibilities for accreditation for professional development spent online. Teachers canvassed at workshops were very interested in at least summary certificates to show hours of involvement in activities on the site.

It has taken two years of research and design for this group to get to the start of what Wenger (1998) describes as the second phase of community development, coalescing.

A group has formed and some small amount of networked activity has occurred but individuals are not yet engaging in activity that will further strengthen the ties between them. There is a marked reluctance amongst the teachers to contribute and to share over the online environment. This may be a cultural issue with teachers and it may be a readiness and availability issue related to use of the technology itself, or indeed a combination of both. Further research is being carried out at this stage to determine the basis of this reluctance to contribute in stark contrast to what we know of teachers as avid consumers of the resources the technology offers.

Activities have been planned to draw teachers into greater levels of contribution and to adopt varied roles in the network. The opportunities to be provided over the next year have been designed to move the group towards forming a community through addressing the four identified hallmarks. These are detailed in Table 42.4.

Clear and shared focus driven by the members		
• Think tanks • On-line tutorials • On-line meetings	• Resource upload/download • Quick Starter pages • Links to professional associations	• Publication area • Member project proposals • Feedback and suggestion forms
Employ appropriate technologies and styles of communication		
• Resource database • FAQs • Listservs • Threaded discussions	• Chat topic and guests • Links • Browser-based publishing • Archives	• Project activities • Template and PDF files • Ideas forums • F2f functions & events
Members feel part of a social network expertise, leadership, content contributions are valued.		
• Groups (k-6, 7-10) • Leadership & mentor program • Buddy activities (novice/expert) • Collaborative project development	• Member moderated/lead discussion • Experts on-line program • Rewards and accreditation for member activity • Promotion of local f2f activity	• Student publishing on-line • Schools link-up for local and International project partners • Publicising and encouraging member workshops and publications
Provides ongoing discussion, sharing of, and collaboration on, commonly valued things		
• Syllabus forums • Links • Celebration of student works & achievements • Teaching programs	• Database to support sharing units of work • Classroom practice forums • Member moderated/lead discussion	• Tutorials • Student research forum • Calls for participation in member developed projects • Workshops & conferences

Table 42.4   Syntheses of community essentials and listing of planned Internet activities and features (Stuckey and Hedberg, 2000)

42.9   What lessons have we learnt to date?

The research study cannot present conclusions at this stage, indeed it has raised more questions than answers. The research to date has raised a raft of issues and areas for further study in order to support this network's move toward true community. These have become part of the research focus for the upcoming year of activity, research and data collection.

At this stage the site hosts a network that has not yet developed the characteristics of community. It lacks the roles and the contributions suggested in the hallmarks to allow it to be labelled a community. It remains to be seen whether it will develop into a true community or whether as a network it might ably meet teacher needs.

Some of the raft of issues that have arisen:

- How does access to technology affect membership and contribution? Teachers do not have access to online technology at their fingertips as members in many of the other studies described in the literature. Many different teaching areas are considered lower priority in terms of access to technology in schools.

- What incentives does it take to elicit strongest teacher involvement? What precedent exists for equating time and contributions online with hours of professional development?

- How much personal and individual contact is required to establish member involvement and is this commitment required across the life and development of the community?

- What professional issues might impinge of teacher preparedness to share and publish their classroom activities and student work samples?

- What level of security and support will support teacher confidence to contribute?

- Is school technology adequate to support teacher involvement in online activities?

- Can such a network or community be used to support teacher standing in the profession?

- Will early adopters of the activities be strong in technology skills and experience or in drama/dance skills and experience or both?

- What parallels can be drawn between the development of this community and other teacher professional associations and groups, on or offline.

- Will student projects serve as the lure to involve teachers in activities that upon reflection they will recognize as valuable professional development?

42.10   References

Brown, J.S., Collins, A.. and Duguid, P. (1989) Situated cognition and the culture of learning, *Educational Researcher* **18**(1): 32—41.

Collins, A., Brown, J.S. and Newman, S.E. (1989) Cognitive apprenticeship: teaching the craft of reading, writing and mathematics. In L.B. Resnick (ed.), *Knowing, Learning and Instruction: Essays in Honor of Robert Glasser*. Hillsdale, NJ: Erlbaum.

Cothrel, J. and Williams, R. (1998) On-Line communities getting the most out of on-line discussion and collaboration, *Knowledge Management Review* **6**, Jan. —Feb. 99 <??>

Clancey, W.J. (1997) *Situated Cognition: On Human Knowledge and Computer Representation*. Cambridge: Cambridge University Press.

CLN Online (http://olt-bta.hrdc-drhc.gc.ca/CLN/clninit_e.html — accessed 03-06-01).

Duffy, T.M. and Cunningham, D.J. (1996) Constructivism: implications for the design and delivery of instruction, In D.H. Jonassen (ed.), *Handbook of Research for Educational Communications and Technology*. NY: Macmillan Library Reference.

Etzioni, A. (1998) In A. Etzioni (ed.), *The Essential Communitarian Reader*. Rowman & Littlefield.

Figallo, C. (1998) *Hosting Web Communities: Building Relationships, Increasing Customer Loyalty, and Maintaining A Competitive Edge*. John Wiley & Sons.

Galston, W.A. (1999) Does the Internet Strengthen Community? (http://www.puaf.umd.edu/IPPP/fall1999/internet_community.htm — accessed 22-11-01).

Grossman, P. and Wineburg, S. (2000) What makes teacher community different from a gathering of teachers? An Occasional paper. Document 0-00-1, Center for the Study of Teaching and Policy, University of Washington.

Hagel, J. and Armstrong, A.G. (1997) *Net Gain*. Boston, MA: Harvard Business School Press.

Hall, G.E., Wallace, R.C. and Dosset, W.A. (1973) A developmental conceptualization of the adoption process within educational institutions. ERIC Clearinghouse ED095 126.

Hedberg, J.G. (1997) Creating motivating interactive learning environments. Paper in Conference on Technological Education and National Development. Abu Dhabi, 6—8 April, pp. 203—18 (http://crm.hct.ac.ae/020hedberg.html — accessed 22-05-01).

Jonassen, D.H. and Mayes T. (1992) A manifesto for a constructivist approach to technology in higher education (http://www.icbl.hw.ac.uk/ctl/msc/ceejw1/paper11.html — accessed 09-01-01).

Joyce, B. and B. Showers (1982) The coaching of teaching, *Educational Leadership* **40**(1).

Kahn, T.M. (1998) Creating virtual design and learning communities (http://www.puaf.umd.edu/IPPP/fall1999/internet_community.htm — accessed 09-11-01).

Kim, A.J. (2000) *Community Building on the Web: Secret Strategies for Successful On-line Communities*. NY: Peachpit Press.

Lave, J. and Wenger, E. (1991) Situated learning in communities of practice. In L.B. Resnick, J.M. Levine and S.D. Teasley (eds), *Perspectives on Socially Shared Cognition*, pp. 63—82. Washington, DC: American Psychological Association.

Little, J.W. (1993) Teacher's professional development in a climate of educational reform, *Educational Evaluation and Policy Analysis* **15**(2).

Mueller, C. (1999) Networks of 'personal communities' and 'group communities' in different online communication services: first results of an empirical study in Switzerland. Paper presented at the *Exploring Cyber Society Conference*, 5—7 July 1999 (http://sozweber.unibe.ch/ii/virt/newcastle.html — accessed 22-11-01).

Novick, R. (1996) Actual Schools, Possible Practices: New Directions in Professional Development (http://olam.ed.asu.edu/apaa/v4n14.html).

Palloff, R.M. and Pratt, K.P. (1999) *Building Learning Communities in Cyberspace: Effective Strategies for the On-line*. The Jossey-Bass Higher and Adult Education Series.

Pennell, J. and Firestone, W. (1998) Teacher-to-teacher professional development through state-sponsored networks, *Phi Delta Kappan* **89**(5): 354–7.

Preece, J. (2000) *On-line Communities: Designing Usability, Supporting Sociability*. Chichester: John Wiley & Sons.

Reingold, H. (1992) *Virtual Communities*. Addison-Wesley, San Francisco.

Reilly, R.A. (1999) EdNet@Umass: providing quality professional development via the Internet, *Journal Technical Horizons in Education* **26**, March: 60.

Spiro, R.J., Feltovich, P.L., Jacobson, M.J. & Coulson, R.L. (1991) Cognitive flexibility, constructivism and hypertext: random access to instruction for advanced knowledge acquisition in ill-structured domains. *Educational Technology Journal*, **31**(5), 24–33.

Stuckey, B., Hedberg J. G. (2000). Building on-line community: the way forward for professional development In R. Sims, M. O'Reilly & S. Sawkins (Eds), *Learning to Choose: Choosing to Learn* short paper presented to ASCILITE 2000 Annual Conference Coffs Harbour, NSW: Southern Cross University Press.

Stuckey, B., Lockyer, L. & Hedberg, J. (2001). The Case for Community: On-line and Ongoing Professional Support for Communities of Practice. In M. J. Mahony, D. Roberts, and A. Gofers, (Eds) *Education Odyssey 2001: Continuing the journey through adaptation and innovation – Collected papers from the 15th Biennial Forum of the Open and Distance Learning Association of Australia*. Sydney: ODLAA/Open and Distance Learning Association of Australia. CD-ROM

Vygotsky, L. S., (1978) *Mind in Society*. Cambridge, MA Harvard University Press

Wellman, & Gulia, M., (1997)Net Surfers Don't Ride Alone: Virtual Communities as Communities. In *Communities in Cyberspace* edited by Marc A. Smith. Smith & Peter Kollock. London (Routledge)

Wenger, E. (1998). *Communities of practice: Learning, meaning, and identity*. Cambridge: Cambridge University Press.

Sue Clegg and Alison Hudson
Sheffield Halam University, UK

Higher education is no longer confined within the boundaries of the traditional post-compulsory education sector. The drivers for exploiting the new capabilities of C&ITs come from an expanded international market of education providers (Cunningham, 1998), policy-driven initiatives to promote lifelong learning (Coffield, 1999), and business investment to meet the needs of the knowledge economy. Policy is being shaped by the perception that new media can extend learning to everyone regardless of location. Any appreciation of new environments for learning, therefore, needs to be understood in the context of the Government's orientation towards globalisation, and its view that the competitive position of the UK can be enhanced through the development of a highly skilled and trained workforce.

One of the clearest statements of UK Government's attitudes to changing learning environments was the made by David Blunkett, then Minister of State for Education, setting out his views on the future of higher education. Blunkett framed the higher education agenda in terms of the likely impact of globalisation:

> this change is related to the fundamental socio-economic development of the last quarter of the 20th century: globalisation. It is therefore with the challenge of globalisation that higher education policy now starts. (Blunkett, 2000, para. 7)

The UK, and other Governments, increasingly view a high skills strategy as being at the heart of 'the productive capacity of the new economy and the prosperity of our democracy'. Universities are exhorted to open up to business in order to play their role in the knowledge economy and to provide students with 'a flair for enterprise' as well as C&IT and other skills.

Delivering this vision involves multiple institutions: especially created institutions such as the University for Industry; an expanded role for traditional higher education institutions using new media to extend their delivery (Laurillard, 1993); companies with their own training programmes e.g. Motorola (Motorola 2000), British Airways (Lancaster University, 1999), British Telecom (Solstra, 2000), and Unipart (UCG, 2000); and newer global market entrants concentrating specifically on e-learning, e.g. Online learning (2001) Hungry Minds (2000). The pressures on universities in the creation of new learning environments are therefore wider than those associated with the traditional higher education sector.

Moreover, learning is no longer conceptualised as taking place at the beginning of a career; rather changing economic conditions necessitate constant updating of skills. As Malcolm Tight (1998) has observed 'Lifelong learning for all is the new imperative'. Universities are not solely concerned with providing undergraduate courses; they are also involved with the provision of a range of skills and courses at various stages in a person's career. This meshes with the Government's widening participation agenda. It is widely accepted that it is impossible to contemplate a future in which only a minority of the population participates in higher education. The need for a highly qualified workforce, widening participation and lifelong learning all fit together as a way of envisaging the future of higher education and the need for new learning environments.

Our key argument is that the main issue confronting all higher education institutions is that of responding to change. We therefore need to understand the drivers and barriers to innovation and reorganisation. In this context we look at how Sheffield Hallam University works in supporting innovation and change by considering a number of case studies. The case studies are not designed to be exhaustive; rather they are a way of exploring some of the complexities the change process involves. Institutions in the UK and internationally have different cultures, purposes and histories. The answer to the question *What Kind of University?* (Brennan *et al.*, 1999) yields no unitary response; however, we hope that by critically reflecting on our experience we can offer readers an insight into strategies that can work, as well as pointing to some of the difficulties. The following chapters draw on the experience of working collaboratively with staff in designing new learning environments. Researchers have worked alongside both lecturing staff and students to document and support decision-making processes among groups of staff by providing data to help shape learning, teaching and assessment strategies. These data provide the basis for Chapters 43–5. Chapter 46 summarises the responses of the participants at the ISL conference to the case study activity on the adoption of C&IT in higher education.

References

Blunkett, D. (2000) *Greenwich Speech*. Department for Education and Employment (http://cms1.gre.ac.uk/dfee/#speech).

Brennan, J., Fedrowitz, J., Huber, M. and Shah, T. (eds) (1999) *What Kind of University? International Perspectives on Knowledge, Participation and Governance*. Buckingham: SRHE and Open University Press.

Coffield, F. (1999) Breaking the consensus: lifelong learning as social control, *British Educational Research Journal* 25(4): 479–99.

Cunningham, S., Tapsall, S., Ryan, Y., Stedman, R., Bagdon, K. and Flew, T. (1998) *New Media and Borderless Education: A Review of the Convergence between Global Media Networks and Higher Education Provision*. Australian Department of Training and Youth Affairs (http://www.detya.gov.au/archive/highered/eippubs/eip97-22/execsum.htm).

Hungry Minds (2000) http://www.hungryminds.com/

Laurillard, D. (1993) *Rethinking University Teaching: A Framework for the Effective Use of Educational Technology*. London: Routledge.

Motorola (2000) Motorola University (http://mu.motorola.com/).

Online Learning (2001) http://www.onlinelearning.net/Index.html

Solstra (2000) Online Learning (http://www.solstra.com/Solstra2000/mnframes.htm).

Tight, M. (1998) Education, education, education: the vision of lifelong learning in the Kennedy, Dearing and Fryer reports, *Oxford Review of Education* 24(4): 473–85.

43 Policy frameworks – entering the labyrinth or 'it's not just the technology'

Louise Thorpe, Madeleine Freewood

Sheffield Halam University, UK

43.1   Introduction

As part of its Teaching Quality Enhancement initiative, in 1999, the Higher Education Funding Council for England required all higher education institutions to produce a Learning, Teaching and Assessment (LTA) Strategy. The aim of this was to raise the profile of teaching by focusing on enhancement activity at a strategic institutional level. In preparing its submission, Sheffield Hallam University (SHU) identified three key priorities:

- flexible delivery with time, pace and, increasingly, place chosen by students;
- support for a diversity of students within a culture of lifelong learning;
- opportunities for realising the potential of the appropriate use of technology to enable and facilitate learning (SHU, 2000a, p. 3).

At an institutional level the decision was made to take a devolved approach in the implementation of the LTA strategies as a way of increasing university-wide ownership and engagement among all stakeholders. This policy sought to create a balance between achieving institutional aims and empowering individual academic staff to drive and embed change. In many ways this has involved walking a tightrope between the need for standards and guidance at a university level, and the risk of over-standardisation that can act to stifle academic creativity and innovation. What follows is an exploration of this tension within the specific context of the devolved LTA model at SHU.

43.2   The devolved approach

With the key priorities as the starting point, each Director of School was invited to produce LTA Strategies for their Schools. These were written in consultation with other members of staff within the School and reflected the institutional priorities in relation to their schools' own objectives, policies, and, importantly, culture. In December 1999, the school-based strategies were submitted to the Pro Vice-Chancellor (Academic Development) who revised the institution's strategy to reflect them, thus creating a loop so that the goals of academic staff and university could be informed by each other.

The next stage in the implementation of these strategies involved the same ethos. Each school was asked to identify two LTA Co-ordinators who were given a specific role to implement and co-ordinate LTA strategy activity, and encourage engagement across the school. LTA Co-ordinators were also identified within central departments, including Registry, Facilities Directorate, the Learning Centre, CIS (computer services) etc. The LTA Co-ordination group meets once or twice per term and is managed and facilitated by the Learning and Teaching Institute (LTI). This provides an opportunity for them to share experiences, discuss common issues, identify areas of common interest for collaboration, and provide feedback on strategic activities to central departments and senior management, either directly or through the LTI. In addition to these meetings, biannual reviews of activity are undertaken by the LTI and reported to the Academic Board.

In April 2001 each school and the LTI completed a self-evaluation of activity over the past 18 months, reflecting upon the strengths and weaknesses of the initiative, the support available to them and their strategic plans for the future. These were submitted to the Pro Vice-Chancellor (Academic Development) who then fed back on the issues raised to the Co-ordination group in person, and steps were taken at institutional level to address some of the barriers being experienced. A report (Thorpe, 2001) of this activity has been circulated to all members of the LTA Co-ordination group, Directors of Schools and other interested individuals within SHU to further promote a culture of openness, encourage the sharing of experience, and provide opportunities to learning from each other. The Learning and Teaching Research Institute have undertaken additional evaluative work. This looks specifically at the way the Learning and Teaching Institute has supported the activities within the schools and how this could be improved in the future.

43.3   Communication and Information Technology

While explicit reference is made to Communication and Information Technology (C&IT) in SHU's third strategic priority, its impact is much wider, as the role of learning technology is pervasive across all three priorities. Emphasis on the technology has not necessarily created new *problems*, but has rather served to accentuate existing issues. The use of technology increases the visibility of all aspects of learning, teaching and assessment, giving them permanence beyond face-to-face contact, and making activities available for scrutiny after the event. This increases the need to address these issues and provide institutional guidance or policy, as appropriate, to staff wishing to incorporate technology into their curriculum design. Thus the university has experienced a tension between its desire to encourage devolution and academic freedom, and the need to offer centralised guidance on the emerging issues. In determining how best to deliver the support necessary without encroaching on academic freedom, there was a consultation involving internal research by the LTI identifying staff perceptions of e-learning (Hanson and Wan, 2000). This was an enabling activity and set out to inform policy decisions at an institutional level to establish an inclusive framework for C&IT development.

The findings of this research were consistent with that of Hodgson *et al.* (1994). Hodgson *et al.* (1994) focused upon the levels of staff IT skills required to undertake their academic duties. The SHU research, coming as it were in a different 'technological-era', focused upon staff attitudes to e-learning. In both pieces of research, key findings include the importance to staff of firm and visible commitment and support at the institutional level. Also important is a clear relationship between the overall institutional strategy, and the necessary staff development and training programmes.

At SHU, the institutional commitment to e-learning was put into effect through the selection of a Virtual Learning Environment (VLE) that would be supported university-wide for the next three years. Models of evaluation and consultation that have underpinned such choices were reviewed, including institutions in the UK, USA and Australia, particularly the

Universities of Bristol, Huddersfield and Coventry in the UK and the University of New South Wales, the University of Southern Queensland and James Cook University, Australia. The latter provided particularly rich information about comparative studies of the various platforms and the way staff have reacted to the decision-making process (http://www.tld.jcu.edu.au/general/survey_re/, 2000). Using the data available, SHU decided to undertake a short pilot of the virtual learning environment, Blackboard© (http://www.blackboard.com), from January to July 2001.

The choice to pilot Blackboard© was based on a number of factors; in particular its ease of use and the low level of technical skills required for staff and students to engage with the environment. The decision drew upon lessons learned through the internal SHU evaluation of the Virtual Campus (2000b), and research into staff views of barriers to e-learning (Hanson and Wan, 2000), together with the earlier works of Brown (1998) and Hart *et al.* (1999). Senior management of the institution and staff in the LTI leading the pilot were keen to provide an environment accessible to the majority of academics, not just the '10 per cent enthusiasts' (JISC, 2000). This ease of use allows academics to effectively 'put the door back on their classroom' and establish their own identity within their course or module, and offers scope for experimentation and innovation. For this level of engagement to be adequately supported, staff development activities had to be designed to avoid the establishment of a dependency culture between the academics and the technologists. The pilot activity was not to evaluate the technological aspects of the environment, but rather ensure that its functionality could adequately meet the specific needs of SHU staff and students.

43.4   Entering deeper into the labyrinth

So far we have outlined how SHU has determined to integrate and embed the use of learning technologies, how policy decisions are informed by research into staff views and how these policies in turn inform practice and activity within schools. Up to this point, the experiences of earlier travellers into the labyrinth, as well as internal consultation with stakeholders have informed the decision-making process. As we travel deeper into the labyrinth, this drives the need for existing institutional policies to be reviewed and refined, and for new policies to be established from first principles. These cover a range of issues such as technology and assessment, content production and ownership, inclusion and widening participation. From these we have chosen the following case studies; electronic submission of assignments, accessibility, and quality assurance and enhancement, to illustrate how SHU has approached some of these issues.

43.4.1   Electronic submission of assessments

While it has been technologically possible for students to submit work to academics as an email attachment over the last few years, this has not previously been allowed by university regulations. This stance was adopted for a number of reasons; concern about level of student access to hardware and general IT competency being primary factors. As the number of students with access to a computer at home has increased (for example 35 per cent of all hits on the log-in page of Blackboard© took place off-campus over the year-long trial period), the anxiety over access has dissipated and renewed the impetus to revisit the issue.

The suggestion that for certain groups of students online submission would bring about some concrete benefits, for example distance learning students, mature students with family commitments and students with disabilities or learning difficulties (Brown *et al.*, 1999) has further added weight to this interest in reviewing electronic submission procedures. The institutional commitment to C&IT enabled learning has increased the opportunity to support a diverse student population because of the increased flexibility. This commitment is reflected in national trends that emphasise a more 'student centred' approach to learning.

Previous resistance to online submission also centred on concerns relating to the potential incompatibilities of format, cost to the institution and the practice of centralised rather than direct submission. Blackboard offers specific functionality for the electronic submission of assignments, maintaining the centrality of submission while allowing students to submit in a place and time convenient to them.

This functionality, combined with the shift in culture described above, has led to, what many staff feel is a long overdue review of the rules and regulations, with regard to submissions of assignments at SHU. A strategic approach to electronic submission also facilitates the exploration of other related avenues in a coherent manner. For example, it has been shown that for plagiarism detection software tools of any kind to be used effectively, a robust and workable electronic submission strategy needs to be in place (JISC, 2001).

Responding to this a working party, made up of representatives from members of the Learning and Teaching Institute, School based academics and Registry, and in consultation with Corporate Information Services (CIS), is currently introducing a draft protocol that will be piloted in the current academic year. The protocol must strike the fine balance between offering appropriate and robust guidelines for submission and not being over prescriptive about what the institution considers to be best practice with regard to modes of submission. From the outset, the protocol states that 'having students submit assessment documentation online is an opportunity which staff *may* wish to exploit. Staff will not be required to pursue this path, it is for the academic member of staff to pursue if they are convinced that it is appropriate to a particular group of students.' (Working party document, p. 2).

While the pedagogic choice of when to require that work be submitted electronically is left to the academic, the protocol clearly dictates the roles and responsibilities of all parties: academic, administrator and student, in the submission process. The institution needs to ensure that students' rights are protected, and that the guidance given conforms to existing assessment regulations. At the same time, however, care needs to be taken of the dangers of creating an administrative burden on course support staff where a cohort may submit in a number of different formats depending upon personal circumstances and learner preferences. It is also important to limit the opportunities for student abuse of the submission process.

The process of negotiation between prescription and guidance is thus ongoing and continually being enacted. How this will translate as the protocol is implemented in the pilot phase, at the individual school and course levels, will therefore be important. What is yet to be explored, for example, is how the institutional support of one type of assessment submission process, with the aims of increasing flexibility, will impact on existing assessment methods that cannot easily be translated into a mode suitable for online submission, i.e. portfolios or other evidence based assessments. An evaluation of this pilot stage is to be carried out by Research Assistants in the LTI, the findings of which will feed back and inform practice at an institutional level, before rolling out the protocol across the whole university. There is a continuing aim to balance guidance and prescription, to help ensure flexibility is achieved for the benefit of a diverse student population, and continue to facilitate academic creativity.

43.4.2　Accessibility

Issues related to student accessibility and parity of experience have long been on the agenda, the permanence and explicit visibility of learning practices and material when part of an online environment refocus and re-emphasise these issues. As with online submission, concerns over physical access by students to hardware and software, and the impact of differing levels of student IT literacy skills, are issues that need to be addressed if learning that takes place online is to be accessible by all. Such issues will be discussed later in the symposium from a student perspective. From a policy frameworks standpoint they are also important in terms of informing decisions about levels of investment in the technical infrastructure, student support and the appropriate accommodation of hardware.

Increasing use of C&IT means that staff development is also an equally important consideration that has to be addressed at an institutional level. This needs to encompass not only practical skills, but also issues around designing accessible and pedagogically sound on-line material. For example, where staff in HE might have at one time been able to 'wing it', responding to the needs of the students present by tailoring their lecturing style on the day, this is not possible in the same way with courses that are delivered online. Ensuring accessibility therefore means moving from the responsive model to an 'inclusive' model. If accessibility is not considered at either the design or implementation stage of the 'e-learning curriculum', sections of the student population can be excluded from taking a full and active part in the learning, teaching and assessment activities planned.

Raising the profile of accessibility, particularly in relation to the needs of students with disabilities has thus become a key issue for SHU over the pilot phase of the VLE. This is made even more pertinent by the influence of a range of new legislation that has come into force, although yet to be tested in the courts. Article 2 of the First Protocol of the Human Rights Act (1998) states 'no person shall be denied the right to education'. The full ramifications of what this means for HE is still to be fully realised across the sector as a whole. The same also applies in terms of the full implications of the SEN and Disability Act 2001, which will be mostly operative from 1 September 2002. The Act will make it unlawful to discriminate against disabled people or students by treating them less favourably than others; and responsible bodies will be required to provide certain types of reasonable adjustments to provision where disabled students or other disabled people might other wise be substantially disadvantaged.

The presence of such external factors, which also includes Quality Assurance Agency (QAA) guidance, adds another dimension to the balancing act between institutional guidance and academic freedom. SHU is responding to this, by undertaking a yearlong project to establish best practice guidelines for the use of Blackboard© as part of the implementation strategy.

SHU already has a well-established reputation for supporting students with disabilities and learning difficulties, and the institutional move to increase the use of C&IT, allows the university to place this experience at the cornerstone of new developments. Expertise in the university's Student Services Centre, in co-ordination with Corporate Information Systems (CIS) is being drawn on to inform considerations in relation to the interface for Blackboard© for example. Specific staff workshops for members of the university's Disabled Student Support Team have taken place to demonstrate the functionality of Blackboard©, so that staff are able to inform strategic practice decisions. Through this process the Disabled Student Support Team are also considering ways of using Blackboard© to support students with specific learning needs. For example, a course is to be designed in Blackboard© by a member of the team to support dyslexic students.

While this type of activity is taking place on a strategic decision-making level, the university is also looking to create partnerships and learn from the experience of other institutions to inform staff practice. For example, speakers from the University of Wales, Cardiff, (UWIC) came to participate in the e-learning week events held for SHU members of staff in May 2001. UWIC, which also uses Blackboard© as its university VLE, shared good practice guidelines with academic staff around accessibility in a series of workshops. Further resources and information for staff are provided on the SHU e-learning website (http://www.shu.ac.uk/e-learning). The experience of the year-long project focused on accessibility will continue to feed into this.

Promoting and enhancing an 'accessible curriculum' is clearly an ongoing process, its impact reaching beyond benefits for set groups of students, such as those with disabilities or learning difficulties. While increased use of C&IT in learning has served to reinvigorate the debate around accessibility and strategies to effectively support the needs of a diverse student population, it also encourages staff and the sector to scrutinise past/current practice in a face-to face environment. For example, ensuring the use of high-quality paper-based material (both in terms of clarity and appearance) is just as important as ensuring the format of online learning is accessible. The Special Educational Needs & Disability legislation and QAA Code of Practice for Disabled Students makes no distinction between technology delivered learning and face-to-face learning. The requirement rather is that all learning be accessible.

43.4.3   Quality assurance and enhancement

It is within the quality arena that the issues of conflict between standardisation and academic freedom, central control and devolution, and the risks around innovative learning techniques are highlighted most strongly. Learning, teaching and assessment, within UK higher education, are subject to a series of Quality Assurance Agency procedures. These involve external reviewers 'judging' performance within particular subject areas, disciplines or across the institution. The use of learning technologies to deliver or support aspects of learning, teaching and assessment are necessarily, therefore, subject to the same Quality Assurance Agency reviews. This external 'policing' can make staff in some subject areas reluctant to make innovative use of technology, particularly where they suspect that their reviewers do not favour the use of technology. This suspicion may not be a reality, but may be enough to stifle innovation where the risk is seen to be too great. Also staff may not wish to challenge a status quo that has in earlier reviews provided them with a high overall score for quality.

At this point, therefore, it is tempting to say that the 'safest' course of action from a quality assurance perspective is to reject the innovative use of technology. In reality, however, the Quality Assurance Agency can be seen as an external driver for the use of learning technologies looking at the quality of learning resources and activities from a perspective of modernity, varied student experience and appropriateness. The issue facing staff is that they are encouraged to use learning technology, but must ensure that this can still be judged as of appropriate quality to perform well in external assessments. From an institutional perspective the issue becomes what policies need to be in place to support staff through this process and offer assurances to the institution itself that the quality of learning, teaching and assessment is maintained.

The institution could take a strong centralised quality stance encouraging standardisation and the use of templates for development of materials. This may involve materials being submitted to central departments for approval before use and to regular internal reviews. This may indeed contribute to ensuring a certain quality threshold, but may also lead to over-standardising, thus stifling academic freedom and creativity. Also within the context of the quality of student experience, such standardisation is likely to conflict with the importance of variety. The concerns about over-standardisation, combined with SHU's already devolved approach to learning, teaching and assessment, make such a centralised approach to controlling the quality of learning technology inappropriate.

SHU has taken the stance that the use of learning technology is no different from using other learning materials, and that the responsibility for approving their use falls within the remit of the school-based Quality Committees. It is possible, and by the very nature of devolution, likely, that this approval can lead to different levels of engagement in different schools. There is a need for Quality Committees to consider the implications of using e-learning upon the quality of the learning experience. It is possible that a less than 'confident' Quality Committee could be wary of approving innovation, not feeling sufficiently well informed to approve these changes. Alternatively they may find themselves approving a use of learning technology based upon their perceptions of the unit leader's IT literacy and expertise, rather than its appropriateness to the learning experience. The institution must, in taking such a devolved stance, ensure that the Quality Committees are confident and comfortable making decisions about the use of learning technologies, just as they would with more traditional methods.

This presents a responsibility to educational developers and learning technology advisers to work closely with Quality Committees within schools to provide guidance about effectiveness and appropriateness of learning technologies to address certain aspects of the learning teaching and assessment experience: for example, which learning outcomes are best addressed via e-learning, how to effectively computer assess higher order skills from Bloom's taxonomy, how to encourage deep learning or independent learning. Equally importantly is the need to highlight where technology is not the most appropriate vehicle. As a result of the Blackboard$copy; pilot, the LTI has offered guidance to Quality Committees in the form of both face-to-face dialogues and documentation, in addition to the guidance offered to individual staff engaging in e-learning activity. There is also a major thread in the project plan for the implementation and integration of the virtual learning environment in the coming year to work closely with Quality Committees reviewing their procedures for minor modifications, major modifications and validations. This research will look at the incidence of changes relating to technology enabled learning, the quality issues and concerns arising within Committees surrounding these and guidance that can be offered centrally on these issues. Again it is intended that the findings from this are shared across the institution so that all schools can learn from each other's experiences.

The emphasis in this case study so far has been on the need to ensure a certain level of quality is maintained. However, it must be noted that the focus of the HEFCE Learning Teaching and Assessment (LTA) Strategy Initiative has been to offer incentives for institutions to *enhance* the quality of the learning experience for students. So beyond the Quality Assurance activities already addressed there is the need for institutions to look at how this can be achieved. The explicit priority in the SHU LTA strategy is to encourage the *appropriate* use of C&IT. It is this appropriateness that forms the basis for university policy-making, ensuring that there is a clear and common understanding by senior management and academic staff of what this means in terms of variety of experience, the balance between face-to-face contact and online delivery, quality and efficiency, and its role within the assessment and feedback process.

The use of learning technology has the effect of making the learning materials and activities not only more visible, as mentioned earlier in this chapter, but visible for a longer period of time and open to scrutiny by those who would normally be outside the walls of the physical learning environment. This necessarily causes anxiety in staff about being willing to take risks in such a public and permanent forum. Consequently staff can be tempted to 'play safe' with materials more than would be the case for face-to-face learning experiences. If this is the case how can this be seen as enhancing the quality of the student experience? Again the institution has a responsibility to make clear its position on innovation and risk taking as a way of pushing forward the frontiers of learning experiences available. It must also recognise the role of champions within this context and the benefits to all of sharing experiences, both positive and negative, through internal staff development events and conferences, these being promoted to staff as valued contributions to the scholarship of teaching and learning. This aspect of internal dissemination is covered in more detail in the paper regarding staff experience later in this symposium.

43.5   Conclusion

This chapter, through the choice of case studies (electronic submission of assignments, accessibility, and quality assurance and enhancement), demonstrates how an increased engagement with learning technologies does not create new 'problems' in learning, teaching and assessment, but rather accentuates existing issues. The visibility and permanence of learning technologies, combined with the need to ensure the use of such technology is pedagogically sound, create a tension between the necessity for institutional commitment and guidance on the one hand, and academic freedom on the other. This relationship is further heightened by the external requirements set by the QAA, legislation and so forth. SHU is responding to this challenge by seeking to implement a devolved model which aims to be responsive as opposed to prescriptive in terms of addressing institutional policy. Inclusive ways of working, consultation, and research and evaluation are at the heart of this process.

43.6   References

A'Herran, A. (2000) *The Search for an Online System for Teaching & Learning at JCU*(http://www.tld.jcu.edu.au/general/survey_re/ – accessed 07-09-01).

Brown, S. (1998) Reinventing the university, *ALT-J* **6**(1): 30–7.

Brown, S., Race, P. and Bull, J. (1999) *Computer-Assisted Assessment in Higher Education*. London: Kogan Page.

Hanson, J. (2001) *Report of the Working Party on Computer Assisted Assessment (CAA) Regulations*. Internal document. Sheffield Hallam University.

Hanson, J. and Wan, S. (2000) *E-learning: Past Perspectives and Future Directions. Internal document. Sheffield Hallam University.*

Hart, G., Ryan, Y. and Bagdon, K. (1999) Supporting organizational change: fostering a more flexible approach to course delivery, *ALT-J* **7**(1): 46–53.

Hodgson, M., McCartan, A. and Hare, C. (1994) *A Framework for the Development of Core IT Skills for University Staff*. CVCP/USDU Publications.

Plagiarism Detection Pilot Project (2001) JISC Committee for Integrated Environments for Learners: Pilot Studies of Plagiarism Detection Software 2001 (http://www.jisc.ac.uk/mle/plagiarism/strandone.html – accessed 07-09-01).

Sheffield Hallam University (2000a) *Learning, Teaching and Assessment Strategy*, AB/5/99/6.2, Sheffield: Sheffield Hallam University.

Sheffield Hallam University (2000b) *Virtual Campus Evaluation and LTA/TQEF Actions and Proposed Actions*. Internal document.

Special Educational Needs and Disability Act 2001, UK. Chapter 10 (http://www.legislation.hmso.gov.uk/acts/acts2001/20010010.htm – accessed 07-09-01).

Thorpe, L. (ed.) (2001) *Schools and LTI Self-evaluations Based on Activity to 27 April 2001*. Internal document. Sheffield Hallam University.

44 Staff attitudes – staff experiences and the dilemmas for practitioners

Julie Hanson and Stephen Wan

Sheffield Hallam University, UK

44.1 Introduction

Recent changes in Higher Education, and the changes in the technology available, have placed increasing pressure on Higher Education Institutions (HEIs) to embrace new media alongside their more traditional means of delivering learning and teaching. The Dearing Report (HMSO, 1997) recommended that 'all higher education institutions in the UK should have in place overarching communications and information strategies by 1999/2000' (Recommendation 41). Increasingly, however, academic staff are coming under pressure from government bodies and university management, to show innovation in the use of C&IT (communication and information technology) in the new educational and political context of a mass education system (Clegg *et al.*, 2000; Scott, 1995).

The desire to embrace new media is far from all pervasive among academic staff. A recent enquiry by JISC (January 2001) into the roles and functions of UK Higher Education staff involved in the development of learning and teaching through the use of new media identified both the growing numbers of staff involved in using learning technologies and the diversity of their work. Among the groups of staff, which the report identifies, it classifies 10 per cent of all academic staff as innovative in terms of their use of learning technologies. These staff are actively involved in:

- delivering, supporting and assessing student learning by means of C&IT;
- adapting existing programmes and modules to incorporate use of learning technologies;
- updating and reviewing learning programmes to include learning technologies;
- supporting, updating and maintaining electronic learning materials;
- providing content for CBL materials or learning environments (JISC, 2001, p. 33).

The study found that this figure was fairly consistent across institutions, and suggested that there are probably around 8,000 such staff working in UK universities. This role may not demand a very high percentage of personnel hours spent on work relating to the use of learning technology. 'Innovation' is also a context-related term – the definition was carefully worded to exclude routine use of well-supported technical applications, and institutions vary widely with respect to which technologies are routinely used.

Beyond this group lays the remaining '90 per cent' of academics who are not deemed to be innovators in terms of their use of learning technologies. For both institutions and educational developers, the key to ensuring that the student experience is enhanced by the appropriate use of innovative media is to reach this '90 per cent'. Indeed, it is this group that is increasingly the focus of awareness raising exercises. The challenge is not to achieve innovative practice among 100 per cent of academics but rather to disseminate the possibilities of what is deemed as 'innovation' among the '90 per cent'. Gibbons and Hillard (1996) argue that:

> although there is a great deal of hype about the impact of new technology, the revolutionary convergence of various strands of communications technology has opened up the potential for radical innovation in the delivery of teaching and learning materials. (Gibbons and Hillard, 1996, p. 2)

Gibbon and Hillard cite George Richardson (1997) in refining the meaning of the word 'innovation':

> continuous product and process innovation as *routine innovation*, thus distinguishing it from radical innovation, where major breakthroughs so change the industrial landscape as to permit routine product and process development to set off in new directions. In most industries, firms now expect routine innovation and will not expect to stay in business unless they can successfully undertake it. Innovation of this kind is a necessary, if not sufficient, condition for earning normal profits. Firms are of course aware of the possibility of radical innovations, which close avenues of development with which they are familiar, while opening up totally new ones down which their own capabilities may or may not permit them to proceed. (Gibbons and Hillard, 1996, p. 2)

This is an interesting distinction when applied to C&IT in Higher Education Institutions, in reflecting on how many academics are able to use C&IT for the purposes of 'radical innovation'.

A recent study into the staff attitudes towards C&IT in Scottish HEIs (Anderson *et al.*, 2000) identified that awareness raising exercises were having some effect: 'Very few staff at any level viewed C&IT as of little or no value to teaching in their subject, most seeing it as being of moderate to significant value, but more for quality enhancement than for efficiency gains' (Anderson *et al.*, 2000, p. 15). Nonetheless, it concluded that 'significant barriers' to the use of learning technology still exist, in particular the lack of time for academic staff to spend developing and embedding learning technologies, and the relative importance placed on research as compared to teaching.

Without knowledge of the attitudes of academic staff as a whole to learning technologies, it is difficult to develop strategies which will encourage these staff to explore and take up the new media available to them. Echoing the above findings, among the staff surveyed as part of the Dearing Report (HMSO, 1997), the most frequently cited reasons for staff changing teaching methods were the availability of new technologies, increased student numbers and resource constraints. Qualitative data resulting from a large number of interviews with staff at Sheffield Hallam University testify to the variability of staff attitudes.

Certainly, the distinction between the '10 per cent' and the '90 per cent' is one to be borne in mind when assessing staff attitudes – but it is clear that the '90 per cent' cannot simply be perceived as anything approaching a monolithic or homogenous group. Indeed, the research undertaken at SHU sought to identify the varying attitudes and experiences of those staff who were not 'innovators'. It also tried to ascertain how these staff could be best informed about, and given the opportunity to explore the use of learning technologies.

44.2 Research on the staff experience of C&IT – enhanced approaches to teaching and learning at SHU

Interviews were undertaken as part of a number of research projects (described below) conducted at both university and school level which survey the attitudes of staff to learning technology. The findings highlighted how some of the issues raised reflected the institutional context of Sheffield Hallam University, but that others were applicable to the Higher Education sector as a whole. In drawing on a number of research projects, it is possible to offer some tentative conclusions as to how staff attitudes have changed over time and in response to specific institutional initiatives. Moreover, we will also explore how a lack of take up in early learning technology initiatives has shaped more recent approaches to encouraging staff participation. Other issues raised were common to both enthusiasts and novices and we were able to discuss how staff perceive the varying importance and relevance of new media. An important element of the research undertaken is that it is inappropriate simply to approach staff as the enthusiasts/experienced and the non-enthusiasts/inexperienced. This research is necessary as a basis for understanding how institutional strategy can disseminate the initiatives which the '10 per cent' have developed to the remaining '90 per cent'.

Factors influencing staff attitudes towards the use and potential use of new media are coming to the fore through continual generation of new data. Our initial research has indicated that staff attitudes are shaped by staff beliefs about students' perceptions of the use, or non-use, of new media. This is linked to the dilemmas which face staff in determining whether to, and how best to, incorporate the new media into their teaching. For example, Stephens *et al.* (1998) comment on the dilemmas that staff can face in introducing Computer-assisted Assessment (CAA):

> It must be acknowledged that no system, technology-based or not, is foolproof. There are advantages and disadvantages to technology-based and paper-based systems. (Stephens *et al.*, 1998, p. 285)

This chapter draws on three significant pieces of research that have been conducted at SHU over the course of two years (1999–2000) in relation to the staff perception and experience of the use of C&IT in teaching.

44.2.1 Research project 1: Evaluation of the Virtual Campus initiative

The first of these research projects came out of SHU's first major university wide C&IT initiative; the introduction of the Virtual Campus (VC) in 1997/1998. The VC was a platform intended for staff to engage with allocated web space that had successfully been provided for every academic in the university. The aim was then for a team associated with the project, staff from the Learning and Teaching Institute (LTI) and Corporate Information Systems (CIS), to provide support for academics. In 1999/2000, an evaluation on the 'Present State and Future Opportunity' (Cashdan and Todd, 2000) of the VC was conducted which included interviews with a representative sample of approximately 30 members of senior staff, VC providers and teaching staff. The interviews with the senior staff and VC providers were open, and sought to obtain the views and perceptions of staff, on the nature, operation, successes and problems of the VC. Interviews with the teaching staff were semi-structured and questions were used to direct the participants to discussing their teaching experience and delivery of their courses using the VC, in addition to more general use of C&IT. The overall aim of this study was to investigate the value that the VC offered as a vehicle for student learning.

44.2.2   Research project 2: Staff needs for a school-based Online Learning Environment

In April 2000, shortly after the evaluation of the VC, the Sheffield Business School undertook a research project to 'inform the School's decision as to the most appropriate commercially-produced online learning environment to purchase to meet the School needs' (Bannister and Freewood, 2000, p. 1). The School had embarked on this study because it was identified that its needs differed from other schools in the university due to their unique and strong links with corporate sector and 'strong cultural emphasis upon enterprise and entrepreneurship' (p. 1). The overall aim of the research sought to identify staff and student requirements of online learning environments as a provision for course delivery and management. As part of the research, 14 key members of School staff were approached, using structured interviews to establish their use of existing C&IT and the functionalities they required from a proposed online learning environment. This chapter will focus on the analysis of those interviews, that provide the basis for highlighting the staff views on the implementation of an online learning environment and appropriate use of educational technology for course management as well as for teaching learning and assessment.

44.2.3   Research project 3: Staff past perspectives on the future directions of e-learning

In July 2000, research was commissioned within the LTI to provide evidence on the opinions and experiences of SHU staff, both academic and technical, with regard to building on the VC initiative in particular, and 'e-learning'1 in general. The research was set in context within the university's Learning, Teaching and Assessment (LTA) strategies with a view to contributing to the evaluation of the VC initiative so that the needs of students and staff could be clearly understood and met. Eighteen in-depth semi-structured interviews were conducted mainly with academic staff across all schools and some from CIS. The evidence gathered from this research formed a major part of a report to the Pro Vice-Chancellor (Academic Development) concerning the development of strategies to build on the VC initiative. This research consolidated a previous study carried out at SHU by Steel and Hudson (2001) which looked at staff perceptions and experiences of educational technology.

44.3   Research findings around the use of educational technology within higher education, as identified through research into staff perceptions and experience of C&IT

The above three pieces of research conveyed a rich source of ongoing qualitative data which provided a strong basis with which to form strategic decisions to support staff in making appropriate use of C&IT in their teaching. The themes identified here were not exclusively derived from each particular research project; some themes were common to two or all three of the studies. The themes are headed under those research projects which most prominently highlighted the theme as an issue.

44.3.1 Themes arising from research project 1

44.3.1.1 *An urgent need for pedagogic advancement*

The VC evaluation report highlighted 'an urgent need for effective pedagogic help at School level (or below) to cover the whole of the university if TEL [teaching enabled learning] is to be rapid and general' (Cashdan and Todd, 2000 p. 33). After the implementation of the VC, much of the research at SHU (Cashdan and Todd, 2000; Hanson and Wan, 2000) revealed an overwhelming view that there was a greater need for focus on pedagogical advancement rather than technical issues by both teaching and academic staff. Issues voiced by staff reinforced the notion that C&IT activities are too often ill-thought through, and as Littlejohn and Stefani (1999) describe as being 'bolted on the curriculum rather than thoughtfully included in ways which fully consider pedagogical parameters' (p. 74). Evidence strongly suggested a general lack of awareness amongst teaching staff with regard to the university VC. Staff who had engaged with the initiative felt that the VC project had lost impetus and needed to be built upon. There was also a recognition that the main focus of the VC had been on developing the technical infrastructure rather than 'hearts and minds' work, which was said to have inhibited the take up of the provision. Although some criticism had been voiced around this issue, it was acknowledged that a positive outcome of the VC work had been placing SHU in a strong position for having a good technical infrastructure to build upon.

44.3.1.2 *Creating 'space' by releasing staff for training*

A recurring theme among teaching staff across all the research, was the lack of time for academics not only to plan and develop technology enabled learning materials, but also 'space' to engage in the pedagogical aspects of their teaching in general. Hudson and Steel (2001) argue that space is important so that sufficient planning and development can occur and an appropriate combination of teaching and learning scenarios can emerge to enhance the student experience. Work from other institutions underlines this point, Clegg *et al.* (2000) reported on significant difficulties with time and work commitments. Other institutions such as De Montford University have in the past made decisions to formally set aside budgets with the specific objective to 'buy out' the time of faculty staff to enable staff to evaluate and embed learning technology into the curriculum (Ryan *et al.*, 2000, p. 164).

44.3.2 Themes from research project 2

44.3.2.1 *Capitalising on existing resources*

From a practical perspective, staff believed that existing resources should be capitalised upon and that any major investment in adopting an online environment should not place the onus on tutors to develop new materials when there was already much in place. An example that was given was a printed 'reading pack', which distance learning students receive, could be replaced with a 'web pack' comprising links to appropriate web-based resources. Subsequently, it was felt important that a chosen online environment should permit easy access to other learning environments such as online databases available through the Learning Centre. In addition to compatibility with other learning environments, both academic and administrative staff emphasised the importance of at least some level of integration between the online learning environment and the existing school administrative system. This was felt necessary so that communication between systems could deal with such time-consuming activities as student data details, assessment results etc. It was acknowledged that, to a large extent, the university's central administration would determine what the possibility of integration of systems would be.

44.3.2.2   *Imperative to maintain face-to-face contact*

The study revealed that staff members felt that the use of C&IT within courses must not be regarded as a substitute for face-to-face contact. In line with the results of the other SHU research projects, there were a number of explicit calls for existing levels of tutor–student contact to be maintained. Many staff believed face-to-face contact with their students was not only an essential part of the learning process, but was also a feature that students, as customers, actively desire. The other research projects at SHU indicate that most staff are convinced that it is better to have a face-to-face element in every course where possible thus providing a mixture of online and direct contact with students.

44.3.2.3   *Student centred ethos*

Consensus opinion among the staff interviewed was that the principal role of a chosen online learning environment should be to promote greater interaction among students, rather than to provide tutor-originated learning material for students to navigate through. Indeed, other universities have identified that student collaborative group working was one of the 'main reasons' for deciding on their chosen virtual learning environment (Cook, 2001, p. 12).

44.3.3   Themes arising out of research project 3:

44.3.3.1   *Current use of e-learning*

Mirroring the findings in Scottish HEIs (Haywood *et al.*, 2000) and from the previous SHU research conducted by Hudson and Steel (2001), the staff interviews showed a positive attitude towards incorporating e-learning and other C&IT in their teaching, albeit with certain caveats. Again, the qualitative data indicated that learning technology ought to be driven on pedagogical grounds that add value to traditional teaching, rather than for efficiency gains. Staff also made a clear distinction between the introduction of e-learning as the sole method of delivery and its use in a mixed mode of teaching, whereby learning technologies are used in conjunction with more traditional teaching methods such as lectures and tutorials. A clear preference for pursuing a mixed mode of delivery was expressed by most interviewees.

44.3.3.2   *Barriers to the use of e-learning*

Again, many of the findings of the report on learning technology use in Scottish HEIs (Anderson *et al.*, 2000, p. 13) are reiterated in our findings at SHU. In particular, the lack of allocated staff time for SHU academics posed the key barrier to making meaningful use of learning technologies in their teaching. Other prominent barriers for staff included the lack of effective fora in which School staff were able to share and generate ideas for e-learning, and other areas of teaching such as assessment. It was also commonly claimed that there was a need for incentives to engage with innovative teaching practice because research is seen as more highly prized within academia (and recognised in terms of output production). In implementing its virtual learning environment, Electronic Campus, De Montford University have recognised from previous experience that whilst buying out staff time in itself is important, incentives and recognition of such work was equally essential:

Aside from infrastructure costs, the major Electronic Campus investment had been staff time, as buyout of staff from other normal duties and recruitment of additional staff. Money is not enough however to ensure adequate human resources. In our experience the faculty staff taking a lead in Electronic Campus have typically been heavily committed to other key activities as well, such as student recruitment, research, university consultancy, administration, etc. It has been difficult for such people to allocate as much time to Electronic Campus projects as they themselves would like. Other rewards need to be put in place such as recognition of the importance of teaching innovation and excellence. (Brown, 2000, p. 82)

44.3.3.3   Provision of resources

There was a general sense that staff in Schools wanted to be kept better informed about the e-learning resources available within the university. Their perception was that staff training and development ought to emphasise the application of technology to teaching and learning, rather than simply the proficient use of technology. However, Clegg *et al.* (2000) found that in their study, staff complained that too much time was spent on the theory of well-considered C&IT use, rather than promoting more hands-on training due to their perceived 'immediacy of ICTs [information and communication technologies] skills acquisition and the urgency of gaining professional ability in technological application' (p. 144). This appears to underline the way that staff conceptualise their C&IT needs in terms of their own immediate motivational agendas. This may in some way explain the fact that the perceived 'ideal' provision of resources at SHU, varied according to personal preference and/or need. This posed a challenge to central departments and Schools in satisfactorily catering for a wide spectrum of desired methods for resource provision. SHU's response to this is discussed later in this chapter.

44.3.3.4   Associated concerns regarding e-learning

A gap emerged between those staff who were most inexperienced and those who were more familiar with C&IT. It became evident that staff who were least experienced with C&IT were apprehensive about e-learning associated issues such as copyright material on the web. While most staff were in favour of a more open access approach to web material, those least experienced with C&IT expressed strong concerns over 'personal' copyright and security of systems adopted for protection against copyright. In addition, these staff invariably felt uncomfortable about the heavy reliance on technology due to previous 'bad experiences' with failing technologies and/or infrastructure and the critical impact that this may have on the student learning experience.

44.4   Implications for new roles and working relationships in the Higher Education environment

As part of the process of being committed to making more appropriate use of C&IT, SHU has manifested a shift in the traditional definitions of roles and working relationships. This has been symptomatic of the need to respond to the change in the demographics of H.E. student population and external drivers. SHU's use of the institution's Learning, Teaching and Assessment (LTA) Strategies (enabled by Teaching Quality Enhancement Funding monies from HEFCE) as a vehicle for achieving an increase in the appropriate use of technology has created a new working environment in which school-based academics work in close collaboration with central department staff such as educational developers (academics and Research Assistants), multimedia courseware developers and information specialists from the Learning Centre. LTA projects are often commissioned that require a co-ordinated team approach by which academics require support from all of these sources. Responsibilities of staff, whether academic, administrative or technical could potentially impact on the embedding of an online learning component to course delivery: 'The nature of staff roles will need to be examined and possibly redefined within this changed context [...]' Bannister and Freewood (2000).

Furthermore, some school-based academics have taken secondments to work directly with educational development initiatives in the LTI. An example of this would be the fractional appointments of academics from different schools who work in the LTI as 'e-learning co-ordinators'. The work conducted by these members of staff include work researching in the area of computer assisted assessment (CAA). As part of this work, a methodology for implementing CAA is currently under development. As school based practitioners in e-learning, these members of teaching staff have a key role in mediating between the policy driven agenda of management and the pedagogic concerns of academics.

44.5   SHU Response

Out of the decision to refocus the Virtual Campus, and in light of research such as that outlined above, SHU adopted a much more staff focused approach to the pilot and introduction of its latest Virtual Learning Environment (VLE), Blackboard©. The role of the LTI staff has been central to this initiative and the shift in provision has been focused in three main areas:

44.6   Resource provision

- Resources to support e-learning initiatives are provided in several forms. For projects which have emanated from the schools' LTA strategies these have included the provision of support in the form of Research Assistants to undertake educational research, and also Courseware Developers to support individual academics in transferring work to, or creating work for their Blackboard©; sites.

- The university now offers the support of two 'At Elbow' individuals who can be e-mailed or telephoned by staff for support on any aspect of Blackboard©;.

- The university has also allocated an 'e-learning room' and this provides a 'drop-in' help facility for staff who may have more general queries or interest in Blackboard©;.

- The seconding of academic staff from schools either on a part-time or full-time basis has provided another resource. These members of staff undertake various activities within the university associated with disseminating and supporting the use of e-learning, as well as having input into the more strategic developments within the university.

44.7   Activities

A number of activities have been undertaken to support and inform staff about the e-learning initiatives in the university. These have been characterised by the following.

- A flexible approach to staff development workshops, some offered university wide, others organised by schools to specific groups of staff.

- Workshops offered a number of formats such as introductory awareness raising followed up by more focused sessions looking at assessment and for communications. Another example would be hands on course building workshops usually run for subject groups or programme teams.

- A series of Blackboard©; workshops have been run on an open basis with all staff welcome to attend, others have been run for a specific group of staff. Workshops were open to academic, managerial, technical and administrative staff. The workshops have been offered in pairs; the first providing a basic introduction to the system and the second in more detail looking at, for example, the assessment possibilities of using Blackboard. The workshops have been run by staff from the LTI, including those seconded from schools to assume 'e-learning' roles as well as the 'At Elbow' people (staff from Corporate Information Systems to support any staff with e-learning and Blackboard© activities). The introductory Blackboard©; workshops proved to be very popular and saw attendance figures of 415 members of staff in total (to July 2001).

- To complement these workshops a second series of workshops has been run on CAA. These have been run across the university and have been open to all. The aim was to provide a vehicle for debate on the role of CAA, and e-learning, in the modern university. The workshops welcomed both the experienced practitioner and the novice, and involved the development of a methodology for the introduction of CAA which can be used by staff in a number of ways when thinking about CAA.

- In addition, the LTI ran an 'e-learning' event over a three-day period to which all staff were invited. The sessions were run by both internal and external personnel, and aimed to raise awareness of Blackboard©; and share experience of staff engaged in the pilot (Jan. –Jul. 2001) to highlight the issues involved in e-learning in general, for example disability issues.

44.8 Evaluation

The last academic year, 2000/2001, was a pilot of Blackboard©. However, the take up of the pilot was three times the level that was expected. In total, over 3000 students used the system in that year and the figure has now risen to over 9000 in October 2001. It was, however, recognised that some form of evaluation of the use of the system was needed to identify how successful it had been. This has been undertaken in several forms:

- Individual units were evaluated. This involved students undertaking both the standard type of course evaluation questionnaire, and in some cases other more in-depth forms of evaluation. The role of the Research Assistant in the LTI was important in providing support for academic staff.

- There has also been an extensive evaluation of staff experiences and this has been undertaken in several different ways. Firstly, a study has been undertaken in which a number of academics with responsibility for e-learning in their schools were interviewed about the progress of e-learning for their subjects and divisions. Secondly, a Research Assistant in the LTI designed a questionnaire to evaluate support structures for Blackboard©; staff users, which will be distributed at the start of the 2001/02 academic year. Finally, there are two focus groups planned for

2001/02. These will be run with staff who have used Blackboard© and will focus upon two areas – assessment and communication. The aim of the focus groups is to present academic staff with an opportunity to share experiences and ideas and also to identify ways in which the use of Blackboard© can be further supported.

44.9   Conclusion

As can be seen from the above the cycle of innovation and evaluation, the process of change management is a complex one. Drivers and barriers to innovation and reorganisation can emerge from a range of sources, from broad economic or institutional factors, to complexities arising from circumstantial or individual dynamics. It is clear that the environments for learning are changing. The way staff have been involved in the research described above can be thought of as a form of action research. The result is a *continuous* process of reflection and re-appraisal. Considerable progress has been made since the introduction of the Virtual Campus, and the uptake of Blackboard© suggests that the university has reached beyond the '10 per cent' and is involving at least some of the '90 per cent'. Success in the implementation of C&IT strategy will not end this process of review, new cycles of evaluation and improvement are already in process. However, we may reach a point where the incorporation C&IT in learning, teaching and assessment is so mundane that it becomes only one element of continuous review, rather than, as at present, meriting the separate space it currently occupies.

44.10   References

Anderson, C., Coyle, H., Day, K., Haywood, D., Haywood J. and Macleod, H (2000) Learning technology in Scottish higher education – a survey of the views of senior managers, academic staff and 'experts', *ALT-J* **8**(2): 5–17.

Cashdan, A. and Todd, M. (2000) *,Present State and Future Opportunity – A Report on the Virtual Campus*. Internal document. Sheffield Hallam University.

Clegg, S., Konrad, J. and Tan, J. (2000) Preparing academic staff to use ICTs in support of student learning, *International Journal for Academic Development* **5**(2): 138–48.

Bannister, P. and Freewood, M. (2000) *Sheffield Business School: Requirements on an Online Learning Environment*. Internal document. Sheffield Hallam University.

Brown, S. (1998) Reinventing the university. In D. Squires, G. Conole and G. Jacobs (eds), *The Changing Face of Learning Technology*. Cardiff: University of Wales Press.

Cook, J. (2001) Choice of VLE for the University of Bristol, *Interact* **22**, March. Published by Learning Technology Support Services, University of Bristol.

Gibbons, M. and Hillard, J. (1996) Virtuality, higher education and workplace learning. Paper presented at the 'Beyond the Learning Workforce', Conference, University of Lancaster.

Hanson, J. and Wan, S. (2000) *E-learning: Past Perspectives and Future Directions*. Internal document. Sheffield Hallam University.

Her Majesty's Stationery Office (HMSO) (1997) *Report of The National Committee of Inquiry into Higher Education – 'Higher Education and the Learning Society'* (The Dearing Report), London: HMSO

(http://www.ncl.ac.uk/ncihe/index.htm - accessed 21-02-01).

Hudson, A. and Steel, J. (2001) Educational technology in learning and teaching: the perceptions and experiences of teaching staff, *Innovations in Education and Teaching International* **38**(2): 103–11.

JISC Committee for Awareness, Liaison and Training Programme, Career Development of Learning Technology Staff: Scoping Study, January 2001. http://www.sh.plym.ac.uk/eds/effects/jcalt-project/final_report_v8.doc.

Littlejohn, A. and Stefani, A. (1999) Effective use of communication and information technology: bridging the skills gap, *ALT-J* **7**(2): 66–76.

Richardson, G.B. (1997) Innovation, equilibrium and welfare. In S.C. Dow and J.V. Hillard (eds), *Beyond Keynes*. Edward Elgar.

Ryan, S., Scott, B., Freeman, H. and Patel, D. (2000) *The Virtual University*. London: Kogan Page.

Scott, P. (1995) *The Meanings of Mass Higher Education*. Buckingham: SRHE & Open University Press.

Stephens, D., Bull, J. and Wade, W. (1998) Computer-assisted assessment: suggested guidelines for an institutional strategy, *Assessment and Evaluation in Higher Education* **23**(3): 283–94.

[1] defined to interviewees as 'where the use of information technology is integral to either, or both, teaching and learning, as opposed to technology serving the administrative process of teaching and learning'.

45 Student experience: novices, surfers, learners

Phil Bannister, Sadie Parr

Sheffield Hallam University, UK

45.1 Introduction

The use of communication and information technology (C&IT) for teaching, learning and assessment continues to increase throughout the higher education sector in the UK; there is high-level government commitment towards the development of e-learning within the sector (e.g. Blunkett, 2000). This chapter focuses on critical issues around the implementation of learning technologies that have been foregrounded through research at Sheffield Hallam University (SHU) on student experiences and perceptions of C&IT-enabled approaches to learning. Our aim is to assert the need for C&IT to be used in an 'appropriate' manner if learners are genuinely to profit through its application.

What do we mean by 'appropriate'? A pertinent starting point in considering the idea of 'appropriateness' in relation to learning technologies is with those benefits often attributed to the use of C&IT in higher education. Education technologies are held to offer the possibility of increasing the effectiveness of teaching and learning processes; enriching the quality of the learning experience; and providing greater flexibility in course delivery, overcoming physical and temporal barriers which have restricted access to higher education for many groups of potential learners (HMSO, 1997).

The technological optimists, who view education technology as an inevitable and essentially positive advance, advocate the wholehearted embrace of new technology. For them, C&IT is appropriate as it is a sign of progress and will ultimately improve education. On the other hand, there are strong opponents of educational technology who believe technology is inevitably antisocial and destructive, and that the above benefits will never be delivered on the ground. The employment of C&IT in HE is written off as inappropriate and a trend that will ultimately devalue the educational process.

O'Sullivan (2000) has examined these debates and discussions about the perceived impact of C&IT on higher education and has identified four perspectives that appear in the popular literature regarding the future of educational technology: Utopian technological determinism; dystopian technological determinism; utopian social determinism; and dystopian social determinism. His descriptions of each are summarised in Table 45.1.

As O'Sullivan argues, there is some truth in each set of assumptions; however, such assumptions are clearly one-dimensional and naive. What this chapter seeks to assert is that educators need not adopt an extreme position on the merits of C&IT in HE, but should adopt more balanced attitudes about the possibilities offered by technology; Technology is neither all good nor bad:

	Technological Determinism	**Social Determinism**
Utopian Determinism	Technology will improve education by reshaping the educational . process, encouraging more and better interaction, and making more useful information available to students	Teachers and students will use technology to improve education by . reshaping the educational process, interacting more with each other in positive ways, and by being able to find more useful information
Dystopian Determinism	Technology will degrade education by reshaping the educational process, discouraging interaction, and making nore unwholesome information available to students	Teachers and students will use the technology to undermine education by reshaping the educational process, interacting less with each other and in negative ways, and by being able to access more unwholesome information.

Source: O'Sullivan, 2000, p. 56

Table 45.1

> Individuals are not hapless victims or beneficiaries of autonomous technology – they can make choices about how to use various technologies' characteristics. In this view, individuals have the ability to evaluate various technology options, select the one perceived as best suited to their goals, and use the technology's characteristics in ways that further those goals. (O'Sullivan, 2000, p. 56)

O'Sullivan emphasises how technology may be used in various ways and has the capacity to produce both positive, beneficial outcomes and destructive, detrimental outcomes. It is only in an ideal world that the adoption of C&IT in higher education will automatically prove worthwhile.

Our conceptualisation of 'appropriate' is therefore compatible with Julian Kilker's understanding of the same term. His definition (in relation to web-based technologies) is premised on the belief that educational technology must be pedagogically and contextually driven:

> The evolving conceptualisation of 'appropriate' with respect to Web-based technologies suggests that the process of reflecting on the form and pedagogical role of technology is more important than choosing a specific technology, and that their challenges and benefits are strongly context-dependent. Educators should start with pedagogical goals and contextual factors ... then choose specific technologies that may include Internet and web-based technology as well as more traditional tools and techniques. (Kilker, 2000, p. 76)

Kilker's understanding of 'appropriate' reinforces the notion that the utilisation of C&IT in higher education does not automatically improve the delivery of courses. He places emphasis on the importance of starting with clear pedagogical objectives and on taking account of the nature of the context in which C&IT applications are to be employed. Henceforth, 'appropriate' may mean very different things in different situations.

Adapting technology to meet pedagogical goals and understanding the context in which educational technology will be used, means taking into account a number of both intellectual and physical matters. Certainly, an uncritical adoption of C&IT in a higher education context is a hazardous step. Those implementing education technologies within programmes of study must consider, among other things, the computer literacy of the potential users; student familiarity with using C&IT in an academic context; student access to the technology; and the possibility of student resistance to the introduction of C&IT into teaching and learning processes.

In what follows, we intend to examine in further detail why it is so important to reflect on contextual and pedagogical factors when employing C&IT within programmes of study. With reference to research undertaken on student experiences and perceptions of C&IT-enabled learning, some key issues will be explored in order to demonstrate why educators must make well-informed decisions about the ways in which they might use C&IT applications. It is important to emphasise that the focus here is on the student perspective, since their needs and concerns regarding educational technology are critical and can not be neglected (Kilker, 2000). Indeed, if technology is to be utilised appropriately there must be some negotiation with users regarding how they have and will interact with educational technology, in order to help educators avoid unforeseen negative consequences. There are also lessons to be learned from the literature on others experiences of success or failure.

45.2 Research on the student experience of C&IT-enhanced approaches to teaching and learning at SHU

In order to take SHU's LTA strategy forward, target outcomes have been developed for the three years 1999–2000, 2000–01and 2001–02. Targets set for the academic year 2001/2002 include 75 per cent of staff to be making educational use of the online learning environment currently being rolled out across the university; and 50 per cent of courses to have learner support materials available online. This means making significant use of C&IT in teaching and learning.

Research assistants from the LTI play an active role in supporting and evaluating development activities emerging from LTA strategy implementation in the Schools, with a significant proportion of the research work undertaken relating to the use of C&IT within programmes of study. The majority of these research studies have focused, to varying degrees, on student experiences and perceptions of the learning technology implemented within a particular unit (or part thereof); and/or on student responses to the possible introduction or expansion of a C&IT-based component within their courses.

This chapter draws on the following examples of C&IT-enhanced approaches to teaching and learning at SHU which have been investigated by LTI researchers.

45.2.1 The delivery of part of a unit through a dedicated computer-assisted learning package

The package in question is designed to teach information management skills to undergraduates. Following the introduction of the package into a social science level 1 core unit, research into the student experience of using the software was conducted through informal semi-structured interviews with a total of 27 students on three different degree routes.

45.2.2 The use of computer conferencing facilities to support and enhance learning

The application of computer conferencing technology was investigated in three units – two in the humanities (levels 2 and 3), and one in the business area (level 2). Across these units, the students were expected to use the conference for different purposes – to engage in seminar-style discussion on set topics; to plan a group presentation; and to discuss and exchange information on a topic not being covered elsewhere in the unit. In two instances, student experience data was collected via a questionnaire survey (involving 39 and 63 students); in the third instance, group interviews were used in addition to the questionnaire (32 students). Some analysis of the messages posted to the conferences by the students was also carried out.

45.2.3 The introduction of a unit website

Student responses to the introduction of a supporting website, containing some content and links to other resources, were investigated within two humanities units (at levels 2 and 3) through focus group interviews involving 23 and 16 students respectively.

45.2.4 The implementation of a virtual learning environment

Research was conducted into the student experience of using a virtual learning environment in a level 1 business and technology unit. The virtual learning environment, which integrates content delivery and communication functions within a single application, was employed to replace one of the two weekly lectures which the unit previously featured. Research data were obtained through analysis of the reflective essays written by the 110 students taking the unit on their experiences of using educational technologies.

Related research has also taken place on student attitudes towards and levels of competence in using C&IT.

It is important to acknowledge the fundamental differences that exist between the various learning technologies investigated. Some centre on learner interaction with the content (e.g. computer-based learning packages), while others facilitate interaction among learners (e.g. computer conferencing). The student experience of using C&IT for learning needs to be understood in relation to the particular technology engaged with, and the precise context of its use. Nonetheless, our research does indicate the importance of a number of *overarching* issues around the student experience of C&IT-based learning, which appear relevant within any C&IT-enhanced approach to teaching and learning in higher education and which must be taken into consideration if the use of new media is to be 'appropriate' for supporting high quality student learning.

The remainder of this chapter will discuss these issues. Prior to this, however, it should be emphasised that our research studies show that many students who have experienced C&IT-enhanced approaches to teaching and learning *do* perceive the technology to confer certain advantages (sometimes concurring with the oft-cited benefits listed above). These include:

- flexibility (e.g. can work at own pace; do not have to be physically present on campus etc.);
- peer support;
- variety in the learning experience;
- accessibility / permanence of the learning resource;
- in some instances, a higher level of appropriateness than face-to-face delivery (e.g. for learning a C&IT-related skill).

However, these positive experiences must be balanced against less favourable responses to the use of C&IT for teaching, learning and assessment purposes which were evident in our research studies. It is not our intention to deny the potential of learning technologies, but simply to stress the importance of 'appropriateness' in their use.

45.3 Key issues around the use of learning technologies within higher education, as identified through research into the student experience of C&IT-enhanced approaches to teaching and learning

45.3.1 Although becoming less of a factor, student physical access to the technology is still variable; the level of access is seen by the students to affect learning

A key motive for using C&IT in course delivery is to provide greater flexibility for the learner, who can be more independent in terms of location, time and pace of learning. However, if students are required to use C&IT outside of formal, timetabled sessions, issues around access to the technology come to the fore.

At Sheffield Hallam University there is considerable ongoing investment in networked computing facilities. Currently, over 1100 desktop PCs are available on an open-access basis, in addition to the C&IT resources of individual schools; during term-time, 24 hour access to computer facilities is offered at a number of locations. Yet in spite of this increased availability, comments from students indicate that there is pressure on C&IT resources within the university campus.

Education technologies in HE are increasingly web-based and accessible outside the University, making it less necessary for learners to be physically on campus in order to engage in study. This development has been simultaneous with, and partly in response to, changes in both the composition of the student body and the nature of 'student life' as experienced by full-time undergraduates. The broader age range and social diversity of students in UK HE (HESA, 2001) means that a significant number of learners have other commitments (domestic, employment) around which they must organise their studies. Part-time work during term-time is increasingly the norm for full-time undergraduates, who previously might not have had this type of commitment Barke *et al.*, 2001 (Tysome, 2001). It has also been observed that increasing numbers of students are choosing to study at local HE institutions (Swain, 2001) and may not be in as close proximity to the campus as their non-local counterparts. All of these groups of learners stand to benefit from being able to engage in learning at a time and location which suits them.

The number of students with computers and Internet access at home seems to be relatively high at SHU. A recent questionnaire survey of all new entrants to one school of the university (which is not highly C&IT-focused in terms of the subjects taught, and has a very varied age profile) showed that 56.3 per cent of the students had Internet access outside of the university. Even though this proportion will undoubtedly increase in the next few years, it is likely that there will remain many learners not connected to the Internet at home. A recent report by the National Statistics Agency identifies a direct correlation between socio-economic status and Internet access:

individuals in households headed by someone in a managerial or professional occupations were the most likely to have accessed the internet (68 to 87 percent) whilst the least likely were individuals living in a household headed by someone in a routine or semi-routine occupation (22 to 36 percent). (National Statistics Agency, 2001)

With the ongoing expansion of HE and government commitment to increasing the diversity of intake (Blunkett, 2000), it is probable that a broader range of socio-economic backgrounds will be represented within the student body. The problem of access to the technology among students in higher education is thus not likely to disappear in the near future.

Research at SHU on units where students have been expected to use C&IT outside of timetabled classes (e.g. communication via a computer conference) indicates that access to the technology affects student perceptions of the learning experience. For example, in a unit where students were required to plan a group presentation through using a computer conference, several research respondents asserted that because some members of their groups did not have easy access to email (e.g. no Internet access at home; living a long way from the university campus), it had been more difficult for the group to make progress; they felt they had been disadvantaged by the requirement to use the technology.

The expectation that students will access course materials and participate in learning activities online outside of timetabled classes, possibly from an off-campus location, also raises issues around the financial burden such a development places on the students (e.g. purchasing hardware and software; time spent online; printing out materials). The negative reaction of a group of students to having to incur a cost which previously would have been absorbed by the course (the unit guide was available only via the unit website and was not distributed in printed form) suggests that in some instances, this financial burden may lead to student scepticism and resentment over the introduction of the technology.

45.3.2 Student C&IT competence is highly variable; this will have some effect on how students engage with learning technologies and their capacity to learn through their use

In one School at SHU, undergraduate entrants (357 in total) were surveyed via questionnaire as to their C&IT competence – their technical ability to use particular software applications (e.g. word processing; spreadsheets; email; a web browser). Student attitudes towards C&IT and levels of personal confidence in its use were also investigated.

In relation to gender, it was apparent that male students were, overall, more strongly oriented towards C&IT (a larger proportion displaying 'positive' attitudes) and were more confident in its use than female students. For most of the C&IT applications examined, levels of competence were slightly higher among male students. That learner orientation towards and ability in using C&IT appears to be gendered is perhaps not surprising, since the realm of information technology has traditionally been treated as a masculine domain: 'descriptions of computing resonate with notions of rationality and power which are discursively projected as masculine' (Clegg, 2001, p. 316). Clegg argues that the introduction of computers into schools in the 1970s was loaded with meanings external to the education system. The development of computers, the design of programming languages and compilers were all funded by the military; computing and computers were therefore imbued with machismo meanings. Computers in the home have also been marketed and targeted at boys and men. In sum, 'as a cultural artefact the computer, in both its actual and fictional forms, existed in a love affair between men and computers' (Clegg, 2001, p. 313). This renders women's relationship with technology complex. This relationship, however, does not render women less able but less attracted to identifying themselves with technology. The centrality of C&IT within teaching, learning and assessment processes thus carries the risk of discriminating against and excluding female learners.

Contrary to expectations, the research survey found much less variation in C&IT skills by age than might have been predicted. Students in the 18–24 age group were *not* massively more skilled in using C&IT than the older students, nor more positively oriented towards it. While one might reasonably expect levels of ability in using email and web-browser software – relatively recent and high-profile 'new' technologies – to be in inverse proportion to age, this was not apparent. For these two applications, the distribution of students in the 18–24 age group across the different ability categories ('below basic level', 'intermediate', 'more advanced') into which the survey respondents were placed on the basis of their responses was fairly similar to that of other age groups; a high proportion of each age group was 'below basic level'. Indeed, among the students surveyed, the most significant variation was by course of study: certain degree routes in the school had relatively high overall levels of C&IT competence among their students, while others had much lower average ratings in comparison. The overall level of ability of the students appeared to relate to the degree to which the subject being studied was 'technical' in its nature, suggesting that different courses attract differently C&IT-skilled learners.

It should be emphasised that this survey was conducted before the students had commenced on their courses. An end of year survey of the same students found much higher levels of technical competence in relation to certain applications (e.g. email, web browser software) indicating, that for many students, ability does develop over the academic year. Nonetheless, these survey findings have clear implications for the use of learning technologies in course delivery. The variations in technical competence and predisposition towards C&IT among learners means that there is a risk of disadvantaging or excluding certain groups through moving towards an online mode of delivery. It is inadvisable to make any assumptions or generalisations about levels of learner ability in using C&IT; student development in this area needs to be actively supported. The level of C&IT competence with which students enter higher education and the rate at which skills are developed may dictate what is appropriate to implement at a particular stage in a course. The complex use of learning technologies at lower academic levels might be less likely to work, with students unable to engage due to lack of required technical ability. Moreover, the variation of C&IT skills by course of study may mean that C&IT-based approaches to teaching, learning and assessment will 'root' more readily in certain areas, i.e. where students are already relatively competent users, than others. The nature and extent to which learning technologies are employed in courses need to be appropriate to the precise context.

45.3.3 Technical competence in using C&IT applications does not necessarily mean that students are able to use these technologies effectively for the purpose of learning

While any lack of technical competence among students can be remedied relatively easily, through provision of appropriate training, other factors which influence how effectively students use learning technologies are not so easily addressed. Learners in HE will engage with communication and information technologies within specific contexts and for particular purposes. Given this, it cannot simply be assumed that possession of the functional ability to use a particular technology necessarily makes one able to *learn* through its use, although technical competence is obviously a precondition for learning to take place.

This view is supported by evidence from one strand of the research on learning technologies at SHU, which has investigated the use of computer conferencing technology for teaching and learning purposes within units delivered to on-campus students. In each research study, students (either 2nd or 3rd year undergraduates) were asked to state their level of ability in using an email system to send and receive messages, with most rating themselves as competent in this regard. While the majority of respondents had experience of using email for leisure purposes, very few had used it within academic study. Levels of email use for leisure purposes were relatively high (e.g. several times per week), and generally there was a positive orientation towards email as a method of communication. However, in each study it was apparent that the level of actual student involvement in the computer conference was highly variable – certain students were very active contributors (e.g. posting new messages, replying to other learners, summarising discussion to date) while others contributed relatively little or did not engage at all. Importantly, there was no correlation between the students' level of technical ability in using email and their level of involvement in the computer conference, although a certain level of ability is obviously a precondition for participation. Other factors appear to be of equal or greater significance in determining how far the application of computer conferencing technology within a programme of study facilitates student learning. For example, in research on one unit where students had used a computer conference facility to plan a group presentation, the survey respondents were asked to indicate problems and drawbacks around using the technology for carrying out this task. Their objections related mainly to the difficulty of engaging in effective dialogue through the medium; difficulty in using the software was not raised as an issue by anyone.

In the same research study, many of these students indicated that they liked the fact that the facility made it easier to stay in touch with one another and to monitor the progress of group members. However, from this and other studies it seems that, in order for learners to experience this type of beneficial peer support, conference participants must maintain a certain level of active involvement. Several research respondents stated that the lack of response to messages they had sent had a demotivating effect, and in some instances led them to stop participating.

> I was quite excited to see what other people in my group had to say about my views but there wasn't any response at all so I got bored.

The nature of messages posted also seems highly significant. In relation to one particular conference, it was commented that the actual dialogue which had taken place online among the conference participants was very limited. This was attributed to the fact that the conference postings were being assessed directly by the tutor: it was felt that students were more concerned with making 'perfect' postings which would receive high marks than with engaging in genuine dialogue. Such an action can be classed as an 'inappropriate' form of online communication. Other behaviours which can be placed in this category have been identified in other research studies of conferencing in HE courses (e.g. Light *et al.*, 2000). These involve participants posting lengthy and overly formal, 'academic' messages; or deliberately antagonising or insulting ('flaming') other learners, with negative consequences e.g. withdrawal of those participants who feel they are being victimised. Clearly, how far students learn through participation in a computer conference is much less dependent on their functional ability to use the software than on their skill in communicating within this specific medium, and possibly on the ability of the tutor or moderator to facilitate productive dialogue. The social rules governing communication in face-to-face settings may not be applicable within an online environment; new protocols have to be developed and learned (Hammond, 2000; Light *et al.*, 2000). For example, what is an appropriate tone to adopt? How formal or informal should one be? What is a suitable length of message?

Similarly, it cannot be assumed that the ability of a learner to use a given technology effectively within one, relatively informal context (e.g. for leisure purposes) makes one able to use it successfully in another more formal context (e.g. for academic purposes). This is suggested by research into student levels of competence in C&IT use, conducted as part of two separate investigations into student perceptions of C&IT and its possible introduction and/or expansion within courses. Focus group research on student usage and requirements of the student section of the main university website found that most of the respondents in the sample (drawn from a range of schools of the university) were technically competent in using the web browser software, although a number did not understand certain functionalities (e.g. how to bookmark URLs). However, the students appeared much less skilled in terms of their ability to use the software to locate relevant information: many tended to have a single search strategy for finding information (e.g. use of a particular search engine). If this did not produce results, they were unable to use alternative strategies. Another focus group study, on student attitudes towards online communication, found that while some of the 21 respondents were 'competent' users of email in that they had a basic ability to send and read messages, they were unable to manage more 'advanced' tasks (e.g. opening and sending attachments; replying to an existing message rather than creating a new one). While such a level of skill in using the software might be adequate within a leisure context, use of these applications as part of academic study may well demand a more formal, rigorous approach. Without further support for development, students may not be able to make best use of this technological resource, and as a consequence their learning will be limited.

The research evidence supports the assertion that C&IT literacy does not in itself make one an effective online learner. The transition from 'novice' to 'surfer' to 'learner' may not happen spontaneously, but rather require active support on the part of the tutors and the institution.

45.3.4 There is often some resistance among students to the introduction or increased use of C&IT in programmes of study

A certain amount of resistance to the use of C&IT in course delivery was evident among the respondents in a number of our research studies; this manifested itself in different ways. In certain studies (e.g. relating to use of a unit website; a computer conference) the student response to the technology was mixed, with a significant proportion of learners stating that they had not used the facility provided. In other instances where students were largely positive about the use of learning technology in a particular unit (e.g. that utilising a virtual learning environment), concerns were expressed over the possible increase in the extent of the C&IT component. Such reluctance is not always attributable to innate conservatism: it sometimes reflects a genuine concern over the quality of the learning experience. Our research at SHU found three main areas of student concern over the implementation of learning technologies:

45.3.4.1 Fear that use of C&IT in course delivery will lead to an erosion of existing face-to-face contact

Research on student responses to a website created by the tutor to support the unit found that while this type of development was welcomed, it was felt important that it did not become so central within unit delivery that face-to-face contact was lost. One respondent asserted that the existence of email had already diminished the level of informal contact between tutors and students. In another unit, the use of a virtual learning environment to replace one weekly lecture was received very positively by the learners. However, concerns were expressed over the possible isolation which learners might experience in a purely online mode of study. It is perhaps telling that in their written reflections on their experience of studying in this, students stated that the aspect they liked was the variety of delivery methods, a combination of face-to-face and online learning. As has been observed in studies in other HE institutions on the use of C&IT in course delivery (e.g. Brown *et al.*, 2000), the students at SHU considered it important that some face-to-face contact was maintained:

> I was pleased ... that lectures were included as part of the course. I feel that through the lectures, the course is given a face and personality. I like to have the opportunity to speak to the tutor in person.

45.3.4.2 Fears that some learners may be disadvantaged by this development

If learning is dependent on the use of a particular technology, problems arise if learners do not have access to the required facilities. Student views on the problems caused by learners having different levels of access have been mentioned above (in relation to the use of conferencing for group collaboration). The reliability of the technology is also an issue; in one unit where the students were required to interact with one another online via a conference, it was commented that problems with the computer network had impeded progress.

45.3.4.3 Concerns over the value of online resources which do not originate from the tutor (e.g. found on the Web; posted to a shared online workspace by other students)

In a research study of student responses to a unit website, the provision of links to Internet resources was received positively. However, the respondents expressed a wish for these links to be annotated more fully by the tutor – it was felt that some commentary should be provided on the relative authority and usefulness of particular sources. Similarly, the idea of past student work being available through the unit website was seen as a good one, but again it was felt that tutor commentary on it would be essential. Without this, the status of the material would remain unknown; the students felt they would be uncertain about how to approach it. In relation to computer conferencing, Light *et al.* (2000) found that, among students who had used a conference for academic discussion there was some doubt about the legitimacy of what other participants said, with some learners saying that they would not use such material in their essays or exam answers. However, a tutor may be able to encourage greater trust among students in the contributions of others – for example, through requiring learners to quote from the conference in a written assignment (Lea, 2001) or through basing the end-of-unit examination on the shared learning that had taken place via the conference (Rimmershaw, 1999). Nonetheless, the research evidence does strongly suggest that many students require the academic authority of the tutor and want guidance rather than absolute independence in learning. The wish for course delivery through conventional face-to-face teaching methods can also be seen as part of this general desire for that which is familiar.

45.3.5 The importance of the use of the technology being perceived as appropriate – students seeing there to be a firm pedagogic rationale for using C&IT in unit delivery

The introduction of learning technology into a programme of study does not ensure that the students will engage with it. A number of the research studies at SHU (e.g. introduction of a unit website; computer conferencing) found that a proportion of learners had made little or no use of the online resource. If students are not motivated to use the technology, they may not engage with it. If that technology is central within unit or course delivery processes, the learning of those students may be impaired.

Our research studies suggest that if the learners are to actively participate in C&IT-enabled learning, it is essential that they perceive there to be a good reason for their doing so; the use of the learning technology must be seen to provide a genuine benefit. In investigations into student experiences of computer conferencing within different units, numerous respondents stated that they could not see the point of their having to communicate online rather than face-to-face, which was perceived as a much more conducive medium for dialogue and decision making. In a unit where the students had been required to prepare a group presentation via a conference, it was commented that such a use of the technology was contrived:

Computer-mediated communication isn't really appropriate in this situation. You'd never use it to plan a presentation in any other circumstance. It's a false situation.

A similar point of view was apparent among the students in a unit where a supporting website had been introduced. Although the majority of respondents in the focus group interview had used the site, opinions of it were largely negative. In particular, resentment was expressed by a number of respondents that the technology was being used so as to make students pay for the printing of course materials, which would normally have been provided for free. The website was not regarded as offering any additional benefits over paper-based resources. Such scepticism about the validity of the use of the technology could easily lead to demotivation and non-engagement.

Littlejohn and Stefani (1999) identify this type of situation as resulting from the limited understanding of staff as to how educational technologies can be used (e.g. seen principally as a mechanism for delivering lecture notes); and also from the lack of dialogue between tutors and students regarding the new teaching and learning framework, which renders student (and staff) responsibilities unclear. This latter point is supported by our research at SHU. The delivery of part of a unit through means of a computer-based learning package received a mixed response from the students interviewed: some found it beneficial while others were more negative, complaining that they had not been given any explanation for the rationale behind the package, its purpose, or why they were being asked to work through it. When the interviewer explained the background to the package and its intended benefits for students, most of the respondents were better able to see the relevance of their package for learning. It was commented by one student that having this kind of explanation at the outset of the unit would have motivated them far more strongly to engage with it.

The perceived status of the C&IT-enabled learning activity within the unit or course is also of great significance in determining learner engagement. For example, the importance attributed by learners to computer conference discussion can be seen to depend on a number of factors, including the relationship of that discussion to assessment; the extent to which interaction through the conference constitutes a formal learning activity within the unit (i.e. how far the technology is integrated into teaching and learning processes); the clarity of objectives set; the role of the tutor etc. It is critical that students regard use of the conference facility as important within the programme of study, since online communication is seen as more time-consuming than face-to-face interaction (e.g. having to log in regularly to see what has been posted; spending time reading through postings and writing own messages; delay in waiting for a response). Indeed, in different units a frequently cited reason given by students for non-participation was 'lack of time'. There is also a certain amount of risk involved in online communication (Searle, 1999) – research on the student experience in one unit found high levels of anxiety associated with communicating in this medium (e.g. because of the permanence of statements made). The initial threshold for participation is quite high (Hammond, 2000); students need to see active engagement as being worthwhile if they are going to invest large amounts of time and energy in using the technology to interact with other learners.

45.4   Conclusion

Placing the focus of research onto the student experience of C&IT-enabled approaches to learning shifts the emphasis away from the technology *per se*, towards exploitation of the technology to achieve pre-determined pedagogic objectives. Technology itself does not improve learning and teaching, but the appropriate management of the technology in HE certainly has the potential to do so. The findings from our research serve to emphasise the necessity of fitting the manner in which technology is employed to the particular context and purpose of its use. As we have stressed, what is appropriate to one educational context will not necessarily be appropriate to another. For this reason it is not possible to produce effective, universally applicable guidelines on how to implement educational technology. However, if factors such as those detailed above are given adequate consideration during the planning process, then potential problems will be better avoided.

If universities are to continue to develop technology in ways that support and enhance current practice, then there also needs to be an institutional commitment to skills development of staff and students in order to enable them to engage productively with the technology. In addition, there needs to be a commitment to the ongoing evaluation of the uses to which technological applications are put. The context does not stand still – learners change; the technology changes; the manner in which the technology is employed changes. An ongoing cycle of evaluation and adaptation means the appropriate use of technology can be continually honed to the demands of the current situation.

45.5   References

Barke, M., Braidford, P., Houston, M., Hunt, A., Lincoln, I., Morphet, C., Stone, I. and Walker, A. (2000) Students in the labour market – nature, extent and implications of term-time employment among University of Northumbria undergraduates, *DfEE Research Brief*, 215.

Blunkett, D. (2000) Speech on Higher Education, 15 February at Greenwich University (http://www.dfee.gov.uk/greenwich).

Brown, S., Hardaker, C.H.M. and Higgett, N.P. (2000) Designs on the Web: a case study for a new language-learning environment, *ALT-J* 8(1): 30–40.

Clegg, S. (2001) Theorising the machine: gender, education and computing, *Gender and Education* 13(3): 307–24.

Hammond, M. (2000) Communication within on-line forums: the opportunities, the constraints and the value of a communicative approach, *Computers & Education* 35: 251–62.

Her Majesty's Stationery Office (HMSO) (1997) *Report of The National Committee of Inquiry into Higher Education – 'Higher Education and the Learning Society'* (The Dearing Report), London: HMSO (http://www.ncl.ac.uk/ncihe/index.htm – accessed 21-02-1).

HESA (2001) Press Release: 1999/2000 higher education student data at: http://www.hesa.ac.uk/Press/pn47/pn47.htm

Kilker, J (2000) When and where appropriate lessons from 'foreign' contexts for the pedagogical use of web-based technologies in the United States. In R.A. Cole (ed.), *Issues in Web-based Pedagogy: A Critical Primer*. Greenwood Press.

Light, P. and Light, V. (1999) Analysing asynchronous learning interactions: computer-mediated communication in a conventional undergraduate setting, in K. Littlejohn and P. Light (eds), *Learning with Computers: Analysing Productive Interaction*. London: Routledge.

Light, V., Nesbitt, E., Light, P. and Burns, J.R. (2000) Let's you and me have a little discussion': computer mediated communication in support of campus-based university courses, *Studies in Higher Education* 25(1): 85–96.

Littlejohn, A.H. and Stefani, A.J (1999) Effective use of communication and information technology: bridging the gap, *ALT-J* 7(2): 66–75.

National Statistics Agency (2001) First Release on Internet Access, June 2001 (http://www.statistics.gov.uk).

O'Sullivan, P.B (2000) Communication technologies in an educational environment: lessons from a historical perspective. In R.A. Cole (ed.), *Issues in Web-based Pedagogy: A Critical Primer*. Greenwood Press.

Rimmershaw, R. (1999) Using conferencing to support a culture of collaborative study, *Journal of Computer Assisted Learning* 15: 189–200.

Seale, J. (1999) Learning technologies and the life long learner: armament or disarmament, *ALT-J* 7(1): 61–8.

Swain, H. (2001) Does home work or is it better to breakaway?, *Times Higher Education Supplement*, 19 Jan. (http://www.thes.co.uk).

Tysome, T. (2001) Students strive to stave off debt, *Times Higher Education Supplement*, 17 Aug., p. 3.

46 New environments for learning: case studies of developments using new media in a higher education setting: symposium summary

Sue Clegg, Alison Hudson, Phil Bannister, Madeleine Freewood, Julie Hanson, Sadie Parr, Louise Thorpe and Stephen Wan

Sheffield Hallam University, UK

46.1   Symposium activity

Following the presentation of the papers that formed the basis for Chapters 43–45 the participants were asked to take part in a role-playing activity looking at the issues surrounding the key themes. They were divided into groups of 6/8 and asked to take on the roles, as a group, of university management, academic staff and students. The groups were given a scenario and question regarding the issues surrounding increasing the use of C&IT to consider for. After ten minutes they were given a further question about how this increase could be implemented effectively. Details of the activity and questions are included in Appendix 46.I. The groups were asked to feedback on their discussions and the themes were noted.

The main issues emerging from the *management groups* were predominantly financial, looking at the implications of costs to the institution with regard to hardware, software and staffing, as well as the potential impact upon research income. They considered how the student 'market' could be broadened through distance learning and continuing professional development (CPD) to offset some of these costs, and the possibility of additional income generators such as hosting external conferences and training events. With regard to the quality of the student experience concerns were expressed about how this should, or indeed could, be measured effectively. The management groups both felt that the increased use of C&IT could better promote access to support services and enhance administration.

The *staff group* pointed out that it is not just students who enjoy face-to-face contact and that this should be recognised when considering the quality of the staff experience as well as the student experience. Tensions were highlighted around the need to deliver more for less and to 'look good' in the eyes of the students. These tensions were felt to exist in a climate where staff are already experiencing significant time pressures, increased administration responsibilities and are required to develop additional skills to be able to use C&IT effectively. The group felt this kind of innovation could potentially change the role of the tutor and broaden out the roles of other staff, most notably administrative and support staff, and the impact of this needed consideration. The staff group were explicit about the need to be appropriately supported by management, and that this should to be demonstrated through time allowances for development work, adequate training and support, and opportunities to share resources. They felt that issues surrounding the quality of the student experience centred upon student expectations, and they debated how these could best be managed.

The focus on expectations was reinforced by the *student group*, who raised a number of issues around equity and quality of student experience, by focusing upon what they needed and expected in order for the increased use of C&IT to be effective and successful. Staying within role, the group produced a long 'shopping list' including:

- provide every student with a laptop;

- give access to learning via a mobile phone;

- free printing;

- maintain some on-campus activity;

- negotiated access to tutors;

- proper training in the use of all required software;

- interesting and well-designed activities with authentic purpose;

- clear and appropriate framework and structure to learning experience;

- resource and time management skills support – to help me manage;

- online submission of assignments, but offline feedback (preferably face-to-face, preferably one-to-one!);

- thorough evaluation with student consultation;

- clarity of tasks;

- confidentiality.

They also stressed the need to enhance student experience through technology, while maintaining the better aspects of face-to-face contact.

The final observation in the symposium was made by a participant who argued that in 'real life' university managers and senior staff draw up a strategic plan which was then cascaded down. They left us with the thought that it would be interesting to see what would happen if a more participative model (as demonstrated by the symposium activity) was adopted.

Appendix 46.1   Symposium activity

Role play

To participate in this activity we would like you to role-play the tasks from the perspective of one of the following people:

- a member of senior strategic management – responsible for making policy decisions regarding learning and teaching developments;

- a member of academic staff – you may be a member of teaching staff or anyone involved with supporting the learning and teaching process;

- a member of the undergraduate student body.

If possible, please choose a role that does *not* reflect your current personal experience.

Background

The university is situated in a large bustling, ethnically diverse city and prides itself on attracting local as well as international students. It offers a wide range of course covering the major discipline areas and courses for continuing professional development for a range of practitioners. It is known for the quality of its teaching as well as its research. Currently it has 20,000 students a third of who are part-time. The university is dependent on state funding for its core teaching and research activity, but also attracts money from commercial and other sponsors for research. While its financial situation is currently sound there are worries across the sector that core government funding is being reduced and pressures for efficiency gains are becoming more intense.

The senior management team recently reviewed their strategic goals for the next five years, and in the light of increasing international competition decided that a key objective was to increase the use of C&IT across all curriculum areas.

Task

As part of this, the senior management team has decided to form a working party with representation from senior strategic management, academic and learning support staff and students. This is the first meeting of the working party. To encourage a full and frank dialogue within the meeting for the first 30 minutes each of the three interest groups are asked to discuss a series of topics from their particular perspective.

Outcome

At the end of this discussion phase each group is asked to feed back to the full working party and possibly take questions on these items. The group will then work together to identify the next phase of activity necessary to make the objective a reality.

Management Group – the strategic managers responsible for making policy decisions regarding learning and teaching developments within the institution.

What are the key issues surrounding the increased use of C&IT for you as strategic managers? (10 mins)

These issues may be with regard to:

- learning and teaching;
- the quality of student experience;
- levels of staff engagement;
- financial and logistical considerations;
- internal and external drivers for change;

- possible barriers to achieving the objective;
- university core mission.

How would you implement this? (10 mins)

Your implementation strategy may wish to consider the following:

- level of resources and funding;
- training and staff development;
- how priorities are set and by whom;
- roles and responsibilities;
- technical requirements;
- reaching beyond the enthusiasts;
- dissemination of information.

Staff Group – members of academic staff, technical staff or anyone involved with supporting the learning and teaching process.

What are the key issues surrounding the increased use of C&IT for you as a member of staff? (10 mins)

These issues may be with regard to:

- learning and teaching;
- the quality of student experience;
- managerial expectations;
- your own roles and responsibilities;
- institutional support;
- internal and external drivers for change;
- possible barriers/problems in achieving the objective.

How would you implement this increased use within your modules or courses? (10 mins)

You may wish to consider the following:

- level of resources and funding needed;
- training and staff development you require;
- development time necessary;
- student expectations;

- technical and physical requirements;
- students level of C&IT skill.

Student Group

What are the key issues for you as a student of the increased use of C&IT as part of your learning and assessment? (10 mins)

You might want to think about:

- the impact among different groups of students, discipline areas;
- the impact upon your learning experience;
- your expectations of higher education with regard to technology;
- external factors that influence the use of C&IT;
- factors within the university that influence the use of C&IT;
- possible barriers or problems you may envisage;
- academic support and contact.

How would you like to see implementation managed on your course? (10 mins)

You might wish to consider:

- the technical resources you may need;
- how you choose to learn;
- on campus attendance and off campus access;
- support and training offered to students;
- level of C&IT skills expected of you;
- what you want the technology to do;
- what you not want it to do.

How would you like the implementation to be evaluated?

This may include:

- what would you consider to be appropriate measures of success and/or performance indicators;
- how would you like your voice to be heard;
- what should happen to the evaluation feedback.